Noside

The Adventures of Ronniehood

AN ACCOUNT OF REMINISCENCE BY

Ron Arold

Copyright 2018 © Ronald J. Arold

*Disclaimer – This book is not affiliated in any way, shape, or form to the Yes logo and its trademark owner. It is used only as a pointer to the story about the band Yes at their concert at JFK stadium in Philadelphia, Pa. and is used strictly for educational purposes only.

Graciously re-edited by Noreen Branigan for grammar, punctuation, and all around excellence.

I would like to give thanks to the following people as without their help this book would have never been written. My wife Jill. My kids Chris, Kayla, & Angelica. My late parents Frank and Joan Arold. My brother Robert Arold. My later brother Erik Arold. My late and loyal pet Sandy for sitting by my side on many nights. Larry Estep. The entire Gulotta family. Alan Lindenbloom for his tips on helping me become a writer. Ronnie & Barney Eskin. Dave, Janis & Archie Genovese. Jesse Kurtanick. John & Tony Velez. Billy Fenton. Cliff Giddes. Phil Maroon. John (Jackie Boy) Geoghan. Paul Barrall. Mickey Blair. Matt & Linda DiLello. Howard, Brian, & Ricky Bernard. Dave Witmer. Reed Holland. John Farrant. Wayne Richardson. Mutah Thomas. Frankie Hajer. Grady Boswell. Melvin Marks. Gus Bodalato. Kevin Halsey. Kenny Leight. Bob Smethers. Pat Connolly. Charlie Catalano. Donna Celi. Bob Manna. Fred Stemming. Ellsworth Hutchinson. Bob, Anthony, & Elena Naccarato. John Kurachick. Mike 'Stogie' Winters. Skippy & Ronnie Guenther. George Caunt. Lance DeLisle. Marc TenEyke. Joe Salgado. Danny Bifano. Ellis Goodlette. Jimmy McVie. Noreen Branigan for being the Little Irish Hussy. Vicky Saragusa. Janet Demers. Lori Sera. Duck Sutton. John Perubski. Wayne Copeland. Vick Farkas. Craig Hendrickson. Vick Northway. George Pyka. Artie Baldwin. Bruce VanDervender. The Melvin Brothers. Steve Fox. Rocco Pepe. Little George Thomas. Larry Fuwah. Dave & Donny Hess. Jim Koye. Ted Miller. Edward 'Steady Eddie' Berlin. Joe Bajer. TonyKoschick. Jeff Sawinski. Pacella"s Deli, for Frank's stories, letting us hang out, & great Italian hotdogs. The Washington Swim Club.

Playmore 1. Romper Room. Sergeant Peppers. Thursday's Place. Dario's. Thomas Jefferson Junior High School, for showing how a school shouldn't be run. Edison Senior High School, for showing me how fools fail at educating students. Bonne Brae School for Boys, for wasting my time when I knew better. The Edison Police of the mid 1970's, for allowing some of their officers to act like Nazis. Linwood Grove. Edison Lanes. The Edison Diner, for great food and coffee 24 hours a day, 7 days a week. Mom's Restaurant, for showing me how employees shouldn't be treated in front of the customers. The Jade Pagoda, for great food and underage drinking. Great Eastern. Carolier Lanes & Skating Rink, for beers and picking up girls. Camp Kilmer, for mini bike riding and crashing cars. The Edison Boat Docks. The Route 1 Flea Market. Lawrence Brook and Farrington Lake. Howard Johnsons. Edison Products, for letting me have a job that was a continuation of high school (a quote from Matt D.), Kilmer Plaza, for Zia Lisa, Grants, Acme, and Pete Tomasino's grandfather's hot dog stand. Mary's Pizza, for having food where I didn't have to walk too far and for my future wife. Raceway Park. Tastee Sub Shop. Burger King. McDonalds. The Rolling Stones. Aerosmith. And lastly, Tom Keifer, Eric Brittingham, and Fred Coury of the rock band Cinderella for influencing me on how to be creative.

Preface

I came to write this book from a suggestion that came from my good friend Jeff Gulotta. Like most friends who gather around at parties telling old stories about their youth, Jeff had been hinting for years that he wished someone would have recorded it all. Since I've been told that I have a bizarre gift of recalling memories in great detail, I decided that it was time. Growing up in Edison, N.J. was very interesting. Starting as a small child, to our wayward teen years, to our introduction as young adults, I never seemed to be bored. My recollections focus mainly on verbatim conversations and experiences taken from actual events that took place in the mid to late 1970's. There are landmarks mentioned, styles of dress, latest music, sexual encounters, drug experimentation, arrests, and bad language. Being that I lived through all of it, I thought I was uniquely qualified to give a real and raw rendition of what it was like growing up under those circumstances. In these tales, you may or may not recognize some of the characters. Some of them are still here, and sadly, some of them are no longer with us. Regardless, they have all enriched my life and showed me how to laugh and cry as a human being. Living through some of these experiences were some of the best times of my life and I carry no regrets. Though some say I was misguided, I wouldn't have changed it for the world. With no responsibilities back then, most of us entertained ourselves with what we saw around us. I took from this what I could as it helped me to understand friendships and camaraderie. Therefore, I have laid it all out here for all to see. Though I don't speak, dress, or have the same attitude anymore, I feel you'll find some of these tales very entertaining. If you feel you may be offended by some of these subjects, please refrain from reading.

NOSIDE

THE ADVENTURES OF RONNIEHOOD

CHAPTER 1

Accident Prone

I was born in Bloomsburg, Pennsylvania on January 17, 1959. I am the only family member including all of my cousins, to be born outside of New York and New Jersey. Therefore, I started out early being the "Black Sheep" of the family. My late mother used to tell me stories about how I was almost born in the back of a taxi cab in a raging blizzard. She added that she was "crowning" with my overly large head and that she barely made it into the hospital for me to be born. My parents had moved to Bloomsburg from New Jersey due to my father being offered a management position at a store named W.T. Grants. Grants were a very popular chain store in the 50's and 60's. After only a year, my father had a bad verbal altercation with his district manager. It seemed that my father was promised a significant raise for moving. But, when my father questioned where his raise was, his district manager refused to comply. My father abruptly resigned. Now, with no job prospects and having to support me as an infant along with my older brother Robert and my mother, my father borrowed money from his dad and moved us to Perth Amboy, New Jersey. I only have faint memories of Perth Amboy. I was swinging on the baby swings at age 3 and of an old woman who babysat me from time to time. Soon, my father secured new employment with Rahway, N.J. hospital as a credit collector. He was elated with his new salary and moved us into a 3-bedroom house he and my mother had bought in Edison, N.J. The house was at 64 Sturgis Rd. It was a typical one-floor ranch house that was popular at the time. What I remember the most was the abundance of fruit trees in its backyard. There was a huge apple tree, a cherry tree, a peach tree, and Concord grape vines intertwined along the fence separating our house from the neighbors on the left.

Picking and eating the Concord grapes was my favorite. This was when I was age 4. A lot of bad things happened to me at that age. So, my parents were convinced I was accident prone. Around this time, my little brother Erik was born and my mother was very busy attending to him. So, I was free, or snuck out free to get into as much trouble as possible. My father worked a lot and had taken on a second job at Montgomery Wards in the Menlo Park Mall. Again, he was a credit manager. I didn't see him much. And, when I did, he was usually too tired to want to do anything else. During this year, 1963 I believe, I got into my first dose of real trouble with my parents. During a raging blizzard outside, I overheard my older brother Robert telling my mother that he was going to walk to Grants. It was ironic as it was the same chain my father had resigned from a few years previously. It was also 5 miles away. Anyway, he had left and I asked my mother where he had gone. My mother told me not to worry about it and to go play in the snow outside. In our driveway was a 1950's blue Plymouth. It hadn't run for a long time and needed repairs. I remember that I loved to play in it and pretended I was driving everywhere.

After a while, I got bored playing imaginary driver. I somehow got it in my head that my brother Robert went to Grants to get candy. I absolutely loved candy at the time. So, I decided to try and find him. I knew how to get from Sturgis Rd. to Lincoln highway (also known as Route 27). Even at 4 years old, I had an amazing, photographic memory. I left the blue Plymouth without telling my mother. I knew if I told her I was following my older brother, she would have said no. So, I did it anyway. As I walked out of my neighborhood and trekked down Route 27, I remember how thick the snow was on my little red snow boots. There were almost no cars in sight. So, I figured I was safe as long as I was able to discern where the sidewalk was. It didn't seem like it was far to me even though it was 5 miles away. I sang songs to myself humming "I'm getting candy, I'm getting candy" and was proud of my 4 year old independence of walking alone.

When I was almost at Kilmer Plaza where Grants was, I was across the street on the sidewalk in front of the 7-11 convenience store. As I was about to attempt to cross Route 27, I saw a police cruiser pull up behind me. A very tall policeman got out of the car and asked me "Where do you think you're going little man? It's a blizzard out here. Where are your parents?" I told him to mind his own business and that I didn't need my parents. He was not amused. He grabbed me up by my waist causing me to scream "Let go of me asshole". I knew a lot of curse words from a very young age. The officer then proceeded to hoist me onto the counter. He told the 7-11 owner "This kid's got a real mouth on him". The cop then asked me my address. I told him "I'm not telling you nothing". I knew if my parents found out, I"d be in for a real beating. He tried to manipulate me with various treats and candies and desperately wanted my address. Being that your address is usually the first thing parents teach young children, I knew exactly what it was. But, I kept holding out due to fear. Finally, after 20 minutes of offering me hot chocolate and everything else the officer could think of, he told me "Welp, if you won't tell us where you live, I guess We'll have to take you to the orphanage". I didn't know what an orphanage was. So, he explained it to me "It's a place bad kids go and never get to see their parents or family ever again". Crying and looking down, I gave it to him.

W.T. Grants In The Kilmer Shopping Center

A few months after this, in the springtime, I had just watched my favorite show The Adventures of Superman. Like most little boys, I wanted to be Superman too. Back in those days, there weren't costumes with capes for children. So, parents had to improvise with what they had. In my case, my mother would take diaper pins from my little brother Erik"s supply. She would take an old towel she didn't really care about and fasten the towel around my neck. That way, in my mind, I was "Superman". I flitted around the house in my underwear with this towel around my neck believing I had powers and could fly. One afternoon, my mother was hanging clothes to dry on the clothes line in our backyard. We had a French style back door and it was the kind with many individual, square window panes. I decided that I would play a trick on my mother and lock the door. After watching my mother through the glass for a while, she approached the door to come in. Seeing that it was locked, she asked me if I had done it. I giggled "Yes mommy, I was playing a trick on you". She then proceeded to scream at me that I had better "open it or else". I tried and tried to push up the little button that would open the door. I even tried on my tippy toes. But, to no avail as I was just simply too short to do so. As my mother became more and more irate, I knew I had to figure out how to open it or I would be punished. Behind me, was one of those old Westinghouse rounded corner refrigerators we owned. It was the kind with the huge handle in the front in the middle. Believing that I had super powers like Superman, I told my mother "Don't worry mommy, I'll get the door open". I backed up and placed my small back against the front of the refrigerator as I wanted a running start. Then, I ran toward the French door with my arms out forward yelling "I'm Supermaaan". I dove head first being thoroughly convinced I wouldn't be hurt by the glass shattering around me. As I fell amongst the shards of sharp glass onto the small, concrete foot path below, I heard my mother scream "Oh my god! Why did you do that?" I was crying hysterically and saw blood trickling down my left arm. It was a lot of blood and I was bleeding profusely. I peered up whimpering and told my mother "Because mommy, I thought I was Superman". My mother called her friend who lived across the street for a ride to take me to Saint Peters Hospital in New Brunswick. It was the only hospital close at that time. My mother didn't drive then. So, her friend obliged. As we were driving to the emergency room, I remember being wrapped in towels with blood soaking through everywhere. My mother was screaming at her friend "Drive faster, drive faster. He's going to bleed to death!" Fortunately, we arrived in the nick of time. I was sewn up with many stitches on my left arm and wrist and sent home. Afterward, my mother hid all of the diaper pins out of my reach. I was banned from playing "Superman" ever again.

Summer time came and my father got me my first bike with training wheels. I would ride it from Sturgis Rd. up Ashley Rd. and back again. One day, I decided that I liked the sound the training wheels made. So, I would look down as I glided across Ashley Rd. There was a house with a big milk truck parked in front of it and it was the kind from the 1950"s. It had a big grate on the front that had sharp edges. As I was pedaling forward and not paying attention, I smacked right into the grate, head first. I was startled a bit and it wasn't really painful but it dazed me. After I got back up, I steadied my bike, and proceeded to cycle back home. As I turned the corner, a teenager came up to me and asked "Do you know you have large amounts of blood trickling down the right side of your face? I replied "No". He then asked "Where do you live? I think you might need some stitches". He took off his white t shirt, wrapped it around my head, and took me home. I remember my mother at the door "Again with this, Ronald?" With my mother's friend in her car like the last injury, I was taken to Saint Peters again. I needed more stitching up. But, this time, 5 across the right forehead. I still have the scar I'm self-conscious about.

As the summer season turned into August, my father decided to bring home a dog from a family that lived across the street. The father of this family was a retired policeman from Jersey City, N.J. The man had a K9 police dog that was very vicious and trained to attack. When he retired, he took the dog with him when they had moved to Edison. After a couple of years, the man and his family decided they wanted to move back to Jersey City without the dog. So, they offered him to my father. The dog"s name was Prince. He was a larger than normal German Shepard and appeared to be very muscular. I remember being afraid to walk passed him in our hallway as he always growled at me for no reason. My mother had tried to talk my father out of taking the dog because she had an uneasy feeling about him. My father built Prince a doghouse for him to stay in in the backyard. He put him on dog chains attached to the doghouse. But, every chain my father attached, he would break and escape. Finally, my dad put a thick boat anchor chain on him. My father convinced said "That"ll hold him". We came out the next day and Prince was dragging his house around the backyard. He was a super strength dog for sure.

One afternoon, my mother was across the street visiting her neighbor friend and no one else was at home. Somehow, Prince managed to get off of his chain again. I guess he broke the hook that held the anchor chain to his collar. As I was trying to enter our house through our front door, Prince came through the left side of a wooden gate that had been left open. He growled at me and showed his teeth. I backed off for a minute waiting for him to go into the backyard again. Every time I tried to approach the front door, he would hear me. He would come between me and the door always displaying his teeth. He was growling and snarling like a rabid wolf. I never did anything bad to this dog and I never teased him, yelled at him, or anything. He was just nasty with a fearsome disposition. It seemed to have been inbred into him and he hated everyone except my father. After playing this game of trying to get in and backing off, I decided that I would try to reverse strategies. When he went to guard the door, I would try the back gate instead. This didn't work either. Every time I tried, he would block that entry as well. By this time, I was getting fed up and was trying to figure out how to get rid of him. I spied some cinderblocks along the bottom edge of the fence that was connected to the gate. I yelled at him "Last chance asshole, or you're gonna get it". I never chastised him before but I was pissed. I then proceeded to pick up half a cinderblock and threw it hard towards him. It missed his rear area by inches. He began to growl and bark loudly in an even more threatening manner. But, I was determined in my little mind not to let him win. I picked up a second piece of cinderblock and threw it at him. This time, it connected and hit him squarely on his hind quarters. He gave out a pronounced yelp. "Big mistake!" I thought. I tried to run away towards a crabapple tree in our front yard. I thought if I could get to it, I would be safe. I found out later, that the worst thing you can do when an animal is threatened is to run. I never made it to the crabapple tree and Prince was upon me like lightning. He pounced and was ripping me apart as I was screaming as loud as I could. I was hoping a neighbor, anyone, would hear me. I was on my back and he was really gnawing into me. He was throwing me around in his jaws like a puppy playing with a chew toy. Being that I was so scared, I pissed myself. But, he continued with his ferocious attack. As I was screaming for help, my older brother Robert appeared as he was on his way home from school. He ran into the yard as fast as he could and grabbed Prince by his collar pulling in vain to get him off of me. It was no use. Seeing that my brother was only 10 years old, he didn't have the upper body strength to restrain him. He simply couldn't stop Prince from mauling me.

    We had a Cadillac in our driveway my father had recently bought for my mother. My mother had finally gotten her driver"s license and had begun to drive. My brother Robert screamed at me "When I pull up on him, run to the car, run to the car! "I was so frozen with fear, I couldn't move. Finally, after a few attempts by my brother with no results, a neighbor named Emil had heard us. He saw the commotion, jumped over our fence, and repeatedly punched Prince in his face until he let go. Then, my brother carried me into the house and laid me on our couch. I told my mother "My pee pee hurts Mommy, my pee pee hurts". Someone had called the police and they had just arrived. Beforehand, someone had covered me with a blanket. The policeman pulled back the blanket and gasped to my mother "There's a lot of blood in his penal region, Ma'am, I don't think your son"'s gonna make it, I'm sorry". I was taken to the hospital in New Brunswick again.

I don't remember having the operation as I was probably still in shock. I was told after waking up that I had lost a lot of blood. It seems after I had pissed myself, Prince zoned in on the urine smell and tore rabidly at my pants. He bit the top of my penis off straight through the material and right through my underwear. It was hanging by a piece of skin and had to be reattached with stitches. About 2 days later, I remember going for a checkup at the urologist. When the doctor removed the bandages for inspection, I freaked out as my penis was all purple and yellow. It was sewn up all around the crown and had a tooth mark in it. I had refused to pee at home out of fear of it stinging and pain. The doctor asked me "Now Ronald, your mother tells me you are afraid to make pee pee at home, correct? You have to try very hard, son". He pointed to my abdomen on my right side. "Otherwise, if you can't do it in a few more days, we will have to give you a valve right here". I told the doctor that I would try. Try I did. The next day my mother held me over the toilet bowl and I pissed all kinds of colors. It also burned very badly. But, I was successful. There was no way that I wouldn't be. Even at that age, I knew it was my manhood.

A couple of days later, Prince was still with us and he was chained in the backyard to his doghouse again. But, this time something was wrong about him. He was lying down very stiff and looked as if he were dead. I poked him with a stick accompanied by my little girlfriend from a few doors down. He was indeed dead. I asked my mother "What happened to Prince, Mommy?" She answered "Someone put Top Job cleaning solution in his dog food. He was poisoned and he died. I think the neighbors behind us did it because they have 4 kids. They were afraid He'd attack them next I suppose". I never believed that story and still think my mother killed him. "How did she know it was Top Job?" I thought. "How come she always said "I" instead of "we"? Even with the injury he had given me, I hadn't wished death upon him. I just wanted him to go away. Eventually, my penis healed up. But, I still have a tooth mark on the right side of its head. Most of the needle marks from the stitches are gone as well. It looks like a faint puncture wound as a scar. Humorously, the girls I've been with can attest to this. Whenever I see a large dog now, I usually try to avoid them. The doctor did a good job though as I have 3 kids with 3 different women. I guess the plumbing still works!

After a few months of my healing process, I was getting into trouble again. This time, it was with a sewer in the street up from our house. Cats sometimes hung out there and I was amazed at how they could crawl inside. I'd watch them as they'd scamper over the grate, and drop down to the pipe below. I foolishly decided to try this myself. I slid down through the opening and into the sewer. Though it was dark, I still found it adventurous and intriguing. "This is great and fun" I thought. That was until I tried to get out and got my head stuck in the opening. As my feet were dangling off the ground and I was terrified, I screamed for what felt like hours. Finally, someone must have heard me as the fire trucks and police cars arrived. The firemen used a tool to pull up the heavy metal grate and set me free. The police took me home and berated my mother. She was accused of not watching me and they seemed like they were getting tired of it. So much for copying cats!

In September of the next year, it was time for me to start kindergarten at Lincoln Elementary School. The school was only a few blocks from our house. Still, I was afraid to leave my mother. But, my mother insisted I was going and demanded that she needed a break from my misadventures. So, I was in the morning session with Mrs. Washington. She was a very rotund black woman and actually very nice. After our introduction, I had a tantrum when my mother left me. Even though it was only my first day, my mother was very worried. She knew that when I was challenged, I would reciprocate with my very bad temper. Mrs. Washington told my mother "Oh, just let him cry honey. They do this all the time. Once he settles down and makes friends with the other children, he'll be fine". She was wrong! I hated school right from the get go and I saw no purpose for it. I was comfortable in my own little world at home and I didn't like being told what to do. Mrs. Washington tried to distract me by offering me toys. She gave me a small scooter to ride that was made of out of wood with metal wheels. I remember some of the kids had erected a wall made out of blocks. It was a pretty tall wall for 5 year olds. I took the wooden scooter, ran up a little speed, and rammed the other kids wall. Blocks fell down all around me and they were thrown to the ground. Its force threw me off balance and I was knocked to the floor. The other children began to cry "He knocked down our wall" they shrieked. The teacher, who had been very pleasant with me up until then put me in something new called 'Time Out'. I went into a rage. Mrs. Washington refused to call my mother to let me go home and forced me to 'cry out my anger'. Though I was incensed by her way of discipline, I couldn't understand what the problem was. I thought "Aren't walls meant to be broken?" After that, I was forced to be good and was never trouble for her again.

After I had turned 6, I met a kid a few houses over from us named Bruce M. Bruce was older than me by about 6 or 7 years and took me to the local Foodtown a lot. He even referred to me as his "little mascot". On the other side of Foodtown was a drug store and a sweet shop. The sweet shop was owned by an old guy and his wife. I remember that the old guy had an attitude and was always chomping on a cigar in his mouth. Sometimes we'd go in there to get candy and he would always yell at us "You kids better have money, this ain't no charity son!" So, unless his nicer wife was around, we usually just avoided him. To the extreme right of the sweet shop was a very large lot that had a Carvel Ice Cream stand. It was placed there after a defunct diner had been removed. I distinctly recall the diner having been placed on some wheels, sat there for a while, and then was pulled away. I had guessed it was moved to a new location. But, I never really knew. Afterwards, Carvel obviously had leased or bought the land and took possession for their business.

On some days when Bruce brought me to Foodtown, he would steal. Bruce loved to steal just about anything and got a real high off of it. In those days, cigarettes were kept at the end of the aisle on the end caps. If you wanted a carton, you took it to the register yourself and paid for it there. Bruce would always take out two cartons from the display, look around to see that no one was watching, and then quickly stuff them down my pants. Since he was a good planner, he always made sure I wore a big coat to put over them. When I asked him "How come you always want me to have the cigarettes? I'm just a little kid?" He would explain "Now Ronnie, what employee will think a 6 year old is stealing cigarettes?" I guess in the more trusting 1960"s he was right. He did this to me with cigarettes and other items many times. Thankfully, we were never caught. So much for having a mentor!

At 7 and 8 years old, I remember all of the truck vendors that came into our neighborhood that sold a multitude of goods and services. There was the fresh vegetable man, the knife sharpener man, the guy who had rides like the whip and the Ferris wheel man, the soda man, the Charlie's chips man, the milk man (who left milk in glass bottles, cheese, butter, and yogurt in a metal box outside the front door) and my favorite, the ice cream man. The ice cream man was named Sugar Boy (though years later, I was told his real name was Michael). These were the days when their trucks used actual bells that we could always hear chiming from afar. To us, it was like radar. We counted on the familiar ching, ching, ching, ching as it reverberated in our childlike ears. It called us, beckoning us "Ice cream, ice cream" the voices would say. "You must have ice cream on this day". All of the children knew it by heart as it was practically drugs for kids. We wanted our sugary treats so bad, we all came running like the lemmings to the sea. Out of backyards, woods, and playgrounds we'd come. We'd shriek to our mothers "Mommy, Mommy! It's the ice cream man, the ice cream man! Can I have some today?" Sugar Boy was born without forearms on both sides of his body. So kids being kids, we made fun of him and thought he had extremities like a T-Rex dinosaur. This didn't stop him from distributing his ice creams or making change for us though. He improvised and had a little step stool that he used to reach into the freezer to retrieve our frozen goodies for us. We would giggle and laugh watching him shimmy his way inside. If need be, he would maneuver his body all the way to his waist, even if it meant climbing all the way to the back. He didn't mind he said and would do anything to make a sale. After all, it was his livelihood. He was a nice man from what I remember and ignored our criticisms as just part of the job.

There was also the DDT truck. Anyone who grew up in the 60"s remembers the DDT truck. They always came right around sunset. They also had a unique hissing sound we were familiar with. We'd hear their noise and our ears would perk up. It was like a signal for fun and programmed from memory. An order would go off in our brains "To your bikes, to your bikes. Mount your bicycles boys; it's time to follow the fog." The truck emitted an immense plume of dense, formidable smoke that was thick, blinding, and we loved it. We'd gather a plethora of riders and chase it as fast as we could. Five or six at a time we followed edging closer while pedaling away. I could hear the others adjacent to me, but could see nothing at all. It was a cloud of bright white that enveloped us and we felt concealed in its obscuring mist. As we finally abandoned our quest, it was like gliding through a vapor of steam. A few minutes passed by, and I began to choke. The killer chemicals were getting to us and my lungs were starting to ache. I heard a friend cry out "Back off, back off. We're all gonna suffocate". Slowly, we retreated. One by one we wobbled away, wheezing at curbside to regain our equilibrium. "That was fun" I wheezed to a friend. "But, I wish it didn't burn so much". "That's the best part" he said. "Not being able to see is what makes it so much fun. Who cares about the poison? We've all gotta die sometime!"

One Sunday, I was walking through Edison High School's football field toward home and was with a neighbor friend named Rodney. Rodney had an annoying habit of always having boogers dripping down off his nose. No matter how much he snuffed it to suck it up; he always failed and looked the same. It was disgusting and made me laugh, but he was still my friend. So, I overlooked it. As we were walking, I thought of a short cut. "Hey, Rodney" I exclaimed. "How about instead of walking all the way around to the gate by the parking lot, we just climb over the fence instead?" "That sounds great" he replied. "But, you go first. I've never climbed a fence that high before and I wanna see you do it before I try". "Ok" I told him. "Just watch and copy me" I said. "I'll meet you on the other side". I approached the fence with much trepidation as its eight-foot height was more than I had anticipated. It was like a barrier that had metal wires interwoven into it with a see-through diamond pattern in its center. It made its chain link palisade very intimidating. I lifted my left foot and inserted the toe of my sneaker delicately. I wanted to make sure it fit before my sojourn to the top. I turned to Rodney "Ok, here I go" I said. "Watch my hands and my feet. This is how you scale it". I placed my right and left fingers in the holes above me and began to lift myself. My right foot was next. I pulled up, set my fingers in the next row, repositioned my corresponding foot, and continued on to the next one. I looked like a crab moving vertically instead of horizontally. When I reached the apex of this steel, foreboding object, I felt instant gratification. "I did it" I thought. "Now, all I have to do is to swing over.

As I straddled the pipe of its frame, I took a quick respite to catch my breath. My proposal was to place my torso over the sharp pointy summit, swivel my legs over expeditiously, dangle with my hands for a moment, and then drop to the sidewalk below. I yelled to Rodney "I made it, I made it. I'm almost over it now". I had made all the attempts as I thought I would and I felt victorious. There was only one small problem though; they were called "shoelaces" and they had become my nemesis. While I was soaring beautifully over of the barricade, the shoelace on my right sneaker had caught a lonely spike at the top. It didn't look too promising as one of its loops had me hanging like a butterfly. I felt taunted by its eye "Let's see you get out of this one" it said. As I was swaying in the wind I was hanging by a thread. I was upside down and was terrified. "Rodney" I cried. "Help me, help me. I can't get down from here. I can't reach. My foot is stuck. Go and get someone, hurry". "I don't know who to tell" he screamed back. "What should I do? What should I do?" While Rodney was frozen with fear, I felt the shoelace begin to give way. "Oh shit" I thought. "I hope this doesn't break". "Rodney" I shrieked. "Get under me in case I fall. That way, it won't be so bad". Just as Rodney was making a dash to assist me, the shoelace became untied and broke.

Unfortunately, I had no time to brace myself. There were no attempts allowed for forward protection, no outstretched arms, no tuck and roll, nothing. Then, my face hit the pavement with a skid. My right cheek ricocheted across the concrete like a kid skipping stones on a lake. I slid forcefully and felt the burn. "Motherfucker" I screeched. "Fuck! My face, my face, my fucking face!" I reached up to feel my injury and as I touched it, it stung like a million bee stings. There was blood dripping down from my fingertips. "How bad is it?" I asked Rodney. "It looks like a scrape like you get on your knee" he squealed. "But on your face instead. I think you better get home and take care of it". "Help me to my feet" I ordered. "I can't believe I got hurt from a fucking shoelace" I said. "You're accident prone Punky" he replied. "You get hurt more than anyone else I know". "Yeah" I told him. "But, fucking why? I can never catch a break"

Not much happened after that until I hit age 9. My father had done so well with his credit collection job that he was able to open his own company. It was called Statewide Credit Bureau and he had offices in Edison, Bloomfield, and Morristown. He was starting to really take off and was really raking it in. Since he was making so much money, my parents decided to sell 64 Sturgis Rd. and move to 37 Price Dr. on the other side of town. It was a major upgrade for us and was a split level house with a den downstairs, 2 bathrooms, 3 bedrooms, a large side yard, and a full basement. Though it was nice, I didn't want to move as I already had friends in Lincoln School. These kids eventually went on to become the LSD"s. The Lincoln School Delinquents. My nickname in Lincoln School was Punky. There were a lot of people who thought it was due to my cursing and attitude problem. The name did fit the description well. But, that's not where it came from. When I was little, my father had said to my mother "Gee, he has a large head like a pumpkin". I couldn't pronounce pumpkin. So, I would say Punky instead. The nickname was born and stuck.

After we moved, I was enrolled in John Marshall Elementary School. I hated it immediately. But, I eventually made friends in Miss Weiff's class with Charlie C., Pat C., and Anthony N. I have a class picture of me giving Pat C. rabbit ears behind his head while Anthony N. was making big head gestures. We thought it was hilarious. But, the principal Mrs. Miller didn't agree. Somehow, she got it in her head that I was the ringleader behind any trouble that happened at "her" school. This was including the class picture. She pulled me into her office many times for interrogations. So, I despised the woman right away. She was a crotchety old krone who spoke through her teeth and tried to run the school like the military. She acted like a drill sergeant in the army and expected us to follow her lead. Of course being "Punky" I would have none of that! So, when she tried to say "We won't have that at "my school", I challenged her. "But, Mrs. Miller?" I asked, "Isn't it the taxpayer"s school and not yours"? She didn't find that funny and was chaffed at why I had questioned her. She couldn't believe I had the gall to confront her. She then went on a personal quest to have me removed. It turned out that she was very crafty and found out I lived on the exact borderline between going to "her" school and Stelton School on Plainfield Ave. So, she sneakily went to the Edison School Board Superintendent to request that I be transferred. My father went to the board to try to fight it and reverse it for me. But, there was nothing he could do. The bitch face won in the end and I was transferred the following year.

At Stelton School I got my first taste of making my own music. I initially wanted to play guitar because I loved The Rolling Stones. So, my father sent me to Lou Rose music center on Route 27 for guitar lessons. The teacher had a flat top crew cut and he always seemed to have dog shit stuck on the bottom of his shoes. My fingers were too small to make the chords I wanted. So, as much as I tried my small fingers just couldn't shape them. I lasted 3 lessons. Depressed about it, my father suggested I take up alto saxophone instead. He had found out that Stelton gave lessons and it was way cheaper than my attempt at guitar. I decided to try it and ended up being very good. I was taught how to read sheet music and different structures of sound. For a 10 year old, I continued to do quite well. My parents even came to a band concert we performed at in the gym. It was one of the few times they came to cheer me on.

I had turned 11. Being brought up as a Catholic, my parents wanted me to make my confirmation. Believing in God I liked, but I've never been into the whole church vibe. My parents decided I had to go to Saint Matthews Catholic School for catechism lessons. I had heard of these classes before from some friends. I was told they were something about Catholicism and that I needed these classes to learn. So, my parents signed me up to go there after my regular studies at Stelton School. I didn't really want to attend as I knew it would cut into my after school play time. Reluctantly, I walked the few miles to Saint Matthews on Thursdays to attend classes from 4:30pm to 6:30pm. I arrived for my first session with no great expectations as I wasn't really interested and didn't care. I only went to satiate my parents so they would leave me alone about it. I had heard that the nuns who taught the classes were strict and believed in physical punishment. "I don't think so" I thought. I have always believed that other than my parents, no one has a right to lay their hands on anyone else"s children. Today was going to be one of those days.

I entered my catechism class and took a seat closest to the door. I've always done this in case I needed an emergency exit. There was the usual blackboard, desk, a picture of the president on the wall, and an American flag on a pole in the corner. But, this time there was competition for the presidential photo. On the right side of the chalkboard there was a picture of the Pope. So, somehow, I knew this was gonna be fun. The nun who was teaching the class entered the room and introduced herself. As it was with most authority figures, I despised her right away. She had an air of disposition of judging us for no apparent reason and carried herself very arrogantly. She was the type of prestigious figure I had grown to annoy as I hated them and their preconceived notions of what was right or wrong. Below the blackboard there was a railing that held the chalk, some erasers, and a pointer with a rubber tip on the end. The nun grabbed the pointer and instructed us to call out our names one by one and row by row. As she did this, she tapped the edge of the pointer on each of our desks. "She wants to ensure compliance in her head" I thought. When we were finished, she went on a diatribe about what we would learn, what was expected of us, and the rules. It always comes down to the rules. She pulled down a graph from a roller attached to the top of the blackboard. These are the type like a shade over a window that are spring loaded with a tassel on its end. On the chart, was some text with a picture of the Vatican. She took the pointer and chose an area to explain. As she turned around sideways she said sternly "Now, children, we are here to learn about God and his forgiveness. He has infinite wisdom we do not understand. I am here to teach you about these subjects on his behalf. You will pay attention at all times. You will not speak unless you are told to do so. During my instruction, you will remain silent and you will remain seated. If you have a question, you will raise your hand and I will answer you. I will only accept a question regarding our religion. I do not give bathroom breaks. Therefore, you must relieve yourselves before the start of each class". "Yeah, yeah, yeah" I thought. Just more of the same authoritarian bullshit I was accustomed to. The usual rules I would ignore.

 Half way through our class of forgiveness, the nun had turned her back to us. She had pulled on the graph earlier and it was back in its home position. Now, while she was writing something on the blackboard, I made the mistake of talking to another student that was behind me. Hearing this, she became enraged. "Mr. Arold" she shrieked "You were to remain silent! What part of the rules do you not understand?" I replied "None of them, I have a hearing deficit". She totally lost it "If you have a hearing problem as you claim, how come you hear me now?" she asked. I countered "Well, you see, it's like this sister. God gave me special powers. So, I can read your lips"! The class erupted in laughter. She was not happy. She went into a drawer in her desk and pulled out a foot long ruler. She approached me with it angrily and stood before me. Then, she screamed to the rest of the class. "Mr. Arold here thinks he's a comedian" she exclaimed. "I will show him what we do to students who interrupt our learning processes". I knew this nun was trying to intimidate me as she was using her body language with the possibility of doing something physical. She wanted to make an example and dissuade me from any further outbursts. As I was foolishly resting one of my arms on the desk with one of my hands facing an upward position, I only half believed the stories I"d heard about crossing the nuns with their temper and I didn't think sHe'd have the actual balls to strike me. While I had partially turned my head to enjoy the laughing of the students behind me, Nazi Nun struck my palm with full force. The ruler let out a loud slap and I felt its immediate sting. "Now, you will obey me" she commanded. The kids in the class all gasped and had instant fear instilled on their faces. I was undeterred. I said nothing and bided my time. I held in my scream and pretended to comply. "Yes sister, you're right sister, whatever you say sister, I'll never do it again sister" I said. She had no idea it was a ruse and I was only wimping out along enough for my revenge.

    After Nazi Nun finished her boasting of correcting me, she made the unfortunate error of stepping out into the hallway. She had to converse with another Nazi about something torture worthy I supposed. While she was out of the room, I turned to the students and gave them the shhhh sign with my fingers. I rose from my desk and made a dash for the blackboard. I grabbed one of the erasers and rushed back to my seat. Then, I hid the eraser under my right thigh as we waited for her to return. When she came back, she continued her hypocritical teachings about peace and love. I was waiting and was stealthily observing her. All I needed was for Nazi Nun to stay with her back to us for a measure of about fifteen seconds. It would be more than enough for my vengeance indeed. When she made her mistake, I was ready. I had my right hand fully on the eraser when it happened. When she was turned long enough for my launch, I raised my arm in a nano second. I aimed, and I fired. The eraser thwacked the back of her head in a thump and a cloud of chalk dust enveloped her skull like a halo. Her habit garb had been dusted. I had won, or so I had thought. She turned with the face of defeatism and rage. She wanted answers and was determined to find out who the culprit was. She zoned in on me as she knew the missile had come from my area. "Mr.Arold"she accused "I know it was you. How dare you do this to a person of the religious faith"! I ignored her. This enraged her further "You will leave this class immediately" she ordered. "I will report you to the church"s administration for immediate expulsion". I stood up and I thanked her. I then bowed to the class and left. A religion of forgiveness my ass!

CHAPTER 2

Characters, Discovery & Sex

It was 1971 and I was about to be in the 7th grade at Thomas Jefferson Junior High School. I liked that I had gotten out of Stelton School as other than music, it had become quite mundane. I also liked that it was closer to home. I merely had to walk about 4 blocks through a hole in a chain link fence surrounding TJ to get there. My first day of indoctrination to this school was a strange one. Instead of one class and a music room to attend, I was now subjected to a myriad of different classes. To a 12 year old, it was a very confusing time. But, once I studied my schedule, I figured it out like a pro. The first incident I saw of teenage angst and attitude was in a bathroom on TJ"s bottom floor. Two teens that I later learned were Rich and Brian M. were about to have a fight. Back then, most of the boys were still dressed in Italian knit sweater shirts, leather pointed shoes, tight black trousers, and leather jackets. I was told this was the "Newarky" style. Supposedly, the look was labeled after Newark, NJ. There were a few kids dressed in "Hippie" clothes, but the transition from Newarky to Hippie had not yet fully transpired. This is when boys still slicked back their hair with Wildroot or Brylcream. My older brother Robert dressed as a Newarky and I never liked it. My father always had that greasy, shiny hair. I found it to be quite repulsive and nasty.

I stood in the corner of this bathroom and watched the two boys grappling ferociously. It was like they were snakes intertwined violently and rolling on the ground. Not many blows were connecting. But, there was tons of cursing and a spectacle on that floor. Eventually, a teacher came in and broke it all up. I was one of the new style Hippie looking kids. My hair had just started to grow out over my collar and it was still parted on the side. This was before everyone parted it in the middle. I found the Newarky style kids alien to me and didn't understand what they were fighting about. I was more into the peace and love concept and it was influencing me more and more. I remember feeling that I couldn't wait for the Newarky style to subside. It felt old and passé to me. It was like a friend who hung around too long and forgot to go home. It was out of fashion now. It was time for a change.

Being that I was new, I got picked on and bullied a lot. It got to the point where I didn't even want to attend school anymore. Neither my father nor anyone else had ever bothered to teach me to defend myself. So, from the bigger kids, I took a lot of beatings. I was too nice of a guy I suppose. TJ at that time was way overcrowded. The hallways and classrooms were like a zoo and every day was like being in Times Square in New York. I guess putting that many juveniles in that small of a space would make any kid pissed off. It was a sea of too much testosterone, anger, and estrogen. The principal of TJ was Mr. DiAquila. I had the unfortunate experience of meeting him when I had mouthed off to a teacher in one of my classes. I was sent to see him in the early morning and I was half asleep. I got the usual "I recognize your last name. Didn't your brother go here?" shtick. It was an ongoing headache I hated. I think all kids have this problem when they attend the same schools as their siblings. No matter how much you try to be an individual, you always get compared to a brother or sister. Its unfair treatment and they didn't care. It didn't matter if they knew you or not as they seemed to enjoy being judgmental. As I was daydreaming, Mr. DiAquila went on and on about adhering to the school's bullshit rules. Peering around the room, I noticed he had a bull whip attached to the wall. I came out of my fog and asked "What is that for"? He laughed "Oh, that's for the really bad kids. Sometimes I have to take it down to administer some fast discipline". I didn't find it funny. I answered him "That's all fine and dandy" I said. "But, if you ever touch me with that thing, my father will be down here showing you how it's really done. And, you'll get to be his first recipient". He called me a wise guy and said "Let's not let that happen now, shall we"? I think he was onto my game. He sent me back to class and asked me to curb my temper in the future. I did the usual "Yeah, sure" to shut him up and went on my way.

A short time after my DiAquila fiasco, I had heard that he had died. He had complications from diabetes supposedly. When I heard about it, I felt a little bad about how I had talked back to him and then changed my mind. As I was soon to be 13, I really didn't have much compassion for authority figures just yet and I thought I knew everything. Shortly thereafter, I found a way out of my persistent problem of dealing with school bullies. Especially with the ones I despised. It turned out that there was a "special" class I heard about for kids with emotional or behavioral problems. I had a bad attitude and I hated authority. So, I figured I would easily qualify. This was even though in grammar school, I was a straight A student. "It was perfect!" I thought. I just had to come up with a scheme and devise a way to get in. I asked around from fellow students on how it could be done. I was told to try to make friends with as many of the kids in the "bad" class as possible and that they would be able to help me. The next day, I was in the boy's bathroom upstairs by the school's back door. This bathroom was known as the "smoking" bathroom. This was where boys would sneak cigarettes between periods and smoke as fast as they could. There was even a secret signal used in case a person of authority came snooping around. This particular bathroom had a large wooden door with a C shaped handle attached to it. It was on the left hand side and the door swung to the outwards direction. On the bottom, there were louvers for ventilation. Before you entered, you were expected to grab the handle and bang the door twice against its frame. You were to use this signal at all times before entering. That way, the kids on the inside would know if it was still safe to keep puffing or stop. As an extra precaution, someone was always peering through the bottom of the door to look for feet wearing shoes. The only people wearing shoes would be a teacher, a principal or a vice principal. If you saw sneakers, earth shoes, or wallabies, you knew it was safe to continue. As we puffed, the head on the cigarettes would light up like an orange and red flare. In between drags, one foot was in the stall, while the other one was facing the door. You would always keep one eye out around the partition. That way, you could drop the butt in the toilet and avoid sneaky teachers looking for easy suspensions. The trick was to satisfy our nicotine cravings while averting being caught at all times.

It was in one of these smoking sessions that I met a kid named Ronnie E. I liked that he had the same name as me and he was very funny. He had a sense of humor like Bill Murray from Saturday Night Live. This was before Saturday Night Live was even broadcast on TV. He had one tooth missing in the front of his mouth and it made him look like Alfred E. Newman who was the mascot on the cover of Mad magazine. He was wearing a green Army coat that was far too big and had a habit of blowing smoke rings through the space from the hole in his mouth. It was quite hilarious. We got to talking and we became friends. I asked him "How did you get in the Special Ed class"? He gave me the low down and knew exactly what to do. He informed me that I had to immediately start failing all of my classes and go from A's to F's. He went on "As soon as that's accomplished, the school will have a meeting with your parents. They'll want to see what's going on with you. You'll then be sent to a meeting with the school's 'Child Study Team'. During this meeting, they'll analyze you and give you a Rorsach test. This is also known as, the 'ink blot test'. When you look at the ink blots, they'll ask you what you see. Use all violent descriptions and tell them you see 'Devils, dead people, murders, and shit'. Then, they'll ask you what you would do if you saw the Beatles Yellow Submarine going down Route 27. Tell them "Why, I'll blow it up of course, with a bazooka!" They'll ask you to draw pictures of your family. Sketch some with your dad being a gangster holding a machine gun, you're mom screaming, your brothers clawing at each other, and make sure you're not included with them in the picture. Draw yourself way off in the corner of the paper some place. That"ll make them think you feel alienated and alone. Make sure you draw shit like lightning, black clouds and rain. Whatever you do, don't ever draw any sun or rainbows. You need to make them think you're depressed and angry. The more fucked up you act; the more believable it'll look". He offered more "While waiting for the test results, cut as many classes as you can and continually come in late. Be very loud in all of your classes and make as much noise as possible. In the end, They'll think you need medication and isolation from the rest of the students". I did just that. Everything he had told me. It was beautiful.

While waiting on the school's decision to see if I got into the Special Ed class, I got into more trouble on purpose. I had a mechanical drawing class with a teacher named Mr. Hall. Mr. Hall was one of the first black teachers to be hired by the district. This man had an uncanny ability to be able to know what you were doing without even looking at you. It was like he had a 6th sense. If you strayed from a task he had asked you to do, he would have his back to you and exclaim "Mr. Arold, I can see that you're not being productive. You are distracting my class. You don't want to be behind the 8 ball, do you?" This would become his signature phrase he was known for. One morning, I had questioned him about the purpose of drawing all of these brick walls. "How will it help us as adults later in life?" I asked. He didn't like me being this inquisitive and he chastised me in front of the class "Now, I'm going to have to lower the boom on you" he said "You have just earned a ticket to the principal"s office".

    I was sitting in the waiting area for discipline once again. Soon, I was told by a secretary to go into the principal's office and to sit down in front of his desk. Being that DiAquila had passed on, I had no idea what to expect. In came a very tall, lanky kind of guy who was wearing a tweed suit and looked like his tie was tied too tight. He reminded me of Lurch from the TV show the Addams Family. He introduced himself as 'Mr. Guzak'. He was maybe in his mid-50's and was wearing reading glasses perched on the end of his nose. He sat in the chair behind the desk and leered at me acting as if he was royalty. I was immediately onto his charade and thought "This guy has got to be kidding, right? He's taking this thing way too seriously". I couldn't help but notice that he had very long fingers and arms that looked like an alien. He was trying to use intimidation tactics against me. He waved his right hand back and forth arrogantly as he spoke and was questioning my behavior "Now Ronald" he said. "We are on to you. We know you were a straight A student before coming here. We know you have great potential. Why do you persist on following this path in life?" he asked. "It will get you nowhere. You will never amount to anything acting this way. Do you want to be a ditch digger all of your life? Don't you want to be a contributing member of society?" He rambled on about how he was "The temporary acting principal" and, since he was already the vice principal, he would be serving in this capacity until a new principal could be found. He lectured me that "I had to learn to obey the rules and his authority". I was chuckling inside and thought "Um, I'm a new generation of hippie kids. I have no inclination of following yours or society's rules". Since this was my first time seeing him, he said he would 'cut me a break' and send me to my next class. He also asked me to behave myself. I laughed as I walked out the door. I was told later on that the kids named him 'Stoneface'. He never, ever smiled. Now, I saw why.

A few months passed by and I was called to the office again. I was trying to figure out what I had done as I hadn't been in any real trouble for some time. To my surprise, I was told "Starting next week, at 9am, you will be in Mr. Stanislaski"s class. We have already informed your parents. He is on the bottom floor across from Mr. Campbell's class. Both of these classes are for Special Ed students. Congratulations, you got what you wanted". I was overjoyed to hear this. I had found out more information about these classes while I was waiting to see if I was accepted or not. It seemed that not only would I be in one class for the entire day, but the Special Ed kids got to start at 9am instead of 7:45am and we were discharged to go home at 2:30pm instead of 3:30pm. Since I hated school anyway, it was a win win situation. But, my parents were not happy. I had meticulously gamed the system and won. It wasn't due to a lack of intelligence though. It was due to bullies, and the sheer boredom of attending school. I was way ahead of any lessons the school had thrown at me and had put on an academy award performance. I passed the audition, and was rewarded with an easier life. I was very proud of myself. I figured, if school was gonna suck anyway; I might as well do it the way I wanted. "Why conform when there was a way out?" I thought. Since I was so successful, this was the beginning of my many scheming ways.

In Mr. S's class, as we called him, every day was like a holiday. There were about 8 or 9 of us with supposed emotional, mental and behavioral problems. From narcissistic, paranoid schizophrenics, to learning and developmental issues, to low IQ, and finally, to the rest of us who were playing the system and simply didn't care. We spent most of our days reading 4th grade English and history books and looking out the window. Mr. S. was big on art. So, some days to keep us busy, he would give us large sketch paper and colored pencils to draw with. I guess Mr. S. had been speaking to the Child Study Team. He didn't think we knew it, but we knew the drawings were only to see into our child psyche. A lot of mental health kid's emotional problems we found out were gauged by children's drawings. This is to see how they really feel. It's a way to see inside their heads to see what's going on with them at random intervals. Of course since we were all hip to this, we made sure no one ever drew anything depicting happiness. We had to keep up appearances, lest we get kicked out of the program. Once we were acclimated to the easy school life, there was no way any of us wanted to go back as we all hated the drudgery of complying with a regular school schedule.

There were a few characters in these Special Ed classes that would drive the two teachers crazy. One of them was Joey. He was a very large kid and was maybe 6 feet 2 and 240 lbs. It was very easy for him to become emotional over nothing. There was an aggressive kid in our class named Leon. Leon was very good looking with long, surfer dude blonde type hair. The little girls we named tiny heinies adored him. But, Leon had a personality flaw. Like most bullies, he loved to torture people. This was especially true if they were as vulnerable as Joey. Joey had a disgusting habit of picking his nose and wiping the boogers under the table. This drove Leon insane and enraged him. Whenever Leon would catch Joey doing this, he would force him to turn over the table and clean it with a wet paper towel from the bathroom. This exasperated Joey's low self-esteem and he would cry, shake, and lose control. He never realized that he was so large over Leon, that he could have pummeled Leon easily. When kids are teenagers, they can be quite cruel. I think Leon knew this and used it to his advantage. It always seemed like he enjoyed it for shits and giggles. Regardless, the rest of us saw this as entertainment and thought it was hilarious. Joey didn't always want to reclaim his boogers from under the table. So sometimes he would scream that we were all picking on him again. He would jump up from his desk and yell "No, no, no. not again. I'm going home Mr. S.!" He would fly down the hallway in hysterics with Mr. S. pleading to stay behind him. When this happened, we would rifle through Mr. S's desk to see what we could steal. Occasionally, Joey would come back. When he did, it usually took hours of Mr. S. coddling and reassuring him to calm him down. Other times, the cops had to be called and he would be found wandering up and down Plainfield Avenue talking to himself.

Some days, Mr. S. and Mr. Campbell would combine our classes for "Championship Checkers Day". This was only if we had been good for a week or two. We would all play checkers until there was a single triumphant team. Mr. Campbell was an older black man with a very good sense of humor. He used this approach to control us more than Mr. S. Mr. S. had a higher degree than Mr. Campbell in child psychology. So, I think he used more of the clinical technique. Mr. Campbell had a rule during these checker games. Once you 'touched' a checker, you had to 'move' it and there was no going back. He called it the "Touch a man, move a man" rule. If he jumped over your checker and took it, he would put it to his lips, blow on it and cry out "Gimme gifts, gimme gifts". He would tease us and proclaim "Keep going, I have your pile right here brother! Don't try to be slick!" Another saying he used was "King me, fool". He especially enjoyed this if you were losing badly. The way he said these phrases made us laugh a lot. We even copied them and used them in our day to day vernacular. Sometimes, these championships would take all day. If we kept the noise down, Mr. S. would go to the teacher's lounge and bring us back Cokes from the soda machine as a reward. I guess he didn't realize that the caffeine in the Cokes made us even louder. I always felt that Mr. Campbell and Mr. S. were always trying to manipulate us. They always seemed desperate to keep us quiet and be reasonable for the day. They didn't understand that most of us came from chaotic families and that being unreasonable was the only thing we knew. Most of us didn't care about their attempts at control as long as we got something out of it. It was part of the game we thought. It was us against them. About once a month Mr. S. would get us pizza. After we had eaten the pizza and made sure everyone got the exact same amount to avoid a fight, we would take the greasy paper plates and play 'Frisbee' with them. Mr. S. hated this game and would do anything to dissuade it. Eventually, he turned it into a competition and manipulated us into aiming for the garbage can. If we did so, we would get an 'extra prize'. It would usually be a pack of gum or another Coke from the teacher's lounge.

On one cold winter's day, Ronnie and I decided to cut school. We walked in the deep snow that had fallen the night before and decided to go to Camp Kilmer. Camp Kilmer was an old Army base that was abandoned by the government. It had a back gate that was no longer functioning on a street named Suttons Lane. A lot of the buildings were in serious disrepair. But, some of them were not. It was always an adventure going there. We would imagine what it must have been like to have been stationed there during its heyday. There was a decrepit laundromat, a jail with wooden bars, a septic field, remnants of a train station depot, an empty PX store, vast buildings with huge doors on rollers, and ramps up one side of the building and down on the other. We decided to keep walking until we got to some apartments we knew of on the outskirts of the base. It was so cold; we went to find a laundry room. We knew there were dryers down there and that we could use them to our advantage. Once in the laundry room, we came upon the idea of using the dryers to warm us up. Ronnie had some quarters and so did I. The first thing we wanted to warm was our sneakers as they were frozen. Ronnie put his sneakers in the dryer along with mine. We dropped some coins in and cranked it up. While we were waiting, we decided to put our clothes in there next. That way, on the walk back home, we would be toasty warm. After we pulled our dry sneakers out, we disrobed down to our underwear. We threw our cold clothes into the dryer and dropped some coins in again. As we smoked cigarettes and watched the dryer's tumbler go round and round, we heard the door to the outside creak open. A woman was attempting to drag her basket into the room for washing. She was aghast at the sight of the two of us sitting there in our underwear with cigarettes dangling out of our mouths. She shrieked "What the hell are you boys doing in here in your underwear? Why aren't you in school?" Ronnie laughed, looked at me, back at her and announced "We're practicing nudists. We're getting ready for the polar swim dance. Would you care to join us?" I was laughing so hard; I was holding my sides and trying not to fall off the table. The woman didn't say a word. She grabbed her basket, turned on her heels, made a face of disgust, and headed back out the door. After laughing loudly for 10 minutes, we calmed down enough to realize the seriousness of our situation. I told Ronnie "I think we better get out of here. You know she's gonna call the cops". We donned our clothes from the dryer and made our way back home.

Things with my father were starting to become pretty precarious. It was still winter and meant I had to spend extra time inside listening to his rants more than usual. He had also become further frustrated with me over my lack of his discipline and my failing grades. It was then I had decided to run away for the first time. When I told Ronnie E. of my plan, he offered for me to sleep over at his apartment he shared with his family. He lived at Marina Gardens below the Morris Goodkind Bridge. There was a rather steep and winding road to get down there and it was close to the Raritan River. It was a scary thoroughfare where drivers had to apply their brakes incessantly to avoid going over the embankment. It was the perfect place I thought where my father wouldn't be able to find me. We decided to cut school for the day and try to find something fun to do instead. Ronnie met me at the top of the hill and already had an idea. His wheels had already been turning. "Hey man" he said "Look down there at the bottom of that slope". "You see that kiddie pool?" he asked. "Yeah, what about it?" I replied. "We can drag that up the hill and use it to slide down in" he laughed. "You know? Like they do with those rafts at the ski resorts". "You mean like snow tubing?" I asked. "Yeah, just like that" he said. "We can slide down and hold onto the sides" he chuckled. "It'll be fun". I had noticed by now that there was a rickety old swing set that was all rusted out at the bottom of the ravine. It looked as if it had been sitting there for years. "What if we run into that fucking thing?" I asked. "I don't feel like getting cut up so I have to get stitches". "We'll just dive out before we hit it" he said. "Worst comes to worst, we can just tip the pool over". "Ok" I replied. "But, if I see us going toward that thing, I'm not helping you trying to direct it. I'm just gonna jump out". "Ok" he murmured. "If you say so. I'll jump out too".

We trotted down the chasm to where the kiddie pool was. It was abandoned and upside down. It appeared as if it had algae growing on its bottom and the edges were chipped and ragged. There were also a few cracks in its center. "I don't know" I told Ronnie "This thing looks pretty beat up man" I said. "What if it disintegrates on the way down?" I asked. Ronnie always being the mischievous one smiled and said "We'll just stay by the sides. The sides look ok. So, don't puss out on me now man. Have some balls". "Ok" I said. "But, I'm telling you, I better not get hurt". He grabbed one side, and I grabbed the other. The wind was making it difficult to climb with and I felt as if we were trying to steady a sail on a ship in a hurricane. Half way up, I slipped and the pool almost took off in a gale. Ronnie was holding on intently with both hands. "Jesus Christ, Arold!" he screamed. Get up and grab the fucking thing or We're gonna lose it". I regained my foothold, spun around, and lunged for a grasp. To my surprise, I was successful. "Hurry up" he yelled. "If We're quick, we can make it". After much twisting, turning and redirection, we succeeded in settling down in our soon to be boat. We laid it down as flat as we could and jumped in respectively. Ronnie was looking around. He was scanning the terrain and reminded me of a surveyor inspecting his coordinates. "I think because of this wind, were gonna have to push this thing to the right a little" he advised. "That way, we won't get blown off course". "I don't give a fuck which way we go" I replied. "As long as we don't hit any big bumps or that fucking rusty swing set". "We won't" he said. "I think I got this down. We'll hold on the sides with one of our arms, and rock it back and forth. I'll count to 3. When I get to 3, give it a big push and We'll slide down nice and fast". "I hope this works" I replied. "I really do". He announced "Are you ready?" "1,2......3". On our last shove, we flew through the air and slid over the ground rapidly and laughing as we went. Ronnie was shrieking "Mahhhhh huhhhhh". It was another of his catch phrases where no one knew what it meant. Suddenly, we hit a patch with no snow that had rocks jutting out of the soil. We ran right over them and I felt bumps hitting my ass. Ronnie was still screaming "Mahhhhhh huhhhh". But this time, there was vibration in his voice. We began to spin around and were losing control. I wasn't ready and hadn't anticipated changing direction as my back was now facing the street. I lost my grip on the edge of the plastic and was rolling. "Jump Arold, jump!" he howled. "We're gonna crash!" Just as I was about to bail out, the pool flipped over spilling us to the ground. We tumbled off our bearings. I went left and Ronnie went right. Suddenly, I felt my left elbow scraping the edge of the curb. Ronnie had just missed the swing set avoiding some serious injury. "That was great" he beamed. "Let's do it again". I glanced over and could see the remains of what was left of the kiddie pool and it was in tatters. "Fuck that shit" I wailed. "My arm's fucked up and that pool is trashed. I told you it had too many cracks in it". "You have to live dangerously if you wanna have fun, Arold" Ronnie smirked. "You can't say that wasn't some fun shit". "It was pretty cool" I replied. "But, my elbow is fucking killing me". I took off my coat, examined my arm, and didn't see much damage. Ronnie continued "There's no blood. You just sprained it. It'll go away and be better in a little while. Let's go find something else to do. Sit down and have a cigarette with me. Then, We'll figure it out".

Some time had passed and my arm was feeling better when Ronnie came up with another suggestion. "You ever been up in Bums Castle?" he asked. "A castle?" I replied "Where?" "There are no fucking castles around here" I said. You're fucking crazy". "Follow me" he said. I shadowed him under the bridge where one of its humungous arched supports was soaring over our heads. It was a very intimidating structure. Ronnie pointed upward. "You see that rope up there on the left dangling from that ladder?" he asked. "Look at the opening on top of that ladder. That's Bums Castle." "Why do they call it that?" I asked. "Because fucking bums live up there I guess. How the fuck do I know? You wanna climb up there with me or not?" he asked. "We can check it out and see what's in there". "It looks pretty high up" I replied. "I'm afraid of heights". "There you go with that pussy shit again" he said aggravated. "Be a man and follow me up there. If I can do it, you can do it too. Don't be a girl". "Ok, I'll try it" I said anxiously. "But, you go first".

"Piece of cake" he said. "Just copy me and do what I do. You won't fall and you'll be ok. I've climbed up there before. It's really not that dangerous". "Not dangerous?" I thought. "The last time you said that, I fucked up my elbow".

He grabbed the knot on the end of the rope and began his accent. I was following right behind him. It was about a 10 foot climb to the first rung with subsequent rungs above him. Slowly, and carefully I reached hand over hand and foot over foot. With each grasp and step I was shaking. I felt like a leaf newly released from a tree. Ronnie looked down at me. "How you doing down there?" he asked. "I'm scared shitless" I replied. "We're almost to the top. Just don't look down" he laughed. "Otherwise, you'll fall". "Gee, thanks a lot" I cried. "I'll try to remember that, asshole". "Don't make me kick you" he blurted out. "It's a long way to the ground". He finally reached the summit, pulled himself over the ledge, and stood up. "I can see New Brunfest" he yelled. "That's nice" I murmured. "I can see your sneakers. Now, help pull me up and gimme a hand". He reached down with his left palm and went to grab my arm. Just as he got close, he brushed it up against my hand. "Psyche" he chuckled. "Don't fall" he said. I wanted to kill him. "Stop fucking around and help me up there" I begged. "I'm gonna fucking lose it". "Ok, for real this time" he said. "Are you ready?" he asked. "Fuck yeah" I screamed. "Get me the fuck off of this thing". Again, he attempted to reach for my hand. This time, he touched my fingers and quickly pulled away. "Oops, you missed it" he cackled as he rubbed his hand over his head. "Come on now fuck head" I shrieked. "This shit isn't funny anymore. It's scaring the piss out of me". "Keep your shirt on pussy" he exclaimed. "This time I'll pull you up. Godamn you're a fucking baby".

When I was finally safe at the top, we began to look around. As I stepped behind me I heard a crunch. I took another step and there were more crunching sounds. "What the fuck is that?" I asked Ronnie. "Pigeon shit!" he laughed. "Look! It's all over the place. They live up here. That's why it's so shitty". I was laughing at his comment. But, I was still nervous. I really didn't want to be there due to my extreme fear of heights. "Aren't you glad you did it?" he asked. "Look at the view man. Just don't get too close to the edge though. Because if a strong wind hits you, it's curtains". While I was looking around and enjoying my steadiness further inside this skyscraper, I heard a chirping sound. It was really more of a peep.

"What's that noise?" I asked. "Do you hear it?" "It's baby birds" he said. "The pigeons roost up here." "Let's see if we can find it" he said. "There are probably lots of them". We strolled around crunching on the dried excrement as we explored the totality of its caverns. "Here it is" Ronnie yelled out. "Look, it's yellow and it's a small one. I wonder if it can fly yet?" he asked. "I don't think so man" I replied. He picked it up from its nest and examined it. "You're touching that thing with your bare hands man" I responded in disgust. "How do you know it doesn't have any diseases?" I asked. "There's shit all over here. I hope you don't catch anything". He began dancing with it in his hand. He started to sing a parody from the play Annie "It's a shitty life. It's a hard knocks life; everything's shitty in the hard knocks life. "As I looked closer, I could see that the chick didn't have many feathers. He was spinning around and getting closer to the edge and I was beginning to get scared. It appeared as if he wasn't paying attention. I didn't want him to lose his footing and fall. Suddenly, he stopped. He threw the fledgling in the air. "Let the pigeons loose" he cheered. "Fly birdie fly, you're a big bird now". The fowl didn't fly and fell to the floor. I wandered over to it to see if it was ok. It was just sitting there stunned. I didn't think it was dead. "That's enough" I yelled. "It's time for me to go". "But Arold" he replied. We can't leave. It's a pigeon circus". "Pigeon circus my ass" I said. "You're fucking crazy. I'm getting out of here". "Ok, killjoy" he said. "But, you go down first. I'm not gonna sit down there waiting on you all day because you're too much of a pussy to get back down". As we were descending, I felt more at ease. Going back down from somewhere has always been easier for me than going up. I got half way down the ladder when I felt a tingle on the top of my skull. It was Ronnie fucking with me again. He was slightly stepping on my head with the toe of his shoe. He'd tap and laugh, tap and laugh. "Don't lose your concentration, man" he giggled. "It's a long way down, bro. And, I don't do bodies. So, if you fall, the animals with have to eat you". "Don't worry about it" I replied. "I'll be fine". "That's because you're a definite shoo" he bellowed loudly. I could hear the echo behind him as we continued navigating down. His voice was reverberating off the concrete surrounding us. "Shoo" he repeated. "A definite Shooooooooo".

When we finally reached the bottom, I had to take a cigarette break. "That was interesting" I told him. "What's next on the agenda that won't get us possibly killed?" "I have to go over to some chick's apartment" he replied. "I'm supposed to baby sit her kid while she goes to the doctor for a couple of hours. She's gonna pay me a few bucks. I need to do it because I'm gonna need cigarette money". "What's this chick's name?" I asked. "Is she hot?" He began to crack up hysterically "Hot?" he said. "Umm, no. Unless you consider rolling her in the dough to find the wet spot hot? It's a girl I know named Marilyn. She's Rocco P's sister" he said. "Her kid is a little girl and she's like 6 months old or some shit. So, We'll go over there for a while. We can get out of the cold that way anyway". I agreed to go and followed him. We got to the apartment and Marilyn answered the door. She was a very large woman and took up most of the doorway. But, she was nice enough and invited us in. I sat down on her couch and listened to instructions she gave to Ronnie about how to watch her baby. She went on about where the diapers and bottles were, etc. It was the usual baby stuff most tenders had to acclimate to. "I'm going to keep her in her baby swing" she said. "She usually stays asleep if you keep it running. Just crank it back up when it runs out and she should be ok. I'll be back in an hour or two after my doctor's appointment. If there's an emergency, call the pediatrician's number on the wall. They'll tell you what to do until I come back". "I can handle it" Ronnie replied. "We'll just watch TV until you get back. Do you have any coffee?" he asked. "It's in the cabinet" she said. "Just brew some up and you'll be fine" "Sounds good Marilyn" Ronnie said. "I guess We'll see you in a little while." Marilyn gathered up her purse, keys, and doctors papers, put on her coat, and left. "Ahhh" Ronnie sighed. "Now, we can relax. Go and make some hot coffee, bro" he demanded. "If I gotta watch this kid, you gotta make the drinks. I'm too tired from Bums Castle". I prepared the coffee and handed him a cup. "Thanks man" he said. "Now, let's see what's on TV". I sat down with my mug and sipped patiently while getting more comfortable. Ronnie had finished his coffee and turned to me "Shit, I forgot something" he said. "I've got to go to my house and get it. Stay here with this kid and I'll be right back, ok?" "What do you mean stay here with this kid?" I asked. "I don't know how to take care of no frigging baby!" "Cut me a break, man" he pleaded. "I tell you what; if I'm not back in 10 minutes, just leave. I promise you I'm coming back. I'm not leaving here without collecting what she owes me. Besides, you'll like it. It's pretty cool". "Ok" I said. "But, if you seriously don't come back, I'm out of here". "Stop worrying man" he replied. "I won't take long". And with that, he flew out the door. Fortunately for me, the baby was sleeping. So, I made some more coffee and continued watching TV.

Around 10 minutes had passed and he returned as he promised. He sat down where he was before and was fumbling with something in his coat pocket. "What do you got there?" I asked. He pulled it out and showed it to me. It appeared to be a spool of white thread and was impaled on its side with a needle. "What are you gonna do with that?" I laughed "Some needlepoint?" "No dickhead" he chuckled. He reached into his other pocket and produced a small container with a black substance in it. "What's in there, man?" I asked. "It's India ink" he laughed. "We're gonna do tattoos today". "Tattoos?" I said nervously. "How the fuck are we gonna do tattoos with that shit?" I asked. "All you have to do" he instructed. "Is wind some thread all the way down the needle until there's only the point showing. Then, you dip it in the jar of ink, and make holes with it really fast in your skin. You do it over and over again, wipe off any ink that's left over, and keep on going until you're done". "Where'd you learn that from?" I asked. "Don't worry about it" he said. "Do you want a tattoo or not?" he asked. He was daring me. "I dunno" I replied sheepishly. "Is it going to hurt?" I asked. "Only a little bit" he joked. "But, if you're gonna be a pussy about it, I'll let you do mine first. Then, you let me do yours". I watched him wrap the thread around the needle and get it prepared for the technique. "There might be some blood" he warned. "But, it'll only be a little bit. All tattoos bleed some". I freaked out for a second "Blood?" I asked. "First you told me pain, and now you're saying blood. I dunno if I wanna do this anymore or not" I said. "Oh, you're doing it, man" he laughed. "You already told me you would. So, I don't wanna hear it and you better be ready after me." "How are we gonna make sure it stays clean?" I asked. He reached in a cabinet and pulled out a white bottle with clear liquid in it. "Marilyn has some rubbing alcohol right here" he said. "So, there's no reason for any more of your excuses". He finished with his preparations, sat down, and rolled up his right sleeve. "As you know, I'm a lefty" he said. "So, I want you to do my right arm in case it gets sore". "Ok" I replied. "Are you ready?" I asked. "Yeah" he said. "Now, the easiest tat to do first I think is a cross. So, take a pen and draw a cross as an outline on my skin first. Make it like the ones you see in church. Then, maybe put some lines over the top corners of it to make it look like the sun"s rays are coming up behind it and shit". "I'll try my best" I replied. "But, I've never done this kind of shit before. So, don't get pissed off if it comes out shitty". "That's why We're only gonna do a small one" he said. "Like a few inches up and down. If it sucks, we can fix it later when We're old enough to get it covered". I took a pen and made the necessary drawing on his arm. When, he thought it was correct enough, I took some toilet paper from the bathroom, soaked it with alcohol, and rubbed over his arm gently. When it was dry, I grabbed the India ink and dabbed the needle in it. "Not too much" he said. "You only have to put the tip in". "Ok man" I chuckled "Here we go". I began poking tiny holes in his skin in fast repetition. I felt guilty. It was as if I was a human sewing machine and he was the textile. I made sure I didn't make the punctures in his flesh too deep. "That's it" he winced "You got it, man". He was obviously trying to hide the sting. "Just keep going until I tell you to stop. Stay with the pattern and don't forget to keep wiping it. I'll know when it's done". When he was satisfied that the image remotely imitated the cross that he envisioned, I stopped. "I think that looks pretty cool. Doesn't it?" he asked. "I guess so" I replied. "But, you're looking at it upside down. Go look in the mirror in the bathroom" I said. You can probably get a better idea in there". He rose from the couch and did just that. "Not too bad" he yelled from a distance. "I can live with that". He came back in front of me, tilted his arm and asked me what I thought. "It won't win any prizes" I grinned. "But, I guess for your first one it'll do". I was feeling apprehensive because I knew I was next. "Ok" he laughed. "It's your turn now. Don't even think of pussing out on me. It's really not that bad. In some spots, it hurts a little. After a while, it got kind of numb. I didn't feel too much after that until the end". I sat down and rolled up my left sleeve as he already knew I was a rightly. Then, he wiped my skin and got ready. "Ok, Arold" he said "Here goes. And, don't move your fucking arm either. If you do, you'll fuck this whole thing up and it'll look stupid. No matter how much it hurts, don't fucking move". "I won't" I replied lying. I was trying to convince myself that I could handle it. It wasn't easy since I hadn't done this before. He started to pierce my skin. "Fuck me" I howled. "That fucking hurts, man!" "Shut the fuck up, you fucking baby" he wailed sarcastically. "I didn't cry, did I?" he asked. "Now, be quiet or you're gonna distract me. The more you interrupt, the longer it'll take. So, suck it up man". I remember trying to think of something else during the procedure. I was wistfully tying to disassociate myself from enduring the discomfort that he had thrown upon me. With each one of his downward jabs, I was gritting my teeth inside. I wouldn't dare let on to him that I was in agony. I knew if I did, he was the type to immerse the needle even deeper just to teach me a lesson. My thoughts went to the permanence of the ink "I'm gonna have to hide this" I thought. "If my parents see this, I'll be punished again". Soon, it was over. "It looks almost exactly like mine" he boasted. "Go look in the mirror like I did". I checked it out in my reflection and was fooling myself. I felt more adult from it but the tattoo sucked. It looked like a jailhouse tattoo and anyone could tell it was very unprofessional. Since I didn't want to hurt his feelings, I went along with it. "Ok, man" I said. "I guess we have tats now". "How long until this thing heals?" I asked. "You can't go swimming in any pools with it, and don't pick the fucking thing" he advised. "Well" it's winter time. So, swimming is out" I said. "Keep it clean too" he replied. "I was told to put Vaseline on it. I guess that protects it. Maybe in a few weeks, we can do another one?" he suggested. "We'll see" I answered knowing full well I wouldn't be doing any homemade ones again.

While we were nursing our wounds, I heard a loud fart. "Was that you, man?" I asked. "No man" he said. "I was just about to ask you if that was your nasty?" "It wasn't me, man" I replied. "Then, who the fuck was it?" he asked. "There's only you, me, and that baby here" he said. We both looked over at the infant at the same time. Just as we did, shit started dripping out of the side of the baby"s diaper and it was beginning to hit the wooden floor below. It looked like dark fudge with grainy material in it. But, it was more of a runny consistency. "Holy fuck!" Ronnie cried out. "It's raining cah cah. I think the kid's got diarrhea". "No shit" I laughed. "You better do something about it man. It's splashing all over the ground. It's going everywhere". "I'm not cleaning that bullshit up" he exclaimed. "Let her sit in it. I'm not being paid enough to put my hands on that". "Come on, man" I said. "It's a fucking baby. You're gonna let a baby sit in its own shit all day?" "It won't be all day" he said. "Marilyn's coming back in about 15 minutes. It's all grainy and shit too. It's gross. It looks like pudding with sand in it. Let the kid's mother clean that shit up, fuck that. "I'll clean it" I laughed. "It's not the baby"s fault" "I don't give a fuck whose fault it is" he said. "If you wanna clean up shit, go ahead. But, I'm not touching it. And, don't think I'm giving you any part of my baby sitting money for doing it either". I went into the kitchen and found some paper towels in a cabinet. Just as I was reaching for them, I heard the apartment door creak open. Marilyn had returned. She couldn't see me yet due to her view being obstructed from the hallway. I raced back to my seat. Ronnie jumped up acting concerned. When Marilyn got to the end of the hallway, he exclaimed "I was just about to clean up her mess. The poor kid pooped herself". By now, there was a large puddle of foul smelling feces under the swing. I was chuckling to myself at how Ronnie was lying. He had always been a great actor. "I'll get it" Marilyn said. "Did she just do this?" she asked. "Oh yeah" Ronnie said nervously. He looked over at me "Right, Ron?" he asked. I nodded my head in the affirmative. I was trying very hard not to continue laughing. "Ok" Marilyn said. "It's not your fault. I guess I shouldn't have fed her so much before I left. She reached in to her purse and handed Ronnie 3 dollar bills. "Thanks" Ronnie said. Again he tried to justify his predicament. "I would have cleaned it up for you. But, she did it like 5 minutes before you came home". "I understand" Marilyn replied. "Thanks for watching her. It's no problem really". We donned our coats, said goodbye, and headed out the door. "Let's go back to my place" Ronnie said. "I'm getting kind of hungry. I know there's some lunch meat in our refrigerator. We'll make some sandwiches and watch some TV. "Sounds good to me" I replied. So, we headed on over.

I slept over Ronnie's just as he had offered. He gave me his step brother's bed and had him sleep with his step sister. It was the above bunk in a pair of bunk beds. The morning came and we were going to cut school again. As we turned the corner to walk up the hill out of the apartment complex, I saw a red Chevrolet Impala barreling down the road toward us. "Hey Arold?" Ronnie asked. "That looks like your father man". "Fuck" I said. "I think that's him too. How the fuck did he find me?" "Mr. S. I bet" he added. "I bet he ratted you the fuck out. He's the only one who would have my address. Fucking rat! You better run man. Your dad looks pretty pissed off. If he catches you, you know he's gonna beat your ass". I was torn between escaping or getting in the car. The old man approached us and ground his car to a halt. He flung open the driver"s side door and stood up. "Get in this fucking car right now, Ronald" he demanded. "If you don't, I'm calling the cops and you're going to Jamesburg". Jamesburg was the Jamesburg School for Boys next to the town of Monroe. It was a detention center for misguided youths. Most teens were afraid to go there as you usually needed a court order from a judge to get out. I had heard stories of even if you managed to escape that the state police would find you. Sooner or later, you"d get pinched and right back in you would go. My father almost never bluffed. So, I got in the car. Ronnie was shaking his head in disgust. "He's playing you" I could hear him say as we drove away. "They always bluff, you'll see". We got home and I stood in our den in my parka waiting for my punishment. I was convinced that I was going to take my licks like a man. My father had gone upstairs to speak to my mother and had returned. As he approached me, I was afraid. "I'm ready to take my beating" I told him. "Oh you are now, are you?" he yelled. "We'll just see about that" he said. He raised his belt and gave me a good 10 bruise thrashing. I was good again for a week or two to satiate his anger. But, I was tenacious and I would not be perturbed.

I was awoken the next day to the sound of jangling in my bed. Every time I moved my legs, it would happen again. I pulled back the covers and couldn't believe what I saw. My father had chained my ankle to the bed frame. It was a strip of metal with holes in it that was flexible and bent around my leg. I could see that he had taken screws and nuts and tightened them through corresponding holes to make it all fit. I remember feeling like a prisoner or a slave. "He must have done it while I was in a deep sleep" I thought. "Otherwise, I would have heard him and felt it". I was beginning to get angry. I spoke to myself "Check this fucking guy out. He thinks he can keep me here so I don't run away again. He doesn't realize that I didn't run away for good. I only did it to get him off of me temporarily". What my father didn't know, was that I had a screwdriver in a cubby hole behind my head in the headboard. I had left it there from when I had been messing around with a CB radio previously. I reached back and opened the door, grabbed the tool and examined it. "Yup, this will do" I thought. "All I have to do is rap on the edges of the nuts at the end of the bolts and it'll eventually come loose". I knew it would work as I had done it before using a hammer when I couldn't find a pair of pliers or a wrench. It takes much longer, but it usually did the trick. I knew that he had gone to work. So, I didn't have to be afraid of my escape attempt with the possibility of him hearing me. I grabbed the chain and banged on the screwdriver end with the palm of my hand. It began to move. Slowly at first, and then it started to spin backwards from its threads. Fortunately, my father hadn't tightened them enough. So, they backed out easily. It was probably because he didn't want to wake me. That was one down, 5 more to go. When I had finished releasing myself from his amateur torture device, I dressed and went downstairs to our kitchen. My mother was there and on the telephone talking to a friend. She cupped her hand over the receiver and asked me how I got out. I laughed and told her "Amateurs can't keep me down". She uncupped her hand, told her friend "I'll call you right back", and told me "You're father said if you escaped, to keep you here. If you leave, I'll be in trouble with him". "Don't even try that guilt trip move, mom" I said. "I'm going out with my friends. You tell the old man, if he hunts me down and chains me up again, I'm calling the cops on him". "I think I can reason with him as long as you come back home, Ronald" she replied. "I'll come back later tonight" I said. "But, he's gotta stop with his temper bullshit". "We'll all talk about it later" she answered. "Just don't rile him up. You know how he gets". "Yeah, yeah" I moaned wryly "I've heard it all before".

Ronnie E. and I had found out that we could sneak swimming at the Ramada Inn on Woodbridge Avenue. It was actually against their policy to let anyone who wasn't a guest swim there. But, some friends had told us that as long as we didn't get too loud or draw attention to ourselves, the management would never be the wiser. So, being the usual scammers that we were, we headed right down there. This time, we took Phil M. with us. On our arrival, we had run out of nicotine. Ronnie was always short of cigarettes and had no qualms about dipping into used ashtrays to retrieve "Buttnicks". He'd reach down into the sand full of filters and exclaim "Look, it's the hairiest. This one was only smoked half way". When I asked him "why would you want to put something in between your lips that was in someone else"s mouth?" He proclaimed "I don't let it touch me, I finger it. It's a gershey mahuh!" When Ronnie's task was done, we sauntered over to the pool area and noticed there was no one around. We loved that we had the entire pool to ourselves including the diving board. A few times, a hotel worker came in and asked us to keep it down. We complied and were quiet for a while. That was until Ronnie decided to do what he called "a triple cannon ball fish". I asked him "What's a triple cannon ball fish?" He replied "You jump off the board as high as you can, flip three times, and then wag your legs toward people like a fin on a fish". "Impossible" I laughed. "There's no way you can do that on a low board like this". "Sure I can" he insisted. "Watch and learn". Phil was at the other end of the pool and yelled out laughing "He's gonna do a belly flop and sting his stomach. He'll cry like a little bitch. I can't wait to see this catastrophe" Ronnie ran and rounded the corner of the pool with great haste. He was screaming "Mah huh" like he always did when he was excited about something. He jumped on the board, bounced a few times, and flew into the air. He flipped once, twice, and then a half roll. He didn't make the third nor waved his legs like a fish. With a loud crack, he landed straight on his back. Phil and I were laughing hysterically. Phil said. "You know when he comes up from under the water, that shit's gonna sting like a motherfucker". "I hear that" I replied. "I think he'll be done swimming for the day". Ronnie surfaced with a grimace on his face. "Don't even fucking say it Arold" he cried. "It wasn't my fault. I slipped coming around the corner because I wasn't fast enough". "Uh huh" Phil laughed. "It looked to me like you slid like a fish instead of waving like one". "Shut the fuck up, Phil". Ronnie said. "I wanna see your little ass try it". "Not me" Phil replied "I'm not that stupid". After listening to Ronnie moan about his injuries, Phil got bored. He asked us to come out of the pool area and to follow him. "You know when I went to the bathroom before when we first got here?" he asked. "Well, I found a sauna room in the back. We should go use it to see how it works. I've never been in one of those before". "Me either" I replied. "How about you Ronnie?" I asked. "The only hot box I've been in is pussy" he said. "But, we can go check it out. Maybe it'll take away the burn in my back". We accompanied Phil to the spa and stepped inside. There was no one in there and we had it all to ourselves. Phil and I sat down on the benches while Ronnie was examining the steam making device. "This thing looks like a barbeque" he said. "I wonder how this fucking thing works" he asked. He lifted its lid and there were permanent type coals inside. There was also a ladle hanging on the machine"s side on a hook. "There's a little trench of water in here in front of these fake coals" Ronnie said. I bet you have to take the ladle and pour water over the rocks and that's what makes the steam". "Brilliant deduction" I replied sarcastically. "Ronnie's so smart" Phil said. "So smart, he can't even do a cannon ball fish". "Fuck you Phil, you little dick head." Ronnie yelled. "You better shut up before I burn your ass with this shit". "Come on man" I replied. "Can't we all just get along?" "Fine" said Ronnie. "Now, leave me the fuck alone. I'm gonna sit down and relax".

It was starting to get very hot in the steam room and I mentioned that maybe it was time for us to go. "Not yet" Ronnie exclaimed. "I wanna try something". "What's he up to now?" Phil asked. "I don't know" I answered. "He's always up to some kind of shit". "Watch this" Ronnie exclaimed. He pulled out his dick and started pissing on the hot coals in the machine. It began to stink. "Wow" Phil laughed "That's fucking gross man. It's steaming piss!" Ronnie was chuckling uncontrollably. "Fuck the Ramada Inn" he said. "This is what they get for making their pool deck so slippery". The more he urinated on the rocks, the more of a piss cloud emerged from the machine. The room was becoming full with egesta tinged steam and it was starting to make us gag. Suddenly, Phil and Ronnie bolted for the door. I heard it slam quickly behind them. I was wondering what this was all about and stood up to follow them. They were laughing through the lone window in the center of the door. "What the fuck are you guys doing?" I asked. They wouldn't answer and continued with their comedy and mocking me by making ugly faces. I pushed on the door to leave. But, it wouldn't budge. They were holding the door closed with the weight of their bodies. "How does it smell in there?" Ronnie asked giggling. "Is it stinky?" "Come on man" I said. "It's getting pretty bad in here. Don't be jerkoffs". I had to put my t shirt over my face to be able to breathe. "Is it rank?" Phil asked. "Don't pass out, man" Ronnie replied. "You guys better let me out of here or else" I warned, "Or else what?" Ronnie asked. "You're not gonna do shit. You can't get out. You're gonna smell like piss though" he chuckled. I knew if I kept feeding into them, that they would continue with their charade. So, I sat back down on the bench and waited. A few minutes went by and they soon lost interest. When I saw that they weren't holding the door anymore, I made my move. I slung it open and escaped. I noticed as I was looking for them, I did indeed smell like piss. I wanted to kill them. I found them back by the pool laughing. "How"s that new cologne working out for you?" Ronnie asked. "I bet all the chicks will love it" Phil remarked. "Fuck you guys" I said. "Why the fuck did you do that to me?" I asked. "You guys are assholes". "You laughed at me when I hurt myself diving" Ronnie exclaimed. "I had to teach you a lesson". "A lesson?" I asked. "What the fuck man" I said. "Fucking Phil was laughing too. What about him? "He's smaller than you" Ronnie snickered. "So, you deserved it more". "Fucking Ronnie logic again huh?" I asked. "Yup" he said "It's never failed me yet". "Don't stand too close to us either" Phil laughed. "We don't want your stink to rub off on us". "He's Old Piss Spice now, Phil" Ronnie crowed. "You'll get yours eventually Ronnie" I threatened. "Yeah, yeah. Same old bullshit, Arold" Ronnie replied. "Now, stop being a baby and let's go home. We're done for the day."

The following year I was "socially promoted" to the 8th grade. I was 14 years old. I've always felt that a social promotion was just the school administration's way of getting rid of the bad kids. It was a way for them to move us along to high school and pass along the problem. During this school year, I met more and more people. Some became my friends and some became my enemies. Most of them I met through Ronnie or from hanging out in TJ"s smoking bathroom. I also made friends with kids who had problems and were relegated to Mr. S's or Mr. Campbell's class. In Special Ed classes, the 7th, 8th, and 9th grade kids were all lumped into the same room and there was no separation of grades. I guess it was easier for the school to keep an eye on us that way. This year I met Billy F. He was added to our class along with a few others. During this winter, Mr. S. was put in charge of ski trips to the Vernon Valley ski area. It wasn't just for us Special Ed kids though, it was for everyone. When Billy and I heard of a ski excursion coming up, we were interested immediately. Billy mentioned to me that he had skied some before. I had also done some skiing on a small hill in Jamesburg at Thompson Park with my parents when I was 11. So, I had some basic ski skills. We were very excited to go on this trip because we knew it would be another adventure and it was something we had never done before. Billy and I had it all planned out. We would bring some joints and a couple of pints of blackberry brandy. Booze was pretty easy to get in the early 70's as the drinking age was only 18. There was always an older friend or a brother who could supply it for us. As we pulled up to the ski resort, we were amazed at how big it was. We knew we could easily disappear from chaperone eyes to smoke weed and drink without the possibility of being caught. Billy and I rented our skis and boots and continued to the chair lifts. We had never seen a chair lift like this before. Each lift chair was covered by a polymer type orb. The park called it the Big Bubble. It closed over you like you were inside a space ship while your skis dangled below. I guess it was designed to keep skiers protected from the harsh winter elements. Billy and I were in heaven. "What better place to get stoned without having to worry about being seen?" We thought. It was flawless and we loved it! Soon, Billy lit up a joint. As we passed it back and forth he inhaled the smoke deeply. He looked at the white tufts of snow below us and was amazed at our altitude. He chortled "Don't get too stoned there bro. I wouldn't want you to fall out of this thing!"

As we came to the top of the mountain, we slid off the lift and chose which way to go. Being stoned, it took us a few minutes to get our bearings. Once we settled on an area, Billy said "Damn, it's cold up here Ronnie Boy, time to whip out that blackberry brandy bro". We downed our two bottles in about 15 minutes. As we transcended down the mountain, I lost sight of Billy as he was a much better skier than I was. He was really flying ahead of me and I tried to keep up with him. I was fairing pretty well until I saw a rock wall approaching on my right. I knew I was going to be forced to maneuver around it somehow. I tried to stop. But, it was too late. About 10 feet from the wall, just as I felt confident that I was going to make it, I fell. And, I fell hard. I felt a sharp pain. I had twisted my left leg around the middle of my back. I was done. Other skiers came by to offer aid. They saw that I was immobilized on the ground and that I was splayed out on my back like a criminal on a cross. One of them stayed with me while his partner went for help. I was put into a red basket by the ski patrol and whisked down the hill to the medical area. After causing the bus to be two hours late, I was hoisted into one of the buses seats for the trip back home. Billy asked "What the fuck happened to you up there?" I mumbled "too much weed, and too much brandy". My skiing career was over.

The Christmas holidays came and went and we were back in school. Ronnie was in the smoking bathroom with me again trying not to get his cigarette hot when in flies a guy with a large afro. "But, he's white?" I thought. I had never seen a white guy with an afro before. He introduced himself to me and said "Hi, I'm Dennis G. Some call me fro bro". He had a very comedic disposition and I liked him immediately. He was a naturally funny guy and the kind of person you"d want to always hang around with. He was that entertaining. He had a gift of making faces that matched the circumstances going on around him. He was very intuitive and I wished I had had half of his charisma. As he smoked his cigarette half hiding in the stall, his eyes rolled up and down and he looked a lot like Harpo Marx. As he passed his cigarette to others so they could get a quick drag in, he exclaimed "Don't get it hot, don't get it hot. And, don't lip it either". It was like watching a standup comedian. What I think drew most kids to him was that he was always this way. I"d piss my pants laughing with some of the rants that came out of his mouth. Dennis G. was the surely the flame and we were the moths.

During this time, I was traveling through Edison a lot and discovering neighborhoods I had never been in before. I was meeting new teens like Phil, Paulee, Jackie Boy, and Mickey. I met them all through Ronnie E. as Ronnie knew just about everybody. Phil looked like a mini Paul McCartney but with much longer hair. Paulee was another good looking kid. He had a very sarcastic sense of humor and had no qualms about speaking his mind to you. If you didn't like it, he simply didn't care. Jackie Boy was known as Jackie the Neat. Of course he didn't know this as we called him that behind his back. This was because his hair and clothes were always perfect. By now, all of us had extended length hippie hair parted in the middle. He was the only one of us with layered; feathered back hair above his collar and half way over his ears. He was also a real ladies man and always somehow got the pussy. Sometimes, I was jealous of him. It was like girls gravitated to him and he didn't have to try. He had the gift.

We would usually meet on the street corner of TJ in the early morning. There, we would decide if we wanted to cut school or not. Once we decided not to attend, we'd sneak down to a luncheonette that a woman named Minnie owned. It was on Route 27 across from the Dunkin Donuts. Minnie was a short, Italian woman who could have a mean streak if she didn't get her way. She also spoke with an Italian accent. Pinball was all the rage then and Minnie had 3 pinball machines placed by the back door. This is where we spent our lunch money given to us by our parents. We'd usually buy a pack of cigarettes shared between us, and enough coins left over to last at pinball for the day. Occasionally, Minnie would want to close up early and would attempt it around noon. She would yell to us from behind the counter "It's time to wrap it up fellas. No more pinballs". We would argue with her until she let us finish our games. I guess since there were hardly ever any customers she wanted to go home.

Dismayed by Minnie closing, we had to find something else to do to occupy our time. When all ideas within walking distance failed, we usually voted for the shopping malls. Out of desperation, we could always depend on them for kicks a few times a month. There was a brand new mall that had opened a year or two earlier called Woodbridge Center. Before Woodbridge Center, we would take the M10 public transportation bus to a smaller, closer mall named Menlo Park. On the bus on the way there, laws were different then. You were allowed to smoke on the bus as long as you sat in the back with a window open. Like most teens trying to emulate adults, we smoked as much as we could. Menlo to us was just an ok mall since it wasn't very large. Therefore, we would get bored easily. We did a few petty crimes like shoplifting small items from there. But, Menlo didn't offer much and had pretty good security.

When Woodbridge Center opened, it was a whole other ballgame. Eventually, we started to bypass the stop to Menlo, and went straight to Woodbridge instead. Woodbridge Center to us 14 year olds was massive! None of us had ever been in a shopping center that large before. On our maiden trip to this new shopping extravaganza, we did the usual teenager traits like visiting the head shops first. They were the ones with their posters, pot pipes, and black lights for sale. We always knew when these stores were starting to get close as you could smell the incense as you approached them. We also hit the big department stores as they usually had the latest technology available. Back then, the most popular items were things like Texas Instrument calculators. They were so expensive; they were tethered by a wire to deter being stolen. The popular style for winter coats then were large parkas with lots of pockets. You can see where I'm going with this. Mickey B. was obsessed with the calculators. He had figured out a way to detach the security cables without store staff or security noticing. These were the days before security cameras. We would all stuff as many calculators in our pockets as possible and slowly walk away. We always tried to be discreet as we didn't want to stand out too much. We would then move onto another store with a jewelry counter. Phil M. loved jewelry. I think he realized it paid the most when he fenced it all for cash. Phil had a system like Mickey but much more ballsy. We would distract the jewelry sales person while Phil went around the other side of the glass display cases. In those days, the sales people never bothered to lock the sliding doors in the back that accessed the trays of jewelry. Phil was a short guy. So, most customers didn't even notice him. He would reach over the counter while lying on his belly, slide the glass door open, and grab as many items as possible. This kid had it down to a science. He was in and out in about 15 seconds flat. He never got caught. Not once! Myself? I was the black light poster pilferer. I loved anything that lit up. Like neon lights, fire, etc. Ronnie E. was also proficient at poster stealing. He's the one who showed me how to stuff a poster down my pants leg, cover it with my parka, and walk out like I had a limp. I also liked pot pipes. The popular craze back then was the metal pot pipes that screwed apart in the center. The pot pipes were a little harder to abscond with though. But, we were still successful occasionally. Jackie Boy G. didn't usually steal anything as he was more of a lookout he told us. He'd usually warn us about nosey people or guards approaching close by. I don't remember Paulee coming with us to the malls. Paulee was a skirt chaser too. He was probably in some teen age girl's bed at the time instead.

In an area of Camp Kilmer, there was a large, square, asphalt driving instruction course. The Army had used it for teaching soldiers how to drive Jeeps and trucks. Across from this was very high, red clay, dirt hill that had a tall tree on its left side on the top. This was the place where everyone rode their motorcycles and mini bikes for fun. As I mentioned before, Camp Kilmer was abandoned. So, it was the ideal spot to ride there. Because it was still federal property, there were no nosey local cops lurking around patrolling. My older brother Robert had a mini bike before me and I was enamored by it. So, I wanted one too. Phil M. had a purple one; Mickey B. had a purple one as well, but with a regular bicycle wheel in the front, and Paulee B. had a motorcycle. When it was my turn to get a mini bike, my father brought home a second hand one. It was brown, rather tattered, and it never ran more than twice. I was never able to get it off of our driveway. A few weeks later, imagine my surprise when my father brought home a brand new one. I still wanted a motorcycle like Paulee. But, this was the coolest mini bike I had ever seen. It was red and white and had a "kick start". I was the envy of the mini bike kids. No one had ever seen a mini bike with a kick start before.

After school had let out for the summer, all of us would go riding (as Phil would always say). We'd gather at Phil's apartment and take the back roads through TJ"s field. One day, we met Paulee on Camp Kilmer's driving course and he was doing wheelies. I think his bike was a Kawasaki. After a while, a black kid came up to Paulee and asked him if he could take his bike for a spin. Paulee agreed and the kid said he would be right back. 10 minutes went by, 20, 30, an hour. Poor Paulee was constantly checking the horizon for that kid who had his bike. All the while, he was hoping the kid would come back. The problem was, he never did. So, Paulee was forced to call the police. We laughed about it but the bike was never found and we secretly felt bad for him. None of us could believe he actually let a stranger take his motorcycle. Especially since how cocky he could be. I guess Paulee had been too trusting that day.

About a half an hour later, I saw what appeared to be a homemade go cart with a large engine on its back. As it got closer, I noticed there were two people riding in it. It was a guy named John K. in the front driving and Bob N. in the back. Bob N. was Anthony N's brother from when I attended John Marshall School. As I peered at the go cart, I realized it had a transmission and a shifter with two gears! I had never seen anything like it before. Amazingly, they had built it themselves! When they stopped for a bit, I asked Bob "Where did you get the engine for that?" He answered "You know that new Pathmark warehouse they are building behind my house on Fairview Avenue? Have you ever seen those cement mixers they are using?" "Yeah, I replied. "I know that place". "Well, you use your imagination" he laughed as him and John drove away. As they turned a corner, I could hear Bob screaming over the engine "C'mon, Hife! Let's roll!" I never did find out what Hife meant. But then again, Bob was known for making up his own language. A few hours later, in the distance, I saw them coming back. I couldn't make out what it was at first trailing behind them. As they got closer and closer, it looked like a huge, rectangular block. Finally, they pulled up and asked "What do you think?" I replied "What the hell is it?" It was attached by a trailer hitch to the back. Bob shouted "It's a trailer, We're going camping. Can't you see? It's obvious!" As they drove away with the sound of grinding gears, I was crying and holding my side from laughing so hard. I thought "I can't believe these are some of the kids I'm growing up with!"

By now, it was the middle of the summer. July I think. Ronnie E. had lived off of Woodbridge Ave. in Edison in the Silver Lake Ave. neighborhood. At the end of this road, was a very large natural gas holding tank that belonged to some natural gas conglomerate. There was a small lake in front of this tank where sometimes teens would congregate. I guess it was the Silver Lake the road leading up to it had been named after. Someone had always left a small row boat tied to its shore facing the street and farthest from the tank. Ronnie must have discovered it one day and he began using it. He told Jackie Boy G. and I a story while at school about how he talked two girls into taking a ride in this row boat with him and Phil M. One of the girls had sunlight blonde hair and the other was a brunette. The brunette lived in Ronnie's section and the blonde girl was visiting. Both of these girls kept teasing Ronnie and Phil alluding to the possibility of giving them sex. After Ronnie and Phil got the girls into the open water into the boat, they demanded "You're gonna give us some pussy or you're gonna swim back. We're tired of you teasing us".

The brunette mentioned she was 13 and so was the blond. Ronnie was 15 and Phil was 14. It was obvious from their talk that the 2 girls were virgins. After much pleading, the girls agreed to have sex with them. Ronnie rowed the boat back to shore while Phil sat toward the bow making rude gestures. After exiting the boat, the girls willingly took off their clothes. Ronnie and Phil then fucked them on the beach ravenously. Ronnie went on about how "We fucked these girls a second time in an abandoned house right next door to mine. It had an old mattress in it. We used rubbers though because they didn't want to get preggers. But, it was still amazing. I could probably talk these girls into giving you guys some pussy too" he said. They like to fuck. So, come by tomorrow in the afternoon". Jackie Boy and I were giddy over the prospect of banging young girls and said "Sure!" We couldn't wait to indulge. We arrived at the abandoned house the next day just like Ronnie had planned and Ronnie was laughing hysterically. "Come and look at Phil getting some pussy. He's really going at it!" We turned the corner to where the bedroom was and could make out a faint outline of a mattress on the floor. As we gazed upward, there was the blonde. She was on her back with her pants down around her ankles and Phil was on top of her pumping away.

Ronnie shouted out "Check out Phil! His ass is like a little motor boat and he comes in 5 seconds, hahaha!" The blonde was moaning "Oh, fuck me baby, fuck me good!" While this was transpiring, Ronnie whispered in my ear "Hey man, her friend is in the other room, bro. I found another mattress with a box spring underneath it and I just finished with her. Go in and fuck her" He handed me a rubber and I complied. She was lying on the bed with her slate blue, button downed shirt opened with her tits hanging out and she was naked from her waist down. Her legs were already spread open and she was waiting. I was very nervous as I was a virgin and I wasn't quite sure what to do. She seductively motioned me over to the bed. She told me "it's ok" and to come and get some. I laid on top of her and began to suck on her tits. I remember that they were very soft. After a few minutes, she asked me to "put it in". I slipped the rubber on and went to town and I came in 2 minutes. Being that I was only 14, I thought it was the most wonderful thing in the world. I mumbled to myself "I had finally gotten some pussy! I can thank Ronnie for losing my virginity!

After we were done, I thanked the brunette and went back to where the other guys were. By this time, Jackie Boy was on top of the blonde and taking his turn. He was a smooth fucker and was taking his time. He liked to "soak in the pussy" as he would say. After he was finished and rolled off of Blondie, Ronnie told her "Now it's time for you to fuck me, and then Ronnie A. I want my friend to get maximum pussy on his second try." The blonde decided she wasn't sure if she wanted to have sex anymore because "it was damp in the room" and started complaining. So, Ronnie and Jackie Boy took away her pants she had taken off back when it was Jackie Boy's turn. They went outside and threw them on the roof. Ronnie came back inside and said "You're not getting your pants back until you give us more pussy". Blondie laughed "If you're gonna be a jerkoff, come back and finish me off then. You're lucky I'm still horny. But, make it quick, because it's getting cold in here". Ronnie snapped on a rubber and began banging away while the rest of us went outside to have a smoke. He was very loud and we could hear him through the windows outside. He was moaning "Ahhh yes, yes, that's right, make me come. You got it. Move those hips, baby!" After he climaxed, he yelled for me to come back inside. He said it was my turn now. By this time, I felt bad for her because of the cold and I was trying to leave. Ronnie would have none of that. He demanded I go back in and "Pump her good. "You probably won't have pussy again for a long time" he said. So, you better get back in there". I went back in and asked her if it was ok and if she didn't mind. She said it was fine and I was cute for asking. She demanded I put on a rubber and motioned for me to get going. I laid on top of her, stuck it in, and gave her my best. This time though, I lasted much longer. I remember that compared to her friend she had very hard tits. They weren't soft like her friend's were. When we were done, we got to talking. Ronnie had brought her pants back in while we were fucking. As she was getting dressed, I asked her if she would date any of us. She said she had to think about it. She asked that I not tell anyone what went on. Though the sex was consensual, she didn't want her parents to find out. Later, I saw her again in school. She never spoke to me again. I guess she was embarrassed.

On our second trip to Woodbridge Center, it was the same crew as our first trip minus Mickey B. Except this morning, we brought along a new guy. His name was David W. Dave W. was a skinny guy, about 5 feet 10, 120 lbs., with freckles on his face and light brown collar length hair. He was the kind of kid who bounced as he walked and was full of energy. Like the rest of us, he was sarcastic, rude, cynical, despised authority, and had a very quick wit about him. "Yup" I thought "He fit right in". As we stepped off the M-10 bus, we negotiated amongst ourselves where we would go first. Phil seemed annoyed and wanted to use the nearest bathroom. So did Ronnie. So, we followed behind them to the nearest lavatory. Jackie Boy and Dave waited outside since they informed us they didn't have to go. The remaining three of us stood in a line pissing into our urinals. It was Ronnie all the way to the left, Phil in the center, and me to the right. Suddenly, Phil moaned in pain "Man, by balls itch" he exclaimed as her peered down at his crotch. Look! My ball sack is huge! Look how swollen it is!" What the fuck is wrong with them?" I asked. "Do you have VD or what? "Phil" I said "I'm not looking at that shit, fuck that you homo!" Ronnie laughed and was giggling at Phil"s misfortune. "Be quiet Phil, you pussy" he said. "Put some calamine lotion on that shit and shut the fuck up". Phil went on complaining and had tears welling up in his eyes. He was trying desperately to hide it "But, you guys don't understand, my balls are enormous! I'm in serious pain, they're sore as a motherfucker! I scratched them so much from itching, they are raw! They look like balloons!"

As I was laughing at Phil"s condition, I asked Ronnie "Why does he need calamine lotion for his balls?" He blurted out "Remember those two girls we fucked at Silver Lake a while ago? Well, it seems while Phil was fucking that one girl, his balls were rubbing beneath her on the grass. It turned out the grass was poison ivy! Hahaha!" After we were done relieving ourselves, we zipped back up and headed toward the exit. Ronnie announced loudly "Phil"s new name is now Itchy". The guys outside asked "Why the fuck is that?" Phil, with a contorted face exclaimed "Shut the fuck up Ronnie, I don't need anyone else knowing about this shit!" Phil then turned to me quietly "Hey Arold, do me a favor; keep this shit to yourself man. If these other guys find out, they won't leave me alone for the rest of the fucking day. I owe you bro". As I tried to hold back my laughter, I nodded in agreement and we went on our way.

We usually spent our time exploring the ground floor of the mall first and the second tier later. As we were walking, we came upon a variety store that had a few pinball machines we could see through the window on the front right side. As we entered and started looking around, Phil called all of us over by a change machine that was about waist high. We thought he was getting quarters for the pinball machines. He became very excited and was insistent on telling us something. "I have the scam of the day" he chuckled. He pulled a piece of paper out of one of his pockets that was about the size of a dollar bill and it had a faded out black and white pattern on it. What's that? Dave asked "That doesn't look like money". "Shhhhhhh, said Phil. "Not so loud. I don't want anybody to see this except you guys". Phil stepped in front of the change machine and slipped the paper into the money slot to get change returned. The bill got sucked in and 4 quarters popped out below. "Look!" he proclaimed "Free money! Scarf!" Ronnie was skeptical of this and asked Phil "How the fuck did you do that? That bill looked fake as fuck!" Phil explained "I photocopied a dollar bill. Some machines haven"t been set to figure that out yet. I think it's because its new technology and they haven"t gotten the bugs out yet. It works on some machines, but not on others. Do you want free money or what?" I asked Phil "How many times can you do that? Phil laughed and said "As many coins as we can get. There's no limit man". While the rest of us were pretending to play pinball, Phil wandered stealth fully back over to the change machine. We were watching his every move. When he thought he had drained the machine sufficiently enough to weigh down his pockets, we left the store while patting him on his back. I asked him "How much do you think you got?" "About 20 bucks" he replied. Ronnie exclaimed "Good job Phil. Now, we have cash for the day".

As the morning progressed, Ronnie kept saying "Charlie fish, Charlie fish". At the time, it was a quote from a popular tuna fish commercial. Sometimes, we had a habit of picking up phrases and comments we heard from the media and used them. Usually, we'd do this for about two weeks before it became annoying or someone came up with a new one. "Fish, fish" Dave kept repeating to himself. "We have to do something with fish!" "We need to find a pet store" he said. In designated areas of the mall, there were monument looking pillars. They were square with maps of the mall inlaid in them under Plexiglas. Most malls have these to make it easier for you to plan where you're going. Dave gingerly ran his finger down the names of the stores on the map "Here, here" he said pointing to a red square with a name next to it. "Right here. Here"s a pet store that probably has fish" he said. It's in the West wing. Let's go there". We all agreed and followed Dave to the storefront.

Upon entering this pet land, Dave saw rows of tanks in the back of the store. They were indeed aquariums laden with various species of fish. He asked us "How much would you give me if I ate a live goldfish?" Right away Ronnie said "Dave you sick fuck, I'll give you a dollar out of that money Phil scrapped up if you do it in front of the customers". Dave walked over to the goldfish tank. As he stood in front of it smiling, he pulled out a two-inch goldfish and remarked "Follow me". He made his way to the front of the store where there were a few people waiting in line to make purchases. Like a carnival barker on a midway strip, he announced "I, the great David will now perform a feat unknown to mortal men". He then proceeded to open his mouth, drop in the goldfish, and swallowed it whole. After a few "Ewwww"s and that's disgusting!" from some of the customers, Dave took a bow, pointed at the cashier, and said "My man Phil over here will pay you now. But, I will require a second goldfish to accompany me for my next trick out of the store". Phil paid the clerk the 50 cents needed for the purchase, grabbed a second fish from the tank, put it in a plastic bag of water, and left carrying it with him.

As we were all laughing while walking again, Phil and Jackie Boy decided they were hungry. Phil spied a hot dog stand close by that appeared to have what he wanted. He bought a hot dog for him, and one for Jackie Boy. As they got to the condiments area, there were four square trays laid out before them. Inside, there were onions, relish, chili, and sauerkraut. They prepared their hot dogs to their liking and wolfed them down expeditiously. While this was going on Dave informed us he had another idea. He declared "With wit (a play on his last name), I have a feature presentation". He explained that he would be taking the lone goldfish "For a swim in Germany". "Germany?" we said. "What the fuck are you talking about Dave?" Dave took the goldfish from Phil, held it up by its tail and told it "Alas my friend, the sacrifices we make for our youth". He then dropped the goldfish in the sauerkraut bin and closed its door.

A portly woman who had just received her order was heading toward the condiments area. Knowing what was about to happen, we stood far to her left for the expected rude outcome. As she scanned the various choices of toppings, the woman asked herself "Should I have chili, or sauerkraut?" Ronnie whispered under his breath "Neither you fat fuck, go for a walk instead". As the rest of us were trying to withhold our laughter, the woman finally decided on the sauerkraut bin. She lifted the top of the container, grabbed the tongs with her free hand, and peered inside. Abruptly, she let out a loud wail "Oh my god, there's a fish in here!" By the sound of this, everyone in the mall was now craning their necks to see. She turned on her left heel while trying to balance her hot dog in her left hand and began to berate the owner "This is disgusting!" she screamed "How could you let this happen with customers in here?" she asked. She became even more agitated. So much so, when she attempted to turn around to point to the direction of the problem, she lost her balance and her hot dog flew to the ground. That is when she really lost it "I want a refund" she demanded. "I want a refund and I'm not cleaning that up! Do you hear me?" she screamed. The proprietor, not wanting to aggravate the scene any further, opened the register and dutifully complied. The plump woman accepted his apology, leered at us as she walked by, and continued on her way.

Finished with this episode of hilarity, Phil decided he wanted to visit a candy store he knew of in the mall. Just like kids to the Pied Piper in a trance for a reward, we strode up the escalator to the second floor following quickly behind him. After we arrived, we waited outside the confectionary for Phil to return. Soon, he came back with a bag full of M & M's. He motioned for us to follow him to the railing. As we complied he asked "Help me look underneath us for a woman with big tits. I have a surprise for her". Not having any idea of what he was talking about, we inspected the people below. One by one we watched trying to find Phil the perfect candidate. "Here comes one" Jackie Boy muttered. "And, she's got some big ones too!" Looking down, Phil opened the bag of M&Ms. "Watch this!" he yelped. We watched as woman with large breasts was traveling directly beneath him. They were like massive balloons with a nice Y cleavage. He took out a few M & M's and aimed for her chasm "Bombs away!" he screamed. The M &M's fell precisely to their intended target. The woman picked at her shirt wondering what was going on. I screeched "Direct hit! You sunk her battleship!" As we spin around high fiving ourselves for Phil"s success, the woman was on to us. She looked up bleating "I'm calling security. "You kids aren't funny". She then sped away out of view.

Not to be outdone by Phil's competition, Ronnie smirked "That ain't shit. Wait here you guys. I'll be right back!" We shrugged our shoulders wondering what Ronnie was up to. Ronnie demanded from Phil "Give me a couple dollars in coins; I have to go get something". Phil agreed and handed Ronnie the money. Ronnie reappeared a few minutes later with a large ice cream cone in hand. It was vanilla with assorted sprinkles on top and was already starting to melt and was dripping down his hand. "Step aside fools" Ronnie said. "Let me show you how it's really done!" We all laughed having an idea of what he was going to do. "Find me a victim" Ronnie said. "But, this time, make it a man". I knew if Ronnie did something to a guy, the guy would probably chase us. When challenged, Ronnie liked to live dangerously. It made me a little nervous.

As with Phil, we scoured the floor below us for the perfect casualty. "Hey, how about that one?" Dave pointed out. "Nah", said Ronnie. "He has too much hair. I want a guy with a smooth landing". "Smooth landing?" Phil asked. What? Like a bald guy?" "Yeah", Ronnie sneered. "It'll be more fun that way". Eventually, we found what Ronnie was looking for. Right there, was a man of about 5 feet 8 wearing jeans and a brown waist length leather jacket, and bald as a baby's behind. He looked to be in his mid 40's. "Perfect" Ronnie whispered. He was like Renfeld rubbing his hands together waiting for the horror to begin. "I have him in my cross hairs" Ronnie said. At just the right position, he dropped the cone right on queue. "Geronimo" he screamed. "Beat that douchebags!" The cone landed directly onto the center of the bald man's head. After impact, he looked like a clown you see at the circus, or one of those party hats you wear at a small kid's birthday party. The cone steadied itself for a few seconds and then it began to slide down the right side of his face. It was dripping channels of ice cream mixed with sprinkles. Like small rivers of white goo and glitter on its surface, it slid off his shirt, then down to the floor. The man looked confused and startled as he shook it off and looked up at us. "You little fuckers!" he screamed loudly "I'm gonna get you!

Since the man was downstairs, he had no choice but to run up the nearest escalator to attempt to apprehend us. While people were watching, he traipsed up the automated stairs while pointing at us and cursing "There they are. I'll get you bastards". As he grew near, Ronnie had a plan. He told us "When he gets close, run with me to the other escalator that goes down. I'll show you what I mean when we get there". When the man was almost to the top of the stairs, he began to huff and puff. This didn't stop him and he started to get closer. I was getting worried. Right when the man was about 20 feet away, Ronnie blurted out "Now! Follow me!" In the 70's, before security and the mall found out, there was a space between all of the escalators where you could slide down to the bottom. This is where we escaped from the ice cream man. We slid down laughing and taunted him to chase us. The bald man couldn't follow us as he was too large to fit into the opening. At the bottom, Dave jumped up and down yelling "We're free, We're free. Bye bye ice cream man!" We waved at the man and then ran to the other side of the mall.

After hiding in one of the mall's bathrooms for about an hour, we waited to see if the coast was clear. I stuck my head out slowly and didn't see anyone of any consequence. I didn't see many people and there certainly weren't any guards or authority figures to contend with. Therefore, it didn't appear as if the ice cream man had called security. "Maybe he was too embarrassed?" I thought. We purposely ran to this particular bathroom as it was close to a large anchor department store where the bus stop was. We knew if the jig was up it would be a lot easier to get outside to escape. We were lucky though, as no one ever came. Dave thought it would be safer for us to linger in the store"s lower level until our home bus had arrived. We all agreed. So, we eventually left the bathroom and lurked around while waiting. He constantly looked over his shoulder as a precautionary measure and exclaimed. "I'm not gonna let that ice cream man catch me, no sir. If I have to, I'll dodge him in the bedding area". "Maybe you can tire him out until he falls asleep" laughed Phil. "I'll suffocate him with a pillow instead" Dave replied. "That should do it if he's brave". While exploring the cellar level, he came upon a display about bicycles that were on sale. Above the bikes was a large sign written in Old English lettering. It read "Ye Old Bike Shop". Dave being another one of my friends that insisted on coining phrases, called everything he saw "Ye Old". He insisted on doing it for weeks. "Ye old TJ, Ye Old Marlboros, Ye Old Burger King., Ye Old everything. He drove all of us crazy!

One afternoon, I was invited over to Phil's apartment. He shared this two bedroom abode with his parents on the second floor apartment house behind the Burger King on Plainfield Ave. After being invited in, I followed Phil and entered his bedroom and I noticed that he had a Quadrophonic stereo system. He put on David Bowie"s Ziggy Stardust album and moved the toggle in all different directions. It was amazing and sounded like the music was going spherically around the room. I was entranced by it. Soon, he asked me to accompany him to his kitchen. On the way, I almost tripped over what appeared to be a small kitten. As the kitten turned to follow us, I saw that its left paw was deformed and turned inward. I asked "What happened to him?" he laughed and said "Oh, that's Woodstock. Don't leave your weed lying around. He'll eat it on you". I laughed at the idea of a stoned kitten with a deformed paw being high and continued on.

He called me over to a dresser in his parent"s bedroom. There, he pulled open a top drawer and stuck in his hand. When he pulled it out, he had a clutch of 100 dollar bills and asked "What do you think of these?" Wow!" I replied. How many of those have you got? Let's go party!" I can't use around here" he said. "Me and Billy F. used one of them at Burger King a few weeks back. I guess they must have caught it because somebody ratted us out". "What did they do to you?" I asked. "The feds came to our apartment and made my father pay the money back. Then, they asked me where I got it from. My family has a bar in New Brunswick that my parents are part owners of. So, the bad bills came from there from when drunks try to pass them off for drinks". "Then, how did you get more of these?" I asked "Well" he replied. "We didn't have any more when the secret service came. But, recently my dad brought home some more". How are you gonna cash them if you won't use them around here then?" I asked. "Oh" he laughed. "I have a new scam that works, bro. But, you can't tell anyone, ok? I take them to Seaside and use them at the games on the boardwalk. There's so many people going in and out of there that they couldn't remember who had what even if they wanted to. Plus, it's all teenagers working the wheels. So, they won't recall who I was and they don't care anyway". "Man" I sighed. "You must make a lot of money that way". "I've made a few thousand" he chuckled. "But, I just can't do it too long or too many times. The cops will due a surveillance sting if I get too greedy". Now, let's go in the other room. I wanna show you something" he said.

I sat down at the kitchen table as he reached into a cabinet and pulled out a large bottle of vodka. Grinning, I could see the mischief in his eyes and I knew this wasn't going to be good. He asked me if I"d do a dare for two packs of Black Cat firecrackers. "It depends on what the dare is?" I asked. "Well" he said. "If you can down an entire glass of vodka" "They're yours". Being that firecrackers are illegal in N.J. and hard to come by, I took him up on it. He then laughed "Ahhhhh, but I set the amount". He then proceeded to pull a large glass out of another cabinet. It was one of those 20 ounce ones from the Shell gas station you got every time you filled up your car with gas. He opened the bottle and poured some to the brim. "I want you to down this entire glass without stopping" he demanded. If you succeed, you can have the firecrackers". Being that I didn't like to be challenged, I stupidly complied. I chugged it down in a few gulps and smiled as I put down the glass. "I did it with no problem" I said.

It didn't hit me until about a half hour after I got home from his apartment. I walked in the door to my parents" house and was yelled at by my father immediately. He didn't speak much then. So, I knew if he was yelling, he must have been pissed off about something all day. My father had a habit of displacing his anger onto innocent people sometimes who had nothing to do with his rage. It was nothing personal on his part. It was just part of his personality and was usually because you were in close proximity when he was in one of his 'moods'. Therefore, I didn't know if I had actually done something wrong, or if he was just pissed off in general. This particular time, he was upset because I had supposedly arrived home late for dinner. This was unusual, as my mother rarely cooked. It turned out he had made something and wanted to know where I was. I told him I was at a friend's house. He didn't appreciate my answer and decided I was to be punished. He had no idea I had a belly full of vodka and it was starting to affect me big time. I gave him the usual yeah, yeah, yeah and took my journey down the basement stairs. I usually went down there to avoid him when I didn't feel like hearing it anyway. As I heard him pontificating from behind the cellar door, I began to feel ill. The vodka was really hitting me and I was beginning to have double vision. Half drunk, I had a feeling that if I didn't puke up the large of an amount in my stomach, I"d probably be dead by morning. I segued to a concrete sink in the back of the basement between the washer and the dryer and stuck my right two fingers down my throat. I began to gag and it was nasty. Up came the vodka mixed with bile. It was acidic and tasted horrible. It was like something very sour and congealed at the same time. After three discharges, my belly was finally empty. I had a single sized bed on the other side of the room for cases just like this. So, I washed the puke off my face and went to lie down.

An hour passed, maybe more. I was so sick from the booze, I couldn't really remember. I had passed out for a bit. That much I was sure of. I rose up off of the bed, stood up, and steadied myself to the best of my abilities. I rambled sideways back up the basement stairs while clinging to the railing. With each step, I had remembered that it was skate night at Carolier Roller Rink and I desperately wanted to go. Carolier was stationed in North Brunswick and they sent buses to TJ to pick us up every Friday night. I guess the money they made off of teenagers for skate rental was worth the trip to retrieve us. But, I had my overly furious father to contend with first. With the usual motes operandi, I had to play his game. I had to jump through hoops with begging, pleading, and promises I"d do better in school to get my way. "I'll be good, I swear I'll change" etc. The usual bullshit I had no intention of honoring. Soon, my father was satisfied with his assessment, and I was free to go.

I staggered through the fence opening of TJ, up the back field, and to the Carolier designated pickup area. Most of my friends were already there waiting. Ronnie, Phil, Jackie Boy and a few local girls. It was the usual crew as always. Some asked "What the fuck happened to you? You look like shit!" I told them "Don't even ask. I'm wasted". After a short ride, the bus pulled up to the rink and we all got off for some skating. I usually liked this place as it was a premium destination to meet pretty young girls. It was also perfect pickings for dating and sexual liaisons. One night, a rather small girl with long blonde hair and blue eyes traversed through the middle of the crowd toward me. She had no qualms of interrupting the other skaters and wheeled right through them. Pushing them aside, she screamed to me "I love you!" I had no idea who she was as I had never met her before. She introduced herself as "Debbie". Such were incidents that happened to my friends and I on a continual weekend basis.

When our skating sojourn was over at about 11pm, Carolier"s bus would pack us in to take us all home. On the way, there was a company we'd pass on the highway named Johnson & Johnson. Yes, they were the maker of bandages. For some reason, J&J had a huge sign that read "Modess………Because". This sign was about 30 feet long and 10 feet high. It was that big. None of us were ever able to figure out what the words emblazoned on the sign meant. Until a guy on the bus named Vick F. claimed he knew. As we drove passed the sign, I heard Vick cry out "Modess………..Because…..It happens once a month!" Some of the girls told him he was disgusting. My friends and I thought it was hilarious. When Vick was done congratulating himself, he started nosing around the bus seats we were all sitting on. To Vick"s amazement, two of the seats had hinges on them which meant that they opened up. He was curious and wanted to know what was in there. "Are you gonna open it?" I asked. "You bet your ass" he replied. "There wouldn't be anything hidden in there if it wasn't important, bro". As he fiddled with its clasps, he asked some of us to distract the driver. He lifted the lid that doubled as a seat and found a compartment underneath. Inside, there were thick iron chains with hooks on both ends. "These must be for towing in case the bus broke down" he exclaimed. There were also some emergency road flares that were two to a pack. He decided he wanted to see if there were more compartments hidden under the other seats. But, there were too many teens in his way. Vick had somewhat of an intimidating presence with his broad shoulders and booming voice. So, when he asked the other kids to move, they didn't dare deny him. After all, he was on TJ's wrestling team. As the kids veered away from him, he went down the buses aisle searching one by one. He eventually stopped and found another stash of chains and flares under a second seat. This is where the real fun began. By this time, the bus had taken its exit off of Route 1 to Woodbridge Avenue. Vick had deduced that the seats with the compartments came loose and could be taken off of their foundations. I turned around as he was lifting one up and noticed that a window on the right side was open all the way down. He and another teen proceeded to shove the edge of the seat through the open window and it was dangling half way out. It was teeter tottering up and down on its center axis point. It was only a matter of time before it fell out. I heard the rest of the kids on the bus shouting "Do it, do it!" Vick and the other kid gave a big shove and the seat flew out the window and onto the road. As it landed on the pavement behind us, I watched it bouncing around like a jumping bean. Cars that were following were leaning on their horns and their drivers were cursing up a storm.

As the bus turned again from Woodbridge Ave. onto Plainfield Ave. heading toward the Route 1 intersection, Vick began to throw the tow chains through the window next. There was a loud jangly sound and sparks as they hit the street below. Drivers behind the bus were swerving and trying to avoid them. As we made the crossing over Route 1, there was an orange iridescent glow behind me. Vick had lit some of the road flares and was holding them out the window. He started bellowing "Tweak, tweak!" and was waving them in a circular motion for all to see. Even though we knew it was wrong, Phil, Ronnie, Jackie Boy, and I were laughing uncontrollably. That was until the bus was pulled over by the police. We hadn't seen the police cruisers flashing lights as the flare"s brightness had out shone them. Inside the bus, there was teen panic and pandemonium. Everyone was clamoring for the exit door and I thought "My father is going to kill me if I get caught up in this one". Suddenly, Phil motioned for me to come near him "The windows, the windows bro. Jump out, jump out! Its only two cops, they can't catch us all!" Me, Phil, Ronnie, Jackie Boy, and a few others, slipped out through the openings and down to the ground. In our desperation, it was almost comical. We looked like inexperienced Keystone Cops attempting an escape trying anything we could not to get caught. Once we were on the outside, we all ran like hell and made it to the safety of the woods behind Edison Lanes. We were relieved not to have been caught by Edison"s finest. "Man" Ronnie exclaimed. "We sure dodged a bullet with that one. We surely would have gotten a beating". Shortly after, the Carolier buses stopped coming. We never saw them again.

    On a balmy kind of day, where there was a slight haze in the sky and a gentle breeze enveloping us, Ronnie E. and I decided to go to the Great Eastern department store in New Brunswick. It was a humongous retail establishment that sat on a hill partially overlooking the Raritan River and wasn't too far across the bridge from Edison. Sometimes, we went there when we were cutting school and wanted something different. I was sitting on Ronnie's handlebars as he pedaled slowly and we entered the parking lot. We were taking our time and just soaking in the scenery. As we cycled forward, we saw what appeared to be a Coca Cola truck. Ronnie blurted out "Look! The side doors are open! The guy's not around. Let's scarf some drinks!" We approached the vehicle slowly, stopped, and I began to load a case of soda onto my lap. Once I felt it was secure and steady enough, we were off! Ronnie pedaled furiously away and was laughing with abandon. "Free soda, free soda" he exclaimed. Suddenly, the bike started to wobble. It seemed during our attempt to be elusive; we misjudged our balance and the weight of the soda in relation to the bike. I jumped off to readjust myself and the effervescent cargo as best as I could.

Just then, I heard a voice in the distance shouting "Hey you rotten kids, I see you. Put that soda back". It was the driver of the Coca Cola truck. He was rounding the corner of his vehicle and was almost upon us. "He's running pretty fast" Ronnie yelled "You better hurry up with that soda". I jumped back on the handlebars, steadied the case of Coke and yelled "Pedal faster, pedal faster, he's gonna catch us!" The case of soda began to teeter again. First it was veered left and then right. Bottles started to fall crashing to the pavement below. As I looked back to see where the driver was, I got a faint glimpse of him trying to navigate through the shards of glass and puddles of Coke under his feet. He was screaming at the top of his lungs "You bastards, you little bastards. I'm gonna get you!". Even though he was getting close, we couldn't help but laugh at his predicament. He kept tripping over the broken glass and righting himself in his futile attempt to detain us. He looked like an ice skater who had never skated before and he kept slip sliding away. He'd bend over, get back up. Bend over, and get back up. It was like wings on a plane coming in for a bad landing. His fingertips would touch the ground as he tried to regain his composure. Then, He'd slide back down again and repeat the same scenario. As much as he tried, he just couldn't stay balanced. Eventually, I dropped what was left of the soda and it hit the ground with a loud thud. With less weight distribution, we were able finally able to escape. The last I looked, the soda man was way behind us with no chance of seeing us again.

After school one afternoon, Ronnie E. and I decided to trek to Dennis G's house. This was my first time going there and he lived close to Route 1 not far from the Edison Diner. To me, it looked like a farm house on a corner lot with wooden stairs in the front leading up to a small porch with two mulberry trees adjacent to the left of the home. There was also a bank of vertical windows that seemed to wrap around its frontal exterior vertically. The house was painted red and white and the stairs were colored gray. I liked it immediately. As we drifted up the front yard toward the house and rounded its left corner, there before us was Dennis. He was smoking a cigarette and laughing. Suddenly, I heard a high pitched womanly shrill. It was very demanding and boisterous "Dennis?" it asked "You put that cigarette out right now. You know you're not supposed to be smoking". I didn't see the woman but I had gathered that it was his mom due to her authoritarian request. Dennis answered her "Just one more drag Ma, just one more drag and I'll put it out" Right before she looked out the window, he handed the cigarette to me. When his mother saw us she chortled "I told you no more smoking!" Dennis pointed at me, laughed and replied "I'm not smoking Ma, Ronnie A. is". This wasn't to be first time I was to laughingly take the blame. Later, there would be many more. We soon left and went to the diner to retrieve some coffee.

    A few days later, on a weekend, I went to Dennis G's by myself. I had never seen anyone inside his house except for his mother. This time, I meandered up the steps to knock on the front door. Dennis answered, "I'll be right out, bro". Behind the light tan wooden door, there was also a secondary screen door. He had left the front door slightly ajar with the screen door open behind him. While I was waiting, out of nowhere came a short, skinny old woman who looked to be in her late 70's or early 80's. She came at me furiously with a broomstick and was trying to hit me in my head. My first reaction was "WTF is this? I don't even know this woman?" As I tried to cover my head with my hands to protect myself from her blows, she was screaming in a very heavy European accent. "You kids, you rotten kids. Get out, get out!" Dennis suddenly flew through the door pushing me out of the way. I fell back against the porch"s railing as he hurriedly closed the two doors behind him "That's my grandmother" he laughed. "She's old and crazy. Don't pay attention to her. Let's go before she figures out how to get outside again".

    I had yet to meet Dennis' other family members other than his mom and grandmother. One Saturday, I went to his house again to see what he was up to. As I approached from the street, I could see a little boy with very long hair playing with Hot Wheels type cars under the porch"s stairs. I introduced myself as Ron A. and he answered back "I'm Dennis' brother Jeff". He then ignored me as he was engrossed in playing with his toys. I asked "What are those? Hot Wheels?" He refused to look up at me and sarcastically growled "Nooooooooo, these are Johnny Lightning cars!" As if I was stupid for not knowing the difference. Out of nowhere, from the side of their house came Dennis. He was running in circles in the yard and yelling at the top of his lungs "I'm Johnny Lightning! I'm Johnny Lightning!" Upon his head was a red helmet. It had a rotating cop light attached to its top and was just like the kind seen on the roof of police cars. Looking closer, I saw that it was held to his head with a chin strap from underneath his jaw. There were wisps of his afro poking out from under the sides and it looked far too tight for his head. The light was undulating around in its casing rapidly while making a clicking noise. Jeff caught sight of this and reacted angrily "Dennis!" he howled "That's my helmet that came with my cars. You better put it back or else. I'll tell mommy!" Still prancing around Dennis screamed back "What? I can't hear you! I'm at the race track! Tell mommy I need more fuel, hahahahaha!" Jeff climbed out from under the porch and started winging toy cars at him. He was aiming for his brother's head. "Gimme back my helmet! Gimme back my helmet, asshole!" Jeff screamed. Dennis yelled "I can't, I'm in first place. Throw me some more cars so I can beat you!" Eventually, and out of sheer exhaustion, Jeff gave up. It was only because Dennis had longer legs and could run faster. There was no way Jeff could have kept up with him. From that day forward, I remember thinking "If this is what it's like at their house every day, this is where I want to be". With the Gulotta family, I had never laughed so hard in my life.

Ronnie E. had discovered Livingston College in the old Camp Kilmer area and was telling us about it at Thursdays in the morning. Listening was me, Mike W., and Phil "They have a movie theater and a TV studio there" he proclaimed. "We should go there and check it out". "Is it free?" asked Phil. "Oh, yeah" Ronnie replied. "We can go there and hang out for the day. Fuck school. I'm bored with TJ." "I'm in" said Mike. "What about you two guys?" he asked Phil and I. "Yeah, I'm into it" I replied. "Me too" said Phil. "Whenever you're ready, let's go". We took the long walk to the large rows of brick buildings out by Joyce Kilmer Avenue and searched for the theater first. "Here it is" Ronnie pointed. "Let's go inside and explore" "I'm not going in there" Mike said. "I have to find a bathroom. I gotta piss" "Me too" said Phil. "You guys go in and we'll catch up with you later" "Ok" Ronnie replied. "Arold and me will go in instead". After they left, we walked into a tight corridor with entrances on each side that led into a steep incline to a screen and some seats below. Flickering around us was an old black and white foreign film with a language that we didn't understand. The theater was virtually empty except for a few film students in the front row. "What the fuck are they saying up there?" I asked. "It sounds like German?" "It's Smogidydoice!" Ronnie yelled loudly. "Everybody knows that!" Unmoved, the people in the first row craned their heads back to us and gave us a pronounced "shush". "I don't speak shush" Ronnie remarked. "That must be another language for you". "They're gonna kick us out" I said. "I think We're pissing them off". "Fuck those people" Ronnie howled looking down at them. "Who wants to see this shit anyway"? Just as I had predicted, a student supervisor approached and asked us to immediately leave. "I'm glad I didn't pay to see this crap" Ronnie said as we walked back up to the exit. "These assholes don't even serve any popcorn." "What kind of movie theater doesn't have that shit?" he asked. "They don't have soda either" I whispered. "Yeah, that too" Ronnie replied. "So, fuck this place. We're out of here. Come on, man, let's go find someplace else to go to". As we departed, I saw a large white building to my left and was wondering what it was. "I wonder what's in there?" I asked Ronnie. "It's one of those older buildings that have those large doors with the rollers on them". "Right" Ronnie said. "Let's go check it out".

We entered through the door and saw two people milling around. It was a very large room with a false ceiling that had lights hanging down and wires everywhere. In each corner of the room were television cameras on large dollies with many cables protruding out and trailing along the floor. A woman approached us and asked us what we were doing there. "You two don't look like college students?" she asked. "What are you doing here?" "We're interested in seeing what this TV studio is all about" Ronnie said. "It looks pretty cool and it might be something me and my friend here might want to learn in the future". "Well" the woman said. "You're not really supposed to be here unless you are a college student. But, We're not busy right now. So, I'll show you a little of how it works if you want". "Cool" I replied. "Can we look through one of the big cameras?" "Yes" she answered. "We have our own television station here. This is the studio where we teach students about the media". She pointed over to a guy that was starting to move one of the dollies around. "Go over by him" she instructed. "And, he'll let you look through the viewfinder". As we strode over to him, the man said "Why don't one of you stand in front of the camera, and I'll let you guys take turns seeing yourselves on TV". "Cool" Ronnie said. "That would be great". While we were having our fun, the girl left for a while and then returned. "I just spoke to one of our supervisors on the phone" she said. "We're intrigued by how you guys are interested in all of this. So, We're gonna talk to you on camera and do an interview outside the building". "We're gonna be TV stars!" Ronnie yelled. "We're gonna have our own show". "Yeah" I laughed. "We'll call it, the two fools who cut school". "I wouldn't go so far as that" said the girl. But, yes. You'll be taped for TV. Now, go outside and wait for us" she advised. "We'll be right out with a microphone and a portable camera machine".

Ronnie and I exited and waited by some bushes next to a wall. Soon, the girl came back as promised. "I'm gonna ask you guys a few questions about yourselves" she said. "My co student will have a camera on his shoulder zeroing in on you. I'll put the microphone in front of your face when We're ready. When the cameraman points at us, that means the film is rolling. So, when you see that cue, that means We're recording. Try not to be nervous and act as natural as possible, ok?" "Sure" Ronnie replied giggling. "Whatever you say". The cue came and the girl began. She put the mic in front of Ronnie's face and asked "How do you see yourself ten years from now?" "I'm gonna be rich, don't you know?" he asked "I'm gonna hit the lottery". She turned her attention to me and asked "What about you? How do you see yourself in ten years?" Before I had a chance to answer, Ronnie stuck his face in front of mine and exclaimed "Oh, he wants to be a garbage man. He loves to play in the dirt". As the camera man was laughing and trying to retain his composure, the girl yelled "cut". She was a little annoyed and told us "If you can't be serious, we can't continue" "Ok" Ronnie said. "I apologize. But, Arold here really does want to be a sanitation engineer". "He's out of his skull" I replied. "I never said any such thing". "Ok" said the girl. "I'm gonna give you guys one more chance. We're not trying to do a comedy show here. Just answer the questions honestly or We'll have to stop again. "We're ready when you are" Ronnie said. "Let's go". Again, she put the mic in front of us and waited for the cameraman"s cue. After he pointed, she started asking questions again. She put the mic back in Ronnie's face. "What would you study here if you attended college here?" she asked. "Biology" Ronnie replied. "Why biology?" she asked. "Do you like to study organisms and possibly save people?" "I wanna save my mother" Ronnie said. "Why?" asked the girl. "Because, she has crabs!" the girl gave the cameraman the cut sign across her throat with her hand again. "That's it!" she screamed obviously frustrated. "You guys aren't serious. So, our session is over" "I didn't know we were having a session?" Ronnie asked laughing. "Are you a psychiatrist on TV?" "You blew it, man" I said. "They're leaving". The girl and the cameraman turned on their heels and began walking away. As they did, I could hear the cameraman laughing. But, the interviewer girl wasn't amused. "Those kids are assholes" she hollered. "They're worthless. And to think?" she asked "I was trying to educate them". "Well, that was fun" I chuckled. "Now, let's go back to those brick buildings and see if we can find Mike and Phil".

As Ronnie and I approached an elevator, Mike and Phil were stepping off the one next to us. "What have you guys been doing?" I asked. "We got to be on TV". "You're too ugly for TV" Mike said. "They must have wanted Ronnie". "Though I am devilishly handsome" Ronnie replied. "Arold here is correct. We were on television briefly until Arold ruined it by being a wiseass" "Me?" I asked. "You're the one who was the fucking wiseass. The girl got rid of us because you couldn't stay with her script". "Script, shipped" Ronnie laughed. "Who cares? It was in black and white anyway". "We found a lounge with a snack machine where we were able to get extra goodies out of" Phil quipped. "You guys should come up there with us and see it". "I am kind of hungry" Ronnie said. "Especially since Arold ruined my chance at TV stardom". "I didn't ruin shit" I laughed. "You couldn't keep your mouth shut, that's all". "Yeah, Ronnie has a tendency to do that" Mike said.

"But, let's forget about that for now and see what else we can get for free". "I have some quarters" Ronnie exclaimed. "Good" said Phil. "We're gonna need them to get the door open on the bottom of the machine". "The bottom door?" I asked. "What does a bottom door have to do with it?" "You'll see" chuckled Mike. "If you're hungry, we're gonna raid the machine".

We took the elevator to the 3rd floor and exited to a student lounge just as Phil had mentioned. "Check this place out" exclaimed Ronnie as he ran for a couch. "All cozy and shit". I watched laughing as he plopped himself down and sank into the cushions. "Where"s those vending machines at?" I asked Mike. "I want some cookies and shit. "Follow me" said Phil. "They're at the end of the hallway". When we stood before them, Phil demonstrated how it was done. Ronnie handed him a quarter and Phil dropped it into the coin slot for payment. "Now, watch closely" Phil said. "After the snack you paid for drops down into the chute below, one person holds open the top half while the other one reaches up and pulls down some more. Mike and I got like $2.00 worth of freebies that way". "Cool" I shouted. "Did Ronnie ever tell you about doing the same thing to get free shit from a soda machine?" "How"s that?" Mike asked. "I gotta hear this one". "Hey, Ronnie" I said. "Clue Mike in on how you and I always get free Cokes out of the soda dispensers". "It's like this" Ronnie laughed. "You pay for one just like Phil did here with the snacks. Then, after the door opens at the bottom and a can of soda drops down, you reach up into the machine. But, you have to squeeze one of the cans so it'll drop out of the rack inside that holds them. The can will be dented and shit. But, who the fuck cares? It's free soda, man". "I knew I could count on Ronnie to supply us drinks with free treats" replied Mike. "He knows all the scams". "How about this one next to this snack machine?" Phil asked. "You think we can do it with this one?" "We can give it a try" chuckled Ronnie. "But, it all depends on how far you can get your arm up in there. Not all soda machines are the same". "I wanna try it" giggled Phil. "Show me what to do". We stood around and watched as Ronnie instructed Phil on exactly where to position his arm. While he was crouched down on the floor attempting to pilfer, Mike made a suggestion. "When We're done with this, I have some magnesium metal I took from metal shop class on me. I saw a phone booth on one of the other floors. I wanna see if I can unroll a strand and fire it up in the coin slot and bust open its coin box. We might be able to get $20 or $30 out of there". "What the hell is magnesium metal?" I asked. "You"ve never seen that shit before?" Ronnie asked. "No" I replied. "What does it do?" "Tell him, Mike" Ronnie exclaimed. "It looks like a coil of solder" said Mike. "Except after you uncoil it and take out a strand, you light it and it burns really bright. It'll fuck up your eyes too if you don't wear protective glasses. It gets so hot; it'll burn right through your hand if you touch it too". "Like a fuse after it's lit?" I asked. "Exactly" Mike replied. "I don't know if it'll melt steel though. But, I wanna try". "If we can get money, I'm in" Ronnie laughed. "I'll just stand back and watch" I said. "Even if it doesn't work, I wanna see it burn anyway".

We followed Mike to the 2nd floor and watched him place the magnesium into the phone where a key was supposed to go. "Stand back and cover your eyes" he bellowed. "I'm gonna light this bitch up!" It took him a few tries to get it right. But, eventually the end lit up and made an intense glow. "Don't look at it" Mike yelled. "It's like looking at the sun!" A few minutes passed by and its flame had finally wound down. Mike walked back over to inspect his work and was grimacing. "Fucking garbage" he mumbled. "That shit doesn't work at all". The rest of us meandered over to see what was going on. Where the key hole was, it was burnt dark black and it smelled funny. "I guess that didn't work out so well" Ronnie quipped. "So, there won't be any coinage for us". "God damn it!" Mike yelled. "The teacher told me this bullshit is supposed to burn through anything". "Looks like Bell Telephone is way ahead of you" I laughed. "Some douchbag probably already thought of it" Ronnie marked. "And, made it burn proof". "Well, this is a wash" replied Phil. "I guess we have to find something else to do now". "Let's go back to those twin elevators and play elevator tag" Ronnie said. "We can have some fun doing that". "You guys go ahead and I'll meet you there in a few minutes" Mike blurted. "I have something I have to do". "What's that, Mike?" I asked. "Don't worry about it" he replied. "You'll see it later".

Ronnie and I took one elevator and Phil stepped into the other. While waiting for Mike to return, we pushed the buttons to go up, while Phil had his go down. While waiting for the doors to open after stopping on each floor, we would peer through the cracks below to see if we could catch Phil. In between our attempts, Ronnie would pursue him by spitting down on him. Phil would quickly close his door while laughing and we would try again. Eventually, Mike returned and our elevators met together once more. As the doors opened I asked Mike "What did you do that's so funny?" "The 2nd floor is about to be flooded" he chuckled. "I stopped up all of the sinks in the bathrooms with toilet paper to make the water overflow". "Why the hell did you do that?" I asked. "To make them pay for using a coin box that I couldn't get into" he replied. "I really wanted that money". By now, some resident students had reported us to the campus police for commandeering the elevators and stopping them from their use. Phil had mentioned that a student was irate and warned him when he was on the bottom floor. "He said he was gonna rat on us if we didn't stop" he said. "But, we were having so much fun, I told him to go fuck himself". We played cat and mouse a few more times, got bored, and decided to leave. On the way out we were suddenly surrounded by college security officers. There were three cars blocking the path and there was no way for us to escape. A campus cop jumped out of a vehicle and screamed for us to freeze. "Don't you kids move" he yelled. "We've gotten a call about you. You're all being detained". "We're fucked" Ronnie whispered. "Fucking Mike" I said. "You had to go and flood that bathroom didn't you?" "Don't fucking blame me" he replied. "Fucking Phil here is the one who told a student to go fuck himself, blame him instead". "We don't care who did what at this point" said the officer. "Get into the back of the cars and We're taking you to processing". We were all transported to a campus station without handcuffs. In retrospect, we could have attempted to run and a few of us would probably have gotten away. They called our parents and we were released. My parents didn't even want to hear the story I made up and just gave me the evil glare. "Ahhh, that look of punishment" I thought. "It was a fun day".

Ronnie E. and I were walking home from TJ and stopped at the hot dog cart that was always on the corner adjacent to the Acme food store. Here, we would order a couple of franks and sodas and wait for the regular session to be released. The old thin man who served us was usually cordial and would even let us get away with being short occasionally as long as it wasn't a quarter or more. When we saw the kids coming down the walk after being let out, a guy Ronnie knew always seemed to be hanging around. "That's

Larry Fuwah" he laughed loudly. "The guy over there wearing clothes like a pimp?" I asked. "Yeah, that's him" he replied. "He likes to come by here and try to act like he's a big man in front of all of us". "What is he? Like 30?" I asked. "I dunno" Ronnie responded. "But, he sure looks too old to be moseying around here". "I bet he comes around to try to scam on the kids" I said. "Nah" Ronnie chuckled. "I think he just likes to pretend he's important. When he walks by, I'm gonna talk to him. If you think his clothes are weird, just wait until you see the way he talks". Why? What's wrong with him?" I asked laughing. "He speaks like he thinks he's black" Ronnie replied. "Just wait, you'll see". As I was sipping the last gurgles from my can of Coke, Ronnie motioned him over.

When the guy got closer, I noticed that he was wearing a purple felt hat with a feather in it, a green long sleeved satin shirt, a yellow crushed velvet vest, brown corduroy pants, and black platform shoes that were worn down at the heels. None of his ensemble matched and I thought it was hilarious. "Hey, Duke?" Ronnie said as Fuwah approached. "How"s it been hanging?" "Shiiiiiiit" Fuwah replied. "Somebody knows my name". "You're the Duke aren't you?" Ronnie asked. "That's right" he responded. "You must know my street name. But, that's right son. They call me the Duke fo" sho". "Nice to meet you, Duke" I said addressing him. "I've heard a lot about you". "Like what?" he asked. "And, I don't knows ya"ll. So, you may address me as Larry". "Ok, Larry" I replied while trying not to laugh. "Do you always hang around here?" I asked. "Some pumpadoodle owes me some scratch" he remarked slightly slurring. "And, imma gonna get it". "Ok, Larry" I said. "I wish you good luck with that". "What chu knows about luck?" he asked agitated. "Ain't no luck in dis life. Only heartbreaks." He turned to walk away and I noticed he had a shuffling gait like George Jefferson from the famous TV show the Jeffersons. His step was a little off while swinging his right hand slightly hidden behind his back. "Why does he walk that way?" I asked Ronnie. "Because, in the ghetto you have to pretend you might have something behind your back like a gun or a knife to protect yourself" he replied. "It's all an illusion to look tough". "But, he looks like he couldn't beat himself up?" I asked. "You know that, and I know that" he laughed. But, he's a legend in his own mind. Maybe that's why he feeds off of scaring teenagers. Anybody who knows him knows he couldn't beat his way out of a wet paper bag". "That's kind of sad" I said.

"To walk around delusional like that". Suddenly, Ronnie dropped down and fell onto his back into the grass on the side of the road. He was lying straight and was stiff as a board. But, his left arm was protruding up from his stomach with his hand and wrist spinning around. "Look" he said. "I'm Larry Fuwah if he got shot in Vietnam. He's riddled with bullet holes. But, his swagger hand keeps on going". Laughing hysterically, I cautioned Ronnie to get back up before the Duke came back. "I'm not afraid of that loser" he said. "Let him see me. I'll drop down in front of him and do it again. I'll take his hat too and tell him I'm Fuwah Hood". After he got up, I was holding my side from crying. He had a way with doing the best imitations.

On a weekday in school, Mr. S. had taken it upon himself to teach us the history of America. Therefore, he booked a bus trip for us to accompany him to the monuments and museums of Washington D.C. This school outing like the ski trip was not exclusive to just the Special Ed classes. Anyone who wanted to go could was invited as long as they paid the discounted fee for the bus and the boxed lunch fee that came along with it. The morning of the outing, Billy F. and I found out Charlie C. was coming with us from Mr. Campbell"s class. Charlie was a tiny little guy who I had known from when he was in my class at John Marshall Elementary School. He was sarcastic, knowledgeable, and everyone loved him. He was especially popular with the girls. He had very long hair and looked like the quintessential hippie. Like me, he hated authority and I loved him for it.

After the four hour voyage to D.C., the bus parked and we all disembarked to explore the government exhibits on the mall. Being how Billy and I were always scheming for some reason or another, Billy suggested we try to seek a bar that would serve us. Charlie stayed behind with a girl and advised us that He'd "Much rather be with the ladies". Billy and I then walked around some side streets to examine what we could find. We eventually stepped into a bar that looked very old and run down. Its interior was obsolete and looked like a 1930"s drinking establishment that had seen better days. The walls were grimy with tattered posters from days long past and the bar stools were all ripped as if someone had taken a switchblade or a razor to them.

We sat down at the bar and tried to act mature. The bartender asked "What"ll you have?" I replied "We'll have two drafts, thanks". He came back with the two beers and set them down in front of us. Just as I was about to take a sip, he looked at Billy and asked to see Billy"s ID. I thought it was strange as he didn't want mine, just Billy"s instead. Billy got nervous and blurted out "I think I left it in the car". The bartender got annoyed and said "Well then, no ID, no beer." He looked over at me and mumbled "That goes for you too". Initially, I thought I was safe. I guess the guy had begun to have doubts after he carded Billy and Billy couldn't produce. Shaken, we looked at each other dumbfounded and wanted to leave. The bartender bellowed "You made me pour those damn beers. Now, you have to pay for them". Billy jumped off his bar stool screaming "Where you think you're coming off at?" The bartender leaned over the bar and got in Billy"s face "You can pay for the beers, or I can call the cops". We paid for the beers and left.

We went back to the mall to see if we could find our school friend's again. We asked the sleeping bus driver where they were and he told us told us they had all went to the Smithsonian Museum. "If you hurry up" he said. "You just might be able to catch up with them". Billy and I entered the Smithsonian and started wandering around. While half seriously searching for the rest of our touring party, we looked at all of the wonders the museum encapsulated. Some of it was very interesting, while some of it we thought mundane. At the end of the tour, Billy found the gift shop. We bought long books of matches with the Smithsonian logo on them and 3 times the size cigars. We didn't get to have any beer for the day. But, we didn't let it dissuade us either. I thought "Sometimes you win, and sometimes you lose". Anything was better than boredom.

My father and mother had come to the conclusion that we needed a travel trailer to spend weekends in. They insisted that it was the proper thing to do and wanted a place to be able to "get away". I didn't care either way until they decided to kidnap me every weekend to be there with them. The place they chose was Tip Tam trailer park in Jackson, N.J. As far as I was concerned, it was so far out in the woods that it might as well have been on the moon. I hated it at first, but learned to adjust once I saw there was a swimming pool, a small store with a pool table and games, a juke box outside, and most of all, young girls.

Age 15 at Tip Tam Trailer Park – Courtesy of Noreen Branigan

While staying at this park I met two brothers named Ray and John. I don't recall their last names, but I do remember that they were 10 and 12 years old. They owned a bicycle like me to get around with, and always seemed to be getting into some form of trouble with the locals. Ray being the smaller of the two would usually ride on the handlebars as John took control to steer. They didn't stay at Tip Tam though as they lived across the street in a run down, converted to an apartment chicken coop. They also had two sisters though I don't remember their names. The entire time I hung out with them, I never saw their parents as they were hardly ever home. So, they were pretty much forced to rely on themselves. By the looks of their surroundings, they appeared to be very poor. Tip Tam let them hang around as guests during the day but always informed them that they had to leave at dusk. These two characters were the best little con men and thieves I had ever seen. They dressed like the Little Rascals in obvious hand me down clothes and had slightly greasy, stringy long hair. They looked a lot like hillbilly children you would see in magazines and news articles from the Appalachian Mountains.

One afternoon, they talked me into a five mile bike ride to a small strip mall that had a gas station across the street. Here they attested was a store that had pipe lighters that lit from the middle that seemed to be all the rage. Since they smoked cigarettes like I did, they wanted them badly and would do anything to make them theirs. Looking at the lighters through the window I exclaimed. "They look like threaded bolts on both sides with a hexagon nut in the middle. Those are pretty cool. Do you think We'll be able to get any of those?" Ray piped up "We're pretty good at getting what we want. So, We'll see what we shall see". As like Phil with his jewelry escapades in the mall, these kids had their thievery down to a science. The older boy John would distract the sales clerk as the younger brother Ray would pilfer the goods. "I'll take anything else I see if I can get away with it too" Ray laughed. "It's all overpriced shit anyway". All I had to do was play watchman for the cops while I was waiting outside. Afterward, I would always be rewarded nicely as we biked away.

Another time, we took a ride back out to the same gas station. This time, John and Ray had concocted a more daring scheme. The plan was for John to take a spill off of his bicycle making sure that the attendant would see him. "I know this scam will work" John said. "Because there is only that one guy pumping gas and fixing cars throughout the day". As I sat on my bike by a corner of woods down the street, I could see everything that was about to go down. "Are you ready?" Ray asked. "Yeah" John replied. "Let's go". Like a flash of lightning in a driving rain, he took off pedaling as fast as he could. As he entered the lot he aimed for an area between the gas pumps and the door. His front tire hit a pump with a loud bang and he slammed to the ground pretending to be writhing in pain. To the attendant inside, it appeared as if he had lost control of his bike and had crashed. With a performance that would gather an Oscar, John screamed out in feigned pain. "Oh my god! My leg, my leg. Somebody please help me!" The attendant rushed out asking concerned "Are you ok, are you ok? Do you want me to call an ambulance?" As Ray was hiding behind a wrecked car at the edge of the lot, he waited for just the right time to implement his plan. I watched as he quietly crept inside the station while the man was comforting his brother's supposed injuries. He was like a stealth cat moving in on its prey. Slowly he slithered to where the cash register was, put a sock over its bell to muffle any noise, waited for the drawer to eject, and precipitously removed 1,5,10 and 20 dollar bills. He did it so fast; it was like watching a blur through a frosted glass window. After he pocketed the cash, he took the same sock, and wiped down any surface he might have touched to avoid fingerprint identification. He was flawless and quick and I had never seen anything like it. After mere seconds, he ran behind the wrecked automobile through a patch of woods back to me. I asked. "What's next, little man?" He replied with glee "Watch my brother, man. He'll miraculously get back on the bike and say he's ok. With fake tears, he'll thank the man for his help and leave". John did just that. He returned and said "The real trick is to get out of there before he discovers his drawer is empty. So, let's leave and go quickly!" I was in awe and I couldn't believe these little kids got away with it. We rode back to where they lived and divvied up the loot. It was $120.00. That was a lot of money in 1973. Amazing!

Tip Tam had a built-in pool that was pretty large. I would say 20 feet across, 40 feet long and 7 feet deep. Most of the time, I went to swim there alone as I didn't want any friend competition when I was trying to mack on the sweeties. The one thing I despised about Tip Tam"s pool was that if your hair was longer than your collar bone, you had to wear a bathing or shower cap to swim. It was some bullshit rule about it clogging the filter and I always felt they were lying for control. My hair was long then, but not long enough where it was obvious to conform. "If caught" I thought. "I'll sneakily tuck it under my wet t shirt collar, and nobody would be the wiser".

I was swimming away one morning and was scanning the pool area for little females. Out of nowhere, a girl with freckles on her face and wearing a bathing cap dove in right in front of me. At first I thought she was kind of rude. So, I decided just to avoid her. But, she came up from her dive facing me and smiled. I thought she was cute and I asked for her name. She giggled and played coy with me and swam away. It intrigued me so I decided to follow her. As I got close, she turned around and began to playfully splash me. So, I splashed back. Suddenly, she turned around and left. Later that night, I saw her by the performance area where Tip Tam had occasional live acts and movies on movie nights. Asking around, I found out she was visiting with one of her friends. I wasn't crazy about her friend. But, I was interested in her. Over the summer season, I had seen her wandering around and struck up a conversation. In the middle of a question she was replying to, I reached over and gave her a kiss. She didn't seem to mind and appeared happy to reciprocate. I soon found out she was from Jersey City. I liked that as my father's entire side was from there and I kept in touch with her until I was 17. I found her again on Facebook decades later. She fits into the narrative in this book in future chapters. I found out many years later that I was her first kiss from a boy she ever received. I was flattered and had no idea. Life was uncomplicated and good back then.

Back at school, the girl's behavior was sometimes worse than the boys. At TJ, in the center of the building, there is a square courtyard. There is not much in there except an access door and a grassy yard. On its inside, it is surrounded by two levels of classroom windows. One morning, some friends and I were walking down a hallway between classes. At the end of the hallway, you can go left or right. The courtyard was directly in front of us and I began to hear a commotion. It was a gathering of fellow students carrying on and shrieking "Ewww, what is that?" they asked as they pointed down disgusted and bemused. A student I didn't know gestured for me to come closer. He motioned to me to look down through an open window into the courtyard for a look. I slowly stuck my head through the window and peered down. As the unknown student joined me, he pointed to the ground asking "Look! Look! Do you see it? It's nasty, just nasty!" On the ground was a 20 gallon drum that was sometimes doubled as a garbage can. It was lying sideways with its rear end facing the windows, and its front end facing the grass. It looked as if it was deliberately dropped from above, hit the ground, toppled over, and its contents had been spilled. As I looked closer, I could see a trail of white, oval shaped objects with dark red stains in their middles. Obviously, they were used sanitary napkins. "Gross!" I blurted. As I was retrieving my head from the window, other kids were scrambling to have a look. Without warning, Stone Face Guzak soon appeared "Keep moving, get to class" he bellowed. "You'll be late for your next period". "Period you say?" I asked. "Take a look. They'll never be late again"!

Back in the boy's bathroom, the usual suspects were there. They were getting in as many drags as possible to satisfy their young body"s craving for nicotine before the next bell rang for class. Puff puff, pass, get it hot, puff, puff pass. Like a teenaged fog supplying a brief respite from the school's unnecessary authority, the heavy smoke engulfed us. Suddenly, I heard the obligatory "boom, boom" of the door behind me. Someone knew the signal. Someone was about to enter. In walks a tall good looking kid who was about 6 feet 4 and maybe 150 lbs. He was very animated and hyper and he couldn't stand still. He had dark brown, wavy hair tousled on his head and asked loudly "Hey? What the fuck is going on in here? What's the scam?" I had heard of this guy before and I sort of recognized him. His tallness was a bit intimidating at first and I asked him "Aren't you Jesse Titanic?" "Titanic?" he asked annoyed "Where the fuck did you get that from? Do I look like a fucking boat?" He then corrected me "Kurtanick, with a "K". Not Titanic fucking dumb ass! Who the fuck are you anyway?" A little nervous, I told him my name. He accepted it and began laughing. Dennis G. was in there with us and he questioned him about me. "Dennis? Do you know this fucking guy?" he asked. "Is he alright or what? He looks like a punk". As he laughed at me hysterically, Dennis nodded ok between heavy drags on his cigarette giving Jesse the satisfaction he needed to leave me alone. Though he made me wary about him, I liked how Jesse questioned everything around him. He had the same "I don't give a fuck" attitude I had, and appeared to have a personality where he refused to take any bullshit from anyone. Though I was more timid and not as gregarious, he fit right into my circle of who I wanted to hang around with. It looked as if I had just made another partner in crime.

TJ"s cafeteria was usually the highlight of the school day. Like a prison chow hall, it was where you sat with your respective clicks learning the recent gossip around and behind you. Engulfed in the din of the background noise, and always on your guard, you listened intently. Which girls would fuck, which ones didn't, which girls gave BJ"s, which girls were teasers, who was scamming who, who got suspended, who had the best drugs, how to get back at teachers and principals, who owed who money, whose parents wouldn't be home for the weekend, where the best parties were, everything teenagers talked about was here.

Most of my friends refused to eat what the school perceived as wholesome lunches. The food served was the consistency and foresight of penitentiary food as it was very bland and barely edible. Once in a while, you could get by with their ricotta stuffed shells or instant mashed potatoes with gravy. But, the rest was substandard trash and was purely for the desperate and famished. Our group would usually give rein instead to the ice cream sandwiches and chocolate milk. We knew that they were prepackaged and not tampered with. Plus, they tasted good and gave us a sugar rush. Sitting at our usual table by the wall facing the hallway, was Dennis, Ronnie, me, and Phil. On the left side of the cafeteria were 30 foot high windows facing TJ"s parking lot. There were three panes in all and they were quite massive. In front of us was a stage where most band concerts and plays were performed. But, during lunch time, if you misbehaved, you had to sit on the stage and be monitored by a teacher while you ate and finished your meal. The lunch line provided us with green, porcelain plates. These plates became problematic for the school on a continual basis. The lunch room tables had legs underneath that were "set" by slides to lock their feet in place. Sometimes, if we felt like being dickheads, we would re-set the legs on one side. That way, if just the right amount of weight was laid on the table, the table would collapse causing everyone"s plates to slide down crashing to the ground. When this happened, it was like kids at a rock concert during an encore. Everyone would stand on their seats and cheer as loud as possible. We liked this prank a lot as it was next to impossible to find out who the culprit was. We felt it was a perfect way to get back at the administration and randomly pestered them when we could.

A girl came by with long, blonde hair. She stopped to speak to Dennis and had what appeared to be a speech impediment. On closer inspection of her face, I saw that she had a hair lip. She kept asking Dennis about something and wouldn't stop. She pleaded "Denith, Denith Lithenth to me!" It was hard to hear her above the racket of loud teenagers amongst us and Dennis was becoming visibly annoyed. Finally, he dismissed her and she left abruptly. I asked Dennis who she was. He said "Oh, that's Puggy. She has the hots for me and won't leave me alone". He asked laughing "Doesn't she have a face like a pug dog?" I shrugged and said "I guess so". Everyone else seemed to know what he was talking about except me. A few minutes later, she came back. Dennis was trying again to get rid of her. "Puggy, blow me!" he demanded loudly. "When are you gonna blow me Puggy?" Puggy whispered something like "Maybe later Den" and walked off in a huff. Phil asked Dennis "Why do you always do that to her Den?" Dennis looked aggravated and said "It's the only way I can get rid of her, bro. She won't stop". Ronnie suggested "Why don't you just get a BJ off of her and be done with her then?" Dennis, looking disgusted grumbled "Ewww, I don't want any sideways lip on my dick. That's gross fellas. You go and do that shit". Our table erupted in laughter. "Poor Puggy" I thought. "All she wanted was to be recognized".

Between the lunch room tables, there was a path by default. This was the aisle Stoneface strolled to do his rounds to watch us. Back and forth he would walk. He would inherently stare down at us as he strode by in willful indignation. Like a jailer on death row, he incessantly spied on us, looking to record infractions for later. We knew he was saving them to dole out his 3 day suspensions. So, we were mindful to avoid him. We wouldn't let him beat us in the end. As we were getting close to the end of the lunch session, Ronnie was attempting to munch on a peanut butter sandwich. He bit into it and made a face "This taste like shit" he exclaimed. This isn't Jiff; this is that natural, oily bullshit they keep trying to pass off as the real thing. Fuck this sandwich." He proceeded to rise from his chair, faced the large windows on our left, stretched out his left arm like a quarterback preparing to launch a touchdown pass, zeroed in on the upper left fenestra, made sure no one was watching, and let the sandwich fly. Up, up it went. Like a glorious seagull returning to its cumulous stratosphere. When it reached the appropriate height, it smashed to the pane with a thud. It didn't slide, it didn't move, it didn't falter. There, like industrial strength adhesive glue, it stayed stuck on its side. It sat there untouched for months. It was a true testament to our juvenile delinquency.

A brother of Dennis named JR, was sitting at a table with his cohorts around him. JR was older than we were and hung around with a more rugged crowd. He was short, with long straight hair, an Al Capone disposition, and resembled a pit bull commanding his arena for the win. Their table was in the first row, on the middle right about 20 feet away from us. These were the kids who got the most respect, the ones who you didn't mess around with. They were the rough and tumble crowd. JR was chewing on the end of a straw that was usually used for drinking milk or juice. Shortly after, he took a piece of the paper left over from the sleeve of the straw and began chewing it in his mouth. He was making "spitballs". As Stoneface sauntered by with his illusions of grandeur, JR put the straw to his lips, aimed, and fired. It was a direct hit. Stoneface now had "spitball back". Each time Stoneface returned, JR would hit him with another one. Eventually, Stoneface had at 25 spitballs to account for. No one said a word and no one informed him. No student cared as we hated him. For his past discretions against us, we felt he deserved it. We wondered if he had discovered them later on. The thought of him picking off individual papers that were soaked in JR"s spit enlightened us. Soon, the lunch hour was over. Mission accomplished.

The dress code at TJ in 1974 was archaic by today"s standards. For boys, you were required to have your shirttail tucked in at all times, no bare feet, and no open shirts. If you were lucky enough to have facial hair, no beards or moustaches were allowed either. The girls had it a little worse than we did. They were not to have any mid drifts showing skin, no see through blouses, no bra straps viewable, no bare feet, and no open toed shoes. Of course, most of us tried to breach this silliness as much as possible. I was one of the school's main offenders. My father had a German Infantry coat that he had gotten from my uncle from when my uncle was in Germany in the Army. When my uncle was discharged from his duties, he had brought home a few tokens from WWII. This coat was one of them. There was no Nazi, Wehrmacht insignias, medals, or embroideries of rank remaining anywhere on this coat. They had been stripped long ago. I found it in storage in our basement one day and thought it looked interesting. It resembled a coat that Keith Richards of The Rolling Stones had worn in a photo shoot I had seen in a music magazine. I wanted to emulate him. So, I decided to wear it to school. As I showed up the next day parading down the hall in my new attire, I received odd stares and grumblings behind my back. Some were even finger pointing behind me. I could hear students whispering amongst themselves and looking away from me with their hands cupped over their mouths. I heard them say "Wow! Look what he's wearing! He's crazy to do that! That looks like a Nazi uniform!" The thing is, in my head, it wasn't really a Nazi uniform. There was no present indication that it was. I didn't understand the problem with it and I was just trying to be cool. After all, I was only 15 years old.

After a few months of wearing my antiestablishment coat of misguided German heritage, I noticed more and more kids avoiding me. Here I was with teens being afraid of me. I didn't like the feeling that I was being perceived as the very bullies I was trying to avoid. It was totally unexpected and I failed to understand it. I was soon called down to Stoneface"s office. And, it was all because of a damn coat. I was berated by him "We have had many calls from parents of students of the Jewish persuasion." he grumbled. "They are very upset. You cannot wear that coat to our school anymore. It's insensitive and anti-Semitic. May I suggest you go home for the day, and return with clothing more suitable for this institution". I was taken aback and challenged him "I don't see the problem with what I wear". I said. "It's an Army field coat. So what? Would you say the same if it was an American, Russian, or Chinese service coat?" I asked. There are no markings on it. So, what's the problem?" Stoneface wasn't moved "You have two choices here son" he demanded "You can come back tomorrow minus your dress, or you can be suspended indefinitely until you do so". I lashed out at him "This is America! I have freedom to write, wear, and speak about anything I wish whether you approve of it or not!" He retaliated "That may be true for adults" he bellowed. "But, you are not an adult. You are a juvenile who must adhere to the rules of conduct of Thomas Jefferson Junior High School. What you are doing is a distraction. There can be no distractions or anti-Semitism while you are attending this school, period". I refused to relent. But, it was no use. He had said his piece and I was removed from his office and sent home. My parents received a phone call later that day advising what was expected of me if I was to return. Though I was unmoved and believed I was right, my father sat me down and explained to me why the school was upset. He pontificated about how people had lost relatives in the war because of the Nazis and how I would feel if it had happened to me. He also offered punishment if I refused to comply. Slightly remorseful and disillusioned, I returned to school coatless the next day.

We found out that a new junior high school was about to open in North Edison. It was to be named Woodrow Wilson Junior High. This was primarily due to years of overcrowding. With this new school, a new principal would be needed. Therefore, a candidate in training was sent to our school to learn the ropes. The person they sent to us was Mr. Lutter. Lutter was a short man with a slightly bald head, a comb over to try to hide it, horn rimmed glass, a plastic pocket protector for his pens, beady eyes, and a severe case of Napoleon complex. It was very obvious from the start that he was gung ho to impress the administration by proving himself as much as possible. He seemed desperate to want the job.

One day, I met Lutter in the hallway outside of TJ"s office. I politely asked him "Why are you the vice principal since we already have one?" Knowing that Stoneface was already the acting principal, I pushed Lutter to annoy him. Like a prisoner in jail testing a new guard for the first time, I wanted to see how far I could go. He insisted that "I am the acting vice principal for now, Mr. Guzak is the acting principal, and a new principal will be with us within a few weeks". "Do you know his name?" I asked. "His name is Mr. Bone" he replied. "I have to go now, I'm busy. What was your name again son?" I quickly walked away saying "Oh, don't worry about that. You'll see later!" Later came quicker than I thought it would. I came to school one morning and my sneakers were frozen from the snow. I tried to make it through as many classes as I could but it had become impossible to bare. "I have to figure out a way to go home" I thought. "My feet are really cold and they are freezing". Knowing that the only way out was through the front office, I decided to give Lutter a friendly visit. "What can I do for you?" he asked. "We'll" I replied. "I walked to school today in a lot of slush. I wanted to know if I could go home for a bit to change my shoes". Throwing a little drama in the mix, I added. "I feel like my toes will fall off soon". "How far do you live from here?" he asked. "Oh, I'm only a few blocks from here off of Central" I responded. "I tell you what I'll do" he said. "I'll let you go home with a pass to retrieve some new shoes and to get your feet dry. But, I'm only giving you a half an hour to come back". "Cool" I said. "It shouldn't take me any longer than that to find another pair".

Trudging through the snow with soggy cold feet with pass in hand, I arrived home to an empty house. The first thing I did was warm my feet in the bathtub under some hot running water. After toweling them dry, I searched around the closets for some shoes so I could return. No matter how hard I tried, I just couldn't seem to find any. "There's got to be an old pair around here someplace" I thought. While still looking, I glanced at a clock and noticed my half hour was almost up. "Fuck" I mumbled. "If I can't find replacements, that asshole"s gonna ream me for sure". Another half an hour went by and I knew I was screwed. "Maybe if I call him and explain" I thought. "He might understand". I picked up the phone and dialed TJ"s number. "Can I speak to Mr. Lutter?" I asked "I think I have a problem". After asking my name, I was connected. "Where are you?" he said with an attitude. "You were supposed to be back here 30 minutes ago". "Well" I said. "I can't find another pair of shoes anywhere in my house. I swear I'm not lying and I really tried. There just aren't any I can find". "You better get back here now" he demanded. "Or, you're going to have to face the consequences". "Consequences of what?" I asked yelling. "For a kid who"s feet turned blue?" "It's not about that" he said. "You promised me you"d be right back and now you"ve broken that promise. I trusted you to return". "I'm doing the best I can" I replied. "I'll even put my wet ones in the dryer if you can give me just a little more time". "How much longer might that be?" he asked. "Probably about 45 minutes" I responded. He suddenly exploded into the phone. "That will not suffice" he screamed. "You come back here this instant or else". "I don't respond to threats" I said. "So, you do what you have to do you cold hearted asshole.

"Did you just call me a curse word?" he asked. "For that, and for lying to me, you're now suspended for 3 days" "Good" I laughed. "It'll give me more time for my feet to dry. Goodbye douchebag" and I hung up.

Through Ronnie, I met another student at TJ. His name was Mike W. Mike was an average height guy but a little rotund in the belly. Mike, like us, had a great sense of humor and hated authority. Before I met Mike, I had heard a story about him. Supposedly, Mike was in the office on Mr. Bone"s very first day. Mike and a few accomplices were there for an infraction that the school decided needed discipline. Mike had no idea what Mr. Bone would be like. Mr. Bone, like Mr. Lutter was a short guy. But, he didn't wear glasses, and was an impeccable dresser. Like a Gestapo agent, he was obsessed with order and perfection. Mr. Bone approached Mike to ask him why he was there. Before Mr. Bone got a word in, Mike asked him "So? You're the new principal huh?" Mr. Bone answered "That's right. Now, what did you do for me to have to meet you under these circumstances?" Mike went on "Well, do you have a family? "Yes" Mr. Bone replied. But, what does that have to do with why you are here?" With a grin on his face, and trying hard not to laugh, Mike chuckled "Well, how"s Mrs. Bone, and all you're little boners?" Mr. Bone exploded "Out, out and don't come back! You're suspended for three days. Effective immediately! Go home, now! Mike rushed out of the office, looked back at Mr. Bone, and muttered "He has a really red face for someone with a hard on". Mike and I became fast friends.

About twice a month, TJ and other establishments had dances. There were many bands playing out with names such as Creation"s End, Hollywood, Extropolis, Freight Train, and others. Most of these social gatherings were in gyms or church halls at night and usually started between 7 and 10 pm. Though they were held to help promote socialization between the sexes, I always thought it was ironic and hypocritical. The schools and churches were so strict with their dress codes, yet it was perfectly acceptable to kiss girls in the dark while gyrating passionately against them. This is where your self-esteem kicks in. Will you be chosen? Will you be attractive enough? Will any girls like you? I hated it. I always equated it to the uncomfortable experience you felt when you were trying to cop drugs. It always felt it surreal and a facsimile of who you really were. A large hall of teenagers trying to be something they were not. What was the purpose? Was it for a peck on the cheek and a possible hard on for the remainder of the night? "No thanks!" I thought. Our elders tried to teach us about morals. But, it was a hypocritical façade they had planned.

On one of these dance nights, I had been at Billy"s house earlier hanging around. Billy lived close to Dennis G. So, it wasn't uncommon for everyone in close neighborhoods to not know each other. Billy had a basement with a pool table, a tool shop, a color TV, and a nice stereo system. And like his father, liked to drink whiskey sours. He had watched his father make them on previous occasions and had his recipe down pat. So, it was only natural for him to have made us some. With his parents being busy upstairs, we sipped them while playing pool. Here is where I learned The Rolling Stones back catalog. I had always loved their music. But, only knew a handful of their songs. Billy helped educate me and turned me onto one of their greatest hits albums names Hot Rocks. I've been a Stones freak ever since. During a game of 8 ball, I had scratched and had lost miserably. Dancing around with a cue stick still in his hand, Billy started teasing me with a Stones song that had come on the stereo. Like most of my friends, he had parodied the lyrics to annoy me. "You can't get no satisfaction. You can't play pool, got no action. But, you try, and you try, and you try, and you try". Suddenly, I heard a bellowing voice from above. "Bilweeee, Bilweeee. You come up here wight now!" It seemed Billy"s dad had a slight lisp. Billy whispered to me "That's my father. Just stay here and be cool. If you hear him come down the stairs, hide these drinks!" When Billy didn't answer fast enough, his father yelled louder "Bilwee, don't make me come down there aannnd uh, uh, uh, uh". His dad"s voice began to waver like he had just run out breath. I was thinking his father must be a little fellow with speech like that. I was very wrong.

Down the stairs lumbered a totem of a man. He was about six feet four and 280 lbs. I could hear the stairs creaking under his weight as he made his way down to the bottom floor. As he descended, I hid the whiskey sours behind a love seat in another part of the room. When he turned the corner, he saw me leaning against the cinderblock wall with a cue stick in my hand. Billy was fast trailing behind him and nervously introduced us "Ron, this is my father. Dad, this is Ron". "Hewwo Won, Bilwee tells me you are his fwend from school. Any fwend of my son is afwend of mine. Just don't get in any twouble wif him or there will be probwems!" He reached out his hand to shake mine. His extremity was huge and swallowed my palm like a giant. It was so large; it reminded me of a swollen catcher"s mitt left out in the rain. It was enormous, calloused, and intimated me. I answered with a tremble in my voice. "Don't worry Mr. F. We won't get into any trouble". Little did he know what was about to come next.

I had gone home from Billy"s to change and to prepare for a night at the dance. I was to meet Billy behind the Edison Library"s garage across the street from TJ at 7pm. When I arrived, he was already there waiting for me. On the ground in front of him was a large brown paper bag. Billy was grinning from ear to ear and looked very pleased with himself. I asked him "What's in the bag bro? He replied sarcastically "Beer! What the hell you think it is?" Beer? I asked. "How the hell did you get beer? Did you get served again?" He went on about "Don't worry about where I got it from. Just drink up with me and hurry up". Like rabid wolves on a famished kill, we tore at the bag in great haste. It was a twelve pack of Budweiser bottles. So, we split it to 6 beers a piece. As we guzzled, we could hear the muffled sounds of a live band from within TJ"s walls. "I guess we better drink faster and finish these" I said. "Or, we might not get in. We're already late you know?" "Fuck being late" Billy replied. "They're lucky we even show up for their bullshit events". After we drank about five beers each, Billy decided he had to shit. "Man" he said. "Beer always makes me shit when I drink them fast. I'm gonna go in now, man. Finish these up and meet me inside, ok?" He put down his last empty bottle and sashayed away toward the school. As he approached the ticket table, I could see him being interrogated by Stoneface. After much scrutiny and body language, Billy was allowed in. I hung around for a bit and drank as fast as I could. Like Billy, I wanted to get inside to flirt with the ladies. When I was finished, I approached the entryway with great confidence thinking "I'm not that fucked up and this should be a breeze". As I slightly staggered to the ticket table, I was accosted by Stoneface himself "Do you have your ticket Mr. Arold?" he asked. "Why yes, yes I do" I replied. "It's right here in my pocket" I said. I was tearing at my jacket with my fingers trying to find it when the alcohol hit me like a wave. I pulled the ticket out and it fell to the ground. "Just a minute" I said. "Let me pick it up for you". I reached down on the pavement attempting to retrieve it. Looking like a court jester who had lost the faculties of his arms and legs, my extremities were flailing about as if they were made out of rubber. "Here you go Stoneface" I said as I handed it to him. "Now, let me into the dance". Stoneface began to size me up. He started asking me questions to discern the gravity of my drunkenness. I started to argue with him about how he was making me late. "I don't have time for this bullshit" I slurred. "Now, let me in". Just then, Stoneface remarked that he smelled a whiff of alcohol on me. "Have you been drinking?" he asked. The effects of the beer were really kicking in now. I answered him "I had a couple of beers with my dad a few hours ago. I know it's legal to drink with a parent if they let you. So what's the problem?" I asked. Stoneface got close to my face. "I am not prepared to let you into this dance in your inebriated condition. Go home and sleep it off" he commanded. I screamed "I know, I know. It's the usual three days" vacation right? Well, fuck you. And, fuck your dance too! I turned and zigzagged down under the overhead walking backwards to the street. All the while giving Stoneface many one fingered salutes.

I looked to my left and Billy was behind a window making odd gestures with his hands. He kept bending over and pointing to his shoes. Being intoxicated, I had no idea what he was trying to say. He looked like a pantomime and I couldn't hear him. Stoneface came down the walkway and kept insisting that I had to leave. He threatened to have me forcibly removed. "I'm calling the police" he howled. "You're out of control now. I tried to be nice about it and you"ve ignored me. So, you"ve left me no other choice". I told him to go fuck himself and started chanting "Fuck this school, fuck this school. Your dances suck anyway! By now, Billy had come to the door to defend me "If Ronnie gets arrested, I'm going too". Soon, the cops came and put me in handcuffs. They drove me home and lectured me about the responsibilities of acting like an adult and wanted to know where I got the beer from. "A leprechaun gave it to me". I told them. "Can't you see I'm turning green?" Luckily my mother was home while my father was away. Unfortunately, my mother liked to play a game called "owesies". She "wouldn't tell my father of my troubles unless she had to" she said. SHe'd keep the peace as a way to control me. I felt she enjoyed her ritual and saw it as a way to torture me if I didn't want to play by her rules. The police released me into her custody and asked her to keep me inside. I didn't know what happened to Billy. Billy told me the next day that he had told Stoneface that I had gone home to change my shoes and that's what his miming was all about. He'd also been arrested and released. I was of course suspended the next morning. Neither Billy nor I ever danced again.

On a slightly foggy, moonlight night, Ronnie and I were hanging around TJ smoking cigarettes and being bored. It was one of those nights where you could look up and see a misty ring around the moon. There was a large, rectangular concrete block with an overhang attached to a wall on the left side of the front of the building. It was about four feet high and ten feet long. It was just to the right of a gate with a path that went to the back of TJ"s soccer and baseball fields. The overhang was attached to the right corner over a locked red door. A lot of teens would sit there to bullshit and pass the time. While we were brainstorming and trying to come up with something to do, Ronnie suggested breaking in. "We need to go on a mission of revenge and pilferage" he suggested. "Let's go in through the bubble skylights on the roof. I have a friend who went in a few times. It's always open and they never lock it. It goes down into a room right above the bleachers too. They're the ones that collapse up against the gym"s wall when they aren't using them. There's a door right above there that's not locked either. We can drop down and explore and see what we can scarf from inside". I pondered his suggestion for a moment. I was intrigued by his idea and asked "How the fuck are we gonna get up there though? It's at least seven feet high?" He stood up on the block from his supine position and said "Watch, like this". There was a three inch metal lip on the edge of the roof that went from the far left of the building to the corner where it met the overhang. Being that he was six feet tall, Ronnie jumped up and grasped it with his fingers pulling himself easily. He then swung his right leg up against the corner of the overhang, straddled the edge, and hoisted himself up. "See?" he exclaimed as he started to stand. "Come on up. You can do it too. You're just as tall as me. If you get stuck, I'll help you. I'll grab you by your arms". Dared by his request, I acquiesced to comply. I heaved myself up and joined him. "You made it" he laughed. "Now, let's go see what we can find".

As we padded across the small white pebbles beneath our feet, the skylights he described came into view. There were three of them. I asked Ronnie "Which one?" "Right here" he said. As he pointed to the first one. "This is the one that drops down to the gym. We'll open it and go in". He lifted the front of the lunette and tilted it back to an open position. Its portal was about 5 feet by 6 feet wide with a ladder attached to the wall underneath. "I'll go first" he whispered. "You follow down behind me". I nodded in agreement. We transcended down to the floor. The room was a gray dark with a hint of faint light shining down from the skylight"s orifice. There seemed to be chairs and tables stacked haphazardly everywhere and appeared as if they were thrown in in a hurry. I could barely make out an outline of Ronnie's silhouette as he was already opening the door to the gym below. "Down here" he said, as the door swung open. "This is where We'll jump to the floor". He stepped out from the exit onto the top ledge of the accordion folded bleachers. "Let's hang down by our arms. It's the easiest way to get down" he said. "But, don't talk loud because there's an echo in here. I don't want anyone to hear us". I didn't say a word. My heart was beating a thousand miles per hour. The same feeling you get when your fight or flight instincts kick in. I followed him to the ground. I asked him "Now what?" Ronnie thought for a second and remarked "Let's see if we can get to the office in the front. That's where all the good stuff is". We lumbered across the floor with our shoulders and heads down, scanning with laser point accuracy back and forth. Slowly, we came to a door. Someone had left it unlocked and slightly ajar. "Bingo!" Ronnie cried. As we slid through the opening toward a hallway, Ronnie added "One down, one to go". We turned left in the direction of the office. At the end of the corridor, we turned right. The office door was before us. Ronnie reached for the door knob. "I hope they don't have cameras" he said nervously. If they record us, We're toast!" Surprisingly, this entry wasn't locked either. I laughed and told Ronnie "These people are idiots. They"ve left every door open for us!" Ronnie cracked up and answered excitedly "I know. What a bunch of dumb fucks. What do you expect? Look who"s running the place! They're idiots!""

As we crept inside, we were familiar with the layout. After all, we had both spent much time here being suspended by the powers that be. Behind the secretary"s front podium, there were thin drawers stacked on top of each other. They slid in and out with about five to a row. Ronnie began opening them left to right starting at the top. When he got to the third one on the left he yelped "Check this shit out" and pulled out a large book. It was maybe two feet wide by two feet tall. I asked "I wonder what that shit is?" Ronnie answered "Let's open this bitch up and see". He lifted the book up onto the top of the rostrum and quietly opened it. "Scarf" he yelled, as he gazed down before him. "It's a definite shooo!" In a stern voice I warned "Be quiet dick head, or you're gonna get us busted". After he remembered where he was, he quieted down and replied "Fuck, you're right. But, look! Fucking lunch tickets! There's red ones and blue ones! Pages and pages of them! We can sell them or eat for free! We're rich, I tell ya. We're rich!"

In most school lunch programs, these tickets are for under privileged students to be able to purchase discounted or free lunches. The red ones were half off, the blue ones were gratis. Steadying the book on our laps, we ripped the ticket pages out of the book, stuck them under our coats, and ran back to the gymnasium with glee. Ronnie climbed back up the bleachers first to the open door we had come in. He entered and waited for me and I chased quickly behind him. Once inside Ronnie remarked "Holy shit! What a score. I can't believe we scarfed so good." Paranoid of being found out I said "That's cool. But, let's get the fuck out of here. I don't wanna go to jail for something as stupid as lunch tickets". When we were back on the roof, Ronnie was laughing hysterically and then mumbling something indecipherable. I think it was a phrase he had made up. He used it sometimes when he got excited and it always made me laugh. It sounded like Smoigelidoysh. At first I thought it was German. But, he never did tell me what it meant. After peering around to be safe, we got down quickly and escaped. The next time we attended school, we were selling lunch tickets at half price or giving them away. Though our names came up from suspicion, we never got caught or detained. Ronnie had another saying he was fond of "We were robbing from the bitches and giving kids riches. It was simplicity at its finest, while we stole from his highness." I guess it was true for that day.

I had met a guy named Vick N. through some mutual friends. Vick was 100% American Indian, 6 feet 5 and weighed about 210 pounds. He was skinny for his frame and had really long jet black hair and high cheekbones. He was proud of his heritage and bragged that he fit the true Injun stereotype. Vick lived in some brick faced apartments that were across from the Edison Train Station. It was a typical sub level abode that he shared with his father. He never told me about his mother and I avoided the subject out of respect. Though he looked much older, he was close to only being 18. He never went to school, had no desire to learn, and thought it was a total waste of time. Discovering this, I related to him immediately. He was a chain smoker with a great sense of humor and had very animated facial expressions that I thought were very entertaining. When he told a story, he made it feel as if you were there.

One day around noon, Vick said he had invited a girl to come over. Excitedly, he chuckled "She's the BJ queen of Edison. Well, one of them anyway. So, I'm gonna get some head. Do you want some too?" I had never had a blow job before and I told him so. He broke out in a loud guffaw "Oh my God, really?" he asked "Well, We're gonna have to fix that!" I replied "Well, I've had sex before. But, with BJ"s, I have no idea what to do. I've only seen them in porno films." He broke out into laughter "Huh?" he asked "What do you mean what do you have to do? You don't have to do shit but lay there. The chick does all the work. You'll see. But, you'll have to go after me because I got first dibs". I agreed to his plan and went farther and asked "Where am I gonna do this?" He replied "In a bed, of course. I'll let you use my dad"s bed with her when I'm done". I wanted more information about the girl and pestered him. "Was she pretty?" I asked. "Is she good at it? Does she have a nice body? Does she swallow? While asking him all of these things he acted as if he was slightly annoyed. "You sure do ask a lot of questions for someone who"s never had a BJ before" he said. He continued laughing "Well, you'll see when she gets here". But, she gives pretty good blow jobs for a young chick. So, I guess that's where she got her name from.

We were lounging on his couch smoking and drinking beer when the doorbell rang. He rose up and answered the door. As he moved aside, a girl who was obviously Hindu Indian strolled in. Like me, she looked to be about fifteen years old. She had a nice body, long black hair, brown eyes, and was wearing black glasses. She wasn't particularly pretty, but not ugly either. She weighed about 100 lbs. and appeared to be 5 feet 3. She was wearing Keds sneakers, white jeans, and a blue blouse. I introduced myself "Hi, I'm Ronnie" I said. "Nice to meet you" She nodded her head and whispered "Hi", and didn't say anything more. Vick interjected and chuckled "She never talks much. But, her mouth will be busy soon anyway". He took her by the hand and into his father's bedroom. I waited what seemed like a long time watching TV and drinking more beer. There was no sound coming out of the room which I thought was strange as I was in close proximity and figured I"d hear something. Some more time went by and Vick had finally emerged. "I'm sorry I took so long" he said. But, I wanted to enjoy it". By this time, the girl was clinging to the open door and watching us. Vick winked and blurted out "Ok Windy, its Ron"s turn. I'm gonna go to the store to get more beer. You know what to do. He's a buddy of mine. So, take good care of him, ok?" She smiled a bit and went straight back into the bedroom. He motioned for me to follow her. "Go on man, have some fun. I'll be back in a little while". I entered the room and she was naked from the waist up. I remember that she had flawless tits and she insisted I come over and I feel them. In a quiet voice she murmured "Lie down and let me take care of you. I do this for Steve F. all the time. I like it". "You know Steve F.?" I asked. "Oh yeah" she replied. "I do him whenever he wants. He loves it. But today, I wanted to do you guys". Before she attempted to fellate me, I got apprehensive and asked if I could fuck her instead. She squealed a little "Oh no" she said. "Vick tried that and I'm too small. And, I'm not trying it with you either. You can take the BJ or I'll go home". I didn't mean to offend her and didn't expect her reaction. "Ok" I said. "Whatever you want to do. I didn't mean to scare you". "It's ok" she replied calming down. "I'm still a virgin and I'm not ready to fuck. So, I take care of guys this way".

After about twenty minutes, she finished me off and was getting ready to go to the bathroom to spit. Vick had returned with the package goods and asked me how it went. "How did you do with that little squaw?" he asked. Suddenly, he saw her fly through the bedroom door and blocked her. "Where do you think you're going Miss Windy?" he asked. Windy with a mouthful and panic on her face, was making mmm, mmmm noises seeking desperately to expel. After teasing her for a bit, he eventually let her free. After she slammed the bathroom door shut behind her, we could hear her retching and cursing under her breath. Vick was laughing hysterically and turned to me "So?" he asked. "Like I was saying. How"d you like it? It was pretty good right?" I smiled and said "Yeah, that was great. Thanks for setting me up with her". "No problem" he said. "You can owe me a favor later". We went to sit back down on the couch and began bullshitting about various topics when Windy came out of the bathroom pouting and buttoning up her blouse. She attempted to sit down with us and was wiping the corner of her chin. Vick stood up, rolled his eyes while rubbing his palms together, took her by the hand, looked at me laughing and proclaimed "Seconds! I need another helping. I'll be back in a bit. Hang out for a little while and drink some fresh beer. I shall return when We're done". They went into the bedroom again and closed the door. This time, I didn't stay and went home. Thanks to Vick, I had gotten what I wanted. It was a good day.

It was a Wednesday in the middle of the week and I was hanging around with Mike W. We were walking toward route 1 and looking for something to do. On our way there, we had to pass Saint

Matthews Church and School. Saint Matthews also has a basement area. I had gone to a couple of CYO dances there. So, I knew its layout well. As we were walking by, Mike decided to check the lower level doors to see if any of them were locked. The one in the front was, but the one in the back was not. Mike whistled to me to get my attention. I looked over and he shouted "Hey Ron. Look, this door is open. Let's go in and see what's in there". I answered, "It's a church Mike. There's no money in there. The money would be upstairs". He quipped "Just come with me asshole, I wanna see what's here". He slowly opened the door and stepped inside. I followed closely after him. Even though there weren't any lights on, we could see from the daylight shining in from the windows. While glancing around to see what we could find, we took a few steps to the right. In front of us were what appeared to be two giant refrigerators. Each one had a handle that was vertical and about a foot long. They looked as if they were almost connected in the middle. They were at least eight feet high and 5 feet wide and their exterior doors were silver. Mike whispered "Hmmmm, let's see what's inside these bad boys". He grabbed the handle on the left container and pulled gently. As the door opened and we peered inside, Mike exclaimed "Viola, This one"s a freezer!" Inside, there were many kinds of frozen food. Like an Arctic blast, the air flow emanating from it was frigid. I told Mike "There's really nothing of value in here bro. It's too frozen. It would be too heavy to carry home anyway. And, even if we did, this shit would defrost before we ever got anywhere". Mike responded "Yeah, fuck that. My hands would freeze anyway" He shut the door and went on to the next portal on the right. As with the other door, he pulled on the handle and it swung open wide. "This is more like it" Mike uttered. "We can eat this shit right now". Inside there were refrigerated items ready to snack on. There were jarred pickles, yogurt, milk, lunch meat, juice, hot dogs, etc. There were also condiments, such as mayonnaise, mustard, ketchup, relish, and chopped onions.

Mike decided that he was hungry "Let's munch on some of these pickles first" he said. "Then We'll move on to some hot dogs." He took down the pickle jar from the top shelf, laid it on the floor and opened it. He pulled out a pickle with his fingers. Then, he passed the jar to me. He took a bite of his pickle and spit it out on the floor "These pickles suck" he screamed. They are too garlicky. Who eats this garbage?" I was in the process of retrieving my own pickle when I stopped in my tracks. I yelled back at him. "Well, if these pickles suck, I'm not eating this shit either" He then reached for the hot dogs on the middle shelf. "These look more edible" he said. "These better be good". He took a few frankfurters out of its package and began to stuff them in his mouth. After a few chews, he spit them out. "Motherfucker" he yelled. "These are like ice!" It seemed that the temperature dial was set too high on the box causing some of the items to be partially frozen. "Who"s the fucking moron who runs the show here?" he asked. I answered "Obviously, stupid asses Mike". He became enraged. "I wasted my time on this bullshit" He howled. "Now, they're gonna pay!"

He started to remove the large commercially sized mayonnaise container from the bottom shelf. "This will be a nice smear campaign" he joked. "We'll make finger paints with this goo". I was trying to keep my composure with the thought of mayonnaise being all over the place at Mike"s expense. I suggested to him "What about the mustard and ketchup Mike? Should we use them too?" He answered "Sure, We'll make a masterpiece each. It's good for texture" While laughing, we put all of the containers on the floor, opened their lids, and closed the refrigerator"s door. Mike reached into the mayonnaise decanter and took out a big scoop with his fingers. "It's time to paint" he mischievously laughed. He aggressively threw the gob on the freezer"s door on the left. Then, he attacked the mayonnaise making circular motions with his right hand. I asked "Are you ready for some sun? He yelled back "Yeah, come over here with some mustard and make a mural with me". I grabbed a dollop of mustard with my right hand and threw it on top of his creation. The liquids were beginning to meld together as he was mixing them in. "Look, Mike said "I made a thingy, a true work of art". I was laughing so hard I was trying not to piss myself. Now, it needs some blood" he demanded. He reached into the ketchup container and got a blob of red. He threw it as his conception and smeared it around some more. "Uh huh, Yup" he said. "It must be just the right base to gel correctly". By now, most of what he was swirling around was beginning to drip to the floor. It was like individual streams of blood that splattered on a wall and then slowly began to weep. Mike insisted it looked more like McDonald"s secret sauce. But, to me, it looked more like blood.

Mike suddenly expressed to me that he had to shit. "Ron!" he said "I have to make a logger really bad." I suggested "Let's try to find the bathrooms. I think they're upstairs". Mike answered frantically "Fuck that. I got no time to look for them. I gotta shit now. I can't hold it in any longer". I asked "What are you gonna do Mike? Shit right here on the floor?" "Precisely" he chirped. "They owe me anyway for having shitty food". I then got a little serious "But Mike, you can't do that. Come on man, it's a church. We already stole their food and made a mess". Mike retorted "I gotta go. It is what it is. Go and find me a paper towel or something for me to wipe with." He unbuttoned his pants, dropped them around his ankles, crouched down, and made the biggest turd I had even seen. It coiled as it came out and looked as if an appendage had rolled out of him. It was like a small canoe and over a foot long. I had found a roll of paper towels in a drawer in a cabinet and threw them to him. He took a segment, wiped his ass, and pulled his pants back up. "Ahhhhh" he smirked "I just made my donation for the poor". I was in shock that he had done this, but laughing hysterically at the same time. I felt a little guilty about it but Mike didn't seem to care. He was non chalant and acted as if it was an everyday occurrence.

While we were standing there chuckling, I heard an unexpected noise. "Mike" I said "I think someone"s here. I think I heard a door opening in the front". "I hear it too" he replied. "We better get out of here!" Just as we turned to leave, I saw a dark figure through the square glass portal of a door by a set of stairs in the front. It appeared to be a tall man and he had stopped to look around. With each step he took, I could hear the shuffle of his gait across the floor and saw his shadow from afar. I gasped at Mike "What"ll we do?" I asked. "He's sure to catch us if we keep standing here!" Mike thought for a second and pointed to the right. There, on an angle, was a food serving area. It was like the ones in most school lunch rooms with a glass partition out front and food compartments behind. For some reason, all of the food trays were stacked up on the corner of the sliding area. There must have been a few hundred of them and they looked like large plastic, rectangular cards.

Mike whispered "Stay quiet, and We'll hide under the trays". We crept toward the serving table, got down on our knees, and slid beneath it. I was facing the area where the man was, and Mike was directly behind me. After a few minutes of hiding and trying to determine if the man was coming our way or not, Mike murmured "Go take a look, see if he's still standing in the doorway or not". I replied "Fuck that shit, I'm not going out there. You're crazy!" Mike sighed and demanded "You can either go out there, or I'm gonna beat your ass!" Suddenly, we heard the sound of keys jangling. It was the type of noise you would hear off a key ring attached to a person"s belt. Back and forth it rang, closer and closer. "He must be the janitor" Mike whispered. He's probably coming to check out the mess we made". I peered out the edge of the food table through a slit between one of its legs. I wanted to see if I could get a glimpse of the man and his proximity to us. He finally got near enough where I could see his feet. He was wearing work shoes and grey trousers. As I got a better look I deduced that Mike was right; he appeared to be the custodian.

As I watched the man"s feet, I saw them amble forward and reverse. They then moved in a circle. It was as if his feet were confused and trying to figure out what to do next. His dance didn't last long though as I heard his under the breath grumble. All the while, Mike and I were about wetting ourselves. We knew if we were caught, it would probably mean a few nights in juvenile hall and the dreaded parental punishment routine. Eventually, the man seemed satiated with his assessment and moved on. His key jangling lessened as he walked farther away until we could no longer hear it anymore. Again, Mike tried to coerce me into going out there. "Come on man, I think he's gone now" he commanded. "Go and take another look". I wriggled out from beneath the table and stood up slowly. I gave a frenzied glance in the direction the man had come from. He was gone and he was nowhere to be seen. I thought "Ahhh, the coast is clear. It's now or never". I stuck my head in back where Mike was still hiding and whispered "Mike, it's time to go. The guy is gone". He flew out from beneath the counter like a runner in a marathon. He didn't utter a word and I had never seen his stubby legs move that fast before. I watched as he sprinted straight to the back door, pushed hard on its horizontal handle, and heard it fly open with a clang. After I caught up with him, we ran through the church"s back parking lot to escape. Frightened, we never looked back until we reached the woods behind Edison Lanes. We were there for some time until we finally caught our breath. Mike, slightly trembling said "Ron, that's the fastest I've ever run in my life. It was also my quickest sin".

I had never been to New York City before without my parents. I met a kid named George C. through some mutual friends. George being a copious drug user was known by the majority of the locals as Georgie Burns. We decided one day to take the New Jersey Transit train to Penn Station. While on the platform waiting for the train to arrive, Georgie informed me that he had some "hits" of acid. I asked him "Like LSD? Georgie replied "Yeah, just some low level blotter stuff. You wanna try some? We can trip in New York City!"

I had smoked a lot of pot and drank alcohol, but I had yet to dabble in harder drugs. "Sure" I said. "Why not?" Georgie took out a piece of aluminum foil from his jacket pocket and gingerly opened it to reveal two square tabs of blotter paper. On them, were printed red bulls eyes. "Here" Georgie said "We'll each take one of these. Put it on your tongue and let it dissolve. It probably won't kick in though until we've been in the city for a while". I put the tab in my mouth, let it dissolve half way through, and swallowed it down. Georgie did the same. Georgie laughed and announced "Let our magical mystery tour begin". A few minutes later, we embarked on our train to New York.

We arrived at the station about forty five minutes later. As we disembarked, I questioned Georgie "Hey man, I'm not feeling anything yet. How long does this shit take to kick in bro?" Georgie replied "It takes time man. Don't worry; We'll feel it pretty soon". We strolled up the stairs from the station to the street. Looking left and right, I asked Georgie "Where do you think we should go now?" Georgie exclaimed "We should go to Central Park. That way, when we peak, we won't be in a large crowd and freak out". I agreed with him and we began the long trek from 34th Street to 59th. As we were walking, I started to feel edgy. It was like someone was tickling me from the inside. I think the acid was beginning to kick in. Georgie? I asked. "Is this the way it's supposed to feel?" Georgie laughed and replied "For everyone it's different. But yeah, sometimes you'll get weirded out that way". I have to admit, I was a little scared as I had never experienced anything that felt like that before. Georgie elaborated trying to reassure me "Don't get too crazy bro, you won't tweak or anything. You'll just see trails coming off of things like light bulbs and shit. It's pretty enjoyable once that ticklish feeling goes away. It's like the coolest light show you"ve ever seen. You'll see".

We arrived at Central Park and sat down on some giant boulders that came into view. In front of us, in the distance, was a stage set up for what looked like a concert. I had never been to a concert before and was excited to see who was playing there. I looked above the stage and could see a banner with a white background and orange lettering. It was draped across what appeared to be the metal framing of the lighting rig. It read "Summer Concert Series with Joni Mitchell". I had heard of Miss Mitchell before from television and radio from when I was a little kid in the 60"s. I turned to Georgie and asked "We don't have to pay for this shit do we? Georgie answered "No man, it's a free show. This is gonna be excellent. Just sit back and go with it". Though I didn't really know much of Joni"s songs, I lay on my back and looked up at the sky. I was watching the clouds intertwine with each other and making different shapes. To me, they looked like ghosts. Becoming transparent, and then melding together again. Some of them reminded me of a fine mist, or steam from when the water in the shower is too hot. Georgie wasn't saying anything for what seemed like a long time. He just kept lying there and giggling to himself. Some more time had passed and Georgie finally spoke up "How do you feel bro?" he asked laughing. "Are you peaking yet? I'm seeing all kinds of shit!" I told him I was ok and that other than experiencing some strange thoughts, I was coping pretty well.

While we were listening to the music, a black guy came stumbling toward us. He climbed up the rocks nearby and sat down. He was talking to himself and incoherent and we couldn't understand him. Georgie took it upon himself to introduce himself. "Hey man". Georgie muttered. What's up with you? Are you enjoying the concert? My name"s George and this is my friend Ronnie". The black guy yelled "Who the fuck are you guys?" he asked. "Was I talking to your ass? What can you do for me? How can two little white boys help me?" I thought to myself "Great! Now, Georgie"s really done it. How the hell are we gonna get rid of this guy now?" Just when I thought there was gonna be a fight, Georgie pulled out another foil packet from his other pocket. "Hey bro! Georgie asked the guy "You wanna trip for free?" The man sized Georgie up and down suspiciously like a cop looking for a bust. "What do you got there little white boy?" he asked. "It better not be any funny shit". Georgie replied "Nah man, its LSD. You'll see all kinds of cool stuff. Just put it on your tongue and swallow it". Georgie handed the man the hit. The guy grabbed it and stuffed it in his mouth in a frenzy. "I hope this isn't bullshit" he exclaimed. "I wanna have a good day, punks".

We continued watching the concert as the black man started to become more and more erratic with his behavior. He was doing all kinds of odd dancing and talking to himself aggressively. After about twenty minutes, the guy reached into a garbage can. It was one of those receptacles made of metal that had rusted over time. The kind that looked like it was more of a bird cage than to hold refuse. In his hand was a page from a newspaper. As he spun it around, I noticed that it was the front page of the New York Daily News. He peered at it in disgust "Mark Spitz?" he screamed "Fuck this guy. He made millions of dollars from doing nothing. Fuck this motherfucker. All he did was swim. Olympics my ass! Anybody can fucking swim!" By this time, everyone in the park was watching him and he was bringing a lot of attention to himself. He looked over at us and pointed at the paper "What the fuck do you kids think of this guy?" he asked maniacally. "We didn't answer him as we didn't want to provoke the situation. He then took the page, waved it around viciously, and started hollering "This is what I think of Mark Spitz. Mark Spitz can kiss my motherfucking ass!" He took the paper, crumbled it up in a half ball, and pretended to wipe his ass with it. The crowd began to laugh hysterically. It was so funny; we were distracted from the music and no longer cared about the concert.

When the laughter was over and the man calmed down, He decided that he was hungry. He asked us "You white boys wanna come get hamburgers with me? I'm hungry as fuck" Georgie said "Sure" and we tagged along behind him. While we were hiking down the avenue away from Central Park, the man was becoming more and more unpredictable and agitated. His eyes were becoming wide and his gait was off. He was very animated and loud. When we finally stopped in front of a Burger King, he gazed inside, back at us, and asked demanding "Do you kids have any money?" Now, Georgie and I had a few bucks. But, we certainly weren't going to part with it for some crazy black guy on acid. We told him "No man, we don't have any money". He became enraged and screamed at us "Fuck you little white boys" he said. "Your shit is worthless. Wait right here and don't you move and you best be here when I get back". We watched as the guy went into the Burger King cursing to himself. I looked at Georgie with concern. "Yo, we better get out of here man" I said. "We don't know anything about this guy. He's nuts. What if he gets all violent and shit with us later?" I asked. Georgia shook his head in agreement and we left.

   By the time we were far away enough from the crazy black guy to feel safe, it was beginning to get dark outside. I suggested to Georgie that maybe it was time for us to go home. Georgie agreed. We took the long walk back to Penn Station for our return and boarded the train to our seats. Strangely, there weren't that many people aboard. I was tired by now and the acid was wearing off. Georgie was on one side of the train in his seat, and I was on the other. Suddenly, I started to feel queasy. I whimpered to Georgie "Georgie, I don't feel good man. I think I'm gonna puke". I lay down across the bench seat trying not to hurl. With every bump of the train, my stomach was starting to churn. "No" I thought. "Don't throw up here. Try to make it to the train"s bathroom". But, every time I made an attempt, my dizziness forced me down again. Georgie was laughing as he watched me go up and down and collapsing with each endeavor. "Just let it fly" Georgie chuckled. "Nobody gives a fuck anyway. It's just a stupid train, bro" Just as he was done with his remark, up it came. It was like a fire hose on full stream. It splashed like a geyser to the floor below me. Luckily, when it came up, my head was turned in a descending direction. It was orange and red residue swirling within a brown dank liquid. It stank terribly and it was putrid. Out of nowhere, the conductor strode by. He grabbed our tickets from the clip nestled in the top of our seats and kept going. He was looking straight ahead and ignored us the entire time. Either he was in a hurry, or he simply didn't want to deal with the puke dribbling on the floor. Georgie never stopped laughing. Even after we stopped and reached our home destination, Georgie just kept on giggling. Finally, between a break of teasing, he said "Ronnie, I guess acid and puke don't mix. The next time I go with you, drink Kool Aid".

A few days later, on a trip to the Gulotta"s house, I was rounding the corner when I heard the booming voice of Jeff. He was screaming something to Dennis about how Dennis had done something to him. All of a sudden, I heard a side window being slammed open facing the street. "I'll show you asshole! Watch this!" Jeffrey shrieked. Dennis was cautioning him "You better not, you better not Jeff! You'll be sorry!" Jeff continued yelling "Fuck that, I'm sick of your bullshit!" As I was trying to contain myself from laughing, Jeffrey flung a box out the window in anger to the ground and was mumbling to himself "Jerkoff, jerkoff!" The box hit the pavement with a clunk, spun on its edge, and coins of all denominations spilled out everywhere. They made a pinging sound as they fell to the street. Sporadically in all different directions they went, some were like little wheels doing pirouettes. Dennis sprinted to the street "My collection, my coin collection" he yelped. I can't believe you did that Jeff!" He was zigzagging behind the coins, trying to scoop up as many as he could before some disappeared forever. Later, when their furor had settled down, I asked him "Den? What the fuck was that all about? He replied "You know I had that coin collection right? I've been saving them off and on for years. I pissed Jeffrey off I guess. I was teasing him and he flipped out on me again. I think I have to find better hiding spots for my shit. He always finds them". When I passed Jeff in the kitchen, I asked for his version of the story. In typical Jeffrey fashion, he blared back at me "Fuck you Ron, don't worry about it. Stay the fuck away from me!" I was starting to learn that if Jeff gets upset, he takes a very long time to calm down.

Around this time, a lot more pinball arcades had begun to pop up. Minnie had sold her luncheonette to a guy who was a former police officer and he renamed it Thursday"s Place. There was also Romper Room, Sergeant Peppers, Darios, and Playmore 1. They were the perfect haunts for teenagers to congregate from within. There, we could socialize within walking distance. From all over town kids came and were like lemmings to the sea. This was especially true on Friday and Saturday nights. We loved it as these places were out of reach of nosey parents prying eyes and ears. Mostly, they were pick up joints for girls and to find drugs. In the beginning, it was usually marijuana or a few pep pills. The pinball games were a cover and a secondary. Thursdays is where Phil introduced me to Black Beauties. Most teenagers loved Black Beauties. They were brown dextromethamphetamine granules stuffed into dark purple capsules surrounded by caffeine and were made by a company named Pennwalt. The first time Phil offered them to me I had no idea what they were. "Diet pills" Phil said. "The ones fat housewives take with a prescription to try to lose weight. "What do they do to you? I asked. "You take a couple of these, and you'll be up for a couple of days" he replied. "They're speed, bro. Take them and you'll be flying!" Since it was a weekend, I wanted to try some. I had taken two of the capsules he offered me and waited for the effects to arrive. About an hour later, I became very jittery and talkative. I went to the bathroom to piss. I glanced in the mirror and I noticed that the pupils in my eyes were dilated. They looked like big black saucers that were lifeless with no soul. But, physically I felt like I had the energy of ten men. I also noticed that I was sweating profusely and my shirt was soaked with perspiration. I finished my evacuation and went back by the pinball machines. Phil was playing as if he was in a tournament. "How do you feel?" he asked. "Did you get off on them yet?" "Phil" I jammered "These fucking pills are amazing. I feel like a million bucks". "I told you" he said. "They are great. Wait to you find some ho and fuck on them. It'll take you forever to come. But, when you do, it's a full body experience. You'll love it!".

I couldn't sit still and everything felt like it was moving in rocket acceleration. As I was standing there watching Phil play pinball, people were coming in and out of the back door. Some were kids I had never seen before. This is where I met Howie B. and Dave G. Dave was the younger brother of Archie. I knew Archie through Ronnie. Archie and Dave also had a brother named Michael who I was in school with. Archie was also in charge of Thursdays at night. The owner usually went home after 4pm and that was when the fun began. Archie didn't see or hear very well. So, the kids took full advantage of him. One night, one of the teens was yelling for Archie to come in the back where there was a bank of machines. This kid was feigning that one of the pinball games was broken. Archie asked "What? What? I'll be right there". Now, Archie was a big guy. He was about five feet ten and 300 pounds. Therefore, it usually took him some time to lumber his way back to where we were. While he was being distracted, another kid would sneak up behind the lunch counter to pilfer the cash register. With all of us knowing that Archie couldn't hear that far, the kid would open the drawer and remove a ten or twenty dollar bill. When the ruse was complete, someone in the back would scream "Thanks Arch, the machines fixed now. We got it bro". Archie would saunter back to his station none the wiser. This went on quite a few nights. Archie never figured it out.

His brother Dave I liked right away. He was a chubby kid who was about five feet nine and a few years younger than me. Though he was an adolescent, he was very bright and wise beyond his years. He also had a fantastic, dry sense of humor. He could be very sarcastic when making fun of people and kind when he wanted to be. I loved the guy. With him standing next to me, he studied my body language and knew I was on something. "Hey Ron?" he asked "What the fuck are you on bro? I noticed you can't sit still and won't shut the fuck up". I replied "Beauties man". He asked "Do you have any left for me?" I told him "Sorry bro, you gotta talk to Phil here. He's the one who hooked me up". As Dave began to ask Phil about a deal, Howie B. walked up behind me "Your name"s Ron right?" he asked. "I think you know my brother Brian" he said. I replied "Yeah, I know him. He's pretty cool. I think my older brother knew your older brother too". "Cool" Howie answered. "We'll have to hang out sometime". Close to the back door was also a juke box. It was usually playing some rock music very loudly. As I looked to my left, I could see a figure dancing sporadically. He turned toward me and I recognized that it was Paulee B. He was singing along to the record very bombastically "I'm going to Kansas City, Kansas City here I come" Just then, a guy named Ellsworth, who was a few years older than us, crossed the path of the back door. He had a wine sack in his mouth and was drinking booze out of it. While doing so, he was bobbing back and forth to the music making peace sign gestures with his hands. The song ended and I asked Ells if I could have a sip of his potion. He replied "Sure, but just a little. It has to last me all night, it's brandy. So, take your time, it's kind of strong". While I was swigging down a shot, Paulee was dropping a coin into the juke box slot for another tune. He chose Kansas City again. Ellsworth yelled out "God damn it! He's gonna do it again. Somebody stop him. If you don't, he'll keep playing that damn song over and over again! He'll drive us crazy!"

On a Friday afternoon, we were all in TJ"s smoking bathroom again. The usual Marlboros were being passed back and forth in the stalls between us. I don't know where the phrase came from, or who invented it. All I do know is that it had to be Phil or Dennis G. as I overheard them talking about pussy. Phil was saying something along the lines of "Hey Den? If you saw so and so walking toward us, would ya?" It was obvious he meant young females. Dennis asked "Would I what?" Phil exclaimed "You know Den? Would you eat it? Ullllllllhhhhh!" "Eat it?" Dennis replied "It all depends if it was clean or stinky". For many years after that day, that phrase spread in Edison like wildfire. Whenever some male would see a pretty girl walk by and he was with his friends, this remark would be made regularly regarding her appearance. We also used it for something exciting. In other words, the guys would yell "Ulllllllhhhhh" to signify that she was hot and "doable". Dennis called it "The clit noise". It remains in use to this day.

While this was going on and I was laughing my head off, we heard the boom boom signal at the door. We thought it was ok and we thought it was one of us. Unfortunately, it was not. Quickly, like a shot from a gun, walked in Mr. S. "You guys never give up do you?" he asked. "No" I said. "We'll give up when you stop pestering us". Mr. S then went off "That's it Arold" he barked. "You're coming to the office with me. I've cut you too many breaks already". He went to grab my elbow at an attempt to escort me outside. Unfortunately for him, I was wearing a baseball cap with a metal snap on its back. I insisted to Mr. S. "Come on man, this is bullshit. How come you're not going after anyone else?" He replied "Don't worry about anyone else, my focus is on you. Let's go!" I refused and pulled back on his grip struggling to break free. He wouldn't stop and I got pissed off. I took off my hat and whipped his hand with it. He backed off cradling his hand and wincing in pain. He yelled "You're in for it now. I'm going to the nurse and I'll deal with you later". He left the lavatory and we all had a great laugh. "Fuck him" Phil said. "He's been on the rag all week". I went back to his class after our smokes and awaited my fate. Mr. S. came to class a while later with Mr. Bone in tow. In his usual Gestapo tone, Mr. Bone informed me "You broke Mr. S's pinky finger with the strap on the back of your cap. Therefore, you're suspended for three days starting now. Leave the building immediately and don't come back until we've spoken to your parents". "Cool!" I answered. "It's another vacation! That sounds good to me!"

A few nights later, I was on my way to meet friends at Sergeant Peppers pinball joint. It was on route 27 close to where the old Grand Union used to be. It wasn't very large and was a small store front in a strip mall with about six machines inside. To get there, I had to take my usual short cut through the back of TJ"s field. On my way, I was seething about how Mr.S. had me suspended unfairly. I wanted revenge. I wanted retribution. I wanted satisfaction. I got to the front of TJ by the cafeteria and was wondering what I could do to teach him a lesson. After some thought, I began to check the eateries doors. I wanted to see if the school was stupid enough to have left any of them open. I checked a door by the main office. No dice. I checked the front door of the lunchroom. Not open. But, there seemed to be a one inch gap between the door knobs plate and its latch holding it closed to its frame. "I think I can jimmie this" I thought. I just had to find something to slide back the locking mechanism.

I searched around on the ground for some possibilities. Soon, I was in luck and found an old Popsicle stick jutting out of some grass. "Perfect" I thought. "I'll be in in no time". After a few minutes of wrestling with the lock, the door popped open. I peered inside and it was dark with not much light. But, I could make out the eerie outline of the ice cream box that was usually by the side door of the cafeteria during lunch time. "They must have wheeled it back here" I pondered. It was plugged in and running so I guessed it was moved at the end of the day to stop kids like myself from stealing from it. "Wrong move" I laughed. "It's mine now!" I reached across its top, slid open the door, and gaped inside. There they were. It was iced creamy goodness just waiting for my pilferage. Boxes and boxes of ice cream sandwiches. Like dry ice being dipped into warm water, there was a frigid fog wafting over my hands as I reached for the treasure below. I thought

"Ummmmm, this is gonna be good. I'm gonna take all of these babies out of here".

Just then it occurred to me, I hadn't the forethought of how I was going to move the bulk of these rectangular gems as I knew I could only carry a few at a time. Plus, they were far too cold for my hands to handle for a long journey. An idea went off in my head like a light bulb. I remembered on the way in, I caught a glimpse of an Acme markets carriage out by a stop sign. Sometimes, kids would take these carts from the store"s parking lot and wheel them up the street for fun. I had a dastardly plan. I propped the door open with a rock I found in the entranceway keeping it's just enough ajar without raising suspicion from passersby. I skipped over to the cart, scanned around for anyone watching, and moseyed the carriage over to the door. I opened the gateway and pushed the buggy inside. After gently closing the door behind me, I positioned the carriage as close to the ice cream freezer as possible.

As the icy mist enveloped my hands and rolled out of the container, it reminded me of a wave you see at the beach. It curled over like a half pipe but was opaque in color and transparent as it moved. It was surreal and I almost felt like I was in a horror movie. I reached inside and began lifting out cases of these frosty treats one by one. I transferred them all to the carriage as quickly as I could. When the cooler was empty and the cart was full, I slowly pushed it back to the door. I hesitated for a moment as I wanted to see if the coast was clear. I pushed the door open a crack with my one hand while my other hand was on the carriage behind me. I took a good look around and saw no one. Therefore, I knew I was home free. Gently, I pulled the cart through the portal and to the outside. Letting go, the door closed behind me on its own. I was so nervous; I didn't even bother to see if it had closed all the way. I just wanted out of there before my delinquency was discovered.

I began to nudge the carriage through TJ"s front lot and to the street and made a right at the stop sign. All the while, the cart was making a slight racket with its wheels underneath. Rattle, rattle, rattle they went. I was desperate not to get caught and was hoping no one would hear them. But, now that I had my booty, what would I do with all these ice creams I wondered? I decided to share them with friends at Sergeant Peppers pinball parlor. After all, it wasn't that far from TJ and all I had to do was circumvent a few left and right turns. It was a quick run passed my old grammar school Stelton, and directly across Plainfield Avenue. I knew if I was fast I could make it without being busted. My biggest fear was the cops. "How could I explain all those ice cream sandwiches?" I thought. Trying not to think about it, I reached the pinball place and parked the cart outside the door. I ran inside and screamed for everyone to come and see. I was yelling "I scream, you scream, we all scream for ice cream". As the kids flew down the stairs to check out the commotion, I reached inside the carriage and began throwing ice cream sandwiches up in the air. They were raining down like frozen bricks of kiddie contentment. I felt like the child catcher in the Chitty Chitty Bang Bang movie. For a moment, I was the guy running around singing "I have ice cream kiddie winkies! Ice cream! And, it's all free today!"

My father had decided that I needed to find a part time, after school job. The thought of it had piqued my interest from time to time as I liked the idea of having my own money. It was suggested that I would go to Edison High School's job counselor Mr. O"Leary for some help. I thought it strange that even though I was still in junior high school, our district made us go to the higher learning building to achieve employment opportunities. After school one day, I made the trek to Mr. O"Leary"s office. I approached his cubicle and gave it a knock. "Come in, come in sonny" he said. "What can I do for you?" I heard a voice ask. Behind an open newspaper, I saw a pair of hands attached on each side and eyes looking up at me. "I'm just looking over this week"s job ads" he mumbled. "Sit down and give me a minute". He eventually dropped the paper from his face and laid it down on his desk. In front of me was a rather large man, maybe in his 50"s, in a suit that didn't fit quite right, and wearing a red tie. "So? What kind of job are we looking for?" he asked. "How old are you? And, have you ever worked before?" "No" I replied. "I'm 14 and have never had a job. "Not even something like delivering newspapers?" he asked. "Nope" I replied. "Nothing". "Well" he said. Sit down for a bit, and We'll try to find you something".

He glanced over the wants ads and circled listings with his pencil one at a time. "No" I heard him murmur "Too young for that one, nope". As he peered down the second column, he hit upon something. "I think I have a position for you here" he chuckled. "Do you think you could handle being a busboy?" "What's a busboy?" I asked. "It's clearing off the tables after people have eaten" he replied. "Haven"t you ever seen kids doing that when you go out to eat with your parents?" "Well" I answered. I never really paid attention to any of that". "Ok then" he said. "If you think you can handle it, I'll draw up the necessary working papers, give them a call, and send you right over. The place is called Mom"s and it's on route 27 across from the fire station. Do you know where that is?" "Yeah" I replied. I think I can find it. Thanks for your help".

The next afternoon, I took my newly printed working papers and arrived at Mom"s for an interview. I was a little nervous but excited at the same time. I walked in the front door and was greeted by a hostess. "Hi" she said. "Are you the kid who"s come here for the busboy position?" she asked. "Yup, that would be me" I answered. "Stay right here" she said. "Joe"s in the back and he'll be out in a second". I nodded my head yes and waited. I could see waitresses getting tables ready for the dinner hour and people going in and out of a swinging door in the back. With each fluctuation of the door, I got a whiff of some kind of food. It wafted to my nostrils like a pizzeria or a tomato cannery. It was a steady stream of obvious Italian faire. Eventually, from the swinging door emerged a tall, thin man with a pencil moustache and an apron around his waist. He approached me and introduced himself. "Hi, I'm Joe. I'm half owner with my brother Tony. Your name is Ronald, right?" he asked. "Mr. O"Leary called me about you. Can you start tomorrow right? The job pays $1.20 an hour and you get 10 percent of the waitresS's tips". "Sure, I can do that" I replied. He continued "Make sure you wear nice clothes and a pair of good dress shoes. No sneakers or T shirts. I see your hair is kind of long. Tuck it in the back of your collar and there shouldn't be a problem, ok? We start about 6:30. Try to be on time" "All right" I replied. "I'll see you tomorrow".

At 6 o"clock the next evening, I strolled in the door. I heard a very deep male voice bellowing out orders to the waitresses and it sounded like he was berating them. "Hurry up and get those tables done" he screamed. "I don't have all night for this bullshit". Like beaten dogs trying to hide in a corner after too many whippings, they were scurrying about in fear. They were acting very subservient and were obviously afraid for their jobs. Just then, a very large man approached me from out of sight and asked me who I was. He was short, dirty, with stubby hands, greased back hair, and what appeared to be a vulgar disposition. "Who are you?" he asked barking. "I'm Ron" I told him. "I'm your new busboy". "Ohhh, our new busboy huh? He asked. "Well, Joe didn't say anything to me about you. But, don't worry, I'll put you right to work. Go see the head waitress and she'll tell you what to do. And, don't let me see you standing around. You're here to work, not to entertain yourself".

I walked over to the lead waitress and asked her what to do. She told me her name and that it was easy. "Just take one of these gray tubs" she instructed. "And, clear off all the dishes from the used tables. Remove the glasses, plates, garbage, everything. When you're done, drop off the tub on the dishwashers counter in the back and start a new table with another one. You don't have to wipe them down when you're finished because we do that for you unless

We're really busy". "Ok" I answered. "I can do that". As I was leaning against a wall waiting for the first diners to vacate, Tony walked by. "What the hell are you doing?" he asked. No one stands around in my restaurant. Get your ass in the back and go help the dishwasher. Don't come out until a waitress calls for you". Usually, I don't stand for anyone screaming in my face. But, he was an intimidating obese man and I needed the money. So, I made a concession. I figured I would get back at him later anyway.

After working there for about 2 weeks, it was Christmas time and I thought I would have the holiday off. When I conferred with the lead waitress, she told me "You have to go ask Tony or Joe". Joe was easier to approach. But, he wasn't around. So, I was forced to ask Tony and I dreaded it. By now, I had learned that Tony was seen as the commandant and all of the employees were afraid of him. He was like a Nazi overseer who yapped out orders just because he could and it appeared to me that he disliked everything. I had begun to hate him. Tony was usually in the kitchen with the chefs while Joe ran the front of the house. So, he was easier to locate. All I had to do was follow his loud, asshole voice. I swung one of the kitchen doors open and stepped inside. Being the disgusting human being that he was, he was behind the chefs table picking his nose. "This guy is so gross" I thought. But, I had to see if I had off or not. "Tony?" I asked. "Do I have to work on Christmas?" He looked at 2 cooks who were with him, rolled his eyes, and began to laugh loudly. "Do you believe this guy?" he asked chuckling "These kids now a days hate to work. Yeah you have to work" he screamed. "And, on Christmas Eve too. Now, get your ass back out there and clean up or leave". "What a scumbag" I thought. "No wonder everyone hates him"

I had worked Christmas Eve and Christmas and made an astonishing $130. $130 in those days for a kid who was only 14 was a lot of money. I was very happy. Until, I went in the next night. I had always done my job very efficiently and mostly kept my mouth shut routinely avoiding Tony whenever I could. When customers were lax and only a few, I had to fake that I was busy even when I wasn't to satiate him. It worked for a while. But, Tony seemed to enjoy berating me for the smallest infractions. He saw me standing by one of the empty tables and commanded me to "Go in the back, get fresh drinking glasses, and stack them on the shelf on the wall". I nodded my head "Ok" and did what he asked. While I was arranging the glassware, I had a tumbler in my hand. I had an itch on my head and scratched it. Tony saw this and went ballistic "What the hell are you doing?" he screamed "You can't scratch your head while holding a glass in the same hand. You can't do that in front of the customers. If you do that again, you're fired." By this time, I had had enough of Tony"s ugly attitude and was ready to quit. "Really? I asked yelling. "Well, maybe the customers watching would like to know how you make me put all of the butter and bread back in the cooler in the kitchen. You know? How you insist that it be used again after they are done eating and have left. Also, fat boy, how about how you pick your nose while preparing food and that if a chef drops something on the floor, you tell them to pick it up, wipe it off, and put it back on the burner again? How about that Tone?"

He was furious. The few customers were craning their necks to listen. They were mortified. "That didn't happen, that didn't happen" he screamed. His face was contorted and red. The angrier he got, the louder he became. He looked like a thermometer that was ready to pop. Finally, he howled "Get out! Get out and don't come back! You're fired! I don't ever want to see you again!" "Fine" I snorted. "Your place is filthy anyway. I'll see you next week for my pay check" then, he really got livid "You're not getting shit" he screeched. "You're banned from here". "We'll see about that" I replied. "Wait till the health department finds out what I've seen in here" He pointed at the door and had one of his waitresses escort me out of the premises. When I arrived home, I told my father about what happened. He drove me to Mom"s the following week to retrieve my last paycheck. My father was not the type to be intimidated easily. When he went inside to collect my wages, Tony was apologetic and told my father it was all a big misunderstanding. A misunderstanding my ass!

I had really liked working and was determined to find another job. A friend of Dennis G."s named Timmy was employed at the Power Test gas station on route 1 south. Timmy lived close to Dennis and was known as "Tight Timmy". It seemed he got that moniker due to the fact that when out with his friends he would insist that he was broke but would have a wallet full of cash. Timmy had told Dennis that Power Test needed a gas jockey for their afternoon shift. So, Dennis sent me over to him. I went to the station and met Timmy and the manager. Timmy told him "Ron"s a good guy. You don't have to worry about him. He's a good worker". "Can you work 3 to 9pm?" the manager asked. "Sure" I replied. "Come in tomorrow afternoon then. You don't have to worry about working papers as it's an under the table job. You don't have a problem with that, do you?" he asked. "Nah" I responded. "Ok, well Timmy"s busy working right now" he said. "I don't want anyone hanging around distracting him. So, come back later on, ok?" I'll see you later then" I replied. "I was happy for the opportunity and left.

The next afternoon I arrived at the station at 3pm. Timmy was by himself and servicing customers and the manager was nowhere in sight. When Timmy was done, I asked "Where"s the boss guy?" Timmy replied "Sometimes he goes home for a few hours to eat and get some rest. I'm going home in a few minutes. Start pumping gas when the customers come in. Afterwards, come in the office and I'll show you how to work the credit card machine". Soon, I followed Timmy to the office desk. On top was the slide back and forth carbon copy machine for credit purchases. After explaining how it worked and he was satisfied I could handle it, Timmy had a scheme. "You wanna make an extra $10 a day bro?" he asked scheming "Sure" I said. "How the hell do you do that?" Timmy explained. "The dummy manager told me he allots $10 a shift for spillage. I just make sure I'm really careful when pumping the gas. That way, I can scarf the ten bucks without him knowing. Nice huh?" "What a scam Timmy" I replied. Timmy added "Make absolutely sure you never go over the $10 though. Cause if you do, and he checks the readings on the pumps, he'll catch us". "Ok man" I said. "I'll make sure". Timmy then left for the day.

After a few weeks of Timmy and I pilfering the extra $10 per shift, we were called into the manager"s office. "What is this bullshit" he screamed at us. "I've checked the figures for the last 3 weeks and each shift there's $20 missing from the till. The numbers don't add up!" Timmy replied "I don't know what you're talking about man. I always made sure the money is right at the end of my shift". The manager turned to me "What about you?" he asked enraged "You work the afternoon shift until closing. There's no way you didn't know anything about this!" I shook my head no and blurted out "How the hell do I know? I just pump the gas, give change, write up credit card receipts, and put everything in the register". The manager became increasingly irate. He yelled "I call liars with the both of you. Since neither one of you will come clean, you're both fired. Now, leave!" I started to walk off the lot toward the exit. I could hear Timmy in the background behind me. He was still with the manager and trying to explain himself. But, the boss didn't want to hear it. Suddenly, Timmy came running up to me and was whispering "Fuck Ron, what did you do?" he asked. "What do you mean what did I do?" "What the fuck did you do? I asked. "That guy's pretty pissed off" I said. Did you take more than the ten bucks a day? "Yeah" Timmy laughed "I took an extra $10. So, twenty bucks a day". "Damn Timmy" I chortled. "You didn't tell me. I was doing the same shit as you were. I guess he was missing forty bucks a day instead". "Oh well" Timmy grinned. "Better luck next time I guess".

I returned to Billy F"s house after school one afternoon to hear his latest scheme. He wanted to show me a sure fire thing. It was something about cars. We were in his father's workshop in the basement across from the pool table area. In there, there was an assortment of tools, paints, bolts, screws, nuts, etc. It was pretty much all you needed to fix or build anything. As I was looking around the room, Billy motioned me over to a grinder. There, there were a set of drawers just beneath. He slid open the top tray and showed me various keys. "This one" he pointed. "This is the one I wanted to show you. This is the one I was talking about!" I asked angrily "What's the big deal about a key, man? You called me all the way over here for a key? "No" Billy said. "This is a special key, bro. I filed it down with the grinder myself." I still didn't get it. "What the fuck are you talking about?" I asked. Billy explained "You know those old cars that take those little keys to start them?" he asked. "The ones like Volkswagen, Datsun, and Volvo? Well, I tested this one on a friend's Beetle and it worked! I put the key in, turned it, and the bitch started right up!"

I only half understood him. I still didn't get the full significance of a small, aluminum key. "How would it help us?" I thought. Billy got agitated "Ron, you don't get it. Don't you see?" he asked. We can use it to steal cars now!" "Oh!" I said. "Now I get it. We can have fun with this. How"d you figure this out anyway?" he chuffed "I'm not stupid man. I ground down the teeth. I was looking through all those keys one day and it reminded me of small keys in people"s cars. I got an idea that I could probably make a key that would fit one of them". "Excellent" I replied. "When do we start?" He went into detail "You know that train station by where you live? He asked. "Have you ever seen how many people park their cars there? That's easy pickings my friend, easy pickings".

The very next morning, we resolved to cut school. I met Billy at Thursdays Place and over our pork roll, egg, and cheese sandwiches, we hatched our evil plan. "Soon as everyone is in school" Billy chirped, "We'll go down to the station and check out some cars". I nodded my approval while munching on breakfast and couldn't wait to leave. As we were finishing up, I glanced at the clock on the wall. I mentioned to Billy "It's nine o" clock bro, you wanna go now?" I asked. "Let's have a smoke first" he replied. "Then, We'll head on over."

We arrived at the station as the last of the nine to fivers had boarded their train. There were still a few stragglers driving around the parking lot. They appeared to be housewives who had dropped off their husbands for their daily commute. As we waited, they queued at the exit for their car ride back home. One after another their autos would turn, left up a hill, and right down a slope. They were taking too long and we were getting antsy. When we no longer heard the hum of their engines, we knew it was safe to go on. Finally, they had left, all of them. It was time for selection, a blank key victim to test out our wares. We traipsed down each aisle to scope out each spot. There were no candidates in the first lane, and none in the second. Billy was getting depressed "What the fuck man" he moaned. "Doesn't anyone own fucking Volkswagens anymore?" Just as we navigated the third pathway, we saw it. It was a white 62 Volkswagen beetle. "It's about fucking time" Billy roared. "I was about to give up on this bullshit". "Ron" he directed "See if one of the doors are open. I'll keep watch bro". "Ok, gimme a second" I replied. I quietly crouched down and tiptoed to the passenger"s side of the vehicle. "We're in luck man" I whispered over the hood. "The door is open". Good! Billy chuckled "Let's get in and give it a try". I slowly opened the door and slid into the passenger seat. Billy was already by the driver"s side and getting anxious "Hurry up!" he demanded. "Open the damn door already!" I pulled on the lever and gave it a nudge. "There you go" I mumbled. "Jump in and let's get rolling". He fumbled for the skeleton key. "I got it right here in one of these pockets. Damn it! Gimme a second!" he barked. While I was waiting for him to remember which pocket it was in, I watched in the rear view mirror for any busy bodies. Finally, he had found it. He took it out, lined it up with the hole, and popped it right in. "Lemme give this sucker a turn" he said. "Don't forget the clutch Billy "I reminded him. "Do I look like a fucking moron Ron?" he asked. "No man" I replied, "I just wanna make sure it starts ok" "Just watch for the cops" he commanded. As the cylinder turned and the ignition connected, the engine roared to life. "Excellent" exclaimed. "Let's back this thing up and see what it'll do!"

We drove backwards out of the parking spot and into the lane facing the exit. With a loud crunch, Billy slid the car into first gear. Moving forward, he decided against taking Central Ave., the main road of egress. On the right, adjacent to the parking lot, was a dirt road. It ran parallel to the railroad tracks and was owned by Amtrak. I knew this road well as I grew up playing there as a small child. Therefore, I knew its lengths and boundaries. Billy lurched the VW toward the thoroughfare and remarked "We're gonna go this way instead. It's less visible, and we can take the back roads after that. We'll go through the neighborhoods off Sutton"s Lane". Knowing the road led to there, I agreed with him and we drove on. When we reached the end, he stopped the vehicle and stared ahead. "Why did you stop?" I asked. "I thought we were going the back way?" Across the street, was another dirt road that went up a slight hill, and curved to the right. "I wanna see what's up there" he said. "I've never been up that way before". "Are you sure Billy?" I asked. "I don't know what's on the other end of that road" "It'll be fine" he quipped. "We can always dump this thing and walk back if we have too"

We climbed the slope with the beetle and rumbled onward. After the sharp right turn at the top, we could see the entirety of our route and it appeared to stretch for at least a half a mile. "Let's get this thing in third gear" Billy howled. "I wanna see what this pig can do!" He ground the shifter into position and it made a loud metallic noise. It was the kind of sound you hear when gears don't mesh properly. "Damn Billy" I said. "You're really beating the shit out of this thing" "Fuck this junk" he replied. "We don't own it, who gives a fuck?" We picked up some speed and he was really starting to enjoy himself. Zig zagging and rocking up and down, there seemed to be a lot of mud holes. With each one it would make a splash and made us feel like a spinning top in a board game. Billy laughed "This road is treacherous bro! I didn't know there was this many bumps!"

We pressed on until we came to an end in the roadway. Suddenly, Billy hit the brakes. "Jesus Christ" he screamed. "I didn't see that shit!" The trail curved to the right, stopped, and edged up to the railroad tracks. There was nowhere else to go. "I guess We're fucked now" I said. The road"s too narrow to turn around in. We might as well get out and leave it here". Billy became incensed "Fuck that bullshit, Ron! We'll just drive the front up over the rails, back up, and make a K turn". "There's no fucking way We'll be able to get those front wheels back up over those tracks Billy!" I cursed. He insisted intently "I'll do it Ron, you'll see. I don't feel like walking all the way back. Fuck that! Watch me!" I didn't want any part of his plan so I stepped out onto the roadway. Though I knew it wouldn't work, I was chuckling inside and said "Go ahead, buddy and give it a whirl!" He put the transmission in first, popped the clutch, and ran the tires over the rails. Suddenly, the undercarriage of the bug made a scraping, scratching sound. It resembled abrasive metal on metal chatter. He came to a stop and tried reverse. Then forward. Over and over he tried while cursing all the way. It wasn't working. It seemed the car was half on the tracks, and half off. It was obvious the frame was stuck. Each time he attempted to dislodge it, he became more and more irate. "Billy" I screamed "The fucking things teeter tottering. You'll never get it off of there. The car"s grounded now. Come on man; let's get the fuck out of here before somebody sees us!" He didn't want to hear it "Fuck this car, fuck this car" he raged. This shit's really pissing me off!" After about ten minutes, he exhaustively gave up. He shut off the vehicle and jumped out the door.

Unbeknownst to us, there was a man coming out of the woods walking his dog. He was on the left and approaching fast. He seemed to be in his mid-forties. When he got closer he asked "What the hell are you guys doing? Is your car stuck? How the hell did you get it on there like that? Do you need any help? I can go back to my house and call a tow truck for you if you want?" Trying to bullshit the guy, I engaged him in some small talk conversation. I was trying to deflect and manipulate him. "Yeah, I just bought this car for like nine hundred dollars" I said "Me and my friend here were just taking it out for a test spin. We misjudged the road and got caught on the tracks". Surprised, the man questioned me "Nine hundred dollars?" he asked incredulously. "No offense Sonny, but I think you paid a little too much for that car. And, you sure spun it up there now didn't you?" After the three of us laughed, I told him "Thanks for your offer to help us. That would be really cool if you called that wrecker. We'd really appreciate it". The man replied "No problem. I'll go make the call and be right back. I'll wait here with you when they arrive to make sure everything is ok" Sure" Billy replied "that would be great". When the guy had left and was no longer in sight, Billy snickered "He's gone now, let's get the fuck out of here before he comes back. I don't think he believed us and I don't trust that guy. I bet he's going to call the cops!" "Trust?" I thought. I'll never let Billy drive again!

I had made another friend at school and his name was Lance. He was a couple of years younger than me and was a scrawny kid who was about 5 feet five and 100 pounds sopping wet. He had long, scraggily blonde hair parted in the middle and he talked really fast and was always asking questions about everything. It was an occasional annoyance, but I liked how inquisitive he was as I've always believed that asking questions was a sign of intelligence. He invited me over to his house and he lived in the Nixon section on

Kenmore Road. I entered his home and there were kids running all over the place. So, I figured it was his brothers and sisters. He brought me to his living room and one of them caught my eye. I asked "Who"s that?" "Oh, her?" he asked. "That's my older sister Belinda. Why? Do you like her or something?" "I just saw her you retard" I sighed "Why would I like her like that already?" "I dunno he said. "Everybody seems to want to date her". Belinda was a skinny girl with long blonde hair and pretty blue eyes. She had one of those looks where on one angle she was average, but on another she was attractive. She had a Stevie Nicks aura about her long before there was a Stevie Nicks. She was wearing bell bottoms, leather sandals, and a peasant girl shirt. She was the epitome of a hippie chick.

In the corner of the room were two short guys with their backs to me who were fumbling around with a record player on the floor. One of them had an afro and the other long, straight black hair. I noticed right away that they looked as if they were tan and had slightly darker complexions. Lance strolled over and introduced them to me "Ron, this is Tony and John Velez. They are friends of Belinda. Tony is going out with her". As they turned around to address me, I noticed Tony had an album in his hand. Being that I loved music, I was interested in it right away. "Hi" Tony I said. "Nice to meet you". "So?" he asked. "You're a friend of Lance huh? Cool! Anybody who"s a friend of Lance is a friend of mine. This is my twin brother Johnny" Johnny stuck out his palm to shake my hand. We exchanged pleasantries with the "bro" shake that was popular at the time. The cupped palm routine. "What's up man?" he responded. He saw that I was staring at the record in his brother's hand. "Do you like Rick Derringer?" he asked. "I don't know who that is?" I replied. "You don't know the song Rock and Roll Hootchie Koo?" he asked laughing. "Everybody knows that song!" "I know the song, man" I replied. "I just didn't know who did it". Tony was laughing "Well, We'll just have to show you then won't we?" he quipped. He turned back around and placed the record on the turntable and dropped the needle. The tune began to scream from the speakers. They started to head bang in unison. "It's a great song, ain't it?" Johnny asked shouting over the blare. I nodded my head to the positive and listened intently. After the track was over, Tony asked me if I played an instrument. I answered "Yeah, I used to play the saxophone in fifth grade, does that count?" "Cool, cool" he said. "We have a band, man. I don't know if we need a sax player, but you should come over and check us out. "Where do you live?" I asked. "Oh, we live on a dead end street" he replied. It's on Sylvendell Avenue. Do you know where that is?" he asked. "Yeah" I replied. "I have a couple of friends who live by there. I'll find it. So, just gimme your address". We exchanged the information and made a date for the following weekend. I was about to become a singer without knowing it.

I arrived at the Velez"s house on the following Saturday in the early afternoon. It was a two floor home with main quarters on the top, and what looked like a basement apartment below. I ascended the stairs and knocked on the front door. After a minute or two, a short, older woman appeared to answer. It was obvious she was related to them and spoke broken English with an accent. "Down, down there" she said as she pointed toward the cellar. "They are in there, por favor". I shook my head ok and descended down the stairs. I rounded the corner of the building and saw a door in the rear. "This is where the entrance must be" I thought. I gingerly opened the portal and peeked inside. Johnny turned and saw my head sticking in. "Come in, come in" he motioned. "We're hanging out in here. We live down here and my mom lives upstairs". It was an apartment with a small kitchenette, large living room, and a small bedroom on the left. I peered along the back wall of the living area and saw that there were two amplifiers, a bass, a Gibson guitar, a small drum set, and a few microphones on some mic stands. "This looks great" I chimed. "How long have you guys been playing?" I asked. "A few months now" Johnny replied. "Right now though, We're a little funk band". I suddenly heard a noise to my left. The back door opened wide and two black guys stepped in. They ignored who I was and walked passed me like I was invisible. "I wonder what their problem is?" I thought. "I'll probably find out later". After Tony and Johnny plugged in, Tony went over to them. "Ok man, let's pick up from where we were last week, alright?" he asked" The taller black kid sat down at his drum kit and began doing triplets with his sticks while the other black guy positioned himself in front of the forward microphone. "Let's do that Kool and the Gang song again, man" the drummer shouted. "You know?" he asked. Hollywood"s swinging". "Ok" Tony replied as he began counting beats "One, two, three, and four" and they went into the song.

They were sounding pretty good I thought, until it was the lead singer"s turn. He had a fairly decent voice, but he couldn't remember the words. No matter how hard he tried, he just couldn't recollect them. It caused the band to start and stop several times. Finally, in mid song, the singer walked over to the drummer and hung the mic in front of his face. The drummer sang instead as he knew all the words from memory. It was comical watching the lead singer go back and forth between his mic stand and the percussionist as he reminded me of a bellboy running to get his tips. After their third attempt, Tony blurted to the singer "Hey man, we've been over this many times before. You gotta start memorizing the words, bro. If we play out, it's gonna look stupid if you can't remember the words, man." I was smoking a cigarette by the kitchen listening, while covering my face and laughing. The singer got pissed "Don't worry about me and the words" he shouted. "I'll get to them when I get to them". Tony, obviously frustrated, yelled back "But, it's been three weeks, man. When are you gonna get it together?" he asked annoyed. The vocalist flipped out. "Let's just play the song again" he screamed. "And, stop harping on me about it. I'll remember it later". Johnny looking over was mumbling under his breath "Fucking guy, he's worthless".

After a few more minutes of arguing, Tony made a suggestion. "Hey Ronnie?" he asked. "We don't have anyone to sing the Hollywood"s now swinging part in the background. How"d you like to take a crack at it for us?" "Sure" I said. "What do I do?" I asked. Tony directed me to the front. "Just stand over there by that second mic. When the chorus kicks in, just sing that part. You know the song, right?" he asked. "Yeah, I replied. "I can do that". He gave the usual four count and the band started over again. As done previously, the singer couldn't remember the words. Frustrated, he went back over to the drummer while making faces and looking over at me. Out of the corner of my eye, I was observing him and trying hard not to laugh. Soon, the time came to do my part with the background vocals. I began to sing "Hey, hey, hey. Whatchoo got to say. Hollywooooood, Hollywoooood"s swinging". Tony and Johnny"s ears perked up. They smiled at me and nodded as if they were pleased. I was on a roll and proud of myself. We got to the end of the song and I had to do the more repetitive part. "Hollywood"s now swinging, Hollywood"s now swinging". Over and over I sang as it was about five repetitions until the tune was finished.

At the end of the day"s session, the lead singer came over to me in a huff. I knew he had seen the brothers smiling at me while I was singing and it had aggravated him. "Don't even think that you're the new lead singer, asshole" he warned. "I'm the singer and you ain't shit. It's mine and my friend the drummer"s band. We say who comes and goes". "Whatever", I replied as I rolled my eyes. I didn't feel like getting into a fistfight with someone I had just met. So, I just ignored him. I went outside in their backyard to have a smoke and Johnny came out a few minutes later. "Don't worry about him" he said. "He's replaceable". Just then, the two black guys came out the door. The drummer flew passed me in a hurry. But, the lead singer wanted to continue his tirade as I guess he felt threatened. He walked up and yelled in my face "Fuck you; you're not the new singer. Fuck this band, I quit". I laughed at him and told him to step off. He looked over at Johnny to see if he would back him up. Johnny didn't say a word. The guy started wailing "So, that's how it's gonna be huh?" he asked. "Well, fuck you guys then. I'm not coming back!" As he walked to his car, Johnny mumbled "You suck anyway, who cares". Tony came out and asked "What the fuck is going on here?" I replied "I dunno man. That dickhead singer of yours just accosted me. He seemed pretty pissed off too". "Oh, him" Tony said. "Don't worry about him. Me and Johnny just voted him out. His drummer said if his friend goes, he goes too. So, fuck them both. We're gonna change from a funk to rock band now. And, guess what? You're our new lead singer". I couldn't believe my luck.

I was back at Thursdays Place on Saturday night and the usual suspects were in attendance. Jackie Boy, Phil, Howie, Dave W. and others. There was also a guy named Bob. Bob was a couple of years older than us and had been left back three times. Hilariously, he was the only guy in junior high school who had driver"s license. Bob was also a consummate instigator. He loved to take opportunities to relish in other people"s embarrassing moments. So much so, that he would egg on a perpetrator"s intentions just to get his kicks. Tonight it looked like Howie was going to be one of his victims. Howie had made the mistake of confiding in one of us about having had sex with a local slut. Her name was Dawn and she wasn't very good looking. But, she did put out easily. Over the background noise of the pinball machines, Bob started his attack. "Howie?" he asked. "Is it true that you ate out Dawn?" "No!" Howie quipped. "All I did was fuck her". Bob went on with his tease "I dunno Howie; I heard you ate her while she was on the rag, man. Did you get your red wings from that pig?" he asked laughing. "Fuck you" Howie shouted. "I never ate that nasty bitch". Bob was relentless "Come on Howie, everyone knows you ate it". The room began to erupt with laughter and Howie was getting angry. His face was getting flustered and his eyes were welling up. "I never did that shit" he screamed. Meanwhile, the laughs were getting even louder. "Ew" I said. "How could you eat that skank Howie?" I asked. He shrieked "Fuck you Ron. You better shut the fuck up about it. It's not true". I began to instigate a chant "Howie ate out Dawn, Howie ate out Dawn." Suddenly, everyone started following me. It was like a chorus at a church service as it slowly rose to a hymn.

Howie was getting visibly upset and losing control. He began screaming at the top of his lungs "I didn't eat that shit! Fuck you! Fuck you!" Just then, something plopped down onto the glass top of one of the machines. At first, we couldn't figure out what it was as it was torn and frayed. Upon closer inspection, we saw it had a hole in the middle and a red spot accompanying its rim. It was also surrounded by thick, burly hairs. It was obvious that Bob had taken scissors from the kitchen, snuck off to the bathroom, and had cut off snips of his beard. He had meticulously put a rim of ketchup around the hole and added the hairs on the edges as an overlay. Disgustingly, it looked just like a menstruating vagina. Thinking it hilarious, I started prodding them on like a ring leader in a Barnum & Bailey circus. "Howie ate out Dawn, Howie ate out Dawn" I cheered. As I was orchestrating the crowd, their wails reached an ever louder crescendo following me. They seemed to be going ballistic. "Howie ate Dawn, Howie at Dawn" they yelled relentlessly. Howie"s face became scarlet and he was even more livid with anger. Realizing his rage, I decided that I should back off for a while. After I retreated for a bit and was sitting in a booth closer to the front door. He ran over to me "You!" he pointed shrieking. "You did this you asshole!" "What the fuck are you talking about?" I asked. "Bob is the one who made the napkin? Not me." Abruptly, he flew over pushing me in my seat while balling up his fist and threatening me. "I should kick your ass for doing this" he yelled. "But, I'll take care of you when this is over". All the while, the chanting was still going on. It didn't appear as if it was going to subside either. Infuriated, Howie rushed passed them for the back door. He flung it open and cursed "Fuck you, all of you." he screamed as he left. "I promise you you'll all get yours later".

While waiting at TJ"s corner, just before classes were to begin, Billy F. approached me from behind. "What's up, man?" he asked. "Nothing Billy, same old bullshit, different day" I replied. "Guess what I have with me?" he asked. "I don't know? VD maybe?" I laughed. "No asshole" he said. "I have that key with me from that Volkswagen we stole a while back, remember? You wanna come with me and get another one?" he asked. "There's nothing going on here anyway. Besides, school is fucking boring". I pondered his suggestion for a moment. "Ok, man" I answered. "But, only if I get to drive this time. Ok?" He replied "That's fine with me, bro. I just wanna get away from this school. I'm not in a school mood today". We turned left and strode down TJ"s hill to the path that led to the familiar train station. "Well, look at that!" Billy exclaimed peering down the bluff. His eyes opened wide like a little kid in a candy store. "There's one right there, right in the front row" he said. "Do you see it?" he asked. "The black one? Holy shit! This one"s gonna be cake bro! It's right by the entrance". We crossed the street to the lot to a parking space. In it, was a shiny VW beetle. This time, there was no one around as the morning train for N.Y.C. had long been gone. Approaching the car, Billy got anxious and began circling the car like a lion sizing up its prey. "See if the door is open" he whispered. I gingerly pushed in the button of the handle on the driver"s side door. "Bingo" I replied. The door sprang ajar. I was in now. I slid into the seat and waited for Billy to join me on the passenger"s side. Quickly, hopped in. "Here" he said. As he handed me the key from his jacket pocket. "Fire this thing up and let's see where we can go". As before, the car started up with a low rumble. Billy was directing me. "Remember, like you saw me do it. Push in the clutch with your foot and follow the H pattern on the stick. It's easy once you get used to it." I did as he asked and we reversed from the space. I ground the car into first and we drove slowly forward. Other than the annoying sound of the gears grinding, it wasn't very hard at all.

I navigated the vehicle to the exit and Billy remarked "This time We'll take the street. We should be fine as long as we don't take any dirt trails like the last time". I made a right to the roadway and off we went. We drove around for a few hours until Billy blurted out "I wanna drive by TJ . They are all getting out right about now. Let's show them all how it's done". "Ok" I said. I steered the car to where the crowd of kids had begun to emerge. As we passed some of onto Sims Rd., Billy was hanging out the window. He stared to yell. "Hahaha, hahaha, look at us! Scarf, scarf, the beetle, the beetle". Everyone watching us was laughing and pointing. Billy acting like a mad child who forgot to take his medication, peered back and was laughing hysterically. "It's ours" he screamed. "It's all ours!" In the background, I heard someone holler. I turned to see that it was Jackie Boy G, Phil, and a guy named Bruce.

"Stop, Stop" Jackie Boy yelled. "Give us a ride. We don't feel like walking". I looked over at Billy for approval and he nodded yes. I pulled the bug over to the curb and the three of them hopped in quickly. Though it was a tight squeeze in the back, they managed to finagle it without too much trouble. "Go, go" Phil exclaimed. "Let's get out of here before somebody sees us". I threw the VW into first and we took off with a chirp. "Where did you guys get this from?" Jackie Boy asked. "We borrowed it from the train station" Billy replied. "We're gonna cruise around for a while and then dump it off later". He laughed and boasted proudly "We did this before and never got caught" he chuckled. "I've got the magic key you know? The magic key starts everything". We drove around a little longer and I mentioned to Billy that I wanted to go home for dinner as I was starving and hadn't eaten all day. "Ok, man" he said. "We'll drop you off at your house. But, I get to keep the car". "No problem with me" I said. "But, come back and pick me up at TJ"s corner at six o"clock, ok?" "Sure" Billy replied. "We can do that". I pulled the beetle in front of my house and jumped out to the driveway. Billy came around from the passenger side and hopped in to drive. "We'll see you later, bro" he chuckled as he waved and they drove away.

I waited by TJ"s corner at the designated time we had agreed upon. Six o"clock came and no Billy. I was staring at my watch with anxious anticipation wondering. "Did they get busted?" I thought. "Did they forget about me?" I glanced at my watch again "Six fifteen, fuckers" I mumbled. Suddenly, I could hear the low roar of the VW engine in the distance. It was getting closer and closer. Finally, I could see them ambling toward me. As they pulled up to the curb with the radio blaring, Billy was singing a Rolling Stones song but had changed the words. "Please allow me to introduce myself; I'm a man, with car and taste". "Billy, you fuck head" I exclaimed. "You guys are late. Where the fuck were you?" I asked obviously annoyed. "We took a detour, bro" he said. "What the fuck do you care? It's not your car anyway. Shut the fuck up and get in". Phil was in the passenger seat now with Jackie Boy and Bruce still in the back. Phil got out and flipped the back seat forward. "Get in the back" he demanded. "Fuck you" I said. "You get in the back. You're a little fucker and can fit back there easier. Plus, me and Billy stole the fucking thing in the first place, not you asshole. So, I get shotgun". After bickering with Phil back and forth for a few minutes, he realized he couldn't win. He got in the back and we left.

Billy had decided that it was his turn to go home now and he wanted to be dropped off. We pulled up to his residence and he got out quickly. I ran around to the driver"s side and took Billy"s spot. Billy giggled "Now Ronnie, don't get caught now bro. Make sure at the end of the night, you dump this thing like we did before. I don't feel like probation again, ok?" he asked concerned "Yeah, yeah" I replied. "I know what to do. I'll see you tomorrow. Don't worry about it". As he was walking up to his house, the other guys waved and gave him their goodbyes. I put the tranny into gear and away we went. After Billy"s departure, Phil had jumped in the front again. He was restless. "Where do we go now?" he asked. "How about Camp Kilmer"s driving instructor area? I replied. "That sounds pretty cool to me" Jackie Boy retorted. While Bruce was looking out the window, he inquired "There's no cops there right, Ron?" "Nah" I acknowledged. "Not at night when it's dark like now. Even in the day time, they rarely go there". "Cool" Bruce said. "Let's go". I made a bee line for Kilmer"s back gate and headed into the night. When we got close to our target, Jackie Boy was asking if he could take a crack at driving. "Sure" I said. "But, have you ever driven a stick before?" I asked. "Yeah" Jackie Boy replied. "I know how to do it. Just let me check it out, man. Don't hog it all for yourself "Ok" I told him. "I'm gonna pull over and have a cig. Take a whirl around the track a few times and come right back". "No problem" he replied. "Who"s coming with me?" he asked. Bruce volunteered. "Let's go Jackie Boy" Bruce exclaimed. "I wanna see how fast you can go". "I'm staying with Ron" Phil said. I'm gonna hang and have a smoke with him". "Don't smack it up too much" Phil yelled. "I wanna take my turn when you get back".

I pulled the bug over and stopped by the course close to the hill. Phil and I got out and Jackie Boy and Bruce switched seats with us. "Ok Jackie Boy, it's all yours" I said. "Don't strip the gears or go too fast man". As Phil and I were laughing, Jackie Boy attempted to put the car into gear. "Crunch, crunch, thud" the car went. Jackie Boy was having trouble and couldn't quite find first. He was grinding the tranny and having a problem coordinating the clutch at the same time. "You can do it" Phil yelled as they pulled away. "Why don't you let Bruce shift the handle and you push the clutch?" he asked. "Fuck that" Jackie boy screamed. "I'll get this junk in motion somehow". With a shudder and a squeal, they were finally on their way. Round and round they went around the course"s square. Phil and I could hear them in the distance arguing about how to drive the beetle the right way. "Not that way" Bruce was yelling. "Let the clutch out. You gotta get it out of second!" Phil and I were laughing so hard we were crying. Eventually, they had come back and Bruce was not amused. "Can somebody else drive now?" he asked. "That shit was fun but nerve wracking". Phil decided he didn't want to drive anymore. He was afraid if we stayed too long, the police would arrive. "Let's get out of here Ron" he said. "I don't trust this place". "You're paranoid"

I told him. "There's nobody out here but us" "Still" he replied. "I just have a bad feeling about this place. I want to go". "All right Phil" I said. "Let's take one more spin around the block. But, I wanna drive again this time. I wanna try something out before we go" "Ok" he replied. "But, make it snappy. I wanna leave". We all got back in the car with our original configuration. It was me driving, Phil shotgun, and Jackie boy and Bruce in the back. As we took off around the course, I screamed out "Watch this! I wanna see how fast I can get this thing to go!" Like most tracks in America, you start out on the right and then circle to the left. While back at the entrance and I was jamming it into first, then second. We were frantically picking up speed. "Faster, faster" Phil shrieked. I slammed it into third and looked at the speedometer. It read fifty miles per hour. "Not fast enough" I thought. Just as we mounted the turn at the first corner, I was shifting into fourth. Abruptly, the car went up on two wheels as we rounded the corner"s edge. I had misjudged the speed, lost control, and went off too wide toward the gully on the right. "Holy shit" Bruce screamed as the bug began to roll. I closed my eyes in fear. We spiraled once, twice, and I opened my eyes. I remember seeing coke bottles and cigarette packs spinning around me. On the third roll, my head went through the windshield while the gear shifter bent over my leg. I heard more shattering glass and a hissing sound. The car finally came to a stop. We were upside down in a field.

"Is everybody all right, man?" I heard Jackie Boy plead. "I think I hit my head" I replied. Phil was so scared; he was already climbing out his broken window. "Hey, Arold, you stupid fuck!" he bawled. "What the fuck was that all about? You're a fucking idiot, man!" As he was outside the vehicle, he was instructing us on where we should climb out next. I wasn't listening to him and crawled out the side I was already on. Jackie Boy somehow made it to the passenger"s side front window and had managed to escape on his own. Bruce was still trapped inside. I was holding my head and complaining "I think I might be bleeding. I have a huge bump on my head". Jackie Boy was yelling "Holy fuck! We gotta get Bruce outta there! What if it blows up and shit?" Bruce was moaning "My fucking arm is stuck under the car. I don't think I'm hurt real bad. But, you guys gotta roll this fucking thing off of me". Luckily, most of Bruce"s arm was only stuck by the long sleeve of his shirt. "Come on" Phil yelled. "Help me get this fucking thing off of him." The three of us grabbed the edge of the vehicle"s body and pushed as hard as we could. We pushed the car up high enough where Bruce was able to crawl out from underneath and free himself. "Gee, that was fun, wasn't it?" he asked chuckling half-jokingly. "Next time, let me drive". As Bruce was holding his arm and examining it for injuries, Phil turned to me. "Hey dickhead" he yelled. "You"ve got a small river of blood trickling down your face. "Fuck" I told him. "I told you my head hurt". Phil informed me "You better cover that shit up, or else it'll never stop bleeding". Fortunately for me, I was wearing a white T-shirt I didn't care about. I took it off, found a puddle of water, got it wet, and wrapped it around my head. "Well, that was a wash" Jackie Boy laughed. "I guess we got lucky and should walk home now". "That sounds like a good idea" Phil exclaimed sarcastically. "But, don't ever let fucking Arold drive again!"

A couple of weeks had gone by and none of us had heard anything about the VW we had smashed up in Camp Kilmer. Therefore, I thought we were scot free. That was until I got home from school one day and my mother was waiting at the top of the stairs. "I got a call from the cops today, Ronald" she said. "A Sergeant Bertha from the juvenile police wants to have a word with you. What did you do that your father and I don't know about?" she asked. "Nothing" I lied. "I have no idea what that's about". My knees began to tremble at the thought of having to face my father's temper again. I got really nervous. "Well" my mom exclaimed. "When your father gets home from work, you'll have to go to the station and clear it up. You better tell him the whole story because I don't feel like dealing with it this time. And, don't even think of going anywhere. Stay home until he gets here". "Yes, mother" I replied. Somehow I had a feeling she knew I was lying. My mother always had the 6th sense. It was uncanny how she could sometimes tell what I had been doing. She used to tell me "I know because you have that guilty look and I can feel it!" But, this time, she said nothing about it. "Maybe I wouldn't get caught?" I thought. I bounded up the stairs to my room and waited. I was doomed!

My father came home and drove me to the juvie office. On the way there, he interrogated me about if I had stolen the car or not. "Now, Ronald" he said. "If you're in trouble, I'm not too concerned about what you did. I'm more concerned if you lie to me about it or not. Did you steal that VW or not?" Out of fear, I lied my ass off. "No dad, it wasn't me. I swear." I said. "They got me mixed up with somebody else". "Ok" he said. "Because, I can probably get you out of it. But, if you lie to me, there's nothing I can do". I shook my head "Oh no dad. It wasn't me. These cops are crazy". Soon, we arrived for my questioning. There, behind a desk, was Sergeant Bertha. I had heard of him before in conversations with some friends. He was a chubby little guy with a nice disposition. But, he could be very manipulative. I thought "I got this guy and this will be cake. He's got nothing on me. I don't know anything. I'll just deny everything and go home". It wasn't as easy as I thought. Bertha railed into me for a good half an hour attempting to use his best child psychology techniques. From good cop, bad cop, to we know everything about you, to get it off your chest. I held fast and nothing was working for him. I thought I had made it. Then, he used a formula I had never heard of before. He told my father and I "I'll be right back. There's someone in the other room I have to speak too. Give me about 10 minutes". My father got annoyed and cautioned Bertha "We've been here long enough" he said. "Let's wrap this up. You either charge my kid, or I'm taking him home". "Just this one more thing" Bertha demanded. "It won't take long, I promise". Bertha left the room. My dad mumbled under his breath "This is bullshit. They always try to pull this crap when they have nothing".

A few minutes passed and Bertha came back in. "I have a question for you Mr. Arold" he asked my dad. "May I interrogate your son in the room alone for a minute?" he asked. "I guess so" my father replied "As long as it doesn't take too long. I have things to do tonight". "Oh, no" Bertha retorted. "It'll be nice and quick". I had no idea what the Sergeant was up to and was perplexed by his mannerisms. I knew he was scheming on something. But, I didn't know what it was. After my father had left the room, Bertha laid into me again. I felt cornered like a wild animal with no place to go. "Do you know Billy?" he asked. "Yeah" I replied. "Well, you know when I left the room a little while ago?" he asked. "Billy was in there with me and told me the entire story. So, you might as well come clean and save yourself. We'll go much lighter on you if you fess up and cooperate". I felt like a convict trying to save himself from the electric chair. "Shit" I thought. "The jig is up! Fucking Billy ratted me out!" I got so scared, I spilled my guts. I told Bertha everything. "Oh yes" Bertha said. He was comparing my facts of my story to Billy"s and gloated "That's just how Billy told us it went down. Everything you just told me is what Billy said". "Really?" I asked. "Yup" he said. "Now, don't you feel better about telling the truth?" he asked. "I guess so" I replied. "But, my dad"s gonna kill me when he comes back". "Don't worry about that" Bertha chuckled. "I'll talk to him for you".

My dad reentered the room with a bewildered look on his face. Bertha pulled him aside and I could hear them whispering. I was shitting my pants and I thought "What the fuck is he telling him? I'm gonna be punished forever over this one". My father came back over to me and roared "Let's go. I'll deal with you on the way home". "Where"s Billy?" I asked Bertha. I wanted to talk to him and ask him why he had caved. "Oh, he went home already" he replied. "His dad wanted to get him out of here". "Ok" I said somehow not believing him. I remember thinking that it was unusual for cops not to put us in the same room after a while to compare stories. I found out later that Bertha had duped me. He used the "your friend is in the room and told us all about it" scenario. And, I fell for it like a junkie wanting a candy bar. Feeling betrayed, I swore to myself that it would never happen to me again. On the way home from my inquest, my father was furious. "Why did you lie to me?" he asked screaming. "You looked me right in my face and lied to me. I could have got you out of it. They had absolutely nothing on you. I don't understand you at all. All you had to do was tell me the truth. You embarrassed the hell out of me in there". "I was scared dad." I replied nervously. "I didn't know what to do". "Well" he said. "Until we go to court over this bullshit, you're not going anywhere. I hope you like staying home a lot. You're to come home directly from school, and stay in the house. You got that?" "Yeah" I answered. "I got it". "Also" he added "I'll never believe anything you ever tell me again"

In the end, Billy and I went to court and our parents had to pay $150 each to reimburse the owner for stealing and wrecking his car. We also were deemed guilty and were given 6 months" probation. In the court"s hallway I approached Billy and asked him what happened. "Why did you rat me out?" I asked. "I didn't even go to the station you dumb ass" he replied. "You fell for the oldest cop scam in the book. I guess you know not to trust cops now huh? I told you bro; they aren't your friends". In hindsight, after I met the car"s owner, I felt bad about for him. He was a nice, skinny little old man in his early 60"s and he used the VW to get to the train station to get to work. We never thought that far ahead and it didn't dawn on us that anyone would miss it. In our delinquent minds, it was just a car. Though I didn't abstain from any more trouble in the future, I never stole cars again.

After a few weeks of my father's punishment, I had grown weary of his strict regimen. Whenever I wanted to go anywhere, he had to drive me to my destination. It was becoming mundane and tedious and I needed a way out. The pinnacle of my disillusionment came one night at Lance"s house. I was dating a girl who was what we called "easy". She happened to be at Lance"s house that night as she was friends with his sister Belinda. We were in Lance"s room on the bottom mattress of his bunk bed necking and doing some pretty heavy petting. I got bold and began to finger her. "You wanna fuck me?" she asked. "Absolutely" I replied. "But, you have to use a rubber" she insisted. "I have one of those in my wallet right here" I replied giddily. "Ok, slip it on" she said. "I'll take my pants off under the covers and We'll do a quickie". Just as I was about to drop my britches and slide it in, I heard a car horn emanating outside. With no warning, Lance burst into the room. "I think your dad"s here to pick you up" he cried out. "Goddamn it" I yelled. "I'm trying to get some pussy here, bro". The girl got pissed. "What the fuck Ron! I'm all hot and bothered here!" she said. "I'm sorry" I replied. "There's nothing I can do. He's already here. I have to go or I'll be imprisoned forever". I pulled up my pants, kissed her goodbye and scrambled for the door. That damn Volkswagen had cost me some serious trim!

    A week after my loss of vagina, my father was getting on my nerves. I kept pestering him about when my punishment would be over. He didn't want to hear it and kept putting it off. All I got was "When I say so". I didn't respond to that and despised not getting clear cut answers. I've always been that way and I don't reciprocate to manipulative head games. On one such afternoon of one of his ploys, I had had enough and decided I wasn't going to take it anymore. I was going to run away from home. He had heard from my little brother of my plan and was scheming to stop me. Like younger siblings, they love to curry favor with your parents to get in their good graces. So, Erik had ratted me out. "Run away?" My father asked. "We'll fix that. I have the perfect device to stop Ronald from doing so." My father had a pair of handcuffs left over from when he had a previous job as a guard at a department store. He fetched them from the closet in his bedroom and stood in front of me. "Get over here" he yelled. "You're not going anywhere". On our first set of stairs coming in our front door, there was a railing attached to the wall. It ran the length of the staircase to the next level to the living room. My father decided this was the perfect place to attach me for safe keeping. He slammed one end of the cuffs on my right wrist, and the other to the iron bannister. "You're not going any place" he laughed. "I don't care if you have to stay there all day. You're going to learn to be good if it kills you".

I was screamed and told him "We'll see about that. The first chance I get, I'm gone". He walked up the steps and told my mother to ignore me. "He'll come around eventually" he said. While I was sliding the cuffs up and down the railing trying anyway I could to release myself, my little brother had gotten ahold of the restraint key. He started teasing me and dangling it in front of my face. It felt like a horse being beckoned with a carrot. Move a little forward, almost get the prize, and pull it out of reach once more. Erik got great joy in this and kept at it for almost an hour. The entire time I kept telling him if he didn't give me the key I was going to kill him. With each of my attempts to grab it, He'd pull away giggling hysterically. "Here it is" he shouted as he dangled it just out of reach. "Nope, you were real close that time though. Try again!" Over and over he did it and I was losing my patience. It was frustrating and exhausting and I hated him for it.

Eventually, when night came my father released me for my bed. I was tired and wanted nothing but sleep as I knew the next morning was a school day. I thought "He couldn't keep me locked up from classes forever. So, that's how I'll get away". With much thought, I hatched my plan for the next afternoon. I packed a few pairs of pants and shirts and hid them outside in a bag by the fence in our side yard. After school let out, I was free. When I didn't show up at home by 11pm, my parents called the police. They reported me as a missing and a possible run away. "I don't consider myself a runaway" I thought. I just needed a break from my father's crippling sanctions of pain. While I was trying to hide hanging out at the local Burger King, there was an off duty police officer there to keep the peace. His name was Fred. He was a foreboding figure with a slick bald head and beefsteak shoulders. As cops go, he could be reasonable or tense. It all depended on if you were acting up and what kind of mood he was in. Most of the time, he was harmless and we pretended to respect his authority. Also, in this culinary fast food establishment, was a kid named Myron. Myron was slightly challenged but had a good heart. So much so, that the police department made him an honorary member. They even gave him an official jacket with his embroidered name and an accompanying hat. Myron got this attention by his supposed unique talent. He seemed to possess the ability to emulate a police siren with great accuracy. He was so good; there were times when customers thought there was an actual police cruiser driving by. The town even gave him a nickname and deemed him Myron the siren. He was so precise; he even landed a spot on a New York City TV show. I never understood how he got away with disturbing customers with his incessant wailing, while we would be ejected for the smallest of infractions. I guess nepotism worked with who you knew.

As I was chatting up some friends while sitting in booth, I heard a guy yell my name. "Hey Ron" they said. "I think your parents are out front in the parking lot, bro. They're asking a lot of questions to the manager about you. They drive a Gran Prix, right?" he asked. "Yeah" I said. "Thanks for the heads up, man. I'm out of here". I grabbed my bag and ran for the back door. Just as I stepped outside, I heard the familiar roar of my parent"s car. There was no mistaking of the low end rumble of that 500 engine. As they grew closer, I heard my mother scream "Ronald, Ronald, get back here. It's time to come home". With my feet barely touching the ground, I ignored her pleas and shimmied through an opening in a fence separating Burger King from an adjacent furniture store. I watched as they drove passed me and turned and went out to the highway. Inside the furniture store lot behind its back doors, were large empty boxes. They appeared to be leftovers from previous deliveries. I wouldn't dare to avail myself to an open area where my parents could capture me. So, I pushed over one of the boxes and crept inside. Peeking out every so often to see if my parents returned, I started to get sleepy. I thought "I guess this is was my bed for the night."

I awoke in the early morning to the sound of chirping birds. I knew from experience that sunrise meant it was probably about 6am. I lay in the box and lit up a cigarette. I was hungry and had no money. So, I was pondering if I should return home or not. I decided that later in the day, I would use a pay phone to make a collect to call my mother. It was always easier to call her first to feel out how my father's temper was. I wouldn't dare attempt reconciliation if he was on one of his tirades again. Eventually, after much coaxing from my mother, and a promise that my father wouldn't attempt any beatings, I reluctantly returned home that night. It was the first of my many family absences.

As I was closing out my fifteenth year, Sergeant Bertha had one more surprise for me. It seemed he was on a kick to annoy me. My mother had received another call from him asking to bring me in for another interrogation session. She was told it wasn't as severe a charge as the last time and that he just had a few questions to ask me. I had a feeling he thought I would become an informer due to the way I had easily rolled over before. He was wrong. Way wrong. My mother drove me to the juvie station that had since moved from its previous location. This time, it was behind the firehouse on route 27. We walked in and I looked around. Bertha wasn't even in the room yet and I remember thinking that that was rude. I could hear him talking to someone in the distance. But, no one was answering him. So, I deduced that he was probably on the telephone. As I gazed about the room, I could see a large hookah pipe against the wall at the end of the corridor. It was at least 6 feet high and 2 feet wide. There was a large burner on top, and hoses transcending outwards below it. It reminded me of an octopus with many arms, hanging there waiting for its slow toking victim to enjoy. It appeared as if it had been placed there on purpose. "It must have come from a big bust"" I thought. "Why else would it be out here like this? One of those raids where some kiss ass narc had gotten a commendation and a promotion". I imagined rows of cops encircling it, and clapping and congratulating themselves. It was like a prize on permanent display to them, a badge for the authorities to brag and to gloat about. I thought it was pitiful and in bad taste. But, this was a cop shop, so it was expected. In their headquarters, they loved to show off confiscated items to stroke their egos.

Suddenly, I heard footsteps coming from down the hallway. Finally, he had approached. "Hello Mrs. Arold and Ronald" Bertha said. His echoing voice brought me back from my daydream. "Could you bring Ronald into the room down the hall to the right please?" he asked. "I just have a few questions for him". I accompanied my mother and we sat down in some chairs in front of him. There was a pad and pencil strategically placed for intimidation on his desk. He had his hands and fingers intertwined and he was wiggling them. They were almost in a praying fashion. It was the type of gesture where they are partially cupped and facing you, so you were supposed to know they were serious. He began questioning me. "Ronald" he said. "I have information that you are the leader of a shoplifting ring. That you are responsible for collecting all stolen merchandise, and fence these items to the highest bidder. You then collect those funds, and distribute them to all your friends who are working for you". I let out the loudest guffaw this cop had probably ever heard. I smiled, looked him right in the face, and exclaimed "You're kidding right? I wish I was their leader. I wouldn't be sitting here, that's for sure. I'd be on vacation somewhere away from the likes of you". My mother chimed in "Sergeant Bertha?" she asked. "Do you really think my 15 year old son is capable of such an endeavor? Do you have proof of this? I want to see evidence. If my husband comes down here and these are false allegations, We'll be filing a lawsuit against you for harassment!" "Whoa, slow down Mrs. Arold" Bertha howled. "We can't prove it yet, but we have informants that have told us it was your son. This is just a formality". I smirked at him. "Rats" I mumbled "Nothing but rats and bullshit. It's a complete waste of time". "Watch your mouth" my mother warned. "But, he's right" my mom told him. "If you don't have solid proof that my son is implicated by law, We're leaving". Bertha got cocky "You can leave Mrs. Arold, but We'll be watching him" he said. "You can watch a football game for all I care". I replied "You cops got the wrong suspect. I think you watch too much Dragnet on TV". "Come on mom, let's go" I laughed "He thinks he's Joe Friday". We got up and left. Bertha was not amused. "Score one for mom!"

Ronnie E. and I were bored again and decided to take another trip to Great Eastern. It was right before it went out of business and eventually became the route 1 flea market. Walking over the bridge, Ronnie engaged me in a conversation about the Native American Indians that had once settled in the area. "Lenny something" he said. "Yes, you mean the Lenni Lenape Indians?" I asked. "Yeah, something like that" he replied. "How did you know about them?" he asked. "I read a lot man" I said. "So, I found an article about them once. They lived on the banks of the Raritan River and had canoes and shit. I also read that they might have lived in caves right along the river"s edge". "Caves?" he asked. "Where? I wanna explore some of that shit". "Right under us" I replied. "Supposedly, they're under the cliffs next to Great Eastern". "That's fucking cool" he roared. "We gotta go check that shit out, man. Fuck Great Eastern, we can go there later. Let's go see if we can find arrow heads and shit. I heard some of that shit is worth some money. We can sell them". "If we find some" I replied. "Let's go down there anyway" he suggested. "What the fuck else are we doing today besides playing fucking pinball again?" "You have a point" I replied. "If you're game, I'll go down there with you".

We finished crossing the bridge and began parading through the parking lot. All the while imagining what it would be like if we had a real find of ancient artifacts. When we got to the edge where the cliff began, we were temporarily dissuaded by overgrown vegetation. "It seems like this place has a lot of trees and bushes growing here since the Indians left" Ronnie chuckled. "But, I bet we can find a trail through them if we keep looking". We turned left and as Ronnie predicted, and found a path between some shrubs that were less overgrown. "Follow me" he exclaimed excitedly. "But, watch out for any drop offs. If these cliffs are as sheer as they looked from the bridge, we could be killed easily". "I'm just following you" I replied. "Since you're going first, I'll just watch you fall" I laughed. "Fuck that bullshit" he yelled. "If I go, I'm grabbing your arm and you're coming with me". We grabbed onto some saplings and rocks on the way down to balance ourselves until we got to the bottom. When we reached the muddy dirt ground of the river bank, Ronnie let out a sigh "Finally" he muttered "That climbing down shit is exhausting. It's time for a ciggie break". "He passed me a Marlboro and asked me what I thought. As I was lighting it, I answered him. "Look at the banks here" I said. "It's weird. They look like layers on top of each other. It's like what you see in the mountains of Pennsylvania, like shale rock". "Yeah, I've never seen shit like that before" he replied. "But, I want arrow heads or pottery. If they're under that water, I'm not sticking my hands under that shit. That water"s polluted, fuck that". "I don't think they'd be by the banks" I replied "Well then" Ronnie said. "Let's get searching for those caves instead".

As we wandered in further at the base of the cliff searching for any evidence of a tribe or an opening, Ronnie found a clearing. "Mah huh" he yelled out. "I think I found one". "You found what?" I asked.

"Any arrowheads or anything?" "Fuck arrowheads" he said. "I found an entrance to a cave!" "Get the fuck out of here" I laughed. "Show me that bullshit. I wanna see it". "Help me clear these leaves and shit" he asked. "It's right behind these bushes". Knowing that he sometimes liked to make up stories to fuck with people, I was skeptical. But, sure enough, he was telling the truth. "Holy shit!" I gasped. "You really did find one". "I told you asshole" Ronnie beamed. "I wanna see what's inside this bitch". Just beyond the last shrub we had pushed aside was a narrow hole. It was about 2 feet wide by 2 feet high and looked like a tight fit. It appeared to have been dug out by hand. "I'm going in this mah huh" Ronnie said. "Hold my ankles for me in case I get stuck" he demanded. "How are you gonna see in there?" I asked. "It's gotta be dark as fuck. "What do you think lighters were invented for stupid ass" he quipped. "Just hold my fucking legs and pull me out when I ask you too, ok?" "If you say so" I replied. "But, I think it's a little unsafe". "Safe, shmafe" he retorted. "I wanna see what's in there". He took out his lighter, held it in his left hand, got on his stomach, and crawled toward the opening. I was watching him wiggle forward as I was holding his legs. He looked like a recruit in the Army trying to maneuver under barbed wire. On my end, I felt like I was pushing a human wheelbarrow. Further and further he went in. When I could no longer see his body and just his ankles I heard his muffled voice. But, I couldn't make out what he was saying. After about a minute, he began to shimmy backwards. I was pulling on his ankles but was losing my grip. When my hands slipped to his feet, I could hear his voice again. "Pull me out, pull me out" he screamed coughing profusely. When I was able to see his head, I let go. He rolled over and looked up at me and his face was full of reddish brown dirt. He stood up, brushed himself off and told me what he saw. "There's a big area in there" he said excitedly. "If I went in a little further, I could have stood up. I bet this is where they lived". "Why didn't you stand up in there then?" I asked. "My fucking lighter went out and I couldn't see anything anymore" he said. "But, it's a big round room in there. It's like 10 feet high and 15 feet around. Why don't you go in next and I'll hold your feet?" he asked. "I don't fucking think so man" I replied. "That opening is pretty tight. I'm not getting stuck in there and you'll leave me here, fuck that". "I wouldn't do that" he laughed. "I'd at least call the ambulance before I went home. "What's the matter?" he asked "Don't you trust me?" "I know how you like to play jokes on people" I said. "So, there's no fucking way I'm going in there. Plus, it's too tight looking. With my luck, I would get stuck". "Fucking pussy" he replied in disgust. All my fucking friends are pussies. I hate to see you when you grow up" he said "None of you guys ever want to do anything exciting". "I'm sorry you feel that way man" I replied. "But, I'm still not going in that fucking hole". "Really?" he asked "Not even for one of these?" He reached inside his shirt pocket and pulled out an object that looked angular. It looked very dirty and old. "What the hell is that man?" I asked. "Let me see that?" "Fuck you man" he said. Pulling it away from me. "I know what it is. I found it on the floor of that cave right at the end of the tunnel. It's mine now fuck head". As he held it up and taunted me, I could see that it was an Indian arrowhead. It even had the point intact and the part at the bottom where the string was supposed to be attached. It was also in very good condition. "Gimme that!" I yelled. "You don't have any use for it. I love history". "What makes you think I don't like history too?" he asked. "Come on man" I cried. "You don't give a fuck about this shit. Let me have it. I pulled you back out, didn't I? Without me, you might have got stuck in there". "Might is the word" he said. "But, you're a pussy and won't go in there to get your own. So, this one is mine". "Unless, you wanna give me something for it?" he asked. "How much?" I asked. "Hmmm, 50 bucks" he replied. "Where the fuck am I gonna get 50 bucks? I asked. "Ask your parents. They"ve got money" he said. "Yeah right" I whined. "Like that's ever gonna happen". "I guess you don't want a bonafide Lenni Lenape arrow head then" he teased. "What are you gonna do with it?" I asked. "I don't know" he laughed "Maybe I'll give it to the smoigelidoyche museum". He put it back in his pocket and I never saw it again.

I was in my last year at TJ in grade 9; I knew it was only a matter of time before I"d be socially promoted again to 10th grade. Soon, I"d be off to Edison High School. Therefore, I had nothing to lose and had no idea that I would be leaving with a big bang. One afternoon I was called into the front office for a meeting. It was between the principal Mr. Bone, my mother, and me. At the time, I had been taking a liquid medication named Atarax that was supposed to slow me down. When you are in the Special Ed class, sometimes this wasn't uncommon. Some of us were put on various drugs depending on how severe your diagnosis was and how the medication would affect you. It was a big hush hush scheme at the school and the parents and administration were discouraged from talking about it. I for one thought their attempt at deceit was hilarious. Playing up to it, I went around telling other students that if I didn't get my spoonful, I"d go around biting them. The added bonus was that with a threat like that, even the bullies left me alone. They thought I was crazy and that I had the potential to really hurt them. The administration's secretary came out and instructed my mother and I that Mr. Bone would receive us now. We were to go into a classroom on the top floor that was currently not in use. I accompanied my mom to the room and we sat down. I asked my mother "How come he wants to see us here instead of his office?" She replied "I have no idea. Maybe he feels more comfortable in a class room setting". Just then, I heard a squeal at the door. In walked Napoleon himself with his usual grandiose, holier than thou attitude. "Hello Mrs. Arold" he said. He completely ignored me and continued speaking to my mother. "We have a slight problem. Ronald here has been refusing to take his dose of medication when he is sent to the nurse"s office to do so. We're going to have to find a solution for that. Otherwise, unless the child study team and the psychiatrist say differently, he'll have to be sent home". "What do you mean?" my mother asked. "I thought the meds were working and there wasn't a problem? The reports sent to my house are that he's been more complacent lately". "Well" Mr. Bone said "It seems he's been fooling us and has been pretending to swallow the liquid when he apparently hasn"t been taking it". My mom turned to me "Is this true Ronald?" she asked. "Have you purposely been avoiding taking your medication?" "That shit tastes like peppermint" I whined "I told you before it doesn't work and it's a waste of time. It does absolutely nothing to help me in any way". "We'll be the judge of that" Bone blurted out. "Oh, so you're a doctor now too as well as a principal?" I asked sarcastically. "How about you drink that shit then instead?" I asked. He jumped up off his chair and wiggled his finger in my face. He yelled "You'll do as you're told young man; we've had it up to here with you. We've given you every opportunity to improve yourself". "Improve myself?" I asked "If you call running this place like a Nazi prison camp improvement". I stood up in my chair and obviously overshadowed him in height. He didn't like it and started to get belligerent. "Sit back down!" he demanded. "I'll do what I want little man" I screamed. I stood my ground as my mother tried unsuccessfully to calm me down. "Sit down, sit down Ronald" she begged. Just then, he made the bad mistake of trying to touch me. He grabbed me by my left elbow and pulled. "I'm not playing with you anymore Ronald" he howled "You're going to leave this school right away and not come back until you take your prescribed medication". I felt like he was a miniature Dr. Mengele and I was one of his test subjects. His demeanor was rubbing me the wrong way. I thought "He just wants me on meds to be able to control me". I wasn't falling for it. It was funny because most of us kids were taking drugs anyway. But, there was one difference. We weren't being forced and were taking them voluntarily.

After I warned him many times to let go of me, I started to become very agitated. He continued to bellow orders at me trying to get me to obey. Unfortunately, he just escalated the situation. The more he pulled, the angrier I became. Finally, I had had enough. With a hard snap, I tugged back on my sleeve forcing him to release me. He lost his footing, stumbled back, and almost fell on his ass. Free from his grasp, I ran across the room to the side with the windows. He regained his balance and began chasing after me. When he was standing between the edge of the windows and the corner of the room, there was a desk separating us. We went back and forth like hockey players trying desperately to make a final goal. He would shift left, and I would shift right. I was really enjoying antagonizing him as I truly hated the man. Suddenly, he lunged to the far left back toward the windows and I saw my chance. He was trying to come around my rear and out flank me. I grabbed the corner of the desk and flung it at him. It slid across the floor like a performer on ice skates. Since he was so short, it hit him in his hip. Upon its connection, he let out a loud groan. "You hit me, you hit me. That's an assault" he cried. "Mrs Arold, your son is now indefinitely suspended if not expelled. Take him home immediately or I am calling the police". All I remember was the high shrill of my mother's voice. She was begging me to follow her. While I turned to the door to escape, he was holding his side and moaning in pain. "Get him out, get him out" he demanded. I took a quick look at my mother and ran out the door. As I turned left for the main exit, I glanced back to see if I was being followed. My mom was right on my heels with Mr. Bone limping behind her. "Ronald! Ronald, come back" my mother yelled. But, I was indifferent. I called back "Let that be a lesson to you, you little asshole. Maybe next time, you'll keep your hands to yourself". I took off for the day and returned home later that night. I don't remember being punished for it. After all, it wasn't my fault. I was on "their" medication. I was however, indefinitely banned from attending school. A few weeks went by and Mr. Bone had calmed down. I returned for the end of the year and thankfully never saw him again.

CHAPTER 3

Bad 16, Musical Chairs, & Thievery

My 16th birthday had come and gone and my hair had grown even longer. This upset my father by gargantuan proportions. He was incessant with his "Why don't you get a haircut" criticism and wouldn't let up. "In his day", he would tell me, "only women and fags had long hair". I tried to explain to him "Jesus had long hair didn't he?" But, it fell on deaf ears. His answer was always "That's a different time. We're in the 20th century now". "Yeah, ok" I thought. And, I"d just ignore him. He didn't seem to grasp that the greatest generation was over, and it was our time now. No longer would we be forced into professions that our parents expected us to do. We wanted to be individuals, not sheep. We wanted freedom to do whatever the hell we felt like doing without being made fun of or overly criticized for following our dreams.

I was glad I was finally out of TJ and in Edison High School into the 10th grade. It was quite obvious that Bone and Guzack had been salivating to get rid of me. Other than wood shop and art class, I didn't find junior high school enjoyable at all. I couldn't wait to be away from its overly punitive atmosphere and the pretend adults that went along with its devious and dubious programs. Of course being that I was already enrolled in the class for troubled students, I was immediately assigned to the same protocol with other kids who had the same supposed problems right away. On the top floor of Edison High School was a small, narrow class room. I walked in on my first day and was approached by a woman who was skinny, had blue eyes, about 5 foot 5, and had long, straight sun blonde hair. She looked very much like the lead singer in the Swedish pop group Abba. Her name was Miss Godynyk. She chatted with me about how she had a master"s degree in child development and that this was her very first job. I remember feeling sorry for her as she had no idea what she had gotten herself into. She was soon to find out why.

I was spending a lot of time between the Gulotta"s house and practice with my band. We had moved Tony and Johnny"s equipment to my house as we had a large basement and it was a better accommodation for rehearsing and privacy. I was surprised when my parents allowed me to, as it was usually a struggle to attain anything of significance from them. We usually performed on Thursdays and Saturdays and it was exhilarating to feel like I belonged to something for once. Being amateurs, we wanted to practice until we felt we were good enough to play out. "Maybe at school dances or parks" I thought. To me, anyplace would suffice. One problem we had though was always lack of gear. Soon, we would fix all of that.

On a dark Friday night, Johnny, Tony and I, hatched a scheme to find some money to support the band. While discussing our needs at their house, a new friend had arrived. His name was Dennis M. and he was a friend of Bob M"s from Thursday"s Place. Though I didn't really hang around with him, I had known DenniS's name from around town. So, it wasn't that much of a stretch to feel at ease with him. We had heard that there was another dance night at the Washington Swim Club and we needed it for cover for our plan. It fit in well we thought as it was open air and less constraining than a junior high school gym. It was also ideal as it had less supervision. Usually, there would be one off duty policeman, and a few 20 year olds watching us. Fortunately, the 20 years olds mostly didn't care. So, we really only had to worry about the cop. It wouldn't be a problem though as there would be so much going on that he was easily distracted.

The Washington Swim Club – Courtesy Of Howard Bernard

We decided to walk to the dance to see what kind of trouble we could get into. We arrived just when the first band was going on. As we approached the gate we spied the price of admission. It was 3 dollars. "Three dollars?" Dennis quipped. "That's way too much for these bullshit bands. There's gotta be another way we can get in there?" he asked. Johnny offered a solution as it seemed he had snuck in before. "Just follow me" Johnny said. "We'll sneak around the back. You know? Where you can see the fence that wraps around the pool. Once We're there, we can just hop the fence and We're in". I asked Johnny "What about that cop? What if he sees us?" "He won't see us" Johnny replied. "We just have to go to the corner where the fence joins together, that's the spot where it's dark. I've done it dozens of times" "My brother knows all the scams" Tony added. "He's just usually quiet about it". Dennis let out a laugh "I love shit like this" he said. "Let's just not get caught. I'll have to hit the cop to escape and I hate to hit cops. They always beat my ass when they catch me later".

We made it over the fence like commandos practicing war games. We were so silent; we didn't even hear each other"s footsteps. There was nary a peep from any of us. We grouped back together in a huddle and then skulked up to the dance area at the top of a small hill. The band playing was named Until. I remember laughing to myself and thinking "Until what?" Until wasn't too bad and many kids were dancing and having a good time. Usually, when we went to these types of venues, we were more interested in girls than the band. But this time we saw something new. Most bands" light shows used cabinets with colored spotlights installed in them. This band was using something we had never seen before. "Fluorescent lights" Tony whispered. "Fuck man" he sighed. We gotta get some of those. They're horizontal and really bright. I want them". "How can we manage that?" Dennis asked. "I have a scheme you guys" I suggested. I know where we might be able to scarf some money. And, it's pretty close by". "Where?" Dennis asked. "You'll see" I replied. "Ronnie's always scheming" Johnny said. "He's always thinking that way. Just look at his face, he's got it all planned out already". "Let's get out of here" I said. "Do you want free shit or not?" Dennis being Dennis was persistent. "Tell me about it now" he insisted. "I wanna know all the details or I'm not going". "There he goes again" Tony chuckled. "He always has to know everything first". "You're damn right" Dennis demanded. "I'm over 18 and you guys aren't. If we get caught, who gets the brunt of the punishment?" he asked. "Me, that's who". "Stop being a pussy" I said. "This shit will be cake and it's in and out in 10 minutes. Could be maybe, 15 tops". "Well, what's the plan then Ronnie boy?" Dennis asked cockily. "Come over here by the stairs to the upper level" I motioned. "I'll clue you all in on the scam".

"Church" I whispered softly. "The church is the scam" "What fucking church?" Dennis asked. "What the fuck are you babbling about now?" "Ok, listen" I said. "Next door is the Lutheran church right? "Yeah, so?" Johnny asked. You hear how loud these bands are? I asked. "Any noise we make breaking into that church will be drowned out by the noise from the music". "Genius!" Tony yelled. "Keep it down man" I laughed. "Let's keep this to ourselves". "Ok, ok Ronnie" Dennis replied. "But, what do we do when we get in there?" "I'll show you once we are by the church" I chortled. "Churches always have money, don't they?" I asked. "Sure" Johnny replied. "But, if we are caught, you realize We'll be crucified, right?" "Fuck that" Dennis replied. "Let's steal from the poor and give to the band. I'm in bro". "Ok, then follow me" I said. "And, all our bands troubles will be over"

We left the dance and strode over to the church a few lots over. As we approached, I peered around the building for entranceways. Tony exclaimed "All I see is two large doors in the front here". "No, no" I whispered. "We have to find one that's in the back. The front is too risky. Someone will see us". "You got that right" Dennis mumbled. "There's no way I'm taking a chance like that". "Be quiet and just follow me" I said. "I think I see a door in the back on the right". Silently, we crept up to a back door on the right side of the structure. "Here it is" I muttered. "I think this one will do nicely". "Ok" Johnny replied. "Show us your plan to get in then". "Easy" I said. "I got in TJ last year with a Popsicle stick I found on the ground. I just happen to have one here with me in my pocket. I've been casing this joint and a few others for a few months. So, I've always kept it with me". Dennis was incredulous. "Bullshit" he replied. "I don't believe you for a minute. You took us over here with a fucking Popsicle stick?" he asked. "I gotta see this shit" "Just watch and learn" I replied. "I'll be in with 2 shakes of a lamb"s tail" "I believe him" Johnny said. "Ronnie's a pretty crafty fucker".

"Watch out for me you guys" I demanded. "I have to keep my eyes on the lock here and it'll take me a little bit. But, We'll get in, I promise". I took the Popsicle stick and jimmied the sliding catch just as I"d done before. "Viola!" I snorted "We're" in". "No shit" Dennis replied "He fucking did it!" "I told you" Johnny said. "Ronnie knows his shit". "Nah Johnny" I laughed. "You just gotta have patience and a steady hand". "Whatever" Dennis responded "Let's just get inside before somebody sees us". "Yeah" Tony chuckled "I wanna see what's in there. So, hurry up and let's go in already. We're wasting too much time". We filed in quietly and slithered toward the podium like snakes winding a way down a path. "Make sure you close the door behind you" I told Tony. "You're the last one in. I don't want anyone seeing any lights coming out of this place" "I got it. I got it" he replied. "Let's just hurry and see what we can find. This shit makes me nervous". "Look" I whispered "No Lutherans go to church on Friday nights. So, you"ve got nothing to worry about. Now, you and your brother go and check out what you can find by the pulpit, and Dennis and I will check out the office on the right at the end of the hallway". "Ok man" he said. "But, don't leave us too long. I get scared doing this shit". "We'll be right back" I said "Stop being a pussy and go and find some loot". Come on Den" I said. "Let's go see what that office might have for us" Dennis and I scrambled down with earnest to the corridor and the office entry. Observing it, we noticed it was a door with a frosted glass center. Dennis reached for the door knob. "Fuck" he howled. "It's fucking locked! What"ll we do now?" he asked. "Hmmm" I replied. "We'll just have to break the glass then, won't we? Go back to where Tony and Johnny are and get me one of those candlesticks from the stage" "Ok" he replied "I'll be right back".

As I was examining the ripples and pits in the contour of the glasS's surface, he returned. "Will this one do?" he asked. "Holy shit!" I exclaimed "That thing"s the size of a fucking baseball bat". It was a sconce that was about 5 feet long with figure S pieces protruding from its top. "I took out the candle" Dennis laughed "You think we can use it?" "Sure" I replied. "Hand it to me and We'll break this window and get in".

I pulled back on the candelabra like an Olympian throwing a javelin for a score. "Do it" Dennis squealed "Let it fly, bro". I marked my target and fired and it hit the door at center mass. Crash the windowpane went with shards of glass flying everywhere. I released the candlestick and it hit the floor with a clang. "We're in" Dennis remarked. "Reach in and unlock the door Ronnie. I sure hope nobody heard us". "I don't think anyone did" I replied. "We're pretty far away from the roadway." I opened the door and pushed the shards aside with my foot. Inside, we saw an office chair, a desk, some religious artifacts, a filing cabinet, and a safe. Dennis got visibly excited. "Look" he exclaimed "A fucking safe. You know we gotta crack that baby open, don't you?" he asked. "I dunno Den" I said "That's gonna take a long time to bust open. I don't think we have enough time for that." "Fuck it" he exclaimed disappointed. "We'll just take it home with us then". I examined the safe more closely. "I don't think so Den" I said "It's bolted to the wall". He got very agitated. "God damn it" he yelled "Every time I want something, somebody else screws it up!" "Fuck it, Den" I answered. Let's go through the desk real quick and see if there's anything of value. We rifled the drawers and came up with some coins and a few pieces of jewelry. "I don't know if any of this is real, man?" I asked. "But, let's take it anyway and figure it out later". Suddenly, we heard noises coming from the front of the building. It was the podium area where we had left Tony and Johnny. "We better go see what those two are up to Den" I cautioned "Before they get in over their heads". We filled our pockets with the trinkets and wandered back to the lectern area to inspect. Johnny was standing on a chair and Tony was disassembling something. Johnny asked "Did you guys find anything worthwhile back there?" "No" I replied. "Just some change and some bullshit costume jewelry" "That sucks" Tony said "But, check this shit out?" he asked. "See those speakers on those hanging shelves from the ceiling? Johnny found a screwdriver in a drawer up here and he's taking the speakers out of their boxes. They're 12 inch ones and we can use them for the band". "Cool" I replied "But, try to be fast. It's bad enough We're robbing from a church. If the cops come, We're toast". Peering around, Dennis saw an organ to his left and mumbled to himself "Hmmm, nice man. I wonder what this bitch sounds like".

As Dennis was toying with the organ"s keyboard, Tony began telling me about a box he was examining from behind the podium. I knew it was electronic because it had wires coming out of it and they were cascading toward the floor. "This is a module for a PA system, man" he boasted. "See those 2 skinny mic stands over by Johnny?" he asked. "Yeah, so what? I replied. "Well" Tony said "This control box goes to those mics. We can use them as monitors with the speakers Johnny"s taking. We'll have a free system. So, I'm taking them. You'll be able to hear yourself sing when we play". "Sounds good to me" I said. "But, we really should hurry shit this up. We've already spent too much time in here" "Well then" Johnny said "Get your ass up here and help me then. Get another chair, here"s another screwdriver, stand up like me, and take that other speaker out on the left". "Ok" I said. "Whatever it takes to get out of here sooner". Just then, a loud pipe organ sound rang out from behind us. Dennis was fumbling around with the keyboard on the organ and trying to figure out what all of the push, pull buttons and pedals did. "I got it, I got it" he screamed. "Check me out! I'm Mozart and shit!" He pushed in another button and began playing chords and notes with his fingers and his hands. It was bombastic and I recognized it right away. "That's not Mozart you dumb ass" I laughed "That's Beethoven"s 5th Symphony. And, if we get caught, that's the song you'll be singing on the way to the county jail". "So, that's that song of doom and gloom we hear in all the movies before bad shit happens to people?" he asked laughing hilariously. "Yup" I replied "Now, shut that fucking thing off before we all get busted". "But, it sounds so cool" he remarked. Tony was getting flustered. "Not cool enough for me to go to fucking jail cause of you man" he said. "Shut the fucking thing off!" By this time, I was laughing my ass off. It was then I realized Dennis loved to make jokes when he was in the most desperate of situations. We collected the speakers, sound module, microphones and stands, and began exiting the building the way we came in. As we were leaving, Dennis got down on one knee and made the sign of the cross and looked upward. "That's not gonna save you, bro" Johnny laughed "You"ve already done the deed. He'll have to speak with you later". "He'll understand" chuckled "I've had a hard life". "Yeah" I answered "So hard that you have to steal from a church, right?" Dennis insisted "It's not my fault man; I'm a victim of circumstance". "And, I'm a victim of being poor" Johnny laughed. "So poor, I can't afford bail. So, get your ass up and let's go". We carried the goods beyond the church parking lot, stashed them in some weeds by Edison High School, and retrieved them later with a car. I guess I had a fetish for churches.

Jeffrey G., Ronnie E., Georgie Burns, and I all decided to go fishing. It was late afternoon on a Saturday as we gathered at the Gulotta"s house for our journey to Lawrence Brook. Somehow, it got back to us that Billy F. wanted to attend. But, there were some rumblings from within that some didn't want him to come with us. "Come on, man. Let's hurry up and leave before he gets here" I heard someone say. "I don't want to deal with him today" I remember understanding why some would want to omit him. He had a habit of sometimes telling yarns that seemed kind of fantastic. Though Billy could embellish the truth, it didn't bother me and I still thought he was cool to hang out with. Eventually, I was outvoted and it was time to go. We ditched Billy and walked quickly to our fishing spot. As we were walking over the route 1 bridge, I recall looking over my shoulder every so often to see if Billy was tagging along behind us. I didn't show it, but I had felt bad for him knowing after he arrived at Jeffrey"s that none of us were there. Our usual place to fish was along the banks of the northern side of the brook and was under the bridge that traversed Route 18. After an hour of trolling with lures, bait, and bobbers and having and no luck, Ronnie decided we should "Crawl across the arches under the highway to a better fishing spot in the middle of the bridge". "How the hell are we gonna do that? I asked. "It starts out wide on the bottom and then gets skinny on the top?" "Just watch me" he replied "You shimmy up to the center, then lie flat on your stomach and slide down to the foot below you. Its cake! I've done it a lot of times. Don't be a pussy; it's not that hard, man". "What about the tackle boxes and poles?" Jeffrey asked. Ronnie replied. "When one of us is up there, just hand him shit when they reach the middle, then they can just drop it down".

As we watched, Ronnie scrambled up the concrete pylon with ferocious determination. As he climbed to the area where there wasn't much room to move, he was twisting his body into weird configurations. His legs contorted first, and then his arms. "Mah huh!" he cried out. "I'm a human pretzel! All I need is some mustard!" "How can you do that without muscle conniptions?" asked Jeff. "I'll get a Charlie horse if I try that for sure". "He only does that with fish" I laughed loudly. "Shut up, Arold" Ronnie said. "I don't say that anymore. So, get your ass up here or go the fuck home". "Oh, the circus performer is testy today" I chuckled. "So, I guess we better do as he says". Eventually, he slithered down to the other side and called out to us "Come on, man. If I can make it, you guys can too". One by one we copied him. In a relay fashion we transferred the poles and the tackle boxes until all of us were where he was waiting. Once we were all safely on the bridges foot between land and open water, Ronnie exclaimed "It's like when you have a boat, man. You always catch fish better when you're out in the open water, right?" he asked. "But, we don't have a boat. So, we improvise". "I guess so" Georgie replied. "I just hope we catch some fish from here". While casting our lines and retrieving our baits, someone inadvertently kicked Ronnie's tackle box into the water. He screamed "Fuck, somebody jump in a save it! All of my good shit is in there!" Out of instinct, I dove in. Since it was only a few feet away, I had no problem going in to search for it. As I swam closer, I caught a faint glimpse of its green plastic top as water washed over its grooved rectangular lid. Just as I reached out my hand to grab it, it was gone. I swam down a little with a faint hope of retrieving it, but it was to no avail. Watching this, Ronnie became livid "Goddamn it, Arold" he shrieked "It took me a long time to collect all those lures. I lost my hooks, my jigs, my weights, everything". "What the fuck do you want from me? I replied "I didn't kick your shit into the water. Next time, you fucking swim for it. I did you a favor". "I know" he replied "But, it still pisses me the fuck off anyway".

I swam back to the land"s edge and stood up. I was soaking wet and dirty. "What should I do now?" I thought. I could stay where I was, or try to ascend the bridge again. Ronnie called to me half apologetic "Don't worry about it man, it's not your fault. Come back up and fish with us." "I don't know if I can" I replied. "I'm pretty worn out from swimming. But, I'll try". I accosted the arch under the bridge and gave it my best shot. But, I was just too exhausted to do so. No matter how much I tried, I couldn't complete the climb. "I don't think I can do it again" I cried. Ronnie asked "Why don't you just swim over to us instead then? We'll make a chain with our arms and pull you up" "I think I can make that" I replied. "I'll give it a whirl". I was thinking "It doesn't look that far from the land to the bridge abutment. It looks like it's about 12 feet and I should be able to do that easily". I entered the water and swam to the bridges base. The area everyone was standing on was about 3 feet above me. But, as I had nothing to push up against, there was no way possible for me to jump up to it from the water below. There were no channels on the base of bricks to latch onto either, it was smooth and there was nothing. As I was treading water, I realized I was surrounded by water striders. They were like spiders balancing on the surface doing a ballet and kept distracting me. I'd splash at them and they'd keep coming back at me. Ronnie came to the edge and said "I'm gonna hold Jeffrey by his wrist and lower him down to you. You grab onto him and We'll pull you up, all right?" "Easier said than done" I thought. Like a human chain, he lowered Jeff down within my reach and I grabbed for his arm. Jeff grasped my hand in his palm while Georgie was behind Ronnie holding him by his waist. "Pull, pull" Georgie yelled. "I can't" Ronnie shrieked "He's too heavy. I can't hold him". Abruptly, and with no warning, Ronnie let go. Jeff fell and spilled into the water directly on top of my head. Unbeknownst to me, Jeffrey couldn't swim. Though we were only 12 feet from land, Jeff began to panic. In his fight for survival, the harder I tried to surface, the more he pushed me down. Each time I came up, I could hear them all screaming for me to save him. "Save him?" I thought "I was drowning myself".

I remember I had panicked as well at first, and then had given up. I was sinking to the bottom and fast. I started to have strange auditory hallucinations and heard the sound of bells ringing. It was like the kind in a bell tower or a ship. Then, it switched to a buzzing sound with a crackling kind of noise. It was as if you were walking under high tension wires after it had rained. Just as I felt as if I was about to float away, I was wrenched by my arm to the surface. Someone was pulling on me lifeguard style to the lakeshore. When we got there, they threw me down on my back and walked away. I could hear yelling in the distance and I was very incoherent and dizzy. I felt like I had been on a boardwalk spinning ride too long and my equilibrium was off. After a few minutes and having come back to reality, Billy was standing over me. "You know, you almost drowned asshole" he said in a chastising tone. "Jeffrey too. I knew you guys were trying to blow me off. But, I knew where you were all going so I snuck behind you anyway. You're lucky I was on the swim team at school once, or you guys would be dead". Jeffrey was just coming around by now and looked at me and exclaimed "What the fuck Ron?" he asked dumbfounded. "You shouldn't have just let go of me, I don't know how to swim you retard". "Nobody told me, Jeff" I replied. "I thought you guys had it down". Ronnie yelled over from under the bridge "Be glad Billy dove in to save your asses. He learned the lifeguard carry when he was on that wimpy swim team bullshit". "No problem" Billy said. "But, I bet you guys never get rid of me again." "No, Billy" I exclaimed gratefully. "You proved yourself, bro. At least you tried to help us while those knuckleheads just stood around. No matter what any of them say, you can always hang out with us now".

As a teenager, we always tried to indulge in the things adults got to enjoy. We wanted the freedoms they had. We wanted to be grown up and to emulate them. We wanted to look cool. It could be a drag from a parent"s cigarette, watching porn films, drinking alcoholic beverages, everything. Most of us started out with cigarettes as they were marginally hard to achieve. My father smoked Chesterfield Kings and there was always a burning stub in the ashtray. A quick puff was always accomplished whenever his back was turned. Porn was the easiest. Most fathers in America had a stash of Playboy magazines. They were usually tucked away from prying eyes and hidden where only they knew where to find them. Booze was another story. It was generally the hardest to obtain and get away with since the drinking age in 1975 was 18. Most kids I knew either had an older brother or sister to supply it, or if you were bold, you"d mosey into a local bar and take your chances instead. Sometimes you"d be carded, sometimes you would not. Sometimes, it depended on what kind of mood the bartender was in. By networking with other teens, friends, and relatives, we learned of all the establishments where we had the best chances to score. My first try was a scheme many of my friends had used but I had been unaware of. I had been hanging around with a new friend named Danny. He got an idea to go drinking but he wouldn't tell me where it was until we got there. I had met Danny one afternoon while walking home from Edison High School on one of the rare days I had decided to attend. He was a year older than me and lived directly behind the football field"s bleachers. Danny had long black hair, a beard and an uncanny resemblance to George Harrison of The Beatles. I asked Danny "So? Where is this mythical pub you"ve been telling me about? Do you think We'll get served there?" He replied "I know I will because I look 18. I'm not sure about you though". I was annoyed and asked "What's the purpose of even going then?" He was teasing me. "I have a way to get you served, bro" he said. "Just do what I say when we get there. It always works, always". He then informed me that we'd have to walk up to Route 1 south. "What for?" I asked. "We're gonna hitchhike to Carolier lanes" he replied. "There's a girl I want to meet there anyway. The bonus is we can drink beer while waiting for her. If she never shows, We'll just get drunk instead". We took turns sticking out our thumbs to secure a ride and it wasn't long until we were successful. After we arrived and walked into the bowling alley, Danny finally laid his scam on me. "I'm going to go sit at the bar" he said. "Go to the bathroom. When you come out, sit next to me and there will be a beer ready for you". "How the fuck are you gonna manage that?" I asked. "Won't they proof me?" "No way" he replied "I look more than old enough. Since you're with me and you're tall, They'll think you're ok". I left him to himself and went to the restroom as he instructed. I wasted a few minutes knowing it would take the bartender a while to serve Danny"s order. On my way back, I scanned the bar to see if he succeeded in pulling it off. As I bellied up to the banister, I sat down next to him. Right there before me, was a tall cool draft. It was bubbling with effervescent joy and its pale yellow hue was beckoning me. I couldn't wait to take my first in bar sip. "Go ahead, man" Danny mumbled. "Drink up. But, don't act all nervous and shit. If you do that, They'll be on to us". "How did you fool them? I asked. "It's pretty easy" he replied. "I just told him I needed 2 beers because my friend was in the bathroom. He asked me if you were cool and of age. I said yeah and the dummy believed me. This is a bowling alley, bro. It's a family place and most family places won't card you". The bartender came by as I was half done and offered us another. We graciously accepted and paid him. I was ecstatic. I had been served!

I was walking along Central Avenue one night by the train station getting ready to cross the tracks. At this time, there were no buildings and only a platform to wait on. On the other side of the live commuter tracks, there was an old rail line. It was a leftover from when Camp Kilmer was in operation. On these rusty tracks, there were occasional box cars loaded with assorted sundries and possible high value items. I usually took this short cut to gain access to a path that went to a lake that was far back in the woods. The lake was named Bare Ass Lake or Eagles Pond depending on who you asked. On this night, I was interrupted by laughing and faint figures in the distance. It seemed they were sprinting up to an open rail car door, grabbing something, and darting to the woods behind them. With suspicion on my mind, I crept up closer to get a better look. "Who are they?" I thought. "What the hell are they doing?" Just then, someone came up behind me. I was startled thinking it might be the cops. It was Howie B. "What the fuck are you doing Ronnie?" he asked. "You scared the fuck out of us. We thought you were the Amtrak police". "I scared you?" I asked. "I thought I was busted for doing nothing". "Nah" Howie chuckled. "Nothing is cheese tonight, bro". "Cheese?" I asked. "What the fuck are you talking about Howie? Fucking cheese? I don't get it. Like a mouse? "No man" he replied "It's box car cheese night. You see these here open rail cars?" he asked. "Me, my brother Brian and a few others cracked one of those bad boys open. Inside are 5-pound blocks of yellow American McDonalds cheese." He started laughing hysterically "They are the traps, and we are the mice. Grab some and eat up man, its cheese night for everyone!" I joined the crowd of kids and stood by the door for the handouts below. A few teens were already inside and dropping down the blocks for anyone to take away. "It's a free for all of pilferage proportions" Howie chuckled. "It's the cheesiest thing we've done today" I took 5 or 6 blocks and hid them in the tall grass at the edge of the woods. As Howie was moving more and more product, he was singing to himself and making squeaky mouse noises. "Cheese, cheese, squeak, squeak, and squeak" he whispered. "Cheese, cheese, tweak,

tweak, tweak". I was laughing so hard, I almost peed myself. After all of us bandits were satisfied, we collected our loaves and headed home. Luckily since I lived close by, I only had to make 3 return trips to collect them all. On my final expedition, Howie was still there finishing up. "I have to close the box car"s door so it's not so obvious" he said. "Now, don't get caught by the cops running home with one of those blocks Ronnie" he cautioned. "I"d hate to see you fall and have a melt down with one of them". "Yeah" I said. "Then, the cops would grill me like a tasty meal. "They'd make a sandwich out of you for sure" he laughed. "Don't worry, man" I said. "I don't like melted cheese with bacon". "You got it, bro" he chuckled. "It's best to avoid pork at all costs". In the coming weeks, all of South Edison had blocks of cheese. There was cheese everywhere and everyone I knew had some. We had created a down low dairy product fest. It was the cheesiest celebration I had ever attended.

Every Wednesday night at Zaffys was The Good Rats night. The Good Rats were a band from Long Island, New York who played the local circuit and had had some marginal success while touring. Most everyone I knew from Edison loved them and rarely missed a performance whenever they came into town. Being that I was underage, my friends and I had to continually come up with schemes to be able to see them. Since the allowable age to enter was 18, it was easier in the realm of reason to procure a copy of someone else"s driver"s license that was only a few years older than you. Since picture ID"s weren't invented yet, an older brother or sister's proof was usually the first we'd try to achieve. Fortunately for me, my older brother Robert had just turned 22. Therefore, he had already been entering bars and clubs for some time. When I pled my case to him, he understood and offered me a ragged copy of his license for a "small fee". "What will you use for yourself if you sell me your old one?" I asked him. "That's no problem" he replied laughing. "I'll just go to the DMV and buy a replacement one. The only problem you're gonna have though is my old one is only good for a few more months. Also, if a bartender or liquor store owner is savvy, They'll sometimes ask you to write your name on a separate piece of paper to match the one that's on the license. And, I don't think you'll be able to copy mine". That's true" I replied. "You have a very ornate signature". "Well, it's up to you" he said. "If you want it, give me 10 bucks. And if any cops ask you, you found it and I know nothing". I paid him the money and he handed it over. It had a blue faded tint to it with the N.J official seal on the top. The only problem I saw was that its edge was frayed and the typeface was faint. "Tell them you washed it by accident a few times" he said. "A few people I know did that and it was accepted. But, I guess it all depends who"s at the door".

I ran into Howie"s younger brother Brian and asked him if he wanted to go see the Good Rats with me. Coincidentally, he had gotten a copy of Howie"s ID around the same time I secured mine. "This Wednesday right?" he asked. "Yeah" I replied. "Who"s opening for them?" he asked. "Being that I was an avid reader of our local music scene paper called the Aquarian, I knew exactly who it was. "The Rockids and some band I never heard of before called Borzoi". I replied. "Ok, cool" Brian said. "I'll go because I love the Rats. And, I think you'll like the Rockids anyway because they dress like the Stones". "Sounds good" I said. "I'll meet you there at 8". I arrived at the designated time and Brian was already there waiting. He was excited as he had somehow gotten in to see the Good Rats before. "You're in for a real treat" he said. "Have you ever seen them before?" he asked. "No" I replied. "But, I heard they are really good and put on a great show". "Great show is an understatement" he said. "Just wait until you see what they do on stage. You're gonna love it". We stood in line, paid the fee, and strolled inside. "Wow" I exclaimed. "That bouncer hardly even looked at my ID". "Well, We're both 16 anyway" Brian said. "He's knows We're close enough. And, We're both pretty tall. So, I guess he believed us". "Excellent" I thought. "If it's this easy, I'm gonna have to try to use this again".

We bought a couple of beers and found the best spot by the front of the stage that we could. It was early. So, we chose a place over by the dressing room entrance to the left. I turned my head and noticed that members of the band the Rockids were standing by a door and their guitar player was arguing with a girl. "How about a blow job before we go on?" I heard him ask her. Amazed, I nudged Brian with my elbow. "Check this shit out?" I asked. "That guy just asked that chick for some head". Brian laughed and replied "That's nothing, bro. You should see what they all do after the show". In between talking to Brian, the guitar player must have pressed the girl more. She blew up in his face "Fuck you!" she screamed. "I told you maybe later. That's not all I'm here for. So now, you're not gonna get anything". She ran back through the door with the guitar player chasing after her. "That was funny as fuck" I laughed. "I've never seen shit like that before". "Is this the first time you"ve ever been inside a club to see a band?" Brian asked. "Because, that shit goes on all the time". "I've read and heard about it" I said. But, never seen anyone blatantly ask for sex in front of a room full of people". "Welcome to the world of rock and roll" he said. "I was glad to indoctrinate you". When the Rockids and Borzoi were done, there was a short break and a stage change. I glanced over in a corner and saw a roadie placing a beat up metal garbage can to the right of the drum riser. Then, he came back out and placed a baseball bat in it. "What the fuck are those, Brian?" I asked. "Are they props?" "You'll see" he said. Just watch because I don't wanna spoil it for you". Next, the stage hand came out with a large cardboard box and placed it on one of the amplifiers. "I wonder what's in that?" I thought grinning. "I guess I'll have to wait and see". Soon, the Good Rats took the stage. I had only known one or two of their songs. But, I was hooked on their performance immediately. I watched as they went through their various numbers while their singer Pepe mounted the shoulders of their guitar player John "the cat" Gato. I was in awe as I had never seen anything like it before and was wondering how he had to fortitude to carry Pepe that way all around the stage. At the close of that song, they started one of the one"s I knew named Injun Joe. The audience flew into a frenzy. I remember thinking "This must be one of their signature tunes". Pepe danced over to where the garbage can had been previously placed and picked it up by one of its handles. With his other hand, he grabbed hold of the baseball bat that had been set inside. He began banging on the trash receptacle with all his might. "Hey Injun Joe" he screamed into his mic. "What you know? Went to the city, to organize". Everyone was on their feet and singing along loudly. Most knew every word. Toward the end of the show, they played the second song I knew named Tasty. During a slight middle break, I witnessed Pepe saunter over to the cardboard box I had been wondering about that had been sitting on top of that amplifier. He reached in and pulled out 10 or 20 rubbery looking black things. "What the fuck are those, Brian?" I asked. "You'll see" he replied. "Just put your hands out to catch one". "Catch what?" I thought. Pepe came to the front and aggressively threw them out into the audience. I didn't retrieve one but Brian did. "Lemme see that?" I asked As Pepe went back for some more, Brian held it up to my face and was smiling "Holy shit" I exclaimed. "It's a rubber fucking rat!" "They throw these out at all the shows" Brian said. "And, I almost always get one. He's gonna throw out more in a second. So, try to get one, man". I never did grab a rat. But, I did attend more of their shows. Eventually, they released an album named Rat City in Blue. It has my favorite song they have ever done called "Advertisement in the Voice". Unfortunately, many years later Pepe passed away. I will never forget them as they turned me on to my very first club show.

A friend of ours named Marc was the neighborhood Evel Knievel. This 14 year old had ramps, custom bikes, outfits, the whole 9 yards. His jumping point of preference was a path that was between 2 lots that belonged to a grumpy old man named Herchui. Occasionally, we'd use one of his domains as a shortcut to other areas of the neighborhood. Sometimes, when we felt ornery, we'd ride past him on our bikes and throw stones at his back while giving him the finger. When we did this, he would usually retaliate swiftly. He had an annoying habit of popping us in the ass with his salt gun whenever he thought we were disrespecting him or trespassing on one of his lots. Fortunately for us, we seldom did. On most weekends, kids would gather around and watch Marc do his daredevil tricks for the majority of the afternoon. He would start at the top of the hill on Jefferson Boulevard. There, he would take his time sizing up his speed to distance formulas until he was ready to fly. He had it all down to a science. Wind velocity, trajectory, weight distribution, acceleration, etc. At the end of the byway, was a cul de sac type of street that had virtually no traffic. Therefore, there was less risk of over shooting the ramp and being hit by a passing motorist. For a bicycle stratagem enthusiast, it was perfect. The neighborhood youths would gather at the bottom of this area to egg Marc on and scream his name. It must have been a real confidence builder for him I'm sure. Marc wasn't particularly a large kid, maybe 80 pounds and 5 feet tall. I'd imagine it was the ideal body specifications for how far he could sail when coupled with the weight of his bike. Since this path was about 50 feet long on a 60 percent grade, he never had any problem tackling his own record. With great ease he would demonstrate his expertise. There were many times where I witnessed him jump at least 25 feet. He would scream down the hill, hit the ramp, and glide through the air like a rocket and was always pushing himself to do more. As far as any of us knew, he was ordained as the local 2 wheel bike champion. His had an obsession to always want to be in the Guiness book of world records. We were sure in adulthood; he would have done that and had been a star. Until, the fateful afternoon of the Fireman"s Fair.

The local Edison Fireman"s Fair was held every year across the street from the old Edison police station and behind the local post office on the corner of Plainfield and Woodbridge Avenue. There, like most other fairs, were various states of vendors hawking their wares for the supposed benefit of the fire department. There was beer, sausage sandwiches, clams on the half shell, popcorn, cotton candy, and games. There were lots and lots of games. It was the classic scenario to keep the crowds entertained whilst manipulating them into spending their money. It was all under the guise of the feel good metaphor. They'd keep you happy for an hour or two, and pick your pockets clean by the end of the evening. I could always tell when I was near due to the loudness of the intoxicated adults in the far west corner of the lot. There, they would stand by the beer truck, leaning on ledges of wood and spilling false yarns about how great they were and how successful their lives had become. It was a smorgasbord of haves, have nots, their station in town based on their income, and who kissed the asses of who for the most favors and nepotism. It was the hypocritical social ladder, and classic gossip machine. These were the so called grownups who preached to us the deviance of underage drinking whilst exceedingly imbibing themselves. It was the parents, the cops, the judges, the teachers, the firemen, anyone and everyone who had even a hint of authority. They were drunken fools in oblivious harmony patting their backs and congratulating each other for conquering their imagined imagery. While the attendees were enjoying their merriment, Marc was travelling on his bike with a friend. He and his buddy Mike decided to visit the fair for a night out of fun and discovery. As Marc straddled his bike and pedaled, Mike walked alongside him. They couldn't wait to partake in the party and were discussing what was new for this year. Would they visit the games of chance first? Would they get a bite to eat and a soda? Would they ride on some rides and see friends? The possibilities were endless. As they approached the intersection of Route 1 and Plainfield Avenue., they stopped to wait for the light. When it was red and safe to cross, Mike motioned for Marc to accompany him. Marc wheeled his bike to the center of the crossway. Suddenly, out of nowhere, came a car careening at high speed. Marc never had a chance. He was hit and thrown to the ground. He died almost instantly. The hopes and dreams of our daredevil friend were shattered. No more would we see our champion perform with charismatic tenacity. We were sad; we were shocked, it shouldn't have happened. We had to do something in his name.

It turned out that Jeffrey had a friend who knew a reporter who worked for our local newspaper called The Home News. Jeffrey was given the reporter"s phone number and told to call him about Marc"s untimely demise. Jeffrey rang the man up and explained the story with great detail. The reporter gave Jeff an appointment asking to bring all who were involved to his office for an interview. It seemed the newspaper was very interested in what we had to say. On the day of the consultation, Jeffrey got me, Georgie Burns, and Dave G. to consort with him for the long walk to the newspaper building. It was from Edison to New Brunswick on Hoes Lane. We knew it was a far hike, but we couldn't refuse in the memory of our friend. Jeffrey insisted something had to be done. We began our journey and were brainstorming ideas while walking. Jeff came up with a scenario. "How come there aren't overhead walkways at that intersection?" he asked. "I dunno" I replied. "It's probably because the township doesn't wanna spend the money. "That's a bunch of bullshit" Dave shouted. "The local government has more money than they know what to do with. I see them piss money away on stupid projects all the time". Georgie Burns agreed. "The government is nothing but crooks" he said. "The more power they have, the more corruption". "True" I replied. "But, let's stay on track. What more are we gonna tell this reporter guy? I asked. "It seems like nobody ever does anything about highways and roads until someone gets killed". "That's what pisses me off" Jeffrey shouted. "We have to try to embarrass them in the newspaper. Hopefully, They'll print our story about it". "I hope so" Dave exclaimed. "Cause this is a mighty far walk and I wouldn't want my friend to have died in vain".

After a two- hour session of fact finding and interviews amongst us, the reporter said it would be a great humanistic story about the honor and death of friends. Jeffrey had decided that a petition was warranted for maximum effect and the reporter agreed. A few days later, a photographer showed up in my front yard and took some stills of Jeff, me, and Georgie Burns. Dave couldn't make it that day but was still included in the story none the less. A week later, to our amazement, we were on the front page. Right in the center staring at us was our picture and the words "Local teens start petition for friend killed on highway". We felt like celebrities, but celebrities for the right reason. Though we continued our petition all over town and received roughly 3 thousand signatures, its purpose was short lived. We dropped the papers off at the appropriate township department for review. They were supposed to be open for possible consideration of a proposed walkway. Being that it was Edison as Edison always is, we never heard back from then again. But hey, at least we tried.

The little red headed girl from the campground had asked me to come visit her at her house in Jersey City. I agreed to it and began searching around for a friend to accompany me. Since I had gone to New York City on the train with him before, I settled on asking Georgie Burns. Georgie volunteered immediately and couldn't wait to go back to a "city atmosphere". "But" he said. There was one condition. He wanted to "trip" on the way there and refused to go unless I would supply some. "I don't know her mother Georgie" I said. "Are you sure you want to trip in front of someone"s mom you"ve never met before?" "Don't worry about me" he replied. "She's your little girlfriend. I'll be in the background like I always am. You're the one who"s gonna have to face her". "What if she looks in my face and knows I'm high?" I asked. "That would be embarrassing". "We can just leave then" Georgie said. "You act like you're married to her". "I just don't want any trouble, man" I answered concerned. "You know how I puked on the train on the way home the last time I tripped with you". "You took too much last time, bro" he replied. "Just be cool and take a quarter". "I guess I can do that" I replied. "But, if it gets freaky and I start acting like a weirdo, give me a sign and We'll go home". "No problem" Georgie said. "I gotcha, bro".

I met Georgie at his house on the set afternoon and called for a cab to the train station. Before the taxi arrived, Georgie was bugging me for his hit. "Come on, man" he said. "Cut that shit up. I wanna peak before we get there. All the lights in the city give cool trails when you peak". "All right, all right already" I replied. "Stop pestering me". As I handed him his dose, I reminded him "You better watch out for me and not like the last time" I said. "I mean it". "I told you, you'll be ok" he replied. "Now, take yours and lets go". As we exited the cab neither one of us were feeling any affects yet and were just happy that we were on time. "Here comes the train" Georgie yelled as it approached. "Let's get a seat by a window". We settled in and discussed how we had to change trains in Newark and how it wouldn't be that long before we were there. "I hope she has a girl for me" Georgie asked. "I hate being the 3rd wheel all of the time". "I'm sure she'll have a friend there" I replied. "So, stop worrying". After changing modes of transportation to Journal Square, we walked down the steps to Kennedy Boulevard. "She lives on Summit Avenue" I said. "It shouldn't be too far from here". "Cool" Georgie replied. "Because it's starting to get dark soon and we don't know this neighborhood. And by the way bro, the acid is kicking in". "I know" I replied nervously. "Me too".

As we approached the girl's home, I was starting to get that dreaded tickling feeling inside again. The one that I despised every time I dropped acid that always seemed to linger longer than I wanted it too. "Here comes the low self-esteem paranoia next" I thought. "I don't know why I even do this shit". "Are we almost there?" Georgie asked. "My legs feel like rubber and I need to sit down". "The next house is her"s" I replied. "Look, they're sitting on the stoop waiting for us. So, be cool and don't say anything about us tripping". "I won't" Georgie said. "But, don't get angry if I started laughing for no reason". We converged on the gate and walked inside. The little red headed girl threw her arms around my neck and gave me a big kiss. I introduced Georgie as my friend and she did the same with hers. Her girlfriend was quiet and wasn't saying much. She seemed to be caught up more in sizing us up and observing us. After a couple of hours had passed and it was night time, the little red headed girl asked me if I wanted to come in to meet her mother. "Oh God, no" I said acting very paranoid and afraid. "I'm really tripping over here and I don't think I'm in any shape to meet someone"s parents right now. I'm really sorry". "That's ok" she replied concerned. "I'll be right back. I'm gonna go up and tell my mom that you don't feel well and prefer to stay outside in the air. She'll understand if I explain it to her that way. I don't want her to think you're disrespecting her". As the 2 girls left, Georgie began fucking with me. "Why won't you go inside, man?" he asked laughing. "So, you'll see her mom for 5 seconds? Big deal, bro. After that, we can all hide in her bedroom". "Leave me the fuck alone Georgie" I howled. "I'm tripping my balls off. That quarter must have been really strong. There's no way I can face her mom while I'm all tweaked out and shit. Look at me man, I'm shaking". "Just tell her mother you have the flu" Georgie exclaimed. "That should do it". "I'll get to it when I get to it" I replied annoyed, "As soon as I come down some, I'll be ok. So, just drop it".

The little red headed girl and her friend returned and were smiling. "I spoke to my mom" she said. "I told her you have the flu and are really sick. She said it's ok and that you don't have to meet her if you stay over. She has to go to work in the morning anyway. So, you're off the hook Mr. Arold". "We're staying over?" I asked. "Who said anything about staying over?" "My mom said there's no way you're going home sick at 10 o"clock at night. Besides, even if you make it back to Newark, you'll miss the last train home anyway. I don't think it's a good idea for you and your friend to stay over in Newark". "Do you?" "She has a point" said Georgie.

"You should listen to her, bro". "So, you're mine tonight whether you like it or not" she said. "And, that's final". "See Georgie?" I asked. "She's the little Irish Hussy. Now, you see why I gave her that name". "I wouldn't argue with her" Georgie replied. "She has the upper hand and you're outnumbered". "You're at my house now" the little red headed girl giggled. "And, there is no democracy". When it came to a point where the acid had finally started to ebb, we all agreed to go inside. "We're gonna stay in my room" said the little red headed girl. "We'll play some records until we fall asleep. I laid down on her bed sweating from the LSD as she was holding me and stroking my head. "Why did you do that stuff when you knew you were coming to see me" she cooed. "I want to be with the real you, not the drugged out Ronnie". "I'm stupid" I said. "And, I never learn". I peered over at Georgie in the faint glow of the night light and could see he wasn't making any headway with her friend. "What's up with the 2 of them?" I asked whispering. "Doesn't she like him?" "No offense" she replied "But, he's just not her type". I had finally come down enough to feel relaxed and was drifting off to sleep. The last song I remember playing in the background was Rod Stewart singing The First Cut is the Deepest. Deep I was, and out I had become.

In the morning, I awoke and was starving. The little red headed girl was asking if I felt better. "Indubitably" I replied. "Good" she said. "I like this Ronnie much better". "So do I" I laughed, "But, I don't get to see him too much". "What would you like to eat?" she asked. "There's some eggs in the kitchen". "If you don't mind" I said "I'd like to cook breakfast for everyone". "Well" she replied. My mom went to work. So, you can cook whatever you want. "Cool" I said. "Go entertain Georgie and your friend and I'll call you guys out here when I'm done". We ate a sumptuous meal, guzzled some tea and coffee, and I was beginning to go back to my old self. As I was helping to wash the dishes afterward, the little red headed girl put her arms around my waist and whispered in my ear "I told you before my mother wasn't home, remember? So, let's go in her bedroom". "Are you sure it's cool?" I asked. "I don't want you to get into any trouble". "My grandmother is downstairs" she said. "But, she doesn't come up here. So, we can be alone now. I told my friend to keep Georgie busy in conversation for a while. Now, come with me". She grabbed my hand and led me to the bedroom and threw me down earnestly on the bed. We began to make out. I got to 1st base, then 2nd; she reached her hand down my pants and began stroking me. I got very aroused. "This is better than tripping isn't it?" she asked. "Why do you want drugs when you can have me?" "Are you telling me you want to go all the way?" I asked all hot and bothered. "You can take me if you want" she murmured seductively. Just then, I was having thoughts of how far away I lived and how many times a year was I going to be able to continue seeing her? I wanted to take her virginity badly. But, if I couldn't see her much, I didn't want to break her heart. Most guys I knew would have taken any pussy thrown at them. But, I really admired this girl and my conscience got the better of me. I stopped our petting and pretended I was afraid. "Why did you stop?" she asked coyly. "I said you can have me". I used a lame excuse. But, at short notice, it was the best one I could come up with. "If we bang" I replied. "I don't want your grandmother to hear the bed squeaking downstairs while We're doing it. So, maybe next time when my friend and your friend aren't here, we can try again then". Visibly upset, she tried to coerce me into continuing. With each advance, I kept rebuffing her. "I just can't do this to this girl" I thought. "She's just too sweet to take advantage of". If she only knew.

At the Gulotta"s house, their mom Dee was always working 6 days a week. I had found out after some time that their father had passed away at an early age and that Dee had become the main bread winner for their family. She worked very long hours at a restaurant named Jacques in Plainfield. Therefore, due to involuntary lack of parental supervision, and circumstances out of her control, their house was the place where most youths would congregate and party. I was one of them. There always seemed to be something going on there from morning to late at night and was definitely the place to be. I had always loved the non-rigid, laid back atmosphere they enjoyed as a family even when hard times would envelope them. On many occasions, I felt like I was watching a non-scripted comedy show. With each visit being a new adventure, I would watch them and then laugh for days. It was as if their entertaining personalities had addicting qualities, and all the kids were drawn to them. It was like sketch comedy without rehearsals. They were naturally gifted whimsically without even trying. A scenario would arise and they'd go with it. While the banter between them was hilarious, sometimes I was even included myself. There were many instances between each other where I would be in awe of what they got away with. I have many examples. Like the time I came to collect Dennis for a trip for some lunch at the Edison diner.

I navigated up the front steps to the sound of Jeffrey screaming "Get off of me. I'll kill you!" "What's this all about? I thought". The door was slightly ajar. "Dennis?" I asked. "Are you here?" Is everything all right in there? Who"s yelling?" "Come on in Ron" he said. "It's just Jeff. He's been aggravating me again and I had to teach him a lesson". With some trepidation, I slowly entered the dining room looking to find where they were. As I peered around the corner toward their mother's bedroom, I could see Jeffrey on the floor. He was wedged between the oven and the doorway. Dennis was on top of him and holding him down by his neck with his right knee. Jeffrey was wearing a dark blue windbreaker. He had its hood snuggly wrapped around his head and tied tight under his jaw. It looked like he had a shiny bald blue skull and his face was beet red. Dennis began rubbing his cranium, "Whittle booberry" he crooned. "Whittle, whittle, booberry." "What's that boo?" he teased "You want to get up? Well, I can't do that yet, cause you're the whittle booberry!" I was trying hard not to laugh. But, I couldn't contain myself. Jeff was becoming angrier and angrier because he hated when people laughed at him. "Let me up, asshole" he screamed. "I'm gonna kill you!" "No, no, no" Dennis teased "Booberries have to be squeezed. And, you're just not ripe enough yet". He rubbed Jeffrey"s head again, stroking it like someone checking fruit at the supermarket. "Booberry" he muttered. "Whittle, whittle booberry!" "Dennis?" I asked. "How long are you gonna keep him there?" "Not much longer" he replied. "I like to wait until his face gets really red. When he's about to pop a blood vessel, I usually let him back up. But, you have to run bro. It takes him a long time to calm down and he gets crazy". Jeff was really fuming now. "Tell him to get off of me Ron" he screamed. "What can I do Jeff?" I responded. "He's your brother. There's nothing I can do". Just then, Dennis let him up. "Run bro, run" he shrieked "He's gonna go ballistic!" Dennis sprinted to the front door like a deer being chased by a hunter. Foolishly, I stood there immobile laughing. Surely, I couldn't be blamed for anything? I thought. "I was merely an innocent bystander". Jeff didn't chase after his brother nor come after me. He ran into his mother's bedroom instead. I saw that as strange. That was until he returned with a fishing pole. "Dennis, you better run you cocksucker" he howled. "I'll kill you". Suddenly, I felt the sharp stinging pain of a whack on my right forearm. It was like when a parent disciplines you with a switch. "What the fuck Jeff?" I asked. "Why the fuck did you hit me? I didn't do anything". "You laughed at me" he cried. "I asked you for help and you laughed at me. Nobody laughs at me, ever!" I grabbed the end of the pole in an attempt to disarm him. Back and forth we went. I was struggling to stop him from hitting me again. Eventually, he lost his grip and fell to the floor and I saw an opportunity to make my escape. As I scampered around the corner for a fast exit, I felt a twinge to the back of my neck. I had no idea what it was. All I knew was that I wanted to get out of there before Jeffrey hurt me again. I turned and heard a rattle hit the floor. Jeff was flinging metal forks at me from the kitchen. Luckily, he had only connected once. I kept hearing him mumbling "You laughed at me, you laughed at me. I'll kill you, I'll kill you".

Accidents with friends resulting in death seemed to become the norm this year and it was becoming quite depressing. There was a guy named Steve we all knew who was unknowingly about to become another one of Edison"s youth"s recent victims. I had hung around with him a couple of times via some friends and like most of us; he had a clownish sense of humor. It made people drawn to him like an addiction. Before he was killed, I have a great recollection of Steve standing in Dunkin Donut"s window exposing himself. As I did on many nights, I had walked in to purchase a large coffee and found him facing the parking lot with his pants around his ankles, a confused look on his face, and furiously pretending that he was jerking off. With each stroke of his hand, he was mumbling something incoherent to 2 women seated in their car outside. He was insisting with his body language that they couldn't wait to have him. "The cops are on their way" a waitress warned. "You better leave. They're gonna be here soon". "Steve!" I yelled out. "What the hell are you doing, man?" I asked. In between motions with his hand, he turned to me. He looked like he was lost and was having trouble balancing. "I'm showing them my grapefruit" he replied. "They all want to see my grapefruit". "No, bro" I hollered. "You're in a Dunkin Donuts, man. You need to pull up your pants and go home". My words didn't seem to connect with him and he seemed to be in another world. He turned back to the window, murmured something indecipherable about games, looked back at me smiling, and went back to jerking off again. "The cops are coming and I can't help this guy" I thought. "So, I better leave". I said goodbye to him but I don't think it registered. I found out later there was more to this story than I knew. It seemed that on that day, Steve had been paling around with JR and they had gotten into some bad drugs. Supposedly, someone had given them what they thought was snortable crystal T. Thinking nothing of this; they cut out their lines and were anticipating a buzz for some fun. Unbeknownst to them, they weren't given crystal T but a drug named Belladonna instead. Unfortunately, Belladonna had a reputation for giving its recipients a 3-day trip without the ability to come down. JR I was told, was so out of it he was found 2 days later walking the boardwalk naked in Seaside Heights with 2 girls on either side of him holding his hands. He was pontificating about his future and the universe he was in. Many months later, Steve was crossing the street by his home near Suydam Avenue and was stuck by a drunken asshole from Franklin by the name of Michael Bradley. This douchbag was so intoxicated; he hit poor Steve, travelled 91 feet with Steve still on the hood, and didn't stop until after Steve fell off 118 feet afterward. For some reason unknown except to Bradley"s attorney, Bradley got away with it and was let go.

There had been more stories of death I wasn't accustomed to. And, some of them were outright weird. I had heard a rumor that Ronnie E"s older brother Barney had taken a part of Mary Moore"s gravestone home and had propped it up against his bedroom wall. Mary Moore was buried in a plot in the graveyard adjacent to the old white church on Woodbridge Avenue. Supposedly, she was a witch from the 1600"s. I had heard that the white church had been used as a hospital for the Minute Men and that there was a rich history there to be explored. The story with Mary was that she had left a curse for anyone who attempted to antagonize the memory of her legacy. If you ran around her grave and shouted her name three or more times, she would thrust her curse upon you from the other side and death would surely await you. There was also another version that said the same fate would occur if you spun around while saying her name into a mirror.

Jesse and I one afternoon were visiting Ronnie E. at his home across from Stelton School. Ronnie was excited and insisted on showing us something he thought was spectacular. "Come on upstairs to my brother Barney"s room" he said. "Wait until you see what he has". We followed him up and watched as he opened the bedroom door. Inside, was a faded, chalky white monolith with a slight description on it leaning under a window against a wall. "Check it out" Ronnie laughed. "It's the top half of Mary Moore"s gravestone". "The witch on Woodbridge Avenue?" Jesse asked nervously. "Yup" Ronnie replied. "That's the one. He took it the other night with a few of his friends. It's cool isn't it?" "What the fuck does he need that for?" I asked. "That shit's crazy!" "Don't tell me you guys believe in that curse bullshit. Do you?" he asked. "I'm not fucking with anything that has to do with the dead!" Jesse barked. "I'm getting the fuck out of here". Jesse bounded down the stairs and ran outside. Amazingly, I found him in Stelton School's own graveyard across the street. "What did you take off for?" I asked. "It's only a grave marker?" "I don't tempt dead people when it comes to that shit" he said. "I don't want to be anywhere near it, bro".

A few years later, I was told that shortly after Barney had taken the marker, three of the people who had stolen it with him had died. Mike P. had been walking on the Route 1 concrete barrier, slipped and had fallen straight into the path of a large semi-truck killing him instantly. Not soon after, a guy named Wayne C. met a similar fate but it was done with a car. Steve F. as I have written previously was run over walking home from Desti"s and killed as well. Some people are convinced that those deaths were completely contributed to by the taking of Mary Moore"s stone. Incidentally, after their demise, Barney was said to have returned the marker back to Mary"s grave. Perhaps Jesse had had a point after all.

Keg parties at the time were the norm. Someone in our Edison circle would always seem to secure a keg or a half keg to satiate the teenage masses. These soirées were usually held in someone"s garage or in the woods. The usual semi forest we'd settle on was by the old train trestle just off Talmadge Rd. and was in the area of

Bare Ass This particular swatch of woods was used for ice skating, hockey, forts, and drinking. There was always lots and lots of drinking. To me, it was also a prime area to party and to pick up pussy. What better place to snag some trim than at a bonfire surrounded by intoxicated, horny teenage girls. On one respective night, I got word of such an event. We called them "Keg Jams". This keg jam was to be close to Bare Ass Lake under the soaring high tension wires that were between a housing development and the train tracks. These 100 foot structures of steel and electricity were in the Walnut St. subdivision. Between these working class homes were the towers that provided energy for entire neighborhoods. I knew a few families that lived there. So, it would occasionally become one of my hangouts for a while. Everyone in Edison almost always had a nickname. Such as the Barnyards, a guy named "Eddie the Rat", the Gootches, and a few others. Howie was a Bernard, as well as his brother Brian and Ricky. Therefore their nickname was the Barnyards. The Gulotta"s were the Gootches, and so on and so forth. When making these alter names, there was always a twist to make them sound more entertaining and memorable. I've always felt that if it was funny, it was easier to remember. My nickname with some was always Arnold. It was from the show Green Acres as per Arnold the DouglaS's pet pig. My last name at first glance usually causes this mistake. But, it was funny and I had to live with it.

Train Trestle Party Spot – Courtesy Of Howard Bernard

While hanging around under the tension wires waiting for the party to begin, I remember gazing upward and thinking of the story of Don Quixote. The towers looked as if they were mechanical entities waiting to snatch us all up. They were like arms with corners that criss crossed with I beams. In my mind, they somehow resembled angled steel rib cages. I imagined that under the right circumstances, we would transcend to another dimension from alcohol and drug intake and be seized by the voltage forces above us. The most unusual of these stationary, frame worked fabrications was their sound of humming adjustment. These could be especially predominant on rainy days. It was the identical buzzing sound of when I had almost drowned in Lawrence Brook. When the party was almost in full swing, I came back from myself. I didn't want to daydream too long, lest I"d miss out on the possibility of picking up some ladies. When I saw more clearly, people were milling around the keg as to not subconsciously miss out on the last drop of fermented, yeasty perfection. While exchanging pleasantries with the attendees, I bumped into Ricky B. Ricky had a slight developmental consciousness problem. But, he knew how to party and had a genuine, great sense of humor. Sometimes for demented kicks, kids would tease him and ask him to repeat sentences that they knew he would repeat back differently. Ricky was also supposed to be banned from nefarious substances because they didn't coincide with the medications he was taking. But, no matter how much Howie and Brian secluded him, Ricky always seemed to find a buzz. Ricky"s signature phrase was "Jam, like a motherfucker". When asked to, he would repeat this expression over and over. Usually until one of his brothers showed up, or he was distracted by something else.

While I was flirting with a neighborhood floozy, I heard the sound of Howie behind me. "Who wants to climb this tower?" he asked. Slightly stoned and drunk from my imbibing festivities, I offered to accompany him with others soon following. Four of us had volunteered for Howie"s wild ascension spectacle to climb to its top of grandiosity. At the base of this monolith were the standard pegs to grasp on to. They jutted out like fingers in the night and were beckoning us to scale them. We mounted them serendipitously, and climbed onward to the level of our next upward challenge. About 12 feet above the fasteners, was the bottom of a welded, permanent ladder. That is where I pussed out. I've never been able to do heights and this was not the ideal time. At first, as I was climbing, I imagined I was a great pirate circumventing a shiP's rigging and struggling to plant my flag atop its mast accordingly. But, it never came to be as I was too scared to continue. By the 50th foot, two of the remaining climbers had relinquished their Howie vows and like me had come down in haste. "Howie"s crazy" one of them said "He wanted us to go to the top. But, the wind was starting to kick up. So, we said fuck that and came back down. I don't know what the fuck he's doing up there, but it's too windy for that bullshit. He's got brass balls, that Howie dude". Suddenly, we heard Howie bellow downward "I can see New York City. You guys are pussies. You gotta see this shit, man. I can see the twin towers. It's fucking amazing!" Almost all of us keg revelers looked skyward as we could plainly hear Howie but we couldn't see him. As I was listening to Ricky and attempting to flirt with some local teen fem bone, I heard female gasps all around me.

"Ahhhhhhhhhh, Ahhhhhhhhh" they screamed. Suddenly, everyone froze in a circle of worried fear and speculation. "Oh my god" I heard girls scream "I think Howie fell off the top of the tower". As I doubted them and gazed loftily, I heard the wave of a whir that was similar to when a bird flaps its wings. If you were lucky enough to have one graze your ear, it would usually have a puttering low hum. The object fell fluttering across from us. "Holy shit!" I exclaimed. "I thought that was Howie. I bet he's fucking with us to scare the chicks". It turned out that as a goof, Howie had thrown down his dark blue windbreaker to simulate his death.

The High Tension Tower That Howie Climbed – Courtesy of Howard Bernard

Chatting amongst themselves, some people accused Howie of being an asshole. Unlike me, they didn't seem to appreciate his goal of funny. He yelled down when he heard the premature wails of young girls below him. "I'm alive" he screamed. "It's was only my coat" he said. "I was just fucking with you. But, right now. I'm Batman! I'll be down in a while. "Not funny, man" A female exclaimed. We really thought you slipped, fell, and you hit the ground dead." "Nah" Howie replied. "You"d know if that was the real deal or not. I woulda turned blue and you woulda had a bar b que". He finally sauntered down and was laughing. I'm glad I don't have acrophobia he exclaimed. Cause the higher I go, the better the view".

Deliveries we loved. They were standalone deliveries with no security around them. In the wee hours of the morning between 3 and 5am, my friends and I would partake in the delicious task of removing food stuffs from local businesses. One of our favorites was the Acme market in the Kilmer shopping plaza on route 27. Here accompanying Acme, was a plethora of various enterprises just ripe for the pickings. These places with deliveries we knew we could always count on for an early sunrise snack. There were usually cakes, Danishes, breads, cookies, and pies. Lots and lots of pies. They were so fresh; we could sometimes see steam coming off the top of them. Being that they had just been dropped off, the heat still emanated from their recent release from the bakery ovens they had come from. When the occasion arose, we would scout out the area obsessively to make sure it was devoid of local policemen.

On one famished night, I was with Dennis G. outside the Acme by the corner. "Dennis?" I asked "Do you see any cops or cars around?" "Nah, Ron" he replied. It looks pretty copacetic to me". "Stand by this corner at the end of the building" I advised him. "Watch for the capers. I'm gonna sneak up to the racks out front to see what goodies they have for us today". "Ulllllhhhhhh" Dennis remarked "I hope they have those angel food cakes. They are always warm and spongy and I love how they fall apart in my hands. That's some good eating, bro". I peered around like a burglar with stealth resolve determining if it was safe to pilfer or not. Behind the delivery racks were rows of carriages. This facilitated a perfect path for me to hide behind as a go between. That way, I could easily weasel up without anyone seeing me. There were almost always 4 to 5 racks lined up with canvas covers enveloping them. As I approached, I could smell the baked confections inside. I gingerly lifted one of its covers and inspected its culinary delights. I was beginning to salivate at the thought of gorging ourselves on these sugary masses of sumptuous satisfaction. "Dennis!" I yelled "Its Danishes this morning. "Uuuullllhhh, fucking Danishes bro! There's Cheese ones, blueberry, cherry, lemon, and ladyfingers man. Fucking ladyfingers and éclairs too! You're not gonna believe it. We've hit the motherload!" "Uuuullllhhh" Dennis screamed. Let me see, I'm starving" He ran over, stuck his head under the tarp, and started pointing out what he was going to take. "I want a tray of each" he demanded. "I'll take as much as I can carry". "Easy Den" I replied. "They are on trays. But, they're all in cardboard boxes. We'll have to wiggle them out of there first". "Fuck that" he replied. "Look! I can see handles on the enclosures. Once we get them out, we can grab them and then run across the highway by Shoe Town. Let's stack as many as we can on top of each other and head for the hills bro". "That sounds good, Den" I replied. "But, where do we go once We're by the shoe store?" "You know that path across from there?" he asked "The one that goes between the houses to Ovington Avenue? "Yeah" I acknowledged. "Well, we can drop our goodies there and come back for more". "I dunno, Den" I said "That's a pretty far run carrying heavy boxes". "We can do it" he insisted. "Let's just take only as much as we can carry, that's all". "Ok, Den" I confirmed. "But, while we are running, if they get too heavy, I'm dropping some" "I don't care" he laughed "As long as I have breakfast for the morning".

We slowly pulled out 5 boxes each and stacked them on top of each other. They looked like pizza boxes but horizontal and longer than average. As we had anticipated, they were indeed still warm. We took a last gander around the parking lot for the authorities and we were off. To not totally stand out for anyone to see us, we ran to the end of the plaza to escape instead of diagonally across the parking lot. Right as we got to the department store named Grants, we took a short rest. I set down the buttery baked items and gazed back behind me. Out of the corner of my eye I saw large manila colored bags. They were 3 of them piled up in front of the Zia Lisa Pizza shop. "What the fuck are those Den?" I asked. "Oh, you saw those too?" he said. "I think they are filled with rolls bro. As I ran passed them, it looked like it was bread on top". "Rolls huh?" I asked. "I love fresh bread and rolls. We're gonna have to come back and scarf some of those before the sun comes up" "Ok" Dennis retorted "But, we only have a little more ways to go to breakfast heaven. Let's get out of here and up to that path before the snorks catch us". We picked our treats back up and headed across the highway. We had made it. Half way up the walkway, Dennis collapsed in exhilaration. "Now, it's time to rest and partake in the opening of the morning meal" he said. He removed the layers of boxes one by one and laid them on the ground. For some reason, he chose the container with red markings on it. "This one" he whispered "I can smell Danishes in this one" with a small struggle, he opened its lid. "Ullllllhhh" he mumbled "Cheese Danishes. What a scarf bro, my favorite". While stuffing his face ravenously, I had opened my own box to discover some ladyfingers. I didn't say a word and dug into them like a prisoner forced to fast after days languishing hungry in a punishment hole. I gazed over at Dennis and he had cheese drippings all over his face. "Goddamn, those were good" he said satisfyingly. "So were mine, bro" I replied "But, I wanna go down and get those rolls. I have a taste for them now, man". "Let's hide these boxes then" he said "We'll put them under these bushes and come back for them later". "Good idea, Den" I quipped "We wouldn't want them stolen from someone who stole them". "Great analogy" Dennis replied "And, true".

We poked our heads out beyond the path to see if the coast was clear. Satisfied there was no one around, we snuck back down the hill the way we had come. Spying the bags again in front of the pizza establishment, we converged upon them quickly. I tore into the first bag I saw and discovered they were sub rolls. They were about 6 inches long and 4 inches wide. As with the Acme baked goods, they were also still warm. We sat down next to them and I handed one to Dennis. I grabbed one myself as well. Dennis split open the middle with his fingers. "Ron!" he squealed "These are so fresh; they are still doughy in the middle". I ripped open mine and it was the same. As I was starting to chew on this crusty creation of glutinous delight, Dennis began to make noises. He began attacking the roll as if he was having oral sex with it. He looked at me, rolled his eyes, stared back at the roll and screamed "Ullllhhhh, ulllllhhh, ullllhhhackie ackie ackie" I asked "Dennis? What the fuck are you doing?" "It's like pussy, bro" he said "This roll is so good, I'm gonna eat it like vagina. Ullllhh, uullllhhh ackkie ackie ackie". He was biting the middle out of it and spitting its contents on the sidewalk like a rabid animal after a hunt. His technique reminded me of an aggressive puppy with a slipper. As he continued, I was choking on my bites as I found this to be quite hilarious. After a while, we realized the sun was coming up and it was time to go. We knew that with daylight the nosey police morning shift would start soon. We grabbed a few rolls each, tucked them under our arms, and headed back to the path where we left our baked items from before. When we got there, Dennis asked "What are you gonna do with your haul, bro?" "Well, you have a lot of people in your family" I replied. "So, I'll keep a few gifts and give the rest to you". "I like that" he said "I'm sure my family is about hungry right about now."

We piled the boxes back in our arms and made the long trek back to DenniS's house. Fortunately, there were many twisting and turning side streets with shortcuts to conceal us. When we got to the park at Lindenau School we knew we were set and home free. As we bounded up DenniS's porch stairs, we could hear his brothers starting to awaken. "Up, up" Dennis howled as he flew through the door. "We have Danishes and Éclairs. All we need is coffee". As we set it all down on his dining room table, Dennis announced "Ron, here"s a few bucks from my drawer. Go to the diner for us. You know what to get, bro. Make it 4 coffees light and sweet". As his brothers were rubbing the crust from their eyes, I heard one of them sleepily moan "Nice haul bro, thank you". "You're welcome, man"

I said. It would be one of many instances of me facilitating Ronniehood.

A Japanese restaurant that was adjacent to the original Edison diner had become a favorite hangout for us. It was called The Jade Pagoda and had a pleasant bartender by the name of Dave. Dave was impeccably dressed and his hair was always perfect. It was parted on the side and was middle of his ear in length. It was a popular style for young adults at the time and he looked very professional. Two of us had gone in there to brave the identification laws to see if we could be served. I believe it was Dennis G. and I. "What will you have?" Dave the bartender asked. "We'll have a couple of bud bottles" I replied. "No problem" he exclaimed". After a few of these drinks, Dennis and I departed and left Dave a generous tip. While we were walking back to DenniS's house, we got to talking. He was ecstatic "Rooooooon!" he yelled out. "Looooook! We got served at the Jade, bro. We got away with it, man. It looks like a new underage place for us now". "Yup" I replied. "I guess they don't care about us drinking under the age of 18. I think that bartender Dave knew were weren't legal. Maybe he just didn't give a fuck. He does work on tips after all doesn't he?" I asked. Dennis replied "He probably does Ron. He probably does."

We had been going to the Jade for so long that we started to bring more and more friends to drink with us. Most of the time, and usually on Friday or Saturday nights, there was me; Dennis, his little brother Jeffrey, Dave G., and a guy I had met through Dennis named Ellis. Ellis had his own language. He was a mulatto. But, he looked more Caucasian than black. He had very wiry shoulder length hair that was parted in the middle and looked like a pyramid. He was about 5 feet 8, skinny and 120 pounds. When he talked about something, he would use words none of knew. Such as, bahoots, porticle skulls, walloots, play it off, a definite shoo, chin ups, skulled, souse puppy and others. We learned much later that a bahoot was money, porticle skulls were Newport cigarettes, play it off was pretend and lie, a shoo was someone who was a fool, chin ups was eating pussy, skulled was being too high, souse puppy was an alcoholic, and too many more here to mention. He had gotten an inheritance before I had met him, spent it all in a short time, and was homeless and living on the graces of others. He would usually crash on someone"s couch for a few days, a basement, or if he was really despondent, you could find him sleeping in a Salvation Army clothes donation box. The only bad trait he had was that he could occasionally be quite annoying. This was due to the fact that he was desperate and had no way to sustain himself. If he wanted you to share something with him such as a cigarette, or food, he would badger you to the point of almost having to hit him to get him to stop.

In between beers, I whispered to Dennis asking "Hey, Den? How does Jeffrey even reach the bar? He's only 12 years old, man?" He replied "Look Ron. Look what Jeff is sitting on. But, be casual about it". I peered down at Jeff and noticed he was propped up and sitting on 2 thick Bell system phone books. I hadn't seen him sit on the chair earlier as I had been busy conversing with Ellis. Just then, I heard Jeffrey call out for a drink. "I'll have a Mai Tai Dave, and don't make it too sweet please". The sight of this made me laugh inside with much joviality. Here was a 12 year old kid, sitting in a bar and actually getting served alcohol. "It was glorious!" I thought. After many more visits and leaving the bartender generous tips, he had learned to trust us. Dennis asked him one night "You know We're all minors, right Dave?" Having overheard this, I cautioned and whispered to him "Hey man, what are you telling him that shit for? You're gonna ruin it for us". "Nah" he said "Dave"s cool. He doesn't care, right Dave?" Dave the bartender replied in accented Chinese "Me no care fellas. In our country, you reach bar, you drink. You have fun, yes?" "See" Dennis replied "He doesn't give a fuck as long as we keep giving him good tips. Stop worrying about it, bro".

On another trip to the Jade, we were all attending except for Ellis. While conversing amongst ourselves, a tall, skinny, 60 something year old Chinese man came into the bar from the large restaurant area in the back. He approached the bartender and whispered something Chinese in his ear in. Then, the man came from around the bar and was facing us. "I am owner" he proudly said. He pointed at us. "You, you kids?" he asked "You no look old enough for drink". "Sure we are" Dennis replied "We've been coming here for months". "I no believe you" the owner bellowed. He walked over to Jeff sitting on his phonebooks. "What about you?" he asked Jeff. "You no look enough 18"s. You come into my bar to drink and you try to fool me. Who you think I am? Your mother? I not your mother. You come back when you enough 18"s. Now, you take monies and go home. No come back until of age, ok?" Dennis had spit out his beer and Jeffrey had a blank stare on his face while Dave G. and I were laughing hysterically. The owner became impatient. It was probably due to us making fun of him and he began to yell "You go, you time to leave now. You no go, me call police". "We're going, We're going" I replied. "Keep your shirt on. You're gonna lose money because of us though". "Me no care about money" he screamed. "Me no want problems. You come back as adult". We learned that when we wanted to keep drinking at the Jade, we had to be cognizant of if the owner was there or not. Since the owner never stuck to a schedule, we'd sneak in the front door quietly and creep up to bartender for the scoop. He informed us that the cops had found out minors were sometimes drinking there and that the owner didn't want to risk a fine. Therefore, he said "If owner not around, you come drink. Me no care about stupid laws". "Won't you get fired?" I asked "No, no fire" he replied. "He have no one else work cheap like me". So, from then on, it was cat and mouse game. Sometimes we'd drink, sometimes we couldn't. Luckily for us, the Jade wasn't the only game in town.

I rang Dennis G. on the phone one afternoon and asked him if anything was going on. "There's a house party tonight" he said.

"Oh, really" I replied. "Where"s it at, bro?" I asked. "It's at Vick F"s house" he said. "His parents are out of town. There's not gonna be any kegs of beer or anything. So, We'll have to bring our own. But, I have a couple of joints here with me. So, come on over. We'll get stoned and see if we can pick up a few chicks while We're there". "Sounds great" I replied. "I'll be right there". While walking to the Gulotta"s from my home, I remembered that Vick was the crazy kid who threw out the bench seats from the buses on the way home from Carolier roller rink. The night we jumped out the windows and barely got away. I was hoping that in his home environment, his party would be more subdued and laid back. My experience was that loud noise brought around the cops. So, I liked to avoid them as much as I could. I arrived at DenniS's in the usual half hour time frame and could hear the sound of the band Yes emanating in the background. Dennis and I had always been singers and had spent many amphetamine fueled nights walking the streets harmonizing to ourselves. We had a few favorites. They were frequently The Rolling Stones Heart of Stone; Time is on my Side, or Jumping Jack Flash. Though I sang Jagger"s part most of the time, we took turns with the lead vocals. Dennis especially enjoyed the Heart of Stone lyric "You're not the kind I wanna meet" and got great joy out of repeating it over and over.

While he did great background vocals of Jones and Richards, his proficiency was singing like John Anderson from Yes. He could hit the very high falsetto notes and master them with ease. I could do them some, but had to work much harder at it. A lot of times, to my ear, I couldn't tell the difference. He was that good. As I knocked on the door, an odor of smoke hit my face and I recognized it immediately. "Come on in, Poke" he exclaimed. Poco was a nickname he sometimes called me and surmised it from a strain of marijuana called Aculpoco Gold. He merely changed the words to Arold poco Gold and there it was. "What's up, Den?" I asked yelling over the concert level sound of Yes blasting on a stereo in the background. "I'm in the kitchen" he screamed "I'll be right in.

I'm trying to dry my clothes". I wandered into his bedroom and turned down the stereo to hear since I was hardly able to hear him over its rhapsodic din. I entered the scullery area and broke out into instant laughter. In front of me was Dennis shirtless, barefoot, and in his boxers. He was toking on a joint and culling his afro with his hair pick. "I just got out of the shower" he said. "Once my pants are dry, we can hit that party I told you about. Everyone is gonna be there". I looked to my right, and the oven door was ajar. In between its opening and the interior, were his green khaki pants. They were hanging on the edge of its door by the waist while the leggings were dangling toward the burner. There was visible steam coming off of them and it appeared as if he was cooking them until they were done. I could smell the aroma of burnt fibers and was wondering if it was safe. "What the fuck is this?" I asked. "I had to wash them in the sink, bro" he laughed. "We don't have a dryer, so this was the best I could do. I won't wear them damp either. So, the party all depends on how fast my pants dry". "You"ve got to be kidding, Den?" I asked amazed. "We seriously have to wait until they are dry enough for you to wear?" "No other way I'm going" he replied. "I hate wet pants. So, it's either that, or we don't go". He spent the rest of the time going back and forth between his bedroom and the kitchen singing a Yes song called Heart of the Sunrise. It was driving me crazy. All I wanted to do was go to the party. I thought it was ridiculous that I had to wait for a pair of pants! After some time went by, and I periodically checked his trousers for dryness, he was ready to go.

"Ron? Ulllllllhhh" he said as he removed them from the oven. "These are perfect now, bro. They're nice and warm too. So, we can leave now. Just let me slip these on and fix my shirt. Then, we can go". "I can't believe you, Den" I said. "You take almost as long as a woman to get ready". "I have to look good, man" he said. "There's gonna be pussy there. If I want some Ulllhhh, I need to look my best" "I guess so" I replied. "But, can we finally go now?" "Let me give you a shotgun off this joint I just lit up" he said. "You"ve been patient waiting on me. So, I think you need to get stoned first. You're poco is coming out, man". He put the joint in backwards in his mouth, cupped my face, forced the smoke into my lungs, retreated, and laughed. "Arriving stoned to a party is the way it should be" he remarked". I coughed a little and nodded my head in agreement. As the THC content hit me, Dennis began mumbling about how some girl who was easy was supposed to be there. He had told me in the past that he had been with her. "I hope she's there" he said. "I need to get my pipes cleaned".

We arrived at the bash and there were many teens milling about the driveway. Some we recognized, some we did not. At the top of the entrance we could hear rock music playing from inside and were greeted by Vick himself. "The party is downstairs in the basement fellas" he announced. "Go through my garage and down the stairs to the left. Everybody"s already down there. There's a few 6 packs last time I looked. But, I don't know if there's any left now. "Cool" Dennis said. "But, Vick/" Dennis asked. "Are there any chicks down there?" "Ahhhhhh, Den" Vick laughed. "I know exactly who you're looking for. Yeah, I think she's down there bro". "Scarf" Dennis whispered to himself. "The cum is on". I followed him down the steps into a cellar of darkness below. We had to light our cigarette lighters to be able to see as there was almost no lighting receptacle available. The only thing we could make out was a single dangling bulb connected by a cable that was slung over a beam slightly above us. As we made our way further, it was hard to see as there was only some slight, natural illumination accompanying it. Some grayish angled luminosity was also coming through a small framed casement on the far back wall. It wasn't much and it might have been moonlight. But, it was barely enough to discern where you were going. "Don't turn on the light" someone bellowed as we approached. "We're all having sex down here". As we followed the person"s voice, I tripped over something. "Jesus Christ" somebody yelled "Watch where the fuck you're going, man". "Sorry" I said. "I can't see shit down here". Suddenly, the light came on with Vick at the top of the stairs. "I'm leaving this on for a few minutes" he yelled. "If you touch it, I'll break your fucking hands". I could see couples intertwined on the ground holding their palms over their eyes to avoid the effects of the light. Most of them were crying for the glare to be shut off and complaining. In the far left corner was a guy I recognized as Craig. His pants were down around his ankles and he was bare assed. He was lying on top of a slut we knew and slowly pumping away. Underneath him, the girl turned her head, looked at us, and smiled as if it was a badge of honor. Dennis let out his signature noise "Ulllllhhh, you get it Craig. Bring that shit home bro". Everybody was laughing including me.

Personally, I was kind of shocked at the time. I had seen couples at other parties in a corner hiding their sex under blankets or coats. But, I had never seen a girl being fucked in front of so many people so blatantly. I knew after Craig was done, other guys would be on her like flies on shit. So, I ignored the situation and looked away. I turned my attention to my left and I bumped into a reclining chair. Dennis had already claimed it and announced "This is my spot for the night. I'm not lying on that cold concrete floor, so fuck that. Now, bring on all the ladies". I didn't see any girls I was attracted to so I moseyed my way back up the stairs and back outside. As I was leaving, Dennis was still in his chair chatting up some girl I didn't know. As I stepped to the driveway, I lit up a cigarette. I inadvertently brushed up against a girl I had heard about but had never met. She was about 5 feet 4, with shag type raven hair, maybe 100 pounds, and had what I thought was a kick ass body. I liked them small anyway. So, I chatted her up. It turned out that she knew Billy F. and was in one of his classes at TJ. "So, what are you doing here?" I asked her. "Oh, I'm with a friend of mine" she said. "But, I'm getting kind of bored". "How about a drag off your cigarette?" she asked. It was obvious there was a mutual attraction and she was flirting with me. "Sure" I replied. "Have you seen the downstairs yet?" I asked. "There are a lot of cool people down there. You wanna come with me and check it out?" "Ummmmm, downstairs huh?" she asked licking her lips and teasing. "That sounds good" she replied. "I'm right behind you". As we navigated down the steps to the cellar, I realized the light was off again. I grabbed her hand and led her so she wouldn't trip in the darkness and fall. As we moved, I could hear the sound of kids kissing and moaning on the floor below. There was low rock music playing in the background which made the atmosphere become surreal. I was slightly stoned and it made me feel like I was fluid cascading down a window sill. Then, I had a horizontal vibe to be with this girl that made my attraction to her more aware. I began to feel sparks and that familiar tickling feeling in the back of my throat. That vibrating nervousness and goose bump feeling you get when you meet somebody new. I imagined that was where Dennis had gotten his Ullllhhhh sound from. His description of that experience was perfect.

As we made our way to an area we could crash in, I spun the girl around and began kissing her. I guess she didn't mind as she reciprocated immediately. I was very pleased with myself as I abhorred rejection of any kind. "Let's lay down here" I said. Scarcely able to see, I pulled her down to the floor with me. I had taken my jean jacket off in the interim and offered it as a pillow to lay her head on. I wanted her to be as comfortable as possible. We began to make out and were necking profusely. I claimed 1st base, 2nd base, 3rd base, and stop. "Not here" she murmured in my ear. "I won't do anything in front of all these people. We can continue like this, and that's it". I was horny as hell and had a hard on like a Sequoia tree. As much as I wanted to bang her, I respected her wishes and kept our petting to a strict 3rd base minimum. I did ask her out though and she gladly accepted. I was happy. I had a new girlfriend. Suddenly, the overhead bulb came on again. I heard a low drone of "Ohhh" from all the attendees. I peered up and saw Dennis with a tall, long haired blonde girl in his lap with her hand down his pants and laughing. She had been obviously jerking him off. "Shut that fucking light off" Dennis wailed. "I didn't finish yet". The girl I was with thought it was hilariously funny. Most girls would have quickly pulled their hand out as soon as the light had come on. But, this girl didn't care. She was easy and it appeared that that was what he liked about her. He could always count on her He'd say "for a quick squirt when he was frisky". Almost all of us boys had a couple of girls like that. They had low self-esteem and would let you do almost anything to them sexually. All you had to do was get them drugs or beer. Sadly, they'd get a reputation as we passed them around from friend to friend. This was especially true if it was at a party or a large gathering. Edison boys were notorious pussy hounds and would even resort to fights to get into a girl's pants for the evening. As the party was coming to a close the girl I was with was telling me it was time for her to go home. Dennis had gotten off and was ready to depart as well. As we rose from the floor he and his girl got up from the recliner and were standing. Dennis gave me a wink while the girls went off by the stairs to converse. He whispered to me "I finally got to cum, bro. She wouldn't finish unless the light was out. "How"d you do?" he asked. "Did you get anything?" "I did ok, Den" I replied. "But, I don't kiss and tell. I like this little girl. She's pretty cool. I asked her out tonight" "Asked her out?" he asked laughing. "You don't even know this chick, bro. She's still in junior high school". "That's the beauty of it, man" I said. The less I know them, the more attracted I am". "If you say so" he replied. "But, you should get some of that as soon as possible". "Duly noted" I said. "Maybe I will the next time".

My band was again rehearsing in my parent"s basement when we stopped to take a break. Tony blurted out "We need a name man. We've been practicing for a few weeks and nobody knows who we are". "Ronnie's good with words" Johnny blurted out. "Come up with something Ronnie. If it sucks, We'll let you know anyway". "I dunno man" I replied. Most bands use colors and descriptions. What colors do you like?" I asked. Steve our drummer replied "Let's use red. Red means danger. I like danger. Red scares people". "I like that" Tony said. "Let's take a vote. Who"s for red?" he asked.

"Well, I have another name for red that sounds much cooler" I replied. "What's that?" Johnny asked. "Scarlet" I said. "Have you ever heard the story of the woman who had to wear a scarlet letter on her dress because she was an adulterer?" "No" Tony replied. "But, it sure sounds cool. Who"s all for Ronnie's new word?" he asked. We all raised our hands in a yes and no vote. The yeS's won out. "Ok" Steve said. "We can't just use the word red though? A red what?" he asked. "Hmmm, let me think for a minute" I said. "If the woman is an adulterer, then she would have an equal as a man, right? So, what could we use?" I asked. "How about a pirate?" Tony offered. "A buccaneer" Steve suggested. Meanwhile, I was going over in my head alphabetically as I usually did when I was confronted with a word problem. What is like a pirate and a buccaneer, but sounds scarier? I thought. I got to the letter R and stopped. I found it. "Rogue" I chuckled. "Scarlet Rogue". What the fuck does that mean? Tony asked. "What's a rogue?" "A rogue is a guy who has no scruples of stealing from you" I said. He doesn't care about anything. He uses everyone and everything. He loves women and leaves them. He makes promises but gives you nothing in return. He'd even steal from his own mother. He has the absolute worst reputation imaginable. Picture a pirate, but with way more balls". "Wow!" Steve said. "Who"s all for the name Scarlet Rogue?" he asked. We raised our hands in unison. "Scarlet Rogue it is" I laughed. Now, we just have to find a place to play.

A few weeks had gone by and Johnny had gotten us booked for a battle of the bands at the YWHA in Highland Park. The band with the most votes from the audience would win a prize of $100. The show started at 8pm. So, we were told to come and set up any time after 6. Johnny and Tony"s sister had a Karman Ghia sports car and helped us move our equipment from my cellar to the venue. It took many trips to move all of the amplifiers, the PA system we rented from Lou Rose, and lighting equipment to get it all there on time. When it was getting close to perform, we looked around and tried to size up the other bands for our competition. There were 4 bands in all. But, only one group gave us anxiety. They had multiple keyboards, the latest amplifiers, and the best drums money could buy. We were quite jealous of them. But, there was one thing they were lacking. They didn't have much of a light show. Most of it was a white spot and a rotating cop light. We knew we had them there. Our lighting was vertical boxes with individual ceramic receptacles and wired to a keyboard that Johnny had made. He had cut tabs that simulated keys into Plexiglas and placed micro switches beneath them. There were sticky tabs on each key that signified which light went with each color. When they were pressed, they illuminated each light accordingly. I remember thinking it was quite ingenious for a 16 year old. Our monitors were made of plywood that Johnny had also made to match the dimensions of the speakers we had stolen from the Lutheran church earlier. We thought we were the shit and acted that way. The other 2 bands were of no consequence we thought. They were jock bands that had sparse equipment, marginal lighting, and the worst boring stage presence I had ever seen. Imagine football players from school with short crew cuts trying to act cool and failing miserably.

The director of the hall came over to us and mentioned that we would go on 3rd. I liked that as the later you go on, the more people remembered you. The 1st group to perform was the stuck ups with the superior gear. They played radio friendly hits and did quite well. And the audience seemed to have liked them. We were intimidated though by their sound. They played very close to originals and had obviously honed their act. While they were on, we went outside to smoke some of Johnny"s Panama Red weed. "What do you think of those guys Ron?" Johnny asked. "The band that is on now?" "Eh" I replied. "They are really good. But, they play pussy ballad songs like Chicago and Paul McCartney Wings type music. They're better than us technically if you want to fall asleep. They chose safe tunes that have no cahonas, bro". No crunchy amps or soaring lead guitars. It's not for me". Dennis M. who had been with us as a roadie chimed in "Fuck those guys" he said "They're a pretty boy band whose parents bought all their shit for them. I guarantee there's no way they could afford all of that on their own". "Yeah" Steve replied. "Did you see that fuckers drum set? Fucking Ludwigs. Big bucks man" "It doesn't matter" Tony chuffed "They look like mannequins and fake. We should be able to wipe the floor with them" "We'll see man" I responded "We'll see". We strolled back into the venue and began to get ready. The 2nd band was up now, so it was just a waiting game. Our rhythm guitar player hadn't shown up yet and we were starting to get worried. "Did you call that asshole Tony?" I asked "Yeah, 4 times already" he said. "He's really gonna fuck us up if he doesn't show" I replied. "Well, we have a backup plan" Tony said. "You know Ronnie G. right?" he asked. "Yeah, that super star guitar player that we could never get. He's the big guy right?" I replied. "That's him, man" Tony said. "Johnny"s been on the phone with him and he's gonna come down here just in case". Annoyed, I asked sarcastically "How the fuck is that gonna help us? He doesn't know the material". "Relax" Tony said "This guy can play anything. If worse comes to worse, you'll sing the first half of the show, and he'll do the 2nd". "That sounds stupid man" I bellowed "It won't look professional at all". "Professional?" Tony asked yelling "Who the fuck are you? Mick Jagger now, Ron? We're fucking teenagers man, just go with it. If not, then we won't get to play at all. "Ok" I replied. "But, if they laugh at us, I don't know you". "They won't" Tony promised "You'll see". I was more willing to reciprocate because I was very stoned. Usually, I wouldn't want anyone else in our band without at least having passed an audition. But, I knew of Ronnie G. and he was well known locally as a consummate guitar master. I bit my tongue and moved on. I was watching the other band when Tony began to tune up. He was playing a little loud and it was noticeable right away. It seemed he was playing the same song as our competition and following along with them. At one point, it sounded like he was playing over them and he was doing it better than their guy. Suddenly, the director came over and was furious. He began berating Tony maniacally. "What the hell do you think you're doing?" he asked screaming. "You can don't that. It's unfair to the other bands. You stop that right now or I'll drop you down a notch after the kids are done voting". "So?" I asked. "You'll punish us by dropping us down just for being better than they are?" "One more word" he howled. "And, you'll be out of here. You'll get to leave first. Do you understand?" "Yeah, yeah" I replied wryly. He turned on his heel and went back in the direction of his office. I gave him the finger behind his back as he walked away. Dennis M. approached me "What the fuck was that all about?" he asked "Just some asshole with a chip on his shoulder" I said. "I'll tell you later" I walked over to Tony to make sure he was ok. "Don't worry man" he chuckled "I shut the fucking thing off. What a douchbag that guy was right?" "Yeah", I answered "But, it looks like our other guitar player isn't gonna show. We got 10 minutes before we go on"

Johnny had disappeared for a while and came back bounding through the door. He made a beeline for us right away. "Ronnie G. is here" he shrieked "We don't have to worry anymore. He'll blow everyone else away". Ronnie G. lumbered in and asked me what was on our set list. After informing him, he told us he knew a little more than half of what we had planned to play. I was fine with that but insisted that I go on first. No one refused. We opened with ZZ ToP's song Tush. It was a popular favorite and was relatively easy to play. Unfortunately, Johnny"s Panama Red was starting to creep up on me. After a few more songs, we segued into one of my signature numbers. It was Midnight Rambler by the Rolling Stones. It was a rather long tune with a nice harmonica solo I got to play in the middle. By now, I was so stoned that I forgot the words to the 2nd chorus. I whispered into Johnny"s ear "I forgot the fucking words, man. I'm high as a kite". "Just do the harmonica thing, man" he said. "We'll just keep playing until you stop and the change comes" When the solo came, I ripped into it like a madman on steroids. I could see a few people"s faces with a "what the fuck?" look when it went on longer than it should have. While I was finishing, I suddenly remembered the words. I looked back at the band, gave a nod for the change, and went right back into where it should have been. I recovered and other than the long solo, most in the crowd didn't seem to care. After the song was finished, I put the harmonica back in my pocket. I turned to Johnny for what number to do next. "Uh, Ronnie" he said. "You have blood dripping all down your lips and chin man". "Blood?" I asked "What do you mean blood? What the fuck are you talking about?" I then realized there were paper type cuts all along the inside of my mouth. I had played the harmonica solo so hard and long, that my lips began to bleed. I had inadvertently sliced them open with the metal edge of the mouth harp unintentionally. Tony was listening in and commented "No wonder everybody kept looking funny at you, you were bleeding all over the place". "Maybe you can do that for every show" Johnny laughed. "You could be Ronnie Alice Cooper".

We did a few more songs and finished our set. While we were watching the 4th and final act, we noticed that they weren't very good. They were the epitome of the worst jock group players we had ever seen. We tried not to laugh at them but it was like watching tone deaf Army recruits at basic training trying to play rock and roll. I still gave them credit though; they still had the balls to get up there. When they were done, the director came over the loudspeaker from his office. I remember what a pussy he must have been that he couldn't confront any of us to announce the winners. I guess he was afraid of long hairs. Of course the band with the new equipment came in first. We thought we should have come in 2nd but it was not to be. It seems the director kept his word about bringing us down a notch. So, we came in 3rd. I was very pissed off, went to find him, and confronted the guy. "Why did you list us as 3rd place? I asked. "Everyone here knows we were better than they were?" "I told you before" he said sarcastically. "To turn down your amps while that one band was playing. You didn't comply. So, too bad for you". "Nice, real nice" I replied "Remind me to never play this dump again"

I wasn't going to school much and was either at my girlfriend's house, or at the Gulotta"s. I was in their basement with Dennis on a cold winter"s day when he showed me some paintings criss crossing the ceiling on some beams. They looked a lot like trademarks in various colors and designs. "What's this writing?" I asked. "Oh" he said "That's our lettering for our new store down here" "A store?" I asked "What kinda store, bro?" "Well" he replied "Jeffrey and I got to thinking that there are no head shops around this neighborhood. So, we drew and painted a few descriptions with hooks to hang items on. It's nothing serious man. We just think it's a cool idea for something to do part time". What are you gonna sell, Den?" I asked. "We have pot pipes, rolling papers, roach clips, and some homemade craft shit we tried to do" he said. "Cool" I replied. "So, Den?" I asked. "What are we gonna do tonight? It's really snowy outside?" "I have a few ideas" he said. "Since this blizzard is really coming down, how about we go bumper skiing?" he suggested. Bumper skiing for people who don't know is when a car goes by and you crouch down, grab the bumper, and slide across the frozen street without the owner of the vehicle knowing. To be safe, we would usually do 2 or 3 blocks and let go. We always had to gauge the speed of the driver, as if they went too fast, you could tumble and get into some real trouble. Unfortunately, for a guy named Craig, the same bare assed guy I spoke about previously at the Vick"s party, he wasn't gonna have a good experience this night. Craig came over and joined Dennis and me. This time, as a friend we knew was stopping by for a few minutes; we didn't have to rely on a stranger"s automobile to facilitate us for a bumper ride. He pulled into the front of DenniS's house and called out to us "Are you guys ready?" he asked screaming. "Give us a sec" Dennis replied "We're getting situated on your bumper. I'll yell for you to go once I know we've all grabbed on" "Ok" the driver said "I'm ready when you are". I turned and couldn't help but laugh at

DenniS's head. He was wearing a tight knit cap with balls of his fro sticking out from the sides. He reminded me of a Brillo pad. Dennis asked loudly "Ullllllhhhh, are you guys ready?" "Sure" Craig and I shrieked. "Ok" Dennis yelled to the driver. "Go!" We were off and skiing. Now, when you bumper skied, it was always wise to wear flat leather bottomed, or platform shoes. This time, poor Craig was wearing sneakers. The reason sneakers are dangerous is that they grab onto a street"s hard surface. It was not an ideal choice for him. We tried to tell him earlier, but he wouldn't listen. As we were weaving back and forth and hollering like drunks in a strip club. Suddenly, we saw Craig go down. "Fuck me" he screamed. He was shrieking at the top of his lungs and it appeared that he was in obvious pain. He had spun around and rolled behind us like a ball. Dennis and I let go and ran back to assist him. I looked a few feet above where he landed and there was a manhole cover jutting out of the snow. "Are you ok? Dennis asked. "No man" Craig yelled "I think my fucking ankle"s broken". "Fuck me" I said. "I guess because of those sneakers you're wearing, you hit the manhole cover. "We tried to tell you, bro" Dennis said. "Call an ambulance" Craig muttered "I gotta get this bullshit fixed".

After Craig had departed for the hospital, I wanted to know what we were going to do next as it was still early in the evening. "Den?" I asked. What's going on for tonight?" "Well, there's a concert type of thing at the high school" he said. We could go there for kicks. That one guy named McDonald is playing and his band is supposed to be pretty good. We could go and see them. Of course, if you don't mind walking in this thick snow. I think Mickey has some trips too. We could buy some from him and have a snow fest". "What does he have?" I asked "He's got that blotter acid" Dennis replied. "You know? Those bulls eye ones that look like a target" "Those freak me out, Den" I said. "Every time I do those, it feels like somebody"s tickling me from the inside" "I know, bro" he said. "But, you have to admit, the part right after you peak is great. We laugh our asses off and see trails of light. I love it. Just do a half or a quarter. That way, you can still manage your buzz" "Ok, Den" I said "I know the real reason is because you don't feel like babysitting me. I'll do a half instead". "Cool" Dennis laughed. "Let's go over to Mickey"s and see what he's got for us".

We arrived at Mick"s and strode up the steps to his bedroom that was situated in his attic. It was a Cape Cod house with the ceilings upstairs that all swept down in angles. Most teens loved that configuration as the walls were perfect for hanging posters. As usual, Mickey had the stereo blasting and the TV running with no sound. "What can I do for you guys?" he asked laughing. "I hear you have trips Mick?" Dennis asked. "Yeah, I have a few hits lying around" Mickey grinned. "How many do you guys want?" he asked. "I'll take 2" I said. "I'm only gonna do a half and save the rest for later" "Cool" Mickey said "Three bucks a piece". "How many do you want, Den?" he asked "I want 4, bro" Dennis replied "I think We're supposed to meet up with Phil and Artie later. I just remembered". "They're coming too, Den?" I asked. "Yeah, I forgot to tell you Phil called me earlier. I was supposed to meet them at Thursdays Place". "Where you guys going?" Mick asked. "To the high school" Dennis remarked "There's supposed to be a pretty good band playing there tonight". "With all this snow?" Mick asked surprised. "Apparently so" Dennis replied. "Why? You wanna come with us. bro?" "It sounds pretty cool" Mick laughed. "Tripping in the snow? Yeah, I think I'll come with you guys. It sounds like fun".

The blizzard had let up significantly which made it easier for us to make the journey to Thursday"s to meet Phil and Art. Art was a hyper kind of guy who had an infectious laugh like The Riddler from the 1960"s Batman TV series. He had a saying he used whenever he became excited and we would anticipate it whenever he was in a good mood. As he would escalate we'd always wait for it. "Ahhhh, 99 hard rocks" he would say. I never figured out what it meant, but in his falsetto voice, it was damn funny. After we met up with the other guys in our group, we started the long trek to Edison High School. It wasn't really freezing out, but it wasn't warm either. It was one of those nights where the moon was bright and it illuminated enough to be able to see everything clearly. As I gazed up at the sky, I could see a ring around its lunar surface. It was opaque in color and almost transparent. Like a fog with a misty halo, it was slightly blurry and appeared sorrowful. As if I was looking at its edges after I had come out of a pool dosed with too much chlorine. When we were about 2 streets over from the high school, Dennis whipped out his tabs. "Who"s gonna trip with me tonight?" he asked. "Den, you got trips?" Phil asked "Where'd you get those, bro?" Dennis peered over at Mickey and chuckled and called him by his nickname "Why, from Milky Bear of course" he exclaimed. "Mickey hooked us up earlier. Isn't that right Milk?" "Yup" Mickey replied. "Give some to Phil and Art" Mick said "Don't be stingy, Den". "I have some too" I blurted. "Give one to Art Den, and I'll split one with Phil" "Fuck yes" Phil chuckled "Thanks, bro". Mick took his own hit out of his pocket and placed it on his tongue. He laughed as he closed his mouth, swallowed it, and opened it again to prove that it was downed. "See? Nothing to be afraid of" he said. As I was splitting one of mine with Phil, Dennis was handing a whole hit to Artie. Phil and I had taken ours and were waiting for them to finish. Just then, Artie screamed out "Motherfucker! I dropped mine in the snow! Now, I'll never get a buzz. It looks like 99 hard rocks for me fellas". Phil was laughing his ass off "Lemme help you try to find it, man. Maybe its right by you, bro." He bent over and was scouring the street amongst the snow with his hands. Artie was right along with him. "Fuck that!" I thought. "That shit's gone". Dennis and Mickey were giggling. Mick came over by Art. "Don't worry about it Art" he said. "You're not gonna find that shit in the snow. It's already melted. I have a few extras I was holding on to. I'll rip a tab in half so you won't be left out, ok? " "Melted is what I wanna get "Art said. "Thanks for helping me out, Mick" "No problem" Mick said. "Now, take this shit and let's get going to that show".

We slipped into the auditorium and took some seats in the back. We didn't want to be obvious when the acid kicked in and we all started laughing. "Those guys look like dirty hippies" Mick said. "They sure do" Phil replied. "I hope they at least sound good". "It's better than standing outside in the cold, man" I mentioned. "You got that right" Dennis said. The band came on, played a few cover songs and stopped. We could see way down on the stage that they were arguing about what to play next. "Cmon man!" Dennis yelled while cupping his hands around his mouth. "Hey, what the fuck is this?" he asked. "You're not supposed to stop. You're supposed to keep going. You guys suck!" He looked over at me in my seat "Ron?" he asked "You're in a band, bro. Go down there and show those weirdo"s how it's done". "Dennis" I whispered. "I'm about to peak on this blotter. There ain't no fucking way I'm going down there to sing man". Suddenly, the band started up again. They were doing the intro to the Deep Purple song Smoke on the Water. Abruptly, the guitar player stopped again. He came up to his microphone. "Is that what you want to hear?" he asked "Hell yeah" Artie screamed. "Play any fucking thing" Dennis shouted. "Just quit with the stopping bullshit". The guitar guy never continued the song. He began fumbling around with non-discernable chords and notes no one knew. "This guy plays like he has broken fingers" Dennis laughed. "This is a total waste of time. This clown is killing my buzz. Let's get out of here and go someplace else. Fuck this!" We all nodded in agreement and followed Dennis to the door.

We exited and decided to walk back to DenniS's house. I remember gawking at some tall evergreen trees off the roadway and was astonished at how they all seemed to look like rock candy. "My trip was definitely coming on now" I thought. The timbers were glistening as if they had glitter glued to them and shone radiant rainbow colors with each turn of my head. It was quite spectacular. While we were walking, I couldn't help staring at the snow on the ground beneath me. It was modulating as if something was making it move. The only thing I could equate it to was the old Little Rascals show where Stymie was making a cake with prizes placed inside. It was the episode where after he baked it, it made a "Wee Wah" sound. Thinking about it, I couldn't control laughing to myself. Dennis came over to me while the others were conversing. "You ok, man?" he asked "Weee wahh, weee wahhh, we" I replied. "Why are you quoting the Little Rascals for, bro?" he asked. "The snow Den, the snow" I laughed. "The snow goes wee wah?" he asked. "Yeah, Den" I said. "Don't you see it? It keeps vibrating up and down". "I don't know about up and down" he quipped. "But, I sure am enjoying these trails. Did you look up at the moon?" he asked "Its luminescent colors". "I'm busy with the ground here, Den" I said. "My legs feel like rubber bands. Let's just keep moving till we get to your house". "Nobody told you?" he asked. "We're not going to my house; We're going to Dunkin Donuts by Phil"s instead. Everybody wants coffee". "I don't care where we go at this point" I said "I just want this ground to stop moving".

We entered Dunkin Donuts and took our seats with our backs facing the street. On the opposite side were what we deemed to be old people. Most were in their mid-50"s to 60"s and looked like senior citizens. They were all over dressed in multiple layers of clothes and coats to keep out the chill. The waitress came over and asked for our order. "Will these be separate checks?" she asked. "Or, will this all be on one bill?" Phil jumped up a little in his seat. "We'll each have coffees" he instructed. "And, Arold"s gonna pay for it. He's on welfare and got his money in the mail today. And, you can't put it all on Bill, because he's not here" The Geritol crowd across from us was not amused. They began to smirk and whisper their "I nevers" to themselves. Phil caught wind of this and commented back to them "I never?" he asked "I never what? What's your problem lady?" "Settle down there syphilis" Dennis said using a nickname I had made up for him previously. "You're peaking now. Let Ron rub your head so you'll feel better". "I'm not touching his nasty ass" I replied. "Let Syph fight his own battles". The waitress finally brought over our beverages and asked if we needed anything else. "Ulllllhhh" Dennis yelled "Just your phone number". She ignored him and walked away. Phil was really starting to get animated now and he couldn't sit still. "This coffee tastes good" Artie said. "It's not bad" Mickey replied. "At least it's nice and hot". Phil was examining his spoon and staring at it like it was the greatest invention on earth. "It's shiny" he said mumbling. "Yeah, we know that Syph" Dennis laughed. "And, they make them in factories too. Now, be cool and sip your drink bro". By this time, I knew Phil was peaking much more rapidly than we were. Maybe it was because he was a small guy. I didn't know. What I did know is that I was about to tease him. "Hey Phil?" I asked. "Look at that lady sitting across the counter from you on the other side, man. She's got snakes and bugs in her hair" Phil was in mid gulp of a mouthful of coffee. Instead of swallowing it, he spit it out like a stream from a fire hose. It flew through the air, over the opposing counter, and landed in a wet surge directly in the woman"s hair. It appeared as if it had ruined her doo and it was dripping down her face like raindrops. She stood up screaming. "You kids think that's funny? That's not funny. I'm getting the manager. You better run before I call the cops. You kids have no respect". "Good one Phil" I said. "Now, we have to leave". "I may not have respect" Phil giggled "But, I sure do have some coffee". "Not anymore!" the waitress screamed "Pay for your drinks and get out! As we rose from our stools, we were trying desperately not to laugh. Passing me as everyone was filing out the door; I got a few dollars from Mick. I added one of my own, and placed the cash on the counter adjacent to the register. "I'm sorry" I told the girl. "Sometimes my friends can't help themselves". "Well, help is what they need" she boasted. "There's something wrong with them. Don't ever come back here again".

Johnny, Tony, and I were looking for hashish. We had heard of a new way of smoking it instead of lighting it up in a pipe. It was to be impaled on a pin stuck in a sponge, lit, covered with a glass, and smoked from underneath with a straw. "What's the purpose of this?" I asked Tony. "It's supposed to give you a better high" he replied. All of the smoke gets trapped under the glass so there's no waste". "Sounds good to me" I said. "But, where are we gonna get some from?" "I know a guy who"s a friend of a friend" Johnny exclaimed. "They're older than us. But, I was told they have blonde Lebanese for sale" "Perfect" I answered. "How much does he have? Does he sell it by grams or what?" I asked. "No" Johnny said. "He'll only sell small slabs. Tony and I don't have any money though. Do you have any coin Ron?" he asked. "I have about 80 bucks in my pocket. How much do you think we can get for that?" "It's 8 bucks a gram". Johnny said. So, 8 or 10 grams I guess". "Good" I replied. "Let's go on over there and get some. You have your mother's station wagon again, right?" I asked. Yup, Tony said. "We have it for the whole night. We should go there and then cruise down to Seaside. We can get stoned on the beach and try to pick up chicks". "I like that idea Tone" I replied. "That sounds great to me".

We drove on over to the dealer"s house, grabbed a slab with the cash, and jumped on the Garden State Parkway. From the back seat I moaned "We can't smoke this shit in the car you guys. How are we supposed to do this?" I asked. "We'll have to wait until we get there" Johnny said. "It's too bumpy to try that shit now". "Well then, hurry up Tony" I complained. "You drive like a little old lady". "You better shut up coño" Tony warned. "Or, you'll walk home". "Hold your colo, Ron" Johnny said. "We'll be there shortly." We pulled off the exit and headed toward the amusement area. This is the place everyone remembers from their childhood. Where their parents took them to ride the rides, play the games, stroll the boardwalk, and stuff their faces until they couldn't eat anymore. As we turned the corner and found an empty parking spot, I was reminiscing more from my youth. It was all familiar to me. Like a favorite warm blanket from the dryer. Its memory always made me feel warm and safe. Enveloping you with that cozy feeling where you felt you belonged. There were many excursions my family had taken there. It was a wondrous, spectacular place to be. It was long before Disneyworld and it was like mini Las Vegas to me. Glitzy lights, neon bulbs, recognizable odors, and sounds of excitement beckoned us. We'd beg our fathers "Daddy! Daddy! Rides! Rides! Can we Daddy? Can we?" It was the draining of our father's wallets that kept his kids satiated from killing each other that day. It almost always did the trick. He would always comply knowing that being this close; He'd have a short respite devoid of the nagging wife and the 3 rotten kids. Rest, relaxation, and revelry were Dad"s order of the day. Even though it was only for a little while, his sanity would be saved.

We were sauntering down the boardwalk enjoying the amusements when it began to rain. It was a slight drizzle with a tad of fog accompanying it that gave us a superficial chill. The area wasn't too crowded to begin with and had now started to resemble a ghost town. "This sucks" Johnny exclaimed "No chicks, no rides, no fun. They're turning everything off, man". "There are still some games of chance we can play Johnny" I replied. "The chance is, we should have stayed home if I knew it was gonna rain like this" Tony complained. "Well" I said "Let's just make the best of it and see if we can win some prizes before we leave." We approached a gaming kiosk and laid down our bets. The attendant spun the wheel and barked out his usual monologue of play more times, win more prizes. We watched intently as we listened to the tick, tick, tick of the device"s revolutions. Its clapper hitting its pegs as we all hoped for a win. "Not this time" the attendant blurted. "Would you care to try again?" he asked. "Fuck this game" Tony yelled. "Let's go back to the car and see if we can smoke some of that hash Ronnie boy has on him". "We don't have a glass or a pin, Tony" I replied. "We don't even have a pipe to smoke it in". "Hash? The attendant asked "You guys have some hash?" "Yeah" I replied. "Why? Do you wanna buy some?" "Why didn't you say something earlier" he said. "I'll let you spin as many times as you want. As long as you sell me some of that shit. I'm bored as fuck working here and my boss doesn't pay me squat. It would sure help me pass the time better if you"d sell some to me, bro". "How much do you want?" I asked. "How much do you got?" he replied. "We'll, I have a tasty slab. I can sell you some nice pieces for 8 bucks a piece off of it". "Sold" he said. "I'll take three". "Do you have a pipe?" Johnny asked. "Sure? You wanna borrow it?" he said. "I can't leave here or I'll be fired. So, you can use it and bring it back if you want. You'll have to sell me some first though. That way, I know I can trust you" "I can do that" I replied. "In the meantime" I laughed. Keep spinning that wheel Johnny. Maybe you'll get lucky and win an overpriced prize for free". I squeezed in between the concession stands, called the guy over, and made the deal. He was a very happy customer. We took the guy's pipe back to the car and smoked up. When we were sufficiently stoned, Tony was griping that he wanted to go home. "It's too fucking cold here" he cried. "Let's give this guy back his shit and go. I'm fucking freezing". "Stop your baby shit" I yelled. "We haven"t even been here that long. Calm down and relax. We'll go back, give him his pipe, and grab a few Cupie dolls and leave. I've never heard anyone complain as much as you my entire life Tony". "You don't understand, Ronnie" he moaned. "We have island blood, we don't do cold well" "Then, you should have worn a coat, pussy" I said. "The next time, fucking plan ahead".

On the way home, the car was starting to have problems. There was a loud squeal coming out from the car"s undercarriage and we hadn't even gotten to the Parkway entrance yet. "What the fuck is that?" Johnny asked. "It sounds like the transmission" I replied. "Fuck" Tony yelled "It's fucking slipping. We're gonna have to pull over in that parking lot over there". "What do you mean its slipping?" I asked. "We better not get stuck here, man. We're 50 fucking miles from home and its raining asshole". "It's not my fault" Tony mumbled "How the fuck was I to know if it was broken or not?" "Did you check the fluids before we left?" I asked "No" Tony said "Why the fuck would I do that? It's not my car, it's my mothers". "Jesus Christ" I screamed. "Now, We're gonna be stranded here". We limped into the parking lot of a strip mall and put the car in park. Tony popped the hood, got out, and inspected for a possible solution. A few minutes later, he returned. "I can't see anything wrong under there" he said. "There's no leaks, nothing"s disconnected, nothing I can see that's broken, nothing". "Try it again" I said "Put it in low this time and see if that works". "Nope" Tony complained "Look, I've tried every shifter position possible. Now, it's even worse. It won't even move at all now." "What the fuck are we gonna do Tony?" Johnny asked. "Try reverse" I advised. "Do that, and rock it back and forth. Maybe that"ll force it back into forward". Tony went from high, to low, to reverse, and back again. "No dice" he replied. "We've only got reverse, man". "Fuck it then" I said. "Let's find a back road and drive fucking backwards home. I don't give a fuck. My older brother was drunk once and this happened to him. He drove 12 miles all the way back to our house that way". "I'm not doing that" Tony yelled. "Its 50 fucking miles man, not 12 dumb ass". "Then, what do we do now, genius?" I asked. "It looks like We're gonna have to hitch hike home" Johnny suggested. "Great" I replied obviously annoyed. "In the fucking rain too. Great Tony! Just fucking great!"

We locked up the car, headed for the highway and I stuck out my thumb. Tony and Johnny waited by the side of the road. They didn't think they would be successful in securing a ride. Since it was the 70's and they were Latin, they thought the mere idea of it was hopeless. I saw their point as prejudice was still alive and well in 1975. So, I was duly elected. A few minutes of us getting soaked and somebody stopped. I was surprised as most drivers didn't pick up long hairs. "Where you guys going" the voice in the car asked. It was a fat man with a comb over on his obviously balding head. He didn't appear threatening and there were 3 of us against him anyway. So, we took the plunge. "We're trying to get to Metuchen at least" Tony said. "Well" the driver exclaimed. I'm going as far as that. So, jump on in". The driver entered the Parkway and began asking us questions. I guess he wanted to feel safe. "So, what brought you guys down here?" he asked. "It's a long way from Metuchen" Tony was in the front seat while Johnny and I chose the back. "We went down to hang out on the boardwalk" Tony said. "But, our car broke down. I think the transmission is shot out". "Shot transmission huh?" the man asked. "Yeah, most of the time, if your car won't move anymore, that would be it" he said. "You guys are lucky I stopped. I don't usually pick up hitch hikers. But, it's raining and you guys looked pretty desperate, so". "We really appreciate it" I said. "Who knows how long we would have been standing there". "You're welcome" the man replied. "I was young once, and I know how it is when you get stranded. I'm obliged to help anyway". How"s that? Johnny asked. "Well" the man offered "I'm a cop. I'm off duty and on my way home. It's my obligation to make sure people are safe. So, that's why I stopped to pick you up. But, like I said, I don't usually do this. If you're safe looking, I will. You seemed ok, so I guess it's your lucky night".

While the man went on about his job and other chatty pleasantries, Johnny and I spotted a box between us on the seat. We were wondering what was in it. "Hey mister?" Johnny asked. "What's up with this box back here?" "Oh that?" the man said. "Those are fresh donuts for my wife and daughter. There's two dozen in there. But, don't eat those ok? Because I bought them for them special". "Ok" Johnny said "We were just curious". As we travelled closer to home, Johnny and I were looking at the box and mouthing words between us. He was nodding his head and pointing for me to take a peek inside. Tony was jabbering with the man and keeping him completely immersed in conversation. So, the guy was distracted. I slowly lifted the tab on the side of the container facing me and I was careful not to make any noise. I peered inside and could see variations of tasty delicious donuts. Johnny and I were ravenous. "Hey mister?" I asked. "Are you sure we can't each have just one donut each? We're kind of starving". The man became visibly annoyed "I told you no. Now, I gave you a ride out of the goodness of my heart. Do I really have to drop you off for not listening? Those are meant for my family. A ride is the best I could do". "All right" I said. "I'm sorry, we won't touch them". As the man went back into talking with Tony, Johnny and I gave each other the "fuck him" look and decided to ignore him. When we knew he wasn't watching us in his rear view mirror, we slowly opened the top of the box. I slipped out a couple of donuts from its perimeter. There was no way we were going to let these baked beauties go to waste on some coP's wife and kid. We each took a donut, ripped off a small piece, stuffed it in our mouths, and pretended we were looking out the window. We were munching away furiously as not to get caught. It was a challenge to not choke on the doughy goodness without the driver being on to us. The last thing we wanted was to go to jail for embezzling some officer"s donuts. After I had eaten about 3 of them, I peered over at Johnny. I lip synched the words "How many did you eat?" It was dark in the back of the vehicle. So, you couldn't really make out much detail of what was going on. We had to depend on glimmers of light from the Parkway"s poles to make out anything discernable. Johnny raised his hand and made a 3 count with his fingers. I was trying very hard not to laugh. Johnny had powdered sugar residue all around his mouth and was making the OK sign while licking his lips. Then, he rubbed his belly in a circular motion indicating the donuts were yummy. When we were a few miles from Edison, I blurted out. "We're almost home, Sir. You can drop us at the Edison exit right?" "Oh, you're going to Edison?" the man asked. "I thought you said Metuchen? I'm going to Linden. But, I'll tell you what. I'll drop you off at the Edison exit and I can take route 1 for the rest of my trip. You guys have been pretty cooperative with me. So, I guess I can help you out". "Thanks" I said. "We just wanted to get as close to home as possible because of this weather". "No problem" he replied. "But, you should really join a towing service like triple A. It can be dangerous out there sometimes. If I didn't come along, who knows what could have happened to you?" "We'll look into that" Tony said. "As soon as we get back home".

When we finally reached our stop, we exited the car and waved the man away. Tony asked "What the hell was that all about man? You guys left me talking to him the entire time. You didn't say hardly anything to him. He was creeping me out. He kept asking me shit about my personal life. That guy was a weirdo, man. The next time, one of you fucks sit in the front". "We couldn't talk" I replied. "We were too busy eating". "Eating?" Tony asked "Eating what?" "Donuts" Johnny giggled. "The guy had a whole box of donuts he left on the back seat. While you were telling him your whole life story, Ron and I had the munchies. So, we stole some of his donuts. We were starving". "You mean you guys were stuffing your faces the entire time?" Tony asked. What the fuck man. I was hungry too. You didn't save me any?" "No" Johnny said "They were kind of hard to squeeze into our pockets. Tony screamed "I can't believe you jerkoffs don't have any for me. I was covering for you the entire time" "Nobody told you to do that" Johnny laughed. "You snooze, you lose bro. Next time, pay attention".

I was over Dennis G."s learning guitar. I had been a lead singer for a while and still wanted to learn how to play. Dennis had an acoustic he had borrowed from a friend of ours named Duck. Duck never seemed to get it returned. Dennis had absconded with it and always seemed to have an excuse not to give it back. He didn't have much money, so I guess he kept is because he loved to play. I came out of the bathroom and I heard a pop. "What was that?" I asked. "I'm trying to get that center hole pickup to work again, bro" he exclaimed. "Yeah" I said "You showed me that before. But, you never told me why it doesn't work anymore". "I was plugging it back in the stereo to see if I could get it to work again" he replied. "Work again?" I asked. "What do you mean getting it to work again, Den?" "Well" he said "My brother Ricky"s really pissed at me. It's his stereo and I don't have an amp. So, I tried and it worked for a little while. Now, all it does is make loud popping noises. I think I might have blown it up". "You can't plug guitars and shit into things like that" I laughed "It's a different kind of circuit".

"Circuit, circuit" he mumbled "I just want to play guitar, bro". "I know, Den" I said. "But, you can't do it that way". "Sure I can" he chuckled. "I got it to work before. Just sit back and watch. It'll work". He plugged the end of the jack back into the stereo convinced he would get the amplification he desired. "Hamm, pop, pop" the speakers went. It was the obvious sound of feedback exploding in our ears. As he was fiddling with the wire and trying to force it to work, smoke began billowing out of the back of the receiver. "Mum, Dennis?" I warned. "I think there's smoke coming out of the back of this thing" "Nah" he said "Just a few more seconds, and I think I can get it to come on". "Dennis" I yelled. "You're going to make a fire" "So", he laughed "It'll be a rock show. All we need are lights". "Dennis?" I asked "Why don't you shut that shit off and show me how to play Mood for a Day again?" "Mood for a Day again huh Poco? I guess I can do that. I guess We'll be technicians with this later.

He showed me a few chords and we practiced for a while. "I'm bored with this now, Ron" he said. "Let's find something else to do". "Like what?" I asked. "Let's go to the rope swing on Farrington Lake and go swimming." The rope swing was a popular area for us to congregate at. We'd socialize with friends and waste the day running up a hill, grab a cord attached to a tree, and launch ourselves over water about 20 feet below. We'd undulate over the basin, dangle for a bit, and let go into a celebratory splash. Rinse and repeat. That was our day of fun. There was one problem though. They were the Rutgers college police. We really weren't supposed to be there because it was considered private property and off limits to teenagers. Being kids with no other place to go on a balmy afternoon, it had never stopped us before and we simply ignored them. Some days they would appear out of nowhere. They always gave us the usual pep talk "You guys know you're not supposed to be here. It's a liability issue. If one of you drowns or gets hurt, the college doesn't want to be responsible". "Yeah, yeah" we told them. The typical "We won't do it again" response when we all knew we were lying. After such lectures, they would let us finish our swim and we'd be merrily on our way. I would take turns, a few others, and then Dennis. Dennis had a traditional maneuver he always insisted on. While gliding through the air, he called it "The Italian Spin". "Watch, Ron" He'd say. He would swing down over the water twirling around like a fro haired whirling dervish. He looked like a top that was spun too tight. An ever increasing form of inertia exerting itself until it was spent and he would fall. We could hear him echo as he left the shore. "Uuullllllhhh" he screamed. "I'm flying to the abyss of epic proportions".

On one previous visit, there had been 5 of us. The Rutgers cops had shown up and decided to chase us. "Stop, stop" they yelled as we all took off running. We thought it was unusual as they almost never acted that way. So, I dove for the water with a friend named Nicky A. Nicky was a large teen of about 250 pounds and about 5 foot 4. Nicky and I watched from the shore as the others fled for the trail through the parking lot. "We'll just float here, Ron" he whispered. "They can't see us way down here by the water. If they come by, We'll just dive under for a few seconds". "But, Nicky" I said. "We're in our underwear. I don't feel like running in them". "It's better than going to jail" he quipped. "At least here, we have a chance to escape". Sometimes, when we didn't plan such an event, we wouldn't have the forethought of taking our bathing suits with us. Therefore, we would just go in our skivvies or swim buck naked for the day. An hour had passed and it seemed like the authorities had missed us. "Whew!" Nicky sighed "I think they left. Let's go get our clothes and get out of here". We climbed up the bank and made a bee line for where we had left them. To our surprise, they were gone. "Our clothes, our clothes" Nicky screamed "What the fuck happened to our clothes?" "I dunno, man" I nervously replied. "You don't think our friends took them do you?" I asked. "No" Nicky said "They were too busy running from the cops to play tricks on us like that" "We'll, who the fuck took them then? "It could only have been those cops man". Nicky snickered. "I guarantee those fucking cops stole our clothes". "How the fuck are we gonna get home then?" I asked. "How the hell do I know" he replied. "I guess We'll have to figure something out". There were no telephone booths by, or any place where we could steal outfits off of someone"s clothes line. "We're fucked Nicky" I blurted out. We're too far in the fucking woods". "I have an idea" he suggested. "I see they didn't get our sneakers. So, at least we still have those. I notice both of our t shirts are extra-large and hang down almost to our knees. If we keep them wet, I bet we can stretch them even further. That way, we can walk home and nobody will see our briefs. "I suppose so" I replied "But, We're still gonna look like fucking idiots walking over the bridge with people driving by watching us. They'll think We're weirdoes and shit". "It's either that, or in our birthday suits" he laughed. "Look, I'm a pretty large guy, bro. I think that would be much more embarrassing for me". "Ok" I conceded. "I guess we have no choice". We pulled our shirts down as far as we could to stop our privates from being revealed. "I feel like I'm wearing a dress, Nicky" I complained. "You think you feel bad?" he asked. "I look like a fag". "Just try to ignore it, man" I said. "We'll just rush across the bridge as fast as we can. That's all we can do. Once we get to the Edison side, no one will see us anyway". "Fucking cops" Nicky muttered. "It's always the fucking cops."

I had slept over the Gulotta"s house and awoke to the sound of chattering birds outside their living room window. There seemed to be hundreds of them. Dennis was already up and making tea in the kitchen. "What's with all those robins outside, Den?" I asked. "It looks like the movie the Birds". "Ain't no Alfred Hitchcock here, bro" he laughed. "It was just JR and his friend Pyka. They stole eggrolls last night from the back of the Jade Pagoda that were cooling on racks. They snuck up real quiet and ran off with a whole metal tub of them. They had an eggroll fight while we were all sleeping. I guess the birds are going nuts over the leftovers". I peered out the window and saw broken egg rolls in pieces all over the landscape. Birds were swooping down and furiously pecking at them. "Are there any left, Den?" I asked. "I don't think so" he replied. "I think they ate their fill and that was that". "Damn" I thought "I like eggrolls. What a waste of food". Dennis called me down into the basement. "Look!" he said. Ellis has been sleeping down here again. That scuff has been taking advantage of us. I told him he couldn't stay down here anymore. He's been sneaking down here while We're all asleep". "How do you know for sure?" I asked. "There's cigarette butts on the floor". He said. "And look! This is disgusting, bro". In the corner, he pointed toward a white bucket. The kind a painter uses. It was a 5-gallon plastic one with dark matter inside. "What the fuck is that, Den?" I screeched. "It's shit, bro". "Shit?" I asked revolted. "Like, in human shit?" "Yup" he replied. "That homeless fucker has been shitting in this bucket as a toilet. He's fucking gross, man. But, I got an alarm system I've been working on. Come over here by the steps, bro. I'll show you". I accompanied him to the edge of the cellar"s stairs. "Right here" he pointed. "See this last step before it hits the floor?" he asked. That's where I'm gonna set up bottles". "Bottles?" I asked. "For what?" I was confused and didn't get it right away. "How is that an alarm system?" I asked. "It's like this, Ron" he said. "I'm gonna set up empty beer and soda bottles in a row. When that scuff Ellis tries to sneak down here in the dark, he'll trip over all the bottles. They'll make lots of noise crashing and breaking to the ground. Then, I got him". I couldn't help but laugh at his homemade system. "Where did you learn this from?" I asked "Why, it's elementary my dear Ronald." he replied. "There will be no scarf from the scuff tonight!"

I ran into Skippy one morning as I was ditching school outside Pacellas Deli. Pacellas was our go to place whenever students wanted to skip school. It was close by and accessible enough to be able to avoid intrusive teachers or nosey truant officers that were searching for us. Also, Mr. Pacella made a mean Italian hot dog. This was the kind of establishment that looked straight out of a village in Italy. You"d walk inside and immediately try to maneuver your way between the hams and cheeses dangling from the ceiling. You could see them in their nets aging gracefully and imagined what they tasted like as you passed them by. There were the added smells as well. It was an added bonus of perfunctory sensations, twilling your nostrils with a delicious mix of seasonings, salts, and sage. Therefore, it was a perfect hangout for disillusioned teenagers. We'd sit at the counter, sip Italian coffees, chew on our delicacies, and execute our strategy of the day. We felt safe there as Mr. Pacella was very hospitable and inviting. He had no qualms or interest in our personal lives either. He was too preoccupied with running his business to care. In between his food preparation though, he was an excellent conversationalist. We'd lounge on our stools listening intently to his slight Italian accent as he regaled us with stories of the old country and his youth. He treated us like adults and we loved him for it. It was a far cry from the overzealous authoritative measures utilized in the building up the road. In between pecks of his frankfurter and potatoes, Skippy acquainted me with a story of his own. "Guess what I found out?" he asked. "What, Skip?" I replied. By now he had a trail of mustard dribbling down his face and was reaching for a napkin to remove it. While I was preoccupied with the hilarity of this, he answered me. "You know that angel dust shit some people are smoking now?" he asked. "Somebody told me if you spray embalming fluid on mint leaves, you'll get the same kind of high". "I've never heard that one before, Skip" I replied. My brain started having images of smoking with dead people and I was trying hard not to laugh at him. The ridiculousness of the idea seemed unfathomable. "Where would we get that chemical anyway?" I asked. "That kind of shit is in funeral homes". "I dunno" he replied. "Maybe we can sneak into one. There's one in Highland Park and one by the Big T truck stop". "It's too risky man" I said. "It's way too easy for people to see us. Let me think about it for a few minutes". With that, I was imagining breaking into a funeral home"s back preparation room. I hadn't known much about them as I had only seen them in the movies and on TV. I pondered the severity and danger of it if we were to get caught. "I don't think it's a good idea, Skip" I informed him. "How would it look if we got busted doing that? It would surely make the papers. They'd lock us up for being gross and throw away the key. Plus, being around dead people gives me the creeps. We gotta come up with something else. But, I have an idea. It's also lower risk and away from any nearby roads. I'll tell you about it on the way to Danny B"s house." Danny"s house?" he exclaimed. "What are we going there for?" he asked. "I have to talk to him about some stuff" replied. Besides, both his parents work and are never home. I like hanging out there. He has a cool stereo system and lets me eat anything I want out of his refrigerator". "But, you just ate" he replied. "I know, Skip" I said. But, I know I'll be hungry again in 2 hours".

What Was Once Pacalla"s Deli – Courtesy Of Howard Bernard

Danny was waiting on his front porch for us and seemed aggravated. "Where the fuck have you been, Ron?" he roared. "You were supposed to be here an hour ago". "Well" I replied. "I stopped at Pacella"s because I wanted a coffee. As I was walking, I ran into skinny Skip here. Why do you care anyway? You quit school and hang out here all day". "That's not the point, man" he complained. "A little courtesy would help you know?" "Stop with your whining" I told him. "Skippy here has a plan for us to maybe get high on the cheap". "What's that, Skip?" Danny asked. As Skip was explaining the formula he had discovered to him, I made a lunge for the front door. Quickly and in mid-sentence, Danny cried out "Where are you going?" he asked. "Did I tell you could go inside yet?" "I'm going to make tea" I laughed. "So, stop acting like your parents" "Ok" he said. "But, make me some too. I can see you already had coffee because you're already hyper. Plus, you talk too much when you have caffeine So, get your ass in there and brew some up". "Yes Sir, Mr. Asshole" I quipped. "But, listen to Skip. You need to know what We're gonna be doing afterward".

When the tea was finished and I called them inside to fetch some of it, Danny was mildly laughing. "Skippy told me what's up" he said. "Now, where you gonna get the formaldehyde from genius?" he asked. "The school" I chuckled. "It's right in your backyard, man". "My backyard?" he asked. "What? Do I have a fucking chemical warehouse behind me?" "Do you, or do you not have Edison High School behind your house, you retard?" I asked sarcastically. "Yeah, so what" he said. "No" Skippy laughed "No fucking way, man. I know exactly where Ron is going with this. It's an easy scarf. Am I right Ron?" he asked. "Very perceptive Skipper" I said. "Wait? What? Danny" insisted. "I don't get it man". "You'll have to excuse him Skip. I have to explain it to him" "Tell me douchebag" he demanded. "You're in my house. So, spill". "Ok, man. It's like this" I said. "In the high school, there's a science lab and class on the ground floor, right?" "Yes" he nodded. "Well, in that class room cabinet, what's in there?" "Tools?" he asked. "And, what else?" I inquired. "I don't fucking know? Books?" he said. "Jars" Skippy chuckled. "Jars of dead animals". "That's right, Skip" I replied. "And, what do the dead animals float in?" I asked. "Formaldehyde" Danny replied. "They are preserved in formaldehyde". "Bingo!" I chortled. "All we have to do is break in and scarf a couple of those containers. We can dump out the dead stuff and use the chemical for a spray". "Ewwww" Danny said obviously disgusted. "You really wanna use formaldehyde that dead shit was in?" he asked. "It won't hurt you" I replied. "It's not like you're gonna bathe in it or anything" "Ok" he said with revulsion on his face. "But, I'm not pulling dead shit out of any jars. You guys have to do that shit". "No problem" said Skip. "That shit doesn't bother me in the least".

We spent the remainder of the day watching TV and waiting for dusk to come. As soon as we felt it was dark enough, we climbed over Danny"s fence with great stealth. We were rabid for a reason, a mission in motion. We wanted that formaldehyde. When we saw that there were no pesky employees or other potential witnesses about, we crawled up along the edge of the building sneakily. The science lab was mid-way and just before the breezeway. As we skulked down, I raised my hand to the window and was checking to see if it was unlocked. "Fools" I whispered. "They left the windows open. All we have to do is climb in and take what we want". "Cool" Skippy murmured. "Who"s gonna go in first?" "Not me" Danny said. "This is your gig. I'll stay here and be the lookout". "Sounds good" I replied. "Skip and I are skinnier anyway. We'll be in and out in a flash. Watch for cops though, bro". "Got it" Danny breathed. "If I see them, I'll knock on the glass. But, I'm running back home after that. So, you'll be on your own". "That"ll work" I said. "But, just make sure to tell us so we have a chance to get away". I lifted open the window and peered inside. "Skippy?" I asked. "Lean over and let me step on your back. I need something to step on so I can lean right in". "Ok" he said. "And, Danny" I instructed. "Once I'm in, do the same for Skip. And, try not to make any loud noises. We're far from the street. But, there are still houses over there." "I got it, I got it" he replied. "Just hurry up and get this bullshit over with. I don't wanna go to jail over dead animals". Once Skip and I were inside, we made a dash for the cabinets in the back of the room. Strangely, they looked like the type of hutches you would see in someone"s living room. Like the kind that the good china was kept in for company. There were multiple shelves with see through glass inside each door frame. Beyond that, we could see the jars waiting for us to capture them. "Which ones?" Skippy asked. "There are so many. They're all dead in suspended animation". "Let's take a couple that aren't too big, Skip" I whispered. "If they're too heavy, we won't be able to run with them". "How about that octopus one?" he asked. "Yeah" I said. "Take that one and I'll take the rabbit" I said. "They're pretty small. So, we can escape with these with ease". We gingerly removed the containers from their shelves and cradled them to the floor. Skippy titled a jar, took a good look inside and let out a snort "Ewww" he said. "These fucking things are disgusting. Why the fuck do they keep this shit in schools?" he asked. "For science, Skip" I replied laughing. "They use them for dissection. "Now, enough talk" I said. Let's get the fuck out of here before somebody sees us".

We whistled quietly to Danny to see if he was still waiting for us. He whispered back asking "Did you get anything? I can't see shit in there" "Yeah" I responded. "We're gonna hand you these 2 jars through the window. Carefully take them from us and set them on the ground, ok?" After he had the containers in his possession, it was time for us to exit from our crime. Skippy went first. I watched as his tall thin frame jostled itself through the horizontal opening. His arms were so long, he looked like a spider monkey attempting to escape its enclosure. When I heard him hit the ground outside, I followed him. It was challenging shimmying sideways without catching my clothes on the sill below my waist. Halfway through, they were laughing at me. "Look at Stretch Armstrong" Danny boasted. "You better get out of there before you break something" Skippy said. As my palms hit the grass, I gyrated in a half circle, like a cheerleader doing a half assed cartwheel before I fell to the ground. "Fuck you guys" I snapped. "As if you jerkoffs could do it any better." "I did" Skippy chided. "It took me 2 seconds to slide out of there" "Well" I replied "You're as skinny as a fucking Biafrain. You can slip out of anything". "Like a rubber?" Danny laughed. "No" Skip replied. "I'm not that much of a dickhead yet".

"You could have fooled me" I said. "Now, let's get out of here before somebody sees us".

Back at Danny house, we set the jars on his rear porch and examined them more closely. "Nasty" I said. "They look like leather". "Duh" Danny replied sarcastically. "That's cause their dead dumb ass". "Not as dumb as you, you stupid fuck". I chuckled. "Skippy?" I asked. "Do you have those rolling papers?" "Yeah man" he replied. "I have them right here". "All right" I said. "I'm gonna open this one with the octopus in it first. I hope it doesn't stink too much". "Octopus?" Danny shrieked. "Yeah" I said. "You know? The one with 8 arms for jerking off and the pussy you don't get". "Hahaha" Skippy laughed. "He got you". "Shut the fuck up, Skip" Danny cautioned. "At least I'm not a fucking twig". "Now, now children" I chuckled. "Fight nice". "Danny" I instructed. "Go in the house and get me that spray bottle we talked about. Fill it with a little bit of water, about a quarter inch. We have to mix it with this horrible shit to spray it on those rolling papers. Skipper here forgot the mint leaves. So, We'll have to wing it and put tobacco in there to see if it works instead. We'll let it dry afterward and then see if it'll light up". While Danny was retrieving my request, I opened the jar. "Holy fuck! Skippy screamed. "That shit is fucking rank, bro. You sure you want to do this, Ron?" "Hand me that cup over there under the window" I said. "And, stop crying like a little girl. It's not like this shit is caustic or anything. We're just doing a little experiment, that's all". I steadily poured out some of the liquid while trying to keep the malformed creature inside. When I had enough from its dribble, I closed it back up. "There" I said. "That should be enough". Danny had returned. His face had a grimace and a turned up nose. "What's that fucking smell, man?" he asked. "Is that fucking embalming fluid?" "Yes" I replied. "Hand me that sprayer you have. I have just enough here so we can finish this bullshit". After my task was done, I asked Skippy to hold a rolling paper up so I could dust it quickly like an aerosol can. I sprayed the paper carefully but it was no use, it kept getting soaked.

"Fuck" Skippy shouted. "This isn't gonna fucking work". "Let it dry, Skip" I said. "Then, We'll see". Twenty minutes went by waiting for the paper to dry and Skip was getting antsy. "I think it's done now" he said. "Let's put some tobacco in it from one of my cigarettes and see if it works". He pulled out some strands with his bony fingers and laid them down in the paper"s crease. "A few more" he said. "And, We'll smoke this baby up". Danny and I watched as Skippy furled up the onion skin, licked its glued edge, rolled it up, and presented it to us. "Who"s gonna be the Guinea pig?" he asked. "Who wants to go first?" "Not me" Danny exclaimed. "You guys try it. Let me know how it goes". "Pussy" Skippy chuckled. "Fuck it; I'll smoke it first then". "Be careful Skip" I warned. "None of us know what that shit will do to you. Take a small hit first. We don't want you to die and turn into a zombie". "Yeah" Danny chimed in. "I don't want you chasing us down the street trying to eat our faces off". "It's a fluid you morons" Skippy chuckled. "I doubt if it'll kill me. It's for dead people after all". I laughed to myself about how ironic that was. Skippy put the faux joint to his lips, lit it, and took in a deep draw. Immediately, he went into a coughing spasm fit and looked like he was having an epileptic seizure. He turned his face toward the pavement and began to wretch. "Are you ok?" I asked concerned. He stretched his left arm out with his palm facing me and was indicating to us to give him a minute. His cough sounded like he had taken in too much marijuana smoke and there was an uncontrollable heaving of his chest accompanying it with a loud hacking noise. It was as if he was expelling on steroids. "Skip! Skip!" I shouted. "Are you all right man?" His spasms were starting to retreat and he began to talk. But, his voice was slightly raspy. "Wow, man!" he exclaimed. "That's some fucked up shit! It burned the fuck out of my throat, man. I don't think We're gonna get high off of this stuff". He threw the butt on the ground and smashed it with his foot. "I'm just glad you're ok" I said. Danny didn't say much and sat there shaking his head muttering something to himself. It sounded like "Stupid fucks" as far as I could tell. I blurted out "So much for experimentation". Skippy replied "I want to go home".

It was time for our band to do another show. Johnny acted as the booker again and secured a gig at the new Woodrow Wilson Junior High School in North Edison. We were to have the stage while another band named Toast of the Town would play on the floor in front of us. It was ironic as that band was Ronnie G"s band. He was the guy who had helped us previously at the battle of the bands in Highland Park. Since they were the main attraction, we were to go on first. Being that we were all minors, the contact at the school insisted we couldn't play without an adult representing us. So, we got Bob M. to be our manager. We were influenced by the band Kiss and We're trying to come up with a spectacle for a show like theirs. During rehearsals in the basement of my house, I got it in my head that I could blow fire like Gene Simmons. I had read his interview in a popular magazine where he had admitted how it was done and that he had learned it from a circus performer long before he had become famous. It was very simple, he said. As he used plain old lighter fluid. It was the kind used to fill cigarette lighters or to stoke a grill or a camp fire with. "How hard could it be?" I thought. I bought some fluid and waited until the appropriate time when the entire band was in attendance.

We had a new drummer and rhythm guitar player by the names of Bob R. and Chip. Bob looked a lot like Billy Joel and had the same bug out eyes and a New York accent. He was also a way better drummer than we had had before. On some songs, the former percussionist just couldn't hack it. So, we let him go. There was one small problem with Bob though. He was AWOL from the U.S. Navy. Since it was a good hiding spot, he lived at Tony and Johnny"s house in their apartment downstairs. Most people never ventured to the end of their street as it was a dead end that went nowhere. So, it was the perfect spot to shield him. Chip was a kid Johnny knew from school. He had a Brian Jones from The Rolling

Stones style haircut and lived with his grandmother. He was a decent guitarist but didn't know a lot of the same material we knew. But, since we fired the other guy, we needed someone to round out our sound. So, we figured He'd learn as he went along. He was also a quiet guy with a good sense of humor and didn't mind taking direction. On one of their early practices with us, I decided to show them my blow fire like Kiss trick. I had bought some fuel earlier and placed it where I could retrieve it easily. "I have something new for our band" I announced. "What is it?" Johnny asked. "You'll see" I replied. But, all of you have to stand way in the back by the wall against the concrete sink. My trick is kind of dangerous". As I watched them all shuffle to the designated area, I reached down for the lighter fluid I had left under a shelf on the floor. "What the fuck arc you doing?" Tony asked. "I'm gonna show you guys something that will amaze you" I said. "So, just stand there and watch, ok?" I raised the can of fluid to my lips and injected a stream into my mouth. Right away, it tasted disgusting and warm. It reminded me of when Jesse and I had been in Camp Kilmer once and had huffed some vapors from a gas tank on a cement mixer. The fluid had the same consistency and smell. I was careful not to swallow any as I knew if I did, it would make me ill. When my mouth was sufficiently filled to the point where I didn't need anymore, I laid down the can and grabbed my Bic lighter from the floor. The looks in their eyes was of panic and fear. Bob yelled out asking "Is he really gonna do that? I think he's fucking nuts". "Go Ronnie, go" Johnny screamed. Tony was frozen still and speechless and Chip was shaking his head in disbelief. I lit the flame from its striker and placed it before my lips. It had to be strategically positioned as to avoid any nasty burn injuries. I pulled back a breath and let the fluid fly. I forced a stream of spray directly out in front of me while holding the flame about 6 inches from my face. The fire had to be far from the funnel for the ultimate effect. As the flame hit the edge of the flow, it ignited into a mushroom cloud fireball at its end. When done precisely, it was a very quick trick and spectacular. The boys were amazed. "How did you learn how to do that?" Johnny asked. "Practice my friend, lots and lots of practice" I replied. "You"ve done this before?" Tony asked. "Only once in my backyard" I said. But, it's too cold out to do it out there tonight. So, I did a smaller one with you guys down here". "Wicked" Johnny commented. "But, it still scared the fuck out of me. You could have burned your house down you know?" It was still really cool to see that in person though. Are we gonna use this in our show?" he asked. "I'm working on it" I replied. "I almost have it perfected". "I have an idea too" Johnny offered. "If you're gonna do that, I want to do that part where Simmons drips and spurts blood out of his mouth. But, I want Dennis M. to take a knife and pretend to stab me with it. I'll put ketchup or something in my mouth and spit it out after he's done". "We can do that" I replied. "I'll run it past him when we see him next. We'll have to let him sing backups though. Otherwise if he's not part of the performance, it'll look stupid if he just runs up from the side of the stage without warning.

The night came for our gig at Woodrow Wilson Junior High. The day before, we went to Lou Rose Music Center on route 27 and rented some PA equipment. Bob M. and I picked it up and loaded it into his station wagon. On the way there, he asked "What are those clothes you got in that bag there?" "These are mine and Dennis M."s stage outfits". "Stage outfits?" he asked. "What kind of fucking outfits? I didn't know you guys were gonna dress up for this?" "We have a few surprises" I said. "You'll see. Just wait until we get there". "Ok" he replied. "Just don't make it anything stupid. I'm your manager now you know". "Don't worry" I said. "We'll make sure to embarrass you". Johnny, Tony, Chip, Dennis M., and Bob R. were already there when we pulled into the loading area behind the stage. They had delivered their amps and the drums way earlier. "Let's get these amps and PA system situated" I said. "Who made you the fucking boss?" asked Bob M. "I'm the manager" he laughed. "You're the guy we "let" be the manager" I said. "Now, either go down to the floor and speak to the person in charge of the school, or get out of the way". He jumped down off the stage and disappeared. After our equipment was all settled and secured, I went down to see how Bob M. was doing with the PA system. It was a slightly complicated task as the speaker cabinets were much larger than what we were used to. I fiddled around with the mixing board to see if our microphones were in sync with their corresponding channels. All of the inputs and outputs looked right, so I was satisfied; until I ran into a guy who was a friend of Bob M"s. His name was Michael and I had known him from high school. "Hey, Michael" I said. "What are you doing here? Are you here to watch us play?" Surprised he replied "Watch you play? Bob M. didn't tell you? I'm running the sound and the mixing board tonight". "That's news to me" I said. "Have you ever run a board before?" I asked. "No, but I think I can figure it out" he said. "It doesn't look too difficult at all". I was pissed! Bob M. was giving our performance over to someone who had absolutely no clue of what he was doing. I walked over to Bob M. seething with resentment "What the fuck are you doing?" I asked. "You can't have a guy who never ran a board before do sound for us! Are you fucking kidding me?" "Relax man" he said condescendingly. "You guys know what you're doing. You can't run it because you'll be performing. I can't do it because I know fuck all about sound systems. So, I figured you can set the controls, knobs, and levels and Michael will monitor it all. Don't worry; he won't touch anything once it's set, he promised me". "He better not fuck this up, man" I warned. "Because we have stiff competition tonight and I want us to sound good". "Stop worrying" he assured me. "It's in the bag, bro". It was a decision I would soon regret.

All of us in the band including Dennis M. were in the boy's bathroom getting ready for the show. I pulled open the bag I had shown Bob M. previously and paraded some outfits around the room. "What's that black shiny shirt there with the silver on the front Ronnie?" Johnny asked. "That's a lightning bolt going down the front" I said. "I used silver glitter and glued it to the material. It's pretty cool, huh?" "Awesome" Johnny replied. "But, what do the rest of us have?" he asked. "Well, I didn't have time to make everyone something" I said. So, We're gonna do it like this. I have tubes of an assortment of different colored paints here. You guys are gonna paint all of your faces whatever colors you like the most. I'm gonna do mine too. "Like Kiss? Tony asked. "Exactly" I replied. Bob R. peered into the bottom of the bag on the floor. "What's that top hat and cape for?" he asked. "That's Dennis M."s" I said. He likes Alice Cooper better than Kiss. So, I figured He'd paint his face like him and wear the hat and the cape". "Why does he get to wear the cooler outfit?" Johnny moaned. "Because, We're in the front and he's singing backup in the back. He doesn't get to stand out as much as we do and I wanted it to be fair. That way, the audience can see him better". "I should have been a backup vocalist instead then" Johnny laughed. "Fuck you, man" Dennis M. sneered "That shit it mine".

We changed into our stage attire while deciding what paint would go with whom. Dennis M. was easy as his was already decided. "I'm gonna do 2 stars on my face over my eyes in purple with a white background" I announced. "I wanna do all black on one side, and all white on the other" Johnny said. "And, Tony and I have decided that since we are twins, he's gonna do the same thing but in reverse". "Is that right Tone?" I asked. "Yeah" Tony replied. "I don't really give a fuck about this Kiss makeup bullshit. I just wanna play". "Ok then, what about you Bob R.?" I asked "Fuck all this time wasting applying makeup crap" he said. "I'm with Tony man. Just put something easy on my face. Like 2 dark circles or some shit. I'm behind my drums and nobody"s gonna give a fuck anyway" "Fine" I said. "You do that". I turned to Chip. "Ok, Chipster" I asked "What about you?" "I kind of like orange" he replied. "Orange?" Johnny asked laughing "You'll look like the great pumpkin". "I don't care. I like orange" he replied. "So, make me orange with white eyes". When all of our get ups were finished, we snuck up on the stage to prepare. While behind the curtain, I came across the school official who was moderating the dance and began asking him some questions. "We have a show that has some fire in it". I said "Is it against the law for me to do a bit where I blow fire out of my mouth?" "Blow fire out of your mouth?" he asked concerned. "How high of a fire are we talking about here, son?" "Just a few feet" I replied. "Well, as long as you have a fire extinguisher, I don't think the fire marshal would mind. But, you have to keep it as far away from the curtains as possible". I thanked him, ended the conversation, and went to ask the janitor if there was an extinguisher available. The janitor brought us one, set it down next to an amplifier, asked us what it was for, told us to be careful and walked away. I turned to Johnny and asked "Do you have your blood thing ready for your mouth? Is the knife ready? Is the lighter fluid and the lighter there with the crystal goblet I took from my house?" "Yeah, it's all here" he replied. It's right behind my bass amp" "You do your fire thing Ronnie during the cover of KisS's song Strutter" he said. "And, I'll do the blood act during my Santana cover of Oye Como Va. Hopefully, we won't burn the place down".

When it was time to go on, Bob M. gave us the cue. We had a really nice intro Bob R. had made up for our very first song, The Rolling Stones Sympathy for the Devil. No vocals, no guitars, no bass. Bob R. started pounding away 1,2 3, - 4,5,6,7,8 -1,2,3- 4,5,6,7,8. As the curtains began parting, about 100 kids ran up to the stage. They didn't know what to make of us. Rolling Stones songs but are dressed like Kiss and Alice Cooper? I went into my best Jagger rooster impersonation and started to sing "Please allow me to introduce myself". I could barely hear myself and something was wrong. "There's no time to contemplate it" I thought. "No matter what happens, the show must go on. We continued playing. ZZ ToP's Tush, Bad Company"s Can't get Enough, and then KisS's Strutter. When it came time for my fire breathing exercise, I reached behind Johnny"s amplifier for my props. I gasped as the box they had been in was empty. There was no goblet, no lighter fluid, no knife, no lighter, no fake blood packets, nothing. The fire extinguisher afforded us earlier was gone as well. I rushed over to Johnny and whispered into his ear "Where the fuck is everything? I demanded "All of the special effects are gone!" Johnny covered his microphone with his hand so no one could hear". "They're not there?" he asked. "They were there before. Somebody must have moved them. But the song is almost over, bro. So fuck it, it's too late now. Just go with it and finish the show". We played a few more tunes and ended with Cream"s Sunshine of your Love. I looked back and noticed Chip wasn't playing anything and was leaning up against a wall. He looked pale as a statue. "This is a disaster! I thought. "First we can't hear ourselves, then someone took our props, and now Chip is just standing there. I couldn't wait for it to be over.

While in the bathroom removing our makeup after the show, I started insisting on answers. "What the fuck was that Chip?" I asked screaming. "You didn't play the rhythm part in that Cream song at all?" "I forgot it" he replied. "Forgot it?" I asked. "How the fuck do you forget part of a song we rehearsed for weeks?" "Ronnie" Johnny interjected "Leave Chip alone, man. Clapton"s band with that song was just a 3-piece anyway. So, it doesn't make a difference". "It makes a difference to me" I bellowed "It's not professional" "We're not rock stars, Ronnie" Tony yelled. "You keep forgetting that. So, leave the fucking guy alone". "And, the sound? I asked "I couldn't hear shit up there. What was going on with that?" "Don't ask us" Johnny said. "Go and see that Michael guy Bob M. hired. "I had a great time" Dennis M. exclaimed. "I couldn't hear shit. But, I didn't give a fuck. I had a fun time singing backups and watching Ronnie run all over the stage. He does a great Jagger impersonation and looks like a chicken with his head cut off". "It's a rooster, Dennis" I said. "Still", he replied. "It was funny as fuck". I finished changing back into my regular clothes and accosted Bob M. by the sound board. "What the fuck happened here?" I asked very annoyed. "With what?" Bob M. replied. "We couldn't hear shit up there" I said. "Nobody touched the board man" Bob M. quipped. "So, I don't know what you're talking about". I peered down at the board and could see all of my settings had been changed. Some were too low, some too high, some were completely shut off. I turned back to Bob M. "Um, all of these have been changed from what I originally set them at". "Like I said, I don't know anything about it." Bob M. said. "You'll have to ask Michael". "Ok then, where is he?" I asked. Bob M. thought for a minute "Oh, he left" he said. I was raging inside. I thought "Of course he did" and walked away.

While packing up to go while Toast of the Town was playing, Johnny and I had found the janitor again. So, we interrogated him "Could you please tell us what happened to all of our stuff that was in a box behind my amplifier?" Johnny asked. "Oh" he replied "You mean that can of lighter fluid and that knife?" "Yes" I said "Where is it?" "Well, you know when you asked those questions about fire with the head guy here? He told me to take that stuff away from you because he said you"d start a fire and he couldn't have it. He also said the knife was gonna be too violent for these kids. So, he made me take it all away". "That's stealing" I yelled "You can't do that and you ruined our entire show" "There's nothing you can do about it" he replied. "You can't prove it anyway. We had to think about the safety of the school. Have a nice night". As he was walking away, Johnny screamed at him "No wonder you're a fucking janitor, you fucking dickhead". We watched the other band play, cursed some more, and went home.

I had broken up with the girl from Vick F"s party and was dating a new girl who lived off of Woodbridge Avenue close to Meadow Road. She had beautiful brown locks and a body that was one of the sexiest I had ever seen. One summer afternoon she was over a guy Brian W."s house with a friend. Brian lived in a duplex off of Sutton"s Lane that was close to where I was living. So, I didn't have to walk very far to be with her when she called. Her friend was kind of chubby with shoulder length blonde hair and I had known her from seeing her at dances at Guardian Angel"s church. Therefore, we all felt comfortable with each other as there were no surprises regarding getting along. Brian had been dating the blonde girl so we decided to hang around as couples for the day.

While I was on the couch necking with my girl, Brain and the blonde disappeared. My girl and I started doing some heavy petting and I had gotten to 2nd base. Hoping for more, I asked her to accompany me to one of the rooms upstairs. She complied and followed me with no reservations. As we delved deeper into sexual attraction on the bed, I asked her if I could make love to her. "As long as you use a condom" she whispered. "I see no problem with that". I reached into my back pocket to retrieve my wallet, took it out, and peered inside. "Shit" I thought. "No rubber. What am I gonna do now?" "I'll be right back" I said apologetically. "I have to go ask Brian if he has a spare". "I'll be right here waiting" she cooed. "But, try to come back quickly if you can". I bounded down the stairs to find Brian. Coming out of a laundry room, I approached him. "Hey, man?" I asked. "Please tell me you have an extra rubber on you?" "I'm sorry, bro" he replied. "I just used the last one on my girlfriend. We did it on the dryer and I don't have any left. She's in the bathroom cleaning up right now, bro. I sure am sorry I couldn't help you". "Fuck" I growled. "My girlfriend's upstairs ready and waiting". "I don't know what to tell you, man" he said. "Maybe you can walk to the store and buy some new ones?" he asked. "The nearest store for those is in Highland Park" I quipped. "I'm not doing that. By the time I come back, it'll be too late and my chance will be over". I walked back upstairs with my head down feeling defeated. "Did you find one?" she asked. "No" I replied. "Brian and your friend just used the last one he had. But, how about if I pull out and go on your stomach?" I suggested. "I promise to be real careful". "I'm sorry" she said "I'm not having your kid. So, that's not gonna work. No way, no how". "I guess our attempt is a wash then" I moaned. "I guess so" she replied. "We can always try again some other time. But, you'll have to be more prepared". I buttoned up my shirt and gave up. It wasn't the first time I was shot down.

A week went by and Ronnie E. and I went to the Saint Mathews carnival. While I was waiting for him by the scrambler ride to come back from doing something, I heard a song blasting from some speakers inside. "What's that tune?" I asked the scruffy ride operator. "You don't know who that is?" he asked. "No" I replied. "But, it sounds fucking amazing. Who is that?" "It's Zeppelin"s new one off of Houses of the Holy" he said. "Yeah, but what's the name of the song?" I asked. "Oh, that" he replied. "Why, it's called Dancing Days. Isn't it great?" he asked. "Fantastic" I yelled. "I'm gonna have to buy that". Just then, Ronnie had reappeared. "Where the fuck did you go?" I asked. "I've been over here waiting for you for like 20 minutes?" "I just found out about something that's gonna piss you off" he said. "What's that?" I asked. "Aren't you supposed to meet your girlfriend here tonight?" he asked. "Yeah, so" I replied. "So, what's wrong with that?" "I have some bad news for you, man" he laughed. "You know Joe S. from our class with Miss Godynick, right? Well, it turns out she's been cheating on you the entire time with him. I know it's gonna hurt your feelings but you're my friend so I thought you should know". "I guess I'll have to confront her about it when she shows" I said. "But in the meantime, check out this new music".

After an hour went by, Ronnie left again and she finally showed up with a different friend tagging along. She could see I was angry and asked what the problem was. "You look really pissed off about something" she said. "Is it anything I've done?" she asked. "Is it true you"ve been cheating on me with Joe S.?" I asked. "Because I have it from a very reliable source that you have been". Looking away from me, she denied it. "I don't know who told you that" she said. "But, I'm not a cheater and I really like you. I wouldn't have gone that far with you at Brian"s house if I didn't". "That was a week ago" I howled. "Some people change from week to week. Now, have you been seeing him or not?" I asked again. "No" she said looking away a second time. "I swear I haven"t". Since she refused to look in my eyes after I had interrogated her twice with the same question, I broke up with her. "You're gonna believe Ronnie over me?" she asked visibly upset. "I'm sorry, but I have to" I replied. "I've only known you for a few months. But, I've known him for years". I turned to walk away to see if sHe'd chase me. But, she never did. I turned to speak with Ronnie since he had just come back and she was gone. I thought "So much for teenage love".

Edison Lanes was another place most of the teenagers hung out at. It was the largest bowling alley in the United States at the time and had 112 lanes. Jackie Boy worked there as a dishwasher on the weekends and I would sometimes meet him there. He was allowed to give me a free soda as long as I bought something to eat. There was also Fred"s pool hall. Fred"s was always crowded with locals who took their chances on wagers of 9 ball, 8 ball or straight shooting games. You could even rent a spot to lock your cue stick in there. That way, you didn't have to carry it around if you didn't want to. Most of the older players I watched had custom made Q sticks and were hustlers who made money from the games. Some of their rods were very ornate with ivory or brass handles and pearl or jade inlays. They always had to open their velvet lined cases to brag to everyone and show how we wished we were champions. A few of my friends were quite good and managed to take a few 20"s from me. Jesse had always seemed to beat me as well as Tight Timmy G. They had their own pool hall language too such as "You gotta have Poe, Ron" meaning positioning your ball for the next shot. "It wasn't about the ball you're shooting at" Jesse would say. "It's was about lining it up for the next shot". Jesse was also particularly good at bank shots. I"d play him and He'd amaze me with table length attempts out of nowhere. "You have to learn bankies, Ron" he said. "It's the only way you're gonna make any money". There were other times where we simply used the lanes as a meeting place. We rarely bowled there as it was usually too busy with leagues anyway. We would use the many banks of telephone booths lining the back wall, or simply play early videos games. We'd play to pass the time or talk on the phone until our friends arrived. Edison Lanes also had a vast parking lot. In the summer months, we could always count on the Clyde Beatty/Cole Brothers Circus to arrive. My friends and I would sometimes sneak under the canvas when circus personnel weren't looking. We'd slink in really low and secure a front row seat right in the center under the big top. Ronnie E. and I even got rooked by them once. One late evening, when it was after the final performance, a worker asked if we'd like to make $10. He wanted us to help break the tents all down. "Sure" we said excitedly. When their trucks were full and they were ready to go, we asked for our pay. "Oh, the paymaster had to leave for a little bit" the worker told us. "Some of us will still be here tomorrow morning though. So, come in the morning and We'll pay you then". Believing him since we were so young, we showed up at the agreed upon time. To our disappointment, the lot was empty and they were all gone. "Asshole" Ronnie said. "He duped us". But, we learned from it and never did it again. It was karma for sneaking in I guess.

One of Edison"s Teen Hangouts And Where I Got Shocked In The Sign

Behind Edison Lanes was a patch of tall trees that everyone called Saint Mathew"s woods. We could never figure out that one as the property belonged to the lanes. Most likely, it was due to its close proximity to Saint Mathew"s church"s parking lot. In the center of this little forest was a perfect spot for drinking beer, smoking pot, and having sex with our girlfriends on the ground. It was one of our perfect enclaves for ultimate privacy. We could hump vicariously and make carnal like noises without anyone being nosey or hearing us. The main trail cut partially through the middle. So, we always had a way to escape. There are a few occurrences about the Edison Lanes parking lot I remember vividly. The first was walking through it with Johnny V. As Johnny and I were traveling to his house from school, we ran into Ronnie E. Ronnie wasn't fond of Johnny at the time and decided it was time to tease him. In front of Edison Lanes was a monolithic tower made from cinderblocks. It had hollowed out S shapes on each side that made a pretty nice pattern and was climbable. Ronnie accosted me "What are you doing with this guy?" he asked pointing at Johnny. "He's a friend of mine. I'm in a band with him" I replied. "I don't like this guy" Ronnie said "You shouldn't be hanging out with him". "That's funny, man" I laughed. "You don't look like my father. I didn't know I needed your permission". Johnny was wearing a blue coat tied around his waist that he had taken it off due to the weather becoming warmer. "Permission this" Ronnie shouted. He snatched Johnny"s coat from his mid-section and began dancing around in the lot taunting him. He had the coat by its sleeves and was whirling around and pretending that it was his dance partner. "Look at me" he screamed. "I'm in a band too. I can dance just like you guys". "Um, people in bands play instruments" I said sarcastically. "They don't do it to dance around, you retard". "Oh yeah" he said. "Well, you dance around like a fag like Jagger. So, I wanna be just like you. "And just for that" he said motioning to the tower. "I'm gonna dance this jacket right up that chimney". He stood before the concrete obelisk and announced. "Here goes your coat". He scaled the tower to the summit, stopped, and stuck the coat into a hole in one of the hollowed out chambers. "What an asshole" Johnny whispered. "I hope he falls". When he descended back to earth, he remarked "Try to get that bitch now. I dare you". I felt bad for Johnny and told Ronnie "Why do you have to be such a douchebag. He's not bothering you. You had your fun. Let him get his coat and go home". "Stay out of this Arold" he cautioned. "You don't have anything to do with this". "Yeah, I do" I said. "He's a friend of mine". "Well, I was your friend first" he complained. "So, you're gonna have to choose". "I'm not choosing anyone" I replied. "I just want you to stop being a dickhead". While we argued, Johnny was attempting to retrieve his coat. He was half way up when Ronnie said "I'll leave him alone if he can make it back down without getting hit". "Getting hit by what?" I asked. "Just a few pebbles" he replied "It won't hurt him" he chuckled. It'll just sting a little bit" He reached down and grabbed a few stones from the ground with his left hand. Then, he whispered to me "I'm not really gonna hurt him. I'm just fucking with him, man. I wanna see his reaction, that's all". "Hurry up, Johnny" I yelled. "If you're fast, he'll miss you". Ronnie whipped a couple of pebbles toward Johnny as Johnny was almost through. Fortunately, his aim was off and only a couple had grazed him. "You're a scumbag" Johnny said. "I never did anything to you". "Did I hit you Johnny?" Ronnie asked. "A little" Johnny replied. "But, I still don't understand why you had to do that". "Stop crying, man" Ronnie chuckled "I won't scare you anymore. You passed the test. In the face of danger, you still went up there to get your stuff. So, you're cool now". "I hope I don't ever have to pass any of your tests, Ronnie? I asked. "You already passed a lot of them" he said. "You just don't remember".

The second instance was when I was hanging out with Phil and a few others. We had been shooting pool in the pool hall and had heard about a party that was going on in some woods off of Woodbridge Avenue. Phil blurted out "Yeah man, I just got off the phone with somebody I know who"s going to be there" he said "There's going to be beer and shit. But, they want a $2 donation. I have $2 left, do you?" he asked. "Yeah, I've got 5 bucks" I replied. "Let's head on over there then before all of the beer is gone". As we stepped outside and were traversing the parking lot to go, we ran into Jesse. "Where are you guys going?" he asked. "We're going to a party" I replied. "Cool, a party huh?" he asked. "How many chicks are gonna be there?" "A few I guess. Just like most parties" Phil replied.. "I'm gonna come with you guys then" Jesse demanded. "You got any money?" I asked. "Because, you can't come with us unless you have some money". "What?" Jesse screamed. That's the last thing I remember hearing before I felt a blow to my upper left jaw. It was painful at first, but then it went suddenly numb. "Wow!" Phil howled. "You're lip is bleeding, bro". Jesse, in a fit of mad rage, had clobbered me and had punched me right in the mouth. "Fuck you, Ron" he yelled "Nobody fucking tells me where I can and cannot go. You don't tell me what to do just because I don't have any money". In between drips of blood, I answered "Smooth move Jesse. Smooth move, thanks a lot man". "You better go back inside the lanes and get cleaned up, man." Phil said. You're whole shirt is full of blood. So, you might as well forget about that party". "Yeah, you guys go on ahead" I replied. "I'm gonna have to go home after this because of this asshole". "Asshole?" Jesse shrieked "Yeah Ron, you better leave before I give you another one" he threatened. "Whatever, tough guy" I said. I walked away to tend to my wound without ever looking behind me. I guessed that Jesse had left with the others. Still, I was fully expecting for him to attack me again. Luckily, he had left me alone. I entered the lanes bathroom and peered into the mirror. I had a ¼ inch tear in my upper left lip that went clear through to the inside of my mouth. I was able to open it up to inspect it and the damage appeared to need stitches. "Fucking Jesse" I moaned. "I'm not going to the hospital, fuck that" I said. I pinched the wound closed the best I could to try to stop the bleeding. It was taking a long time and it was more time than I had patience for. I took some paper towels from the dispenser, balled them up into a makeshift bandage, held it to my mouth and headed home. On the way out, all of the patrons were staring at me. I got the usual "Are you ok?" questions of concern accompanied by sad, funny looks. I ducked out the back door and thought to myself "Remember to never argue with someone who is 6 foot 4 ever again".

Ronnie E, Joey S., and I sometimes had a lot of fun in our bad kid's class at Edison High School. One day, Miss Godynyk mentioned to us that she had brought some brownies to class for a snack. But, just like Mr. S at TJ, we were expected to "be good" before we could have them. We had figured out that even in high school, each Special Ed teacher had their own technique of trying to keep us in line. But with Miss Godynyk, we just wondered why it had taken her so long. In high school, there was no more Child Study Team, fewer parent/teacher conferences, less observation, less progress reports, and a pull back on disciplinary actions. Therefore, we made the assumption that the educational system had given up on us. Joey S. had been absent on this day and we were wondering where he was. As Ronnie and I were finishing our assignments, we were fully expecting to be compensated with a treat. "Very good boys" Miss Godynyk beamed. "I'm very proud of the both of you. So, I'm going to open the locker now and give you guys what I promised. Keep up the good work and I'll bring you even more rewards later on". Ronnie and I were salivating at the thought of it. "Treats for doing nothing?" he whispered with her back turned to us. "Yeah, these lessons are cake, we can do that". "After all" I thought". "These lessons are far below par of what normal students are expected of. This shit is easy!" We sometimes resented that the curriculum thought we were stupid by giving us text books 3 to 4 grades below our intelligence level. We had a feeling that their teaching methods were all a ruse designed to keep us calm rather than to educate us anyway. So, the joke was on them. Most of us were smarter and more cunning than the administration and the teachers were. We never showed it though as we were consummate actors. It was all in trying to secure an easy day. As Miss Godynyk opened the door to the locker, she let out a high pitched shrill "They're gone" she gasped. "They're all gone. All of my brownies are gone!" "What do you mean they're gone?" Ronnie asked. "You promised us. I didn't answer all those stupid questions in that book you gave us for nothing". "Miss Godynyk?" I asked. "Are you sure you locked it? "Yes, I'm sure" she replied. "I checked it twice". "Well, apparently not" Ronnie complained. "Because now me and Arold are fucked out of our brownies. "Stop cursing" she demanded. "I've told you before Ronnie, cursing doesn't solve anything". "It makes me feel good though" he laughed. "How else am I supposed to be when I got ripped off?" "Stories of our lives, right bro?" I asked. "You got that right" he said. "We're always getting shafted". Just then, Joey S. came rambling through the door and had an obvious brown stain on his chin. "Joey S.?" Miss Godynyk asked. "You are late. Where have you been? Class started an hour ago". "I was in the bathroom" he replied. "I was washing my face". "Washing your face for what?" Ronnie asked. "I had brownie frosting all over my mouth" he proudly exclaimed. "And, man, were they good!" "Ronnie was becoming very upset. "How the fuck did you get brownies you asshole?" he asked. "The fucking locker was locked" "I came to class early and nobody was here yet" he said. "I knew there were brownies in there because Miss Godynyk had told me she was bringing them yesterday. I was starving because I didn't have any breakfast. So, I took a broom handle I found in the closet and I broke it open". "You're a scumbag Joey" Ronnie howled. "You didn't save any for us!" "What the fuck did you want me to do?" Joey asked. "It was only a small tray anyway". "You never think about anyone else, you selfish fuck" I said. "No wonder you have so many fucking problems". "The cursing, the cursing" Miss Godynyk exclaimed. "You guys have to stop. I can't have that in here. I'll get in trouble with the administration". "Fuck the administration" Ronnie chided. "Tell them to get us some fucking brownies". "Joey" Miss Godynyk commanded. "Leave this class room immediately and don't come back until tomorrow. You have to learn to share and it's not right that the rest of the students have to suffer because of your behavior". "I'm not going any place" Joey chuckled. "It's not my fault there was no food in my house". "You"ve got 5 seconds to get out of here" Ronnie warned. "Or else, you won't have to worry about eating anymore. Because I'm gonna give you a knuckle fucking sandwich". "No violence, please" Miss Godynyk begged. "Just go Joey, go". "Ok, I'll leave" he said. "But, fuck you guys; I'll be back here tomorrow".

A third time I was cutting through Edison Lane"s parking lot when I passed their lit up sign. I noticed right away that its maintenance access door was open and it had always been locked before. "I wonder who broke in there?" I asked myself as I stuck my head in to see. Gazing upward, I saw that there was a ladder that went up to the top. "I think I'm gonna go up and check it out" I mumbled. "It looks like somebody"s been up there". As I ascended the rungs I noticed that it was very warm with hot air surrounding me. "It must be from these hundreds of light bulbs that are on?" I thought. I turned behind me and saw that someone had laid a mattress in there. "Cool" I said. "A new place to hang out in if I'm drunk to take a rest". I turned to hold onto a rail to prop myself up so that I could take a break and sit on the bed. As I reached with my other hand to steady myself, I got the shock of my life. My body began to tremble and I thought "Holy shit, I'm being electrocuted. I must have grabbed an open wire. I have to break this thing or I'm gonna die". I swung myself to the left as hard as I could and miraculously was able to let go. Unfortunately, that meant falling down the stairs. After I reached the bottom, my face was contorted with fear. My right shin I hit on the way down was aching and I was gasping for air. "Oh my god" I whispered shaking. "I almost got fucking killed up there". It became obvious to me that whoever had been sleeping up there had set an open wire as a booby trap. "Fucking homeless cocksuckers" I screamed after I calmed down. "I wonder if it was that scuff, Ellis?" Stepping back to the outside, I regained my final composure, slammed the door shut, and walked away. Feeling for change in my pocket, I reached for a coin for a call. I went into an Edison Lanes phone booth and called the cops anonymously. I was all for a secret hideaway, but I thought it ridiculous that I could have died. I hung up the receiver and whispered nervously "They'll be no more traps and They'll pay".

I was walking through the field in the back of TJ one night when I heard some people laughing. I recognized one of the voices right away. It was Howie B. Where the small hill of grass met the bottom of TJ"s back brick wall, he was struggling with what appeared to be a ladder. As I grew closer, I could see that he was attempting to get it into a vertical position but he wasn't really having much luck. Upon closer inspection, I could see that it was a painter"s ladder and that his brother Brian was trying to help him. He was standing there and suggesting directions. "Do it this way, Howie" Brian said. "Maybe that"ll work". At first, I had wondered how they had gotten it there. Then, I remembered that they were pretty easy to carry. I approached them and they recognized me immediately "Hey? What's up Ron?" Howie asked. "Nothing" I replied. "I was just on my way to Dunkin Donuts to get a coffee". "A coffee huh?" he asked. "Well, I'm gonna do a thingie" he said. "And, Brian"s gonna help me." "A thingie?" I asked" What do you mean, a thingie?" He pointed to one of the feet at the bottom of the ladder. There was a can of paint sitting there with two large brushes on top of it. "Now that I got this fucking thing stable" he said. "I'm gonna climb up on that ledge just under the roof and paint a Yes logo". Yes was a progressive and popular rock band of the 1970's and most hippie kids like us loved them. Therefore, the logo from their albums was very recognizable. The ledge Howie was describing was about 8 feet below the roof. It was 4 feet wide and maybe 6 feet long. It jutted out from the midway point of the wall and cascaded down another 5 or 6 feet to the ground. "You wanna help me, bro?" he asked. "Brian doesn't feel like going up there. But, it's cool though. He can stand watch for us in case anybody comes. I'll do the outline and you can fill in the rest. It'll be cool." "It'll be so large" he said "That you'll be able to see it forever". "Ok, that sounds fantastic" I replied. "But, first?" I asked "Do you wanna smoke some Thai stick? We can paint while we get blown away." "Wow!" he exclaimed. "You have some Thai stick?" he asked. "That sounds awesome. Help me get all of this shit onto the ledge. Then, I'll get the paint ready while you roll a joint" "You got papers, right?" he asked "Of course" I replied "Painters always come prepared". I asked Brian "You don't mind do you, Bri?" "Nah, fuck that" he said. "As long as you got the weed, I'm good down here, bro. But, we gotta make this fast. If one of those neighbors in those houses sees us up there, They'll surely call the cops". "He's got a point there, Ron" Howie said. "So, let's get this show on the road".

I held the ladder against the wall, steadied it, and watched Howie ascend to his position. "Hand me the can of paint and the brushes, man" he said. "Then, you come up. But, watch that third step bro, it's kind of rickety". "Thanks for the warning, man" I said. "It's dark out here and I don't think I would have seen that". "No problem" he replied. "We can't have anything happen to you; you have the goods" he laughed. I got half way up the ladder and Brian handed me our tools. First it was the paint, and then the brushes. "Thanks, man" Howie said. "Now, you stand over here to the left of me. That way, you won't be in the way. While I'm doing the outline, whip out some of that bodacious smoke. After you light it up, we can pass it between us and get silly". "Sounds like a plan" I said. "Let me crouch down here and twist one up" I soon realized that I couldn't see as it was far too dark. "I have to get down" I said. "I can't roll up here. I only have 2 hands. Somebody will have to hold the lighter so I can see". "I'll do it" Brian replied. "It's probably better for Howie anyway. He'll have more room up there that way". "He's right, Ron" Howie said. "I can probably get done faster. Why don't you and Brian take a few tokes, and then bring it up to me. I can wait a few minutes to get stoned. It's no big deal. Just make sure you save me some". I descended down the ladder and handed Brian the Bic. "Let's go against the wall, man" I said. "That way, there won't be any wind messing up the flame. We'll be able to see better". "Sounds good" Brian replied. "I'll stand right over here in front of you too. That should block everything". I pulled out the bag, sprinkled some weed in a zig zag, and rolled it on up. "Now, We're ready" I said ""Let's light this sucker". I grabbed the lighter from Brian and touched its flame to the joint. I breathed in deeply, held it in for a second and gave a slight cough. "This shit is potent, bro" I gagged. "But, it tastes really good". "Let me check it out" Brian asked. "Bonzai" I laughed as I handed it to him. Brian took a few tokes. As with me, he coughed some of it up. "Damn, this shit is good" he exclaimed. "We're gonna get very stoned I think. "I hope so" I said. "Maybe We'll paint better that way" Howie was singing a Yes song to himself and suddenly stopped. I could barely see the outline of his silhouette in the night. "That shit sure smells good" he said. "Now, don't Bogart that stick bro. Bring some of that up here. Don't forget about me". "Howie"s always paranoid he's not gonna get any" Brian whispered. "He's always that way". "You're goddamn right" Howie blurted. "I heard you Bri. I'm doing most of the work here. So, you know I'm getting fucking stoned". "All right, all right Howie" I assured him. "I'll be right up". Brian and I were already sufficiently high. So, we didn't really care. We shrugged our shoulders and wandered back to Howie"s project. "I'm coming back up, Howie" I announced. "How much of that shit do you have done?" I asked. "All of it" he replied. "Now, hand me that half a joint of that Thai stick and get busy. It's your turn now, bro". He took the joint from my fingertips and began to drag on it profusely. "Ahhhh, that's much better" he chuckled. "Much, much better". I dipped the clean brush into the paint can while Howie stood on the other side of me toking away. "Aren't you going to get down?" I asked "Nah" he said. "You only have to paint the inside now. It's a lot easier and I won't be in the way. The outline is a pain in the ass, bro. To do that, I needed ultimate room. That's why I needed you out from here". "Ok, man" I said. "But, don't get pissed at me if I splatter paint on you". "I don't give a fuck about that, Ronnie" he boasted. "I'm high as a kite now. And. I got fucking paint all over me anyway". I painted the logo starting from the center and was careful to stay in the lines. Howie was watching me intently. I felt like he was a teacher making sure I was doing it right in a coloring book. "That's it, Ronnie" he said. "Just stay inside the lines, bro. And, it'll be prefect". Brian wasn't saying much and was mentioning how he was looking at the stars. "Howie thought it was funny and was laughing at him. "I"d see stars too little brother. Ronnie's Thai stick stars. We're all seeing stars tonight. "Right, bro?" he asked. I was so encompassed in my painting, that I was only half listening to them "Stars" I mumbled. "Yeah, We're all gonna be stars". After we were finished, we dropped down to the ground and examined our work. "It's a master piece!" Howie yelled. "A goddamn master piece!" "It's pretty cool" I replied. "That thing is huge" Brian said. "Everybody"s gonna see it". "That's the point, man" Howie laughed. "Everybody should see it". As Howie was packing up the ladder and turning it sideways for its trip back home, I noticed that there was some paint left in the can. "Can I use the rest of that paint Howie?" I asked, "Or, are you taking that with you as well?" "Why?" he asked. "Do you wanna do your own thingy?" "Yeah" I said "I wanna do an Aerosmith and a Blue Oyster Cult one". "That Aerosmith logo is pretty ornate, bro" he replied. "I don't think we have enough paint left and time to do that. But fuck it though, man. Just do it in regular letters. If you spark up some more of that Thai stick, Brian and I will watch out for you" "Ok, man" I said. "But, I'm not going back up there to do anything. There's no room left anyway and the Yes one took up the entire wall. So, I'm gonna do it at ground level instead". "Sounds good" Brian replied "But, like Howie said, can you pass around another bone first?" "Yeah, I guess I can do that" I said. I twisted up a fresh one, took one hit, and let them smoke the rest. I didn't really need any more as I was already quite inebriated anyway. I did the Aerosmith logo first, and accompanied it with a BOC logo on the right. When I was done, the 3 of us stood back and took a long, final look. "The school's gonna be pissed about this one" Howie bragged. "But, you'll be able to see it from real far away. Good job fellows" he said. "We did our perfect Picasso". Many years after our artistic endeavor, our artwork was still there. I would pass it from time to time until the late 1980's. I used to embellish thinking of the administration's embarrassment trying to explain to students and to the parents of how it might have gotten there. The talk around town was that most people knew it was us and that we were the main criminal offenders. But alas, they could never secure enough proof to arrest us. Without witnesses, it was all here say. Sadly one day, the school district had the entire thing sandblasted into oblivion. I didn't mind though. It was all for teenaged Edison and lasted a decade. "It's all good" I thought "Until, the next time".

On a clear crisp morning Ronnie E. and I were standing in the senior parking lot smoking cigarettes. "What's going on with you for the rest of the day?" I asked. "Nothing much" he replied. "Just, tennis anyone?" he said "Tennis anyone?" I asked. "What the fuck is that?" "You know those tennis courts in the back of the school behind the track?" he asked. "That's where we have tennis anyone" he laughed. "It's my favorite class of the day". "How did you get that class?" I asked. "They won't give it to me". "You just have to refuse regular gym" he replied. "I told them tennis, or nothing". "Wow" I said. "I have to try that scam". As I was finishing my last drag of my cigarette, I spied a figure past a few rows of parked cars in front of us. He was bobbing and weaving back and forth. It looked like a person doing surveillance. Since we weren't supposed to be outside, we figured it was a teacher trying to snag us and report us to the office. As he popped up from behind a bumper we could see it was one of the vice principals named Mr. Poskaitis and he was trying to catch us violating the rules again. Ronnie whispered "Let's fuck with this asshole. We'll play cat and mouse with him. It'll be funny as fuck. Are you in?" "Yeah, I'm in" I said. "Let's give this clown a run for his money". We crouched down so he couldn't see us and peered under the cars. We were able to see his feet shuffling from one position to another. Ronnie began laughing "This shit is easy, peasey" he said "His socks don't match and they're bright as fuck. What a dumb ass. All we have to do is track him". As we tried to contain our laughter, it became a game similar to Whack a Mole. We'd pop up our heads, Poskaitis would see us for a brief second, and He'd retreat back down again like in a hole. He'd reciprocate and we'd do the same. He would move up an aisle thinking he was getting closer to catching us, find nothing, and go back again. It went on for about a half an hour. Ronnie and I kept whispering "Oops, there he is. Go this way. Nope go back. Shit, there he is again". Every time he would go to the rear of a vehicle, we'd dodge him and go to the front. It was great fun to tease this guy that we couldn't stand. After his obvious frustration of not being able to capture us, he began to plead "I know who you guys are" he yelled. "Even if I don't catch you, I know your names. So, you're going to be suspended anyway. You might as well come out and surrender yourselves". "Mah huh" Ronnie screamed back "You'll never catch us asshole, don't try to be slick. You'll get tired soon anyway because you're old. Then, We'll win". "You won't win anything" Poskaitis replied. "Except a 3-day suspension". "Good" I yelled back "I just love vacations. They're everything I've always wanted, you know?" Ronnie motioned for me to come closer. "This is what We're gonna do" he whispered. "The next time this jerkoff sticks up his head, We're gonna throw dirt bombs at him. I bet he'll leave us alone after that?" he laughed. "You think it'll work?" I asked. "It should" he replied. "But, if it doesn't, We'll have the satisfaction of knowing we won't have to come back for 3 days".

We gathered up a few balls of compressed dirt from the ground and waited. When Poskaitis made the mistake of standing up too long, we let him have it. Our missiles didn't connect but came very close to him. We could see clouds of dirt when they hit emanating from the nose of a car that he was attempting to hide behind. With our next volley, he made a bee line for a side door. Like the coward that he was, he didn't say anything or make any threatening movements. He simply ran away. "What a pussy" Ronnie exclaimed. "He talks so much bullshit and leaves. "You know

We're fucked because of this right?" I asked. "Yeah" Ronnie replied. "But, who gives a fuck, its only school".

The next day Ronnie and I were in the breezeway enjoying a few cigarettes and engaging in some socialization. Fortunately, smoking by the students was allowed in the 1970's. Suddenly, we heard our names ring out over the loud speaker "Ronnie E. and Ronnie A., please report to the vice principals office immediately". I turned to Ronnie "You know what this is about, right?" I asked. "Yeah" he replied "Our dirt bomb attack from yesterday". "Do you think we should go see him?" I asked. "He's just gonna send us home anyway". "Fuck him" Ronnie said. "Let's go see what this asshole has to say. It'll be fun. It can't be any worse than the trouble We're in already". "True" I replied. "Let's go". We treaded down the hallway and discussed all possible scenarios. "Should we admit it was us?" I asked. "Nah" Ronnie replied "Never admit anything man. Make them work for it". Upon entering the vice principals office, we were confronted by worried Mr. Moretti. For some reason, they always had 2 vice principals. No one ever explained this to anyone or the reason why. We just thought it was just the way it was. It wasn't important to us to question it. So, we never did. We called him worried Moretti because he always had a worried look on his face and always appeared as if he was about to be fired. I thought it was unusual that he had a unique writing as well. His hands always shook very violently that forced him to have to write with a ruler. As he put pen to paper he could never keep them quite steady enough to finish. Later on, I was told it was due to his severe alcoholism. But on this day, he said, "I won't be the one seeing you. That would fall to Mr. Poskaitis. So, have seat gentlemen. Mr. Poskaitis will be with you shortly". It didn't take long until Poskaitis showed up. "I have letters for the both of you" he said. "You are to give them to your parents as soon as you return home". "What are they for?" Ronnie asked. "You know what they are" Poskaitis replied. "You're both getting 4 days suspension instead of 3. I saw you both yesterday. You weren't fooling anyone"

"Fooling anyone?" I asked "The only fool is you. You have a case of mistaken identity". "Regardless" he warned "You're both being suspended effective immediately". He handed us our letters and I stuffed mine in my pocket. Ronnie wasn't so impressed. "Now, now Mr. Po" he said. "Before I give this to my parents, I have to inspect it first. I don't trust what you may have written in here. I have to make sure it's correct and official". He grabbed the corner of the envelope, ripped it open, pulled out the paper and started reading it. "Hmmmm, let me see here" he exclaimed. "No, no, and no" he said. "Well Mr. Po, we have a problem here." he said. "What is that?" Poskaitis asked. "It doesn't seem like this is warranted enough for you to suspend us. Therefore, Arold and I fully reject your reasons for such suspensions." He turned to me and asked "Isn't that right, Ron?" He handed me the letter and I scanned it quickly. "I must say Mr. Po" I replied. "Ronnie here may be right. It doesn't seem like you have any clear evidence here against us". "See Mr. Po?" Ronnie asked "You don't have any witnesses to attest to the fact of what you"ve accused us of. So, We're not gonna accept this and We'll see you tomorrow." I was trying not to cry as I was laughing so hard. "Give me your letter" Ronnie asked. I took it out of my pocket and handed it to him. "What do you need mine for?" I asked. "It's going in the garbage with mine he said. "There's no proof. So, in the can they go. He dropped the letters in, leaned over PoskaitiS's desk, looked him squarely in the eye, and said "I don't think so". "Are you threatening me?" Poskaitis asked "No, I'm telling you" Ronnie said. Mr. Poskaitis became enraged. He stood up from his desk and started shouting "Call the police, Call the police. I want these 2 hoodlums off school property immediately! If you 2 refuse to leave, I'm having you arrested!" Ronnie turned around, laughed and said "He's bluffing man. We'll see you tomorrow Frank. Have a nice day". As we were leaving the office, I asked Ronnie if he thought Poskaitis was really gonna call the cops. "Nah, he won't do that" he said. Don't worry about it, man. He's a bullshitter like all the rest". We walked to the front of the building intending on having another smoke. Just as we rounded the corner by the cafeteria, we could see a police cruiser entering the school's driveway. "I guess he was serious this time" I said. "I guess so" Ronnie replied. "Fucking Poskaitis, he finally got a pair of balls!"

After our suspensions we were back in Miss Godynyk"s class. It was raining outside and we were bored. Ronnie mentioned that he was hungry. Suddenly, Miss Godynyk made a suggestion. "Why not take my car?" she asked. "I have a Datsun B 210. Here are the keys. Go and get pizza and come tight back". The only one of us who had a license was Ronnie. He had just turned 17 and was more than eligible. "I'll take those keys" he laughed. "You stay with her Arold". "Joey and I are going to get the pizza" he said. "We'll be back as soon as We're done". As I doodled some artwork to pass the time, an hour and a half had passed. "Miss Godynyk was starting to get nervous. "Why have they been gone so long?" she asked. "I dunno" I replied. "Maybe they stopped at the store or something?" Ronnie finally appeared at the door with Joey trailing behind him. He laid a box of pizza on a desk adjacent to my right. "Pizza baby" Ronnie exclaimed. "Pure, unadulterated pizza". "Where did you go?" Miss Godynyk asked. "We went for a spin" Ronnie replied. "Why do you care anyway?" he asked. "We have premium pizza. Don't worry about what We're doing. Worry about the pizza". "You don't understand, Ronnie" she cried "I can get fired for letting you use my car". "No one saw us" Ronnie replied. "So, stop crying. We met up with some girls, and then went to get cigarettes. That's why it took us so long. Now, do you want the pizza or not?" he asked. "Yes, it is nice that you brought back food" she said. "But, I don't think I'll be letting you use my car again. You took way too long and you shouldn't have stopped at a store. You were supposed to come directly back here with no side trips. Now, I have to worry about my job because of you". "Well, here"s your keys back" he said. "And, don't ever ask me to do you a favor again. The next time, drive your lazy ass there yourself. I'm eating my slices and I'm out of here for the day". "If you leave" she warned "I'll have to report you to the office". "As if I care" he chuckled. "Coming here is just to break the boredom when there's nothing else to do, or to meet up with our friends who want to cut class." "You got that right" Joey laughed. "I don't know anybody who comes here voluntarily". "Well, since I'm not part of this" I said "I'm just gonna feast on my share and be done with it". Ronnie turned to me and said "Joey is coming with me when I go. Are you gonna come with us?" he asked. "Or, are you gonna wimp out and hang out here with her angry ass?" "If all of you leave, I won't have a class to teach" Miss Godynyk said. "Teach?" Ronnie laughed. "You don't teach shit. You get paid to babysit us. So, you're only fooling yourself if you think that. You don't understand that none of us give a fuck. We've been in classes like this so long, we gave up. So, go ahead and report us, We'll just laugh at them like we always do. Suspensions are just official vacations for us". "I guess I could use another few days off" I chuckled. "So, I'll be coming with you guys after all.

Another Saturday night and I was at the Gulotta"s. Dennis and I were wondering what to do when he mentioned he was hungry. "Well then, cook something up, Den" I said. He opened his fridge and made a scowl on his face. "There's nothing in here but old milk and some moldy cheese" he replied. "Try the freezer, bro" I said. "There's gotta be something in there, no?" He closed the bottom half and opened the top. Peering inside, he pushed an ice tray aside and exclaimed "Fuck, there's nothing in here either. All I see are icicles hanging down from inside. "What are you gonna do then, Den?" I asked. "There's gotta be something you can scarf?" "I have an idea" he said. Remember when my brother JR stole those eggrolls with Pyka from the Jade?" "Yeah, so?" I asked. "Let's go there and see if they left anything to cool by the door again" he said. "They're cooking all the time there, bro. We're bound to get lucky and find something good. My stomach is gurgling. So, let's go get some food". "You think We'll find anything?" I asked. "Because, I don't feel like going there for nothing". "Come and help me out" he begged. "I can't do this shit alone. Besides, your one of the only ones who can run as fast as I can. It'll be cake man. We'll grab something and run through Raritan Oil, go through the trailer park, and right back to my house. It'll be so quick; I guarantee nobody will see us". "Ok" I said. "But if anybody spots us or We're chased, I'm dropping it". "That's fair" he said. "But, I don't think anything"s gonna happen, man"

We strode over to the back of the Jade Pagoda and surveyed our surroundings to be sure. We could clearly hear food workers speaking in their native Chinese. "Look , Ron" Dennis whispered. "The back door is open". We could see through the breach as the door was propped ajar leaving only the screen door exposed. "You smell that?" Dennis asked. "They're cooking everything in there tonight" he gasped. As we grew closer, we could see short Chinese men scurrying back and forth preparing and cooking dishes. "It smells delicious, Den" I muttered. "But, how are we gonna get anything out of there?" I asked. "JR told me to look for the racks with wheels on the left hand side. They have shelves with trays in them. That's how they scarfed those eggrolls, bro." unexpectedly, a worker shot past us close to the door. So, we ducked out of sight of his view. When he was gone, we slowly moved back in again. Like raccoons lurking behind a telephone pole, we peeked along the edge of the screen door. I pointed to my left and asked whispering "Is that the rack, Den? It looks like there's something on one of those shelves. But, there's tablecloths over it." "I think they always cover the trays" Dennis said. "It probably keeps the bugs off while it's cooling" "That makes sense" I exclaimed. "But, we need to take a peek first" "Fuck peeking under that" he mumbled "Let's just grab a tray and split. We can see what's underneath it later. It's too dangerous to pussyfoot around trying to see what's under it right now. If we hang around too long, They'll see us. We need to quietly open the screen door, tip toe over to the rack, grab that shit and run, man". "So, what's the plan?" he asked. "Do you feel like running?

Or, holding the door?" "I like to run" I replied. "So, you hold it open" "Ok" he said. "I'm gonna pull it open like a thief in the night. Make sure you're real quiet when you step inside though. It's only like 3 steps to the left. I'll keep it open until I see you run past me, then I'll let go and We'll run together, capiche?" "Whenever you're ready, man" I replied. "Just be careful" "Careful as a church mouse at confession" he laughed. "Now, let's go".

When the workers were far enough away that we felt no danger of being caught, we executed our scheme. "They're all the way down on the far end of the kitchen" I whispered. "Get the door". Dennis grabbed the handle gingerly with his right hand and gave it a soft pull. There was hardly any sound. In the background, we could still hear the Chinese cooks chatting away. They were speaking so loudly, it ended up being a good cover for us. Ever more gently, Dennis dragged at the door. When it was open far enough for an escape, I shuffled to a shelf on the rack. "Grab it, Ron" he whispered "Pull it out by its edges. It'll slide right out". I grasped at the tray and seized it with my hands. It was heavier than I anticipated. "Fuck" I mumbled "This damn thing weighs a ton". "Balance it against your gut" Dennis replied. "Once it's out the door, we got it". I felt like a weightlifter at a body building competition trying to distribute the poundage versus gravity. When I had made it outside, Dennis slowly put the screen door back in its place. Struggling, I was having a hard time balancing and attempting to run at the same time. "A little help here, bro" I cried. "Let me grab one end" Dennis said. "And, you can handle the other. "You think we can run like this?" I asked. "What other choice do we have?" he replied. "We can do it, if we don't run too fast" Looking back, there was no one by the door and it appeared we had escaped. I felt confident we were in the clear. After a couple of unsuccessful attempts, we decided we could only walk fast and that running was out of the question. Still, we wrangled with the tray and it's teetering through the paths back to DenniS's house.

When we got to DenniS's dining room, we laid the tray mildly on the table. "Let's unveil this shit" he laughed. "And, see what we've got". He pulled back the tablecloth and his eyes opened wide. "Ullllllllllhhhhh" he shouted. "Fuck yes! Absolute victory, bro. Fucking ribs man! 5 fucking racks of ribs! Ronnie, you're the fucking man bro!" Just then, his mother entered the room. "Dennis?" she asked. "Where did you get that food from?" "Ronnie stole it" he shrieked. "It's pork ribs, mom. The Chinese barbeque type ones". She leered at me and I thought I was in trouble. "Ronnie?" she asked "Did you steal those ribs?" "Why, yes" I replied. "Yes, I did". "You know Ronnie?" she asked "You shouldn't steal. But you steal with good taste. Let's eat!" I've been a favorite at their house ever since.

One early evening as I entered Thursday"s Place, there was a commotion just inside the back door. It seemed that Jackie Boy was in a verbal altercation with a guy named Brendan. Brendan had a speech impediment and was sometimes hard to understand as he had been partially deaf since birth. It turned out that Brendan had been picking on Jackie Boy for most of his life and tonight he was at it again. But now, Jackie Boy had turned 16 and had being working out and lifting weights. He was no longer a skinny target and had bulked up strong. Brendan wanted a quarter from Jackie Boy to play pinball. So, he grabbed Jackie boy by his ear "Gib me noney for bin ball" he demanded. Jackie Boy replied "I don't have any money. Fuck you, let go of me". Suddenly, the situation changed. Jackie Boy was no longer going to take beatings from him. "I'm fucking sick of you" he screamed. "So, get the fuck outside because I'm gonna beat your ass". "You ain't donna do dit" Brendan teased "I'll beat duh dit outta you". The door swung open and Jackie Boy was beckoning Brendan to come outside. "Take your first swing" he demanded. "I'm older now. So, let's see what you"ve got". Brendan lunged at him and attempted a right hook. Jackie Boy danced back and Brendan missed terribly. "Dand dill" Brendan said. "Dop moving away fum me". He grabbed Jackie Boy around his waist and they tumbled to the ground. After a slight scuffle, Brendan was able to right himself and gave Jackie Boy a punch to the face. Jackie Boy became furious. He jumped up and plucked a tree branch next to a dumpster from the dirt that had been lying there while they were fighting. He wielded it over his head as Brendan came back returning for another attack. Brendan lunged at Jackie boy again. Jackie Boy swung the branch down hard and connected squarely on Brendan"s back. Brendan let out a sound like someone had just had their wind knocked out of them and was lying motionless on the ground. "I gib up, I gib up Dacky Boy" he cried. "That will teach you to never fuck with me again" Jackie Boy exclaimed triumphantly. We all patted him on the back, congratulated him, and went inside to buy him a soda.

It must have been a strange moon that night as there were many odd things going on in the course of a few hours. After Jackie Boy's victory celebration at the counter of the luncheonette, I wandered to the back by the bank of pinball machines. I saw Phil standing there laughing. "What's so funny?" I asked. "Look down behind the bannister" he said. "George T. is at it again". George T. had lived not too far from me and had been in and out of jail since the age of 11. I had hung around with him a few times but he was 5 years older than me. He was living in his sister's basement and making no attempts to straighten out his life. It was if he enjoyed his life of crime and just didn't care. He was all about making short term, easy money whenever possible. He was a pretty good fighter for a lean guy and had no qualms about defending himself. He was another character who had a unique saying. When he became irate, he liked to launch hard items at people. His signature oratory was his phrase "Gimme a rock, any rock". He also spoke with an accent as if he was speaking like James Cagney. I found it to be very entertaining.

I leaned over with my head facing the floor below and there was George T. He was on his back with his feet propped up against a crowbar jammed into the coin door of one of the pinball machines.

He was trying desperately to pry open the door. I laughed and asked him what he was doing. With his James Cagney voice he said "I'm getting some coin, see. If you don't wanna be my lookout, get lost. I'm busy here". I left him to his crime and went back outside. I saw a guy talking to someone I didn't recognize who was walking with a cane. He went inside and I stood there with a few others smoking a cigarette. Out of the blue, a guy named George the Greek showed up and started asking a lot of questions. "Where is he?" he shouted. "Where is who?" I replied. "That pussy, Ted" he demanded. "Oh, he's inside" someone said. "He just went in there". We watched as he ripped open the door and ran up toward the front past the pinball machines. A few seconds later, he emerged grabbing Ted by his throat. "I'm gonna beat the fuck out of you" he said. "And, I don't give 2 shits if you're a cripple or not". George the Greek tore into him. Ted immediately headed for the ground covering up his head with his hands and was trying to protect himself. I guess he knew more was coming. George the Greek began to kick him fiercely. "You mother fucker" he screamed. "You think you can pay someone to protect your ass from me?" he asked. With each kick Ted winced and let out a yell. "Please, please!" he begged. "It's all a misunderstanding" "Misunderstanding my ass!" George the Greek replied. "Where"s your fucking savior now?" he asked. "Bring him, and I'll beat his ass too".

Just as George the Greek was taking his final blows, a guy everyone knew named Bruce V. arrived. Bruce V. had a reputation of being a local tough guy and had spent much time in the county jail. One reason for his intimidating image was his callousness regarding a woman"s life after an accident he once had. An elderly woman had been once on the telephone in the front of her house at 3 a.m. It seemed that Bruce had lost control of his vehicle and crashed through the woman"s wall killing her instantly. When asked about the occurrence, he had no remorse and simply stated "Too bad for her. The bitch shouldn't have been on the phone that late". Hence, the reason most of us were afraid of him. He had just rounded the corner and was yelling asking "What the fuck is this about? This guy Ted is a friend of mine. Leave him alone or you're gonna have to deal with me". "Deal with you?" George the Greek asked. "I can deal with punks like you with one hand tied behind my back". "Oh really?" Bruce asked. "Don't you know who the fuck I am? "I don't give 2 fucks who you are douchbag" George the Greek said. "I'm gonna keep beating this creeps ass until I feel satisfied". "You'll have to go through me then" Bruce threatened. "And, I don't think you're gonna like the outcome". "Say where and when?" George the Greek asked. "I'm ready when you are". "How about now?" Bruce asked. "But, we have to go behind TJ because I'm on parole" "We can do that" George the Greek replied. "Meet me there in 20 minutes".

"A fight, a fight!" everyone screamed. "There's gonna be a big fight behind TJ!" Bruce had left first with a couple of friends trailing behind him. A few minutes later, George the Greek followed. It seemed that George the Greek had more supporters than Bruce did. I think because no one liked Ted at the time. There were about 15 of us kids in a semi-circle facing one of TJ"s back doors. Inside was Bruce and George the Greek. They were facing each other. "Take your best shot" Bruce exclaimed. "I'm ready". George the Greek said. George the Greek threw a punch but missed. Bruce spun around and reciprocated. But, Bruce"s attempt made its mark. George the Greek went reeling to the grass with Bruce towering over him. "Fuck with me now, huh?" he asked screaming. "I bet you didn't see that coming?" George the Greek"s face became crimson red and he looked like a bull being teased by a matador. Suddenly, we could hear heavy breathing coming out of his nose. He didn't say a word. He jumped up, tackled Bruce to the ground, and began pummeling him with his fists. He was connecting to Bruce"s head blow after blow. Bruce was obviously beginning to lose. "Time out, time out" Bruce yelled. "Let me stand up, man". Bruce"s face appeared as if he had seen stars. He looked out of it and confused. "He snuffed me, man" he screamed. "He snuffed me". "I didn't snuff shit" George the Greek" replied. "You just can't fight anymore". Stumbling, Bruce pulled out a knife. "I'll teach you to snuff people mother fucker" he shrieked. One of Bruce"s friends I recognized as John P. grabbed Bruce V by his arm. "You don't want any of that shit" he said. "You're always in trouble for small bids. Don't be an asshole and make this a lifetime achievement award". Bruce began to calm down. "Maybe you're right, man" he said in a conciliatory tone. "I think I'm getting too old for this shit". To everyone"s surprise, Bruce extended his hand and proclaimed "George, you won man. Fuck it, let's just be friends. I'll tell you the story about Ted and We'll deal with him later". George the Greek shook his hand, smiled, and we all went back to Thursday"s to celebrate".

Brendan Byrne was our governor and was supported by the Edison Democratic Party. To gain voter support, the Democratic Party liked to have barbeques once a year. My friends and I called them "bribes". But, the food and drinks were free, so we'd always attend and pretended that we cared. They were usually held at the old Mirror Lake Swim Club adjacent to Raritan Center. Mirror Lake was nothing more than an abandoned rock quarry that was filled with water and had a beach manufactured specifically for it. I remembered it due to my parents having once had memberships there and recalled how I thought even then that it was antiquated and run down. On a scheduled day for one of these galas, Jeffrey G, his brother Dennis, Phil, and I were munching on some subway sandwiches at the Tastee sub shop on Plainfield Avenue. Phil had seen the flier about the picnic and asked us if we wanted to go. "Everybody"s gonna be there" he said. "There's gonna be free food and shit. We can sneak in through the back way off of Meadow Rd. Everyone I know does it and no one"s ever been caught." "Let's go swimming first" Jeffrey suggested. "We can't go swimming without paying for a badge" I said in between bites of my sandwich. "That part doesn't come with the deal if we sneak in, bro. And besides, you can't really swim anyway, remember?" "I'm not talking about Mirror Lake" he replied. "You know where Hidden Lake is right?" he asked. "Yeah, the one with the rusted out crane in the middle everybody jumps off of. "Exactomundo" Dennis added. "We've been there before Ron, remember?" "Yeah, I think so" I said. "But, we only went there once. "That's right" he replied. "But, Jeffrey wasn't with us the last time. So, I think it's a good idea. We can go right to the picnic afterward". "What do the rest of you guys think?" he asked. "Should we go to the party first? Or, swimming?" "I think we should all go swimming first" Phil suggested. "It's gonna be hot as balls out today. That way, we can all stay cooled off until later in the afternoon. Plus, We're eating now. We'll all be hungry later again anyway". "Phil"s corrcct" Dennis said. "So, I think we should all do what Phil says". Everyone agreed. We finished our meal and started walking.

After a long journey over old railroad tracks and small mountains of dirt, we arrived at Hidden Lake. We were slightly exhausted from the heat and sat down to take a rest and to rejuvenate ourselves. In the distance, we could see that the rusted out crane was still there. "Hey, Den?" I asked "How long do you think that thing"s been sitting there?" "I dunno bro, maybe since the 1920"s. "I've seen pictures of cranes that look like that in magazines" he said. "All I know is, when you dive off that fucking thing, watch you don't cut yourself man. Because, you might get tetanus. That shit can give you lock jaw. Fuck that noise". "I'll be sure to be extra careful" I laughed. "But, you better watch out for Jeff. He's kind of little and he's never been here before. The last time I attempted to swim with him, he almost drowned my ass" "I can handle myself" Jeffrey claimed. "You just worry about yourself, man. And, the last time wasn't my fault, jerkoff. Ronnie E. let go of me. So, blame him." "Spoken like a true Gulotta" Phil replied. "Don't let anybody fuck with you. You tell them Jeff" "You're only saying that cause you're short like him" I laughed. "All you little fuckers stick together"

"We have to" Jeff said. "Because we have assholes like you guys always picking on us". "He's got chutzpah" Dennis chortled. "I'll give him that. He'll stay on the shore though. But, enough of this chit chat bullshit. Let's get in the water and swim. I'm sweating my balls off!"

Dennis, Phil, and I swam out to the crane and pulled ourselves up while Jeffrey observed from the shore. It was orange in color and looked like a beat up erector set that was purposely left to die. "This thing has sure seen better days" Dennis said. "Watch your hands when you climb up, man. This steel is so brittle; it flakes off in my hand. This orange shit is hard to get off too". "I'm climbing up to the top where the bucket is" Phil exclaimed. "It's the highest point to dive off of". "Be careful, Phil" Dennis warned. "There's empty 55 gallon drums submerged in that water. If you hit one hard, you'll bleed out fast. And, there's no phone around here to call an ambulance. We won't be able to save you." "I'll be all right" Phil replied. "I think I can handle it". Phil dove off the scuttle into the light blue water below. Like parts on a conveyor belt, we followed right behind him. Fortunately we suffered no injuries. In between jumps, I saw that Jeffrey was playing in the sand. Suddenly, he started waving to us but we couldn't make out what he was saying. He's was yelling something brutally in a panic. "What the fuck is he doing?" Phil asked. "I dunno" Dennis replied. "He's always pestering me with something. But, we better swim back and check on him just to make sure." As we swam closer we could hear him screaming "I'm stuck" he howled. "I'm stuck in this pussy mud! Help me; I can't pull my legs out!" "Pussy mud?" I asked laughing. "What the hell is pussy mud, Jeff?" "Worry about that later, asshole" he screamed. "Just get me the fuck out of here". I gazed down where his feet were supposed to be and could see that he was entrenched up to his ankles. "Every time I try to pull my legs out" he cried. "The suction won't let me go and it keeps holding me down". He was beginning to have terror in his voice. "Dennis, get me out of here now" he demanded. "There's 3 of you. So, there's no reason why you guys can't get me out of here". "I dunno" Dennis laughed. "That shit looks like quicksand. We're gonna have to really grab onto you for this one". "You better try Dennis" Jeff yelled. "Ok, Jeff" Dennis said. "Me and the boys will give it a try". "Grab his waist, Ron" Dennis instructed. "And, me and Phil will pull on his legs. That should be able to get him out nice and quick". I extended my arms around Jeff and locked my hands together waiting while Phil had his left calf, and Dennis had his right. "Are you guys ready?" Dennis asked. "Pull!" Soon, Jeffrey"s legs began to move and we heard a sucking sound as we rocked him back and forth. When we had almost gotten him to where we could see the top of his feet, he toppled over and fell in again. "Pull fucking harder" Jeff yelled. "It's hard suction and you have to try more." "Wiggle your toes as we pull on you" Dennis said. "It might release the water that keeps rushing back in. "Ok" Jeff replied. "But, it feels disgusting" "Are you worried about getting out?" I asked. "Or, are you worried about how it feels?" "Shut the fuck up, Arold" Jeff yelled. "And, worry about getting me the fuck out of here" Dennis counted to 3 and we tried again. With some more severe pulling and rocking back and forth, we released him. "It's about time" Jeff screamed. "I thought I was gonna be stuck in there forever" "Forever is a long time, bro" Dennis laughed. "Just be lucky you weren't here alone. You guys see why he can't go any place by himself?" he asked "Because he always gets into trouble". "No I don't" Jeff chastised. "It's not my fault its fucking pussy mud". "Just exactly what is that stuff Jeff?" I laughed. "You were screaming that before. What do you mean by pussy mud?" "You see how it's all gooey and wet once it pulls you down?" he asked "Well to me, it sounds like a pussy when it's being fucked. So, from now on, it's pussy mud". We all got a great laugh out of Jeff's description and couldn't believe how he had come up with it. After we were all sufficiently recuperated, Dennis suggested that Jeff clean off his legs. "You better wash off your legs before we leave" he laughed. "Or else you might smell like dried pussy on the way home".

We waited for Jeff to finish and we were off to the Democratic fiesta. On the way there, we ran into a kid I knew named Kevin. He was leaning into a car and chatting with the driver about sneaking to get in. The driver saw us approach and greeted us. I didn't recognize him nor the other occupants of his vehicle. "How"s it going guys?" he asked. "Fine" we said. "Are you trying to get in too? I asked. "Yeah" he replied. But, Kevin here was asking me for a ride down the dirt road. As you can see, my car is full up. But, you guys can lie on the top of the car and hang onto the sunroof if you want. I'll try not to go too fast". "This guy is cool" Kevin said. "You don't have to worry about him, he'll drive slow. He promised me". "Sounds good to me" I said. "What do the rest of you guys think?" I asked. "You want to hop up there so we don't have to take that long assed walk?" "Yeah, that sounds kosher to me" Dennis replied. "Are you and Phil gonna come with us?" he asked Jeff. "Yeah, We'll go" Jeff said. I just hope none of us fall off of that thing". "It'll be ok" the driver assured us. "So, climb on up. Just make sure you hold on real tight, ok?"

It wasn't the best of configurations to grapple with the sun roof by any means. But, we gave it our best try. "Hold on" the driver insisted as he hit the accelerator. "We're gonna move now!" At first he was travelling at a reasonable speed until he hit a few bumps and began to fishtail. It was obvious that he had bogged down and was attempting to get out of a hole. He rocked the car forward and it fishtailed again. But this time it was more violent and we felt like spaghetti noodles whipping in the air. With each turn of the car, we'd fly left and right while struggling to hold on. Abruptly, I saw Kevin lose his grip and sail tumbling to the ground. I remember thinking "Shit, this asshole is going faster than he said he would. I hope Kevin is all right". I yelled for the driver to stop. "Hey man, Kevin just flew off the back of the car. I think you better stop and go back for him." "I'm not stopping now" he said. "We're almost there. If you wanna go back for him, go ahead. But, I'm parking and going inside". As the vehicle came to a halt, we all jumped off to the ground. I laid into the driver and told him how much of a dick he was and that my friend may have been hurt. He didn't seem to care. "What the fuck do you want me to do?" he asked. My car was caught in a hole. If I didn't speed up, we would have gotten stuck. I'm sorry for your friend, but that's just the way it is" I called him a scumbag and I walked away. "You guys go ahead in" I said. "I'll catch up to you later". "Are you sure?" Jeff asked. "I don't want to just leave him there" I said. "I know him the best out of all of us. And, he lives by me. So, I'll take care of it" "Ok, man" Dennis replied "We'll see you inside then". I turned around and ran back to Kevin who was lying on the ground rolled up in a ball. It was obvious he was in pain. He was grasping at his right arm and yelling. "He broke my fucking arm, man. That asshole broke my fucking arm. He drove too fast after he told me he wouldn't. That guy's a fucking asshole". I tried to calm him down. "Right now, I think you need to go to the hospital" I said. "Can you walk?" I asked. "Yeah, I can walk" he said. "Thanks for coming back for me when nobody else gave a fuck" "Well, I've known you the longest. So, I thought I should help you out. Let's see if we can get you to the back gate. I'll sneak you in and call an ambulance, ok?" "Yeah, let's do that" he replied "Because, I think the picnic for me is over". I got ahold of someone of authority and informed them of what happened. I waited with Kevin until some help had arrived. "Thanks man" he said "Thanks for staying with me, man. I guess I have to put this in a cast now. So, I'll see you later on". "I hope you feel better" I said. "Tell them to give you some painkillers. That should take the edge off for few days". Before they closed to door of the ambulance, I waved goodbye and turned back to my find my other friends. I felt bad but there was nothing else I could do.

I searched around for their familiar faces and spied Jeffrey with a hotdog in his hand. Phil and Dennis were next to him munching on some hamburgers. "Is your friend ok, man?" Dennis asked. "Yeah, he'll be ok" I replied. "I think he broke his wrist. So, he'll be out of commission for a while." That sucks" said Phil. "But, it's not like he didn't know the risks by hanging on the car like that" "True" I said "But, that asshole guy is part at fault for going too fast". "We'll, there's nothing we can do about it now" Phil replied. "So, we might as well try to enjoy the rest of the day. It could have been much worse for him". "Yeah, I guess you're right." I said. "But, I still feel bad for him". "Have some free food" Jeff advised "It'll take your mind off of it". I grabbed a few burgers and fries and was walking over to the condiments table when I saw Dennis and Jeffrey"s brother JR doing the conga in a line. There was a middle aged guy out in the front with 2 bodyguard looking men on each side of him. As they got closer, I saw that it was the governor Brendan Byrne himself. People were walking behind trying to speak to him while taking pictures and asking for autographs. For some reason, JR and his friends were dancing in the rear. He was smiling and waving us over. "Come on" Dennis said. "Let's go over and see what he wants". As we approached, JR motioned for us to join him and said "Watch this!" Suddenly, he and his small group started yelling "Legalize pot, legalize coke. Legalize pot, legalize dope". We thought it was funny and joined in right away. The chant only lasted a short time and was maybe 5 minutes at most. It seemed the governor"s body guards had heard us and felt embarrassed. We saw them point to the NJ state police. They ordered them with hand signals to disperse us. Quickly, they sprinted over and surrounded us. "Get the fuck out of the line right now you little ingrates" one of them demanded. "Were only going to ask you once" he said. "If your little asses don't comply, you'll face severe consequences. This is the governor of NJ and we won't have it. You will learn respect or we will show you how". We all knew what their "respect" meant from previous altercations with the police. When they spoke to you like that, it only had one meaning. "A beating". Therefore, we broke out of line fully expecting to return to the festivities. Not a chance. We were rounded up like prisoners fleeing the Gestapo. "You are banned from any more Democratic barbeques or parties here from this day forward" we were told. We were escorted to the back gate and turned around, banished from celebrating there ever again.

On the radio, there had been many announcements of a custom van show at Englishtown"s Raceway Park. I hadn't been there before, but my older brother had spoken about it many times. He was what we called a motor head. He and his friends were always somehow repairing, customizing, or building various hot rods from street cars the best that they knew how. It was all about power and speed with them. There were days where I saw them hoist an engine on a chain using the crux of a tree, and install it in a car such as a Chevelle or a Camaro. I guess they lacked funds for rental of a cherry picker I had supposed. Some of these cars even had names. They were usually emblazoned on their tail ends or the back panels and had such names as The Golden Komotion, If You Can Beat Me, You Can Eat Me, Thrill Seeker, etc. I listened to long conversations of technical car jargon mixed in with parts descriptions such as Thrush pipes, cherry bombs, wheelie bars, transmissions, Hurst straight shifters, dual quads, etc. I had a feeling about them similar to how I felt about being in a band. I wanted to be a rock star, and they wanted to be famous race car drivers.

Some of my friends who were older than me had recently acquired their driver"s licenses. Mickey had a white 72 box Nova that he had sold to tight Timmy G. Mickey ended up with a 72 Chevy van with a bed in the back, a round table made from a left over spool of wire, and on its opposing side, a short comfortable velvet chair. Vans were in vogue then and were very popular. A lot of them had ornate paintings on their sides that were airbrushed by local professionals. They looked like rolling living rooms and appeared very self-sustaining. Somehow, I had been in touch with tight Timmy and was invited to attend. The van show had camp sites, running water, toilets, naked girls, drugs, and booze. On the morning of our departure, Timmy called me and asked me what I could bring to contribute. "I have a Coleman cooler" I said. "As well as some end tables, and a flashlight or two". "Perfect" he chimed. "I'll be around to pick you up about 11 o"clock." We took the short drive up route 18 to Raceway Park"s entrance and paid the fee to get in. We drove around for a while until Timmy found a small plot of land as a camping spot. Right away I saw people that I knew. Billy F. was there, as well as Mickey and his van. Mickey had brought along Dennis G. and Phil for company. There was also DenniS's brother JR and his friend Pyka who like Billy had arrived in different vehicles. I stepped out of Timmy"s car to greet Billy and immediately realized I had made a big mistake. I had thought it would be cool to be the quintessential hippie and I would walk barefoot at the event. I didn't realize the ground at the park was either muddy, or had tiny jagged gravel as surface materials. I was forced to succumb to dirty caked feet, or walk on my tip toes to avoid annoying pointy rocks digging into my heels. I had no recourse to secure some shoes, so I was left to my own devices. Bravely, I had to maneuver around it to the best of my ability. As my friends watched, they got a kick out of the way I was forced to walk. With Billy tagging along, I told tight Timmy "I'm going to see who else is here, man. I'll be back in a little while". "I'll be here" Timmy said. "I have all the drinks and food we packed in the cooler. So, you can come and find me".

Billy and I approached Mickey"s van and they were all already laughing. "What's so funny?" Billy asked. "Check out Ron" Dennis said "He forgot to bring his shoes. He walks like a deer stepping over a creek". "It's those fucking stones" I replied. "I didn't know this shit was gonna be this sharp". "You're gonna have some sore assed feet when you go home" Phil laughed. "Why didn't you wear sneakers or something?" he asked. "I thought it would be cool to go barefoot" I replied. "Cool is painful" Mickey laughed. "I guess you'll learn the next time". We conversed for a while and passed around a joint or two. Billy announced "I'll be right back. I have something that's really cool. Wait till you see". "Ok" I said. "But, I hope it's something good". "Yeah" Phil replied "Bring us back some naked women and shit. "Uuuuullllhhh" Dennis shouted. "They go good with beer". "You'll like it" Billy chuckled. "Just wait until I get back". A short range of time passed and Billy returned. "What's that in your hand, bro?" Mickey asked. "It looks like a pipe or something". "It's a pipe bomb" Phil laughed. "Billy enjoys extreme violence" "Nah" Billy replied with a mischievous grin. "I don't like to hurt people. Just things like buildings and shit. "Billy the Kid" I blurted. "Always up to something". "If you guys must know" he laughed, "It's a blockbuster firework I brought along with me from home." "Isn't that a ¼ stick of dynamite?" I asked. "You bet your ass" he replied. "And, I'm gonna blow shit up with it". Where you gonna do this shit at?" Dennis asked Billy. "Well" Billy said. "There's a small grass field way in the back by the highway with a tall fence behind it. I figure nobody will see me light it off there. So, that's where I'm gonna shoot it off at. You guys are all welcome to join me to see it if you want". "Cool" Phil replied. "We're all coming with you". Billy gently set down his explosive, yelled to us "Step back" and lit the fuse. He galloped back to where we were and we waited for the boom. We heard the final fizzle of the fuse and a spark began to fly. It came from the top and then nothing. "What the fuck, Billy?" Dennis asked. "Is this thing a fucking dud or what?" "Just wait" Billy screamed "Just give it a fucking minute". Just as Billy turned back for another view, the device went off. "Kerrang!" it went with a large plume of smoke and sounded just as Billy had described. "That was cool as hell, Billy" I said. "You got any more?" "Not with me" he replied. "But, let's get outta here before somebody comes. It was really loud and echoed a lot. I don't feel like dealing with the cops today".

By now tight Timmy had joined us as we were roasting hot dogs and hamburgers on a campfire. It was dusk and about to get dark. "Did you see the parade of the vans coming down the avenue yet?" he asked. "I thought that doesn't start until after the nicest tits contest is over" Phil replied. "I don't think that contest started yet" I said. "We should all go down to the area where the stage is and see what's going on". "Is it time for that already?" Dennis asked. "I feel like we just got here". "That sounds cool to me" Mickey said. "There's never a bad time to see titties". We shuffled over to the entertainment area half stoned and slightly drunk. As we got closer, we could hear the MC over a loudspeaker announcing the winner of tonight"s best tits contest. "Damn" Mickey said "We got here too late. Now, we only get to see the winner"s titties". "But, she's got nice ones Mick" I said. "Some tits are better than no tits, right?" "I guess so" he replied. "But, they better have more entertainment than this bullshit". "Listen" Dennis said. "The MC just said this chick is gonna ride on the top of a van displaying her tits and smoking a joint. She's gonna be in the front as the first one in the van parade." "Move out of the way" Phil laughed "I gotta see this shit".

We jockeyed for position to get the best possible view and waited. Suddenly, we could hear various kinds of car horns blaring in the outskirts behind the stage. "Here they come" Mickey said. "It's a tittie parade!" Around the corner she came, standing on the roof of an expensive custom van with a joint the size of a football in her hand. "How about that?" the MC yelled. "It's a ¼ pounder!" In between small tokes of its end, the girl was waving and cajoling as they drove by. With each turn back, she appeared to be teasing us and wiggling her breasts in our direction. Between hoots, hollers, and cat calls, Billy chuckled "Man, look at the rack on her. Whoever gets her will need a lot of money". "You got that right" Dennis said. "None of those people will let any of us get anywhere near her". As we watched the procession of vans reach its peak, Dennis asked me "Hey Poco? What's the band that's supposed to play tonight?" "I think it's Nasty Lass" I replied. "But, I heard their singer is sick with a cold. So, I don't know how They'll sound tonight, man". "Fuck it" Dennis replied. "Let's hang here for a bit. We'll check them out and then find something else to do". The band came on and did a cover version of a Mott The Hoople song. I wasn't impressed. I knew the guitar player and they were usually pretty stellar. Unfortunately, on this night the singer was having trouble and was struggling. In the meantime, Billy had gone to the bathroom and heard some information on his way back. "There's a keg party with the people right next to your van Mickey" he said. "We should all go back now and see if we can join them". "Excellent" Mickey replied. "I can stay right by my van if I get too drunk".

Back at Mickey"s van, we became friendly with the neighbors. It seemed there was going to be a keg contest that was supposed to ensue. Their keg didn't have the usual spout that travelled down from its tap; but a rubber hose folded over for the competition. As they were taking names to join in, I stupidly volunteered. "What's the prize?" I asked. "Twenty bucks to whomever can keep their mouths on the hose and swallow beer the longest" one of them said. "We have a stopwatch with us. If you can beat everyone else"s time, you'll win. "Sounds easy" I said. "When do we start?" I asked. "You'll be going 2nd" I was told. "So, get ready. We're starting in about 5 minutes". "You can do it, Ron" Dennis said. "I've seen you piss, bro. "You must have a large stomach. I know because you have a big bladder and you always pee longer than anyone else. So, go for it man". "I'll see what I can do" I replied. "I've never done this before. I hope I can make it". The contest started and the first participant was on it. 5 seconds, 10 seconds, 15 and he was done. "You're up, buddy" I heard someone say. The guy in charge of the keg was motioning to me. "Are you ready?" he asked "As ready as I'll ever be" I replied. I bent over and took the bended rubber hose in my mouth. I took a deep breath and let it go. The liquid shot down my throat like a fire hose and I was amazed at the sheer force of its amplitude. Suddenly, I immediately felt the urge to puke. "Keep going, keep going" I heard people cheer. "You're at 30 seconds. Try to do more" they screamed. Along with them, I was also keeping time in my head. I was counting seconds going by with each forced gulp while beer was starting to shoot out of my nose. I heard "100 seconds" and I dropped to my knees. One of the keg people came over running. I thought it was to see if I was all right. I was wrong. They only wanted to make sure the hose was clamped over again. They didn't want to lose any beer for their subsequent victims and seemed like they didn't care.

After I was told to "get out of the way", I stood on my rickety feet and attempted to regain my composure. I was surprised how fast the alcohol had hit me and I was very intoxicated. So much so, I turned around to go back to the campsite adjacent to us and I began to spew. Like a reverse fire hose, beer was shooting out of my mouth and through both of my nostrils. I wasn't able to stop it and it refused to subside. I took a few steps, and it would shoot out again. Another few steps and it was the same. I was in alcoholic anguish. Finally, after about 4 or 5 episodes of this, I found a spot and laid down next to the campfire. There was a pillow I grabbed and I cradled it under my head. I passed out for what seemed like a short amount of time and when I awoke I looked up and saw 3 rotating DenniS's. His head was bobbing up and down over the fire and looked like revolving faces in a kaleidoscope. Each time I tried to raise my head, I couldn't regain by equilibrium. It felt as if I was on a ship and I was attempting to stand on its deck during a cyclone. Nearby, I could hear Dennis laughing "Hey, man" he said. "You didn't win the contest, bro. You puked it all up afterwards. So, they ain't giving you no money". I mumbled "I don't give a shit, Den. I'm really fucked up. I think it's best to just lie here for a while". "You do that, man" he said. "Maybe you should check out until later". I laid my head back down and passed out again. I awoke to a loud boom like a firecracker going off and felt a sharp sting under my left wrist. "Holy fuck" I heard someone yell. "Why the fuck did you do that to him?" they asked. "That's fucked up, man". I looked up and saw Jesse"s older brother Tom. He looked straight at me from Mickey"s van and said sarcastically "Fuck him, I was trying to get a BJ from this chick once at his house. He wouldn't let me use one of the bedrooms upstairs. So, I tried to get the chick to blow me in the basement. The chick wouldn't do it down there. So, she went home. He gets what he gets man, too fucking bad". I knew Tom was angry at me from the night he spoke of. But, I never figured he would do something like this and carry a grudge until 6 months later. If I would have known he was attending, I would have stayed home instead. After he received a verbal thrashing by festival goers telling him what he did was uncalled for, he disappeared into the night. I didn't see him again. I examined my wrist a second time and could see it was beginning to swell. It was also starting to blister badly. I was so drunk I didn't feel any pain. I wanted to sleep it off desperately. I fell back into a micro sleep and was jostled by Dennis. He was demanding the pillow. "That pillow"s mine, man" he said. "I need it to go to sleep in Mickey"s van. So, you'll have to get another one". I was too tired to fight him for it and released it. I was told later that I was lying in a pile of dirt. It was the drunkest I had ever been.

Morning came and the sun was coming up. To my surprise, I didn't have much of a hangover. I imagined it was due to up chucking up all the booze from the night before. I sighed and felt lucky to be alive. I peered around and saw all of the vans doors were closed. This was including Mickey"s. So, I imagined they were all asleep and I decided to take a walk to see what I could find. I had a dry mouth and was craving water and was looking for a source to drink from. I looked down at my hands, arms, and feet and discovered that I was filthy. My long hair was also matted in the back like a Rastafarian. "Jesus" I thought. "I must have been really, really fucked up last night". Coming up the path, I heard a voice behind me and I recognized it as tight Timmy right away. "There you are" he said. "I was wondering where you went last night, man. After we ate, you were supposed to come back to my car. You look like shit, bro. What the fuck happened to you? The back of your shirt looks like somebody lit it on fire with a lighter and shit. Part of its burned up too, man". I hadn't noticed it yet. But I guess Tom had tried to burn me by setting my shirt on fire too. "It's a long story, man" I said. "I think I got too fucked up. But, right now, I need some water". "We still have some soda and juice in the cooler" Timmy said. "But, the beer"s all gone, man". "Beer is the last thing on my mind, Tim" I replied. "Just lead the way". As we were walking back to his Nova, a guy in a row of tents called us over. "Hey, man" he said. "One of you looks like shit. You wanna get stoned for breakfast?" "Sure" I said. "It can't be any worse than how high I was last night". We took a couple of tokes, thanked the man, and proceeded to Timmy"s car. "You should stay here with me tonight and recuperate, man" he said. "Tomorrow morning it's over and we have to leave anyway. So, why don't you just go to sleep in my front seat?" he asked. "I'm gonna crash in the back with some chick I met here" he said. "You can rest that way and give your body a break". "That's a good idea" I replied. "I'm exhausted. Wake me in the morning".

The final van show dawn had come and Timmy mentioned he was hungry. "We don't have any food left" he said. "It was all gone the night you disappeared. I know of a sandwich place on the way home though. We can stop and get a coffee and a bite to eat." "I'm broke, bro" I said. "I have no money left on me". "Well, I have a couple of bucks I can spot you with" he said. "You should be able to get a small sandwich with that and a drink". "Thanks, man" I replied. "I'd appreciate that". We pulled into the shoP's driveway and found a spot to park. We walked in and stepped up to the counter. "Can we have a table or some stools we can sit down on?" Timmy asked. The waitress looked at us up and down and stared at my face with disgust. "You can stay and eat" she told Timmy. "But, your friend here has to wait outside". "You can't discriminate against me just because I'm dirty" I retorted. "Sure I can" she said. "It's our restaurant and we can do whatever the hell we feel like doing. If you don't like that reason, here"s another one." she scowled. "See that sign on the wall?" she pointed. "Tell me what that says, sonny?" "It says no bare feet on the premises". She turned to Timmy "You're friend can read!" she exclaimed. "Now, order something to go or leave our establishment. You're lucky We'll even serve you looking like that". "We'll have two egg sandwiches and two coffees please" Timmy said. As he was reaching in his pocket to pay the woman he whispered to me "Go outside and wait in the car man, if we piss this lady off anymore, I don't think We'll get to eat". Though I felt resentment and discriminated against, I went outside and waited for Timmy"s return. When he came back, we wolfed down our food and drinks, called the woman a dick and left. It was another exhilarating experience.

One of our town"s premier spots for alcoholism was Linwood Grove. It was already an ancient meeting place by our standards and the back building was in total disrepair. I had heard stories about how the old folks frequented its ballroom during the music of swing"s heyday. Artie Shaw, Glen Miller, and all of the big wigs had played there. Now, it sat as a faint reminder of its past glorious days. Sometimes, trying to get served at this establishment could be tricky. Like most taverns, it all depended on who was tending bar, how busy they were, or just the general mood of the day. Being that Linwood was one of the harder places to attempt a purchase, we would wait patiently outside for the possibility of patrons to buy for us. Most successes were made by asking drinkers who were closer to our age. They would sympathize and tell us "Oh, I remember when I was a kid and wanted some beer. So, how much do you want?" They wouldn't give us any idea of what their price was for the favor and usually waited until the deed was done to collect their fee. They'd come out afterward and say "You know, I could still get in a lot of trouble for this because you guys are minors. Because of that, I'm charging you 4 bottles from your case". We rarely argued and accepted it as a part and parcel tax for the transaction.

Linwood Grove Fire

Once we secured the hoppy beverages, we'd trek back to a huge tree in the back of the property where we'd party with other teens from entire neighborhoods. Sometimes, if we felt nervy enough, we'd light a small bonfire and converse about the latest gossip, styles, or music on the radio that we played. Some of these characters could be quite astounding and tenacious. For instance, there was a guy named Animal. Animal was about 6 feet 4, 200 pounds and had long blonde wavy hair with a small tinge of beard on the edge of his chin. He was nice enough to talk to unless you upset him. Otherwise, he could be very intimidating. When it came time to retrieve some more firewood, most of us would collect small kindling from a wooded area behind some houses far in the rear of the acreage. That was not Animal"s usual routine. He would wander into the trees and come back with something similar to a log. The branches would still be intact as he carried it effortlessly and didn't have a care in the world. One night, I asked "Hey, Animal? How come you always bring back big assed tree trunks and not branches like everybody else?" He never spoke much and gave me small sentences. "Easier that way" would say. I guess he figured "Why all the fuss with so many people? A log would suffice and last a lot longer". I never pushed him further and he stayed to himself all the same.

At a time where most of us were intoxicated, I got into an altercation with JR over something trivial. He didn't like my answer to a question he had given me. So, he grabbed me in a head lock half pretending to hurt me. "You're lucky you're friends with my brothers" he said "Or, else you would get a good beating". Upon his release, I thought "He was just warning me as he's very big on respect". I looked down and saw a little drop of blood on my hand. I thought "How could he have hurt me? He only snagged me for a second?" Someone cried out "You're ear is bleeding, man". "My ear is bleeding? How the hell did that happen?" I reached up to my left lobe and noticed my earring was missing. I had pierced it a few weeks earlier at Skippy"s house with the old school ice and needle technique. It was a hook with a dangling gold star attached to it and now I couldn't find it and it was gone. As I scoured the ground in a desperate attempt to recover it, I heard the familiar roar of a big block V8 engine. "Fucking cops" I thought. "Here we go again!" All of us knew the sound from previous keg parties and were especially sensitive to what the police cars looked like as well. Foolishly, someone made the decision for the Edison Police Department to purchase baby blue light colored cruisers. None of us could fathom the stupidity of this agreement and we laughed at them with impunity. "Don't they realize we can see them from 100"s of yards away?" we'd say. "How dumb can they get? There's no way they can catch us using those? They're just giving us extra time to escape".

They'd fly down the dirt path toward us accelerating in the most intimidating way possible. They loved the rush of stroking their authoritative egos I supposed. As they approached, some of us would run, while others would freeze and stand still. Depending on the officer and what kind of mood he was in, you could either expect a beating or be forced to pour out your cans of beer onto the ground. They'd laugh us and tease "Look? There's 2 more unopened cases in the dirt here" they'd say. "What do you think we should do about that?" "I dunno?" The first officer replied "Let's ask these kids" said officer 2. "What do you think we should do here?" asked officer 1. Of course to avoid any implications, we would always stay silent. "You have two choices here kids" said officer 1. "Spill out the beer, or we all get to take a ride to the station tonight". Again, no one said a word. But, the ego officers weren't finished with us quite yet. Officer 2 insisted on teaching us more. "Oh look" he said "Someone popped the trunk on my patrol car. I wonder how that happened?" he asked." "I see" Officer 1 chuckled. "It must know we need beer for this weekend's game, right officer 2? And, everyone knows free booze goes great with football. Now, don't we? None of you guys object right?" "I didn't think so" he laughed. "Just be glad it wasn't a keg with rented taps this time around" Officer 2 teased. "Because, the keg would be ours and you wouldn't get you deposit back. You know how much that sucks when that happens don't you?" he asked. When they got no response, we watched them load up the cases, close the trunk door, jump back in their cars, and drive away. We hated them with a passion that would make a torturer blush.

Knocking on Dennis G"s door one afternoon, I saw a girl come into view. I knew her right away as she had been dating Dennis for a good couple of weeks. She opened the door and recognized me immediately. With an expression as if I was annoying her, she scolded me "Dennis isn't coming out tonight". "Why not?" I asked. "He's staying home and doing clit" she replied. "Doing clit?" I thought. It was hilarious and I began to crack up with serious facets of amusement as I didn't expect a phrase like that coming out of her mouth. Just then, I heard a voice emanating from behind her. I knew it was Dennis and it was coming from his bedroom. "Is that Ron?" he asked. "Yes" she replied. "Well, let him in" he said. She stepped aside and I stood in the dining room listening. "But, I thought you were spending the night with me?" she pleaded. "I've been with you all day since this morning, babes" he said. "I'm gonna hang with my friends tonight and I'll call you later, ok? Now, don't give me any grief. That's just the way it is. I have to have my me time once in a while. We talked about this before, remember? "I guess so" she said. She was obviously distraught. "So, go home and think about me and I'll see you later" he said. "I will" she replied. She gave him a kiss, gathered up her pocketbook, and left for home. After she had left, Dennis jumped up zestfully. He had been lying on his bed the entire time. He ran to the door, peeked out the window, and started to laugh. "Cool" he said. "She's gone. "Come here, Ron" he laughed. "I have to show you something." "What?" I asked. You'll see" he said. He reached down under the covers on his bed and began screaming "Ron! Look?" he exclaimed. Uuuuullllllhhhhh!" Out of the blanket and in between the tips of his fingers, he was dangling what looked like a used rubber. He was swinging it back and forth wildly in front of my face. "I don't wanna see that shit" I gasped. "That's fucking gross, bro". "But, Rooooooon" he sang. "Look? It's full! I was doing clit, bro. Looooook! Looooook! Uuuuuullllhhh! Pussy bro, pussy!" "That's nice" I replied. "But, get that shit away from me, that's nasty". "You gotta soak in it, bro" he said. "First, you gotta eat it so you get it ready". He held up his hands with his palms facing upward demonstrating. "You have to hold it like pads. Pads Ron" he said. "I was in that shit all morning, Uuuuuulllhhh!" "Put that fucking thing in the toilet already" I said disgusted. "I told you, I don't wanna see that shit". "All right, all right" he chuckled. "I'll take it in the bathroom. But, take one more look Ron, look at the hairs? Loooook! The hairs, Ron. The hairs!" "You're fucking demented" I replied. "Now, go flush that thing and get the fuck away from me". While dancing to the bathroom he was excitedly flinging the condom back and forth across his fingers. "One thousand babies down the drain" he laughed. "Hey Ron?" he said. Looking back from the bathroom doorway "This flush is for you".

As he was finishing up, I heard Jeffrey come through the front door. "I'm home" he announced. "Is anybody here?" "I'm here" I replied. "But, you're sick and twisted brother is in the bathroom making a deposit". Which brother?" he asked. "Dennis" I laughed. "He's doing population control". "Population control?" he asked "I don't get it". Dennis exited to the dining room. "I was getting some" he said. "Getting some what?" Jeff asked. "Something you don't know about yet" Dennis cackled. "Are you talking about pussy again Dennis?" he asked. "I've had pussy before, Den. You know that already. So, stop teasing me". "Oh yeah, you"ve had some, Jeff" he laughed. "With that cocktail wiener of yours". "I'm just a kid yet" Jeff yelled back. "But, at least I got pussy for the 1st time when I was younger than you were". "You didn't even stick it in" Dennis teased. "All you got was a nubby". I was trying not to laugh because I remembered Jeffrey"s explosive temper and it was only a matter of time before Dennis goaded him enough where Jeff would explode. Trying to change the subject, I saw a purple bruise on his arm and asked him about it. "What happened to you, Jeff?" I asked. "There's a nasty mark on your arm. It looks like a dog bite". Oh, that?" he replied. "That's from that fucking German Shepard from across the street. Every time I try to come home from school, that fucker tries to bite me. This time he did. But, that was a few days ago. He stays in his yard now". "I was wondering what happened to him?" I asked. "I haven"t seen him around" "Jeff's got rabies" Dennis laughed. "He's gonna go crazy and foam at the mouth any minute now". "Rabies?" I asked. "What the fuck are you talking about Dennis? Your brother looks fine to me". "Tell him Jeff. Tell him how you"ve got rabies?" he asked. "I don't have no fucking rabies Dennis" Jeff yelled. "So, you better shut up before you piss me off". "Oh", Dennis replied "Big man on campus today, huh?" "Let me tell the story, asshole" Jeff replied. "Ron wants to hear it" "Ok, ok" Dennis said "Continue". "That fucking mutt has always been after me" Jeff said. "So, I got sick of him. He came running after me and I stood my ground this time. As he was biting me on my arm, I grabbed the fucker"s fur on his neck and I bit his ass back. After that, that pussy dog ran home yelping". "You actually bit the fucking thing?" I asked. "And, he didn't attack you more? Most wounded animals will keep coming after you after that" I said. "Fuck him" Jeff replied. He's learned his lesson not to fuck with me anymore" "Rabies" Dennis yelled. "UUUuuullllhhh, my brother's got rabies!"

Later that day, in the evening, we were all watching TV in the living room. There was Dennis, Ellis (who had come over a little later), me, and Jeffrey in the kitchen. Jeff was making macaroni and cheese from a box and was shaking his head. He hated the dry mix of the powder, so he always added 2 sticks of margarine or butter. Dennis exclaimed "Hey that smells good. But, Jeff won't give us any, so let's see what else is out there. "Whatever"s good, Den" I said. "It doesn't matter to me". "Ellis, you sit here and We'll be right back". Dennis said. "Let me know what happens on that Rich Baby, Poor Baby show?" he asked. "Make me something too" Ellis begged. "I need a tasty scarf. My fundage is low and my intesticles are groaning". "We'll see" Dennis said. "Just hang out until We're done". Dennis and I sauntered over to the kitchen and headed for the fridge. "Jeff?" he asked. "What's left inside the freezer? Me and Poco are hungry too". I think there's some English muffins left in there, Den" Jeff said. "And, some shredded cheese and tomato sauce. Other than that, just some milk. But, I'm about to add what's left of that to my mac and cheese". "You know the rule, Jeff" Dennis exclaimed. "You have to save me some milk for my tea". "And, you know my answer" Jeff replied. "As long as you're not an asshole, I'll save you a few drops". "Fair enough" Dennis said. "Just don't get on my nerves". While Jeff went back to being preoccupied with stirring his meal, Dennis and I went on a gathering spree. "We're gonna make mini pizzas" Dennis said. "How are you gonna do that?" I asked. "I've never seen shit like that before?" "Watch and learn Ronnie boy" he replied. "Watch and learn". He took a cookie tray out of the oven and laid 9 English muffins upon it in rows of 3 across. "Hand me that shredded goombah" he said. "You have to make it rain cheesy goodness, bro. You see what I'm doing here?" he asked. "First, you take a large spoon, and slather the sauce on the muffins like so. Just like they do at the pizza shop" he said. "Then, we bombard this bitch with cheese. When it's done, We'll stick these babies in the oven for a few, and Uuullhhh! Mini pizzas!" "Incredible" I said. "That's pretty smart, man" "When you don't have much money" he laughed, "You don't economize bro, you improvise". We went back to the living area and Ellis clued us in on what we had missed. A few minutes went by and Dennis mentioned "Time to check those pizzas". While he went to retrieve them, I stayed behind and was talking to Ellis. "The tall guy with the blonde hair is skulling out" Ellis laughed. "He thinks he's gonna get some clit". Dennis had come back with the pizzas and was offering me some. "Here, bro" he said "Take a few of these, they are really good" "Where"s mine, Den?" Ellis asked. "You're not getting any" Dennis said. "Because, you keep trying to sneak into our cellar and think you live here". "That's boosh" Ellis cried. "I haven"t been down there in weeks". "Only because Dennis set up that beer bottle alarm system on the steps" Jeffrey yelled from the kitchen. "So, you don't get anything". Seeing that Dennis wouldn't bend, Ellis made a bee line for Jeff and his now full bowl of macaroni. "Gimme some, Jeff" he pleaded. "I'm fucking starving, bro" "Nope, nope, and nope" Jeff said. "I can't do it, man. Go and sit down and stop bothering me" "Come on?" Ellis begged annoyingly "Just gimme a little bite" "That was fast" Dennis yelled. "Usually Jeff throws shit at you if you try to get his food". "A quick answer is better than a long silence". Jeff replied. "So, fuck that. You're not getting any, now go away". Ellis came back by us pouting and sat down. Dennis and I had 2 pizzas left a piece. "Come on, Den" Ellis grumbled. "How come Ron gets to eat?" he asked. "And, I don't?" "Because Ron brings us cakes and ribs for my family" Dennis laughed. "And you bring us nothing". "Ellis was beginning to be a pest. He had a bad habit of repeating himself over and over and aggravating you until he got what he wanted. "It's not gonna work" Dennis said. "So, stop begging before I punch you in the head". "Please Den, please" Ellis pleaded "I'm so hungry. I'll do anything for a bite. Just let me scarf one of those bad bahoos and I'll leave you alone" "I tell you what" Dennis said. "You see all those dirty dishes piled up in the sink for the past 3 days? If you go and wash all of them, including that sticky assed pot that Jeffrey just used, I'll think about giving you some". "Ok, man" Ellis said with glee. "I'm gonna go in there right now and take care of it". "You do that" Dennis said. "And then, get back to me". "What a pain in the ass" Dennis whispered. "I don't know why I put up with his bullshit". "Come on, Den" I said "You know he makes us laugh with his stupid shit and his crazy language". "True, bro" he replied. "But, sometimes he pushes it too far. So, I have to make a mockery out of him and teach him a lesson. Otherwise, you see how he is? He'll stay like that forever. Plus, I keep him around to do the shit none of us wanna do. So, I'm doing him a favor. He has to learn somehow, doesn't he?" "Well" I replied "At least you feed him once in a while" "It's like the zoo, bro" he chuckled "You have to feed them sometimes to keep them happy. Otherwise, They'll turn on you". When Ellis was finished, he came back and Dennis pointed to the cookie tray with the 2 remaining pizzas. "There's your dinner" he said. "I hope you enjoy it. And, maybe tomorrow We'll have other tasks you can barter for" "I guess hunger and annoyance will make you do silly shit" I thought. I was happy not to have been in that position.

I was with Danny B. again and we somehow ended up in front of the Howard Johnson"s Motel on Route 1 in New Brunswick. We had been drinking MD 2020 for most of the afternoon and were already pretty drunk. But, we wanted more booze and hate to come up with a place that was an easy target for underage drinkers. "Where is that store again, Dan?" I asked. "You know" he said. "It's the one that's up on Edgeboro Road. We've been there once before, bro. Its cake to get people to get us stuff there". "Oh, yeah" I replied. "Now I remember. But, that's a few miles away. Do you really wanna go there? I asked. "It's kind of far". "Do you wanna drink some more or not?" he groaned. "Because, if you don't wanna walk to East Brunswick, We'll have to turn around and go back to

Edison. It's the same amount of distance really". "That makes sense" I replied. "I'm not drunk enough yet. So, I guess we have no other choice". "No, we don't" he said. "So, stop you're crying and let's start walking".

In front of the liquor store we waited patiently for someone who could procure us alcoholic delights. The anticipation was the part I always hated. Since I had done this many times, I asked Danny to try and go in first. "Go inside and see if you can scarf" I said. "You got served at the bowling alley and a few other places before. So, you look old enough". "Not around here" he mumbled. "That's only been in a few spots. And, the last time we came here, we got somebody else to go in. So, We'll have to try with a customer like the last time. And, I don't feel like getting shot down or busted either". "Come on, man" I said. "Don't be a pussy. The most they can do is card you and say get lost after you can't produce it. What's the problem?" I asked. "I'm not going in and that's the end of it" he said. "I'm always the one that has to try first. It's your turn now or no more drinks". "Fuck me" I yelled. "You always have to be difficult". Just then, a Chevy Impala with a black guy came driving up. He appeared to be the right age for package goods. As he strode past us, I gave him the eye. "Hey, bro. What's up?" I asked. "Do you think you can help us get some booze?" "First of all, I'm not your brother" he said. "And secondly, aren't you little white guys old enough to get that shit yourselves?" "Why the fuck would we be asking you if that was the case?" I answered acerbically. "You"ve got a point there skinny boy" he replied. "But, I tell you what, you"ve got some balls on you, son. So, I'm gonna help you out. What kind of booze you boys want from in there?" he asked. "We've been drinking Mad Dog 2020 all day" I replied. "So, here"s some money. Just get us some more of that". "Mad Dog 2020?" he asked laughing. "No wonder you guys are drunk. That stuff's for winos. That's like Night Train and shit. "Don't you want something tastier?" he asked "Taste equals cash" Danny said. "And cash, we don't have a lot of". "Broke white boys" the man chuckled. "Broke white boys who want in on the game. Ok broke white boys" he said. "I'm going in with your 4 dollars and I'll be right out. Just wait here, man"

We watched him intently through the liquor store window as we wanted to make sure he didn't try to abscond with our money. We had been ripped off before by old men lushes and knew to keep an eye out lest they skip out the back door. "Here he comes" Danny said. "I think he got us what we wanted". As the man approached, we could see he had a large paper bag with 2 bottles protruding from the top. "Ummm ummm" he sang. "Pink colored Mad Dog. You boys are sure to get fucked up tonight". "That's the point" I said. "Now give them here" "Slow down skinny boy" he warned. "Let me take my pint bottle of vodka out the bag first". "By the way, son" he said. "My name"s John". "What's your names?" "My name"s Ronnie" I replied. "And this is Danny". "Nice to meet you" he said. "Where are you little white boys from?" he asked. "We're from Edison" Danny replied. "Edison?" he exclaimed "You boys walked all the way here just to get liquor from Edison?" "Yup" Danny said. "And, after we drink this shit, We'll probably be walking back". "You fools are gonna be too fucked up to be walking back later" he chuckled. "You guys should ride with me". "Ride with you?" I asked. "Why? Where are you going?" "You guys wanna go to a party?" he asked. "Sure" I replied "Where"s the party at?" "It's over my friend's house and it's a mixed party. You don't mind hanging out with the brothers and sisters now do you?" he asked. "Nah" Danny said. "As long as there's weed and booze, We're ok. Right, Ron?" "The brothers have made some of the best music" I retorted. "Oh, so you like Motown?" John asked "Because if you like Motown, you'll get along at this party just fine" "Sounds great" I replied. "I can even sing some soul high notes too" "You can huh?" he asked. "I gotta see this". "Maybe later" I quipped.

"Take us to the party first". "Jump on in" he said. "And, We'll leave right now"

As we were cruising down Edgeboro Road, Danny was riding shotgun and I was in the back. I was sipping on one of the newer bottles of booze and beginning to get really fucked up. As I was leaning into the doorframe peering out the window, it had begun to rain and the glass looked funny. I didn't know if the image was from being drunk, or from the drips cascading down the pane. When we came to a stop light, I saw a cop in the rear view mirror. "Hey, man" I slurred. "There's a cop behind us". "I know, man" John said nervously. "Just be cool". As the signal changed to green, I heard a loud thud. It was as if something heavy had hit the ground. "Fuck!" John yelled. "The fucking muffler fell down again". "What do you mean, again?" Danny asked. "What the fuck is wrong with it?" "It's got a hole in it" John complained. "So, I have to hold it up with wire. I have to twist it back up once in a while because it comes loose". "I wish you would have told us you rigged it up that way before we got in the car" Danny howled. "Now, if you get pulled over, they're gonna fuck with us". "It's either that, or walk man" John said. "But, if they make us, just let me do the talking. If I show respect, maybe he'll let us go". Suddenly, I saw the police cruisers lamps light up behind us. "Fuck" I mumbled "He's pulling us over". "Just be quiet" John said. "I'll handle it". He drove the car over to the side of the road and parked as many cars passed by with people staring. He rolled down the window awaiting the officer"s arrival. "License, registration and insurance card please" the cop asked. "And, what is that metal hanging down under your car on the road?" "I'm sorry officer" John replied. "It's the muffler and it just broke, sir". "I rolled down my back window and began shouting in a slur "What the fush you pulleded ush ober for copper?" I asked. The policeman looked back and became agitated with me. He asked John "Who"s the intoxicated kid sprawled out in the back seat?"

"That's just a friend of mine officer" John said "I'm taking him home. He's very drunk". "I can see that" said the cop. "What can you seesh?" I yelled. "I'm perfectly fines". "Fines is what you're gonna get" the cop warned. "If you don't shut your friend up there in the back seat". "And, Sonny" he said peering at me "I'm not addressing you. I'm speaking to the driver of this vehicle. Therefore, I"d keep quiet if I were you". Danny leaned over the back seat facing me "Shut the fuck up, you asshole" he whispered. "You're gonna get us all busted". "Busted, smusted" I murmured. "You're fucking wasted" Danny said. "So, please just go to sleep for now and be quiet".

I laid down across the seat in a horizontal position and was singing a Stones song softly to myself "This ain't no place for, a street fighting man". Danny mumbled under his breath "You're gonna be in the street if you keep up your bullshit. That's for sure, you drunken fuck". I heard John get out of the car and it sounded like he was trying to negotiate with the cop. It was something to the effect of "if you can fix it, you can go". Then, there were strange rumblings coming from under my seat. "What the hell is that noise?" I thought. And was wondering what they were. "Monsters" I mumbled. "There are monsters amongst us. We're all doomed, Dan". "We're doomed if we all go to jail tonight too" Danny said. "And, if we do, I'm leaving your ass in there". After a few minutes of scraping sounds and bumping beneath us, John returned. "The cop cut me a break" he said. "But, he told me to fix it as soon as possible and to take skinny Ronnie home, or else he'll get me next time good". "Cool" Danny said. "Now, let's go to that party you told us about". "Oh, there ain't no party no more, bro" John replied. "I ain't taking no chances on the man pulling me over again. "Wush the fuck?" I asked. "Whersh the fuck are we going to now?" "You're too fucked up to know where you are anyway" Danny laughed. "So, sit back and enjoy the ride". "I'm gonna drive back to my house" John said. "You boys can sleep in my car tonight if you want. In the morning, I'll have more time to fix that damn muffler. I don't wanna try to rig it now as it's too dark outside". "That sounds like a good idea" Danny replied. "Ron is too drunk to walk home anyway".

I fell asleep in John"s car parked in the front of his home. I awoke a while later and had no idea where I was. I could see that I was still with Danny though who was hunched over in the front seat and was snoring. I reached over and jostled him. "Hey, man" I said. "Where the fuck are we?" "We're in front of that black guy John"s house" he replied. "Don't you remember?" "The thing I remember last was some cop fucking with me" I said "That was hours ago" he laughed. "You"ve been asleep for some time" "Well, what the fuck are we gonna do now?" I asked. "This place doesn't look familiar to me". "I think We're in Old Bridge" he said. But, it's kind of cold outside. So, I figured we'd stay here until the morning like John said". "Fuck that" I shrieked. "Didn't he leave the key?" "No" Danny replied. "I guess he didn't know us enough to trust us". "Nice one, Dan" I complained. "We'll freeze our balls off with no heat. You could have at least asked him for the keys". "What the fuck did you want me to do?" he asked. "It's his fucking car". "Well, I'm not sitting here all night waiting" I griped. "I'm coming in the front and I'm gonna hot wire this bitch". "You know how to do that?" he asked. "Of course" I replied. "That shit is easy". I straddled the front seat and scampered over into position. "Fuck" I blurted. "I don't have a knife to cut the wires. I need something sharp to trim away the outside". "I don't have anything" Danny said. "All I have are a set of keys". "A set of keys?" I asked. "Let me see those". He pulled them out of his pocket and handed them to me. It was a small circular key ring made out of metal with 3 keys attached to it. Two of them were bronze in color and the other one was silver. The silver one was worn down with barely any teeth on it. "What's this silver one for?" I asked. "That's for a lawnmower I think" he replied. "It's been on there for a long time, I'm not sure about that one". "Do you remember when Billy F. and I stole those two Volkswagens?" I asked. "Yeah" he said. "That shit was funny".

"Guess what kind of key we had for that?" I asked. "I dunno, a Volkswagen one?" he replied. "No" I said. "The one we had looked blank with hardly any grooves in it and smooth like the one you"ve got here". "So, what are you gonna do with it?" he asked. "I'm gonna try to start this car with it dumb ass" I laughed. "You think that"ll work?" he asked. "Well, I sure as hell am gonna try" I said. "I'm not gonna stay here in a place I don't know in the fucking cold". "Go for it" he replied. "But, I hope we don't get caught".

I entered the key into the ignition and gave the mechanism a spin. To Danny"s surprise, the car started right up. "No shit" he chuckled. "The fucking thing works!" "Now, we put on some heat" I said. "And, drive home". I grabbed the wheel and put the vehicle in gear. It was an automatic, so it didn't make much noise. I turned the car toward the left and headed for top of the hill. "Wait a minute" Danny said. "If we take this out on the highway, we might get pulled over like we did earlier. Since its John"s ride, we should think about this for a little bit. The cops will say it was stolen. Then, We'll go to jail for sure". "Well, what the fuck do you think we should do then?" I asked. "Let's really think about this" he replied. As we pondered our next move, I turned the car back around and was driving in circles in front of John"s house. "I say we keep the fucking thing and drive home" I said. "But, if you wanna leave it here, you better make up your mind soon, bro. Someone will eventually hear us and then They'll wake up. We'll surely be caught then". "We're not that far from Route 18" he replied "I remember that for sure because I wasn't as fucked up as you were." "So, you want to walk back home then?" I asked. "Yeah" Danny said "Because, the sun is coming up soon. It's really not that far away for us to hoof it". "Ok, man" I replied. "But, don't bitch at me if you get cold". "I won't" he promised. "Besides, I still have that second full bottle of Mad Dog left. It'll keep us warm". I gave him back his keys, locked the doors, and we left. It was a longer walk to Route 18 than I had anticipated. All the while, we were sucking down more booze.

Other than walking, I don't remember how we got there. I woke up in a cemetery with my head facing a tombstone and it seemed I had fallen asleep on somebody"s grave. I saw that the sun was up and there was no one else around except Danny. I rolled over onto my left side and I could see him still asleep on the plot next to me. As usual, he was snoring loudly. So, I picked up some pebbles and threw them at him. "Wake up, asshole" I yelled. "Stop throwing rocks at me you fucking dickhead" he replied. "Where are we?" he asked. "How the fuck do I know, genius" I said. "You're the one with the bright fucking idea to walk home last night, remember?" "I don't remember shit" he replied "All I recall is us slapping each other in the face to see if we were still alive" he said. Maybe it's because we thought we were dead when we first got here?" he asked. "After all, it is a cemetery" "Yeah, I know" I said "But, I had no plans to sleep on top of dead people. What the fuck, Dan?" "Well, it's too late now" he said. "We might as well walk back home". We plodded our way down the side road leading out of the cemetery to Route 18 and headed to our homes. "Let's go to my house first" I said. "I don't think my parents are home. Then, after some breakfast, We'll cruise on over to your house". "Sounds like a plan" Danny said. "Let's go"

As we arrived to my street, I could see that my parents" cars were still parked in the driveway. "Fuck" I said. "What are they doing home?" "Your folks?" Danny asked surprised. "That's my dad"s car. What the fuck is he doing here?" he asked. "I bet they snagged us doing the "I'm sleeping over your house, and you're staying over mine" I said. "I didn't think they would check on us. Fuck, now We're caught". "Nothing we can do about it now" Danny replied. "But, face the bullshit. We might as well go in and see what we can get away with". We opened the door and our parents were in the den already waiting for us. "Where the hell have you two been?" Danny"s father howled. "You're only 17 Daniel and Ron is only 16. We've been worried sick about you all night." "How could you do this to us?" Danny"s mom cried. "Not a phone call, nothing". "I'm sorry, mom" Danny said. "We went to a party, that's all". "Don't you realize there are bad people out there?" she whined "You could get killed if you're not careful". My mother joined in "Ronald, Danny"s parents are right. You're wrong for lying to us at where you were staying and you should have called us". "I was gonna call you" I said. "But, it got late and I forgot". "You forgot huh?" said my father. "It seems you always tend to forget when it doesn't affect you". "Sorry dad, I'll try not to do to again" I replied. "Oh, there won't be any more trying with you two" he barked. "Danny"s parents, your mother and I have come to a conclusion. You kids won't be paling around with each other anymore. Danny is banned from any contact with you what so ever and you'll be doing the same. We've decided that until you can act more responsible, that's how it's going to be" "Oh really?" I laughed to myself. "Fat chance". Danny said his goodbyes and his parents thanked my parents for their cooperation. Like most parents, they made a bigger deal of it than it needed to be. Keeping Danny and I from hanging out with each other lasted a grand total of about 2 weeks.

CHAPTER 4

Concerts, Acid & Crank

I had turned 17 and still didn't have my driver"s license. So, I was at the mercy of my friends for transportation or I simply had to walk. I saw no reason to procure my driving privileges as I couldn't afford a car anyway. My father had bought my older brother his first automobile, but I got nothing. Whenever I asked, I was reminded by my father "Remember the money you cost me when you and your friend stole that Volkswagen when you were 15?" he asked. "How could I forget old man, you bring it up constantly" I thought. "That's why you're not getting a car" he said. "You don't deserve one". This was perfectly all right of course in my father's eyes as my brother was a perfect angel. He didn't ever bring up the fact that Robert had gone on a criminal spree driving bulldozers and road graders around a construction site illegally with his friends. "That was a one-time thing" he said. "He doesn't bring me as much trouble as you do". "Maybe if you paid more attention to me I wouldn't have to do that" I thought. Hanging around a small patch of woods behind Playmore became a place we frequented to get stoned. One afternoon, Dave G. had scored an ounce of weed and was dipping his hand into the bag to stuff his pipe. "What kind of weed do you have there, Dave?" I asked. "I scored this nice bag of Acapulco Gold for 40 bucks" he boasted. "It's supposed to be some of the smoothest pot out there right now. It makes you laugh your ass off too I'm told. It came around in my travels. So I couldn't resist." Phil M., standing behind me asked "Pack us a nice bowl, bro. So we can get really, really high". "Oh, you're gonna see stars with this" Dave chuckled. "Just wait and see". As Dave asked me for my lighter to put some flame to make smoke, a baby blue cop car rolled up screeching its wheels. A police officer we knew named Jimmy K. ran out of the vehicle and got right in our faces. "I see you guys were about to fire up?" he asked. "We weren't doing anything" I replied. "Was I asking you, asshole?" he asked. "I was asking your friend here with the pipe in his hand. I saw all of you as I was coming down the street. You put that bag in your pocket just before I pulled up on you." "What bag?" Dave asked. "I see no bag here?" "Maybe I'll search you then" he said. I bet I would find it then?" he asked. "You can't search anybody here without probable cause" I said nervously. "I know my rights". "You're a funny guy" he chuckled. "You must be a lawyer?" he asked. "Well" he said. I have a statute for you you'll all enjoy" he said. "You're all under 18, right?" he asked. "Therefore, you have no rights. That's right? None. You know why? Because you're all juveniles, that's why. He turned back to me and asked "So, do you know what that means Mr. Attorney? Tell these fine friends of yours here for us please?" "Fuck" I thought. "This prick"s got us". "It means you can do whatever you want" I replied. "And, there nothing we can do about it". "You see that?" he asked sarcastically. "I can take your weed, and there's nothing you can do about it. How about that?" he laughed. "So?" he asked. "This is what we can do. You can give me the bag of weed right now that's buried in your pocket, and you can keep your pipe. Or, I'll take the pipe and you can keep the weed. But then, you all get to come with me". I looked at Dave"s face and he was gritting his teeth and almost crying from his anger. "I'll give you the weed" Dave mumbled. "Smart, very smart" officer Jimmy K. said. "So, hand it over and go home". Dave reached into his pants and pulled the weed out handing it to him. "Put the pipe in your other pocket" officer Jimmy K. said. "I wouldn't want you to lose it after you left here". "Yeah" Dave smirked. "Thanks a lot for nothing". "Happy birthday kids" he yelled as he walked away. "I hope you liked your present". He backed into the street in a hurry and we watched Dave become depressed. "How come shit like this always happens to me?" he asked. "Nobody else gets to go free and get their shit taken away from them?"

Skippy had called me out of the blue and asked me to meet him at Playmore. As I arrived, I could see that he was playing pool and using a cue stick to mime a guitar solo to Queen"s song Bohemian Rhapsody. He was really getting into it and sliding his long skinny fingers up and down as if it were a fret board. "What's up, Skip?" I screamed over the blaring music. He turned to me singing the lyrics loudly into my face "So, you think you can stone me and spit in my eye" all the while still mimicking the guitar parts. I watched laughing at his body swaying back and forth as if he actually thought he was on stage. "What are you doing?" I asked yelling. Along with the song, he screamed at me more "Just gotta get out, just gotta get right outta here". When the tune was finally over, I was able to grab his attention. "I've been trying to get you to listen to me since I walked in the damn door" I said. "Do I have your attention now, or what?" "I'm sorry, man" he replied. "But, you know how that song always gets me going". "So, what did you call me down here for?" I asked. "We have to come up with a scheme, Ron" he exclaimed. "I'm broke and need some money really bad. I'm sick of being out of cash, bro". "You aren't the only one" I answered. "I've been without any for weeks". "Do you have any good scams we could do?" he asked laughing. "Because, I'm fresh out of ideas and you always seem to come up with something quick". "I'll have to think about it for a minute" I said. "So, just give me a few". Just then, my mind started racing and was remembering how someone had told me that the best crimes were done in the rain. It was along the lines of "there won't be any footprints because the rain washed them all away, the roar of the raindrops covers up any sound, and there's usually not that many witnesses outside during thunderstorms" "Perfect" I thought. "Now, how can I use that information for what I need?" When I came back from my thinking, I asked "How important is the parka you're wearing when you go back outside, Skip?" "You mean the one I have hanging up over there?" he asked pointing at a coat rack. "I really don't give a shit about it. It's only a coat, why?" "Because, you're gonna need it and I'm gonna need mine to pull it off" I replied. "Pull what off?" he asked. "Where are you going with this, man?" "I have a really easy scam if you want" I replied. "It's been raining out all day too. So, come with me to the A&P up the road and I'll show you what it is". "What could we possibly scarf at A&P?" he asked with a puzzled look on his face. "Cases of food?" "Much easier than that" I replied. "What We're gonna be doing is gonna be outside of the place". "Outside?" he asked. "Are you crazy, Ron? It's coming down like cats and dogs out there, man". "That's the point" I chuckled. "It's the perfect cover for us". "Well" he said "I've still got my jean jacket I on I wear under it. So, I guess it won't be too bad to lose the other one" "Exactly" I said. "We're gonna do a bait and switch". I had already had my parka on and asked him to do the same. Before we left I said "Just do everything I say when we get there". "And, We'll do just fine".

When we arrived at the A&P, it was a torrential rainstorm. Barely being able to see in front of our faces, we stood by the exit door. "So, what's the deal?" Skip asked. "Are we just gonna stand out here and get soaked or what?" "Take the string on your hood of your parka and tie it real tight around your head". I said. "That way, no one will be able to see your face". "Why am I hiding my face?" he asked. "You're really not making any sense to me, man". "It's like this" I replied. "We're gonna wait until a woman comes out after she's done shopping and grab her purse. You grab it, and then hand it off to me like a football. I'll run into the woods behind Linwood Grove with it, and then you go the other way. The lady and any witnesses won't see our faces because we have them wrapped up in our coats. They'll also be confused due to us going in different directions. After I'm done in the woods with her pocketbook, I'll meet you back at Playmore to divvy up the cash". "But, They'll still have our descriptions" Skip exclaimed. "If the cops come, They'll recognize us". "I have a scheme for that too" I laughed. "Across the street from the Edison bank is Bells drugs, right? Behind there is a large garbage dumpster that them and the bakery use to put their trash in. As you run back to Playmore, simply take off your parka and throw it away into there. The coP's descriptions of us won't match. Therefore, it's flawless". "That's pretty smart" Skip said. "So, who do we go after first?" "The best ones that most likely won't fight back are middle aged, chubby women" I replied. "They can't run far and run out of breath easily". "Ok, man" Skip exclaimed. "But, we better hurry up as its starting to get dark and it's really wet out here". "The darkness is even better" I chuckled. "The more elements to hide us, the more successful We'll be".

As we waited, we watched to zero in on a perfect victim. Soon, a woman came rolling out with her carriage full to the brim. In the cart"s seat was her slightly open pocketbook. She was also gray haired and portly. "A perfect mark" I thought. I turned to Skip and whispered "This is it, bro. She's the one". "Are you sure?" Skippy asked nervously. "What if she's parked way in the back?" "We're only gonna do this if she's in the front row" I replied. "If we follow her too long, she might have time to look back at us looking suspicious". We stared with anticipation as she wheeled herself in the direction of her vehicle. She hit the first row and stopped. "Get ready, Skip" I said. "But, wait until she's distracted and is putting her groceries into the car". Suddenly, a huge gust of rainy wind came down partially obstructing our view. "If we can't see her clearly" I thought. "Then, she can't see us either". I turned to Skip and yelled "Now!" As the woman was bent over the back seat placing bags, she was slipping on the wet pavement struggling to right herself. With her back to us, we struck. Like a spider snatching a meal, Skippy grabbed her purse and began to run. I immediately had a crisis as my parka"s hood string broke loose. Unfortunately, it revealed my entire face. The woman turned back and stared right at me. "Oh my god" she screamed. "They"ve stolen my purse". No longer wanting to wait for Skip to give me the hand off, I ran the other way. Skip not knowing what else to do, put it under his coat and kept running.

As I ran, I could hear the lady screaming for help behind me. All I could think of was "She saw my face, she saw my face. I hope I don't get busted". I stopped at the dumpster, stripped off my parka, threw it in, and started walking toward the bank to find Skip. It was raining so hard that I had trouble seeing and had to keep rubbing my eyes with my hands. Soaked to the bone, I crossed the back of the bank"s parking lot and saw Skip coming into view. He was drenched and bouncing down the road toward me very nervously. As he approached, he started explaining "Ron?" he asked. "I saw that the lady looked right at you, man. So, I didn't wait for you to take the pocketbook because I knew she saw your face. My instincts kicked in and I said fuck it. So, I ran instead" "That fucking woman looked right in my face" I said. "The godamn string on my hood broke just as I was about to run with you. It snapped out of nowhere". "Yeah" Skip replied. "I saw that and it scared the shit out of me. Anyway, I took her purse into the woods and opened that bitch up. I found a stuffed bank envelope. So, I guess she just got paid. I don't know how much money we got, but I think we did good". "What did you do with your parka?" I asked. "Because, it's obvious you never made it to the dumpster and you're in your jean jacket now?" "I figured I"d just do the same thing we planned but leave it there instead" he replied. "She's got descriptions of two crooks in parka"s" he laughed. "So, I don't think They'll be looking for us". As we stepped over a curb to the street, a police cruiser came to the corner and stopped. The cop rolled down his window and started asking questions "Where are you kids coming from?" he asked. "From my friend Skippy"s house" I replied. "Why officer?" I asked. "Did we do something wrong?" "How long ago did you leave his house?" he asked. "About 5 minutes ago" replied Skip. "We were just going over to Playmore to play some pool". "Well" the cop said. "There was just a robbery by here. But, you two guys don't fit the description. So, it couldn't have been you. Have you seen anyone else come by here since you"ve been walking?" he asked. "No" I replied. "What did they look like officer?" I asked. "Don't worry about that" he replied. "It doesn't concern you. So, you two go have fun playing your games and get out of the rain". "Ok, officer" I said. "I guess We'll go do that now". He spoke something into his radio, rolled up his window, and left.

"That was a close one" Skip said. "He almost busted us". "Busted us for what?" I asked. "Even if he patted us down and found money on us, he has no proof of where we got it from. He would have had to let us go anyway". "They still make me nervous" Skip replied. "It's just their bullshit intimidation tactic" I said. "They're all taught to do that so you'll rat yourself out. Now that he's gone, let's just go to Playmore and see what we've got". "You sure know how to scheme, Ron" he said. "I would have never thought of just changing my clothes". "They always go by what you look like or what you are wearing" I exclaimed. "So, all you have to do is think like the enemy and you"ve beaten them". "You're a funny guy" Skip said. "You always have all the solutions, man". "Drastic measures call for drastic decisions" I replied. "If you want something, you have to plan for it". As we entered Playmore, we immediately headed for the bathroom in the back. Skip went into a stall and began counting "100, 200, 300, 300 and 50 dollars, Ron" he shrieked. "We hit the jackpot, bro". "I guess that's 175 a piece" I said. "Not a bad haul for a quick job". After we were done dividing up our booty, we went back to the pool table area to calm down. Suddenly, a guy we knew named Drew came running in. He was also an employee of the A&P. He looked around at about 15 of us kids and announced. "The cops are outside. Somebody robbed a lady at the store I work at up the street and took her pocketbook. They wanna know who did it. Does anybody in here know anything about it?" he asked. Everyone in the room including us shook their heads no. "Well, the only description she gave was two people in winter coats with hoods. If anybody here sees them come in here, call the police right away, ok?" "I thought laughing "Yeah, right. Like I'm really gonna rat myself out?" "How do you know they don't have your face as a description?" Skip asked whispering. "Because, if that were true the cops outside would have grabbed me by now" I answered. "All they have are the parkas and they're gone". "She must have not got a good look at you then" Skip said. "Yeah" I replied. "I was worried about that. But, not anymore". "What if the cops come back and search us and find the money?" he asked. "They'll lie and keep it even if they can't pin it on us? "You have a good point there" I responded. "Maybe we should find someone here to leave it with until tomorrow?" "That would be smart" Skip said. "So, that's what I'm gonna do". While we were preparing to play a game of pool and I was racking them up, Bruce V. walked by and approached me "I just heard what you guys just got away with" he said. "That's more money than I make doing stickups, man. You little motherfuckers are good. Very, very good. Maybe one day you can both be on my team?" he asked. "Thanks, Bruce" I said. "But, I prefer to work with just one or alone". "Well" he replied. "If you ever change your mind, you know where I am". "Yeah" I thought. "As if I"d score with a guy who has a record that long". Soon, I had found someone to hold my money for me. It was the tasty girl I had broken up with previously at the Saint Mathews carnival. I wasn't sure if I should have trusted her as she had already lied and cheated on me. But, there was no one else and I didn't want to get pinched. "I'll hold it for you" she promised. "How do I know you won't screw me and keep it all?" I asked. "Simple" she replied. "If something goes wrong, I'll be implicated as an accomplice. I don't want anything to do with that and I still like you a lot. So, your secret"s safe with me". I gave her the money reluctantly and told her to meet me there the next day. Surprisingly and to her word, she arrived at 4:30 pm. "Here you go" she said as she handed back my cash. "I told you you could trust me with it". "I really appreciate that you did this for me" I said. "Well then" she exclaimed. "How about a tip for taking the risk for you?" "A tip?" I asked. "Like, what kind of tip?" "How about 20 dollars?" she asked. "That seems fair". I gave her the 20 and a kiss on her cheek. "You may not be able to be trusted as a girlfriend" I laughed. "But, I guess you do ok with other people"s money". Two days later, I spent most of the funds on a quarter pound of weed off. I bought it off a girl whose parents were the leasing agents for Playmore. Unfortunately, she ripped me off and shorted me. I guess the rippers get ripped off in the end.

It was New Year"s Eve and our nation was celebrating its Bicentennial. A few friends and I had decided that we would go to Times Square for the festivities as we had never seen the ball drop from there except from on TV. Accompanying me were Dave G., Jeffrey G., Cliff G., Danny B., Mickey B. and Jimmy M. Most trains at the time rarely stopped at the Edison station as its completion was still far into the future. So, we took a gamble and hoped we'd be lucky enough to catch NJ Transit's schedule anyway. Dave insisted we were in the right place. "Trains leave here all the time" he said. "You just have to find one at the right hour". "Dave" I replied. "You know there's no platform here, right? They almost never stop if there isn't a platform." "So what?" he asked. "They still leave from here". "Ron"s right" blurted Jeffrey. "We don't even know the timetable. We could be hanging around here all night". Dave was unmoved. "I don't give a shit what you guys say" he groaned. "I'm staying here and taking my chances". "Ok" I said. "But, We're all gonna blame you if we miss Times Square". "We won't" Dave insisted "You'll see". "I hope you're right" I said "Or else We're wasting our time". "Don't you have a bunch of blotter acid hits on you?" Dave asked trying to change the subject. "Yeah" I replied. "What about it?" I asked. "Why don't we do some of them now? That way, We'll all peak by the time we get there". "Yeah, Jeff said. "Let's all do some acid. I've never done any acid before". "Who"s gonna babysit Jeff?" asked Mickey. "I'm not the one who"s gonna watch him. It's not my turn" I laughed. "I'll make sure he's all right" Danny replied. "I have no problem with that". "Just hand out the tabs" Dave demanded. "And, get on with the show". "Oh, you'll get a show" I said "I can guarantee that.

I handed out a hit a piece and watched as they put it on their tongues. Jeffrey wasn't sure of what to do. "Let it dissolve on your tongue first" Dave said. "Then, you swallow it, Jeff". "I better not freak out on this shit, Ron" Jeff said. "Because if I do, I'll come back to kill you later". "Be cool little bro" Danny chuckled. "It's not that big of a deal, man. You'll just see shiny colors and shit. When you turn your head away from any lights, there will be trails following them. It's actually pretty cool to watch. But, in the beginning, when it first affects you, you might feel a little tweaky". "What do you mean tweaky?" Jeff asked. "Am I gonna flip out and shit?" "No, Jeff" I replied. "With some people, when it first starts it sometimes feels like there's somebody inside your body tickling you. You might get a little jumpy, but that's expected". "I can't wait until Jeff gets to the part where you get all philosophical and shit" laughed Cliff. "His ramblings should be interesting". Jimmy added "If it makes you feel any better Jeff, I've never done any either. So, it'll be the first time for the both of us". "Great" I replied. "Now, We'll have to babysit two of them". "Stop complaining, Ron" said Cliff. "He's my friend more than yours and I'll watch him too if I have too". "I'm gonna hold you to that, Cliffy" I said. "Because, I'm gonna be tripping too and I can barely watch out for myself". "Always complaining" Dave sneered sarcastically "Ron is like an old fucking woman. He's never satisfied with anything". "I may complain sometimes" I said. "But, only when people do dumb shit". "Everybody does stupid shit" Dave replied "So, just roll with it". "I'm not gonna hang out with you if you're gonna complain all night either" said Cliff. "So, I'm with Dave. You better get mellow". "Jump off my balls" I yelled. "If it wasn't for me, none of you would have trips to begin with". "This is true" pronounced Mick. "Let's leave the guy alone". "Smart move and Thank you, Mick" I said. "I just don't have patience for inconveniences". "Well, don't inconvenience us tonight with any of your bullshit" said Cliff. "And, We'll get along just fine. Like Dave said, just go with it man. You let little shit bother you too much". "Bad parenting" Danny laughed "I see it all the time".

An hour had passed and the acid was beginning to kick in. "Have any of you guys started tripping yet?" I asked. "I'm feeling something" said Danny. "Does anybody else?" he asked. "Nothing here yet" replied Cliff. "How about you, Jeff?" Cliff asked. "Nope" said Jeff. "How long does this shit take to take effect?" he asked. "It's different for each person" Mick replied. "But, it's just starting to hit me too" "How about you Jimmy?" Mick asked "You"ve been pretty quiet over there". "I feel weird" Jimmy replied. "Is it supposed to be this way?" "I told you before, man" I cautioned. "You're gonna feel strange at first". "I don't know if I'm gonna like this or not" Jimmy mumbled nervously. "I've never felt anything like this before. I don't feel like myself". "That's the point" Dave laughed. "It's supposed to open your mind". "I hope he can handle it" said Danny. "I wouldn't want him to see cartoons and shit". "I'm not gonna turn into a cartoon am I?" Jimmy asked. "Only if you listen to Ron" said Dave. "Don't listen to anything he says while you're tripping. He tries to use big words and he'll fuck with your head". "You're not gonna do that to me, are you Ron? Jimmy asked. "Dave is full of shit" I replied. "He's just saying that because I'm smarter than him". "We'll see how smart you are at the end of the night" laughed Dave. "I've seen you in some compromising positions and you weren't so smart then". "Always challenging me intellectually, right Dave?" I asked. "I'm just busting your balls, man" he replied. "You need thicker skin". I pointed at my crotch "I have your thicker skin right her, bro" I laughed. "Anytime you're ready". "Look guys" Dave laughed "Now, he wants to go moe on me". "Let's came down, man" said Cliff. "I think it's time we find an alternate way to get there. Because it doesn't look like any trains are coming this way soon". "See?" I exclaimed "I told you not to listen to Dave. He's making fun of me and we've wasted an hour here now for nothing". "Hey, I tried to do the right thing" Dave said. "It's not my fucking fault fucking NJ Transit is fucking retarded". "I guess We'll have to go to another station. Like the one in Metuchen" Cliff suggested. "If we pool our money, we can probably take a cab". "That sounds good to me" said Mick. "It's getting kid of cold standing out here anyway". Cliff went to the pay phone by the other side of the tracks and called a taxi. Soon, we would make the transfer.

As we arrived and hopped out of the cab, I began to feel withdrawn and a little paranoid. We went inside to see if we could procure some train information and to see if the journey was still worth it. "Right here" Dave announced loudly. "Right here on the fucking wall". "Look?" he asked. "What does that say?" Behind a glass door attached to a long cork board was a flyer indicating various train times, transfer options and fares. Dave was pointing to it with his finger and sliding it down the pane. "Metuchen station to Penn station" he said. "In 15 more minutes". "Looks like we made it just in time" I replied. "For once, Dave has redeemed himself. "We should leave you here" Dave said. "You're already starting". "I'm gonna be over here in this alcove in the corner" I replied. "I don't feel like being by people right now". "Ok" Dave said "If you're gonna be good, I'll leave you alone. For the time being anyway" he laughed.

When this part of the plateau came along, it always made me feel very vulnerable. Meanwhile, the rest of the party was standing around conversing while I stood there immobile, ashen and silent. Slightly shaken, I was mortified and felt like a victim of a car crash on a gurney. I had seen a TV episode once where a man who was thought to be dead was only able to move his pinky finger. The entire time he was paralyzed but could hear everything going on around him. Though he was fully conscious and aware, he could not cry out or make a sound. I related to him with this experience but on a more philosophical level. Like the man, I desperately wanted it to end. But, I wouldn't dare let on to my friends. How would it look if I was losing it and I had been the supplier of the drug? Therefore, I stood my ground. As I glanced around the room the dreaded tickling effect was starting to kick in and I felt like everyone was staring at me. The paranoia was becoming real. Having had past experiences with this feeling, I had specifically chosen the corner to give the illusion that I didn't want anyone behind me. Dave didn't know the real reason for my isolation and would soon press me to find out. He came over to me and began his questioning. "Hey, Ron?" he asked "How come you keep looking up toward those people over there and then you look back down? You look like you saw a ghost, bro". "I don't know what you're talking about" I whispered. "I don't know anyone over there. Now, leave me alone Dave". "I don't know" Dave said. "I have a feeling you know one of those girls over there and that's why you're over here hiding. He was very intuitive and correct. I didn't want him to know, but there were two girls with men who were much older than us standing by the stairs. They were joking and cajoling each other for what seemed to me like hours. Everything felt like it was in slow motion when I realized it was one of the girl's I knew. She was someone who I had been in a past relationship with and it had ended badly. I was wondering why she was with a guy who looked as if he was in his late 40"s. "You keep staring at that one girl over there" Dave chuckled. "What's the connection, man?" he asked. "You're just being paranoid, Dave" I replied. "Now, go away". Dave, not being the type to let you off once he had you on the hook announced "Hey everybody, Ronnie over here has a crush on that girl over there in the fur coat. He keeps eyeing her up". My heart fell to my knees as I felt ultimate embarrassment. I knew Dave wasn't going to quit so easily. The girl and her friends looked over at us and began laughing. Again, I was the brunt of someone else"s joke. "Hey, you over there" Dave yelled out. "The girl with the long blonde hair. Do you know my friend Ronnie over here?" he asked. "He's over here in the corner with us pretending he doesn't know you". The girl and her friends continued to glance over and chuckle but gave no response. "Dave" I moaned "Stop man, just fucking stop. You're being an asshole". "Not until I get to the bottom of this" he said wryly. "I wanna know what's going on here. Did she break up with you or what?" he asked. "I know you, man. You don't avoid people unless something bad happened". "Yeah, Dave" I mumbled. "We broke up, ok? I don't want to talk about it. Are you happy now?" Dave yelled over to the girl again "Hey chick, don't worry about it. It was a mistake; Ronnie says he doesn't know you". "Thanks a lot, Dave" I said. "That was just what I needed". "I'm happy to help you, man" he laughed. "I did it for your own good. If We're going to Times Square, there's going to be thousands of people there. We can't have you being overly paranoid, man. Its better you face it now, instead of later on". "Thanks, dad" I said "I didn't know I needed another father". "Just looking out for you, bro" he exclaimed "Just looking out for you". "Yeah" I thought. "But, like always, at my expense instead".

We boarded the train and were on our way to Times Square and party town NYC. The acid was still prevalent in my system and I was doing my best to cope. As we were walking down the aisles between cars and trying to find some empty seats, I noticed that it was a very full train. People were either staring at us, or the acid was forcing me to think that way. I turned to Mickey who was behind me and exclaimed "Mick, it looks like it's a full house in here tonight, man. Maybe we should just hang out in between the cars". Dave who was behind Mick was laughing "There goes Ronnie trying to hide again, he'll do anything not to mingle. "Fuck you, Dave" I yelled back "I don't need any asshole analyzing". "I'm watching you, Ron" Dave blurted "Even if you hide, I'll find you". We finally settled between some cars and waited for our half hour ride to Penn station to end. I remember facing the window and watching the blur of trees pass by as the acid took over my brain. I could see my reflection in the glass and my long hair rocking back and forth. I felt weightless and in a breeze. I thought "Was it from the train? Or, were my locks melting?" Everything felt like suspended animation. Suddenly, I wasn't afraid or paranoid anymore. But, like Jimmy had asked earlier, was I in reality or was I in fact becoming a cartoon? I started to think I was a caricature of myself. I had a lot of questions. Was I the real Ronnie? Or, was I watching myself as a clone of who I wanted to be?

Fortunately, Dave had stopped pestering me and my trip was becoming more peaceful. If he would have let off of me, I probably would have been harmonious with myself much sooner. I had started to come out of my turn inward and my jumpiness began to subside. The humorous and fun part was starting to flow in. To me, it was always the best part of the trip. The peak was ebbing and everything you saw was comedic and entertaining. "How you doing over there, Ron?" Mickey asked. "You look a lot better than you did before at the train station". "I'm ok now, Mick" I replied. "I'm in a better place now". "The better place will be the city" Cliff said. "I can't wait to get there. It's New Year"s Eve 1976. You guys know it's gonna be crazy". "I can't wait" Jeff cackled. "I wanna see the ball drop like on TV". "The only balls dropping will be mine" Danny laughed. "If I get too fucked up". "You'll be fine, Danny" I replied. "Just make sure we all stay together. NYC is not the type of place you wanna get lost in on a night like tonight". "Ron"s right" Cliff said. "Let's just all stay together". The crackle of the train"s loudspeaker had begun and was announcing the next upcoming station. "Next stop, Newark" it blared. "Next stop, Newark, New Jersey! With continuing service to Penn station in New York City. Next stop, Newark". "That's the one" said Mick. "After the next one, We're there". "New York City" Jimmy exclaimed. "I can't wait".

As we pulled into Penn station, most of us were feeling the effects of slight hallucinations and giddiness from the low grade LSD. We stepped off the train and gathered together deciding on which way to go. I turned around and saw the steps that led up to the main concourse. "I think we go this way" I said. "We have to go up there and find the escalator. And from there, we can go to the street". "Sounds like a plan" said Mick. "Let's follow Ron". While disembarking the escalator, Jeff was looking around in amazement. "Wow!" he yelled out. "Look at the size of this fucking place!" "It's rather large, isn't it Jeff?" asked Dave. "Just like Ronnie's fucking head!" "He does have a rather large cranium" laughed Cliff. "I hope he knows where he's going!" "A bigger head means smarter brain" I laughed. "So, let's just stop the insults and concentrate on where We're supposed to go, ok?" Jeff began to sing a part of a song from a TV commercial. "Cause his head is bigger than his body". Everybody began to laugh. "So, you think that's funny, huh Jeff?" I asked. "Not as funny as if it was the Thanksgiving Day parade" he said. "If we were here for that, Ronnie's head would be one of the balloons". "He's got a point there" said Danny. "You're forehead should be in a museum". "We could turn him over and play golf with him" laughed Jeff. "His head is like a 9 iron". "Are you guys done?" I asked. "Because this is getting boring". "Lead the way" replied Dave. "Just make sure you duck if you see any rafters". "I should have left you home, Dave" I groaned. "What fun would that be?" he asked. "Without me to pick on you and to keep you in line, imagine how mediocre this trip would be". "I could say some stuff about you too, Dave" I replied. "But, I"d rather not get into a pissing contest with you". "There he goes again fellas" Dave chuckled. "Don't you know why everybody picks on you, Ron?" Dave asked. "Because you're mister serious all the time. Its fun to fuck with you and you let us". "I guess I'll have to work on that and get back to you" I replied. "Now, let's go find Broadway and Times Square".

We made it to our destination and were looking for a liquor store. When we found one, there was a multitude of people loitering outside just beyond the door. Inside, the place was packed. It seemed like everyone and his mother was attempting to purchase alcohol. "How the fuck are we gonna get in there?" asked Dave. "I don't know" replied Jeff. "But, let's ask Ronnie. He's always good at scheming". "What do you think, Ron?" asked Mick. "You think you can come up with something so we can get in there?" "Who has change?" I asked. "Like, in coins?" asked Cliff. "Yeah" I said. "All of you reach into your pockets and hand me as many coins as you can". "What the hell is this all about?" asked Danny. "What? Are you gonna buy all the liquor with coins now?" "I think I know what Ronnie's gonna do" laughed Cliff. "This is gonna be hilarious!" I looked at Cliff, winked, and collected about $3 worth of change. "Watch this" I exclaimed as I made my way to the door. I struggled through various arms, bodies, and legs and reached for the handle. As I opened the portal, I took the handful of coins and threw them to the floor. They bounced, pinged, and swirled around like gravel in a cyclone. Suddenly, everyone in line was clamoring for their share. As they lay crouched desperately attempting to retrieve their revenue, I motioned for my friends to come inside. "We've got them now" I yelled. "Now, We're first in line". "Fuck these people" Cliff howled. "They can all wait. Let's get some booze bro". I instructed the clerk behind the Plexiglas divider to retrieve a bottle of Night Train and 2 bottles of Mad Dog 2020. I slipped him the required currency through the slot in the tray and he reciprocated by pushing through the bottles accordingly. Grabbing them, I handed one to Cliff, and the two others to Dave. "Now, we have drinks" I laughed. "Don't ever underestimate me again".

We were meandering down Broadway sipping on our libations while discussing how to get to the best spot for the ultimate view for the festivities. When I had been to New York City before, most people wouldn't make eye contact with me and were not very cordial. On this night, when a stranger passed, I said "Happy New Year" and they would immediately return the greeting. It was refreshing for once to see that everyone was on the same page. Braving the cold, Jeffrey was beginning to be a handful. He was rolling his head from side to side and jabbering incoherent sentences about how beautiful everything had become. In between sips of Night Train I exclaimed "It's ok, Jeff. Just stick with us and you'll be all right. There's a lot of us here with you tonight. So, we won't let anything happen to you". Just then, he reached for my sleeve forcing the bottle of booze to spill all over my coat and dripping down my leg. "Nice one, Jeff" I screamed. "Thanks a lot, bro. This jacket is fucking expensive, man. I don't even know if I'll be able to get out the cheap booze stains now!" Cliff yelled back at me defending Jeff aggressively "Don't blame him asshole" he yelled. "You know you were gonna get fucked up tonight well before we even came here. Who the fuck wears an expensive jacket to a place like this that has the potential for that to happen knowing he was gonna be surrounded by this many people?" he asked. "Besides, didn't you tell me a few weeks ago some chick stole that coat for you from Macy"s in Menlo Park Mall? You didn't pay for shit. So, you can leave Jeff alone before we all jump your ass. It's not his fault. He's never been this fucked up before. Cut the kid some fucking slack!" "He may be right" replied Dave. "Don't you remember being that fucked up yourself a few times?" he asked. "I suppose" I replied. "But, it's the nicest jacket I've ever owned". "Then, you shouldn't have worn it here" said Mick. "Nice shit should stay home". "Ok counsel man Mick" I replied. "I guess I'll just have to deal with it. But, now I'm gonna stink like booze the rest of the night". "You fucking stink anyway, Arold" laughed Danny. "Let's just drop this bullshit and have some fun for once. We all do enough fighting at home". "I hear that" replied Jimmy. "Let's just enjoy watching the ball drop". "Ok" I said. "I'll drop it. But, can everyone just try to be careful not to spill anymore alcohol on me the rest of the night?" "Typical Ronnie" Dave chortled. "He's always worried about his looks". "Believe me, Ron" Dave said "Nobody here gives a fuck".

The countdown for 1976 had begun and the crowd was going wild with anticipation. Finally, the glistening, mirrored red ball began to fall while everyone did the predicted screaming of 5, 4,3,2,1. After it had slid to its base, the flashing 1976 numerals were hitting us like an automated glittering strobe light. Then, a plethora of confetti was dropping from the rooftops of the skyscrapers surrounding us. Jeffrey was enamored by this and was mumbling to himself about how the shreds of paper falling were very "sparkly". "Yes, Jeff" I laughed. "They do look pretty cool, don't they?" "Wow" said Jeff. "Just, wow!" "I think he's seeing a lot of trails right now" laughed Mick. "The problem is" replied Dave. "Is that by tomorrow, he probably won't remember any of it". "We'll just ask Ronnie" chuckled Danny. "He fucking remembers everything". "It's what I do" I said. "It must be my overly large head you guys always make fun of". "At least it comes in good for something" Dave said. "I'll give you that". "Somebody has to remember these events" I joked. "Because, years from now, none of you will". When the crowd began to disperse, we took our time strolling down the avenue and back to Penn station. "That was fun as fuck" Jeff mumbled. "We have to do this again". "In time" replied Dave. "But, the next time We'll have to make sure your eyes aren't rolling back in your head".

On the train back home, Jeff had become very out of it and belligerent. He refused to listen to any of us and insisted we were all negative. He was going up to passengers and telling them he "loved" them. None of the commuters were amused. "Tell your friend to leave his hands off of me" cautioned a woman. "There's something obviously wrong with him. Tell him to back off before I call the conductor". "Oh, shit" I said. "Somebody better babysit his ass, before he gets into trouble". As we were traipsing down the aisles trying to keep Jeff under control, a conductor came up from behind us and gave us a stern lecture. "Listen kids" he said. "You're friend here is obviously very intoxicated on something. If you can't stop him from bothering the other passengers, I'm going to force all of you to get off at the next stop". "I'll take care of him" proclaimed Danny. "You better" demanded the conductor. "Because, I'm not going to tell you again". As the conductor left, Danny grabbed Jeff around his waist and picked him up off the floor. Jeff's legs were dangling like a puppet who was about to be removed from the stage. "We're taking you in between the cars again" said Danny. "It's the best place we can watch you without you trying to touch anymore people". When we arrived inside, there were two girls standing in there alone. One of them I recognized right away. She lived behind my house and was a couple of years younger than me. She knew most of us and asked where we were coming from. "Hey" I said. "We're coming from Times Square". "You know Jeff here, right?" I asked. "Yeah" she replied. "I know him. But, he looks really fucked up. What the hell did you guys give him tonight?" "Just some low grade acid" I replied. "But, he was drinking too. So, I guess he got obliterated". "I need a break" Danny shouted. "Someone else needs to take a turn watching him. This shit is exhausting". Feeling pity for Jeff and his precarious state, the girl and her friend offered to console him. The girl took Jeff is her arms and began stroking his head to calm him down. "It's ok, Jeff" she murmured. "Everything"s gonna be all right now. I'm here". Jeff peered up at her face like a baby seeing its mom for the very first time. "I love you" he replied. "I know you do" said the girl. "I love you, too". "No, you don't understand" he cried "I really, really love you". I never saw him do acid again.

A new pinball arcade named Romper Room had opened next to the Hess gas station on Route 27 just before the Highland Park border. It contained one lone pool table in the front and 6 or 7 pinball machines in the back. On some evenings, the place was so packed; and you couldn't fit anymore teens in there with a shoehorn. Out of all of the pinball joints, this is the one that had kids selling the most drugs. Available were Black Beauties, Christmas Trees, Quaaludes, Tuinals, pot, cocaine, acid, etc. If you wanted it, it was there. This summer, I was hanging around with Jesse a lot. Jesse thought a lot like me and trusted almost no one. We also liked the same kind of music and understood artist"s lyrics that related to our lives. We did a lot of tripping there and planned a lot of schemes. One of our favorites was my purchase of sheets of low level LSD that was also known as acid. I would pay $17 for a strip of 25, cut them up into little squares, bring them to Romper Room, and Jesse and I would make bank. We had it down so well, we could even afford to keep a few hits for ourselves. There were many types of imprints on these squares, such as Snoopy wearing sunglasses sitting on his dog house, red triangles, and bull"s eyes just to name a few. The bull"s eyes must have been good because almost everyone wanted them as they were popular. Jesse and I would pop a couple of hits and wander the streets until the sun came up. Sometimes, when he was peaking, Jesse would come up with some profound philosophical statements about the universe or why we were here. On one of those nights, he did just that. "Ron?" he asked. "What would you do if you picked up a rock and it talked back to you?" "A rock?" I asked. "What the fuck does a rock have to do with tripping, bro?" "Cid" he said. "Cid?" I asked "What does cid mean?" "Acid" he replied. "If the rock yelled back and said "Cid" he asked. "What would you do?" "I"d take a valium and try to come down" I laughed. "Because I would think I was going crazy". "Ron?" he yelled "I'm seeing a little guy lifting up a rock over there. He's telling me to do more cid. What should I do, bro?" "Talk to him" I replied "And, tell him about the trails of light that take you to never land". "But Ron?" he asked. "The little guy looks like you". "Squish him with your foot" I said "There's already too many fucked up people like me around". I watched as he picked up the rock, threw it across the road, stepped down like he was smashing a bug, and yelled "El Cid, you will never get me". "Nobody is after you Jesse" I chuckled. "But, it's the Cid Police" he said "They are watching us everywhere" "Ok" I replied "Just tell me when they handcuff you. That way I don't have to worry about you wandering the streets" "I won't wander anywhere" he said. "You know why?" he asked. "No Jesse, why?" I said. Before I had a chance to answer, he started singing. "Now it's time, to say goodnight to you. Now it's time, to bid you sweet adieu". It was an Aerosmith song from the Rocks album called Home Tonight and it was his absolute favorite song. "You're gonna be going sweet adieu soon if you keep that shit up" I laughed. "Because, if anyone sees you acting that way, they're gonna take you to the nut house". "Sing it with me Ron" he screamed. "You're a lead singer bro, belt that shit out". If I told him no, he would subject me to more imaginary creatures. As I was having my own problems trying to navigate between light trails from cars whizzing by, I complied.

"Where should we go?" I asked. "We've been walking around seeing shit for the last couple of hours". "I think I'm getting hungry" he replied. "If you're hungry" I said. "Then, you must be coming down". "I guess we should go see the Hamburglar" he laughed. "Because, I need to burgle some meat" "You better watch how you say that" I said "Someone might get the wrong idea". "The only one I let burgle my meat are little sluts" he muttered. "But, maybe if I find one named Patty she can add to my onions". "Will you tickle her bun?" I asked. "Only if Mayor McCheese watches us" he said. "I gotta get away from Officer Big Mac". I knew I was in for a long night. "I'll be Captain Crook" I replied. "You steal the meat, and I'll sell the shakes". "Shakes are what you get with the shit you sell" he said. "So, mix them up good". As we arrived at the golden arches, I could see that Howie was there with a few of his cronies. Jesse and I greeted them and went inside to order. "I'll have an Uuuullllhhh burger smothered in skank sauce" Jesse said. "With a side order of smegma". "Umm, we don't serve that here" the girl said. "You'll have to order something else". "What's smegma?" I asked. "It's cheese" he said. "I've never heard of any cheese like that, sir" the worker replied. "That's because its dick cheese" Jesse laughed. "Now, go in the back and get me some". In between trying to hold down my composure and laughing at Jesse"s comments, I suggested I"d get the food and bring it to him outside. "Ok" he said. "But, don't forget my feel you up fries". "I'll get them for you" I said. As soon as you sit at a table and look at the moon". He turned to walk away and I could hear him rhyming to himself "Moon, spoon, room, poon, boom". I had no idea what he meant. The girl behind the counter asked me "What's wrong with your friend? He's acting kind of out of it". "Oh, he's on some special kind of medication" I replied. "He sometimes gets his words mixed up". She didn't know it, but I was really trying to distract her from calling the manager so we wouldn't get kicked out. She seemed pretty agreeable to my plight and offered me some advice. "You should give him a milkshake" she whispered. "Maybe it will calm him down". "Thank you" I replied. "I'll do that, please give me a large one with the rest of my order".

I paid for the food, grabbed the bags and drinks, and went out to investigate where Jesse was. He was sitting at a table with a guy we knew named Mike L. Like Jesse, Mike was pretty tall and had a great sense of humor. "Jesse tells me you have some hits for sale?" he asked. "Can I get a couple of them from you?" "Sure" I replied. "They are 3 bucks a piece" "Can't I get a discount?" he pleaded "I spent most of the last of my money on hamburgers". As Jesse was taking sips of his milkshake, he turned to me and asked "He's a friend of mine, Ron. Do me a favor and give him the scarf, ok?" "All right" I replied "But, only for you. And, don't tell anyone else. For you, 2 bucks each". "Fantastic" Mike said. "I'm gonna have fun tonight" I took the small glass bottle I kept the blotter hits in, turned it upside down, opened it, and shook out his purchase. "Here you go, Mike" I said. "Don't get too crazy". "Crazy is my middle name" he laughed. "It's what I do". He took the hits from my hand, opened up his half eaten hamburger, placed them on the pickles, and then closed the bun back up. "What did you do that for?" I asked. "You're supposed to wait until after you're done eating". "I don't see a problem" he replied. "This way, I get my nourishment and my buzz at the same time" He wolfed down his food in a flash, shook our hands, and went on his way. "What was that all about?" I asked Jesse. "Oh, he's always like that bro" he said. "Mike believes in efficiency".

While we were smoking our cigarettes after our meal, we heard a loud commotion coming from the roof. There were teens gathering around and yelling "Jump, jump". It seemed like someone was up there and dancing. As the figure got closer, we could see it was Howie. "How the hell did he get up there?" I thought. "Who wants to see me try to jump down from here?" Howie asked. "Us, us" the crowd screamed. "I'm gonna do it. Are you guys ready?" he asked. Yes, yes" they replied. "On 3" he yelled. "1-2-3" and jumped. Just below the roof were the hard plastic umbrellas that covered the tables. They looked to be made from very tough resin and could easily hold Howie"s weight. As he hit the top at the point, we could hear a loud wallop. His feet landed with one foot on each side and he was in a crouching position. He was balancing between umbrellas and starting to slip. "I'm the king of the French fries" he howled. "No fry shall possess me". A man came flying through the door that appeared to be the manager. "What do you kids think you're doing?" he screamed. "You could get killed jumping off of that roof" "Get down from there son, right away", he demanded. "And, I want all of you kids to go home. This isn't your playground for god"s sake". "You don't have to bring god into it" Howie retorted. "I'm only cloud surfing". The man became extremely angry "You have exactly 5 minutes to disburse. If you don't, I'm calling the cops" he threatened. As Howie was climbing down he mumbled "Next time, I'll have to bring my poles. I could have gotten better speed with those."

I was walking home by the Edison Bank one afternoon and I heard many fire truck sirens in the distance. I was wondering where they were coming from and knew they were pretty close. As I turned the corner, I could see a large plume of smoke billowing into the sky. I looked to my right and saw that the Linwood Grove bar was on fire. I thought "Holy shit, that place has been there forever. It doesn't look like anyone will be drinking in there anymore". My older brother had hung out there sometimes and told me a few stories about it occasionally. Since I was underage, I was never allowed much past the front door. The only think I knew about the place was that other than waiting outside to try to get people to buy me booze, was that there was a moose head they had over the bar and that their sandwiches were supposed to be pretty good. Other than that, the right building was falling apart and it was a fire trap waiting to happen. I watched with some others from across the street and could feel some of the heat emanating from the building as it was collapsing in on itself. As I have mentioned previously, it was just a place my friends and I drank behind and its significance was of no importance to us. But, I understood how it could have been to others. It was after all, a local known landmark that had a rich history and was frequented by many locals. Eventually, as the fire raged and became more intense, we were ordered to move away and to find another place as a viewing point. I lost interest by then and decided to go to the Gulotta"s house instead.

As I walked up the Gulotta"s stairs, I could hear laughing going on inside. This wasn't unusual I thought as there was always something comical going on in their house. The door was slightly open and I could hear Dennis singing part of Led Zeppelin"s song called Whole Lotta Love. But, part of it didn't sound right and was off to me. "Dennis" I yelled. "Can I come in?" From his bedroom, he called back to me. "Who is that?" he asked. "It's me, Ron" I replied. "Come on in" he said. "I'll be right there". I entered and waited by the dining room table as I had always done many times before. Just then, Dennis came flying out of the room shouting "Gulotta Whole Lotta Love" and was repeating the words over and over. "Gulotta Whole Lotta Love, whirrrrr" he sang as he imitated the sliding guitar part with his voice. He was gyrating his hips and singing into an imaginary microphone. I immediately saw the humor in this and was cracking up hysterically. "Dennis?" I asked. "Where did you come up with that?" "Well" he said in between gyrations "I give women a lot of loving. So, instead of a whole lotta love, I give them Gulotta whole lotta love. It makes perfect sense to me. Don't you think, bro?" "If you say so, Den" I replied. "All I know is, that's damn funny how you changed the words to fit your last name like that". "It's gonna be my new signature song" he replied. "Every time that song comes on the radio or I hear it someplace I'm gonna sing it that way". "Ok, Den" I laughed. "What else do you have for me today?" "I have others" he yelped. But, I'll show you later. Right now, I'm putting the King Biscuit Flower Hour on the radio. Yes is gonna be on. It's a full concert and I wanna hear it. Why don't you hang out for a while and join me, bro?" he asked. "I can do that" I replied. "And, I have some pretty good weed with me too". "Ulllhhhh" he cried. "Excellent! We can get stoned and listen to Yes. But first, I need you to do me a favor, man" "What's that, Den?" I asked. "I need you to run to the diner and get us some coffee. I'm all out and I'm craving some bean. I'll give you a few bucks and you go get some, ok? You know how I like it, right bro?" he asked. "Yeah, yeah" I replied. "I know, I know. Light and sweet, right?" "You got it" he replied. "And, hurry up too, because the radio show"s starting soon. I don't want you to miss any of it". "I'll go as fast as I can" I said. "Run" he laughed. "And, try not to spill any". "Duh" I said mockingly "It's got a plastic top and it'll be in a bag". "Just checking" he said. "Just checking".

When I returned with the scalding java and reentered the house, Dennis was screaming something again. As soon as I traversed the front entryway, he was standing right in front of me bent over and blocking my way in. It looked like he was trying to touch his toes in some kind of exercise maneuver. Then, he reached back, cupped his hands over each butt cheek and was pretending to gape his ass crack open and closed. "Dennis!" I yelled. "I have your coffee here. What the fuck are you doing, man?" I asked. "Sodomy" he shrieked. "Hey, Ron" he said. "Don't economize, sodomize". "Have you been watching that Hertz rental car commercial on TV again Dennis?" I asked laughing. "I changed the words to that one too" he replied. "Isn't it great?" "Is this what you have to do all day since you quit school?" I asked. "I have to do something to be entertained" he said. "What else is there to do all day around here except play guitar and watch TV." "Well, we can start by drinking these coffees" I replied.

"And then, I'll roll up a bone and we can listen to some music". "Weed and Yes" Dennis said. "For now, that's all we need, bro".

The concert on the radio was two hours long and was coming to an end. It was beginning to get dark outside and I was wondering what we were going to be doing next. "What's on the agenda, Den?" I asked. "There's no food in this house again" he replied. "You wanna hit the Jade and see if we can get ribs like the last time?" "Do you think it's safe?" I asked. "Don't you think by now those guys would be on to us?" "Nah" he sneered. "Those guys are foreigners. They're morons, bro. All they know how to do is cook and take orders. We should be ok". "If you're sure we can get away with it again" I said. "I don't want to go to jail for stealing food. My parents would wig out if they had to come and get me from that one". "We'll be extra careful" he replied. "We gotta get some eats. Help me out again, bro. I'm starving!" "Ok, Den" I replied anxiously. "But, you're gonna owe me big time for this one" "Don't I always let you hang out at my house after I kick everyone else out?" he laughed. "I know how you help us. Its copasetic, bro. You have nothing to worry about, man". "Just make sure we don't get caught" I blurted. "That's all I ask" "Mission accomplished" he replied. "I can taste those ribs now".

Just like the first time, we snuck up to the back door and did our recognizance. Silently, with a lot of whispering and hand signals, we approached but were leery about anyone seeing us. I prowled up to the screen door and gave Dennis the high sign to hold it open for me. Like before, we could see that the cooks were busy and distracted and it was the perfect time to pounce. "Grab a tray on the bottom. Just like we did before, bro" Dennis whispered. I tip toed up to the rack, slid the platter out, balanced it against my hip, and made off into the night. Just as we were running and approaching the border of the properties between the Jade and Raritan Oil"s back parking lot, I heard a whoosh behind my right ear. "Holy fuck"

Dennis screamed. "He's got a fucking cleaver! Run bro, run". I turned slightly for an instant and could make out the gleam of the edge of something metallic and shiny. It looked like it was very sharp. "Whoosh" I heard again. I heard a voice cry out "I keer you, you fucking kids. I keer you. You no steal from me" It seemed one of the Chinese cooks had seen us at the last minute running from the door and he was trying to cut me with his tool. "Under the tank truck, Ron" Dennis screamed. He was ahead of me and could see the man better than I could. Like a contestant doing a limbo competition, I had to see how low I could go to escape. I desperately wanted to see if I could make it while still holding on to the tray. As I slid down underneath the truck, I handed the tray to Dennis. He took off between the other side of the oil tankers and the trailer park. This left me to deal with cleaver man chasing me from behind. Unbeknownst to him, the oil tanker trucks were almost always lined up in sequence and parked at the end of the day. Since they had already been sitting for some hours, I used this ploy to my advantage. Its configuration made a maze that wasn't an easy navigation unless you had known of it beforehand. Experienced with this, I merely had to circumvent the puzzle easily, leaving the cook far behind. I watched as he attempted to follow me. He skidded under one truck after another while trying to keep a grip on his cleaver. Fortunately for me, he was not successful. As I hit the exit curb of the mobile home park, I could still hear the man yelling in Chinese. He seemed to have been caught under a tank, ran out of breath, and had given up. When I rounded the corner, Dennis was there waiting for me and had the tray lying on the ground in front of his feet. "He almost got you, bro" he said. "I thought for sure you were a goner at first. But, I knew once you got to the maze, he never would have caught you. He doesn't know the neighborhood like we do". "Yeah, I'm glad I was quicker than him" I replied. "Did you see the size of that fucking cleaver?" Dennis asked. "If he would have gotten to you, he would have taken your fucking head clean off, bro". "You took the tray after I shimmied under that first truck. So, that helped me out a lot. I'm glad you did that. I don't think I would have gotten away without you helping me. "I didn't plan it that way" Dennis said. "It just happened, bro. My adrenaline was flowing and I just grabbed it and ran. I thought since I had the tray, he was gonna change direction and come after me. I guess since he thought you were closer, he was gonna chase you instead. Anyway, I'm glad we got away from that psycho fuck. Who chases kids with cleavers anyway?" "People who have their things stolen?" I replied laughed. "I think we pissed them off" I said. "I think you may be right" Dennis replied. "But, let's get out of here in case that guy catches his breath and comes back. He'll be hunting for us and I don't need us getting cut up by some Asian murderer".

We took turns carrying our pilfered wares back to the house and laid it on the dining room table. "Dennis?" I asked. Didn't you check to see what we got after you got away?" "Nah" he said. "I was so nervous that crazy guy might cut you that I froze. I figured either way, I"d find out what was under this table cloth once I got home anyway". "Ok then" I replied" I'll let you do the honor of unveiling this shit to see what we have underneath it then". He grasped a corner and gave it a tug. "What the fuck is this bullshit, man" he gasped. It was a large mountain of white goop in the center of the pan. "Look Ron, its rice. Fucking rice! I can't believe we risked our lives for some fucking rice. I can't believe this shit!" "Well, it's still food, Den" I replied. "But, it's not ribs, bro" he said. "I had my heart set on some tasty barbeque ribs. We got ripped off, man". "I think they were on to us" I said. "Fuck!" Dennis shouted. "I know what happened! I forgot. JR and Pyka climbed up onto the roof of the Jade last week. They went up the fire escape and in through the window to the rooms upstairs. They have illegal immigrants who work downstairs in shifts and then sleep and live up there. JR told me him and Pyka stole their wallets from their pockets from their pants hanging up on pegs on the wall". "Now you tell me" I complained. "If I would have known that shit, I don't think I would have stolen from them again. How the fuck could you forget something like that, man?" "I was hungry, bro" he laughed. "My stomach knows no bounds".

It was a Friday night and Dennis M. was complaining that he was hungry. He was living in the Velez"s apartment below their mother's house and he never seemed to have enough money to feed himself. So, I came upon the idea of breaking into soda machines to help him out. Coke machines were mostly easy prey as they were usually secluded enough where people wouldn't see us and entering them was a breeze. "What are we gonna use to get into them?" Dennis asked. "Well" I replied. "I've used screwdrivers in the past, but a crowbar usually does the trick and is way faster". "I have a small one that I can hide right under my coat" he boasted. "Stay right here and I'll be right back" he said. "Johnny has one he left here in the closet from when they were fixing this place up". "Ok" I replied. "Go and get it and bring it back here. I wanna see if it's strong enough". "Oh, it's strong enough" he said. "It's made out of forged steel, bro". As I waited, I began thinking of the best places that had obstructed views and were easy pickings. We settled on the Howard Johnson Motel in New Brunswick by the Morris Goodkind Bridge and walked up there to have a look around. "There's a Coke machine right here" Dennis quipped. "It's inside this little alcove too. No one will see us cracking open this thing". I peered around to see if there were any nosey motel guests about and asked Dennis to hand me the crowbar. "This looks like it's gonna be a piece of cake" I said exuberantly. "Gimme that thing and lets hurry up and do this" I said. "I don't see anyone? Do you?" I asked. "The coast is clear as of right now" he replied. "But, let's do this as fast as possible. The Coke machine is kind of hidden and We're sticking out like sore thumbs". "30 seconds" I said. "Just gimme 30 seconds" I inserted the tool in between the machine"s creviced edge trying to look for some leverage. When I got it in the perfect position, I leaned my body weight into it and gave it a pull. "It's coming" Dennis whispered. "Give it a few more tugs, Ronnie". I yanked and yanked as hard as I could. But, the door wouldn't budge. "I'm running out of breath here, man" I said exhausted. "You're bigger than me. You're gonna have to take a turn". "Gimme that fucking thing" he said annoyed. "You're always making everything difficult". I stepped away and gave him a handoff of the cold steel apparatus and passed him while I was laughing. "What's so fucking funny?" he asked. "I've gotten into machines like this one before, man" I replied. "This fucker"s not gonna budge". "We'll see about that bullshit" he remarked. "I need money. So, I'm getting in this fucker by hook or by crook". "Just don't crook your back trying" I said. "Because, I'm not carrying you home".

Dennis gave it all he had. So much so, that the machine was starting to rock back and forth. "Come on, you little scumbag" he howled. "Give it up, bitch". "I'm telling you, that sucker"s not gonna open" I chuckled. "It's like a virgin on prom night". "I've had many virgins before" he laughed. "I'm gonna stoke this slut until she opens". Just as he was finishing his sentence, the door to the machine finally gave way. It opened with a clang and swung to our left with a whoosh. "I told you I"d get this clammy bitch open" he howled. "It's just a matter of weight distribution". "Well, you weigh more than me like I mentioned before" I said. "So, put that crowbar down and let's get to the coin return box". We looked down and saw a vertical and metal container where the change was supposed to be. "Slide that fucking thing out, man" he demanded. "Let's see if there's any money in there". I slid the box out, turned it to the light, and glanced inside. "You're not gonna like this, bro" I said cautiously. "But, there's only like 50 cents on the bottom". "Get the fuck out of here" he screamed loudly. "All that work for 50 fucking cents? What kind of motel only sells 50 cents worth of soda?" he asked. "Look around you, Den" I said howling with laughter. "A cheap one". "Dirty, white trash, cheapo motherfuckers" he bellowed. "I can't believe none of these fucks drink soda". "Well" I replied. "Since we got beat on the money aspect of it, let's take a few Coke"s instead". We grabbed a few cans, stuffed them in our pockets and were intending to walk back home. As we strode up the path away from the concession area, we have to walk up a small hill to get back up to the bridge. Dennis was trying to juggle drinking his Coke with one hand, and balancing the crow bar under his coat. He had its tail end tucked in the back of his pants and the hook under his arm. Just as we turned to climb the last turn, we heard a loud voice behind us. "Freeze" the voice said. "And, you fuckers had better not move". "Who the fuck is that?" I asked Dennis nervously. "I have no fucking idea" he replied. "But, we have two choices. We can try to run for it, or turn around" "Fuck it "I said. "I'm gonna turn around to see who it is". I spun on my left foot and whirled around facing him. It was a short overweight man who was partially bald with a comb over and was wearing horn rimmed glasses. "Who the fuck are you?" I asked demandingly. "I'm the motel detective" he replied brazenly. "We've had break ins in some of our rooms and some of our TV sets have been missing. I don't recognize either of you" "Are you guests here?" he asked authoritatively. Hearing this, Dennis turned around. "Not me" he replied. "I would never stay in this dump. And, as far as stealing TV sets, you"ve got the wrong people, sonny boy". "Never the less" the motel cop replied. "I have to check the both of you out". As he was reaching for me, I gave Dennis the wink. We knew if this guy went too far, we would just run and try to out fox him. That was until his partner showed up. The 2nd detective showed us his badge and demanded that he be able to frisk us". "Go ahead" I said. "I have nothing to hide". As the 1st cop was patting me down, the 2nd one was doing the same to Dennis. We both knew that Dennis still had the crowbar hidden in the back of his coat. With nervous anticipation, I watched as the cop reached under DenniS's open pelage and ran his hands down over his waist and to his ankles below. "I've got nothing here" said the 2nd detective. "I don't either" mentioned the 1st cop. "I guess we have to let them go" "You guys have to understand" the 2nd cop said. "We've had a lot of burglaries here lately. One of you fit the description of a guy who pulled up in his car yesterday and loaded up 3 TV"s. So, we have to question everybody". "Yeah, yeah" I replied. "We get it. Can we go now or what?" I asked. The 2 officers turned away from us and were whispering with each other. Dennis and I were cracking up thinking about how we were about to be released. "My partner here wants to frisk you guys one more time" the 2nd cop said. "Just to be sure". "Fuck that!" Dennis howled. "You guys aren't even real cops. So, We're leaving. You"ve had your little game, now it's over". "Well" the first cop said. "You can either let us try again, or we can call the city police and we can do it in front of them. So, I would comply if I was you". "Don't do it, Den" I yelled. "Fuck these rent a cops". Dennis must have felt confident as he had fooled them with his shake down from the first time. "Go ahead then, asshole" he screamed. "But, make this shit fast". Just like with the initial pat down, I stood like a stone and waited. "This one is ok like before" the 1st cop said. "What do you have?" he asked the 2nd cop. As the 2nd officer turned his head to answer, the crow bar fell out and extended itself right in front of him. "What the hell is this?" the senior cop asked. "This little fucker has a crow bar!" "Turn around and don't move" he barked. "You two hoodlums are being held until a township cruiser arrives." They put us in handcuffs and were talking on a handheld radio to someone about how the grounds needed to be searched and secured. "I don't think you're the TV thieves" the 1st cop said. "But, you must be up to something. Because you have a crow bar on you". "I have nothing to say" Dennis replied. "Do whatever you need to do". "What about you, Sonny?" he asked me. "Would you like to cooperate?" "I'm not saying shit" I answered. "And, you can't prove anything either". Suddenly, I heard a voice over the walkie talkie again. "We have a situation over here by the concession stand" the voice said. "It seems the soda machine has been pried open and broken into". "We have you now" said the 1st cop with glee. "You're going to juvenile hall". Dennis and I looked over at each other and gave the "we don't give a shit" face. We already knew when the one cop saw the tool that it was over.

As we were escorted into a New Brunswick police car, we made jokes with the transporting officers and asked them if they could help us. "You know" I said. "It would be really easy for you guys to just pull over on the side of the road and let us out. Those rent a cops told you themselves that they couldn't prove anything on us anyway". Laughing, the driver cackled "We could do that. But, only if you admitted to it that you two were stealing from that motel"s Coke machine". "I'm not admitting to shit!" Dennis blurted. "I didn't do anything". "I know" said the passenger cop. "Everybody is innocent. We hear it almost every day". "I'm serious" I replied. "How can you arrest us without enough proof?" I asked. "You had the crow bar, you were in the vicinity of the soda machine, and the soda machine was broken into. That's all the proof we need. All you guys have to do is fess up. If you do, We'll take you right back to the bridge and you can walk home" "Will you put that in writing? I asked. "What's the matter?" the driver cop asked chuckling. "Don't you trust us?" he asked. "Fuck no" said Dennis. "You guys lie more than the prisoners". "Your loss" replied the passenger cop. "Because, We're almost there". We pulled into the driveway, were pulled out to the reception area inside, and taken to the medical area. "We're going back out on the road" the two cops said. "You'll be processed from here and They'll go from there". "Thanks for nothing" Dennis said. "Now, get lost". "Be glad you're not 18" replied the driver cop. "Because, this would have went another way". "Well, I'm not" Dennis yelled agitated. "So, you can piss up a rope".

As we waited to take our turn in the nurse"s chair, I was pondering what story I would need to tell my parents. The nurse came back over with a needle and told me "We're going to have to take some of your blood for medical testing". "I'm not letting you take shit" I said sarcastically. "Not without talking to my parents first". "So be it" the nurse replied. "Give me their number and I'll ask them on the phone and be right back". "See how sneaky they are trying to get your telephone number? Dennis asked. "They are all the same". "You're staying here tonight until court tomorrow morning anyway" said the nurse. "It makes no matter to me". I complied and gave her my phone number as I wanted some advice from my father so as not incriminate myself. The nurse left and came back with a telephone. She plugged it into a wall jack under her desk, dialed my number, spoke a few words to my dad, and handed it to me. "What happened now?" my father asked. I told him a brief expose" of the story and waited for his plan. "Don't tell them anything" he said. "They'll try to use it against you later. Let them take the blood if they want. But, nothing else. I'll see you in court in the morning. Now, put me back on the phone with that nurse". I handed the phone to her and watched until she was done. I held out my arm and told her to go ahead. She took my specimen and motioned to a corrections officer standing against the wall to take me away. "Ok" the guy said. "It's time to go into your cell now". I looked back as Dennis, gave him the thumbs up sign and headed down the hallway. Dennis and I spent a sleepless night wondering if we'd be going home the next day. In the morning, we were served a disgusting cold breakfast and corralled into a department of corrections bus to the kiddie court in New Brunswick. When we appeared together in front of the judge, his honor reviewed the paperwork and demanded that we be released immediately. "Why do you officers continually bring before me cases with teens like this when you clearly lack the necessary evidence?" he asked the prosecutor. "Case dismissed!" Upon my release, I skipped down the court house steps singing "I beat the rap, I beat the rap". "Maybe this time" my father replied. "But, one day you won't be so lucky and I won't be able to help you". His prophecy was soon to be revealed.

Jesse and I were hanging around Romper Room again and shooting some pool on their lone pool table situated in the front room. "Look at that" I exclaimed pointing to a poster on the wall.

"What?" Jesse asked. "It's just a fucking poster, man. What's the big deal?" "Look closer" I replied. "It's Jesus. Look what it says in the inscription underneath him. I should show this to my father. Maybe then, he would get it" I laughed. "What does it say?" asked Jesse. "It says, if anyone tells you can't wear your hair long, tell them I said so". "That's hilarious" Jesse replied. "But, your father will never believe it". "I know" I said. "But, isn't it ironic?" Just then, Phil came whizzing by us like he was late for a train. "Where you going, Phil?" I asked. "Shhhh" he whispered. "I just found out from someone that the little brown house across the street is full of cops and they"ve been watching us for a month". "Get the fuck out of here!" Jesse chuckled. "How the fuck do you know that?" he asked. "I know somebody who works with the cops" said Phil. "Those narcs are using telescopic lenses and they are taking photographs. They supposedly have pictures of all of us smoking pot out front and handing drugs back and forth. They're supposed to raid this place soon. It might even be tonight". "Fucking Phil"s paranoid again" laughed Jesse. "I doubt they even give a fuck about any of us here. We're small potatoes to those clowns". "Don't be so sure" Phil replied. "My sources are always dead on". "I guess We'll have to wait and see" I said. "But, now that you told us Phil, each one of us better have an escape plan. I'm not being busted again". We I finished our pool game and decided to go in the back where the pinball machines were. In all, there were about 10 people in the place with an equal mix of males and females. "Who"s got the Cid?" asked Jesse. "Ron"s all out and I feel like seeing colors tonight". "I have a few hits" replied Phil. "But, you'll have to wait until I'm done with this game before I can show you". "Sounds good" said Jesse. "But, hurry up, bro. I feel like tweaking". "Keep your shirt on" Phil chuckled "I'm almost done". Suddenly, we heard the familiar sound of wheels squealing to a stop and a loud bullhorn. It was resonating with orders demanding that everyone stay still and to not move. There was only one entity that used that approach that we knew of and it was the police. They always insisted on making a cacophonous entrance thinking they were the grand masters of intimidation. Like most teenagers distraught at the sight of this, we all tried to escape. I glanced around for an exit as the fear grasped my legs insisting that I run. "Shit!" I thought. The cops will be at the back door too. How the hell am I gonna get out of this one?" As I peered over at Phil, he was pushing hits of acid down the quarter shoot in a pinball machine. "Why are you doing that?" I asked. "We should be trying to get out of here. The cops are almost in the door". "I'll come back later for them" Phil shrieked. "I'm not getting busted with those, bro. They carry a long jail time". "Jesse leaned over us and exclaimed "I know a way out of here. But, we have to act fast. They're almost in". "How?" I asked. "There's only a front and back door". "The bathroom" he replied. "It's chaos in here, man. It's now or never". "But, that window is really fucking small" I said nervously. "Fuck that" Jesse said. "We're all skinny. We should be able to make it. Especially Phil here, he's a tiny little fucker". "I'm game if you are" Phil said "So, let's go".

As the police were hitting the office in the front of the building, we were already in the rest room prying open the window. "I locked the door for extra protection" laughed Jesse. "Fuck those cops. But, hurry up, man. We have about 30 seconds before they break down this door". "Let Phil go first" I said. "He'll be fast because he's the smallest". Phil stood on the tank of the toilet bowl, pulled himself up by his hands, balanced himself on his belly, and dropped down outside to the ground. I whispered to him "What do you see out there, man?" "Hurry up, hurry up" he mumbled. "They can't see us from this side and we can get away. But, We're running out of time". "Go Ron, go" screamed Jesse. "I'm the tallest. So, hurry the fuck up". I hoisted myself up as Phil did, and balanced myself on my torso. I wasn't quite in position to finish dropping down when I felt something grabbing my ankles and pushing. The next thing I knew, I was on the grass looking up at Phil. "Come on Jesse" Phil yelled "You got about 10 seconds left, bro". We could see Jesse through the opening as he backed up against the bathroom door. "Fuck this" he mumbled. "I'm out of here". With a running start, he launched himself through the window like a projectile and never looked back. As he hit the ground, his shoulder dug into the earth and scraped his shoulder. "Wow, man" I chuckled pointing at the window. "You flew right through that fucking thing". "I didn't have time to balance my shit on no fucking ledge" he said. "I'm way too big for that bullshit. Let's talk about this later and get the fuck out of here".

As we walked the back streets to avoid the cops in their pursuit for some easy arrests, we ran into Jeffrey G. "Where are you guys going?" he asked. "I'm going to Romper Room to hang out". "You don't want to go there, bro" said Jesse. "There's a big bust going on in there right now. Phil knew it was going down and we barely got away, man". "That's right" replied Phil. "The cops were watching the place. Somebody told me it was gonna happen. Plus, I was told some of the kids who hang around there are rats". "You didn't tell us that part, Phil" I said. "So, who"s the rat?" asked Jesse "I hate fucking rats". "Yeah, Phil?" I asked. "Tell us who it is and who tipped you off". "I can't divulge my information" he said. "Let's just leave it at that and be glad we all got away. Now, I'm going back to my house because I have some shit I gotta do. I'll see you guys later". "Like hang around with rats?" asked Jesse. "He's not a rat Jesse" I replied. "No, but he hangs out with them. Same shit, man". "Whatever, man" said Phil. "I'll check you guys out later". Jesse, Jeffrey and I decided to walk to the park in front of Lindenau School. While we were there swinging on the swings and contemplating our next move, Jesse came up with a scam. "Hey, man" he said. "I know a good scarf where we might be able to make some money". "What's that?" asked Jeff. "Yeah, Jesse I said. "I'm intrigued". "You know the Beauty Rest Motel on Route 1 right?" he asked. "Sometimes, the guests leave their doors open while they go to the diner or Stewarts Root Beer across the street. We can go there and check it out. If they leave their door open, we can scarf some wallets or booze or something". "I like that idea" replied Jeff. "That sounds like easy money". "Yeah" Jesse said "It's in and out in a few seconds. Even if they call the cops, by the time they get there, We'll all be gone and can run across the highway through Edison Lanes woods. They'll never catch us". "Never say never, Jesse" I replied. "But, I'll give it a shot. Let's go".

We reached the end of the motel"s parking lot and hunkered down by the fence at the corner of the pool. "We'll have to look in the windows first" exclaimed Jesse. "We have to see if there's anybody in any of the rooms before we try the door". "That's the way to do it" I said. "There's no use trying if it's occupied". "I'm gonna stay here and be the lookout" whispered Jeff. "I'm too short to see through those windows. You guys scope it out. And, if you find a good one, give me a sign and I'll watch for the cops". "Sounds good" said Jesse. "Come on, Ron. Let's go". Jesse and I started on the far left side of the building. There were 5 rooms in all. Therefore, it wouldn't take us too much time to investigate. We peered into the first room and it was empty. Jesse reached down and turned the door knob quietly. "Fuck" he mumbled "This one is locked. Let's try the next one". We glanced inside the second one and saw nothing. Jesse once again gave the door knob a whirl. "This fucker"s locked too" he said. "There better be an open one on the next one or I'm gonna be pissed". As we crept up to the third room, we could see a shadow of light coming off the screen of a TV. It was flickering off and on like a late model set in gray and black tones. We persisted anyway as Jesse and I were insistent on finding something valuable. As we stood up to inspect and peak through a bend in the curtain, Jesse became hysterical. He had looked first and fell down to his knees. He made the shush sound with his index finger and was cracking up with laughter. "You're not gonna believe what I just saw, bro" he giggled. "Go on and take a look, man. Go ahead, you're not gonna believe it". As Jesse sat crouched and was trying not to draw attention to himself, I stood up slowly and glowered into the room. There, on the bed, was a man lying half naked on his back. He had white underpants down around his ankles and was wearing black socks. His T shirt was also white and was rolled up above his belly. His head was facing the television and he was jerking off profusely. As he spanked himself, his right hand looked like a jackhammer trying to dislodge a piece of concrete. He was beating it so fast; it looked like a blur in some weird orgasmic competition. He was moaning quietly to himself and murmuring "Oh yeah, that's it baby. Give it to me; you know you want it like that. Oh yeah baby, yeah!" Jesse stood up behind me close to my ear and whispered "Look at that fucker go! He's one horny bastard". While this carnal occurrence was taking place, Jeffrey got wind of what was going on and kept asking "What's so funny you guys? Why are you laughing so much? We're supposed to be robbing people. I don't get it?" "Should we tell him?" Jesse asked. "He might be too young to see this". "See what?" asked Jeff. "I wanna see, I wanna see". "Be quiet Jeff" I replied. "We don't want to scare the guy away. It's funny as fuck". "Ok Jeff" said Jesse. "Come over here and I'll hold you up. Wait till you see what this guy's doing, man. You're gonna piss yourself laughing". Jeffrey crept up slowly and Jesse grabbed him by his waist. He lifted him up just at the edge of the windowsill. "What do you see through the curtains, Jeff?" Jesse asked. "Holy shit" chuckled Jeff. "That fucking queer is jerking off. That's fucked up, man!" "What should we do about it Jeff?" I asked. "Yeah" said Jesse "We'll leave this one up to you". "Pick me back up a little higher so I can see his ass better" Jeff replied "I'm gonna scare the fuck outta this weirdo so he never does it again". Jesse hoisted Jeff up to a position in the middle of the window so there was no way the man would not see him. Just as the guy was getting into it and looked as if he was about to come, Jeff banged hardily on the window and screamed "Hey, you fucking faggot. We don't jerk off around here. You better go back home to your mother and get a blow up doll. You sick fuck!" The man was so startled; he jumped off the bed like a recently opened clown in a jack in the box. After steadying himself and leaning on the wall, he ran to the bathroom while tripping over his underwear. "Get out of here" he yelled. "Can't a person get some privacy?" he asked. I paid for this room". "Fuck you, and fuck your hand" Jeff screamed. "You"ve got 5 minutes to get out of here you fucking perv. Or, We're gonna beat the shit out of you! Fortunately, with the glare of the TV and the way we were bent down, we escaped without him being able to identify us. Running across Route 1 and joking between ourselves, Jeffrey boasted "I wish I would have had a camera. I would have taken a picture of that guy and blackmailed him". "Too bad" Jesse laughed "He could have been your Polaroid perv".

One night I was bored and went over to the Velez brother's house. While discussing what we could do, I got the bright idea of taking my father's car for a ride while he was at the camp ground in Jackson. He had a 4 speed 67 Cougar he kept in the garage and barely used it. "Let's go to my house" I suggested. "We can borrow my dad"s car. Him, my mom, and my little brother are gone for the weekend". "What about your other brother, the older one?" Johnny asked. "Isn't he gonna be around?" "Nah, I replied. "He comes and goes a lot. He's not usually home anymore". Bob P. asked "Do you have the keys, man? Or, do we have to hot wire it?" "I know right where he keeps the keys on a hook in the kitchen" I answered. "So, I can grab them and go". "Well, let's go then" laughed Tony. "We can take it and cruise around town". "That's the exact idea" I said. "We'll cruise around for a while and bring it back. My dad will never know". "I hope you're right" exclaimed Johnny "You know how his temper is when you aggravate him". "I'm not worried about it" I said. "He's far away and won't be back until Sunday. So, stop being a baby and We'll go for it". "Ok" Johnny replied. "It's your funeral".

As we approached my house, I could see my older brother's car parked by the curb. "Fuck!" I whispered. "What the fuck is he doing home? "He's almost never here on the weekends". "Looks like your plan is foiled, Ronnie" said Tony. "We're gonna be walking tonight". "Fuck that" I replied. "You guys stay by the side of the house. I'm gonna sneak in quietly to see if he's here or not. Maybe he left his car here and one of his friends picked him up". "Wishful thinking Ronnie" replied Bob. "But, I hope you're right". I approached my front door, creaked it half way open, and slowly stepped inside. Fortunately, our dogs recognized me and didn't bark which made it easier than I had anticipated. After getting the pets to calm down, I crept up the three flights of stairs being careful not to make a sound. If my brother wasn't sleeping, all bets were off. I gingerly pushed open his bedroom door and could see he was in a deep slumber. "Ahhh" I murmured to myself. "He's got the air conditioner on in the window. He sleeps really deep too. With the noise of that thing running, he'll never hear us". Desperate not to awaken him, I closed the door quietly and squirmed back down the stairs. I made a pit stop in the kitchen and being careful not to be noisy and grabbed the keys from a hook that was embedded in the wall. Next, I went down to the side entrance to the garage and was fortunate it wasn't locked. So, I slithered inside and peered around. "I'm gonna have to shimmy between the car and the garage door" I thought. "Then, I'll lift the door slowly so my brother doesn't hear anything". As I raised the portal open, it began to squeak. "This is gonna take some time" I whispered. "This door is really old".

I tugged up on the door"s handle every 5 minutes trying to avoid making noise. Since my brother's room was directly above the garage, I knew it would be a challenge to continue. A row of panels at a time I pulled. Quietly and meticulous, I was relentless and eventually got it completely open. Waving my friends over from the side of the house, they were praising me for being successful. "You got the keys, right?" Johnny asked. "Because, I know you wouldn't have went to all that trouble to open that rickety door unless you got them". "Is your older brother here?" asked Bob. "How did you get around him?" "He's in a dead sleep" I replied. "The air conditioner blocks out everything. I don't think he heard much. If he was gonna hear me, it would have been when I was opening this door". "Fantastic" Johnny chuckled. "What do we have to do next?" "I'm gonna go to the front of the car and put it in neutral" I said. "Then,

I'll get it rolling down the driveway real slow. Once it's backed out into the street enough, you guys help me push it forward. I want to make sure when I start it, We're out of ear shot of my brother. Close to the house, the engine makes a lot of noise. So, just to be careful We're gonna do it that way". "Sneaky Ronnie strikes again" laughed Johnny. "He's always thinks of everything". "I have to" I said. "Great crimes have plan A, B and C. I go all the way to D, E and F if I have to. I try everything imaginable not to get caught. You have to plan these things out carefully, bro". "I wish I could do that" Johnny replied. "I just don't think that way". "My mind is always going full tilt Johnny" I said. "You know that. I get bored if I don't read everything I get my hands on or lay in bed all night trying to figure shit out. It's just the way I am". "I hope you"ve thought of everything with this caper". Tony said. "You know your dad will throw away the key for taking his car if he catches you" "He'll get over it" I replied. "Because, he's never gonna find out". "Overconfident Ronnie" laughed Bob. "I hope it's not your day".

As the car rolled down into the street, I steered it to the right enough so its rear end curved and became straight in the direction I needed it to be. Suddenly, I heard someone yelling. "Ow, ow, ow". "I leaned out the window to ask what was going on. "What's all the noise about?" I asked. "You're gonna wake up my brother". "The back bumper hit Bob in his shin" Johnny replied. "He wasn't paying attention I guess and it rapped him pretty good". I was having visions in my head of my brother bounding down the stairs and coming out screaming asking where we thought we were going". "Well, tell him to bite his tongue and shut the fuck up" I said. "If my brother comes down here, it's over". I looked in the rear view mirror and could see Bob holding his ankle and jumping up and down. "What a dumb ass" I thought. "I can't trust anybody". I waved Johnny over to me and exclaimed "Ok, man. I have it in neutral with my foot on the brake. You guys stay in the back and start pushing. Once We're down the block and far enough away, I'll stop and you guys jump in". "I'll tell them" Johnny said. "I think

Bob is ok now. The bumper only grazed his shin". "Good for Bob" I smirked. "But, we need to get going". I watched them in the rear view mirror as they laid their hands on the back of the car and began to exert some pressure for the run. The faces they were making I thought were comical. It was as if they were all lifting weights at the same time. "It's starting to roll" I yelled out the window. "Keep it going. Just a little more and We'll be good to go".

After we had passed a few of my neighbor"s houses, I brought the vehicle to a stop. In the rear, I heard multiple thuds. Tony let out a scream "You fucking idiot. You didn't tell us when you were gonna stop. Now, we all hit our shins on this fucking thing". Laughing to myself I replied. "You should have paid more attention you crybaby fuck. The next time, watch what you're doing". "Stop complaining and get in the car" Johnny said. "Bob fucked up his leg too. You don't see him being a pussy about it". "Exactly" I said. "There's no time for little injuries right now. We're far enough away where we can escape. So, all of you get in and let's ride". Tony and Bob jumped in the back and Johnny was riding shotgun. "Are you sure you know how to drive this thing?" Johnny asked. "No, man" I replied. "I'm a fucking moron. Of course I know how to drive it. It's just like those Volkswagens Billy and I stole. It's a simple H pattern. How hard could it be?" "Well" Johnny said. Put it in drive and let's go" I started the car, pressed in the clutch, put it in first and let my foot off of the pedal. With a quick jump, the car went a few feet and then stalled. "He doesn't know what the fuck he's doing" Tony chuckled. "You should have let somebody else drive". "Shut up, asshole" I shouted "It's a little bit different than a VW bug. I have to get used to it first". "It's all the same" Tony insisted. "I can see We're gonna be sitting here forever until you figure it out". "We can't do that" Johnny said. "The longer we sit here, the more of a chance his brother will see us". "Ronnie?" Johnny asked "Just for the sake of argument. I'll put it in gear for you. That way, you can pay more attention to letting out the clutch slowly and we can get out of here". Feeling stupid with a bruise to my ego, I complied with Johnny"s request. I started the car again, let out the clutch gingerly, Johnny pushed the shifter into first, and we took off. The engine was whining and begging for a higher gear. "Ok, Ronnie" Johnny instructed. "I'm going into second, bro. Press in the clutch again, man". I pushed in the pedal and went into 2nd gear. "Ok, man" said Johnny. "I think you're getting the hang of it. When we round the corner to Central Avenue, We'll pop it into third. After that, wherever you want to go, man".

After we cruised around Edison for a while, I had mastered the clutch versus the shifting into gear and was asking for suggestions of where to go next. "How about Seaside?" asked Bob. "It's an easy straight run right down the Parkway. You wouldn't have to do much shifting driving down there". "Bob thinks he's funny" I replied. "Maybe we should leave him in the Pine Barrens". "He's just fucking with you" Johnny said. "But, that's a good suggestion. He's right about it being a straight drive, bro. There's less cops to worry about too. Since none of us have our drivers licenses". "Yeah, well" I said. "I figured there was no use in getting one because I can't afford a car. So, I do shit like this instead". "Driver"s licenses are stupid anyway" replied Bob. "It's just another way for the state to control us". "So, We're all in for Seaside then?" I asked. "You sure you wanna take your dad"s car all the way down there?" Johnny asked. "That's a long way from home, man". "We're not gonna stay there" I replied. "We'll just walk on the boardwalk for a little bit and then come back home". "All that way for that?" asked Tony. "It's your call, bro". "Fuck it" I said. "We'll be ok as long as we get back before the sun comes up. It's only an hour each way. We should make it fine". "I have coins for toll money" said Bob. "So, let's get going then".

I drove the car to the nearest Parkway entrance and steered for the Jersey shore. While we were traveling, I got the dumb idea of driving passed where my parents were staying in their trailer at their campground. "I wanna get off the exit for Lakewood" I said. "I wanna show you guys where my parents have their vacation spot at". "Why do you wanna do that?" Johnny asked. "You'll have to take back roads there. It's way off where We're at now, man". "Ronnie likes to tempt fate" Bob remarked. "He likes to live dangerously". "I wouldn't go anywhere near my parents if I robbed their car for the night" Tony said. "But, it's your idea. I'm just along for the ride". "You sure you wanna do this?" asked Johnny. "It's kind of late already". "I'll make it real quick" I replied. "It'll be in and out. I'll take us right back to the Parkway" "Ok" Johnny said. "As long as we return that way I guess its fine with me". As we drove down Brewers Bridge Road in Jackson, I asked my friends to keep an eye out for the trailer park"s sign. Since the street wasn't very illuminated, it was the kind where we could ride right passed it. "There it is" Johnny cried out. "It's right there on the left". On top of a pile stones was a tattered old sign that read Tip Tam RV Park. "Maybe we can see your dad?" Bob asked laughing. "I bet He'd love to see you driving by in his car. "You do have balls, Ronnie. I'll give you that". Tony said. "But, just in case, you better not stop here. You know how people are. If anyone there sees you, They'll probably rat you out". "How the fuck will anybody see me this late at night with no street lights?" I asked sarcastically. "You guys crack me the fuck up". "Just keep driving, man" Johnny suggested. "We need to get back to the highway.

Satisfied with my accomplishment, I kept driving and didn't stop until I go to the next bend in the road. As we turned left, I saw signs for the Parkway in front of me. "There it is" Johnny exclaimed. "Turn left, bro. I wanna get out of this place, man. This area looks like a place where people dump bodies". "That's only because it's really dark out here" I replied. "But, we should be heading back in the direction of Seaside soon." Just as I had released my hand from the blinker, I saw red, blue, and white colors in the rear view mirror. "No fucking way!" Bob screamed. "It's the fucking cops, man. I think he's pulling us over, Ronnie". "Motherfuckers!" I yelled.

"They just can't leave any of us the fuck alone". "You better pull off right here" Johnny said. "There's no use in trying to run. We don't know this area and They'll beat our asses once they catch us if we try". "Yeah, yeah" I complained. "I'm telling you guys right now. This is gonna suck big time. I guess We'll have to be nice to the cop and wing it to see where it goes". "Just don't piss him off with your mouth" Tony said. "You know how sometimes you can be an asshole". "I'll try to be cool" I replied. "That's about the best I can do". As I was reaching for the registration and the insurance card from the glove compartment, Johnny was fidgeting with something in his pocket nervously. "Don't turn around, Ron" he said. "Try to keep the cop occupied in conversation. I have a slab of hash in my pocket. I have to get rid of it somehow, bro". "Now you fucking tell me" I replied annoyed. "You didn't tell any of us you had that on you before we left tonight?" "What the fuck?" Tony asked. "I'm your brother and you never even told me?" "We'll talk about it later, man". Johnny said. "The cops almost up to the car. So, let Ronnie talk and be quiet".

The officer approached the car and asked for my documents. I handed them to him and he got a grimace on his face. "I see you have your insurance and registration, son" he said. "Whose car is this?" he asked. "Umm, it's my father's" I replied. "He let me use it tonight". "Where is your license?" he asked sternly. "Umm, I don't have one" I answered. "I don't think your father would have let you use his vehicle without a driver"s license" he said. "All of you stay right here until I get back" he demanded. As the cop was walking back to his cruiser, Johnny leaned his arm out the window and threw something under the car. "What the fuck was that?" I asked. "I hope that porker didn't see it". "It was that small slab of hash" he replied. I don't think he saw me throw it though". "I sure as fuck hope not" I said. "Because, I think We're in enough trouble as it is". I watched the officer in the rear view mirror and could see he was on his radio and checking us out. "What do you think is gonna happen?" asked Bob. "You think he's gonna bust us?" "As long as he didn't see Johnny throw that shit." I replied. "I think we should be ok". The cop came back to our car and began asking more questions. "Who here has a license?" he asked. "None of us" I answered. "Well" he said. "There's going to be a real problem then, boys. I can't let you move this vehicle unless someone has a license. But, I tell you what; if one of you even has only a permit, I'll cut you a break and let you go". After turning around and talking over each other trying to see if any of us had one or not, I had to answer the cop in the negative. "That's too bad" he said. "I have no choice than to impound the car and take all of you to the station. You'll have to call your parents or someone who can be a guardian for you to take you home". "Come on, officer" I begged. "We were going right back home on the Parkway. We just got lost, that's all. Can't you just cut us a break this one time?" I asked. "It's already late and no one would know". As the officer was pondering my request, his partner pulled up in another cruiser. We watched restlessly as he exited and strode up to us. "What's going on here?" he asked. "It's just a bunch of kids with no license" the first cop said. "I'm thinking of letting them go. They"ve been very cooperative". Hoping for the best, we glanced over as the two cops retreated to the back of our car. We sat helplessly as we peered at them from behind the rear window and saw their heads shaking back and forth as if they were trying to figure out what to do. The second cop started to swing his flashlight back and forth with its beam just touching under the edge of the bumper. Just then, he got a strange look on his face and a changed demeanor. "Did you see this?" he asked as his light shined further underneath. "There's something under here". "Fuck!" Johnny whispered. "I think they"ve found it". "Kick it over here" the first cop remarked. "Let's take a look see". He reached down between his legs, picked up the rectangular object, put it to his nose, and gave it a sniff. "We definitely have a problem now" he announced. "This smells like hashish". "Well" said the second cop. "We were gonna let you go. But, this changes everything". "I think this means we've changed our mind" said the first officer. "Unless one of you admits that this is yours, you're all going to jail tonight". "It's not mine" I said abruptly. "I'm only the driver". "What about the rest of you?" he asked as he waved the hash around diligently. "Nobody owns it?" "You know what they're going to say" blurted the second cop. "They're all gonna deny it and tell us they don't know where it came from". "Isn't that right, fellas?" he asked. None of us said a word and kept looking straight ahead. "Ok" said the first cop. "Let's get them all in the back of our squad cars and take them to the station. Opening the doors and motioning for us to exit, I couldn't help but think how much trouble I was in. "What's gonna happen to my father's car?" I asked. "Oh" the first cop replied. "That's going to the impound yard". The officers separated us with Johnny and I in one car, and Bob and Tony in the other. As Johnny and I were being transported, the officer we were with began ribbing us "I hope you guys have someone to come and pick you up" he said teasing. "Otherwise, you'll be going to the detention center". Knowing my parents weren't home and my brother was asleep, I started to get worried even more. "Fuck" I thought. "If these clowns can't reach anyone, I'm toast".

We pulled up to a large metal garage door and waited for it to open. "We'll be going inside in a minute" the cop said. "Are you sure you two guys don't want to tell me anything?" "It would be a lot easier for you in the end". Knowing this bullshit tactic from previous encounters with the police, I replied "We really have nothing to say". "Have it your way" the cop said. "I'm just trying to make it easier on you". "Easier my ass" I thought. "You just want to do as little work as possible writing up the paperwork". Eventually, the entrance opened and the patrol car rolled inside. It was a sally port design so it was impossible to escape. A few minutes went by as Johnny and I languished in the back seat trying to come up with a plan. While conversing, the vehicle Tony and Bob were in drove up next to us. Bob was leering out the back window shrugging his shoulders and making faces with his tongue sticking out. Johnny for some reason thought it was funny. I did not. "Enjoy laughing, bro" I said. "Because once We're in there, it's all gonna suck". "Don't be so serious, Ron" he replied. "You'll go home eventually" I hope you're right" I answered. "But, you guys got your mom and Bob has his dad". "Me?" I asked. "I'm doomed. Finally, some intake officers came out from behind a side door and escorted us inside. They shackled us to a bench with our handcuffs behind us and we waited. After what seemed like hours, one of them came back with a clipboard in his hand. "Velez Jr., John" he said "You're coming with me." He unlocked Johnny"s handcuffs from the bench, relocked them, grabbed him by his elbow, and escorted him down the hall. "Where are you taking me?" Johnny asked "Don't worry about it" the cop said. "You're going in a cell until later". I couldn't help but think to myself that the place had the most pronounced echo I had ever heard in a building before. It must have been the antiseptic atmosphere of the painted over cinderblocks that comprised the jail that caused sound to resonate off the walls so swiftly. "They make these places miserable like this on purpose." I thought. "No wonder why everyone hates the police".

Soon, it was my turn. The same cop came back and used the same monotonic procedure on me and guided me down the hallway. I looked to my right and was counting the lines between the bricks in the wall. I knew that each block was 16 inches long. So, I wanted to know how many feet it was to where we were going. We came to a stop in front of a door that said "E2". It was one of those security looking doors with a sliver of a vertical window in it that had wire mesh imbedded in the glass. The cop held my arm with one hand, placed his clipboard on the ground, unlocked the door, opened it, and abruptly threw me inside. "Sit on the bench on the back wall" he demanded. "And then, turn around". I did as he ordered and he removed my cuffs. When I went to turn back around, I heard the sound of the door booming closed behind me. "So, this is it? I thought. "I'll have to wait here and hope that these pigs get someone on the phone". Hours passed and all I could hear was the echo of doors opening and closing. "Johnny, Tony, and Bob have all probably gone home by now" I thought. "I guess I'm fucked". I fell asleep for a while and was awakened by a different officer than the one who originally put me in my cell. He was barking at me as I heard him put the key in the door. "Wakie, wakie" he said. "It's time to come out now" he laughed. "Am I going home now?" I asked. "Oh, no" he chuckled getting pure pleasure out of taunting me. "We couldn't get anyone on the phone number you gave us, so you're being transported to the Ocean County Juvenile Facility. You'll stay there until you either go to court, or we can reach one of your family members". "Fucking detention center?" I asked. "Is that really necessary officer?" "First off, don't curse at me" he replied. "And secondly, it's out of my hands, its protocol, son".

I was briskly whisked away in the back of another patrol car again to a destination I knew nothing about. I was treated with the same procedure as before and locked away in a cell in the rear of a long, freezing cold building. It had the same resonating echo of foreboding doom and I had begun to get depressed. "I wonder how long I'll have to sit in this shit hole". I thought. "Someone better come and get me soon". I laid down for a few hours on the marginal bed they supplied staring up at the ceiling and started to become very agitated. "Fuck this place" I mumbled. "This shit isn't fair. Just because of no driver"s license and a tiny bit of hash?" I questioned. I was beginning to lose control. My hate and resentment for the cops was brewing at an ever increasing pace and I was becoming fixated on revenge. "I'll show these fucks" I said. "Watch this". I rose from the mattress and ran for the door. The door was made of wood and not as sturdy as the steel one from my earlier excursion. My anger had taken over and I went ballistic. "Boom!" the portal resonated as I kicked at it. I had connected with my right heal attempting to smash the lock in. "Again" I thought. "Fuck these guys". Over and over I did the same routine, trying anything to get attention or a slim chance at escape. "Boom!" the door went.

"Officer!" I screamed. "Get me out of here, officer!" no one came which made me even more incensed. I wanted attention and I wanted to go home. "Boom, boom, boom". With each kick of the door. Soon, I became exhausted and was running out of breath. "Fucking cops" I said. "They don't fucking care". I went back to the bed and leaned against the cold, dank wall. My rage was spent and I finally fell asleep. I was awoken to the sound of keys jangling and someone shouting the words "Breakfast, breakfast in 10 minutes, breakfast". Breakfast I wasn't in the mood for. I was still fixated on doing anything to go home. Suddenly, I heard a key turn in the lock on my door. The door was pulled open and a fat, short man wearing a white pressed shirt motioned me to accompany him. "Come over here and sit on this chair, sonny" he said. "He handed me my sneakers they had confiscated from me earlier and directed me to put them back on. "It's your lucky day" he chuckled. "We finally got a hold of your brother. Since he's over 21, he's coming to get you soon. He's on his way here now. So, it shouldn't be long. Just sit here quietly and I'll come back to get you after he arrives". "Thank God" I replied. "Because, this place sucks". "Yes it does" the man said giggling as he walked away down the hallway. "But, you must have done something to have ended up here". When he was out of sight, I heard a voice coming from the cell that had been adjacent to me "You think you so cool beating on that door last night keeping us all awake, don't you?" he asked. "You won't be so tough after breakfast when we get ahold of you". "Fuck off!" I yelled. "You have one problem". "What that be?" he asked. "It be that you get to stay here, and I get to go home. So, obviously nobody gives a fuck about you and you're not going anywhere. "You be a real wise guy, huh?" he asked. "I be wise enough more than you to get out of here, asshole." I said. "Have a nice day with your incarceration".

On the way home in my brother's car, he wanted to know everything and gave me the third degree. After I told him how I snuck the car out of the driveway and the rest of the story, he started with his "Wait until daddy gets home" bullshit. "I spoke to the old man this morning" he said. "He told me to pick you up and not to let you out of my sight. Under no circumstances are you to leave the house. He's really pissed off at you. He said it's gonna cost him a small bundle to get his car out of the impound yard. You also have to go to court in a few days too. So, I wouldn't try to run away again if I was you". "Don't worry about it" I replied. "I'll deal with the old man after he gets home". "I don't know" he said "He's really on the war path with this one. You better lay low for a while. If I was you, I"d hide in the basement until he wasn't pissed off anymore". "Yeah, yeah" I replied. "Here we go again". When we reached our home, I went down into the cellar as my brother had suggested and fell asleep in my bed. I awoke to immense pain in the calves on the back of my legs and the sound of my father's voice screaming at me at the top of his lungs. "You little inconsiderate bastard" he yelled. "You ungrateful tenacious bastard! How dare you take my car without my permission?" He had what was left of a pool stick in his hand and was swinging it wildly standing over me. "Jesus Christ" I howled. "I was asleep. You broke that fucking thing over the back of my legs" "What the fuck is wrong with you?" I asked shrieking in pain. "You better not move from this bed" he shouted. "The next time I see you, I'll kill you". "If you hit me with that damn cue one more time" I said "The only one dead in this house will be you". That remark made my father even more enraged and he lunged for me again. But this time, I hobbled up and deflected him. "You better go back upstairs before you hurt yourself" I said. "Because, if you hit me again, I'm calling the cops. I'm not taking this beat me in my sleep bullshit from anyone". Just then, I heard my mother descending the steps. "Leave him alone, Frank" she screamed. "He's bigger than you now. He can hurt you". I wiped the tears from my face and blurted "Listen to Mom; you can't go around disciplining your kids this way. Its abuse". He had finally settled down and was starting to come back to reality. My father had told me stories about how when he was in the Army, he was a Golden Gloves boxer and that when he got really angry, his eyes would glaze over and he would go into another world. I knew that look and this had been one of those times. It could be quite scary. But in my opinion, there were better ways to punish your kid than to pummel them with a pool stick in their sleep. A few hours later, he came back downstairs with my mother in tow and set his grounding rules. "I didn't like hitting you like that" he said half apologetically. "But, you have to understand Ronald that you can't do things like that to us. It enrages me and costs me a lot of money. Therefore, until you can act like a civilized and mature human being, you'll have to stay down here until I say you can leave". I shook my head in the affirmative without saying anything as I didn't want the situation to go back to being out of control. I thought about what I had done and how the old man had had a point. Since I had an aversion to beatings in my sleep, I never took anything of his again.

The next few months were full of turmoil and headaches for me. At Edison High School, I was socially promoted to 12th grade but it was rescinded by Mr. Poskaitis after a mere 3 weeks. I was attending my 1st class in the early morning when I was approached by the home room teacher. "Mr. Arold" she said. "I received a message this morning that you are to report to the vice principal"s office immediately. "What for?" I asked. "I have no idea" she replied. "But, you have you go right away". As I lazily sauntered down the hallway, I was trying to figure out what he had in store for me. It had been some time since he had pestered me with more false allegations and administrative nonsense that had always gotten on my nerves. I walked in and sat down on my usual waste of time seat and waited for my name to be called. Poskaitis did his customary habit of making me wait while fiddling about in his office over nonsensical subjects and pretending that he was busy when he was not. He seemed to enjoy this game of looking down at his papers and randomly glancing at me from the corner of his eye. He wanted to observe me to see how upset I would become. Of course I was onto him and remained emotionless until I supposed he got bored. I refused to play into him and would not give him the satisfaction of a reaction, period. Eventually, he called me in. "You can go in and see him now" the secretary said. "He's ready for you".

"Sit down Mr. Arold" he growled. "I have some bad news for you. It seems there's been a mistake with your grade assignment sheet. You were supposed to be left back to the 11th grade. I'm sorry, but someone made a clerical error. Starting next week, you will no longer be a senior and will be reassigned to where you were supposed to be originally. I stood up and yelled in his face "I don't think so, Frankie! You"ve had almost a month to rectify it. So, I'm refusing your downgrade. You can stick your reassignment right up your ass! You think I don't know what this is all about? You like to play games with the people you don't like. Well, guess what? You lose. You're insane if you think I'm going backwards. This is my last year dealing with your crap. I'll be back in the same classes I have tomorrow. Have a nice day dick head!" "You can get as angry as you want" he replied. "But, the decision has been made. You"ve also gained another 3 day suspension for cursing at me". I turned around and laughed "As if I give a fuck about your free vacations. I never come here anyway. Have you ever looked at my grades? I asked. "I cut for 2 months, never study, and always get straight A"s on all of my tests. Tell me Frankie? Why is that?" "I don't know" he replied. "Perhaps you're cheating?" Cheating? I asked. Your administration put me in regular classes as a junior this year mixed in with Special Ed. How the hell could I cheat? That's the stupidest thing I've ever heard. Did you ever think to yourself that maybe, just maybe I'm a little smarter than the garbage you teach in this school? You know why I never show up? Because there's no challenge and it's boring, that's why. I learn more than the teachers know reading on my own. "We already know you can read on a college level" he exclaimed. "But, to pass, you have to show up as well". "The same old nonsense answer you always give me" I said. "If I'm so smart, than why are you leaving me back a grade?" He looked away and had no answer with a dumbfounded look on his face. All I could do was turn, laugh, and leave. As I was exiting the doorway, I yelled back "Like I said Frankie, I'll see you tomorrow. Same class time, same 12th grade".

When I got home at the end of the day, my mother approached me with some news. "The school called me this afternoon" she said. "You"ve been reassigned to a school in the mountains". "What school in the mountains?" I asked. "Who made that stupid decision?" Apparently, Poskaitis went over your head to the supervisor of our school district and complained about your threatening behavior" she replied. "You start new classes at the Bonnie Brae School for Boys in Watchung next week". "Watchung mountains?" I asked. "And, exactly how am I supposed to get there, mom?" "They are sending a special bus for you to pick you up with other students" she said. "They come at 7am; you get there by 9, and leave to come home at 2pm. There's nothing we can do about it. Your father tried to argue with them like we did when they switched you from John Marshal to Stelton. I'm sorry, but our hands are tied. "Great" I howled "I get to go to school on a tart cart. My friends will have a field day when they find out about this one". "Who says you have to tell anybody?" she asked. "No one will know unless you say something". "Mom" I exclaimed. "You don't understand. This is Edison, teenagers here find out everything". "It won't be so bad" she replied. "You'll be 18 eventually. You can deal with it legally then". "Yeah" I said. "But, in the meantime, I have to look like an idiot". "It's not forever" she replied. "I know you, you'll adjust".

On top of this predicament, I received a phone call from Johnny V. about our band. "I have some bad news, bro" he said. "Tony and I are moving to Florida next week. So, we have to break the up the band. I'm really sorry. There's nothing we can do" "Get the fuck out of here with that bullshit!" I screamed. "We are just starting to get good. The plan was to play clubs next and see if we could get a label or a management company to sign us. Where the fuck did this crap come from?" "My mother wants us to move out of state" he said. "Tony and I got caught doing a few B & E"s. If we go to court, they want to lock us up in Jamesburg until We're 18. So, we wouldn't be able to have a band anyway. We have no other choice, man". "I can't believe this" I replied. "I was just beginning to get into it. My voice was getting better and better. This shit is fucked up". I took a pause and yelled into the phone "Have a nice fucking life, man" and slammed down the receiver with all of my force. "Fuck those guys" I mumbled. "More disappointment". I was so upset and incensed by their decision, I never said goodbye and didn't see them again. 32 years later, I found Johnny on Facebook. We reconnected and I see him from time to time. He's still apologizing for it. I still wonder and think to myself "If they just didn't steal".

I was walking to Mcdonald"s to get something to eat when I ran into Jesse. He was pale looking and appeared ill. "Ron!" he said "I'm sick as fuck, bro" "What's wrong with you, man?" I asked. "I drank Rolling Rock beers that were boiled in the Linwood Grove fire." he said. "I think it fucked my stomach up". "From Linwood?" I asked. How did you get beer from Linwood?" You don't know?" he asked. "Know what? I replied. "Everybody in town we know went into the basement after the fire, bro. We stole cases and cases of beer, kegs, and bottles of wine. It was crazy man!" "Fuck me" I exclaimed "Nobody ever told me anything". "You gotta stay on top of shit, man" he said. "Yeah, I can see how on top of it you are now? I asked. "You're sick as fuck from it". "But, Ron?" he begged. "What can I do to make this stomach ache go away? It's fucking me up big time." Since I had a physician"s desk reference at home, I knew exactly what he needed to quell his nausea. "You have to go next door to the convenience market and buy a quart size carton of chocolate milk" I replied. "Guzzle it all down as fast as you can all at once. After a little while, you'll start to feel better" "Are you sure this is gonna work, man?" he asked. "I don't feel like puking any more than I have already". "Just do what I say" I replied. "And, you should be good to go". He came out of the store, tore open the lid, and proceeded to drain the container in a few large gulps. I laughed as half of it ended up dripping down his face. "Ahhh" he said. "I sure hope this works". A few minutes passed and I could see a marked improvement. "Wow, man" he mumbled. "That shit really fucking worked, bro. You know your shit, man". "I tried to tell you" I replied. "I read a lot". "Well, in that case" he laughed "From now on, your name is Dr. Ron. I owe you, bro". "You don't owe me anything" I exclaimed. "Dr. Ron says just don't drink anymore of that shitty, boiled beer".

I had kept in touch with the little red headed girl in Jersey City and decided it was time for me to have another visit again. Danny B. had never been to Jersey City before and asked to accompany me. During this time, one of the fashion crazes was waist length jackets and high platform shoes. Usually, we would augment this look with polyester button down shirts that had large collars and cuffed pants with pleats. For teens with long hair, sometimes when we went to a big city we would try to assimilate to look sharp and to blend in. When we arrived at Journal Square, it was a short walk to her house on Summit Avenue. I remember passing by a very old run down theater on the way that enchanted me with what it may have looked like in its heyday. I imagined it packed outside with customers waiting to get in dressed in their best formal wear and anticipating a show they might have waited on weeks to attend. I marveled at its architecture. Especially with the handmade designs carved into the fascia and its columns cascading down from its roof to the street below. "It must have taken hours to build this" I thought. "It's too bad they let it all go. What a shame". Being a stickler for building design, I've always wondered in awe whenever I had the opportunity to gawk at such historic structures.

As Danny and I turned the corner on her street, the little red headed girl and her friend were waiting for us on the stoop in front of her home. She ran up to me and gave me a big hug and a kiss. "Finally" she said. "I thought you"d never get here". "We had to switch in Newark" I replied. "You know that. Then we took the PATH to get here. We got here as soon as we could". "Well, you're here and that's all that matters." she said. "So, who"s your friend?" she asked. "Oh, that's Danny" I replied. "Doesn't he look like George Harrison?" "Actually, he does" she said. "What's with the new clothes you're wearing. Ronnie?" she asked. "You hate disco. You almost always wear hippie type clothes. You look kind of ridiculous" she teased. "Your long hair doesn't match it at all" "Hey, don't laugh at us" I replied. "We're in the city compared to Edison. We figured we'd try to blend in" "Nobody cares about that on the street" she giggled. "That's only for the clubs. I love you better when you look like yourself". "Well" Danny said. "It's too late to change now. I think we look kind of snappy" "It is what it is" I chuckled. "So, I guess We'll just have to deal with it". "I'm just teasing you" the little red headed girl said. Now, wait here and my friend and I will be ready in a few minutes. We're gonna go get dressed and We'll all go to that CYO dance I told you about over the phone". "We're going to a dance?" Danny asked. "You never told me anything about going to a dance". "You never asked" I replied. "Besides, We're dressed in disco gear. So, we should fit right in". "I can't wait to see this bullshit" Danny howled. "This will certainly be crazy". "Crazy is what I do best" I exclaimed. "So, sit back and enjoy the ride".

The girls came out and the little red headed girl introduced her blonde friend to Danny. "Oh, I'm sorry Danny" she said. "I didn't mean to be rude. I was just so excited that Ronnie is here, I completely forgot about it" "Don't worry about it" Danny replied. "I get over looked all of the time". "Only when the cops think he's handsome" I blurted. "And, he has his hair up". "Do you like breathing?" Danny asked "Because, I've had about enough out of you" "But, Dan" I quipped. "I've just begun to fight". "We have a real comedy duo here" said the little red headed girl. "But, we better hurry up or We'll be late to the dance". "Lead on my love" I said as I took her hand. "Lead on and show us the festivities". As we approached the door to the basement of her church, the little red headed girl exclaimed "This is where they have all of our dances and its $2 to get in". "I have enough for all of us" I replied. "So, I'll be paying". "You're so sweet, Ronnie" she said. "But, you don't have to do that". "Chivalry is not dead" Danny whispered. "Let Ronnie pay so he doesn't have to be a cheap ass". "I'll cheap ass your ticket back home into the garbage" I replied. "So, you better leave me alone". "Ronnie's so sensitive" Danny laughed. "That's why all of the girls love him". "You're just jealous" I said. "Now, stand behind me in line and let's go into this place". As the 4 of us approached the table to offer our entrance fee, a priest came over and was sizing us up. "You can't come in here looking like that" he said dismissively. "Like what?" I asked. "With your long hair and those clothes. Your kind aren't allowed in here". "And, exactly what kind is that?" I asked sarcastically. "You look like hoodlums" he said. "We don't let hoodlums in here. This is a Catholic run event and we don't want any trouble from the likes of you". "Wow! I screamed. "How Christian of you, father! So much for thou shalt not judge eh?" "What a hypocrite" Danny said. "No wonder I don't like religion". "It does not negate the fact that you are not getting in tonight" said the priest. "And, if you persist, I will certainly call the police to have you removed from the premises". I turned to the little red headed girl who by now had a sad expression on her face "We're leaving" I mumbled. "Your forgiving priest here doesn't think we look Jesus enough". "It's not that" the priest replied. "Don't try to turn this around on me. We've had trouble with kids like you before. We just cannot take anymore chances". "I'll make sure to tell God that next time I speak to him" I said. "With a special invocation just for you". "What a loser" Danny muttered. "Let's get out of here". I was so pissed off at the priest"s prejudice that I stormed out the door in a temper tantrum down the street. I was walking very fast and simply wanted to go home. As Danny was beside me and keeping up, the little red headed girl came running up behind us. "Come back! Come back" she screamed. "I spoke to him and told him you were my cousin. He said if you come back he'll let you in now". "Fuck him" I protested. "I'm never going back in there. I can't believe how rude that guy was. And, he's supposed to be a man of the cloth? What a joke". "The only cloth he kisses is the one of judgment and ridicule" Danny replied. "I hate institutions like those. They're all fake". "We're going home" I told the little red headed girl. "And, I'm not changing my mind". "Please stay" she said with tears dribbling down her face. "I don't want to have to wait forever to see you again". "Forever isn't such a long time" I replied. "Will you still call me though?" she asked. "Of course" I said. "But, don't ever bring me near a church event again".

Jessie and I had been hanging around Playmore again playing pool and trying to conjure up some more schemes. About 3 tables over from us was Ellis who was shooting pool directly across from the main office door. Just inside to the left of it was a desk with a chair, and a small safe that was almost always closed. Most of the time the owner Natasha kept a small amount of petty cash in the top drawer to be able to make change for her customers. While we watched, Ellis was purposely trying to get the cue ball to jump off the table and bounce onto the floor. "I wonder what he's doing?" Jesse asked. "I dunno" I replied. "But, it looks kind of funny". "Go over there and ask him what he's up to" Jesse said. "Something with him doesn't look right". I laid my pool stick on the table and wandered over with an inquisitive look on my face. I couldn't help laughing to myself about what Ellis might be doing and couldn't wait for his answer. "Hey, Ellis?" I asked. "Jessie and I wanna know how come you keep making that cue ball jump off the table to the floor?" "I need some bahoots" he replied. "I'm at maximum brokage, bro". "How does knocking a pool ball off a table going to get you money?" I asked. "I have to get it just right" he grinned. "It has to go into Natasha"s office. Then, you'll see. Now, leave me alone. I have to concentrate". As he was setting up for his next shot, I walked back over to Jesse and reported back to him. "Well, what did he say?" Jesse asked "He says he has to get the cue ball into Natasha"s office for some reason" I replied. "And then, he told me to go away because he had to concentrate". "Concentrate?" Jesse asked "Concentrate on what?" "I have no idea, man" I said. "But, that's what he told me". "We're gonna have to watch this guy" Jesse laughed. "Because, I know there's no way he's doing that for nothing".

After Ellis made about 10 or 15 attempts to force the ball into the office, it finally skipped in and made its mark. It bounced twice and landed directly in front of the desk and underneath the accompanying chair. We watched silently as Ellis laid down his stick, rounded the corner of the table, entered the office, and bent over the chair toward the back wall. He was reaching for something and we couldn't see what it was and his body was obscuring our view. Then, we heard a metallic sound like a drawer opening. All we could discern was that his right arm had reached into a space and he retrieved it very quickly. Next, he turned around and stood up while frantically stuffing his pants pocket with something from within the palm of his hand. "What the fuck is he doing?" Jesse asked. "I bet he's thieving Natasha"s petty cash drawer". "It kind of looks that way" I replied. "I hope Natasha doesn't catch him. She's from Russia and she has a ferocious temper". Just then, Natasha came walking over to the door to right where Ellis was standing. He was in her way and she wanted to know what he was doing there. "Vot are you doink in mine office?" she asked in her thick Russian accent. Ellis, being the homeless street scammer that he was, had an immediate response. "I was playing pool" he said. "And, I went to make a shot and the cue ball jumped off of the table. It went under your chair and I was retrieving it. See? It's right there" he said pointing. "My office ist off vimits" she warned. "You arev not allowed inst here. Zee next time zat happens; you must comv and gets me". "Ok" Ellis said. "Can I just get my ball back and go back to my game then?" he asked. "Dos ist fine" she replied. "But, don't vet me sees you doov it again". "It's cool" said Ellis. "I'll be more careful next time". "Son of a bitch" Jesse mumbled. "Ellis has balls, bro. He just scarfed a handful of cash. I wish I would have thought of that scheme". "He just got there first, that's all" I replied. "We've had better ones than that, man. Sooner or later, she'll get wise to it anyway. As soon as she realizes her drawer is always short, she'll start locking the door". "She's a dumb ass" Jesse chuckled. "She should have done that right from the beginning" "But, Jesse" I said. "She's not from Edison". "True" Jesse laughed. "She's just beginning to learn from us now".

As The Rolling Stones song Memory Motel was blaring away on Playmore"s juke box, Ellis was attempting to leave with his ill begotten gains. "Where do you think you're going? Jesse asked. "How much loot did you scarf from Natasha"s drawer? "None of your business" Ellis replied. "Come up with your own scarf". As I watched laughing, Jesse dragged his foot across the tile floor and made an obvious black mark from his shoe. "Ellis, you scuff!" he yelled "You see that?" he asked as he pointed down to the ground. "That's you, man. You're the scuff of my heal. That's what you are. So, you better tell me how much you got from her, or I'm gonna take it all and you're gonna have nothing". "That's boosh" Ellis shrieked. "I made these bahoots not you. So, I shouldn't have the give you anything. You need to go find your own tasty waloots and leave mine alone." "Technically, those weren't your waloots to begin with" I said. "Just tell Jesse how much petty cash was in there, and he'll leave you alone. It's not that hard, man. He just wants to know what's usually in there, that's all". "I scarfed about 50 skulls" Ellis said. "Now, let me go". "Listen you homeless fuck" Jesse yelled. "The next time I ask you something, you better answer. Otherwise, I'll make your scuff ass regret it". "Ok, Jesse"

Ellis said. "You don't have to freak out about it, man". "Check this guy out?" Jesse asked as he turned to me. "I give him a break, and he still has to be a wise ass." "Ahhh, let's just leave him alone" I replied. "We got what we wanted out of him. He's not that bad of a guy really and he makes me laugh sometimes. He's not always a dick head you know?" "You're lucky your Ron"s friend" Jesse said. "So this time, you get a pass. Now, get out of here you scuff, before I change my mind".

I was hanging around Lindenau Park again when I ran into a guy we knew who went by the nickname Duck. He was a small guy but a scammer like the rest of us and had an acerbic laugh that was sometimes entertaining. His only flaw was, like Ellis G., if he wanted something from you and you didn't want to give it to him, he could be tenaciously annoying. Fortunately, and smartly for him, he didn't needle us as much as Ellis did. So, he got cut a lot of breaks. "What's up, Ron?" he asked as he approached. "What are you doing sitting here all by yourself? "I'm going over to the Gulottas in a few" I replied. "You wanna come with me?" "Sure" he said. "Is there anything going on there though?" he asked. "You know how their house is" I said. "There's always something going on there. I'm sure once We're there, We'll be able to conjure a situation that's entertaining". "You have any weed?" he asked. "I have a small joint here" I replied. "Let's take a few pulls before we get there". "Life is always funnier when you're stoned" I laughed. We took a few tokes, waited for it to kick in, smiled and went on our way.

As we bounded up the stairs of the house of Gulotta, we could hear Dennis singing again as he usually did during the day. "Sooooon, oh sooon the light" he sang. It was one of his favorite songs by Yes. Duck mentioned "Man, he really likes that band. He sings them almost every time I come over here". "He's pretty good, man" I replied. "But, let's knock on the door and see what's up". As I gave the door a knock, we could see Dennis coming into view. In his hand was a huge pickle jar that had strings with tags attached to them hanging over its edge at the top with a tan colored liquid inside. "What's that in your hand, Den?" I asked as he opened the door. "It's tea, bro." he exclaimed. "I don't have any money for coffee from the diner. So, I had to compromise". "How many tea bags do you have in there?" I asked l. "It looks like a lot". "About 10" he laughed. "You want a sip?" he asked. "It's like rocket fuel. You know me, bro. I need caffeine to wake up". "Wake you up?" Duck chuckled. "You'll have a heart attack drinking that". "Nah" I replied. "Dennis makes some fantastic tea. He knows what he's doing. He lets it seep for a long time too. Isn't that right, Den?" I asked. "Other than letting it sit in the sunlight, that's exactly correct" he replied. "There's a science to making good tea. And, I'm the professor". "The professor of tea leaves" I laughed. "He's really got it down". "Down is what you won't be if you drink that shit" chuckled Duck. "So, I'll pass". "Pass if you must" replied Dennis. "It'll be your loss, not mine. Me and Ron will polish this off and be running. It's the best way to start the day, bro". "I'm fine here" Duck said. "But, I'll smoke some more weed if you"ve got any". "Phil"s coming over here in a few" Dennis said. "He's got some new shit called Maui Wowii and it's supposed to annihilate us. So, let's finish this tea before he gets here. Then, We'll check out what he has and move on from there". "I like the idea of that" I replied. "That must be that new shit from Hawaii" Duck said. "I hear it makes you laugh all day long. I'm ready for that too". "I guess We'll have to see what Phil has when he arrives Dennis replied. "Just don't freak out when we smoke it, Duck. You know how all of you little people get when you're stoned" he teased. "Worry about yourself, Den" said Duck. "I'll be ok".

Phil finally showed up and entered the living room where we were all lounging around. "Did you bring it?" Dennis asked. "What? Did you tell everybody already? Phil asked. "Man, I can't keep anything from anybody with you guys around" he laughed. "But yeah, you goofs. I have it with me". "Let me see, let me see" exclaimed Duck all excited like in a toy store. Phil took out a sandwich bag from his pocket and laid it on the dining room table. "It's blue" I said. "I've never seen anything like that before". He picked it up and unrolled it and held it up to the light. "It has color in it like a blue ocean" Dennis said. "This shit is expensive" retorted Phil. "Now, who has papers?" he asked. "And, I'll twist one up". "I have some Zig Zag"s on me" I replied. "You can use those". "Give them here" said Phil. "Just give me a minute and We'll be high in no time". Dennis began to sing YeS's song Soon again. But this time, he was changing the lyrics. "Soooon. Ohh, sooon We're stoned. Pass within our buzz and sooth the night. Our Phil will lead us, our reason to be here. Long ago, stoned in our time". We found it to be hilarious and couldn't stop laughing. "He's already got me crying from laughing so hard" Phil said. "And, we haven"t even smoked any of this yet". "Imagine what he'll be like once it's in his system?" asked Duck. "I think We're in for some real comedy tonight" I replied. "Once Dennis gets rolling, you never gonna know what's gonna happen". "I prefer it that way" expressed Phil. "Or else, I wouldn't hang around with him". Just then, Jeffrey came through the door. "What's up with you guys tonight?" he asked. "We're gonna smoke some weed" I said. "But, you're gonna have to ask Dennis if you can have some. I'm not gonna be responsible". "Fuck that" he exclaimed. "He's not my mother. I can do whatever the fuck I want". "If I feel like letting you" Dennis chuckled. "But, I'm in a good mood tonight. So, you win". "Good" Jeff said. "Because, you're not stopping me. These guys are my friends too. "They were all my friends first" Dennis replied. "So, you have to go through me if you want to party". "Nonsense" Jeff yelled. "I'll hit you in the fucking head". "You don't want to try that again" Dennis said. "I'll have to school you, again". "Just don't get me mad, Dennis" Jeff replied. "You'll have to run once you let me back up". "He's serious" Phil laughed. "He likes to whip shit at you when he's angry". "Let's not worry about my temper" Jeff said. "If We're gonna smoke weed, we better do it pretty soon. Because Mommy"s getting out early tonight from work, Dennis. And, you know how she doesn't like a lot of people hanging around the house. "Mommy, shmommy" Dennis replied. . "You let me worry about that". "Ok" Jeff said. "But, don't tell me later I didn't warn you. You know how she gets". "Hey, Phil?" Dennis asked. "Spark up that bone and let's get this party started".

In a haze of pot smoke accompanied with a slight sweet smell, we all became very stoned and disoriented. "This stuff smells like candy". I said. "Give me another shotgun, Den" I asked. Dennis went around the room with the joint placed firmly backwards in his mouth. Then, he held his palms over our faces forcing smoke into our lungs until we gagged. "I can't do any more of those" he said. "The end of this thing is too fucking hot". "I think We're all high enough already" I laughed. "Even Jeff is gone". "He always gets stoned quickly" Dennis laughed. "That's why I have to watch him". Sitting on DenniS's bed, Jeffrey had a book of photos on his lap that he was slowly flipping through. "What do you have there, Jeff?" I asked. He looked up at me with very stoned eyes and was acting in awe of it. "It's a picture book about the assassination of JFK" he replied softly. It's a very sad story. He was a great president". "Jeff's on another one of his trips again" laughed Dennis. "He wasn't even born yet when JFK got killed. See what happens when he gets high with us? He gets all emotional and shit". "Maybe he just likes a good story?" I asked. "All of our lives are a story, bro" Dennis replied. "JFK was just in the wrong place at the wrong time". "I agree with that" said Phil. "I would never put myself in a place to get my head blown off". Dennis went over to his stereo and put on YeS's song Soon again. As it got to the middle, I peered over to Jeffrey and saw that he was crying. With each turn of the page, there were visible tears streaming down his face. "So tragic" he whispered. "It was so fucking tragic for us. Look at his poor wife, man. That was some fucked up shit". When the song was over, I asked. "Why did you start crying when Dennis put Soon on, bro?" "You don't understand, Ron" he replied. "That music goes perfect with this book. Seriously, just play that sometime and look at the photos in this book while it's going on. It's a very sad turn of events". "Jeff, it's only a song". I said. "It came out way after JFK was gone". "I know that" he quipped. "I'm not stupid. But, some of you guys don't get it and are heartless. Maybe one day, you'll understand". "Don't let him smoke anymore of that shit" Dennis laughed. "Next, he'll be comparing Queen to Viet Nam. "Shut up, Dennis" Jeff yelled. "Go and learn some empathy". "I have plenty of empathy" Dennis chuckled. "Enough to know what fantasy is and what's real". "Come back to earth" laughed Duck. "I spoke to Dennis while you guys were discovering the universe. We're going to the diner. I have some cash and if you guys are cool and stop acting like assholes, I'll treat everybody to a Cheeseburger Deluxe". "The diner it is" Dennis replied. "But, Phil has a funny idea I think we should all know about and be in on". "What's that, Phil?" I asked.

"I think we should do something funny at the diner" Phil said. "Dennis told me he found some bandages in a cabinet and there's like boxes and boxes of them. They're the kind that you wrap around a wound like an Ace bandage too. He's got tape and everything. We want to dress up one of us as a mummy and go in the diner that way. It'll be hilarious. Just imagine the looks We'll get on all the customers faces?" "Are you in on this, Den?" I asked. "Sure, why not" he replied. "But, who"s gonna be the victim?" he asked laughing. "Don't look at me" I said. "I'm always the one that gets picked on, fuck that". "I tell you what" Dennis said. "We'll flip a coin for it. Whoever loses has to be the mummy". "I guess that's fair". I replied. "I just hope it's not me again". "No crying" Phil laughed. "We already had enough of that with Jeff a minute ago" "Fuck you guys" Jeff yelled. "Go and make fun of somebody else". "So, you're not in this with us?" Phil asked. "No, I'm gonna stay home until my mother gets here. I have shit I wanna watch on TV anyway". "Good" said Dennis. "No babysitting for me tonight". "You're gonna get a baby slap to your fucking head if you don't leave me alone" Jeff cautioned. "Just ignore him" Dennis said.

"And, he'll slowly go away". "Ok, Den" I replied. "Let's stop teasing your brother and flip a coin". Who"s got a quarter?" I asked. "I do" said Phil. "I'll go first" I said. "Flip that baby". Dennis yelled as Phil chucked the coin into the air. After a few seconds, we watched as it dropped to the ground. "Call it, bro" Dennis said. "Heads or tails?" "Heads" I screamed. "It looks like you're off the hook, bro" Dennis howled. "Who"s next?" he asked. Phil volunteered, then Dennis, then Duck as last. Dennis and Phil were victorious while Duck was beginning to get nervous. "It's all on you" Dennis laughed. "The final spin". As Dennis threw the coin in the air, Duck yelled out tails". "Tails?" Dennis asked. "Nobody ever chooses tails". The coin hit the floor, danced for a second, and landed on its back. "Heads" Dennis chuckled. "It's heads, bro. You're the mummy for the evening". "Fuck!" Duck exclaimed. "This is gonna suck". "No it won't" Phil giggled. "We're all high as fuck. It's gonna be fun. Just wait until we get there.

As I sat in a chair and watched, Dennis and Phil began wrapping Duck in gauze from head to toe. They were especially vigilant with the detail to his face. They wanted to make sure he could see correctly and that his mouth had a space for talking and eating. "He looks like one of those guys in that revolutionary war picture." I laughed. "The one with the one soldier carrying the flag while the other one beats on the drum" "Let's put some ketchup on him" Phil chuckled. "It'll make him look more realistic". "Fuck that" Duck exclaimed. "I'm not a fucking hamburger". "You're lucky, Duck" laughed Dennis. "Because, we don't have any". "We'll just wrap him up as tight as we can" said Phil. "It won't look real if it starts to come apart". "Hurry up with this shit" Duck begged. "I'm getting hungry" "We're all hungry, bro" said Dennis. "But, it's gonna be worth it. We'll be laughing about it for days". "I hope so" Duck retorted. "Being a fool is time consuming" "Just sit still" said Phil. "We're almost done". When Duck"s costume was finished, we paraded him around the house to see every angle. We wanted to make sure nothing came loose and he looked original as possible.

"What do you think?" Dennis asked "Does it look good or what?" "It looks good enough to me" I replied. "There's only a few spaces where you can see through. But, you did the face really good. And, that's what counts. It looks pretty believable. "Duck"s not wrapped too tight anyway" laughed Phil. "So, he'll fit right in". "I can't believe you guys are doing this to me" complained Duck. What did I do to deserve this?" "You're our friend" Dennis said. "That's enough. You should already know that over here, we need an occasional scapegoat. So, tonight, you're it". "Are we ready to go?" he asked us. "Let's roll" I said. I can't wait to see this".

We cut through our usual way through the trailer park and arrived to navigate the diner"s stairs. People caught sight of us and were glaring through the windows. "They're already staring at me" Duck cried. "Grab onto the handrail" Dennis whispered. "Pretend you're having a hard time walking up the stairs. We have to make it look real if you want to convince them". Duck grabbed the rail while Phil was holding his elbow as if he was guiding him. A man and a woman were coming out the door as I reached for its opening. "You poor dear" the woman said. "I hope your friend will be all right?" "He'll be ok" Dennis replied. "He was in a bad accident and We're taking care of him". "Well, I wish him the best" she said as they wandered away to the parking lot. "Let's get him inside" I said while trying hard not to laugh. "I can't see too well in this thing" Duck cried. "You gotta help me to go and sit down" "We got you, bro" said Dennis. "You're almost inside". As we approached the host station just inside of the door, everyone in the diner was craning their necks for a look. Since the hostess was busy, we decided to sit down at the counter on some stools. I was on the left, Phil was to my right, Duck was in the middle, and Dennis was on the end. "Everybody is staring at me" Duck said. "I think it's going to work" Dennis whispered. "Be quiet, or you're gonna ruin it". Finally, a waitress came over and asked us for our order. "What the hell happened to him?" she asked. "Oh, he was in a bad car accident" replied Dennis. "But, he nodded to us that he was hungry a little while ago. So, we took him out for a bite to eat". "Well, that's unfortunate" she said. "I'm sorry to hear that. Can he talk?" she asked. "Oh no" Phil said. "We'll be ordering for him". "Well then, what will all of you have?" she asked. "We're all gonna have the same thing" said Dennis. "Cheeseburger Deluxes for all of us with Cokes. Except for our friend here. He's going to have chicken noodle soup with no noodles and a straw". "No noodles and a straw?" she asked looking surprised. "I don't know if we have soup like that?" "Just drain the noodles and give him the broth" replied Phil. "The straw is so he can suck it up". "He's like that movie the fly" Dennis said. "It's the only way he can eat. Isn't that right buddy?" Dennis asked as he looked at Duck"s face. Duck looked at the waitress and made a buzzing sound while nodding his head yes. "If that's what he really wants, I'll see what I can do" she said. So, she took off for the kitchen. When she came back, she had a large bowl of soup and a straw just as Dennis had ordered. She set it down in front of Duck and said "I hope you feel better honey, and enjoy it. You look like you have way worse problems than eating from a straw. I'll be right back with the food for the rest of you guys". We thanked her and were goading Duck to starting slurping. "Maybe its duck soup" Dennis laughed. "You're favorite". Dennis put the straw in the hot mixture and lifted the bowl to Duck"s lips. While making sure the other customers could hear he said "Here you go, bro. Take a few sips. You need your nourishment". Duck extracted some liquid from the straw and made a mumbling sound. "What's he trying to say?" I asked. "I think he likes it" Dennis laughed. "Give him some more" I suggested. Duck began to make gurgling sounds and shook his head no from side to side. "I think he's done" said Phil. "I guess We'll all eat while he sits here and watches us". One of the customers behind us was listening and became enraged. "That's so cruel" she said. "How can you just sit there and eat solid food like that while he suffers with soup?" "We didn't make him have an accident" Dennis chuckled. "We're only trying to do him a favor". "You need to mind your own business, lady. We're doing the best we can. He's an orphan, you know?

We're doing this as charity for him". "Well, you should charity him a better meal in my opinion" the woman replied. "Because, I think its ridiculous". "Ridiculous is sticking your nose in where it doesn't belong" said Phil. "Our friend here stuck his nose in where it didn't belong, and look what happened to him?" The woman sighed and went back to her meal. As we were finishing up our burgers and drinks, Duck decided he needed to go to the restroom. I think he had grown tired of our farce and wanted some relief. After a few moments, he came back and sat down minus the bandages. The waitress came by collecting our empty plates and handed us our bill. "I thought he was hurt?" she asked concerned. "Oh, I got better" Duck replied. "You got better in that short of a time?" she asked. "It's miraculous" Dennis laughed. "It must have been your soup!" "Yeah, that was it" I said. The diner makes the best duck soup. Right, Duck?" Duck stood up and yelled "It's a miracle everyone, I'm well!" The manager of the diner saw this and came over in a huff. "It's a miracle your meal is over" he snarked. "Because, 5 more minutes of this and I'm calling the cops". "It's time to go fellas" demanded Dennis. "The show is over".

We got back to DenniS's house and his mother still hadn't come home yet. Coming from the basement, we could hear the sound of music playing loudly. "Is that Kiss?" I asked Dennis. "It sounds like the song Firehouse?" "Yeah, that's JR" he replied. "I guess he's hanging out down there". "Let's go down and see what he's doing" I asked. "He's probably working out with those weights again" Dennis said. "He likes to stay in shape". "I'm gonna head home" said Phil. "I'll see you guys later". As Phil was trotting away down Redwood Avenue, Duck was complaining that he had to use the bathroom again. "Ok" Dennis said. "But, hurry it up. Any minute now my mom"s gonna be home". "Mrs. What?" Duck asked. "Yeah, that's the one" Dennis laughed. "She'll flip if We're all here when she comes home from work". DenniS's mother was known as Mrs. What due to the fact that when her kids wouldn't listen, she would scream "Whaaaaat the fuck is this?" at the top of her lungs to get rid of us. Being that we were all snot nosed teens at the time, we underappreciated that the poor woman only wanted a rest from her long, drawn out work schedule. We were so self-absorbed with ourselves that we had no clue that she had been on her feet for 12 hours serving customers all day. In retrospect, we should have all treated her much better. As Dennis and I descended the cellar steps to the level below, I looked up and could make out sets of hooks that were screwed into the rafters. There was also painted letters of descriptions to sell from a store that they had attempted in the past. Most were in orange and yellow lettering with names such as "beads, cups, clips, pictures, knick knacks, and miscellaneous". "What are those hooks all about?" I asked Dennis. "Oh, that was out head shop" he replied. "We never really sold anything and close it though". JR was just finishing up his exercising and was on his way back upstairs. "What's up, bro" he asked slightly winded from his set. "Nothing" Dennis replied. "We were just having fun with Duck at the diner. We dressed him up as a mummy. It was hilarious". "That sounds like a funny story" JR said. "But, I gotta jet. I have to go upstairs and take a shower before mommy comes home. I have a lot of things to do. So, tell me later, ok?" He bounced up the basement stairs leaving Dennis and I to figure out what to do next. "I have a few Miller beers here I left in the corner from yesterday" he laughed. "You wanna guzzle a few of these with me?" "Sure" I replied. "Hand me one". "Ok" Dennis said. "But, we have to drink them fast. Because, I don't have enough for Duck. I've been using his guitar for 6 months and he keeps bugging me to give it back to him and I keep putting it off. If he sees we didn't save him any beer, he's gonna flip out and want it back again". "I'm not saying shit" I chuckled. "Let him worry about that". Just then, we heard a car door slam shut. "I think my mom"s home" Dennis said. "Duck better leave the house or he's toast". "I thought your mother liked Duck?" I asked. "She does, usually" he replied. "But, it all depends on what kind of mood she's in". "I see" I whispered. "Perhaps we shouldn't make too much noise then?" "Nah, we can play some music and talk down here. I don't think she's gonna go to bed for some time".

As we drank and started to feel the alcohol"s effects, we grew louder in our conversations. So loud, we were louder than the music playing in the background. After an hour, we heard the TV being switched off, several footsteps, and then the creaking of a bed. It was obvious DenniS's mother was getting ready to go to sleep. "Dennis?" she yelled. "I can hear you guys down there. Duck went home and it's time to turn down the noise. Go someplace else to hang out with your friends". Dennis completely ignored her and put his fingers to his mouth indicating for me to not make a sound. When he heard there were no more voices above us, we began to speak again. Again, his mom yelled down to us "Dennis?" she asked. "I told you once already. Don't make me come down there and kick you out". Dennis having worked for a local landscaper, screamed at the ceiling. "I worked 6 days straight this week with no break. This is my only day I get to relax. So, cut me a break already". Suddenly, we heard Jeff's voice booming down to defend her "Dennis!" he hollered. "Mommy"s tired from work. Have some respect. She needs her rest to help support us. Call it a night, bro. Enough is enough!" "Ahhhhhhh" Dennis howled back. "Be quiet and go rub mommy"s back. I'm drinking my last beer here. Then, We'll leave". "Who"s with you down there?" his mom asked. "Nobody you know" Dennis chuckled. "Then, I want you out of the house even more" she demanded. "I don't like kids in my house I don't know". "It's Ronnie Arold" Jeff retorted. Dennis is down there with him, mom". "Fucking rat" Dennis whispered. "He ratted you out, man". "Ronnie" she screamed. "I like you. But, you should know better. Could you please take Dennis with you and go someplace else?" I didn't say a word. I was laughing at the situation but I didn't want to get on her bad side. "We're leaving now" Dennis replied. "So, go take a snooze, the both of you". "Good" yelled Jeffrey. "And, don't come back either"

Another pinball joint had opened up behind a local barbershop named Darios. I had gotten my hair trimmed there once but had never gone back. Dario was a middle aged guy with a crew cut who somehow thought all young boys deserved to have military style haircuts. He was straight out of the 1940"s and it showed. No matter how you asked him to style your hair, he would ignore you and do whatever he wanted. Every young guy I knew avoided him like the plague. We had grown our hair out on purpose and were wary of his "happy, snippy, fingers". If you complained about him cutting too much off, he would use one of his favorite monikers "Just a little more" as he snipped and cut away. Word got around not to trust his services as we felt he would try to coerce us into "conforming to the norm". Dario had hired a short, bearded, and longhaired hippie type guy named Greg to run his pinball enterprise while he was away. Greg was a nice enough guy in his early 30"s who had a pretty good rapport with the teenagers and was slightly trusted over most others. Somehow, he had gained press access to major rock concerts and was permitted to record them with his tripod and his Super 8 camera. Every Friday to keep the kids coming in; he would have "Concert Night". He had footage of bands such as Queen, Yes, the Grateful Dead, and others. He even supplied drinks and snacks at a nominal cost just to keep everyone happy.

While I was playing a game of pool there with Dave G. one afternoon, Dave had come up with a scam. "I know where Greg keeps the keys, man" he whispered. "There's no alarm on this building so nobody would catch us". Catch us doing what?" I asked. "What kind of scheme are you talking about now?" "He keeps all the money in a cigar box under a table in the back" Dave said. "I know there's at least 75 bucks in there every night". "But, what do keys have to do with it?" I asked. "Listen" he said. "I have a great plan. I've been thinking about it for days, bro. I want you in on it because you know how to keep your mouth shut and you're smart enough to get away with it with me". "Clue me in" I replied. "Here"s what We're gonna do" he said. "Remember that story you once told me about how you and Skippy robbed an air conditioner from the neighbor"s house behind you once after they moved out?" "Yeah" I replied. "I remember that. That was last year and I sold it to my ex-girlfriend's relatives". "Exactly" Dave exclaimed. "Well, it got me thinking. I remember how you told me how you and Skip pushed in the air conditioner and were able to get inside so you could carry it out, right?" "Yup, that's about how we did it". I laughed. "We can do the same thing here. Come outside with me and I'll show you". "Ok, Dave" I said. "Let me see your crazy idea". We finished our game and nonchalantly made our way outside to a corner of the building where a room air conditioner was hanging from a window. It was larger than the one I took with Skippy and appeared much more rusted out and older. "How the fuck are we gonna move that thing?" I asked. "It's huge!" "There are only 2 bolts holding it in" Dave said smiling. "I've already checked it out. It's really wobbly too. We only have to shimmy it back and forth a little and then kick it in with our legs. We can disconnect the bolts real fast with a ratchet wrench and just give it a push". "What about noise?" I asked. "The neighbors next door might hear it. It's bound to be loud with how heavy it is". "Not a problem" he said. "I've been watching it for months. Doug has no idea it will break the fall. It's perfect, bro. Are you in or not?" he asked. "Oh, I'm definitely in" I laughed. When do you wanna do this?" I asked "I was thinking this Friday night after one of his concert movies" he said "About 10 o"clock should be good. He closes up at 9. So, it'll be empty for an hour". "Ok" I replied. "We'll do it then".

Friday came for our devious plan and I met Dave just as we had spoken about. "Do you see anybody around?" he asked. "It's looking pretty good". "I don't see a soul" I whispered. "Do you have the ratchet set with you?" he asked. "I have it right here, man" I replied. "It's all ready to go". "Ok, man" he said. "I'm gonna stand over here just at the edge of the air conditioner. Go and loosen all of the bolts. When you're done, call me over and We'll push that pig through the window". "You got it" I laughed. "Just make sure you give me a signal if anyone suspicious like the cops comes by. I wanna be able to hop the fence and get away"."I will" he said. "Just hurry up and get this shit done. The longer We're out here, the more visible we are". I slithered down to my waist height, pulled out my tool case, and matched a socket to one of the bolts on the frame. "Ahhh" I thought. "A 5/16"s. This one will do". Quickly, I snapped the socket to the ratchet and backed out the first 3 nuts. When I got to the last one, it wouldn't budge. The threads on its bolts were rusty and appeared older than the previous ones. I motioned to Dave to come over to see. "Dave" I whispered pointing. "I think the first 3 were newer bolts. This last one is a bitch, it doesn't want to move". "Let me help you" he said. "We'll both pull on the handle at the same time. We have to use leverage". He grabbed the top of the handle while I positioned my hand on the bottom. "Pull" he demanded. "Pull on this fucker with all you"ve got". After 2 attempts with no success, I suggested that we quit. "Dave" I said. "Unless we can get this last nut to come off, there's no way We're gonna be able to move anything". "I can see that" he replied. "We have to find something to give us a lot more leverage than just our hands". "Go out into the parking lot and see if you can find a pipe or something?" I suggested. "I'll wait here until you come back". "Oh, sure" he complained. "Send me out there so somebody sees me". "It's the only way, man" I replied. "Or, you can forget about getting inside". "Forget about nothing" he exclaimed. "I know for a fact there's money in there, bro. I never walk away from easy money. I'll be right back. So, sit tight and let me see what I can find, ok?"

As I watched him wander the gravel road beneath him, he found something in the grass in the berm close to the highway. He picked it up vicariously and was smiling. It appeared to be a square piece of metal that was hollow inside and was about 3 feet long. He looked around 360 degrees to make sure no one was watching and made his way back while carrying it in his hand. "What do you think about this?" he asked chuckling. "It's hollow inside and looks long enough to do the job". "What is that thing?" I asked. "I dunno, man" he replied. "It looks like it came off a clothes display or something. Who gives a fuck, let's just try to use it and get this shit done". "All right" I said. Slide the end over the handle and take the top part like you did before. I'll grab the bottom and let's see if we can yank this bitch out". With both our bodies" weight on it, and attempts by bouncing up and down, the nut finally broke. "Whew" Dave blurted. "That fucking thing was brutal. I guess they wanted to make sure nobody could get in through there". "I guess they were wrong" I laughed. "Now, let's finish the job". I pulled the last bolt from its mounting and got ready to push. Dave got on the left side while I got prepared on the right". "Ok, Dave" I said. "Are you ready?" "Let's shove this thing in as hard as we can. Once we get it in halfway, it should fall in the rest of the way on its own weight". "Ok" he replied. "But, be careful man. If this thing falls on us, it'll fuck us up". "Just push when I count down" I said. "And, don't stop in the middle. It shouldn't fall back on us if we do it that way". "1,2….3" I grunted as we pushed. As it moved, it was squeaking and making a racket and we had to wiggle it back and forth to force it free. Finally, as I had predicted, it started to sink down on an angle. "One more push, Dave" I said. "Then, I think we've got it".

With a loud and thunderous scrape, the air conditioner fell inside to the ground. "Shit" Dave said. "That made more noise than I thought it would. I hope no nosey neighbors heard us". "It wasn't as loud as it could have been" I muttered. "Since those boxes that were under it made a nice cushion. I wouldn't worry about it right now." I laughed. "But, there's a gaping hole in the wall where that air conditioner was. So, we better get inside real fast before somebody sees us". "I'll go in first" Dave ordered. "And, then you come in after me. But, stay by the window looking for cops. I'm gonna go in farther because I know exactly where the money and the keys are. Don't worry, I'll be quick". I lifted him up and over the sill and watched him drop down to the floor. "Hurry up and get in here" he whispered back. "Before somebody sees you". Once I was inside, I could only make out a faint glow coming off of some emergency backup lights attached to the celling over my head. My adrenaline was flowing and I felt like an escaped prisoner. "Come on Dave" I whispered in his last known direction, not knowing if he could hear me or not. "This shit is taking too long". He didn't answer me which contributed even more to my nervousness and I began to become paranoid. I started having visions of police arriving in my head. I was imagining us in handcuffs being paraded by the side of the road as if we were specimens being made an example of. When my thoughts got to the part where the cops were about to put us in their cars, I heard Dave"s voice behind me. I suddenly I snapped out of it. "I got the cash and the keys, bro." he said. "So, let's get out of here before somebody sees us". "What the fuck did you take the keys for?" I asked. "It's not like we can lock the place up for them now?" I laughed. "Insurance" Dave replied. "I'll tell you about it later. Now, either jump back out that hole, or get the fuck out of my way. You always talk too fucking much, Ronnie. Save your comments for later. Let's go". I hurtled back out of the opening and waited for Dave following close behind. "I got about 80 bucks" he said. "Let's go back to my house and We'll divvy it up. Then, I'll tell you about my insurance plan".

A few days had gone by since our Dario"s caper and it seemed like we weren't going to be caught. Dave and I had made sure not to brag to anyone and had kept our mouths shut. A rare occurrence when it came to teenagers. I was much more wary than Dave and had kept my distance avoiding the subject as to not arouse any suspicion. Dave on the other hand being the person of bravado and balls that he was, didn't seem to care. He told me he had gone by there the very next day. When I met up with him again on the street he was laughing uncontrollably. "That dumb ass Doug thinks I'm a friend of his" he chuckled. "Now, he's asking me if I know who robbed the place? He said he doesn't care about the money. But, that Dario is worried about the store"s keys and wants them back. He asked me if I know who has the keys and they can give them back anonymously with no questions asked. He's even offering a reward of 50 bucks. These people are stupid fucks, bro. Do you wanna make some more cash?" he asked laughing. "How?" I asked inquisitively. "Remember, I have the keys right?" he said. "I told him a guy named Mike has them. Of course there's no such person as Mike. So, I'm gonna have you call Doug from a pay phone saying your Mike and admit that you were in on it. But now, you're scared and you"ve got remorse. You're gonna tell him you're giving the keys to me, and I'm gonna give them back to him. After that, I'll collect the 50 bucks and split it with you. It's a perfect scam, man and They'll never know". "What if he gets the cops in on it and they trace the call?" I asked fearfully. "No, retard" Dave replied. "You won't be on the phone that long. It takes them 3 minutes to trace you. As long as you keep it under that, you should be fine. I've timed it already, bro. It will take you under a minute". "If you're sure we can get away with it" I said. "Then, I'll do it". "It's foolproof" he insisted. "Do you want the 25 bucks or not?" he asked. "Because if not, I can find someone else who does. "When do you want to do this?" I asked. "Right now" he said. "There's a pay phone right down the road at the gas station close to Shoe town. We can call from there".

I called Doug at Dario"s as Dave had suggested and waited for the phone to pick up. After a few rings, I heard Doug"s voice come on the line. "Darios, can I help you?" he asked. Trying my best to disguise my voice by making it sound much deeper, I spoke. "Hello Doug?" I asked. "This is Mike. Dave told you about me. I have your keys. I'm gonna give them back to Dave, and we can forget about this right?" "That's right" he said, "But, I want to know your last name". He was already trying to be sneaky and attempting to break Dave"s agreement with him. "That's not part of the deal" I howled back agitated. He kept pressuring me with more questions and was trying to get me to incriminate myself. Each time, I spoke over him. "Not gonna happen". Finally, after getting tired of his constant badgering, Dave gave me the hang up the phone sign. "Fuck this guy" he whispered. "End the call, Ron". I put the receiver back in its cradle quickly and turned to Dave. "Man, what an asshole" I quipped. "He doesn't know when to stop". "He's just being a douchebag because of his boss" Dave said. "Dario is going fucking ballistic wanting to know who robbed him". "Well, that's too fucking bad" I replied. "He should have installed an alarm system". "Exactly" Dave laughed. "But, he was too cheap too. Everybody told him, but he wouldn't listen. So, it's too late now and it'll be an expensive lesson for him to learn. But, his ignorance is to our advantage. Now, go home and I'll call you later after I get the reward money. There shouldn't be a problem after this". "Sounds good" I replied. "You're a master scammer". "Nah" he chuckled "I just take advantage of stupid people who aggravate me". "Welcome to the club" I replied. "You're apprenticeship is over".

Ronnie E. had finally gotten his license and was driving around in his mother's Ford Galaxie 500. He dropped by Thursday"s and picked me up. "Where did you get this?" I asked. "My mom lets me use it once in a while" he said. "I have to use it anyway, because I moved to Old Bridge last week" "Old Bridge" I asked surprised. "Why all the way the fuck out there?" "I had to" he said "That's where she moved to and I had no other choice. But, I'm coming back to Edison to hang out. I'll be here whenever I get the car". "Cool" I replied. "Do you have gas and shit?" I asked. "Yeah, I have a half a tank" he replied. "Do you have any money?" he asked. "I have 10 bucks" I added. "Maybe be we can buy some beer or something and wing it from there". "I have a 12 pack in the trunk" he laughed. "Let's see if we can pick up some chicks and go to the route 18 drive in. Ten bucks should be enough to get us in plus snacks. If we can find a couple easy ones, we can get them drunk and bang them". "Where are we gonna get girls at?" I asked. "Most of them have boyfriends already" "Not the sluts" he cackled. "Let's drive around and find one. They're always around if you know where to look". "Where should we go first?" I asked. "How about

Edison Lanes" he joked. "There's always some ladies of the evening there.

We pulled into the Edison Lanes parking lot and went inside. Ronnie was insistent and had the sex gleam in his eye. He smelt their pheromones and was on the prowl. "Look all the way down the aisle in the back" he said. "Doesn't that look like that chubby chick we know? The one with the long blonde hair?" "Yeah, I think that's her" I replied. "I heard she puts out easy too". "Just what We're looking for" he said. "It's time to sink the sub". We sauntered past the bowlers until we got to the end of the long hallway and the girl was by herself. "How you doing?" Ronnie asked. It was obvious that he knew her pretty well. I already knew her name and knew she had a reputation. "I'm just hanging around here talking on the telephone" she said. "What are you guys up to tonight?" "We're going to the movies at the drive in. You wanna come" Ronnie asked. "Come, huh?" she laughed. With two Ronnie's? I bet that would be a lot of fun". "Oh, you know it will be" Ronnie chuckled. "Me and my friend here always take care of the ladies" "Isn't that right, Arold?" he asked. "She turned to me and giggled "Yeah, I know about you Mr. Arold. And if you're hanging around with Ronnie here, We're all bound to have a good time". "A good time is my middle name" Ronnie replied. "Now, do you wanna come and hang out with us or what?" "Do you have beer?" she asked. "Plenty enough for you" he said. "And, I think Arold here might have a joint with him. He's always got pot". "That I do" I replied. "Well, a half a joint anyway". "That's enough to get stoned on" he laughed. "And, We'll even let the lady here toke first". "How gentlemanly of you" she boasted. "Ok, we can do that" she teased. "Let's go. But, don't get any ideas until I'm buzzed. And, if we do anything, you're not both doing me at the same time". "You mean you're not gonna fulfill my fantasy of a threesome at the drive in?" Ronnie asked. "You're fantasy will be if I feel like going down on you" she laughed. "But like I said, I gotta be fucked up first. I like it a lot better that way". "Well" Ronnie whooped "You have the beers and We'll do the pumping".

As we settled on a parking spot somewhere in the middle, Ronnie reached for the speaker that hung on the door. The girl was in the front seat next to him and I was in the back. "These things suck" he grumbled. "Half these fuckers never work. And when they do, they sound like somebody talking under water" He hung it on the glass and rolled the window partly up. "What do you care?" the girl asked. "In a little while, We're not gonna be watching the movie anyway". She's got a point there, man" I said. "But, at least we can watch half of it". "Half isn't what I'm gonna give her" Ronnie said "I'm going for the full 9 inches. Go in the trunk and pull out some beers, man" he demanded. "And, let's get this party started". About an hour went by and I noticed that the girl was cozied up next to him. "You wanna smoke some of this shit, or not?" I asked. "It's not gonna smoke itself". "The only thing Miss America here is gonna smoke is my pole" Ronnie chuckled. "But, light it up anyway. I'm sure she'll want some". I have a few beers in me now" she said. "If I smoke that, I'll get really horny". "H is the word" I joked. "So, toke up baby". We passed the joint back and forth until there was only a small roach left. As I rolled down the window to throw it outside, I noticed the girl's arm going up and down. Ronnie turned to me and whispered "She's jerking me off, man. Let me use your coat. She won't blow me if you can see. She wants to have her head covered" He was talking about my long Navy coat with tails I was wearing. It had a lot of material in it. So, I understood what he was getting at. "Hurry up, man" he begged. "She just told me she's really hot and wants it". "Ok" I said. "I'll let you use it. But, don't you dare get any come on it" I laughed. "I won't" he said. "I think she swallows anyway". I took off my coat, handed it to him, and instructed him to get on with it". "She's the one who"s gonna get on with it, bro. So, sit back and watch the movie until she's done. And then, it'll be your turn".

In between gazing at the film as it was playing, I couldn't help but laugh as Ronnie covered the girl's head. In moments, I could see the outline of her going up and down on him. He kept looking back at me and making faces. He took his tongue in his mouth and made the universal sign for a BJ. "That's it" he told her "Just keep polling it". After 10 minutes, I heard her voice from under the canopy. "Hurry up" she said. "My jaw is getting tired". "Just keep bobbing" he said "I'm almost finished". As he was climaxing, he grit his teeth and rolled back his eyes and was pretending to shake. "It's an earthquake" he howled. "A drive in earthquake. Everybody come!" I heard the girl gag a little and then she stopped. She came out from under my coat and was wiping her chin" "That was pretty good" she said. "It was even better for me" Ronnie laughed. "Now, it's Arold"s turn. So, get in the back, I wanna watch the rest of this movie". "As soon as I have a few more beers" she said laughing. "I have to clean my palate". Eventually, she jumped in the back and asked me if I wanted the same. "My mouth is tired" she said. "But, I'll do it if you want me too". "I"d rather fuck" I said. "I have a rubber in my wallet". "Good" she replied. "Then, fuck me. Because, I'm kind of wasted" "Go ahead and fuck her" Ronnie laughed. "You can take your long assed coat and cover your ass as it goes up and down. Nobody will see you that way". "She laid down on her back and rolled down her pants. I whispered to her "I wanna suck on your tits first, I love tits". "Go for it" she said. But, be gentle. My period is next week and they are kind of sore". "No problem" I replied. "Thanks for the advice". I lifted up her bra and cradled one of her breasts in my mouth and began to suckle on it. They were pretty big and I felt like a baby feeding in a new born nursery. Suddenly, I felt something odd with my tongue. "What the fuck is that?" I thought. "Is that fucking hair? Holy shit? This chick's got hairy tits!" I had never been with a girl who didn't shave her tits before. I dropped it out of my mouth almost immediately. "Let's just fuck" I told her. "I think I'm ready now. "Pop on that rubber then" she directed. "And, away We'll go". I did as she asked and slid it in gingerly. She gave me a few moans, but they sounded fake" "Are you going to get into it or what?" I asked "You need to roll those hips back to me". "Pump Arold, pump" Ronnie laughed. "Give it to her". "If it makes you get off faster, I'll pump back" she said. But, be quick. I'm kind of drunk and I don't wanna puke". "Don't puke on me" I replied. "Yeah, don't throw up in my car" Ronnie cautioned. "Or, else you'll have to walk home". "I won't" she said. "But, hurry up and come". I relieved myself and finished her off. Ronnie asked. "Are you guys done yet? The movie"s almost over". "I'm done for the night" the girl said. "Could you guys take me home now?" "Yeah, I guess you"ve earned it" Ronnie joked. "You were great". We thanked the girl, dropped her off and headed to my house so I could go home. "Did you know she had hairy tits?" I asked Ronnie "Yeah" he replied. "I knew she had those. One of her nicknames is gorilla tits" he laughed hysterically. "Why didn't you tell me?" I asked. "What fun what that be?" he said. "It's funnier if you found it out for yourself".

This was the year of many concerts for me and I was already lagging far behind my friends. Other than the Joanie Mitchell at Central Park in New York City with Georgie Burns, I hadn't been to any others. At Dennis G"s house, there was talk of a big event coming up at JFK Stadium in Philadelphia with the band Yes and Peter Frampton. Yes had released their album Relayer and Frampton was having great success with his new one called Frampton Comes Alive. I asked Dennis if he was going as almost everyone I knew wanted to attend. "I've got my tickets already, bro" he said. "But, I'm going in Mickey B"s station wagon. I'm not sure if there's any more room for you though? You'll have to call him and ask". I made a mental note of this and asked Dennis of the date for the show. "When is it?" I asked. "June 12th"he said. "And, it's being billed as the bicentennial show. You better get a ticket soon though before they're all gone. You know me; I start partying and getting ready 2 weeks before they even get here". "I plan on doing that" I said. "As soon as possible". In a few days, I conjured up some cash and bought 2 tickets hoping another friend would accompany me. After calling up Mick, I was told "I'm sorry, man. You should have told me earlier, I have a full boat now. Maybe you can catch a ride with somebody else". Undeterred, I made more phone calls. But, everyone"s car was full. Hanging around McDonalds, I ran into Skippy. "Hey Skip?" I asked. "Do you wanna go see Yes with me? I have an extra ticket and I'll give it to you for free. I just need somebody to go with me so I don't have to go alone". "When is it?" he asked. "June 12th in Philadelphia" I replied. "But, I can't find a ride. We'll have to take the train and then the Septa subway to the stadium." "It looks like We'll be there for a couple of days if we do that" he chuckled. "But, I'm cool with it if you are". "Absolutely" I said "We'll have a great time".

June 11th came and Skippy was supposed to meet me at the New Brunswick train station. We had decided to beat the mad rush of other concertgoers and get there the day before. He was a half hour late and I was beginning to get anxious. "I hope he shows and doesn't blow me off" I thought. "Otherwise, this is gonna suck". Just as I was about to call him, I saw him bounding up the stairs. "It's about fucking time" I yelled sarcastically. "I didn't think you were gonna show". "I had to wait around for my mother to give me a few bucks and drop me off" he said. "You know how that goes, man". "Oh, yeah" I replied. "But, at least you are here. The train is gonna arrive in about 15 minutes". "I hear there's gonna be thousands of people there" said Skip. "I hope We'll be ok". "Skip" I said sternly. "Who cares, man? I've never been to a stadium one like this either. So, it's gonna be new for the both of us". "Ok" he said. "But, don't lose me after we get there. I'm not too sure of how to get back home". "Don't worry" I replied. "I'll make sure you don't go anyplace. Now, I'm gonna go downstairs and get a quart of beer. I still have my brother's ID. So, I'll be right back. Don't go anywhere". "I won't" he said. "Just hurry up and get back". I skipped down the stairs to the street below and procured a quart of Bud from the adjacent liquor store. When I returned, Skip was sitting by himself and sneaking tokes off a joint. "You better hope nobody smells any of that shit" I warned. "There's Amtrak cops around here sometimes, man". "Fuck those rent a snorks" he laughed. "Come over here and get a hit before I put it out. And, give me a few guzzles of that beer. If we have to sit on some lame train for a couple of hours, I wanna be stoned enough to relax". "Here you go" I said as I handed him the bottle. "But, don't drink it all. Save me some". "Just drag on this bone before it burns out" he chuckled. "And, don't worry about it".

We arrived at JFK stadium in the late afternoon. But, there weren't many attendees yet. "Let's pick a spot we can camp out at until tomorrow" I said. "How about under that tree sticking out of the pavement over there?" Skippy asked pointing downward. "That looks like a good area". "The tree it is" I replied. So, we sat down, got comfortable, and began looking around. "This fucking place is massive" Skip said noticeably intimidated by its size. "How many people do you think will fit in there?" he asked. "I dunno, Skip" I said. "It's a football stadium from 1920 something I think. So, probably a lot". "I hope we don't get crushed" he replied sheepishly. "I've never been in big crowds like that. I don't know if I'll like it or not" "It's a little late too worry about that now" I laughed. "So, I think it's better we just mellow out until the morning". As I was glancing around and taking in the surroundings, I caught a guy from the corner of my eye with 10 or 15 people around him. "Hey, Skip?" I asked. "Do you see that guy over there?" I think he's selling something. Maybe he has some Black Beauties for sale. I'm gonna go over there and check it out". "You want some if he has any left?" I asked. "Sure" he said. "But, you better hurry up, man. There's a lot of people going up to him". I made my way over to the guy just as people were walking away. "What have you got there?" I asked. "Anything good? Like Black Beauties perhaps?" "I just ran out, man" he replied. "How could you do that?" I asked. I saw you here for only about 5 minutes tops". "Speed goes quick buddy" he said. "They always do". "But, I can see you still have 3 or 4 left in your bag in your hand" I said.

"Sell me those". "I can't do that" he mumbled. "That's my head stash". "I'll pay you double whatever they're worth" I begged. "I'm gonna be here with a friend for 2 days and we need something to keep us going". "Sorry, buddy" he grinned. "Like I said, these are for me. I can't help you". As I turned to leave I muttered to myself "Fucking great, these people here are a bunch of fucking scuffs. They're like goddamn cockroaches". By the time I got back to Skippy, he was already half asleep. I didn't want to disturb him so I bundled up my jean jacket into a pillow and fell asleep myself. I didn't realize it at the time, but we both slept the entire night until early morning.

As we awoke, there was an orange haze in the distance and many buses rambling down a long, winding hill. People were spilling out and approaching the stadium like termites escaping their mound. It was at least a 10 fold increase from the night before. Skippy was getting nervous "Look at all of those fucking people, man" he said with worry on his face. "There's thousands of them! You didn't tell me it was gonna be like a large city, Ron!" "What the fuck do you want me to do?" I asked. "I told you there would be a lot. So, stop crying and relax. You'll be fine, man". "They look like bugs" he replied. "Tons and tons of bugs". As the morning turned into early afternoon, we could hear the melody of the sound check by Yes. They were testing their equipment and preparing for the evening"s show. Around noon, fans were starting to queue for the gates and the lines were getting longer. "Maybe we should get in line?" I asked Skip. "If we want to get a decent seat inside". "Ok, Ron" he replied. "But, try to stay by me. That line looks crazy". Surrounding the stadium were arched entranceways with painted green gates and what looked like waist high turnstiles. As we stood in line, the portal we were standing in began to open. Suddenly, there was a mad dash to enter and there were arms flailing everywhere. People were holding their tickets in their hands and shoving them in the face of the ticket takers. "Hold onto my jacket, Skip" I screamed. "That way, we won't lose each other". Skippy hadn't taken my advice to don his windbreaker and had tied it around his waist instead. So, I had nothing from him to grab onto to reciprocate with. While I was watching, it reminded me of a third world country where relief vehicles come into a village and hand out food. I was having visions of desperate people clamoring with their arms extended and begging for scraps to quell their hunger and despair. "These people are animals" I thought. "All of this just to get into a rock concert".

Just then, I felt a push from a wave of concertgoers behind us. I was off my feet and being launched through the turnstile sideways. The attendant was making a futile attempt to grab as many tickets as possible. But, he couldn't rip and return them fast enough. Half of the ticket stubs he returned, the remainder fell to the floor. It looked like large pieces of confetti in a mish mash of falling bodies, yelling, and a frenzy of forward only attempts As I got through the gate and was about to hit the floor, I saw Skippy in the distance in front of me. He was attempting to right himself and was shaking his head profusely. I stood up, rushed over, and confronted him. "Are you ok?" I asked. "I lost sight of you for a minute. These crazy fuckers pushed me through sideways. They lifted me right off of my feet. The guy didn't even take my ticket. Look! I still have it in my hand". "They did the same shit to me" he said. "But, he ripped my ticket and gave me back the stub. I'm pissed though". "Why"s that?" I asked. "Because, I should have listened to you." he said. "My jacket got pulled right off of me as I was being sucked through the line. I looked around for it for a minute or two. But, the fucker"s gone". "Some asshole probably stole it" I replied. "We can't do anything about it now. There's too many people over there. You'll just have to take it as a loss, bro".

We made our way through a tunnel that connected the gate area to the stadium field and discussed which way to go. Already, most of the choice viewing areas by the stage were taken. "I see a clearing over by the middle over there" I said. "Let's try that area".

"That sounds good to me" Skippy replied. "I just want to sit down for a while. I'm still a little shaky from that line bullshit". "We'll be ok" I responded. "Let's look around and see if we can find anyone we know?" I remember from talking with Dennis G. that if I wanted to find him at this show, all I had to do was search for his fro. I thought "How hard could it be to find one white guy with an afro?" Little did I know what I was in for. As I gazed around the stadium"s field, side stage seats, and bleachers, it appeared as if DenniS's hair style was more popular than I had known. There were many more white guys with afros than I had anticipated and I was having a very hard time connecting them to DenniS's. "I can't find him, Skip" I said frustrated. "Are you still looking for Dennis?" he asked. "Yeah" I replied. "But, it's pointless. With all of these fros, it looks like a sea of dandelions. There's just too many of them to search". "I'd give up if I were you" he said. "You'll just drive yourself nutty if you keep trying". "You have a point" I replied. "I guess We'll just have to see if we bump into him by luck".

While lying on our backs facing the stage and waiting for the first act to arrive, I saw someone I knew rushing down the stadium stairs to my immediate right. He was carrying a cooler on one side with his friend holding the other in tow. It was obvious they were struggling and trying desperately to navigate the steps to avoid spilling its contents to the ground. "Skip?" I asked shaking his arm. "Look over there, isn't that tight Timmy and his girlfriend?" "I do believe it is" he replied. "I didn't know they were coming here". "I didn't know either" I said. "I'm gonna wave them over". I stood up, caught Timmy"s attention, and motioned him to our direction. "He's coming over" I said. "I wonder what's in that cooler?" Skippy asked. "Because, I'm not standing in that fucking line and I'm thirsty". "Knowing Timmy, it'll probably be something good". Tim shook hands with us, situated himself, his girlfriend, and his friend and laid out a blanket that was large enough for everyone. "Funny running into you guys here" he said. "We were gonna stay in the bleachers. But, my girlfriend wanted to try to get a better spot closer to the stage. I figured we'd run into people we know. But, I didn't imagine you guys would be the first". "It's better than not knowing anybody" declared Skip". "That's true" Timmy replied. "But, how did you guys get here?" he asked. "Oh, we took the train" I responded. "We've been here since yesterday afternoon". "Yesterday afternoon?" he asked dumbfounded. "Fuck that. We chartered a bus from Middlesex where we live now. We have like 30 other people who came with us around here somewhere. But, they know where the bus is to go home. So, I'm not worried about them". "Nice" I replied. "It must have been comfortable". Just then, he opened up his cooler. "What do you have in there?" I asked. "Have you ever eaten watermelon with gin in it?" he asked. "No" I replied. "But, it sounds very refreshing". "How did you get the booze into that thing?" Skippy asked. "Simple" replied Timmy. "You just cut a plug in the center on its side and pour that shit in. You shake it up and let it rest for a few days. I have oranges with vodka in them too". "Vodka oranges?" I asked perplexed. "Just how did you manage to get vodka into those?" "Needles" he said. "Needles?" I asked "How?" "Well" he answered. "You take a syringe, fill it with vodka, and then shoot it into the fruit. It works on grapefruits and peaches too". "No shit!" I exclaimed. "I'll have to experiment with that sometime". "You wanna try some?" he asked. "Sure" I replied. "That would be cool". He reached under the ice in the cooler and retrieved an orange in each hand. "Here"s one for you" he said. "And, one for Skipper. Don't get too drunk now" he laughed. "I wouldn't want you to miss any of these bands". "We'll take our time" I chuckled. "But, can we try some of that watermelon drink as well?" "We're not cutting the watermelon open until later" he said. "But, here"s a Dixie cup with the gin and watermelon juice in it. Don't drink it too fast though, or you'll get fucked up". "Thanks" I replied as he handed one to me. "I'll be careful". Not being known for listening, I started out sipping Timmy"s concoction, liked the taste, and wolfed the rest down expeditiously. It tasted more like a shot of grain alcohol than a mixed fruity drink. Then, I peeled the orange and tore it open.

Again, it was very strong. "How much fucking booze did you put in these things, Timmy?" I asked. "These fucker"s are loaded". "More than enough, bro. I tried to tell you". By the time the artist Gary Wright came on, I was passed out from the booze and was snoring. I awoke just at the end of his hit song Dreamweaver and had a very bad headache. "Did you have a nice snooze?" Skippy asked. "I think I drank that orange shit too fast" I mumbled. "Timmy told me while you were out that he put like 5 shots in each orange" laughed Skippy. "No wonder you have a headache". "I guess I got fucked up" I replied. "But, it was better than standing in that damn concession line". "That's why I sipped mine" he said. "But, I guess you like vodka".

Suddenly, and out of nowhere, I got hit in the head with an empty half pint orange drink container. I stood up to investigate and began to get pelted with various forms of garbage from everywhere. Above us, people were throwing items down from the bleacher seats and causing a raining refuse effect. "It's fucking raining down garbage" Skippy howled. "This is fucked up". "Watch your heads" yelled Timmy. "You don't want to get boinked". Though some surrounding me were aggravated by this, I found it to be profoundly funny and threw the garbage right back at them. Skippy agreed with me and felt the same. "Fuck these jerkoffs" he screamed. "Pick that shit up and fling it back". When most in the field were sufficiently splattered with sticky orange drink residue and the fight had subsided, I laid back down with my suffering and listened to the announcements to the crowd from the stage. They came periodically about subjects such as where the bathrooms were, the medical tents, and for the asshole "selling bad drugs to please discontinue". Looking to my left, I saw stagehands with giant water hoses cooling down spectators from the oppressive heat while most of them danced and didn't care. Again, an announcement came over the PA "People? Oh, people. The ones hanging and sitting on those towers up in the back? We really suggest you get down off of them because We're going to be turning those lights on there pretty soon. If you insist on staying, there's a possibility that you may be burned like Kentucky Fried chicken. Thank you!" I heard him once more mentioning something about the heat and how the substances didn't mix forcing some fans to pass out be escorted to doctors to be revived. As the sun was beginning to set, Peter Frampton hit the stage and the crowd began jumping to their feet. Though I still had a slight headache, I was itching to get a closer look at him. Skip and I forced our way through some people by the front and climbed up on the fence to get a better view. After his 5th song, I felt a tug on my shirt from behind. A large, burly type man was pulling on me and demanding I come down from my perch immediately. "You took my girlfriend's spot" he yelled bruskly. "We waited all day to go there. So, you need to come down". "There is no spot" I screamed back. "You snooze, you lose". "We went to the bathroom and that's why we left" he continued. "You either come down from there, or I'll make you come down". I glanced over to Skip beside me and he was shaking his head no. The guy taunting me was pretty large and about 6 feet 4 and 280 lbs. So, I guessed Skippy didn't think two skinny 6 foot 140 pound guys could take him. "I'm gonna ask you one more time" he threatened bellowing. "Then, I'm gonna rip you off of there and beat your asses". Reluctantly, and with Skippy pleading not to get into a fight, we relented. "Why did you make me give in to that caveman? I asked Skip. "As soon as he started with us, security would have taken him away?" "How do you know they wouldn't have kicked us out as well?" he replied. "You may be right there, Skip" I said. "I wasn't thinking about that". We went back to our spot with Timmy and sat down. "Fucking bullies" I thought. "You can't get away from them anywhere".

Darkness had fallen and YeS's crew was preparing their stage. Above it, were 3 large crab head looking creatures that Yes had contracted as special effects for their show. Testing them, I was amazed at how each one moved independently with a fluidness resembling a ballet. Up and down they slid gracefully appearing to mimic creatures not yet seen in our lifetime. "Those are supposed to have a surprise for us I was told" Timmy exclaimed. "Something about them and some lasers". "There's supposed to be lasers at this show?" I asked. "You didn't know?" he asked. "Yeah, it's supposed to be something no one has seen before" "I can't imagine what it's gonna be" I said. "I just hope it's good. Skip and I didn't come all this way for something lame". "I just heard that there are 110,000 people here" Timmy said. "It's the most people to ever come to a show at JFK. So, I doubt if it'll suck". "That's true" I replied. "But, you never know". Just then, the stage went dark and we heard the opening notes to the song Apocalypse. As their set segued from one song to another, laser beams appeared to be shooting out from the crab heads and over the high walls at the rear of the stadium. The 3 lasers shown in one line and then separated into 3 individual cords lined up in an iridescent glow. It looked like a green upside down pyramid that was in a horizontal position and kept changing from flat, to 3 dimensional, and then back to flat again. Eventually, a large vat of smoke was released from the right side of the stage. As it wafted its way over the crowd, it mingled with the lasers and made it appear as if there were clouds shaking inside of a tunnel. "This is amazing" I yelled to Skip over the music. "I've never seen anything like this before". "Me neither" he said. "But, look over there to the left" he motioned. "Check out those glow sticks. Watch what happens when someone holds it into the laser". Glancing over, I witnessed some fans raising their arms and immersing their sticks within the laser just as Skip had described. To my amazement and awe, the tips of the glow sticks were crackling like a sparkler on the 4th of July. "Did you see that shit?" I asked excitedly. "It's like green glowing miniature chips flying in the air!" "It's pretty cool" replied Skip. "I bet We'll never see anything like this again".

At the end of the concert, and immediately after the last encore, Skippy and I were talking about how we were going to get home. "I guess We'll have to walk back to Broad Street and wait for the Septa in the morning" I exclaimed. Overhearing us, Timmy offered a solution. "You guys can come back with us on the bus" he said.

"But, I can't get you to Edison. The bus will only go as far as Middlesex where we contracted it from. You're more than welcome to ride with us though. But, after that you'll be on your own". "What do you think, Skip?" I asked. "It's better than sitting around until 5 in the morning and taking another train after that". "I think we should jump on Timmy"s offer" Skip replied. "That's more than 80 percent home. We can hitch hike the rest of the way. The worst thing that can happen is We'll have to walk back a while. I"d rather be closer to home than 2 hours away". "Gotcha Skip" I said. "So, I guess We're with you Tim". "Ok" replied Timmy. "But, don't say anything to the bus driver, ok? He's gonna count all of us and you guys don't have any tickets. So, I'm gonna tell him some sob story about how you're stranded and you're friends of mine. I'll give him a few bucks as an extra tip. Don't say I never did anything for you guys". "Thanks, bro" I answered. "Skippy and I really appreciate it".

As the bus entered the parking lot in the wee hours of the morning, we said our goodbyes to Timmy and his girlfriend and thanked him once again for being so generous. "I hope you guys had a great time" he said. "We certainly did. I'll see you guys around. It was nice seeing you again. Take it easy". Skip and I made our way to the nearest highway and begrudgingly stuck out our thumbs. "There's no way We're gonna get a ride this late back to Edison" Skip lamented. "No fucking way". A few attempts had passed and a car had suddenly stopped. The driver rolled down his window and asked "What are you guys doing out here at this ungodly hour?" "I don't know how ungodly it is" I replied. "But, we sure could use a ride back to Edison". "I'm not going to Edison" he said. "But, I'm going as far as the Metuchen exit if you want?" "Close enough for us" said Skip. "That"ll work". We hopped in the vehicle and began to tell the driver about our concert adventure and how fortunate we were to have experienced it. He seemed to be genuinely interested and was impressed by our independence. "That's a really cool story" he replied. "I tell you what" he said.

"How far do you guys live from the Metuchen exit to your house?" "About 3 miles" I replied. "I can do that" he offered. "Because, that was a damn good story. Just show me where to go". Skippy gave him directions and we ended our journey there. "You should write a book one day about your experiences growing up" he chuckled. "But, I have to go now, my job awaits. You guys made me laugh, take it easy now and have fun". We watched him pull up the hill and make a left steering back to his original destination. "I hope you had a blast, Skip" I said. "But, I'm wiped out and the sun is coming up. So, I'll catch you later". "I had a great time, bro" he replied "I owe you one. I'll see you at Playmore, later man".

I was walking over the bridge to the flea market in New Brunswick to meet Bob P. Bob had been our roadie from when I was in the band with the Velez brothers and I occasionally stayed in contact with him. I was to meet him inside the flea market where he told me he had some girls lined up and that they were very eager to party with us. As I breached the door of the market, I passed by the familiar sounds and smells I was familiar with. A few years earlier, the flea market had come to fruition after Great Eastern stores had gone bankrupt and went out of business. After sitting abandoned for some time, it was converted and repurposed into an alternative bargaining center to overpriced, snobby style malls and was a prefect catalyst for budget conscious customers to stretch their dollars as far as possible. Every weekend, the place was packed with patrons exploring deals, tax free items, food, and entertainment. My first defining memory will always be of the peanut man. The peanut man had a large iron roasting machine that sat caddy corner right outside the front door that was rarely, if ever missed. As you approached, you could smell the odor of roasting nuts that made your mouth water and coerced you into reaching straight for your pocket as your first purchase of the day. It always made me feel comfortable knowing he was always there and that his image would be forever etched into my memory. There were also the announcements. Mr. Pillow comes to mind as his was the one I remember the most. Once inside, there was a plethora of venders selling everything from hubcaps, to vintage records, to fast food, to vegetables in the back. I met Bob at the preplanned spot and asked him if we were still on. "So, what's happening, man? I asked. "Are we still going to meet those chicks, or what?" "They're gonna meet us under the bridge" he replied. "But, they want some booze for when we get down there". "I'll get the booze" I said. "I get served at the liquor store here. So, that's not gonna be a problem". "What kind of drinks do they want?" I inquired. "They like that shit that tastes like Tang breakfast drink" he said. "Tango?" I asked. "That shit's nasty". "They don't care" he said. They want it anyway. As long as it gets me some pussy, I'll get them whatever they want. Besides, it's cheap, bro." "Well, if you're gonna pay for it" I said. "It's no problem for me".

We procured a large bottle of Tango and walked down the long, muddy road to a clearing outside a small patch of woods parallel to the river below. There were 2 girls, Bob, myself, and some other kid I didn't know. After passing around the bottle and smoking a couple of joints, Bob decided to take the better looking blonde into the woods to see if he could score. I was left to entertain the brunette and the stranger with jokes and stories until he returned. After they left, the brown haired girl began flirting with me, but I simply wasn't interested. I wanted the skinny blonde with the blue eyes we had met upon our arrival. But, Bob had earmarked her and I didn't want to step on his toes. An hour had passed and Bob and the blonde had returned. He whispered in my ear "Hey man, this chick's too fucked up to get it on and keeps telling me no. Maybe you'll have more luck with her than I did. She doesn't seem to be interested in me". "Why do you say that?" I asked whispering back. "All she did was keep talking about you" he said. "She has a crush on you I think. I tried man, but I'm not gonna let her fuck up my party. I'll try with the other one instead". "I'll give it a shot" I mumbled. "Maybe I'll have better luck with her than you did".

We took a few more swigs from the Tango bottle as I grabbed the blonde girl by the hand. I muttered in her ear "You're coming with me". "Oh, I am, am I?" she replied visibly intoxicated. "And, what makes you so special Mr. Ronnie?" she asked. "I have something in the woods I need to show you" I laughed. "We can watch it as the fireworks go off". "Like a missile?" she asked. "Oh, it's much more than a missile" I replied. "It's something truly amazing". "As long as I'm back within a half an hour" she demanded. "I'm supposed to be watching my little brother. But, I left him up at the flea market and I have to get back pretty soon". "Oh, it won't take long" I chuckled. "I'll have you back in plenty of time". As we turned to leave, Bob gave me a smile and a wink and made the ok sign with his fingers. "Don't do anything I wouldn't do" he laughed. "We'll wait for you until you get back. Make sure you make a lot of fireworks". "Oh, there's gonna be a lot of booms tonight" I said. "My pre celebration has just begun". The girl and I walked through the small patch of trees to a clearing not far from the edge of the river, but close enough to where the ground was still dry. I spun her around, grabbed her by the hips, and began making out with her. "I'm really kind of drunk" she giggled. "But, I think you're good looking. So, let's lay down in this area here. I need to sit down for a little bit because my head is spinning". "Sure" I exclaimed. "Whatever you want. We'll hang out until you feel better".

A few minutes went by and I could see that her eyes were closed and she was mumbling something incoherent to herself. I couldn't quite make out what it was and I was wondering how long it would last. She suddenly reached out for me, turned her head, and began to give me very passionate and succulent kisses. I grabbed for her breasts under her shirt and started feeling her up. "Do whatever you want" she murmured. "I'm really into you". "Really?" I asked. "So, you wouldn't mind if I did this?" as I reached down inside her pants. "Not at all" she whispered excitedly. "You can make love to me too if you want. As long as you wear a rubber." At that moment, that's all I needed to hear. Fortunately, I had a spare Trojan for such occasions in my wallet waiting to be sprung. "Help me take my jeans off" she said. "And, you have to make this quick. I'm already in trouble for being here this long". I complied with her request, slapped on my Jimmy hat, entered her, and went to town. In the heat of our moment, the fireworks show from the flea market"s parking lot had begun to shoot into the sky. I could hear the familiar snap of its descending firecrackers whistling after each launch resonating over my shoulder as the girl was moaning my name. Just as I was about to orgasm, she clinched her legs around me in a wrestling type hold. "Happy 4th of July" she laughed. "I just came". "So did I" I chuckled. I guess we made our own fireworks here tonight, huh?" I asked laughing. "We sure did" she exclaimed. "By the way" she replied. "In case you didn't know, I'm a virgin. And, I was watching the fireworks over your shoulder as we were making love". "I hope I didn't hurt you" I said. "You should have said something" "Not at all" she replied. "I'll always remember it". "That's pretty cool" I said. "But, we better get you back now before you're brother thinks you disappeared". "Yeah" she answered. "And, you better ask me out soon. I wouldn't give myself to just anyone like that". "I'll see what I can do" I chuckled. "We'll talk about it later. We have to go now".

I took her by the hand, skipped back through the woods, and rejoined our friends closer to the road. As we arrived, Bob was laughing and making fun of us. "How was it?" he bellowed loudly. "Was she any good?" "Bob, be cool" I replied sternly. "Have some respect, man. Besides, we didn't do anything. All we did was make out". I could see that he was obviously jealous of and was trying to embarrass the girl. "Yeah, right" he cried out. "And, the pope smokes dope". He was acting as if he was bothered by her rejection. "This isn't a competition, Bob" I said trying to protect the girl's reputation. "Check out Ronnie trying to be all chivalrous and shit" he laughed. "You don't even know her, man". "You didn't care about her before, and now all of a sudden you do? I asked.

"Whatever, Ronnie" he replied. "I've got this one over here with me now anyway" he said trying to save face. "So, you just do what you got to do". "I will, man" I replied. "And, you need to stop being an asshole". Ignoring me he took his girl and her friend, turned, and started walking back up the hill. I didn't hold it against him and walked silently behind knowing it was probably just the booze talking. Therefore, I let it go. "That was very cool that you stood up for me" the blonde girl whispered lovingly. No guy has ever done that for me before". "Then, I guess you"'ve been with the wrong kind of guys" I replied. "I've been picked on my entire life. I hate that shit when people bully others". "I knew I liked you for a reason, Ronnie" she cooed. "I hope to see you again".

Ronnie E. had lost the use of his mom"s car. So, we started driving around in Archie G"s blue Ford E150 box van. For some reason never known to me, Archie had drilled a child sized wooden chair into the engine cover in between the front seats making a 3rd forward seat. When Archie and Ronnie came to pick me up, I was always forced to sit there and I hated it. No matter how much I would beg and plead, Ronnie was undaunted. "You're picked up last" he said. "So, you get to sit in the middle like always. If you don't like it, you can sit on the bare floor in the back. But, there's no seats back there. So, it's that or nothing". After thinking about how boring and sterile it would be back there, I usually capitulated. Most of the time, we would drive around looking for something fun to do or visit places we had never been to before. For kicks, Ronnie always liked to start out in downtown New Brunswick. Usually with the windows down, he liked_to berate passersby as we drove by them. One night, we stopped at a light and were waiting for the signal to change. A black man in a beat up Ford Mustang pulled up in the lane adjacent to us and had his radio blasting. Ronnie began taunting him about how his music sucked and that the guy should "turn it down". As the signal turned to green, we pulled away laughing. "That guy has bad taste in music" he exclaimed. "But, it was so loud; I don't think he heard me". "Why do you fuck with people like that guy?" Archie asked. "He'll never change anyway". As we pulled up to the next light, there was the black guy again. This time, the blare of his radio was off and he was screaming at us. "Which one of ya"ll wanna start some funny shit?" he asked. "What?" asked Ronnie. "Speak fucking English". The guy repeated himself. But, this time he was much louder. Ronnie yelled back to him "Are you a definite shooo?" he asked. "What the fuck is that shit?" asked the man. "Spoigideydoish" Ronnie replied. "You look like a definite Samoan". "Is you calling me an islander?" the guy asked. "Mahh huh" Ronnie replied. By now, the man was getting frustrated and began threatening us. "Pull over at the next light and I'll show you guys a Samoan motherfucker, shiiiiit". "What are you gonna do Ronnie?" I asked. "I'm gonna get out at the next light and beat that guy's ass" he laughed. "And then, I'm gonna take his radio". "No you're not" exclaimed Archie". "I'm not having the cops come and have to answer all kinds of bullshit questions. Fuck this guy, We're gonna take a ride to New Hope". "New Hope?" I asked. "You mean, like New Hope, Pennsylvania?" "You're not gonna take him there? Are you Arch?" Ronnie chuckled. "Why?" I asked. "What's the matter with New Hope?" "Nothing" Ronnie replied. "You'll see when we get there".

After the long drive to Pennsylvania, we were travelling down US 202 when Ronnie suddenly became excited. "Here we are Arold" he laughed. "The New Hope diner. Do you have any money?" he asked as we pulled into the parking lot. "No, I'm broke man" I replied. "Well, I have some money" he said, "But, only enough for a few coffees. We won't need much though, because what we wanna show you will only take a few minutes". "What could there possibly be to see in a diner way the fuck out here in no man"s land?" I asked. Ronnie trying to contain himself from laughing replied "Oh, you'll see". "Archie?" he asked. "Go ahead and tell him". "I'm not telling him shit" Archie said. "Let him see for himself". "You're gonna shit yourself" Ronnie said. "You'll see". We greeted the hostess and she asked us if we preferred a booth or a table. Settling on a booth, we sat down, ordered coffees and I began to look around. Ronnie then asked me "Hey, Arold? Do you see anything unusual about this place?" "No, why?" I asked. "Is there supposed to be?" "Do you see any women?" Archie asked. Ronnie chimed in "Look around us, man. It's all guys". Almost spitting out my coffee, I blurted out "This better not fucking be what I think it is!" Ronnie replied "Oh, it's that and much more. Just wait until the lights go out". "The lights go out?" I asked. "Is this place queer or something?" "You'll see" he replied. "It's funny as fuck". "Why the fuck would you take us to place like this if We're all straight?" I asked. "Because" he replied. "You"ve never seen it before. Archie and I think it's hilarious and it's like a carnival ride". "Obviously, a dark and demented ride" I replied annoyed. "Just shut up and drink your coffee and wait for it" he said. "It starts in just a few more minutes". "The night owl" Archie whispered laughing to himself. "He's gonna get to see the night owl". "Shut the fuck up, Arch" Ronnie warned. "Don't give the shit away!"

While slowly sipping on our drinks, time was passing by and I was getting bored. "When is this event gonna start?" I asked sighing. "They don't announce it" Ronnie replied. "It just happens". Just then, the entire place went dark. "What the fuck happened to the lights?" I yelled out. "Shhhh" Ronnie replied. "Be quite or you'll ruin it". "Just give it a few seconds" Archie said. "The lights will be back on pretty quick". "Make sure you look up from the table and take a good look around once the lights are back on" Ronnie laughed. "And, tell us what you see?" "You guys are fucked up" I mumbled. "What could it possibly be?" As the flash of lamps came back on, I glanced around and saw gay men with their tongues down each other"s throats. Ronnie was laughing so hard it was echoing toward the front. "Mah huh" he rang out. "Queer guys!" Though I saw the humor in it and was chuckling along with them, I couldn't believe they had dragged me all the way out there to see. "All the way out here for 5 minutes of this?" I asked. "Shut the fuck up, man" Ronnie said. You know you think this shit is as funny as we do. Now, stop complaining or We'll leave you here. "The fuck you will" I howled. "There's no way I'm fucking staying here alone". "Come on, Arold" he laughed. "You can't say this shit ain't funny?" "It is" I replied. "Especially since I didn't expect it". "Well, We're all out of coffee and the shows over" Archie exclaimed. "So, let's go".

Adding insult to injury, Ronnie had another of his many tricks up his sleeve. I should have learned by then that he was never finished when it came to his humor. On the way out, we had to pass the hostesS's podium to pay our bill. When the woman had given us our total, he whipped out a bank roll of pennies and broke it in half on the counter in front of the register. Watching the coins spill out before him, he tallied them out one by one. After he handed the woman the sufficient amount to cover his part of the bill, he handed me the rest. As I reached for them, the remaining pennies unfurled from the roll and were falling to the floor. All I could hear was the sound of plinking coins darting everywhere. "He'll pick those up for you and pay the rest" Ronnie roared. "We'll be outside when you're done". Abandoning me, they both left me to clean up the mess. "Don't worry about it, honey" the hostess replied. "As long as you hand me most of them, it's not a problem. I can see that your friend's joke was on you. But next time, please don't bring us anymore pennies". "Thank you for being so understanding" I said. "You wouldn't believe what these guys do to me". "I was young once too" she blurted. "But, it looks like they are just funning you. You'll probably remember this later on in life. So, go have fun dear and return to your friends".

I bounded through the parking lot and was happy that the woman wasn't angry with me over the tedious amount of time it took to use coins instead of bills. As I approached the van to get in, Ronnie screamed out "Now, Archie now!" Amazed by this behavior, I thought "What the fuck are they going to do to me next?" With the sound of them laughing out the windows, the van spun gravel back at me as it took off down the highway. "Fuck" I murmured to myself. "They better not fucking leave me all the way out here. I'm pretty far from home". I stood on the edge of the road and watched as they turned around and back toward me. Just as they were within a few feet and I thought they were going to stop, they'd laugh and take off again. It felt like one of those cruel tricks I had seen in a movie about how hitch hikers would have a ride stop, and as soon as the hitch hiker grabbed for the door, the driver would take off again. Over and over the hitch hiker would try, but every time they'd approach, the motorist would leave. Up the highway and back again they taunted me. All the while Ronnie would yell from the window as they passed by "It's a mighty far walk back to New Jersey" Or, "I hope none of those queers make you their bitch". Like usual when it came to Ronnie, I had to play his game. The trick with him was never to answer him back. I had to show no emotion and pretend I didn't care. If I did, he would poke me and tease me for hours. After he had seen that I wasn't giving in, they finally stopped and opened the door. "Jump in, asshole" he said. "You're no fucking fun, man. But, you should have seen your face in the beginning. You looked like you lost your best friend". "How come nobody ever does shit like this to you?" I asked. "Because, I'm the teacher of fools" he replied. "And, somebody has to learn you. I have to toughen you up. It's my job, man". "More like you are the fool" Archie laughed. "Shut up, Archie" he warned. "Or, the next time, it'll be you"

Cliff G. needed to go for a ride in his Vega and asked Dave G. and I if we'd accompany him. His girlfriend was in the front, while Dave and I rode in the back. Travelling up route 1 north toward Woodbridge, Dave lit up a joint. I took a few tokes and handed it back to him. "Hey, Cliff?" Dave asked. Do you and your girlfriend want a hit off this or what?" "Stupid question, bro" Cliff replied. "Pass this shit up to me". When we were almost at our destination, I looked over and saw a guy in a car next to us waving his hands and pointing at us. "What does this retard want?" Dave asked laughing. "He's yelling something?" "Who? Cliff asked turning his head. "There a guy next to us, man" I said. "And, it looks like he's insisting that we pull over". "Screw him" Cliff exclaimed. "I'm just gonna keep on driving. So, just ignore his ass". The more we looked away laughing, the more the guy kept speeding up to us. Finally, he was showing us something out his window and pointing at it. "What the fuck is that?" I asked as it was gleaming in the sun. "Shit" Dave said. "It looks like a fucking badge, Cliff. I guess maybe you should pull over?" "Get the fuck out of here?" Cliff asked. "Why would a cop with no lights follow us this long? That makes no sense, man?" "I don't know?" his girlfriend asked. "But, it looks like he's serious. So we better do as he says". Annoyed and cursing to himself, Cliff veered to the right and pulled into a Shop Rite parking lot. "This fucking asshole better be a cop" he said. "Or, I'm gonna beat his ass for aggravating us".

After we came to a full stop, the guy with the badge pulled in next to us. "Why did you pull us over?" Cliff asked. "And, who the fuck are you, anyway?" The man got out of his vehicle and began to laugh "I was tailing you all the way from Edison" he said. "I saw you guys smoking pot the entire time". So?" Dave asked. "Does that make you special?" "Special enough to pull you over" he replied. "Because I'm an officer for the N.J. DMV". "Get the fuck out of here?" Dave asked. "You don't even look like a cop. You look like a business man. And, what's with blinding me with that shit you had in your hand?" "Oh, this?" the guy said as he reached into his pocket to show us. "That's my badge. See? I tried to get your attention with it while I was driving. But, you ignored me. So, here we are". "Fuck" Cliff exclaimed. "He is a cop after all". "So, what do you want with us?" I asked. "Don't you have some drunk drivers to go bust?" "That's for later on" he replied. "But, since you guys were so blatant with smoking dope while driving, I had no choice but to see what you were up to. Now, all of you get out of the car and stand next to mine. I'm calling back up since there's so many of you". "Fucking typical pussy cop" Dave whispered. "They never interrogate us alone". "What was that?" the officer asked. "Nothing" Dave replied. "I was just clearing my throat, that's all". "Well then" said the cop. "Since you don't feel too well, you get to be first. So, turn around, spread your legs, and put your hands up on the car". As Dave was being frisked, the backup car arrived. "What do we have here?" the 2nd officer asked. Reaching inside Dave"s pants, the 1st cop didn't find anything. "Check his ankles inside his socks" the 2nd officer suggested. "Sometimes, they like to hide their marijuana there". We watched as the 1st cop did just that. "Here it is" he boasted as he pulled out a half ounce bag. "You were right. I knew it had to be here somewhere". He took the weed and placed it on top of his car. Dave was pissed off and whispering "Fucking jerkoffs took my weed again. They always seem to find it on me". As the two cops were searching Cliff"s car and then deciding what to do, I asked "Maybe he'll let us go. He was laughing when he stopped us and thought it was funny". "All I know is" Cliff remarked. "Is that I hope my car doesn't get impounded. It'll be a hassle to get it back". Just then, the original cop came walking over. "My colleague and I have decided to give you a break" he said. "Luckily for you, we didn't find anything else. But, you friend here is going to have to leave his weed with us. That's the only way We're willing to let you go. I'll give you guys a few minutes to talk amongst yourselves to make a decision. When I come back, let me know, ok?"

"What should we do, Cliff?" I asked. "It's your car, man?" "What the fuck do you think We're gonna do?" he asked. "Dave"s gonna give him the weed, man. I'm not losing my car over this bullshit". "Hold on a second" Dave replied. "Maybe I can talk him into giving me back the weed and letting us go?" Yeah, right!" I laughed loudly. "As if They'll let us do that?" Cliff looked over sternly at Dave and said "Listen, man. I'm dead serious here. You don't even know if he'll let us go yet and not take any of us to jail. You know how these pigs always lie, right? So, I suggest you let him have the weed and I'll hook you up with a little to replace it later on, ok? My main concern is my car here, man. I don't wanna lose it and if we walk, its far way back to Edison". "Ok, ok" Dave said. "I'll give him the fucking weed then". The officer came back for out answer. "What"ll it be boys and girls?" he asked. "I don't have all day to stand here on the side of the highway". "Take the pot" Dave said. "And, leave us alone". "Smart decision" the cop said. "And, I'll give you a bit of advice. I can understand that you guys like to get high, right? Well, that's fine with me as drugs aren't my main priority. But, find another way to smoke that shit instead of doing it while driving down the highway. It's too visible and not too intelligent, ok?" He grabbed his evidence, threw it onto the front seat, and he and the other officer left. When we could no longer see them, Dave of course went ballistic. "These fucking cops must have fucking Dave radar" he screamed. "Every time I buy some weed, I smoke like one joint and they keep busting me. I never get to finish the bag". Cliff turned to Dave and exclaimed "I'm sorry I got a little raw with you back there, bro". "Yeah, man" Dave replied. "What was all of that about? You"ve never gotten loud like that with me before?" "I had to" said Cliff. "I was trying to get those two cops away from the inside of my car". "Why"s that?" I asked. "I wanted to deflect them from my ass tray" he replied. "What was in the ash tray, bro?" Dave asked. "Oh, about 50 hits of double barrel mescaline" he laughed. "I'm sure glad those stupid cops didn't find it". Holy shit!" Dave remarked. "If they would have found that, they would have thrown away the key on us!" "Exactly" Cliff said. "I wonder why they didn't if it was right there in front of them?" I asked. "It would have been a nice bust for them?" "Well" Cliff laughed. "I purposely put my shit in there because it's really rusty to pull out. Unless you put some real effort into it, most people give up. Knowing that most cops I've encountered are lazy, I took a chance he wouldn't bother opening it. I guess I got lucky". "Man" I said. "We would have gotten a long sentence for that shit". "The next time I hang out with you, please let me know about any stashes beforehand?" asked Dave. "Actually, I forgot all about it" Cliff said.

"It was already in there for a couple of days". "A couple of days?" Dave asked. "Remind me to frisk you later".

Some of my friends had begun to experiment with harder drugs and began to introduce them to me. Over Dennis G"s house one afternoon, I had knocked on the front door but had not gotten a response. From previous visits, I knew that sometimes Dennis or Jeffrey would be downstairs doing something in their basement. As I walked around to the cellar door, I called out to see if anyone was down there. "Dennis? Jeff? I asked. "Is anybody home?" "Down here" Dennis replied. "Come on down here, bro". As I transcended the stairs, I looked to the back wall and I could make out a silhouette of him puffing on a cigarette and looking down at something on a table. I grew closer and could see it more clearly resting on its side. "That looks like a syringe, man" I exclaimed. "Whose is that?" I asked nervously. "The clouds Ron, the clouds" he said. "What the hell are the clouds?" I asked. "There's no clouds in here?" "Some people sneak down here and use those" he replied. "They tell me when they pull on the plunger, they see rolling clouds in it from Tuinals". "That's fucked up" I said. "You gotta really figure out a way to lock that basement door, bro". "I know, man. I know. But, somehow it always ends up open again". "Somebody is very clever then" I replied. "We've tried everything" he said. "And, none of us are here 24/7. Otherwise, we would have caught them already". "We'll, I hope you do soon" I responded. "I don't think you"d like to see anybody OD down here". "I'll get to it soon enough" he said. "It is getting kind of ridiculous.

As we turned to go back outside, I peered at something plastic looking in a corner. It had a glint of an amber color and appeared to be made out of cellophane. "What is that?" I asked. "They look like wine bottles". "Oh, those?" he replied. "Remember the fire at Linwood Grove a while back?" he asked. "Those are holiday wine gift baskets. They didn't burn up in the fire so we scarfed them all back here". "Holy shit, Den" I laughed, "You have tons of them"

"Yeah, there's a few dozen with about 4 bottles in each" he chuckled. "We'll be able to get drunk for some time". "I didn't get to scam anything from there" I said. "I wasn't around when you guys did that". "There were a whole lot of people there" he replied. "Us Edison kids will be drunk for months". "Yeah" I said. "I helped Jesse with some beer that came out of there a few weeks ago. So, I know exactly what you're talking about". "Billy is coming over pretty soon" he said. "He's supposed to have some crank for us". "Crank?" I asked "What the hell is that?" "You know those black beauty capsules of speed Phil used to get us?" he asked. "Well, this shit you snort up your nose like coke". "I've never done coke yet, Den" I replied. "I can't afford it. It's too fucking expensive". "You snort this shit up your nose just like if you had coke" he said. "It's way cheaper and lasts a lot longer too. But, it burns real bad and has a nasty drip. Once it's in your system though, you'll be flying for days". "I guess I can try some" I said. "If it makes us feel like beauties". "I did it once before" he replied. "But, it's a bit stronger than pills. Knowing how hyper you already are, bro" he laughed "You'll be a fucking talking head for days".

Billy eventually arrived, sat down, and pulled a piece of folded foil out of his top jacket pocket. "You"ve never done crank yet, Ron?" he asked. "Well, I'm gonna do you a favor and turn you onto some for free. I think you're gonna like this shit too. I know how you like to write songs and sing all the time. So, if this doesn't help you write lyrics, I don't know what will". He took out a razor blade from his other pocket, opened the foil container, and scooped out a small mound of pink stuff and laid it on the table. "I'm gonna chop up a few lines for each of us" he said. "Dennis can go first, then me, then you, Ron. After the burn stops, let me know what you think?" After they had taken their turns, I put the straw from my left nostril to the line and inhaled. Immediately, I regretted it. Holding my nostril closed, I started to scream. "What the fuck, Billy!" Inside my nose, it felt like someone had injected battery acid into it and I was raging with pain. "Dennis told you it was gonna hurt" Billy replied.

"So, don't be a pussy about it. Besides, it gets better once that part wears off. In about 15 minutes". "This shit dripping down in the back of my throat is disgusting" I howled. "Is it always this way?" "Yup" he replied. "But, it's cheaper than coke. So, deal with it, man". "I'll deal with it" I said. "I just didn't know it was gonna affect me that way". "Everybody seems to say that" Dennis chuckled. "But, once the buzz starts, I think you'll enjoy it. Plus, Billy gave it to us for free. So, there's no complaint from me".

About 20 minutes went by and the drug had begun to take effect. I was starting to sweat profusely and I couldn't sit still. My mouth was dry and it felt like it had sandpaper in it. "Godamn, Den. I'm really thirsty" I said. "It's just like those beauties" he replied. "But, a little more potent. There's some juice in the fridge, bro. Go and scarf a glass. That should get rid of the dry mouth". I drank a glass and then realized I was grinding my teeth. As the day progressed, none of us could stay in any position resembling calm and were getting up and down every 10 minutes. We were having vast conversations in very fast speech and incessantly talking over each other. It was words pouring out of our mouths while we were already thinking about what to say next. The problem was our mouths couldn't keep up with our thoughts. So, everything came out in rapid fire language. Finally, Billy got agitated "Jesus, shut the fuck up already Ron. I know you're speeding your balls off. But, you don't let anyone get a word in edgewise. Don't you have a fucking off button?" he asked. Dennis laughing chimed in "Ahh, man. Leave Ronnie alone, bro. You knew he was hyper before you even gave him any of that shit. He's always talked fast. But, sometimes he has a lot of knowledge. He just can't articulate that quick". "You're exactly right, Den" I replied. "It's like I have a trillion thoughts in my head going as fast as a locomotive. But, my mouth just can't keep up with them". "Well" Billy said. "I'm getting off this train, bro. I have to split. I have some other places I have to go before it gets too late". Dennis and I walked Billy to the porch, shook his hand, and thanked him for the party favors. "No problem, man" he said. "I just hope Ronnie comes down before the sun comes up and doesn't drive everyone crazy". "I'll be all right, Billy" I replied. "If I tweak too much, I'll just drink a few of DenniS's wine baskets in the basement". "Yeah" Dennis chuckled. "He'll go from a drug addict to a drunk". As Billy was leaving, Dennis suggested we watch some TV. "Whatever is on is fine" I said. "But, I can't guarantee I won't talk through some of it". Just then, Jeffrey had come out of the bathroom. "I heard what's going on here you fucking tweakers" he shouted. "You're more than welcome to stay, Ronnie" he said. "But, if you get too mouthy, We'll put you on the porch like we do with everybody else". "He'll come down out there quick" Dennis laughed. "It's cold out there. It's amazing how cooperative people become when subjected to the cold". "I'll hold my thoughts for in between the commercials" I chuckled. "How about that for a compromise?" "We're just fucking with you" Jeff replied. "But, seriously. If one of our favorite shows is on, you really have to not talk so much".

Some TV shows had come on and it had gone past the 11th hour in the evening. Saturday Night Live was still playing and Dennis was emulating the cheeseburger diner sketch featuring John Belushi. For the next half an hour, their entire house was subjected to Dennis running around the house asking for "Coke, not Pepsi". At the end of the program, Jeffrey insisted that everyone had to be quiet as his favorite TV show called Animation was coming on. Animation was on PBS and included stop action photography, pencil sketches, charcoal, and just about anything that could be manipulated into movement artificially. We'd watch as Jeffrey would focus in like a horse wearing blinders. "I don't wanna hear any fucking noises coming from you guys" he exclaimed, "Or, there's gonna be real trouble". He was so obsessed with the program, that any sound, blockage of view, or distraction would agitate him to the point of insanity. "Don't listen to him" Dennis whispered out of Jeffrey"s earshot. "If he gets too crazy, I'll just go down in the cellar and pull the fuse like I always do. By the time he gets a flashlight and goes down there and figures it out, We'll have control of the TV again". Laughing at this, I had images of Dennis in my head unscrewing an old fashioned fuse, holding it up to his eye, checking it, and then depositing it in his pocket knowing full well Jeffrey would never find it. "What if he comes back up and does get control again, Den?" I asked. "The fuse will disappear" he laughed. "And, even if he gets ahold of it, he doesn't know how to put a penny across the little terminals to get it to work again like I do". "You"ve got it all figured out, huh Den?" I asked. "It helps that I'm older than him" he quipped. "I learned it way faster".

When the TV shows were all finished and the national anthem began to play, Dennis suggested we sit at the dining room table and write lyrics and draw. He always had an ample supply of large cardboard squares tucked away somewhere that he would pull out for such late morning occasions. He also had a plethora of writing tools. He had a plastic box with typical marker stains throughout and appeared as if it had been used hundreds of times. Their mother had come home a few hours earlier and was now fast asleep. Dennis laid out his cardboard piece and announced "Look, Ron. I'm gonna draw the city". "You always draw the city" I replied. "Why don't you draw something else?" "I don't always draw the city" he exclaimed. "I just keep adding to it. I could say you write the same lyrics over and over. Couldn't I?" he asked. "That's true. I usually have bits and pieces of songs floating around in my head". "There you go" he replied. "It's like my masterpiece here, bro. It's never finished". Just then, I heard his mother's voice bellowing from the other room. "You're gonna be finished if I have to come out there" she yelled. "It's 3 o"clock in the morning, Dennis. I have to go to work at 7. You and Ronnie have to wrap it up and go someplace else if you want to keep talking". Knowing myself and how there was no way I was going to be able to, I offered to go home. "You can stay" Dennis whispered. "But, We'll have to keep it down". "I don't wanna piss off your mom" I replied. "So, I think its best I leave" "If you insist" he said. "If that's what you wanna do". I walked home in the chill and waited for the 4am freight train to come by. It always arrived like clockwork and I could always depend on it to block out any impending noise. I used it as a sound barrier for entry so the dogs and my parents wouldn't hear me as I pried open our front door. I tip toed down the cellar steps, laid down in my bed in pool of sweat, and waited for the sunrise. I knew it would be hours before the drug wore off. Eventually, I came down enough to fall asleep.

I was with Mickey B. and driving around Edison in his sky blue Dodge looking for something to do. Mickey glimpsed over at his gas gauge and noticed that it was almost on "E". "You got any money, bro?" he asked. "Otherwise We'll be walking soon". "Sorry Mick" I replied. "I'm broke". "Then, We'll have to come up with a scam" he said. "I think I have a good one" "What's that?" I asked. "You know where we can get free gas?" "I saw a gas pump by Edison High that has a fence around it" he said. "I was driving by there one day, and I saw that one of the employees had opened the gate with a key and filled their car. I bet one of us could shimmy under the gate and get in there". "You think so?" I asked. "But, it's pretty open out there, man. I wouldn't want anyone to see us". "Nah", he chimed. "We'll pull up and use the car door to block anyone"s view. We can be in and out in a minute or two easily". "I'm for it if you are" I replied. "But, you're right. We need fuel or no more cruising around. Let's go by there and check it out" I said. "If it looks safe, we can scarf a few gallons". "That's exactly what I was thinking" Mick said. "We'll go there now". As we drove down the Boulevard of the Eagles and turned right into the parking lot, on the left I could see exactly what Mick had been talking about. There was a red and white gas pump enclosed in what appeared to be a 10 foot high fence, a gate with a padlock, and about 2 feet of space surrounding the machine. It appeared like Mick said to have just the right amount of wiggle room. I looked down to the bottom of the fence and I could see that there was a small trench large enough for someone thin enough to navigate under. "You think one of us can get under there?" I asked. "The hole looks deep enough". "It should be a piece of cake" Mick remarked. "Who"s gonna go under?" I asked. "Me? Or you?" "I'll go" said Mick. "But, slide over here from the passenger"s side and keep the door open with your foot so nobody sees me". "Will do" I replied quietly. "But, hurry up Mick. The longer We're parked here, the longer We'll look suspicious".

I watched as Mick shimmied under the gate wiggling and squirming on his back like an eel moving itself through some saw grass. "I forgot to open the gas tank door" he cried. "Get out real quick and open it". Once I had it opened, I called back asking "Now that you're in there, how are you gonna get the pump handle under the fence to get the gas into the car?" "Well" he replied "I was gonna try to push it under there and have you grab it". "But, guess what?" he asked. "I just leaned on the gate and the fucker"s open. These idiots forgot to lock it. If I would have known that shit, I wouldn't have had to crawl under this fence". Laughing, I replied "Well, it'll be a lot easier now. You can just lean out and slide the nozzle in". "I was only gonna take a few gallons" he said obviously annoyed. "But, since these assholes made me have to go under the gate for no reason, now I'm filling this bitch up". "Fuck them" I chuckled. "Take as much as you can". Mick pulled the handle back on the reset, put the spigot in the car"s tank, and waited. I heard the familiar ding, ding, ding of the numbers on the measuring wheel as the price reading and gallons edged ever higher. "I think it's almost full" Mick chimed. "So, We're almost done". "Maybe you should take the hose out now, Mick" I said. "It should be close enough. We should really get out of here before somebody rats us out". "You're probably right" he replied. "Let me put this bitch back and We'll leave". After he had closed the gate, I slid back over to the passenger side and scanned around me to see if it was safe to go. "I think We're good" Mick said. "So, let's go back to my house and hang for a little while. We can smoke a little weed and put on some music".

We weren't at Mick"s house for more than 15 minutes when his mother came knocking on his bedroom door. "Mickey" she said. "The police are here and want to speak with you. It's something about gasoline at your school". "Fuck, Mick" I whispered. "Some scumbag must have ratted us out". "I guess they saw us, bro" he replied. "You stay up here. I'll go downstairs and deal with this bullshit". "Fucking cops" he mumbled. "I can't fucking stand them". While he was descending the steps toward the police below, I put my ear up to the door to try to make out what they were saying. I could hear muffled and faint voices about how if Mick paid for the gas, the school wouldn't press charges and would let him go. A few minutes later, he came back up and was complaining. "I have to give them 5 bucks in change I have up here" he said. "If I don't, They'll take me to jail. But, I'm gonna fix their asses" he laughed "I'm gonna hand them 5 bucks in nickels instead". "You sure They'll take that?" I asked. "You might piss them off more". "Fuck those cops" he replied. "They have to take it if they're pissed off or not. It's still money". "Let me know how it goes" I crowed. "I wish I could see their faces when you hand it to them". "Come and stand at the top of the stairs, bro. They don't know about you, they think I did it by myself". "No thanks, man" I replied. "That's ok. I don't want them to even see me". "Well, I'll be right back" he said. "I'll try to get rid of these pigs as soon as I can".

After the cops had gone and we relaxed laughing for a while, Mick decided it was time for us to take a drive. We stopped by Thursdays Place and picked up Phil and a few others. "Let's cruise around by Livingston College by Camp Kilmer" he said. "We can park by that thing that looks like a handball court wall and get high. I have some of that really good weed with me in the chamber of my pipe. We can spark it up and tell these guys about the gas story from today". "Gas story?" Phil asked. "What gas story?" "You'll see" I replied. "It was hilarious. Mick made some cops take some change for some gas". A guy named Kevin interjected. "I gotta hear this one" he laughed. "Anything having to do with embarrassing cops is all right with me". As we leaned against the wall sufficiently stoned and laughing, a cop came driving by and had spotted us. He aimed his spotlight toward our direction and was blinding us with its glare. "Why the fuck do they always have to do this shit" I grumbled. "Always right in our fucking eyes". "He's turning around" Mick announced. "Here we fucking go" Phil replied. "Get ready. It's shakedown time". The cruiser made a K turn and pulled in right behind Mick"s car. The officer steadied his light on us, stepped out of the patrol vehicle, and told us not to move. "Put your hand where I can see them" he warned. "I'm going to walk over to all of you. Keep your arms up until I get there" "Yes, fuck head" I whispered. "Whatever you say". "Did you just say something wise ass?" he asked. "Because, I can make up something custom made just for you". "Not me officer" I replied. "I am only here to cooperate". "Oh, a fucking comedian huh?" he asked. "Well, you'll be the first one that I search". "Arold" whispered Phil. "Shut the fuck up, man. You're gonna get us all busted or he'll beat us with those fucking flashlights". "You" the cop demanded as he pointed at me. "The comedian. Get over by this car right now and empty all of your pockets". "Yes Sir" I chuckled. "Right away, Sir". I stood next to the car door while the cop watched me turn my pockets inside out and place by wallet on the hood of the vehicle. "You're clean" he said. "Now, go back by the wall and don't move". After he searched the rest of our party one by one, he told us to get back into Mick"s vehicle and wait for further instructions. It was then that I realized my billfold was missing. "Officer? I yelled. "I've seemed to have lost my wallet after I placed it on the hood of your car. Can I come back out and look for it?" I asked. "Well, since you"ve stopped being a wise ass and you guys pretty much cooperated, come out here and I'll help you look for it". Elated, I jumped out and accompanied him scanning the ground with his flashlight hoping to find it. "Well, well, well" he suddenly cried out. "Look what we have here". My heart sank to my knees as I knew from previous experiences with the police that it could mean only one thing. He had found something illegal. He bent down under the middle of

Mick"s car and reached for something underneath. When he stood up, he turned back laughing with an object in his hand that was silver in color and shiny. "Whose is this?" he asked. "This doesn't look like any damn wallet to me. If it is, it must be a new one I've never seen before?" "I don't know anything about that" I replied. "I've never seen that" "Of course you haven"t" he said. "And, I bet when I ask all of your friends in that car, they're gonna deny anything to do with it either". "I'm just looking for my wallet officer, that's all I know" I said. Pointing his beam at the tail end of Mick"s car, he spurted out "Your wallet is right over there by the driver"s side back tire. Go and retrieve it and get right back here". I took a few steps, did as I was told, and stood in front of him motionless. He was making us sweat and not saying anything to intimidate us. Finally, he spoke "I'm gonna do all of you guys a favor" he said. "Since I opened this pipe and there's only a little in it, I'm gonna let you all go. I could hold all of you for paraphernalia and residue if I wanted. But, I'm not gonna do that because I"d have to call another car to come and pick you all up and I don't feel like doing that tonight. I'm also not in the mood to do paperwork this close to my shift ending. So, it's your lucky night boys. Back up the car after I leave and go home. If I see you here again, you know what that means, right?" he asked. "Yes, officer" we chimed. "What was that again?" he asked. "Yes, officer" we said. "I can't hear you?" he asked. "Louder" "Yes, officer" we screamed. "Good boys" he replied. "Now, remember after I leave, get the hell out of here". After the cop was gone, Mick put the car in reverse, backed out of the path, turned east and went forward berating me. "Fucking Ron, man" he said. "Why the fuck did you have to get back out of the car to go find your stupid fucking wallet? When he was checking your pockets when you went up to him first, I threw my pipe under the car. He never would have found it if you didn't get out to look for it". "Well, how the fuck did I know you were gonna do that?" I asked. "You didn't say anything". "I couldn't" he replied. "I had to get rid of it. He might have busted me if I had it on me". "Didn't we just smoke from that before that cop arrived?"

asked Phil. "Yeah" Mick replied. "I wanted to keep that pipe, man. It had some wicked resin in it I was saving for later". "I'm sorry, Mick" I said apologetically. "I'll buy you a new one". "You gonna fill it with weed to replace the resin too?" Phil asked laughing. "Mind your own business, dickhead" I replied. "I'll fix Mick up with something later".

It was summertime again and I was looking for a full time job. School had let out for the season so I figured it was a good time to try to make some extra money. My friends and I decided to start out in Raritan Center as that was where most of the manufacturing was at the time. It didn't take us long to find an easy warehouse or factory job as there was an abundance of them to choose from. The pay almost always sucked, but it was better than inconsistent scheming or taking the chance of getting busted dealing drugs again. A few of us met up at Dennis G"s house and discussed what companies we would try first. There was Phil, Dennis, myself, and Georgie Burns. "Uuullllhhhh" Dennis howled. "Are you guys ready to go job hunting? I read in yesterday"s paper that there's a few jobs down there". "I saw the same thing, Den" I replied. "So, I guess We'll have to take a crack at it". After the long walk to the center, we happened upon Schwinn Bicycle Distributers. Inside, we asked for employment applications and sat down at a table to fill them out. As I was almost finished, I could hear Dennis laughing at another table in the corner. "Education" Dennis said. He looked up at us, put his pen to the paper and recited "Ain't never went to no school". "Dennis" I whispered. "Why are you writing that? I asked. "Don't you want a job here?" "I'm not interested in putting together no frigging bicycles, bro" he replied. "So, I'll just write some bullshit stuff instead". "I think he's trying to sabotage us" Phil laughed. "If the receptionist hears us laughing, she's probably gonna throw all of our applications in the garbage". "Come on, Den?" I asked. "Some of us might really want to work here". "Work, shmerk" he chuckled. "Now, let me finish this damn thing". "Job?" Dennis asked. He put his pen on the answer line again "Ain't never had no job". "Georgie was cracking up and could barely contain himself. "Criminal history" Dennis said. "5 years at the dome, in Rahway. Rehabilitation resulted in failure". Even I was beginning to laugh and was losing focus while listening to him. "Dependents" he mumbled "Ain't never had no kids cause the court system took them all away". "Dennis?" I asked. "What are you gonna write for your signature at the bottom?" "Why, I'll mark it with an X of course" he laughed. "Because, I don't know how to write". "Do you believe this guy?" I asked. "I bet he'll turn it in too". "I wanna see the receptionist"s face when he does that" said Phil. "It'll be a riot". "Hey, Den?" I asked. "Are you really gonna give that lady your application like that?" "Sure, why not?" he said. "I doubt if she'll even look at it anyway". "I have an idea" said Phil. "When we go to turn them in, I'm gonna help him". "Help him do what?" I asked. "I'm gonna tell the woman he's disabled" he replied. "It'll be fun, watch". "I think you guys are crazy" I said. "If you do that, you'll ruin any chances of me getting a job here". "You don't wanna work here anyway, Ron" Dennis replied. "This place is a bullshit job, I can tell". "Well, I'm done with mine anyway" I said. "But, I'm gonna turn mine in last". Georgie returned to the receptionist"s window, thanked her, and handed her his form. "Who"s next?" she asked. "I need to file these all together". "I am" said Phil. "But, my friend here next to me will need some assistance because he doesn't write very well". I was trying very hard to not laugh and it was killing me. I had to turn around facing a wall so the lady wouldn't see my face. "What's wrong with him?" she asked. "Oh, he's kind of retarded" Phil exclaimed. "But, he's a good worker and never misses any days". She turned to Dennis and asked "Is that true, son?" Dennis mumbled and said something about "Me sign X, me sign form, me sign X on form". "Ok, I'll give your applications to the hiring manager" she said. "They'll call you if they're interested". "What about mine?" I asked "I have it right here completed". By this time, Dennis, Phil, and Georgie were almost out the door. "I'll take yours too" she said. "And, tell your friend I'm sorry". "Sorry about what?" I asked. "I'm sorry about his condition. I think it's touching that your friend is trying to help him secure employment with his condition". Stuttering and trying not to laugh, I replied "Oh, uh, uh that. Oh yeah. Well, thanks for everything. I have to go". I left to meet them outside and they were pointing at the door hysterical as I was exiting. "That was a great act, Den" I said. "What do you have for an encore?" "The day is still young, bro." he chuckled "I have just begun to fight. Let's go to the next one".

A company we heard of named American Multifoods was hiring and we were told that they would hire people on the spot immediately. We trekked down to them, filled out applications, and were all hired within an hour. The place was a factory that had assembly lines that made sandwiches for underprivileged kids in New York City. So, on my first visit a few days later, I was assigned to the bread preparation area. Mine and Georgie Burn"s job was to take loaves of bread from stacked up plastic trays, slice the plastic tops open with a razor blades, flip them all over, and have them lined up for production to be taken away. Almost every kid I hung around with from Edison was working there and it felt comfortable knowing I was surrounded by familiar faces. As the work days wore on, I ran into Jesse. He had just been hired and was working in the freezer room. "What's up, Ron?" he asked. "Hey, man" I replied. "Georgie and I have one of the easier jobs playing around with bread. When did you start working here?" I asked. "Me and Skippy started yesterday" he said. "I didn't see you until now probably because We're in that damn box all day". "Well, at least you're not in the heat" I replied. "Yeah" he said. "It's not too bad and it's a cake job actually. Sometimes, we scarf the chocolate milk from the back too. But, don't eat any of the meat for the sandwiches, bro. Most of that shit they give to those ghetto kids is rotten". "Rotten?" I asked. "You mean all of those sandwiches for the poor kids they make over there on the assembly lines are bad?" "You bet your ass" he replied. "That shit is all rank" he said. "I wouldn't feed that garbage to my dog." "Really?" I asked. "All of it?" "All of it, bro" he replied. "Have you ever seen the salami?" he asked. "That shit is green" "Green?" I asked. "No shit, man. That's fucked up". "Nobody cares" he said. "Because they're all city kids". "They"'ve got a good scam going" he laughed. "They bill New York City all kinds of crazy money and give them bullshit food. Too bad we didn't have enough cash to start it up, bro. We'd be rich".

A week or so went by and my older brother's girlfriend was hired as our immediate supervisor. I couldn't believe my luck as I knew I"d have an easier time and would probably be able to get away with murder. She approached me one day and asked "Aren't you and Jesse pretty tight friends?" "Yeah" I replied "We've hung around a lot in the past". "Well" she said. "I notice that you and Georgie Burns stack up like 8 of those trays 6 feet high and when you're done you stand around doing nothing the rest of the day. I also see Jesse wandering around a lot because he finishes his orders early in the freezer. "Yeah, so?" I asked. "What does that have to do with your job?" "Well, it's like this" she said. "If my boss catches you standing around all day not doing my job, he's gonna be on my ass. So, I have a proposition for you". "What's that?" I asked inquisitively. "I've heard from the higher ups that this place is gonna be shut down soon anyway" she said. "The health department is all over their asses for rotten food. Therefore, I don't really give a shit about this place anymore. But, I don't need them giving me headaches until it's closed. So, why don't you, Jesse, and Georgie come in at 7am, leave at 11 for lunch, not come back, and I'll punch you guys back in and out for the rest of the day. That way, you'll still get paid even though you're not here. Nobody will notice for weeks anyway". "Wow!" I said. "You"d do that for us? That would be fantastic. But, what about Skip?" I asked. "Can't you help him too?" "I can only do 3 at a time" she replied. "I have to space them out from different departments." "Welp, I guess it'll be the 3 of us then" I said. "I'll go and tell Jesse later. Thanks for the scarf". "Well, I'm dating your brother" she laughed. "So, it's no problem for me" she said "Just don't tell anyone else, or We'll all be fired". "I'm not saying shit" I replied. "I love free money".

Georgie never really got to enjoy our ongoing scam as he got caught one day coming back late from a bathroom break. He was fired by a different boss and my brother's girlfriend wasn't able to help him. Jesse and I though took full advantage of it until the end. We called it "Our part time, full time paying job at multiscrub". Eventually, about a week before the plant was closed, my brother's girlfriend was caught clocking our time cards in and out by a sneaky supervisor. He had been watching her without her knowing and reported it to one of the owners. We got phone calls asking us not to come back and she was gone before lunch time. At most jobs, after you are let go or resign, there is a reserve check that you pick up a couple of weeks later. Jesse, Skippy, and I rode down there in a friend's car to pick up our last pay checks. We walked in the door together and were greeted by one of their owners. He was a very effeminate guy and tried to explain to us that the manager who wrote the checks and was unavailable until another day. "Bullshit!" Jesse screamed. "You better have our fucking money or there's gonna be a problem". "That's right" I replied loudly "We heard from the grapevine that you guys are closing soon". "What? Do you think We're stupid?" Jesse asked. "Do I look stupid to you, Ron?" "Not at all, man" I replied laughing. "You better get somebody higher up than you" Jesse growled. "Or else, you're not walking out of here". "Give me a few minutes to talk to someone" the guy said nervously. "I'll see what we can do". He went into some back offices where we couldn't see him and we waited. As Jesse was glancing around the room, he noticed an expensive IBM copy machine on wheels by the door. "I wonder what this is worth?" he asked laughing. "Probably a few grand" replied Skip. "We should take it if he doesn't come out with our money" I said. "That's a good idea, Ron" Jesse replied "If this asshole doesn't come back with some checks, We'll scarf this bitch right out the door. I bet somebody would buy it off of us cheap". The man appeared back in the room and was stalling with excuses. "I can't find the guy who signs the checks" he remarked. "You'll have to wait a while until I find him". "Fuck that!" Jesse yelled as he sauntered over to the copy machine. "You see this bitch?" he asked. "You have 5 minutes to come up with our money, or We're wheeling this thing out the door." "You can't take that" the man exclaimed. "It's rented". "I don't give a fuck if it's yours or not" Jesse yelled. "No checks, no IBM machine. "Wait here, and I'll be right back" said the man obviously terrified by Jesse"s attitude. This time, he came back much sooner and was whispering down the hall to another guy "These guys mean business" he told his colleague. "If we don't pay these kids, We'll be on the hook for a couple of grand for the rental". They went into a side office and we heard a ripping sound that was like checks being torn from a ledger. They soon returned smiling. "Good news" the effeminate one said. "I found the guy who signs the checks". "Good for you" Jesse chuckled. "You just got back your copy machine".

Aerosmith was on tour and I desperately wanted to see them. It was the Rocks album that was a huge hit and everyone and anyone was clamoring to purchase tickets before they were sold out. Fortunately, I got tickets to see them at the Spectrum in Philadelphia and got to attend with no problem. My mother was working at Macy"s in Menlo Park. So, I had the hook up as one of her coworkers worked at Ticketron. I went with Kevin S. and a few others and waited outside smoking Jamaican tops and swigging on a bottle of tequila in the 97 degree heat. Kevin soon became ill. "I don't know if I'll be able to make it inside, bro" he cried. "Every time I stand up, I feel like I'm gonna puke". "You can make it, man" I said. "Just don't ingest anymore party supplies". Soon after, the arena"s doors opened and we strode inside to try to get a seat. It was general admission and every man for himself. I glanced over at the stairs on each side of the building and people were streaming in in droves. It reminded me of an ant mound after it was disturbed. Once they got down on the floor, they were focused in like rabid wolves salivating for a prime spot in front of the stage. Fortunately for Kevin, the air conditioning was on and he quickly began to recover. After the band hit the stage and performed a few numbers, we noticed we were too far back to really see much and decided it might be better to go up into the permanent seats instead. We found a few empty ones by the side of some scaffolding and sat down to watch the rest of the performance more comfortably. Suddenly, I heard a commotion to my right and noticed there were some people yelling at a man who was teeter tottering by a railing. "Get back here and sit down" they screamed. "You're too fucked up to be standing by there. You're gonna fall, man". Oblivious to their requests, he continued his intoxicated dancing as if he were alone. "Watch that guy" I whispered to Kevin. "You think you"ve got problems being too fucked up earlier? I bet in a few minutes, he's gonna fall right over that railing and hit the ground". "Nah" Kevin replied. "He looks ok, he's just a little drunk, that's all". The band took a short break between songs and we could hear the guy hooting and hollering in slurred ecstasy. "Yeah" he howled while pumping his fist. "Aerofuckingsmiff!"Just then, he lost his footing too close to the railing and flipped over to the floor below. He looked like a carnival target spinning around on a bolt at the gun game. "Splat" we heard loudly. He had obviously landed on his back and was now unconscious. "Somebody call security" I heard someone shout. "That guy looks like he's hurt real bad". By the time I left my seat in an attempt to find someone to assist him, he was already surrounded by the venues employees. We watched as he was put on a stretcher and removed. Aerosmith continued playing until we saw Steven Tyler fall over holding his head. Someone in the audience had thrown a Heineken bottle at him and hit him squarely in his temple. He was stumbling toward the back of the stage and attempting to remain upright. The band stopped mid song and we awaited his return. A short lull went by and Tyler walked up to the microphone. Most fans were cheering since he wasn't hurt more severely and was more conscious than we had thought. "Guess what, Philadelphia?" he screamed to the audience. "You guys just fucked up. The show is fucking over and you can thank that asshole who threw a bottle at me on the stage. We don't put up with that bullshit. So, see you next time". After many boos, I peered over to my right again and could see that the guy who had fallen over the railing had returned. He was standing next to his friends and was asking loudly "When is the show gonna start, man?" "Buddy" his friend replied. "The show is over and it's time to go home. Tyler called it. He got hurt too". "I didn't see any of that shit" he yelled. "You"ve both got head injuries now, you're done" said his friend. "In that case, I want a refund" he demanded. "You don't get refunds for being stupid" said another friend. "So, grab your jacket and let's go".

 I was hungry for pizza one afternoon and decided to purchase a few slices at Zia Lisa in the Kilmer shopping plaza. Other than Grant"s department store, I had always liked this particular strip mall as it was convenient and had mostly everything I needed. My parents had always frequented Sav On Drugs there for their prescriptions and Robertson"s Sporting Goods for baseball equipment and skis. I was especially fond of the little old man who had a hot dog cart on the corner next to Acme and I ate there frequently. There has always been a debate over the best pizza in Edison but I put it down to personal taste. One of those places that fit into my life in my future was Mary"s Pizza. Mary"s was a tiny pizzeria that was once a restaurant and sat in the lower level of a house about a block from the Highland Park border. I have vivid memories of going there and seeing a pretty little girl of about 7 years old in a white lace dress, patent leather shoes, hair tied back in a French braid with a bow, and playing with a mixture of flour that she was just about to roll. As I watched, she was kneading it as if a substitute for Play Dough. She was continually giggling frantically while making shapes and sizes to satiate her imagination I supposed. I found out later that the elderly woman named Mary was her grandmother and that the little girl's name was Jill. Her significance fits into my narrative in this book later on as I would see her sporadically and had no idea at the time that there was a reason for us meeting. Other pizza places were just as equally good. There was Edison Pizza on Woodbridge Avenue, Scortino"s for a short time on Route 1 North, and Veils who eventually became Destis".

Where Mary"s Pizza Once Was And Where I Met My Future Wife

I ran into Skippy at Playmore and he was excited claiming he had to tell me something. "Guess where you're going in a few days?" he asked. Puzzled, I asked back "Where?" "I didn't forget how you took me to see Yes" he said. "So, I'm returning the favor, bro. My older brother got tickets to see Led Zeppelin at the garden. He was in the ticket lottery and won. He gave me 2 tickets. So, I chose you to go with me. Is that fucking cool or what?" he asked. "Fuck yeah" I replied excitedly. "How much are the tickets?" I asked. "Just give me 10 bucks, man. And, We'll call it even". "That won't be a problem" I replied. "Not a problem at all". Returning home that afternoon, I knew I had to scrape up some money fast. I didn't want to let on to Skip that I was broke and take the chance that he would give my ticket to someone else. I asked my mother "Hey mom, there's a concert I want to go to in New York City. I need 10 bucks for the ticket and another 10 for the train". "Stop right there" she said. "I don't have any money. You'll have to find another way". "Come on, mom". I replied. "I know you stash away some cash to get your hair done". "That's my money" she shrieked. "I bet the old man doesn't know about it though, right?" I asked. "I see you're going to aggravate me again today" she said. "What do I have to do to get rid of you?" "20 bucks will do it" I replied laughing. "Go outside and cut the grass" she ordered. "And then, We'll talk about it. But, if I give you the money, you can't tell your father". "I'm always willing to negotiate, mumsy" I said. "I wouldn't ask you if it wasn't important" "What's important to you isn't necessarily important to me" she replied. "But, if you do as I said and leave me alone, I'll give you the money. Don't ever say I didn't help you". With my mother, I always knew how to get her in a spot if I had too. I just had to push certain buttons to get what I wanted. Plus, I always kept evidence on her. She didn't want my dad to ever find out about her extra money pilfering. So, I would save up my information for situations such as these.

Skip and I got to the garden to see Zep and took our seats in the orange section. After thanking his brother for helping us get into the sold out show, he passed down a wine sack to Skip. "What's in that thing?" I asked. "My brother told me its electric wine" he replied. "Wine with acid in it?" I asked. "Cool". "Yeah" said Skip. "What better way to see Zeppelin than to trip?" he asked. "I can go along with that" I replied. "How many hits are in there?" I asked. "I don't know" she answered. "But, who cares? It'll be great". He took a few guzzles and handed the pouch to me. I took a few like he did and passed it back up over my shoulder to his brother. "Now, don't get too freaky" his brother warned. "I don't wanna see any bum trips". "We'll be ok" Skippy replied confidently. "We've tripped before". "Just making sure" said his brother "Just making sure" Moments were passing by and Led Zeppelin was extremely late. The show was supposed to start at 8 PM and there was nothing. Usually there was an opening act to keep audiences occupied. But this time, it was lacking. "It's 9:30 Skip" I said. "What the fuck is going on here?" "I have no idea" he replied. "They better not cancel this shit". Suddenly, Robert Plant walked out onto the stage and the crowd erupted. "I'm sorry We're late" he announced. "I couldn't find my jeans. Please be patient with us and We'll be right back. Soon, the band returned as he promised and went right into their song Black Dog.

The electric wine began hitting me and I remember staring up at the ceiling and seeing a large disco mirror ball hanging down. "Skip" I yelled in his ear pointing upward. "Check out the shimmering lights from that thing. It's all over the place". "You're peaking, bro" he replied. "Isn't it great?" he asked. A while later, the band segued into their song Kashmir. Some very thick beams of light were launched up from the base of the stage and looked like wide bars in a prison. "Look at that shit" I exclaimed. "He's a prisoner of the lights". "It's in your head, man" replied Skip. "So, just go with it" When it was time for Jimmy Page to do his solo, he came out with his guitar and large bow. It looked like one used for a violin, but oversized. At first, he had a single spot light on him and seemed to be enjoying himself. Then, the spotlight dimmed and changed color to a purplish hue. Page beat his guitar with the bow making reverberant sounds that swirled around the arena. Down from the lighting rig above came a single green laser in front of him. It started to separate and eventually turned into three. Page stepped into the middle and I saw it take the shape of a pyramid. The cenotaph began to quiver and spin around his body. Faster and faster it moved causing trails of glow from within my eyes. "Fucking fantastic" I mumbled to myself. I was electrified by the performance and couldn't move. After the last song was played and the house lights came on, the band waved goodbye and left the stage. Not satisfied with this, fans began to stomp on the ground and roar for their return. Page came back out first and reached down into his instrument case on the drum riser to retrieve his guitar. Suddenly, there was an explosion. He stepped back in a daze and ran to the back of the platform. I could see that he was cradling his hand, shaking his head, and he appeared to be in pain. The audience started to boo. It wasn't due to Page leaving; it was because some asshole had thrown an M-80 at the stage. Unfortunately, it had landed in Page"s guitar case just before the encore and detonated at the worst possible time. "Who"s the fucking scumbag who did that shit?" I thought. "These people are idiots!" "Holy shit!" Skippy exclaimed. "Did you see that shit?" he asked. "Yeah, I saw it" I replied. "I bet they won't even come back out again after this". A few minutes went by and Robert Plant had returned. He moseyed up to the microphone and asked "It seems we have a comedian amongst us this evening? He must be seated next to someone?" Across the way, I could see a male being dragged away by security. He was being kicked and taking blows to his face. It was obvious the assailant had been apprehended. Plant looked backstage to someone, turned back around to the audience and exclaimed "We'll be right back after we take care of the Physical Graffiti". It was evident he was trying to make a joke out of the occurrence and attempting to get the fans to be at ease. The band came back out and Page had two of his fingers wrapped up in some gauze. They played two numbers very fast and appeared as if they just wanted to get out of there as quickly. When the show was finally over and the house lights came on, Page came back out, walked to the edge of the stage, raised his non injured hand, and gave the crowd the finger. I guess he wasn't amused. On the way home, I mentioned to Skip "You know, if Page didn't get hurt, they probably would have played a lot longer since it was their last show in New York". "Yeah, that sucked" he replied. "But, at least they got the guy and beat his ass. That moron deserved everything that was coming to him". I read later on that because of this, the band would skip the garden on any future tours. Sadly, their drummer passed away. So, We'll never really know. All I remember thinking was "Why ruin it for everyone else?" I guess some people felt the need to be selfish. I never understood that thought process and never will.

While gobbling down my pizza, I was approached by Mickey B. He had come into Zia Lisa for a few slices himself and was telling me about some party that was coming up and if I was interested in going with him. "Where is it?" I asked after gently wiping pizza grease from my chin. "It's gonna be up on Fairview Avenue" he replied. "Supposedly, everybody"s gonna be there. It's a good place to have a party I think because the woods face the train tracks. That way, we don't have to worry about any nosey cops". "I don't know anything about the cops possibly showing up, but I'll go with you, sure" I said. "Cool" he replied. "We can go in my van. I'm not gonna use my parent"s Dodge this time. But, we have to pick up Dennis G., Phil, Jackie Boy, and maybe a few others. We'll go get them as soon as We're done here, ok?" "Sure" I replied "It sounds like this might be a fun party. I have a little weed on me too. So, that will probably help". "Well, I'm bringing some cold beers in an ice chest" he said. "So, it should be pretty cool. Pretty cool I found out later was an understatement.

After we picked up our friends, we arrived at the party and it was in full swing. All along the avenue were cars parked on either side of the road and the wooded area next to Anthony N."s was overrun with teenagers. "Where you gonna park, Mick?" I asked. "Fuck it" he replied. "You see that clearing over there? "I'm gonna sneak into there while slowly driving through those people". "But, Mick?" I asked. "What if they don't move? There's hundreds of them". "Oh, They'll move" he chuckled. "Or, They'll get run the fuck over". Gently, Mick lurched forward with the van. He nudged them like a mother lioness showing its cub how to hunt. Phil came up from the back to the middle and was yelling through the open windows. "Get the fuck out of the way you fucking weirdoes; We're trying to park here". Confused and half intoxicated, most moved out of the way. Finally, Mick succeeded. "Now, we can shut this off and sit here" he said. "I'll open the side doors so we don't even have to get out either. It'll be like our own little partying apartment". After the doors were open facing the trees, kids from all over came over to visit. One girl came by who I had always thought was attractive. She was Anthony"s sister and I had a slight crush on her. She was leaning over into the van and I made my move. In mid-sentence and half drunk, I leaned over and started kissing her. To my surprise, she didn't pull back or resist. She reciprocated very passionately and seemed to be into it. While we were interlocking our faces, everyone around us began to whoop. "You go for it, Arold" they yelled. "We didn't think you had it in ya, man". "Check out Ron scarfing on the chicks" laughed Phil. "He's really on the prowl tonight". "Let's take a walk" she whispered in my ear. "There's too many people here for this party". I hopped out of the van, took her by the hand, and we strolled to a secluded area away from the noise and the party goers. Standing up, I began grabbing her breasts. At first, she didn't stop me and conceded. Eventually, I attempted to go further when I was rebuffed. "We're not doing anything here" she said. "It's not private enough". Frustrated, I offered to go farther back into the woods. "Ron" she said. "I really like you, but it's not happening. My brothers are here and so are all of my friends. I'm not gonna take the chance of getting caught. Maybe next time we can fool around some more, ok? So, I think we should go back now". Undaunted, I pressed up against her. "Come on now" I begged. "Who"s gonna see us? I seriously doubt if anybody"s gonna come back here". "You're a little drunk and so am I" she replied. "It wouldn't be any good anyway" Try as I might and using every manipulating tactic imaginable to convince her, she kept refusing and rejected my advances. "Ok" I groaned. "Fuck it, let's go back". "You're not mad at me now are you?" she asked. "Nah, like you said. I'm too fucked up anyway. We'll go back and enjoy the party". "Wow" she replied. "You're pretty cool about this. Most guys would be assholes". "I'm not gonna try to force you into doing something you don't want to do" I said. "It's all good. We'll just go".

After we returned to Mick"s van, she said she had to leave. I thanked her for her company and went on partying. Of course once she had left, I had to be subjected to my friend's ribbing. "Uuuuullll" Phil teased. "Did you do her, bro?" he asked. "I bet he did" said Jackie Boy. "He tore that pussy up". "It's none of your fucking business" I replied angrily. "Why the fuck do you guys even give a shit about my sex life?" I asked. "Ron ate her bat wings" Dennis laughed. "He motor boated that shit". "He does smell a little bit fishy" chuckled Phil. "Maybe we should get him some cocktail sauce? Then, he can dip his shrimp". "Funny you guys, really funny" I said. At least I got a girl for a while. What have you guys been doing other than playing with your hands?" I asked. "Oh, he's got us there fellas" Dennis quipped. "The bat wings took him over". "Can we just continue having a good time and stop this bullshit?" I asked. "But, it's so much fun teasing you" Phil replied. "You always take everything so seriously". Suddenly, and without warning, we saw the familiar image of blue and red lights floating up the road in the distance. "I hope that's not the fucking cape crusaders" Dennis exclaimed. "Because if it is, this party is over". "Fuck me" Mick replied. "It was just getting started". "You better back this puppy out of here, Mick" Jackie Boy remarked. "Or, we might all get busted".

As Mick put the van in reverse, I went outside to try to push people aside. "Watch out of the way" I yelled. "The van is coming through". Just as we backed out to the edge of the street, the police arrived. And there were 5 or 6 cruisers surrounding us. One cop who appeared to be in charge had a bull horn. "The party is over" he screamed. "It's time to disburse or face arrest". As panic set in and most revelers abandoned their fun to run for their freedom, one guy I knew named Ronnie Gun was unmoved. We watched him and the cops from the van"s front window as he was being harassed "Fuck that!" he yelled. "This is a private party on private property. We know our rights. So, you can't make us leave without a warrant". "A warrant, huh?" the cop asked. "We don't need anything. So, you can leave now or else" "Or else, what?" Ronnie Gun demanded. "You clowns ain't gonna do shit. You're outnumbered". Amazed by

Ronnie Gun"s behavior, Mick began to whisper. "Wait for it, a few more seconds, wait for it". "Wait for what?" I asked. "What's gonna happen?" They're gonna beat his ass. Just watch" Mick said. "You really think so?" I asked. "Oh yeah" Dennis added. "His ass is toast". Ronnie Gun moved more forward trying to intimidate the police even more. "Bad move" Phil said. "Bad, bad move". After his final warning with Ronnie Gun ignoring him, the cops pounced on him like bees protecting their queen. We watched as he was thrown to the ground and beaten. All we could see were blue uniforms over him and elbows jutting out in unison. Blow after blow they beat him. "Fucking punk" one cop yelled. "We'll teach you to question us!" "Cuff him" another cried out. "Cuff his ass, now!" As he lay helplessly on the ground with no way to defends himself, his girlfriend got involved in the fray. "Let go of my fucking boyfriend you fucking scumbags" she shrieked "There's no reason to treat him that way". "Step the fuck back, bitch" the cop in charge screamed. "Or, you'll be going with him". "With him for what?" she asked defiantly. "For defending my boyfriend from an illegal arrest" "That's it!" screamed the commander. "She's going too, grab her!" One of the officers began to approach her. "You're coming with us, honey" he said. "Whether you like it or not". As he approached, there was a steel rake lying on the ground between them. It was the type with a long wooden handle and forged steel tongs on its opposing end. In his haste, the cop wasn't paying attention and stepped on the rake as he got close to her. As his toes hit its teeth, it flew into the air. Its leverage made its head spin and it hit the girl squarely on her cheek. She yelped "You bastard" as she coddled her face in pain. "You fucking bastard. You did that on purpose. I'm gonna sue the piss out of you". "Time to leave" Mickey blurted. "Next They'll want me. So, fuck that shit, We're out of here". Mick leaned out the window asking the other cops if we could go. "Sure" a lone cop replied. "As long as you didn't see anything". "We didn't see shit" said Mick. "In that case" the cop replied. "You are free to go". Driving forward past former partiers who were trying to avoid further interaction with the police, Phil chimed out "Did you see that shit?" he asked. "They fucked up Ronnie Gun"s girlfriend's face pretty bad back there." he said. "I saw blood trickling down here face" "Yeah" I replied. "Her face looked pretty bloody and swollen". "They'll just throw her in the back of the cop car and take her to the hospital" Dennis said. "Then, They'll arrest her for attacking them". "That's why I try to steer clear of those pigs" remarked Mick. "I fucking hate them". "We all do" I replied. "But, they are a necessary evil". A few weeks later, we heard that Ronnie Gun had stacked up charges from the altercation and that his girlfriend was arrested for interfering. She also had to have many stitches to repair the damage to her face.

Jesse had come over my house on his Suzuki RM 250 dirt bike to pick me up to go riding in Camp Kilmer. He motioned for me to hop on the back and we were off down Central Avenue. "Watch this" he shouted. "This fucker is pretty quick. So, hold on tight bro" I grabbed around his waist to secure myself so I didn't bounce off and end up rolling down the street. Suddenly, I felt heat on my right leg. I looked down and there was fire. "Jesse!" I screamed. "Holy shit, man. There's fucking fire coming out of the back of this thing!" He turned his head and asked "Fire? What fucking fire? What the fuck are you talking about, Ron?" "Look down, man. Look down" I yelled. Sure enough, the flames were now creeping up his thigh and were burning his jeans. "Ahhhh" Jesse screamed. "I'm burning up!" "Jump, jump!" he shrieked. "I'm dumping this fucking thing". Luckily, he slowed down long enough for us not to retain any injuries. We hopped off and watched the bike wobble and crash to the curb. It landed on its side and the engine slowly petering out. "The seat is on fire" I exclaimed. "Look man, its fucking melting". "Motherfucker" Jesse grumbled. "How the fuck did this happen?" "Check the fuel line, bro" I suggested. "Maybe it came loose". When the flames settled down and were finally extinguished on their own, Jesse got close to inspect it. "The fucking fuel line hose came disconnected" he screeched. "I can't believe this bullshit, Ron" "It's not your fault, man" I replied.

"Sometimes shit like this just comes apart on its own". "I've had it with this fucking thing" he said disgusted. "You wanna buy it from me?" he asked. "I don't feel like dealing with it anymore. I bought it cheap, bro. I'll sell it to you for 80 bucks. "But, the seat"s melted" I replied. "So fucking what?" he asked. "Just put some tape over that shit and chop a plastic line for a new fuel flow. Once you rig that, this bitch will fly again". I picked the bike up while it was still smoking and we began laughing at it. "Ok" I said. "I'll buy it from you. I guess I can fix it up". "Come on, Ron" he replied. "Where else are you gonna get a motorcycle this cheap?" he asked. "I'm doing you a favor, man". We wheeled it back to my house and placed it in my garage. I got so far as replacing the fuel line and took one ride on it with the melted foam rubber seat. It was so fast, it intimidated me. I sold it later to Mickey B. for what I paid Jesse for it. Mick taped up the seat, painted it, and rode it all summer.

Dennis G. and I decided to go to Lawrence Brook to meet up with his brother Jeff, Cliff G., and Jimmy M. "Jeff and his friends are camping there" Dennis said. "I don't feel like camping out, but We'll go and hang out with them for a while if you wanna come with me". "Are we gonna go fishing?" I asked. "Nah" he replied. "It'll be too dark by the time we get there for that, bro. We'll make a big fire and get stoned and drink beers instead. "Did Jeff bring a tent with him?" I asked. "Yeah, they wanna sleep over there tonight and go swimming by the Rutgers swing in the morning I think" he replied. "Sounds like a plan, man" I said. "Let's go". As we took the journey from DenniS's house across the Morris Goodkind Bridge, he was regaling me with stories about how he was crossing the same bridge alone one day and found hundreds of coins under his feet. "Yeah, man" he exclaimed. "I was looking over the edge down at the Raritan River because it's such a cool view. All of a sudden, I kicked something that went "ping". I watched it as it rolled down the sidewalk and into the gully on the side of the road. On closer inspection, I shuffled some dirt away on the ground under my feet. And right there man, were hundreds of silver dimes. I couldn't believe my luck that day, bro". "I guess somebody dropped them" I replied. "Yeah" he said. "I spent a half an hour scooping them up and getting my hands dirty". "Dirty money" I chuckled. "I wonder where they came from?" I asked. "I didn't care" he answered. "As long as it was money, I had no qualms in retrieving it".

Soon, we approached Jeff's campsite and greeted everyone. "What going on?" Dennis asked. "Are you guys taking good care of my little brother?" "I'm fine, Den" Jeff replied. "We're just hanging out and put up this tent. Cliff brought some beers and they're in the cooler" "Is that right Cliffy?" Dennis asked. "Can we have some?" "Sure" Cliff replied. "Just don't be drunks and drink them all. We have a long night ahead of us". "We'll sip them" Dennis said. "And, tell scary stories like rich people in summer camp" he laughed. "Help us get some firewood" Cliff requested. "We can't do all of this work on our own". "Hmmm" I remarked. "Firewood gathering for beer?" I asked "That seems like a good trade". "Get some kindling, Ron" Cliff instructed. "Because, we've already got the big logs before you got here". While we were finishing and had gathered up a substantial amount of wood, it started to get dark. The sun was setting fast so we had to make a pile quickly. "We need to make a fire" said Jimmy. "Or else, we won't be able to see much longer". "Don't you guys have a flashlight?" Dennis asked. "We have a small one" Jeff replied. "But, I don't know how long the batteries are going to last". As night fell and our fire began to rage, Dennis wasn't satisfied with the height of it. "Did you guys bring any lighter fluid or accelerant?" he asked. "Because, this fire is pitiful. I wanna see a bonfire and shit". "There's some lighter fluid by the tent" Jeff exclaimed. "Go and grab it and throw some on if you want, Dennis". He retrieved the yellow can of fluid and sprayed it vicariously around the fire"s perimeter. "Uuuullllhhhh" he screamed as the flames ascended in a glow "Now, this is a fire kids!" "Take it easy with that stuff, Den" I said. "I wouldn't want you to burn yourself". "Listen to Ron" he replied. "The guy who blows fire like Kiss". "Ron blows fire?" Jeff asked. "Yeah" Dennis chuckled. "He used to do it in the band he sang in". "I only did it in my basement a couple of times" I said. "The one time we were supposed to do it at a dance, but the asshole janitor stole our supplies". "Show them, Ron" Dennis demanded as he pointed at the can. "Show them how you do it". "Not tonight, man" I replied. "It's kind of dangerous". "Don't be a wuss" remarked Jeff. "We wanna see it". "I dunno, man" I replied. "Come on, Ron" Dennis begged. "It's cool looking and everybody wants to see it". "Jeffrey started chanting "Fire, fire, fire! We wanna see Ron do fire!" While I stood there contemplating if I should do it or not, the rest of them chimed in. Dennis began doing an Indian war dance and started spinning around waving the lighter fluid in a teasing fashion in front of my face. "Uuullllhhh" he screamed. "Fire, fire, fire! You know you wanna do it. Come on now, Uuuuullllhhh!" "Ok, Den" I replied. "Hand me the fucking can" "Ron"s gonna do it! Ron"s gonna do it!" Jeffrey yelled. "I can't wait to see this" chuckled Cliff. "I wanna see if he burns himself" "I hope he doesn't" lamented Jimmy. "I don't feel like running to get an ambulance". "He knows what he's doing" shouted Dennis. "He wouldn't still be here if he didn't from before. If Ronnie sparks up, We'll just throw him in the brook!" "Ok, kids" I howled. "Step back. I have to take a long stick and put some fire on the end of it like a small torch. Then, I'm gonna squirt some of this shit in my mouth. I have to do it real fast because it tastes nasty. So, watch closely because it happens real quick". I rose up my head, opened my mouth, tilted the can, and shot in a large squirt. It was just as I had remembered and tasted horrible. With my eyes opened wide for effect, I pitched my head down, pursed my lips, put the torch a few inches from my mouth, and spit the fluid in a spray into the fire. Just like it had done previously in my cellar, the flames cast out into a mushroom pattern and looked like a small atomic bomb. It only lasted a few seconds, but always made a great spectacle for a small audience who were attracted to danger and intrigue. "That was cool as fuck!" shouted Jeff as I bent over spitting out fluid and retching to the ground. "Do it again, do it again!" he urged. "Give the guy a few minutes to recover" demanded Dennis. "He's almost puking his balls off". "I'm ok, Den" I replied as I waved him away. "Just give me a beer to wash this shit out with". He handed me a half full brew and I guzzled a few ounces swirling it around in my mouth. "Pwuah" I yelled as I voided it. "And, you guys want me to do this shit again?" "You can do it, Ronnie. One more time, bro" Jeff nagged. "It's up to you, Ron?" Dennis asked. "But, I'm telling ya, it looks fucking cool". "I guess I can be the circus act one more time" I replied. "Ron?" Cliff asked. "If you do it one more time, I'll get you stoned with this primo weed I have on me. I was saving it for tomorrow. But, Dennis is right. That shit is cool as fuck to watch". "All right, all right" I said. "I'll do it one more time. But, that's it! After that, no more.

I gave them a similar performance and watched their faces as they stared in awe. When it was over, Dennis was telling me I had balls but that I was "crazy". "I may nuts" I replied. "But, it's something to do". "Just so you know" he whispered. "I didn't really think you were gonna do it the first time. But, Jeffrey called you out. So, what was I gonna do?" "Umm, tell him no?" I asked. "You"ve seen when someone tells my brother no" he said. "I came here to party. Not to fight with him". "I get it, I get it, Den" I replied. "I have a little brother too, remember?" After we smoked Cliff's reserved weed and it began to get late, Dennis decided it was time to leave. "We're going back to the house, Jeff" he said. "Stay out of trouble and We'll see you later". "Ok, Den" replied Jeff. "And, thanks for the show Ronnie. That was amazing" "You're welcome" I said. "I'm glad you liked it". A few days later, I found out that after we left, a man who had escaped from a psychiatric ward had accosted them. He had been lying in wait behind some trees and was watching us the entire time. He must have felt outnumbered and was waiting for Dennis and I to leave. The man turned out to be a pedophile and was known for stalking children. The guy came down off the hill, grabbed Jeff around his neck, and put a knife to his throat threatening to cut him. It was only when Jeffrey distracted the man that Cliff had taken a tent pole and whacked the criminal"s arm forcing him to let Jeff go. They eventually chased the man back up the hill and lost sight of him. The police eventually came, scoured the woods, and locked the perpetrator up again. The guy didn't know Jeffrey"s temper. If he did, I firmly believe he would have passed and found another victim. The aggressor never should have messed with a kid who was known to scream "I'll kill you!" when aggravated. It just wasn't the psycho"s day.

Six months later, I was dating the skinny blonde girl I banged under the bridge from 4th of July. I took her to see Aerosmith"s Rocks tour but in New York City instead of Philadelphia. It turned out to be a great show at Madison Square Garden and I enjoyed Rick Derringer opening immensely. The only problem I had was that some asshole sitting behind us decided it would be "fun" to light a very long candle and kept waving it behind our heads. A few times he came close and we felt the heat coming off of it without any warning. I very nearly got into a fight over it warning him to stop. He confronted me and asked "Do you wanna have a go or what?" He didn't realize it with his mouth, but I was much taller than him. When I stood up, he immediately sat back down and clammed up for the rest of the evening. I guess telling him "If you wave that fucking candle behind our heads one more fucking time, I'm going to stick it up your fucking ass" deterred him.

During this time, I was having difficulties attending school in the mountains and I couldn't wait for the day to come so I could quit. My 18th birthday was fast approaching and I would no longer need my parent"s signature to withdraw. In the meantime, I still had to deal with riding on the tart cart and had to waste my days at a place that had no beneficial attributes to me what so ever. Some mornings though, I got a kick out of riding on the short bus and goofing on others as they stepped on. There was one little guy named Stanley that a larger kid named Mark always seemed to pick on. Most days, the driver of the bus would stop at a local convenience store in

Plainfield to retrieve coffee and cigarettes. As long as we promised to behave ourselves during the ride, he had no problem letting us join him. Once inside, Mark always made Stanley steal for him. Being so small and thin, Stanley was deathly afraid of repercussions if he declined. Before we went into the store, Mark would bark out his order. "Stanley, you little weasel. You know what you have to do. I want the same as the last time. You get me 3 candy bars, a soda, and one of those cupcakes I told you about". "I don't know if I can hide all of that" Stanley complained. "It might be too much and I might get caught" "Stanley" Mark demanded "You know what will happen to you if you disappoint me, right?" he asked. "I know, I know" he replied. "I have to kiss the spare tire in the back again?" "Then, get in there and get me my stuff" warned Mark. "I'll distract the clerk while you steal my shit". After we entered the store, I purchased a coffee and went back on the bus. Waiting, I asked the driver if it was always this way. "Sometimes yes, sometimes no" he replied. "But, I have more trouble with the bigger kids than I do with Stanley. So, I try not to get involved unless they get physical with him". "Nice" I replied. "But, what do you do if it gets out of control?" I asked. "I don't say anything" he replied "I don't want to encourage them. I just find the nearest telephone and call the cops. That's what administration told me to do. So far, I haven"t had to do that. You don't know them as well as I do. After a while, you get a feel what they're really like. I know how to handle them".

The kids came clamoring back on the bus with Stanley leading the way. "Hurry up, Stanley" Mark said. "It's cold out here. Move your ass before I move it for you". With fear erupting in his face, Stanley jumped up the steps and returned to his seat in the back. As the bus drove away with kids laughing, Mark demanded that Stanley give up the goods. "Let's go Stanley" he barked. "Empty those pockets and give me my stuff". Stanley exhibited nervousness and his hands were visibly trembling. "I have everything right here" he said. As he handed Mark his goodies, Mark began to chastise him. "What the hell is this shit Stanley?" he asked. "You're missing the cupcakes I asked you to get". "I'm sorry Mark" Stanley said shaking. "The guy was really watching me this time. So, I couldn't get them". "Bullshit" Mark screamed. "I specifically told you to get me those cupcakes. I don't wanna hear it, you little wimp. So, get on your knees and get to kissing that tire. And, don't get up until I tell you too". "Come on, Mark" Stanley begged. "Can't you cut me some slack just this one time?" he asked. "Just for that, I'm making you do it longer" Mark chuckled. "Don't even think of getting back up until I tell you too". Obviously shaken, Stanley got on the floor and assumed the position. "Purse those lips" Mark commanded. "I wanna see some kissing". Stanley put his mouth to the treads. "Keep them there" said Mark. "And, if you take them off because of a bump, you're starting all over again". For a while I thought this entertaining and then got bored with it. In poor Stanley"s defense, I stuck up for him. "I think he's been on that tire long enough. Don't you think Mark?" I asked. "He comes off the tire when I say so" he replied. "He won't learn any other way". "I don't give a fuck" I said. "I'm the oldest here now and I say he gets to go back to his seat. You made your point. So, it's over now". "Oh, so you're the new leader now? Huh, Ronnie?" he asked. "That's right fuck head" I replied. "And, I'm bigger than you. So, if you won't let Stanley get back up, We're gonna have a problem. I'm leaving school soon. So, you can go back to teasing him then". "I'm all for a joke, man". I said. "As long as it's not taken too far. You're going too far. So, that's it". "Ok, ok" he replied. "If you're leaving anyway, I don't give a shit". He looked down at Stanley and waved him back up. "It's your lucky day today, buddy" he said. "Ronnie here has given you a reprieve.

Danny B. had called me up and told me he had tickets to see Kiss at Madison Square Garden for their Love Gun tour. I liked KisS's show but was never impressed by their musicianship. Other than a few fast runs on lead guitar from Ace, I felt all of their stuff was easy to play and was not hard to copy on guitar. Still, the ticket was free as he was treating me and he really wanted to go. We arrived at Penn Station under the garden and searched for a bar. A band named Piper was opening for Kiss and since we didn't know any of their music, we were in no hurry to get to the show. We looked around and settled on a bar called the Iron Horse. Before we left on the train, I had a printed picture in my pocket from a magazine of the band Piper accompanying me. So as they played, I would be able to use it as a reference to identify them. I usually liked to do research beforehand on bands I went to see so I would know everything about them. Danny and I bellied up to the bar, took our seats on some stools, and waited for the barmaid to serve us. She was a short girl with dark wavy hair and sultry brown eyes. "What"ll you guys have?" she asked. "Two drafts please" I replied. "You guys are old enough, right?" she asked. "Don't we look old enough?" Danny asked snarkily. "I'm just trying to be sure" she said. "I don't want any headaches from the ABC". "The only ABC you'll have to worry about is at Rockefeller Center" Danny replied. "And, Ronnie is too pretty to be on TV. So, We'll sit in here instead". "Speak for yourself George Harrison" I said. "You have a lot to say for someone so old". "At least I bought the tickets" he quipped. "So this time, you get to buy the beer".

A half an hour went by and the barmaid started asking us questions. "Where are you guys from?" she asked. "You look familiar" "My friend Ronnie here is from beauty school" Danny said. "And, he's about to graduate with curlers". "You better shut up, bro" I replied. "Before I tell this woman you're wearing a wig" "A wig?" she asked laughing. "Does he really wear a wig?" "Only on Sundays" I chuckled. "So, he can fool the priests into being their favorite altar boy". "I steal change from the pass around plate too" Danny said. "That's how we got the money to be here". "You guys crack me up" she said. "The next draft is on me". She poured us 2 more and disappeared to the other end of the bar to service more customers. "Let's fuck with her" Danny suggested. "How?" I asked. "What scheme do you have going on?" "You know that picture of Piper in your pocket?" he asked. "Remember how I told you look like the singer Billy Squire on that?" "No, I look like me" I replied. "Listen, do you wanna drink beer mostly free before we go to the show or not?" he asked. "Just do what I say, man. Follow my lead and pretend you're him. I'm gonna say I'm your road manager and we ducked in here so as not to get noticed so we could relax and have a few drinks, ok?". "Brilliant" I replied. "As if that"ll ever work", "I'm telling you" he said. "I think this chick digs you. It's just a feeling I have". "Ok, man" I replied. "But, don't get depressed if you fail". "It won't" he said. "You'll see". The barmaid came back and was asking us how we were doing. Danny explained why we were hiding. "I have a surprise for you" he said. "Do you know who this is sitting next to me?" The girl tilted her head looking confused and was guessing. "I know I know him from somewhere" she replied. "I just can't figure out from where?" "Show her, man" Danny demanded. "Show her that picture of you in your pocket". "Ok" I replied. "But, you have to keep it quiet. Or else We'll have to leave". I retrieved the photo from my pocket and handed it to her. "Look as the guy in the middle" Danny prompted. "What do you see?" "Wow!" she giggled. "Is that really you?" she asked. "In the flesh" I remarked bullshitting her. "We open for Kiss in an hour". She inspected the picture more closely and convinced herself it was me. "And, what do you do if you don't mind me asking?" she asked Danny. "I'm his road manager" he chuckled. "I'm the guy who keeps him out of trouble". "This is so cool" she said. "I'll be right back". "Remember" Danny cautioned. "Don't tell anyone else, or We'll be forced to leave". "I won't" she said. "Don't worry"."You sneaky fuck" I whispered. "You got the poor girl believing it's me" "It's only the power of suggestion" he replied. "People are more gullible than you believe". "We'll see when she comes back" I said. "I guarantee you she'll give us free booze" he laughed. "Because all chicks want to hang around with rock stars". Soon, the girl returned. "What are you guys doing after the show?"

she asked. "Do you have to go right away to travel to another city?" "Nah" Danny replied. "We're off tomorrow". "Why don't the both of you come back here after your show is over?" she asked. "I get off work around then". "We can do that" I said. "That sounds like a good idea". Like a school girl excited for prom she went on "I tell you what" she whispered so no other customers could hear. "For every beer you buy, I'll give you guys two. But, drink them slow and don't be obvious about it. No one will figure it out that way". "That would be great" Danny said. "We would really appreciate that. I'm gonna have Billy here autograph that picture and give it to you. Sign the photo Billy. She deserves it" he said. Pretending to be Billy Squire, I asked her for a pen. "I'll be right back with one" she offered. "So, don't go anyplace". "I can't believe you're making me dupe this girl" I complained. "Just to get a couple of free beers". "Be quiet" he whispered. "She's coming back. Just sign the fucking thing and be done with it. We're leaving soon anyway". She handed me the pen and I fake signed the rock star"s signature. She put it in her pocketbook and thanked us both. "I've never met any famous music personalities before" she said. "Thank you so much". "Thank you for the beers" I said. "They're tasting good". Danny looked at his watch on his arm. "We have to go in a few minutes" he said. "We have to get ready for the show". We guzzled a few more beverages and told the girl we'd be back after the performance was over. Waving as we walked away, I quizzed Danny if that part was true. "Fuck no" he replied. "We won't have time to go back and meet her later. We'll miss the train home if we do that. Too bad for you, because she was kind of cute". "I didn't think you were that cunning, man" I said. "Oh, when it comes to free beer I'm all full of tricks up my sleeve my friend" he replied. "Just wait until we have to do it again"

We entered Madison Square Garden just as Piper was finishing their set. They were just ok and I wasn't really impressed. Danny was excited and couldn't wait until Kiss came on. After a 45-minute stage set change, we heard the announcement over the P.A. "You wanted the best and you"ve got "em, the hottest band in the land, Kiss!". Queue massive explosions from both sides of the stage and mass teenaged hysteria. Danny and I had seats in the green section and weren't really that close. Kiss was so loud I couldn't make out half the words they were singing. Danny turned to me and was saying something undecipherable. I couldn't make it out over the bombastic sound from the band. When there was a short lull after their first song, he turned to me again. This time, I could hear him. "Aren't they great?" he asked shouting. "Check out this pyro and shit". "Yeah, it's pretty cool so far" I replied. "I can feel the heat from the explosions from here". "Let's go see if we can sneak down closer" he said. "I bet we can jump the rail to the floor into the red section". "There's a lot of cops here, Danny" I replied. "We can try. But, don't be surprised if they catch us". Just as Kiss was starting their song Hotter than Hell, Danny ran down, hopped over the divider, and fell to the floor. Trailing behind him, I attempted to do the same. I looked up and saw that Kiss had stopped dead after the first verse and wondered why. Without a hitch, the band looked at each other, laughed, shrugged their shoulders, and started the song all over again. I guessed they had lost their way. But, at least they were professional about it and continued without saying a word. After the first chord hit, as I dropped to the ground, I felt a terrible sting on the back of my neck. Someone was grabbing me by my hair and my feet were dangling off the floor. Then, I heard a loud, angry voice. "Get the fuck back up here you little asshole. I saw what you did. You don't have the right ticket to be down there. So, come back up here, or you come with me". I twisted myself to the left and could see it was a New York City police officer. He must have seen my scam. "But, my friend's down there" I replied shouting. "I don't give a rat"s ass who it is" he replied. "You have 5 seconds to climb back up here and return to your seat. If I have to come down there to get you, you're gonna regret it". Saying nothing, I crawled back up over the railing, gave him a dirty look, and did what he requested. After a few more songs, Danny had somehow returned. "Did you see that? Did you see that?" he asked.

"I was 10 feet from them. It was fantastic". "Yeah, well" I replied. "I got close too. For about 10 seconds. A fucking cop snatched me up when I was trying to follow you. He was gonna beat my ass too and arrest me if I didn't go back". "Wow man, that sucks" he said. "But, at least he didn't bounce you".

We went back to our original seats and watched Ace Frehley do his solo. While mid shooting of some rockets out of the headstock of his guitar, I lit up a bowl of hashish. Choking back some smoke I turned to Danny and asked him if he wanted a hit. Without him saying anything, he grabbed the pipe and put it in his mouth. While taking his first draw, a man seated next to us started complaining. "Hey, fellows" he said. "Could you do me a big favor and not smoke that in front of my 2 little boys? I don't really like the idea of exposing them to drugs". Surprised by this, and thinking the man should have known better and that teens tend to smoke marijuana at rock concerts, we capitulated to his ignorance. "Sure, man" Danny replied. "I'll put it down and We'll go up the stairs to use it the next time". "Thanks so much" the man said. "I didn't mean to inconvenience you". "No problem at all" I replied lying. "I hope your kids enjoy the show". After the last song and a return for an encore, we left for the train back home. "I can't hear shit" I exclaimed. "I'm fucking deaf!" "Yeah, those guys are loud aren't they?" he asked. "I can't hear shit either". "What the fuck was up with that guy bringing his little kids to the show?" I asked. "He almost ruined it for me. I couldn't even get stoned. And, don't even get me started on that asshole cop that grabbed me". "I thought that was stupid too" he replied. "Those kids were too young to have been there, they should have stayed home". "Well, at least you got to see your favorite band" I said. "Yeah, man. Thanks for coming with me, bro. I had a really good time". "The free beer made up for the annoying guy with his kids" I said. "So, we can't really complain". After we returned home, I had a hearing deficit for 3 days.

CHAPTER 5

Eighteen & Arrests You've Got It

I had finally turned 18 and didn't feel the need to have to listen to my parents anymore. The Bonnie Brae School in the Watchung Mountains was becoming tiresome and I was only staying a few more weeks to satiate my father's opinion of me not securing an education. I knew it was only a matter of time before I became fed up and signed myself out to quit anyway. One morning, another student named Greg had decided to cut classes and asked me to come with him. I accepted and accompanied him. "Most of the day" he said. "I meander around the mountains on the edge of school's perimeter". Once there, we went deeper into the woods where we found an old abandoned farm house. There were no longer any windows and the front door appeared as if it had been propped open for some time. "Let's go inside and check it out" he exclaimed. "Maybe we can explore and find something cool in there". Since the building was only one floor, I complied and followed him in. "I wouldn't have come in here if it had been two levels" I replied. "The two leveled ones have a tendency to have loose shit that can drop on your head". "I wouldn't have gone in one either" he said. "The stairs are the first to go. I've heard stories where kids try to walk upstairs and the steps collapse. Then, they get all cut up and shit. That's not for me". I glanced around and saw abandoned furniture, old clothes in piles on the floor, and broken ceiling tiles strewn about in every direction. The place appeared to have been deserted for a long assed time. "I wonder what the people were like who once lived here?" I asked. "I dunno" Greg answered. "But, this house looks like the great depression". "They probably lost it to the bank" I said. "Banks suck and love to foreclose on people". "I'm glad I don't own a house then" he said. "Because, there's no way I could pay for any of that bullshit". "You're only 17" I chuckled. "You still have a long way to go".

As we were examining our surroundings in greater detail, I reached into my pocket and pulled out a joint. "No exploration is complete without one of these" I said laughing. "It gives a whole different perspective for the rest of the day". "I didn't know you had one of those with you?" he asked. "Fire that shit up, bro". I reached for my Bic lighter, and gave the joint some flame. As I took the first toke, I began to asperate terribly. Greg was giggling and pointing at me. "What kind of weed is that?" he asked sarcastically. "It looks like you're having convulsions". "Don't worry about it" I replied choking while completing my sentence. "Just take a hit and shut up, man. This is some strong shit and you'll get really stoned". I handed it to him and watched him put it to his lips. He took a deep draw and began to wretch. "See?" I asked. "Just like me. I told you this shit was potent". When we were finally done smoking and recovering from many more coughing fits, the room became silent. We were both exorbitantly stoned. I looked out one of the bare windows and was marveling about how vibrant the colors of the trees were. "What's so fucking beautiful about bare tree branches?" Greg asked. "There's no leaves on them, bro. It's winter time. You have a morbid view of the world, man". "I see beauty in all things" I replied. "And right now, I see the allure of getting out of here and seeing what else we can find". "You want to leave already?" he asked. "Where else do you wanna go?" "Follow me down that trail we saw on the left from when we first arrived" I suggested. "I saw a road over by there in the distance". "I don't know if that highway goes any place" he said. "But, we might as well go toward it. There's nothing else around here I can see". "All roads lead to paradise eventually" I quipped. "So, let's go see what's there".

At the end of the path, we could see cars whizzing by and it was starting to rain. We were getting sprinkled with the vehicles rain aftermath and I began to curse them. "Fucking assholes need to slow down" I complained. "I'm getting all wet here". "They don't give a fuck about us" Greg said. "People in cars are always in a hurry". "We need to find a dryer place than that abandoned house we just came from" I said. "There's got to be something along this road out here some place". "I hope so" he replied. "Because, I'm getting cold and hungry". As we walked down the shoulder of the road to avoid being hit by any high speed travelers, a building that looked like a small cottage came into view. "Holy shit! I yelled excitedly. "That looks like a fucking bar". "We're saved Ronnie, We're saved" Greg remarked. "Provided you have any money?" "I have a few bucks on me" I replied. "Let's go in and get a few beers and some sandwiches". "But, I'm not old enough" he said "They'll card me". "Just follow my lead" I said jokingly. "These clowns don't have a clue. We're way in the mountains, man. I can play these people like a fiddle. You have to walk in like you own the place and don't give a fuck. Otherwise, if you appear nervous they won't serve you. You'll be too obvious". "Well" he said sheepishly. "I'm just going to stay behind you then. You can make the grand entrance and We'll see how it goes". "All right" I replied. "But, it usually works. Find a spot in the back of the bar where they can't see you real good and I'll go up and get the beers. If we get that far, then we can order something to eat".

We stood in front of a huge solid oak door that looked like an entrance to a small pub in a forest. "Look at the size of this fucking thing? I said. "It's thick as hell and massive". "Maybe they're trying to keep people like us out" Greg chuckled. "Most places hate long hairs." "Not once you wave money around" I replied. "Green replaces hair". I pulled on the giant door"s handle and peeked inside. There was no one in there except an elderly bartender beyond a lone pool table in the middle and he was polishing glasses in his hand with a rag. I motioned for Greg to follow me while the door was ajar. As I let go and we stepped forward, it closed behind us with a pronounced boom. "Welcome to my pub" the old man exclaimed. "What can I do for you?" While I was motioning toward him, Greg went over by the billiard table and was pretending that he was checking it out. It was a very dim light and it was hard for him to be seen correctly. "Perfect" I thought. "As long as Greg doesn't get closer to him and stays where he's at, this old guy will never figure it out". When I was near enough to order, the bartender scanned my persona. The scowl on his face was telling as I watched him imagining my age. "You look old enough to drink" he said. "But, what about your friend over there by my pool table?" he asked. "Can you vouch for him?" "He's ok" I replied. "You don't have to worry about him. He's my younger brother". "Well, if you take full responsibility for him" he said. "I'll let you both have a good time in here. The coppers almost never come by. So, I guess it'll be ok as long as you guys don't stay too long". "We'll only be an hour or two" I remarked. "We just want some food and a few drafts". "Drafts it is fellas" he laughed. "And, we serve sandwiches as well. You probably knew that already though by my sign outside". "That's why we came in" I grinned. "Because, We're hungry". "Well, I have two kinds of items to serve you" he said. "Roast beef, and turkey. Take your pick". I wasn't sure what kind of meat Greg liked and I didn't want to tip my hand walking over to him in case the old man changed his mind. "We'll have two turkey sandwiches on rye bread with mayo" I ordered. "While We're waiting, We'll be over there playing a few games of pool. Just call over to us when it's ready, ok?" He retrieved two upside down bell shaped glasses, put them under a tap, and I watched as it poured. When he was finished, he laid them on the counter and slid them over to me. "Drink up buddy" he said. "There's a jukebox back there as well. You can play some music if you want. But, it's not set real loud because sometimes it gives me a headache". "I'm old now" he laughed. "And, more headaches I don't need".

After we had played 3 or 4 games of pool, drank 3 beers each, and wolfed down our lunch, it was time for us to leave. I wanted us to get back to school before someone noticed we were missing. I walked over to the old man and asked him for our bill. When I was done paying him, he thanked me for stopping by and told me we were welcome to drop by anytime again. "Other than you guys maybe needing a few inches cut off of your hair" he laughed. "You were very respectful in here. So, if you're by these parts some more, don't forget to come back and see us". "We'll do that for sure" I replied. "But, I don't know about the hair?" As we waved goodbye to him while sauntering out the door, we noticed that the rain had stopped. "What a nice day" I mentioned. "Weed, booze, sandwiches, and no more rain. It doesn't get much better than that". "Except for girls, maybe" Greg said. "I can't help you with those" I replied laughing. "You have to do that one on your own". "You know, Ron?" he asked. "It's one o"clock. We were supposed to be in gym class an hour ago". "So what?" I asked. "What can they do? Suspend us? They can't do shit" I said. "You worry too much. I'll think up some kind of insane bullshit story if anyone questions us. We'll be fine". "If you think so?" he asked. "You know me? I'm not gonna say nothing". "You won't have to" I replied. "Just ignore these teachers and let them chastise you. Turn your head and think of something else until they're done ranting. I tune them out, man. I just pretend they're not even there.

We arrived at the gym while other students were engaged in a game of basketball. We walked over to the bleachers on the right side and sat down. Suddenly, a tall muscular black man dressed in shorts, a sleeveless t shirt, and wearing white socks and sneakers approached us. I had seen a different gym teacher before and I didn't recognize him. Immediately he made the mistake of getting in my face. "Where have you boys been?" he demanded shouting. "This period started an hour ago. You are late! So, you better have a good excuse for your behavior!" "First off" I bellowed back. "The only one here who has their period is you! So, you can take a step back away from me and calm down". By this time, the entire gym had come to a standstill as the players turned their heads to gawk. "You don't tell me to calm down, you hoodlum" he hollered. "I tell you what to do. I can smell alcohol on your breath from when I first approached. You can be suspended or expelled for that". The volume of our voices was escalating. The echo from within the room was becoming more noticeable. "I have news for you, asshole" I said. "I turned 18 not too long ago. I've seen how you grab the other kids when you're pissed off at them. If you grapple with me, I'll hit you in the fucking head with a chair. And after that, I'll have the cops to charge you with assaulting me." Are you threatening me?" he asked. "No one threatens me!" "I'm old enough to drink if I want now" I replied sneeringly. "Therefore, you can't touch me. I can legally press charges on you". He started to stutter as if he was looking for the right words and seemed as if he was dumbfounded. I knew I had him right where I wanted him. "What a dumb ass" I thought. "He can't do anything except send me to administration. As if I care?" "But, but, but you are setting a bad example for your friend here" he said as he struggled hard to save face. "You don't understand. I have to worry about him and the others around you". "You need to learn on how to approach people" I chuckled. "You're testosterone is way too high". Seeing that he was beaten and he had no way out, he became complacent and tried to back pedal. His tone turned to conciliatory. He backed off of me and tried to berate Greg instead. I wasn't having that either. "I think you need to get back to coaching that game" I suggested. "Before it gets worse for you than it already has. Look around you, buddy. Everyone in this entire gym is laughing at you. "I'll deal with you and Greg later" he replied defeated. "Now, I still have the authority to kick you out of my gym. So, I want you both to leave the premises immediately". "If you feel the need to try to throw your balls around one last time to look important" I laughed. "Go right ahead. Because I already made up my mind that we were leaving when you ran over here like a little girl who lost her tampon". "Out, out, out" he shouted loudly as he pointed at the door. "Out of my gym!" "There they go again with the "my" shit again" I thought. "You give them authority, and they think they own everything". "Let's get out of here Greg" I said. "There's nothing else for us here". Two weeks later, I signed the forms to formally resign from school.

Since I was still dating the girl from under the bridge from the 4th of July, she had asked me to be a chaperone for one of her class field trips. "You're 18 now" she said giggling. "So, what better way to get back at the system than to pretend to be one of them?" I didn't know I was allowed to do that at the time and I graciously accepted. She attended my former junior high school's nemesis Herbert Hoover that I knew little about. The Velez brothers had gone there and had told me that other than the school's colors, it was pretty much the same deal as TJ. I had a feeling then that other than being her boyfriend; she looked up to me and was proud to parade me around in front of her friends. I had heard young girl whispers of "Wow! He's older than her and an adult now. She's got it made". I didn't understand it nor did I care. But, from a teenage girl's perspective, I imagined it must have been a real ego stroker. For the trip, she handed me a form with a few pages on it pretty much asking for everything about my life since I had taken my first piss. I filled it out the best I could, handed it back to her, and she submitted it to Hoover"s authorities for review. A week went by and she called me excited "Guess what, baby?" she asked cooing into the phone. "You"ve been accepted for my class outing. We're gonna have such a great time". "Of course" I thought, her mother's signature from her permission slip had a lot to do with it.

The morning came for the journey and my girlfriend and I gathered on a corner a short distance from her home. As we were waiting for the chartered bus to arrive to retrieve us, I was summarily surrounded by mostly pubescent females and was thoroughly enjoying the attention. All the while, the girlfriend was hanging on my arm marking her territory to show I was hers. I remember thinking I got a buzz out of it and thought it was cute though it slightly annoyed me at the same time. As the bus showed up and came to a stop, its door popped open and out came a woman who made it clear that she was in charge. "Ok kids, everyone on the bus" she commanded. I corralled the teens as best as I could and waited for my orders. "Hello" she said. "You must be Mr. Arold?" I nodded yes and tried to keep a pleasant look on my face. But, by her tone, I immediately hated her from the get go. She reached out and waved a clipboard close to my neck. "Take this" she barked. "The list of all the kids you'll be in charge of on this trip is on there. You will be solely responsible for them as you have already indicated by the form you signed previously. Do not deviate from the rules listed from within the form, and keep your eye out for any inconsistencies with the children's behavior. If you encounter a problem, you are to report directly to me. Do you understand these rules, sir?" she asked sarcastically. "I sure do" I replied. "I've read the form before I signed it many times". She stepped closer and whispered to me in a threatening manner "I don't approve of this" she said. "I feel that you are too young for the supervision of these kids. But, I was over ruled. So therefore, I'm going to be extra vigilant in keeping my eye on you. Just because one our students is your girlfriend doesn't mean you'll get special treatment from me. Don't mess this up, Son. Because if you do, They'll be hell to pay". I stood there emotionless and said nothing more than a quick yes and a nod of my head. After her addicted to power self stepped back on the bus, I looked at my girlfriend in disbelief. "What the fuck was that all about?" I asked. "I feel like she sees me as an enemy or something?" "She's just nervous" she said. "Because no one"s ever been a chaperone for us this young before". "Well then" I replied. "She'll just have to get over it or I'll have to make her life miserable". "Let's just get on the bus and enjoy our day, can we please?" she asked. "I don't need you going to war with anybody. Can't you do it for me? Please?" She was using her blue eyes to persuade me like she had always done. I couldn't resist and capitulated. "All right" I said. "We'll stay in the back of the bus. That way, I don't have to see her". "You know how I am? I asked laughing. "I love to provoke the majority".

We found a few seats in the rear and settled in for our trip. The first stop was going to be the New Brunswick Vocational School. Most of the kids were excited and were making fun of the teachers and telling stupid jokes as most aggravating teens were known for. I joined in with a few, and ignored some others. I was fortunate that somehow they remained well behaved. As we disembarked in New Brunswick, we strode in single file and were escorted by the school principal into the building"s basement. "Why are we in the basement?" I thought. "Isn't that a strange place to start a class excursion?" My curiosity was satisfied when we were informed that "This is the place where we have the beauty classes and the bakery shop. We will take you around and let you meet some of the students while they are performing what they need to learn. It's all hands on and we think you'll enjoy it. You may ask as many questions as you deem necessary. We are showing you this as an alternative to college if you wish and it is always nice to have two choices". "Sounds like more bullshit to me" I thought. But, I was interested in how food was baked. So, I went along with the plan. As we turned to walk to the bakery, my girlfriend grabbed my hand. The woman in charge from the bus saw us and became livid. She whisked herself over and cautioned. "Mr. Arold" she said softly as to avoid embarrassment. "We can't have you showing any signs of affection between the two of you. We have a certain amount of decorum to uphold. You are not here in the capacity of being her boyfriend. You are here to be an adult chaperone. Therefore, could you please abstain and show more discretion?" When the woman walked away, my girlfriend was giggling hysterically to herself. "She really needs to get laid" she said. "She acts as if you and I were gonna actually fuck standing here". "She's just being that way to protect her job" I replied. Just agree with everything she says. It's easier that way. If you don't answer, there's no argument". "I guess I can't fondle you until we get back on the bus" she chuckled.

"Rules are rules" I said. "They are made to be broken. We just can't be so obvious about it here". "If you want" she replied. "But, I'm jumping on you later".

The stoic woman in charge returned and ordered all of us to separate. "I want the girls on this wall" she demanded. "And, the boys on the other. You Mr. Arold will take all of the males to the bakery down the hall, and I will escort the females to the beauty school area". "Ya Voll" I thought in a pretend Nazi accent. "I vill do as you please vight avay". "I'll see you later, baby" my girlfriend whispered jokingly. "Don't get into too much trouble". "I won't" I replied. "Unless you see the cops coming for me". I had the boys follow me down a ramp and turned left into the bakery shop. It had all of the trappings of a genuine patisserie and it looked as if they really knew what they were doing. We met the teacher of the class and he went over the particulars of what the kids would learn and what was expected of them if they had decided to enroll later. While listening to his spiel, I felt the need to take a piss. "I'll be right back" I said. "Is it all right for me to leave my students with you?" I asked. "I have to use the restroom". "Why of course" the teacher replied. "Nature calls. We should be fine. Go right ahead, Sir". "You boys be good" I exclaimed. "I'll be back soon". A few boys raised their hands and asked to accompany me. "Sure" I replied. "If you really have to go". I entered the boy's bathroom with 3 of them in tow. They immediately ran for the stalls instead of the urinals. Upon closing the doors, I heard the familiar sound of a lighter going off. Laughing to myself I announced. "I know what you guys are doing in there. You're not taking a wiz at all. You're trying to get in your nicotine fix while you can". One of the boys unlatched a portal and came out with his head down. "You're no gonna rat us out? Are you Mr. A?" he asked frightened. "Nah" I chuckled. "It hasn"t been that long since I was in TJ. So, smoke "em up boys. You don't have to get it hot while I'm in here either. I don't care and you can smoke as much as you want. But, keep in mind we only have a few minutes before that teacher will start wondering where we are. If that happens, the lady with the attitude will come looking for us. "Wow, man" one of them said. "Your girlfriend told us you were pretty cool. We didn't know you were this cool though". "Yeah" another one replied. "We need to get you to go on all of our class trips". "I'm honored" I said. And, you have nothing to worry about. I smoke cigarettes too".

When the grand finale of the principal"s speech had come and gone, it was time for everyone to get back on the bus. While the woman in charge was counting teens to cover herself and to make sure the kids were all in attendance and safe, I sat down in the seat I had taken from the beginning. My girlfriend was next to me and was cuddling on my shoulder complaining that she was cold. Someone heard her and had handed her a blanket. "Let's put this over us, baby" she remarked. "I'm freezing". As we began to warm up under the covers, she whispered in my ear. "There's something else that needs warming up under here" she teased. "And, I'm hot". "You better cut it out" I warned. "I don't want anyone to see us". She grabbed for my crotch and slipped her hand under my pants attempting to stroke me. "Cut that shit out" I said annoyed. "You're gonna get us into trouble. Wait until we get home. We can mess around then". "Having a chaperone as a boyfriend turns me on" she cooed. "But, I'll wait and get on you later".

Once again, I was hanging out at Thursday"s Place with the usual suspects that always seemed to be there. Howie B. approached me and was telling me about how he knew where we could take a stereo system from a car close by. "There's a few cars in Meineke Mufflers lot parked out back" he said. "It's behind a flimsy gate. So, it's easy access for us". "You want to be in, or not?" he asked. "I could use some cash right now" I replied. "I already have a buyer" he remarked. "And, I have a screwdriver and an adjustable crescent wrench, man. It shouldn't take us too long to pilfer that shit at all". "Ok" I said. "Let's go over there as soon as it gets dark". "That was my plan all along" he mentioned. "And, I have an escape plan too".

"What's that, man?" I asked. "You know where that short brick wall behind Tastee Sub Shop meets Meineke"s property?" he asked. "Yeah, I know it" I replied. "The one where it comes to a point and it looks like a funnel?" "Yeah, man" he said. "That's the one, bro. If we get chased, we can hop right over that thing and get away easily". "If you think it's worth the risk?" I asked. "I'm all for it".

When darkness came, we crept over to Meineke"s back lot and stopped to take a look around. "Do you see anyone, Ron?" Howie asked. "Nope" I replied. "The coast looks pretty clear to me". "I'm gonna jump over this gate first" he instructed. "Then, you follow me. I'll go in the front seat and start working on taking out the stereo receiver. In the meantime, you get in the back seat and start removing the speakers". "Ok, man?" he asked. "Yeah, I got it" I replied. While we were engrossed in our tasks, I neglected to look up and check our surroundings. I was confident there was no one else close by and we were safe enough to finish what we had come for. "I've almost got it" Howie said. "Just a few more twists of these nuts". "How are you doing back there, man?" he asked. As I was replying, I mentioned the words "I'm doing pretty…" But, I never got a chance to complete my sentence. Where Howie was, I heard the driver"s side door lurch open with a screech. I looked behind me to my right and he was jumping over the wall like a Gazelle being chased by a hyena. I glanced back at the rear window and I saw a man with a key unlocking the gate. "Fuck" I whispered. "He must be an employee or the owner. I better follow Howie and get the fuck out of here before I get caught!" Just as I departed the vehicle, I stumbled and fell to the ground. Luckily, my fingertips caught me and I was able to right myself. "Don't you fucking move" the man screamed. "I knew I"d catch you kids robbing us sooner or later. Stay right there!" Ignoring him, I vaulted over the wall with him hollering behind me. I sprinted across Plainfield Avenue, through the back of Burger King"s parking lot, and made a dash towards home. I knew if I made it to TJ in the time it took for the cops to show up, there was no physical way for them to apprehend me. As I bolted through my front door, I ran down my basement steps and was trying to catch my breath from running. Fortunately, there was no one else at home. Therefore, I was immune from any explanations. I laid down on the bed, put on some music, fell asleep, and forgot about it until the next day.

In the morning, I returned to Thursday"s Place to see if there was any gossip about what we had done the night before. I ran into Phil and was told "Hey, man. Did you hear about Howie?" "No, what happened?" I asked. "He got busted last night trying to take a stereo out of some guy's car". My heart ran up to my throat wondering if my name had been mentioned. "Was anyone else busted with him?" I asked. Knowing full well I was an accomplice. "Not as far as I know" Phil replied. "But, I guess We'll find out sooner or later. I think he's still in jail though. I don't know if he got bail or not?" My adrenaline began to flow and I was getting very nervous. "What if Howie told them I was with him?" I thought. "What if the Meineke guy gave them my description?" A myriad of paranoid thoughts was polluting my brain. I had to come up with a plan. I decided to call the police station anonymously to see if Howie had been released or not. "Hello?" a detective asked. "How may I help you?" "I don't want to give my name" I said trying to disguise my voice. "I"d like to know if Howie was released from custody this morning." I asked. "Because, if he wasn't, I have some information about another person who was with him that might change the case". I was feeling out the cop to see how severe Howie"s charges were and to see if the charges would be lowered if someone had been with him. "Oh, he was released early this morning" said the officer. "Now, tell me who you are? What's this about more info on the case? Were you with him? Who are you?" he asked. "Click!"

went the receiver as I placed it down in its cradle. "Sneaky fucking cop" I mumbled. "Always trying to get more information".

Later in the afternoon, Howie came waltzing through the door. Of course my first concern was if he had ratted on me or not. "What happened to you last night?" I asked perplexed. "I was unscrewing the bolts to the speakers in the back of that car. And then, "poof" you were gone". "I'm sorry, man" he said. "It happened so fast; I didn't have time to warn you. I just saw that big guy standing there with keys in his hand and I freaked. So, I ran as fast as I could. I didn't mean to leave you behind. But, at least you got away too". "How did they catch you if you ran?" I asked. "Somebody recognized me when I was coming over the wall" he replied. "They told on me to the cops. So, the pigs grabbed me as I was walking down the street toward home". "You didn't tell them anything about me, did you?" I asked. "Come on, man" he said. "I'm not a rat, Ronnie. They held me for a few hours and let me go. I denied everything". "You know how that is man?" he asked. "They try to get you to confess. You know there's no way that was happening. So, since they lacked enough evidence, they had no other choice but to release me. They tried to tell me they'd get me later and I told them good luck with that and I left. Don't worry, man. We probably won't hear from them again". "I hope so" I said breathing a sigh of relief. "But, it sucks that we didn't make any money though". "Such is life" he replied laughing. "There are always more opportunities in the future".

On another usual Friday night of debauchery, I was hanging out with Cliff G., Jeffrey G., and Jimmy M. Since I was the only one who was of legal drinking age at the time, I was elected to purchase some beer. We pooled all our money together and decided on a case of Budweiser nips. Seeking a place to guzzle our concoctions, Jeff suggested some buildings that were being erected by the path across from Lindenau Elementary School on Jefferson Avenue. This was the same path I had mentioned earlier that was owned by Mr.

Herzcui. It seemed he had passed away and his relatives had decided to sell the property to some developers. In its place, were being built 10 or 15 townhouses. Since they were only partially constructed with a completed roof and wood framing that were bare of any sheetrock, we decided we would party there. "I don't think anyone will see us partying inside any of these" Jeff said. "It looks pretty safe". "As long as no cops come by" I replied. "Because, I'm the only one who"s over 18". "I think if We're quiet" Cliff exclaimed "We'll be under their radar". "What do you think, Jimmy?" I asked. "Do you think We'll be ok in here?" "If we don't talk too loud, I can't see anyone noticing us" he replied". "Ok, then" I whispered. "But, I have a better idea". "What's that?" asked Jeff. "Look above you" I said. "What do you see?" "I see beams and shit" he answered. "What do beams have to do with drinking these beers?" he asked. "Actually, those are trusses Jeff" quipped Cliff. "They're crossbeams to hold the weight of the roof up". "Precisely" I chuckled. "If we climb up there, we can sit on those rafters, drink our beer, and no one will see us. It seems much safer to me". "That's a good idea, Ron" Jeff replied. "Because, there's no doors or windows here and they are all open. If We're all up there, We're safe from nosey neighbors".

We all agreed to clamber up the framing and continue our escapade where the rafters met in the middle. "I'll go up first" I volunteered. "I have longer arms than the rest of you. That way, once I'm up there, I can reach down and you can hand me the case of nips". I scampered up toward the roof like an alley cat pursuing a meal. Once there, I had Cliff hand me up the box. I found a corner off to the side and balanced the container as best as I could. "Don't let any of those bottles fall out of there, man" Cliff ordered. "If they do, none of us down here feel like running so we don't get hit in the head". "Don't worry about it" I replied. "I have them in a good spot. I made sure they aren't off balance". "Good" laughed Jeff. "Because like Cliff said, I don't want to have to do the glass dance or get cut up by any of that shit". "Ok, man" I said. "Have Cliff help you guys up. He's tall enough where you can stand on his shoulders to reach". I watched as Cliff bend down, stood half way up, and balanced Jeff so Jeff wouldn't be out of reach. When Jeff slung his leg over the crosspiece between his legs, I grabbed his arm and pulled him up the rest of the way. Afterwards, I did the same for Jimmy. When Jeff and Jimmy were comfortable and secure, Cliff was strong enough to come up on his own. Finally, we all sat in our spots as I handed out the beer. "I hope I don't get too drunk up here fellas" chuckled Jeff. "I"d hate to fall down from here and break my leg". "You'll be all right, man" I replied. "Just don't guzzle too fast. If you feel like you're getting too fucked up, just get down instead".

Some time had passed while we were drinking when Jeff decided he had to take a piss. "Why don't you just piss from up here?" I asked. "It seems like a lot of work to have to climb all the way down to pee and then have to come back up again". "Fuck that" Jeff said. "I have a nice buzz going now and I was gonna get down anyway. When you guys are ready, I'll be down there instead." Jimmy was feeling the same "I have to piss too" he said. "So, I'm gonna get down with Jeffrey". "Fine" I replied. "But, me and Cliff are staying up here". It also had to do with us having possession of the beer I thought. To me, it was just a formula of easier access and I didn't feel like lugging the case back down to the floor. Cliff and I were starting to get slightly intoxicated and we began to sing loudly and laughing in between songs. It became obvious by being high up in the beams, that there was a pronounced echo. "You guy better cool it with the loud singing" Jeffrey warned. "You guys are being too noisy and the neighbors behind us are gonna hear you". Cliff and I began to taunt him and started yelling down at him. "Ahhh, be quiet" I joked. "Nobody"s gonna care". "We'll be down in a little while, Jeff" bellowed Cliff. "Yeah" I said sarcastically. "Because the beer is almost gone". "Stop being assholes" Jeff yelled. "You're gonna get us all busted". Cliff and I kept making fun and berating him. After a while, Jeff went quiet. We heard some mumbling but thought it was him and Jimmy conversing. Suddenly, Jeff screamed up loudly to us. "Hey, man. The cops are here you guys. You better come down they said or you two are going to jail". Thinking that Jeff was pulling our legs, Cliff and I quickly answered him. "Fuck you, and fuck those cops too" I yelled. "Yeah" Cliff replied. "What Ron said. Those cops can kiss my ass". "I'm serious" Jeff shouted. You guys better come down. They are right here next to me". "So is Mary Poppins" I laughed. "Tell her I'll be down with my umbrella since it just started to rain". Cliff was cracking up and added "And, I'm the Mad Hatter and this is our tea party, bro. Come back when you have more beer with the rabbit". I looked over at Cliff and mentioned "I don't believe him for a minute. Let's climb out onto the roof and look over, man. If the cops are really here, We'll be able to see them parked out front". "You're absolutely right" Cliff said. "Then, We'll know for sure".

Through an unfinished hole where a skylight was going to be, Cliff and I scaled the trusses like primates playing on a set of monkey bars. Once outside, we laid down where two parts of the roof met and sloped down in an angle. Like soldiers in a basic training camp, we crept up slowly to the peak on our bellies to get a view. As we peered down at the street, I saw two familiar police cars with their red and blue lights on. "Fuck me" Cliff whispered. "Fucking Jeff was telling the truth". "What"ll we do now?" I asked. "I don't think those cops will climb up all the way out here" he murmured "And, it's raining pretty hard now too. I think we should both crawl over to the crux of where the roof meets and wait them out. Even if one of them has the balls to come up here, I don't think They'll pop their head out much. It's really dark up here and hard to see". I shook my head yes and followed him over to the area he was talking about. I positioned myself at the top, with him just underneath me. We started to hear commands from below. They were telling us if we didn't come down right away, we'd be in bigger trouble than we already were. Cliff and I ignored them. Then, I heard Jeff yelling from the street. "Last chance you guys" he said. "They're coming up to get you now". Still not believing a police officer would make the climb in the rain, we stayed silent. A small amount of time went by and we heard creaking in the wood. We knew a cop was ascending on us. The opening for the intended skylight was far enough away where we didn't think He'd see us. We watched as the cop stuck his head up out of the hole and went down again. I was laughing to myself as he appeared as if he was in the nursery rhyme "Pop goes the Weasel". He did this once or twice and then stopped. I breathed a sigh of relief as it looked like we had beaten him. Just as we thought we had escaped arrest, he shot his head back up again. But this time, he had a flashlight. He directed his beam toward our way and missed. I still thought we were safe. That was until I heard a different voice from below. "Check all around in a 360 degree circle" he said. "I heard those kids when we first got here. I know that they're up there somewhere" "Ok Sergeant" the cop with the flashlight said. "I'll check one more time". He turned his beam toward us again and slowly dragged it from the apex downward. I felt like a prisoner in a spotlight trying to except a concentration camp. "He's got us" Cliff whispered. "I give up". "I have them" howled the cop. "I can see them now, Sarge". "You guys better come down with me right now" he demanded. "The Sergeant is real pissed off at you guys" As I stood up to obey his order, I couldn't help but see a large mound of sand on the ground just over the edge to the right of a gutter pipe. I was contemplating jumping onto it and running to escape. We were up pretty high though and I knew that it had to have been at least 20 feet. If I would have made it, there was a possibility I could have broken one of my ankles or a leg. Since the cop was watching our every move, he saw my body language leaning over. "Don't even think about it, buddy" he said. "Even if you made it, We'll send the dog after you. He'll tear you up when he catches you too" "You don't want that, do you?" he asked. Harkening back to my childhood and my remembrance of being chewed up by Prince and almost dying, I abstained from my flighty idea.

Once down on the ground and escorted to the front of one of the patrol cars, we were handcuffed and Sergeant Q. began to grill us. "We told you to come down immediately and you disobeyed us" he snapped. "If you did, I may have been more lenient. But, since you made us chase you, now you're all going to jail". I glanced down and could see that he had a few inches of thick, crusty mud on his pant legs. He walked over to me and started rubbing it off on my ankle. "You see this, you little fucker?" he asked. "I had to walk through that nasty shit to get to the inside of that building. So, I'm going to rub all of this shit back onto you". I didn't say anything and went along with his game. I knew if I questioned him, I would have gotten a beating. Then, he went over to Cliff and said "And, this other leg I have full of mud is for you. You can thank your friends for that". After he felt he had cleaned his trousers sufficiently, he began asking us our names. When he got to me, his ears perked up. "Do you have a brother named?" he asked. "Yeah, so?" I asked. I already knew that my older brother had gotten into trouble and beat a charge with this Sergeant over a prank regarding some patrol car headlights. "Your brother only got away because your father hired a good attorney" he chuffed. "My brother was found not guilty" I replied. "And, what does that have to do with me?" "Oh? A wise guy?" he asked sarcastically. "We have a wise guy here just like his brother". "Well, guess what?" he asked. "You're coming to the station with me. We'll see how your father likes it this time". I didn't say anything and just stood there waiting to be placed into the back of a cruiser. One of the Sergeant Q"s subordinates approached him and remarked "Hey Sarge" he said while pointing at Cliff. "I found out this one is a juvenile. What should we do with him?" Sergeant Q. replied "He's a big boy. So, just leave the handcuffs on him". He turned to me again and asked "How old are you? You don't look like an underage monster like your friend here?" "I'm 18" I replied. "Well, now I'm gonna charge you with contributing to the delinquency of minors then" he said. Because it's obvious that you're the one who bought the beer and we have the case with all the empty bottles in it". "I hope you have bail money?" he asked laughing. "I'll be out in a few hours" I answered. "So, do what you"ve got to do. I have nothing more to say". "Good" he remarked. "Then, take a seat in the car behind mine until We're ready to leave."

When we arrived at the police station, Sergeant Q. was going through my wallet and examining its contents in front of us. "Look what we have here" he said. "A pack of marijuana rolling papers! I might be inclined to add an additional charge of drug paraphernalia". "Drug paraphernalia?" I asked. "I think you need an education". He screamed back at me "Now, you just got that added charge" he said. "Keep talking back and you won't be able to afford any bail. By the way, your friends are going home because they are all minors. But, not you. You're going downstairs into a cell". "Whoopie" I whispered under my breath. "I can't wait". "What did you say? What did you say?" he asked sternly. "I lied and said "What's my court date, officer?" "You better watch your criminal mouth" he warned. "Because, I've had just about enough out of you". Surprised by my behavior, my friends were looking at me with amazement and were giving me the shush attitude with their body language. Soon, it was time for me to be escorted to my holding pen below. As Sergeant Q. grabbed my elbow to guide me in my descent, he gave me a slight push and I rolled down the stairs. One by one I hit each step and I felt like a bowling ball in a hurricane. As I hit the bottom after the last tread, my legs were still lying diagonal facing upward against the wall. Sergeant Asshole was standing at the top of the steps guffawing with his corrupt cohorts and making fun of me. "It looks like he took a spill" he chortled. "I guess he should have paid better attention. One of you guys will have to go down there and pick him back up though". "I'll do it" said a kiss ass patrolman from behind him. "Good job" replied Sergeant Q. "I have too much rank to have to go clean up my mess". Moaning in pain from my abrasions, I mumbled back "The only rank is the smell of you". "Did you hear that?" Sergeant Q. asked howling to the other officers. "He thinks I stink. We'll see how much I smell when you're handcuffed to the bars you punk. Have a nice time trying to lie down on the bench until you make bail". A lone patrolman came down toward me and raised me up by my belt loop. He dragged me by my waist and threw me in a cell. Then, he unlocked my cuffs and instructed me "Stick your hands through the bars behind your back. And, if you don't comply, the Sergeant said you're getting the Billy club". I did as he requested and he locked my wrists to the bars. It was awkward and uncomfortable. "Maybe I'll take pity on you after the Sergeant"s shift is over and readjust them" he said. "But, it all depends on your attitude. "Yeah, yeah" I replied arrogantly. "Just tell me when I've made bail".

About 4 hours went by and my friends had already gone home. My father finally showed up and I was released. "They're releasing you on your own recognizance" he said. "And, they dropped the paraphernalia charge". "Good" I replied. "Because, it was a bullshit charge anyway". "Did they treat you ok when you were arrested?" he asked. As I was signing paperwork for my court date, I whispered. "Dad, they pushed me down the stairs on purpose. Check out the scrapes and bruises on my elbows?" After he took a look, his demeanor changed and he went ballistic. "I want to speak to the person in charge right now!" he demanded. "I'm not leaving here until I get some answers". "Answers to what?" the duty officer asked. "What's the problem?" "My son says your Sergeant threw him down the steps" he screamed. "I want to talk to who"s responsible!" "Oh, that?" the officer asked grinning. "The Sergeant told us to keep an eye on your son because he was drunk and lost his footing. He fell down those steps on his own. He probably doesn't remember because of the alcohol". "Is that true?" my father asked. "Is that how it happened?" "Um, no" I replied. "These cops are liars". "I want to register a formal complaint against your department for your mistreatment of my son" my dad demanded. "Well" the officer said. "You can do that. But, you're wasting your time unless you have proof or witnesses. Does your son have either one of those? And, you can't file anyway. Your son has too. After all, he's 18 now you know?" "My father asked "Did anyone who wasn't a cop see it happen?" "No" I replied "No one". "Well then" he said. "There's no way we can win and they know this. So, We're shit out of luck. But, I'll get you an attorney and We'll beat them in court anyway. Let's cut our losses and go". I retrieved my belongings and we left.

While waiting on my court date to arrive, I left Automatic Catering where I had been working and procured a job at a company named PFI as a forklift operator. After working there for about a month, I got Dennis G. a job in the factory. He wanted to drive a forklift or work in the warehouse like me but there weren't any more openings. So, he was hired for the compounding department lab instead. On his first day, he was a hilarious sight with his afro sticking out from underneath his paper disposable hair net. "What do they have you doing in there?" I asked. "They"ve got me mixing all kinds of granular shit in these big vats, bro" he replied. They"ve also got me playing around with samples in test tubes. I smell like a Chocks chewable vitamin". "Yeah" I replied. "I thought more on the line of a Flintstones one. But, I get your drift. Unfortunately, each day after work, you're gonna have to take a shower to get the odor off". "That doesn't bother me" he said. "Because, I found something cool in here when my boss wasn't looking" "What boss is that?" I asked "The one in the white lab coat?" "Yeah, him" he replied. "He's from India and doesn't understand English real well. Watch when I ask him to come out here by this door. I'm gonna ask him a question. He'll have you rolling". He motioned for the man to come over to us and introduced him to me. "Pashwa" he said. "This is my friend Ron who got me the job here. I was telling him about you before". Dennis whispered in my ear "Watch this, bro" "Pashwa?" he asked "Do you have any bat wings? (Alluding to DenniS's nickname for pussy labia)" Pashwa had a confused expression on his face. "Batwings?" he replied. "Maybe we make some" he said. "Cool" said Dennis while laughing. "I'll be back in in a little bit. As soon as I'm done talking to Ron here". "Ok" Pashwa replied. "But, you no take long ok? Boss make angry if you disappear". "Dennis then reached down into one of his pockets and pulled out a glass vial with a yellow liquid in it". "Ulllllhhhhh" he screamed. "Guess what this is, bro?" "I dunno" I replied. "It looks like yellow piss". "I was messing around with those test tubes and I found all kinds of vials like these" he said. "I took off the cap and smelled it. After I sniffed it, I got dizzy. It gave me a rush like that shit they sell in head shops called Locker Room. Give it a snort, man". He opened the top briskly and set it under my nose. I inhaled deeply and started to lose my equilibrium for a second. "This shit smells like bananas" I said. "But, you're right. It's just like that head rush stuff". "I'm gonna take home a whole bunch of these" he chuckled. "They aren't paying me shit and didn't give me the job I wanted that's like yours. So, too bad on them". "Don't get caught" I warned. "Because, it'll make me look bad". "Nah, bro" he said. "Don't worry. I only take them when no one is around at lunch time". While asking him more details about these formulas, a guy walked by who worked in the computer room. He had a very hairy full faced beard and long slicked back hair that looked as if it was combed back over his scalp with Brylcreem. "Who"s that?" I asked. "Do you know him?" "That's Woof Woof" Dennis replied. "You mean the doll that Eddie Munster carries around with him?" "Precisely" he laughed. "Doesn't he look just like him?" I turned to take a 2nd look and almost fell off of my forklift.

Dennis didn't last long after the plant manager asked him to clean the stalls in the bathroom. He wanted him to use big rubber gloves, a brush, and some very strong bleach. Someone had drawn graffiti inside of them and for some reason; they thought Dennis had done it. After the manager had the equipment dropped off at DenniS's feet, I watched as he donned the gloves up to his elbows, examined the brush, went into the bathroom, and stood there shaking his head. "I'm sorry, man" he said. "I wasn't hired to clean no frigging bathrooms" "How come they don't make you do it?" he asked. "I dunno, Den" I replied. "All I was told was that somebody said they saw you coming out of the toilet last. So, I guess they"ve got it into their head that you're the one responsible". "Well" he snorted. "I'm not doing that bullshit. So, fuck that jazz. It's almost lunch time anyway. When you come back from break, tell them I quit". He peeled off the gloves, threw down the brush, and walked away. He kept to his word and never came back. I returned to work each day after and was putting some stock away in the racks with my reach truck. My supervisor came up to me and asked me to place some cases of bottles outside the sliding metal door adjacent to an assembly line. I had had trouble with my forklift before and it had been continually in the shop for repairs. It was an old truck that had a consistent problem with its dead stop braking mechanism. If I let my foot off of the pedal, the machine was supposed to halt immediately. I was rounding a corner toward the metal door when I stepped off the pad but the vehicle kept on going. I heard a loud boom as it connected to the edge of the portal and felt a violent shake. The forklift had crashed into the door. Getting my bearings, I attempted to step off the machine and fell over instantly. As I lay on the floor, I was dumbfounded at how my left leg had collapsed underneath me. "What the fuck is this?" I thought. "I can't stand up?" Suddenly, I felt my left leg go numb. I unlaced my sneaker and pulled back its tongue. Wiggling my toes, I slipped out my foot to examine the damage. Big mistake! I watched in disbelief as my foot swelled up like a balloon instantaneously. I began to get scared and I started to scream. "Help, help me!" I shrieked. "I can't walk, somebody please help me". Several people came out and consoled me as an ambulance was called. I had to spend 4 weeks on crutches healing.

My court date came and my father and I met my lawyer in the hallway while waiting for my case to be called. It was disconcerting that I was still on crutches and I didn't want to be there. The attorney advised us he was going to attempt to strike a plea deal with the prosecutor to lower my charges. He came back with a smile on his face and looked pleased with himself. "The prosecutor wanted to give you 10 days in the county jail as punishment" he said. "But, I pointed over to you as I was speaking to him and apprised him of your situation. Therefore, your charges have been downgraded to simple trespassing and a $150 fine". "Ok" my father replied. "Motion us over when our time comes". "I will" the lawyer said. "It shouldn't be too much longer". When my time came to approach the bench, I looked over to my left and could see Sergeant Q. "The scumbag who arrested me" I thought. He didn't look too concerned and was yakking away to other police officers. The court clerk called out the usual docket procedure with my name on it to appear before the judge. As I stood before him I had heard stories about this magistrate before. Such as, he usually had made up his mind after reviewing your case before you had even entered the court room. Also, I was told that he was a raging alcoholic and was known to fill his water decanter with vodka. I peered up at him and could see that he had a very red nose. I remember laughing to myself and thinking that he reminded me of an overweight Rudolph the red nosed reindeer. But, there would be no presents or empathy today. "Mr. Arold" he bellowed down to me from his podium. "I see that you have had a mishap and an injury? How long have you been on crutches, Son?" he asked. "4 months" I replied. "We'll" he howled. "My original intention was to incarcerate you in the Middlesex County Correction Center for 10 days". I wanted to advise him that that was a little harsh for my 1st offense. But, I glanced over at my father and he was giving me the "shut the hell up and be silent" look. The judge went on "Due to your circumstances and the conversation between the prosecutor and your attorney, I am inclined to suspend your 10 days sentence and to fine you $150". "Do you understand, Son?" he asked. "Yes, your honor" I answered in a soft voice. "Therefore" he said. "I will now release you from this court. But, be advised Mr. Arold that I may not be so lenient the next time. If I see you again, pack your toothbrush and your underwear. Because, you'll be going to the big house". "Yeah, yeah, yeah" I thought. Now, I have to thank this asshole. "Thank you, your honor. I appreciate your decision". "It's not about appreciation" he blurted in between taking sips from his water glass. "It's about respect for other people"s property. The owner is here tonight and he wanted you to be tried for burglary. He says some sheets of plywood were missing from his project. But, since he has no witnesses and cannot provide proof, I have downgraded your charges to misdemeanor trespassing and I have found you guilty". "I don't know anything about stealing any wood" I replied angrily. "Like I said, son. Your case is now over. If you"d like to continue to waste the court"s time, I can certainly entertain and revisit the burglary charges if you"d like to continue to argue". I looked over to my dad again and this time the lawyer was shaking his head and motioning for me to come over to him. "No, your honor. I'm finished here" I said. "Good" he replied frustrated. "Now, leave this court room and be on your way". I walked back to my father, got the required fine from him, paid it, and stood by my attorney as he tried to advise me about proper court etiquette in the future. "Ronald" he said. "You simply must show the judge more respect. When he addresses you, never interrupt him and stay quiet unless he asks you a question". "But, he was wrong" I replied. "We didn't steal any plywood. That owner was just trying to scarf some free money. I don't like being accused of something I didn't do". "Be it that it may" he said. "You can't win against him. That is what you pay people like me for". "Well" I whispered "That rule needs to change and is a bunch of bullshit". "The attorney turned to my father. "You"ve got a real firecracker here" he said. "I hope he changes his ways". Yes, he can be quite tenacious" my dad replied. "I'll have a talk with him at home about it later. The talk never came. What I learned from that encounter was, the people in power are sometimes hypocrites and to always question authority. I had many more inquiries that remained.

Jesse, Dennis and I were riding around in Jesse"s older sister's car. She had a prescription for black beauties. So, we rode with her to her doctor in South Amboy to pick them up. She came back after a half hour and handed us some. "You're only getting 2 each" she said. "Because, I don't need anyone tweaking and I didn't get as many this time". She handed them to Jesse and Jesse doled them out Dennis and I. We thanked her and we drove back to Edison to cruise around. Along the way, after we had gobbled them down, I announced that I had some tabs of acid on me. "Who wants to trip tonight?" I asked jokingly. "You have Cid on you, man?" Jesse asked. "Of course" I chuckled. "We're gonna be up all night anyway. So, we might as well add to the beauties". "What do you think, Den?" asked Jesse with his arm hanging over the back seat. "Do you think we should do some or not?" "I'll take a hit if you guys do" Dennis remarked. "Because, I'm not tripping alone". Jesse asked his sister while still driving "No" she said. "Somebody has to babysit you guys if you're on that shit. It's not my thing anyway. Plus, I'm not gonna attempt to drive while seeing shapes bending all over the place. You guys go ahead and have fun". I reached into my pocket I allocated one blotter paper each. "Let the games begin" Jesse laughed. "It's gonna be a long night fellas. If he only knew.

At about 11 o"clock that evening, we ended up cruising down a street in Piscataway. It was Mischief Night and the evening before Halloween. We saw the occasional toilet paper strewn over homeowner"s trees but we didn't think anything else about it. Suddenly, we heard a loud thud. "What the fuck was that?" asked Jesse. "I think it was a rock" his sister replied. "Stop the car, stop the car" he howled. "I wanna see if anything hit us or not?" When the vehicle came to a screeching halt, he hopped out to the rear. "Motherfuckers!" he shrieked. "There's a dent in my sister's car now". He turned his head forward and exclaimed "I see them! I see those little scumbags jumping over a fence back that yard!" He vaulted back into the car and demanded that his sister chase them. By now, we were tripping our asses off and Dennis and I couldn't stop laughing. "Get them, Jesse. Urrhhh" Dennis said making a sound like someone goading a dog. "Get them and beat their asses".

As we got closer, Jesse motioned for his sister to stop. "Right there" he screamed. "Stop right there by that log looking fence". As he flung open the passenger side door, he yelled back at me and Dennis "Come on you guys, let's get these kids". Since my leg still wasn't completely healed from my forklift accident, they ran way ahead of me. I limped as I ran as best I could to keep up with them. When I got to the curb in front of the barrier, Dennis was standing there and looking around. "What the fuck"s going on?" I asked. "I saw you guys running, where'd Jesse go?" "He jumped over that fence chasing them" he replied. "I decided to stay here. I didn't feel like going on someone else"s property". Just then, I heard the sound of a child crying and it sounded like a little boy. "Owww, owww. Please stop, we didn't mean to do it, owwww!" After a half a minute or so, Jesse returned and hopped back over the fence toward us. He had obvious blood stains on his knuckles. "I beat that little fucker"s ass" he said triumphantly. "Him and his jerkoff friends were throwing rocks at cars. They picked the wrong car tonight to try to do that shit." "What did you do to him?" I asked. "I punched him in his fucking head a few times, bro" he replied. "He deserved it. He could have broken the glass in my sister's car and really hurt one of us. So, I had to teach him a lesson". "What about his friends?" Dennis asked "Did you slam them too?" "Nah, man" Jesse answered. "The other ones got away. But, this one was too slow. So, too bad for him. I bet he'll never throw rocks at cars again though". "Well, I think we should go back to your sister and get out of here" I warned. "Because, someone might call the cops". "Good idea" Dennis said. "We better go".

After we had driven from the scene and were travelling back to the direction of Edison, we heard sirens in the distance. "Maybe an ambulance is coming to pick up that little asshole" Jesse laughed. "He might need a few stitches". "You must have really hammered him, huh bro?" Dennis asked. "He'll live" Jesse chuckled. "It's the price you pay for being stupid. All kids need to learn how to take a beating". As we came to a red light to stop, the sirens were getting closer. "You better floor it" Jesse instructed his sister. "They might be after us instead". At the border where Piscataway and Edison converge, we were suddenly surrounded by police cars. "Stop the car and shut off the engine" a voice commanded from a cruiser. Looking out from the back window, I could see we were about to be detained. "What the fuck do these clowns want?" Jesse asked. "I bet that kid's parents called the cops on us, bro" Dennis replied. "Don't say anything" Jesse"s sister cautioned. "These idiots are just looking for an arrest". As the cops came closer to the vehicle, they screamed for us not to make any sudden moves. They swung open each door and pulled us out to the ground. "Stay right here" one of them barked. "Until we tell you to stand up". I glanced over to my left and saw Jesse"s sister being treated slightly better than we were. She was allowed to sit on the curb instead. Another officer came over and demanded that we stand. "Here they are Lieutenant" he said. "I have them lined up for you". Before us, stood a short, slightly overweight cop wearing a white polyester shirt with a gold badge affixed to it. "Do you know who I am?" he shouted. "I'm the head honcho of the Piscataway police department and we received a call that a young boy was battered by some older kids. Your car fits the description. The boy was assaulted badly and had to be taken to the hospital for medical attention. We're going to find out if any of you were involved or not, ok?" None of said a word and stared down at the street ignoring him. "Stick out your hands" he demanded. "I want you to stick out your arms and show us your hands. Hold them out so I can see them. If I see blood on any of them, I know it was one of you". "I don't have any blood on my hands" I blurted. "Well" the Lieutenant said. "You are one of the people who chased the kid, so you're still involved". "I didn't chase anyone" I replied. "My foot was crushed in an accident. So, there's no way I could have chased after anybody". "I'll be the judge of that" he remarked. "Now, stick out your hands and shut up"

Like a scene from a 3 Stooges comedy film, we stuck out our limbs for inspection. Jesse was on the left, I was in the middle, and Dennis was on my right. The Lieutenant examined us one by one. Dennis was first. "Nope, no blood stains here" he said. "Next". He got to me and grabbed my right hand up to the light. "Are you right handed or left handed?" he asked. "I'm right handed" I replied. He peered at my left hand and remarked "Nothing here either". Then, it was Jesse"s turn. "Bring that flashlight over here" he howled. "I think we've got him". Jesse held out his hands while the cop looked closely. "You"ve got that kid's blood all over your right hand, asshole" he screamed. "You're coming with us". "I don't know what the fuck you're talking about" Jesse said. "I cut myself earlier today fixing a car". "Bullshit!" hollered the Lieutenant. "You picked the wrong kid to beat up on. He was sleeping over my son"s house in a tent in the backyard with his friends. There is no reason why you had to beat him up so badly". "You fucking cops are crazy" Jesse yelled. "I wasn't anywhere near there tonight". Seething with anger and visibly shaken, the cop instructed his cronies to seat us in the back of a patrol car while they took Jesse away. "Where are you taking my friend?" I asked. "Don't worry about it" a patrolman said. "You'll see later". While shackled together with cuffs behind us, Dennis and I could hear someone screaming in the distance. "I wonder what that is?" Dennis asked. "I dunno" I replied. "But, I'm tripping my balls off". "So am I" he said. "This shit is kind of funny". Due to the intense effects of the drug, we began laughing hysterically. Suddenly, the back door swung open and Jesse was thrown in on his side. We couldn't help ourselves and laughed even harder. "Ron" Jesse moaned obviously in pain. "The cops handcuffed me to a tree and beat the fuck out of me" "Holy shit" Dennis exclaimed. "I hope We're not next, bro". "No" Jesse replied. "They blamed me because they found the kids blood on my hand". "Straighten that bastard up" the Lieutenant demanded. "He needs to be sitting straight up in his seat". After settling Jesse in, we were driven to the police station for interrogation.

After being dragged out of the back of the police car, we were escorted to a holding area in front of a large desk. There was an officer on duty that started asking us questions. "You guys are in big trouble" he said. "That kid who you beat up? His father is on his way down here. I"d hate to be one of you if he got ahold of me". "I don't know what you're talking about" I replied. "I said it before, and I'll say it again. I didn't chase anybody". Just then, another cop strolled in and pointed at me. "Check out this one"s shirt" he chuckled. "It's got a big marijuana leaf on it. What do those words say around it, sonny?" he asked. "It says Marijuana Pickers Local Growers Number 13" I answered. "Why?" "Number 13?" he asked. "Didn't you know that's an unlucky number? Because, you hit the big one tonight. All of you are going to jail". The first cop guffawed "You should have picked a better number". "Take them into the search area" the duty officer instructed. "We have to strip search them for drugs". We were stood up, told to walk in single file, and entered a changing room with lockers against a wall. "Take off all of your clothes until you're naked" the cop demanded. "And then, lean up with your palms up against one of those lockers and spread your legs". "I wonder if they're gonna molest us" Dennis whispered laughing. Another cop entered the room to assist. "This one"s a wise guy" the first cop said. "So, make sure you run your fingers sufficiently through his afro". "This one wants to be a hairdresser, Den" I chuckled. "You better guard your privates". I suddenly felt a hard smack to the back of my head. "Shut the fuck up, hippie" the 2nd cop warned. "You're here to be frisked, not to talk". After we were forced to spread our cheeks and cough to prove we weren't hiding anything, we were ordered to get redressed. "Come with me back to the holding area out front" the 1st officer motioned. "We have to process you and then put you in a cell". We sat down where we were initially and the duty cop addressed us again. "Two of you got no bail because you are juveniles. But, Arold here is over 18. So, you have to sit inside until the judge grants you your bail. You other two can go home after your parents arrive to get you". "Lucky me" I thought. "My father's gonna love me again with this one". An hour went by and I kept looking back at the clock over the duty officer"s head. "It feels like we've been here for a long ass time" I said to Dennis. "I hope we don't have to sit here forever". Then, I heard a commotion going on outside the station"s entrance. There was a lot of yelling from someone asking "Where is he? I'm going to kill that fucker!" The door opened and in came a short little boy of about 10 years old with a gauze bandage wrapped around his head. It had blood stains on it and he was crying. His father was accompanying him and he was wailing with anger. He glanced over at us and was screaming "Show me that kid who beat up my son?" he asked "I want to see him right now!" "We have to take you into another room" the duty cop said. "Let us have your son identify who it was first. Then, We'll come and get you". When the father was absent from the room, the Lieutenant appeared again and was holding the little boy's hand. "Now, tell me" he asked. "Which one of these kids is the one that beat you up? Was it one of them? Or, all of them? The boy shook his head as if he was agreeing with all of them. "Me?" I asked. "Tell the truth kid" I said. "You didn't see me do anything to you, did you? I couldn't have beaten on you because I wasn't even there. I can't even run!" The Lieutenant was unfazed. "Do like he says" he said. "Point to the one who did this to you?" The little boy lifted his right arm and stuck his finger out at Jesse. "Good, good" the Lieutenant said. "Don't be afraid. I'm gonna take you back to your dad now". Visibly upset and still crying, the Lieutenant took the boy and left the room. "Fuck that kid" Jesse whispered. "What the fuck was he doing out so late at night throwing rocks at cars with his friends? Bad fucking parenting, man. But, these jerkoffs blame me though, right? He wouldn't have gotten his ass beat if he was in bed where he should have been. Fucking assholes!" "You better be quiet, Jess" remarked Dennis. "They"ve got his dad in the other room". "Fuck these cops and fuck him too. I didn't do anything except defend my sister's property". "Where is she anyway?" I asked. "They took her into a separate area because she's a female" Jesse replied. "But, it's better this way anyway. That way, they can't fuck with our stories".

I heard the door creak open and the Lieutenant had returned. "You're coming with me" he pointed at Jesse. "This kid's father wants to have words with you". He grabbed Jesse by his arm and got him to his feet forcing him back through the door. Jesse didn't say a word. While Dennis and I were still seated and making small talk about our situation, we could hear bumps and muffled talking sounds from afar. "I bet they're beating Jesse"s ass again" Dennis said. "That was a smooth move interrogating that kid about you" he laughed. "I didn't think of that one, bro". "My dad as you know can be a strict disciplinarian" I replied. "So, sometimes I have to think fast to avoid getting a beating". "True enough" he answered. "I just hope they don't kill Jesse".

Some time passed and we no longer heard anymore sounds coming from beyond the door. The door creaked open again and they were bringing back Jesse in a heap. His face was bruised and he appeared as if he had a slight black eye. The cops escorting him left and Jesse sat once again moaning. "The kid's father punched me in the face a few times" he mumbled. "But, I told him his kid deserved it and to go fuck himself. So, they held me down again and that fucker railed on me. It's ok though, man. Because, I can take a beating and that guy hits like a pussy". "Damn, Jesse" I said. "Why didn't you just keep your mouth shut on this one?" "Fuck that shit" he yelled. "These fucking cops abuse their authority. If that kid wasn't sleeping over the Lieutenant"s son"s house, none of this bullshit would have happened. Fuck the police" "Simmer down now, sonny" the desk cop commanded. "You shouldn't have done what you did to him. That's why you're here" "Oh yeah" Jesse remarked sarcastically. "Well, fuck you too".

Eventually, we were taken to our cells and separated. When we arrived, Jesse"s sister was already in her"s across the hall and we could see and talk to her from about 10 feet away. The cells we were put in were shaped like an "L" with Jesse and Dennis on the right and me on the left. After the cop clanged the doors shut, he began making fun of me. There was a passed out man with a huge egg shaped bump on his head lying on the lower bunk bed sleeping underneath me. "Don't wake that guy up, fellas" the cop chuckled teasing. "He was real drunk last night and very angry. We beat his ass to get him to comply. I"d hate to see him come after you when he wakes up if you piss him off". The cop left and Dennis and Jesse started to make whooping sounds. "Hey, man. Wake up!" they screamed. "Ron here wants to fight you". They were getting much pleasure out of irritating me and thought it was hilariously funny. "Shut the fuck up, you guys" I said. "I'm stuck in here with this guy with no way out. And, you know if we fight, the cops won't come back here to break it up" "Ahhh, hahaha!" Jesse laughed "Check out Ron being all scared and shit". "I'm not afraid of anything" I replied. "It's just that I'm coming down from that acid and I don't feel like grappling with some old guy". "We're only gonna fuck with you a little while longer, man" Dennis said. "We just wanted to see you freak out". "I hope you guys are having fun then" I said. "Because, I have all of the cigarettes and the lighter and you have none." "So, who"s laughing now?" I asked. "We better leave him alone, Den" Jesse said. "Or else We'll be Jonesing for smokes". "Ok, Ron" Dennis remarked. "You give us a couple of ciggies each and We'll stop". "What about me?" asked Jesse"s sister from across the hall. "I need some too". "Gimme a couple of extras, Ron?" Jesse asked. "I'm gonna see if I can roll them over to her". "Are you serious?" Dennis asked. "I gotta see this!" Jesse bent down on one knee and carefully positioned a cigarette so that with one tap of his finger, it would roll down the floor"s incline. Incredulous at this venture, I murmured "It'll never make it; you're wasting your time, man". "You won't know unless you try" Jesse replied. "Give it a shove" Dennis said. "If it makes it, I'll be shocked".

Jesse gave the ciggie a light tap and it slowly began its descent. It was sluggish at first, but picked up speed as it moved. "Go ciggie, go" Jesse remarked. "You can do it". Finally, and with many a bounce, it landed within reach of his sister. "Slide the lighter over next" she said. "I gotta have something to spark it with". "This will be much easier" Jesse said. "Just make sure you give it back when you're done". After Jesse got the lighter back, Dennis was examining the ceiling. There seemed to be many soot burns from previous prisoner"s lighters that they had made their initials with. ""Ullllhhh" Dennis exclaimed. "Hand me that torch, bro" he asked Jesse. "I'm gonna make sure these clowns know I was here". "Cool" Jesse replied. "I'm gonna do mine next. I need to leave my badge of courage". "Save some fuel for me" I suggested. "I wanna do one too". When all of our monograms were inscribed and in place, a new officer came in with some news. He was facing Dennis and Jesse with some kind of paper in his hand. "You guys get to leave" he announced. "DenniS's mother is here to release him. Fortunately for Jesse, DenniS's mother is also willing to take responsibility for him. So, you're both coming with me and you will be leaving together. "Adios, Ronnie" Jesse chuckled. "I guess We'll see you later. My sister will still be here though at the end of the hall. So, you can just talk to her instead". "Ok fellas" I responded. "I guess I'll see you guys later. "Whatever you do" Dennis said. "Don't wake that guy up with that enormous bump on his head". "Yeah" said Jesse laughing. "He might wake up really pissed off. Don't try to aggravate him, bro". "Fuck that!" I said. "I'm gonna go to sleep until my father gets here to bail me out". They wished me luck and left.

Jesse"s sister didn't say much afterward other than to ask me for an occasional cigarette. Eventually later in the afternoon, she too had been granted bail and was released. Her boyfriend had shown up to retrieve her. I was beginning to get worried and was wondering what was taking my parents so long. I had fallen asleep for a while and the attending cop came back to give me a message. "Wake up!" he said. "I have something to tell you". "What's that?" I asked. "My father is here to bail me out, right?" "No, sorry" he replied. Unfortunately for you, we haven"t been able to get a response from them, so if we can't get in touch with them by 5 PM, the bus will be coming here to transport you to the workhouse in North Brunswick". "I thought you had to hold me for 24 hours first?" I asked concerned. "Not on the weekends" he responded. "It's Friday night now. So, I suggest you get ready for your move. I'll be back later to come and get you once the bus is here". "Great! Just fucking great" I thought as he left. "This is gonna suck big time". To add more insult to my grave predicament, the guy below me with the egg sized boil on his head was starting to come too. I could hear him stirring and he was mumbling to himself. "Jesus Christ" he moaned. "Where the fuck am I?" Trying to break the ice and not exasperate the situation, I leaned over looking down at him acting concerned about his condition. "Hey, buddy" I said. "Are you ok?" I asked. "You"ve got a pretty large bump there on your head. Are you gonna be all right?" "All I remember was that I was at a party last night" he replied. "And, I've got a hell of a hangover right now. I think I got into a fight with some cops. I got a few swings in I can recall. But, that's about it". "Yeah, no offense" I said. "But, it looks like they got the better of you" He then laughed and began to smile. "I think I got my ass beat last night" he chuckled softly touching his head. "Anyway, what's your name?" he asked. "My name"s Charlie" "I extended my arm and we shook hands. I told him my story and how the both of us were gonna be going to the corrections center in about 15 minutes if we couldn't secure bail. Suddenly, the duty officer came back in. "I have good news for the both of you" he said. Mr. Arold, your father is here. He paid your $150 bail and you're being released". "Mr. Charlie?" he asked. "You won't have any bail and are being released on your own recognizance. It seems you were very intoxicated last night, got into a fight defending a friend, and you only got injured by us because you refused to let the other guy go. Therefore, you"ve only been charged with public intoxication. Now, I have to remove Arold here first. So, I'll be back for you Charlie later". "Well" I said. "It was nice meeting you briefly Charlie. I hope I never have to see you under these circumstances again. "Likewise" he replied. "I'll see you later".

A few months in the future Dennis and Jesse had to appear in juvenile court to face the charges. Dennis told me the kid Jesse had given a beating to had never shown up to testify. The story supposedly was that the boy didn't want to relive the episode and his parents thought it would have been too traumatic for him. When I spoke to Jesse about it, he said "Traumatic my ass! I'll tell you what really happened, bro. They thought about it for a few months. Then, the kid told them more truthful details and they figured out the little fucker was lying. So, we got arrested and went to court for nothing. Now, you know why I hate the fucking cops, man". Jesse"s sister was summoned to court to face the same. But, I hid out and never appeared. For some reason a warrant was never put out for my arrest and Jesse"s sister was forced to forfeit her bail money. She blamed me but I never knew why. Jesse told me not to worry about it because they dropped her charges anyway. Dennis told me later about something that night that none of us knew. "Remember when they had us naked up against those lockers, bro?" he asked. "Yeah" I replied. They were checking out your fro pretty thoroughly from what I saw". "Well" he laughed "I had a joint hidden in there and they never found it". Amazed at this I asked "How come when we were in the cells you never took it out?" "I simply forgot about it" he chuckled. "Jesse and I were having too much fun joking about other things". "You're a good hider, Den" I replied. "Imagine what they would have done to you if they would have found it?" "I don't wanna even think about it" he replied. "After that ordeal, I never want to go back to Piscataway again".

I came home from being out carousing one day and my mother had said she had some bad news. Apparently we would be moving soon as my father had lost his business. It seemed all of his clients closed all at once and there was nothing he could do about it. Soon, our cupboards were just as bare and I had to pilfer deliveries for myself and not just for my friends. My father made sure there was an ample amount of hotdogs, hamburgers, and chicken. But, there would be no more extravagant vacations, steak dinners, going out to eat, or seafood. "It was time to tighten our belts" he said. Being hit with this out of the blue, I knew exactly what had to be done. Knowing we could no longer purchase higher luxuries, I knew damn well there wouldn't be any more cakes, Danishes, rolls, milk, orange juice, breads, or pies. I would have to rely on the same schemes I afforded my friends and was resigned to do so. Like a bi pedal contortionist, I tied heavy test fishing line to the back of my bicycle"s banana seat and made lightning fast trips to the back of the Acme supermarket. There, I would scan the crates with my eyes for the best selection possible. Usually, I"d have 2 gallons of milk on my left side, and 2 of orange juice on the other. It was sometimes time consuming to tie up the containers without cutting up my fingers from the thin monofilament line. That was the part that frightened me the most. If the capers were going to apprehend me, it would have been then. Fortunately on these many trips, my timing was exquisite and I was never caught. Just as the sun was peeking its head over the horizon, I would pedal as fast as I could toward home. It must have been comical to be seen as I looked like a top heavy whale bouncing around in the ocean and trying to get my bearings at the same time. I remember feeling like a cork or a bobber trying desperately to keep my center of gravity lest I"d fall over and have to start all over again. The gallons weighed heavily dangling off my legs as I pedaled furiously attempting my escape. It was a struggle to keep my bike level, but I did it all the same. When I reached TJ I knew I was safe. It was a short cycle to the other side of the field where I knew I"d be free. Once home, one of my parents would usually be awake and would give me the obligatory speech about how I shouldn't steal and that sooner or later I would be captured. I would shrug my shoulders and lie and tell tall tales about how "All of my friends have been doing it and they simply divided up the booty for my services of being a look out and nothing more". I would get no reply and silence as they climbed back up the stairs and back into their bedroom. I guessed concessions would be made now that we were poor.

On a slightly rainy night, Georgie Burns and I were leaning on the bumper on the back of a delivery truck in Desti"s parking lot and were deciding what we were going to do. I glanced over and saw a parking spot with lettering spray painted on the fence behind it. It read "This spot is for Frank M. only. No one else is allowed to park here. Don't get caught!" I thought to myself "Well, that's kind of arrogant. But, if anyone knew the M. brothers, it was best to steer clear of them anyway". My older brother had told me stories about how one of the brothers had held up the Chestnut bar with a shotgun. Supposedly, the owner of the bar reached for something and one of these brothers had shot him dead in retaliation. He had also shot the owner"s dog. Later after he was caught and there was a lengthy trial, the shooter was adjudicated not guilty and walked away. On the court house steps, when he was asked by a reporter if he had really done it or not, he exclaimed "Yeah, I fucking did it, so what? The owner reached for a gun. What was I supposed to do? Stand there without protecting myself? I don't care as I can't be tried twice due to the double jeopardy law. The owner could have avoided it if he would have just given me the money". Another brother I had heard had died in the Middlesex County Correction Center. I was told his liver had exploded and he wasn't afforded medical attention in time to save him. When I came back from reflecting on this, Georgie had conjured up an idea of the possibility of seeing what was inside of the truck. He pointed at the shiny metal clasp that had been threaded through the hole in the locking mechanism and asked me how hard it would be to remove. "It's flimsy aluminum" I replied. "They put these here to show they"ve been inspected". "Let's take it off and see what's in there?" Georgie asked. "Maybe it's something good. It doesn't look like the driver is coming back any time soon. He's probably in the bar drinking". Before I had a chance to attempt to open it, a car came careening into the lot straight for us. Its driver flung open the door and screamed "freeze". He had a gun in between his hands and was aiming at our heads. "Don't move" he yelled. I knew right away he had to be a cop. "I was observing you the entire time from down the street" he said. "I saw you guys trying to break into that truck". "You're crazy" I replied. "We weren't doing anything" "Bullshit!" he howled. "I saw you trying to open that lock. You were about to twist that thing so you could get in". "Wow!" Georgie replied. "Someone didn't eat their Wheaties this morning" "Shut up, you punk" the cop yelled. "You're both under arrest".

As he approached and got closer, I recognized him right away. It was Sergeant Q. from my rooftop escapade earlier. He was familiar with me as well. "Look who we have here" he laughed. "It's Arold again". "You just can't stay out of trouble can you?" "Trouble for what?" I asked. "For leaning up against a truck?" "You weren't leaning up against anything" he said. "You were trying to rob it". "You're out of your skull" I said. "Good luck proving that shit". "And, what's with pointing your gun at us?" I asked. "Do we scare you that much?" "Just turn around and assume the position" he barked. "You know what to do" As Georgie and I were placed into the back of the unmarked patrol car, another vehicle showed up for back up. "What We're they trying to steal?" asked the driver of the patrol cruiser. "It looks like the truck is full of Brillo pads" laughed Sergeant Q." "So, we've got The Brillo Pad kid and his cohort tonight". Sergeant Q. got in behind the wheel and began to tease us. "You're going down for multiple charges this time kids" he chuckled. "And, I'm gonna make sure this time it sticks. You're not gonna get away with it like the last arrest. No expensive attorney from your father will save you now. I've got you both by the balls. Burglary one, which is a felony, loitering to commit a crime, malicious mischief, and anything else I can dream up against you. You're mine now". "Yeah, yeah, yeah" I said. What's the matter? I asked. "Are you still pissed off about the mud you got on your pants from the last time?" "You're lucky I'm not on patrol alone tonight" he jabbered. "Because, there would have been a lesson to be learned for you". Georgie was apprehensive about talking back and was whispering to me to be quiet. "If you keep it up" he said. "He's just going to keep on stacking up charges, man". "Georgie, We're already fucked" I replied. "This cop is an asshole. He's on a power trip and doesn't care".

After being held for a while, Georgie went home first and I was released later. To my surprise, I wasn't thrown down the police station stairs this time and was granted bail much sooner. When my court date came, for some reason Sergeant Q. kept postponing and I felt he was doing it on purpose to aggravate me. Finally, on the 3rd go around, he decided to show up. My father still had a little money and hired me an even better lawyer than the one who had defeated Sergeant Q. before. Unbeknownst to Sergeant Q., my attorney had gone to Desti"s parking area and had taken pictures and measurements as evidence to disprove the officer"s claims. It had become abundantly clear we had caught him lying. Not surprised by Sergeant Q"s corruption, we waited in court for our chance to make a fool out of him once again. Since one of my charges was a felony, we were forced to wait until the court"s docket was cleared before we could finally be heard. When my name was called, my attorney approached the podium and set up an easel with a storyboard and graphics. He was to present my side of the story and evidence to prove the same. I was called to testify first and rightfully denied everything I had been accused of. Frustrating the prosecutor, the alcoholic judge asked to move the trial along faster. My attorney called Sergeant Q. to the stand and interrogated him at length. "Tell us Sergeant Q.?" he asked. "Exactly where did you see the defendant as you claim while you were sitting in your patrol car observing the situation?" "I was 10 feet behind the stop sign on my right" he replied. "So?" my attorney asked using a pointing device as reference. "Here, right here is where you claim your vehicle was parked? Is that right, officer?" "Yes, yes" Sergeant Q. replied. "That's correct. I was able to observe everything the defendant was doing right up until his infraction". "Alleged infraction your honor" my lawyer corrected. "Yes" Sergeant Q. replied visibly agitated. "His alleged infraction". Where are you going with this counselor?" the judge demanded. "You need to get to the point, sir" he said. "It's getting late and we need to finish this". "All right your honor" my attorney chuckled. "I'll get right to the point". Sergeant Q.?" he asked smiling. "Please tell us by the obvious measurements on this graph I am pointing at, how you were able to observe my client? When there's no physical way you could have seen him as there is a corner of a building to your left as indicated here that would have obstructed your vision on that night from where you say you were sitting?" "I was 10 feet behind the stop sign as I have listed in my report" Sergeant Q. responded. "Impossible your honor!" my attorney quipped. "Sergeant Q. is grossly mistaken. From where he was, the stop sign is not 10 feet from the parking lot, but it is actually 20 feet. If Sergeant Q. was indeed at those coordinates, the left side of this building from that far back obstructed his view. "The counselor is correct" blurted the judge. "Do you have anything to refute this evidence Sergeant?" he asked. Sergeant Q. was now fuming "No your honor, not at this time". "In that case, the charges against Mr. Arold are dismissed. You can all go home now". Sergeant Q. left the witness box and was walking by us sulking. I looked him straight in the eye and winked. My father was making some comments and made sure the officer heard him "Maybe he should have kept a tape measure in his trunk" he laughed. "So he wouldn't have to go to so many lengths the next time". It was the funniest court appearance I had ever made.

Eventually, the day came when my parents were forced to give our house back to the bank and we had to move. My father rented a house at 87 Brookhill Rd. not too far from our original location. Since my older brother had moved out months before, I would finally have my very own bedroom and would no longer be relegated to sleeping in the basement. I liked my new bedroom as it was large and had one big window facing the backyard. After we made the move and my parent"s bank took possession, Jesse and I would sneak back to my old house and enter through a broken cellar window that hadn't been repaired for years. It had become our favorite "party house" and I had become comfortable using it behind the lending institution"s back. I had many memories there and felt it was my personal revenge to get back at them. We didn't wreck the place, but we didn't care if we tipped over a beer or burned the carpets with cigarettes either. It was also a great place to hide out from the cold weather and have some privacy when we wanted to bang some girls. Jesse had brought along a young girl one night and had brought her to my parent"s old bedroom upstairs. I waited down below singing songs to myself and sipping on some Michelob beers. Sitting on the bare carpet where the furniture used to be, I looked up at the ceiling and could still see the faux beams my dad had installed there earlier. Now, they were a remnant of themselves and just a memory. Like a bad hand dealt in life, one of them was hanging down disconnected and dangling just above the floor. I felt sad that my parents had paid for the house for so long and didn't think it fair it was being taken away from them. "Fucking banks" I murmured. "I fucking hate them!" Just then, Jesse had come back downstairs with the girl in tow. Right in front of her he exclaimed "This chick is worthless, bro. She doesn't want to do nothing. I'm leaving, man. Have at her if you want. I'll see you later". He promptly went out the back door and left."What happened with him?" I asked. "You didn't like him?" "It wasn't that" she said. "I was giving him a hand job, but he wanted me to blow him. I'm still a virgin and I don't know how to do any of those things. I was embarrassed that I wouldn't be able to do it right the first time. So, I told him no. That's when he got angry with me and told me he was leaving". "Well, why don't you sit down here next to me and help me finish these beers" I said. "You'll probably feel better after you relax". "That sounds like a good idea" she replied. "As long as you don't try anything". "Nah" I said. "I'm just sitting here reminiscing. I used to live here you know?" I proceeded to tell her the entire story to the point where she had forgotten about her tryst with Jesse. She began to sit closer to me and started to rub my leg. "You listen really well" she said. "You seem like a pretty cool guy. After what happened with Jesse, I was gonna wait to have sex. But, I like you a lot". "Well, thanks" I replied. "I just like to help people out sometimes". "How would you like to help me some more?" she asked. "Like how?" I questioned. "You wanna fuck me?" she asked. "But, remember? I'm a virgin. So, you're gonna have to go real slow". I don't know what it is with virgins. But, they have always been attracted to me. "It must be the empathy" I thought. "If you're sure that's what you want?" I asked. "And, it doesn't mean I'll be your boyfriend or anything after" "No, it's ok" she replied. "I'm gonna have to do it sooner or later anyway". "Ask and you shall receive" I chuckled. "You have a rubber though, right?" she pleaded. "Why certainly" I joked. "I never leave home without it". I deflowered her as she requested and walked her home. A couple of days later, Jesse asked me "Did you get with that chick? She was too tight and I couldn't get it in, bro. That's why I left". "That's not what she told me" I laughed. "She said you got mad because she wouldn't give you a BJ". "What a liar" he chuckled. "I must have hurt her trying to go in. Anyway, bro. I'm glad you got some. I wasn't in the mood to argue with her". "Well, thanks for the misguided opportunity" I replied. "I love being handed seconds". "It couldn't have been seconds cause you got to be first" he said. "I merely opened her door for you". "Thanks for the key, then" I laughed. "What are friends for" he said. "You owe me one".

Georgie Burns had called me up and said he knew some guys who had a band and they needed a lead singer. He had told them about me and my previous group and that he thought that I was a pretty good vocalist. They wanted to know if I was interested and if I would audition. I asked where the band was from and who the members were. "I don't think you know any of them" he said. "But, Paulee B. knows them and went to the same high school when he moved to North Brunswick for a while. So, it should be a breeze. Why don't you let me make the arrangements, man?" he asked. "If you feel funny about it, I'll come with you as I've met some of these guys before". "I think I can do that" I replied. "As long as they're laid back, I''d be willing to check it out". "Ok" he said. "I'll call them back and We'll go over there this Saturday". I agreed and hung up. The day came and Georgie and I managed to get a ride to check out the gig. We knocked on the front door and a middle aged woman answered instructing us to go down into the basement adjacent to the 2 car garage. "My sons Dave and Donny are down there" she said. "They are waiting on you. So, go ahead down and tell them who you are" "Thank you, maam" we replied and walked down the outside stairs. There, I met a guy named Dave the lead guitar player, his brother Donny the drummer, Jim the rhythm guitarist, and Ted the bass player. Dave came right up and shook my hand and it appeared to me that he was their leader. "Georgie here tells me you have a pretty good voice" he said. "What kind of tunes do you know?" "The Stones, Aerosmith, Kiss, Bowie, Lynyrd Skynyrd, you name it" I replied. "Well, we won't be playing any Kiss" he laughed. "But, if you sing Aerosmith, Aerosmith we like. So, let's give it a whirl and see what you"ve got. If we feel you can handle it you're in, ok?"

We played a few Aerosmith covers along with a few others and I felt I aced it. "You"ve got some fucking voice" Dave said. "And, you can scream too. Give me a few minutes to talk to the other guys. Go outside and wait for us. We'll be out in a little bit with our decision". Georgie and I waited as I bit my fingernails in anticipation. "Did you see all of the gear and amps those guys have?" he asked. "Yeah, I saw it all" I replied nervously. "They"ve got a hell of a lot nicer equipment than the last band I was in". "I hope they let you in" he exclaimed. "I think this is just what you need. These guys are really good, man". In my mind, Georgie had a point to a certain extent. Dave was a way more accomplished guitar player than Tony had been and was on a whole other level. Even on my first visit, to me he was a virtuoso. Where Tony sometimes struggled, Dave was playing songs with ease. It was as if he was naturally gifted and could copy anything he heard with just one review. "Still" I thought. "It has to be a good fit" I thought "I need to have the same camaraderie I had with the other guys before they moved to Florida". Soon, Dave and the rest of the band came outside. As each one came over to congratulate me and shake my hand, Dave announced. "Welcome to our band, man. It looks like you're our new lead singer. Practice is twice a week. It's usually every Thursday and Saturday. I'm gonna give you a list of songs we already do. Take the list home and rehearse them and try to memorize as many as you can. When you come back, We'll be ready for you". As I was thanking them for the opportunity and gazed down at the list, I thought "Memorize them? They don't know I have a photographic memory and I already know more than half of this material". Even so, I was relieved with the tunes they had chosen as it pretty on par with what I wanted to do. "Thanks, man" I said. "I guess I'll see you all next week". "You got it" Dave said. "And, thanks for coming by".

I was hanging around again with Dave G. a lot and sleeping over his house on the weekends. One Saturday night, Georgie Burns accompanied us for a sleepover and we bunkered down in Dave"s living room. At the time, Dave"s house was the only one on the block that had the new cable channel called HBO. Georgie and I were ecstatic as no one else we knew had cable services and we couldn't wait to watch the latest full length movies on TV. While staring at the screen and lounging in a reclining chair, Dave blurted out "I wanna go through my mom"s medicine cabinet in the bathroom to see if there's anything in there worth taking. Which one of you guys will volunteer to be the guinea pig?" he asked. "It all depends on what it is" I replied. "If I recognize it, I'm game. If I don't, no way". Georgie the ever curious spoke up "I'll do it" he said. "I'll check out whatever you"ve got. I don't care, I'll take it". "Ok, Georgie" Dave laughed. "The experimenter you will be". Dave got up from his seat and wandered off to his bathroom as Georgie and I sat and waited. While playing around with the TV channels, I noticed on a table next to Dave"s recliner there was a telephone that looked strange. It appeared as if it had the shape of a tulip flower on both ends and its base was the color of gold. When Dave returned, I asked him about it. "What kind of funky phone is that, man?" "Oh, that thing" he replied. "That's a French style aristocratic type phone". "When you speak into it, do you have to talk in French?" Georgie asked. "No, Georgie you dumb fuck" I laughed. "Just because it's in a French style it doesn't mean you have to do that". Dave finding this comical cackled "Now you know why we call you Georgie Burns, bro. Your brain is toast". Georgie with an incredulous look on his face asked "What? Did I say something funny?" "He just doesn't get it, does he, Ron?" Dave asked. "Ahh, leave him alone" I replied. "It's not his fault. He's Georgie Burns, he's always this way". "Well in that case" Dave said. "It won't hurt him to try any of these" Dave held out his hand and produced 3 pill bottles. "I don't know what any of these are" he said "But, feel free to open these babies up and try them". "Let me see those" I demanded. "I wanna see what names are on them. I might recognize a few before any one of us takes any of them". Dave handed the containers to me and I read their descriptions and examined them carefully. "Nope, don't know any of these" I exclaimed. "Ok, Georgie" Dave said. "Then, it's up to you". I held out the bottles in my palm and asked Georgie to choose one. "Eeeny, meiny, meiny, moe" he sang. When he got to moe, he picked up the jug and opened it. "Ohhh" he said "These are yellow ones". "Yellow ones?" I asked. "If those are yellow capsules, they are probably uppers". "My mom takes diet pills from the doctor"s". Dave giggled. "But, I didn't know which one of them are the right ones. So, that's why I brought back all of them to you". "Let's not take any of these until I find out what they are" I suggested. "I have a physician"s desk reference book at home from when I worked at that vitamin plant. I'll write down what it says and let you know tomorrow". "Fuck that!" Dave howled. "I'm gonna take one of these right now then". "Let's wait until right before we go to sleep.

After we watch a movie" Georgie suggested. "That way, we can take some and see how we wake up".

Georgie tilted the vial gingerly and spilled a few capsules out into his palm. "Ok, man" he exclaimed. "Two each, right?" he asked. "That's right" laughed Dave. "Hand those suckers out". After we each took our required dose, we held them to ourselves until it was time for bed. "Welp" Dave announced. "That movie"s over. It's time to play pop goes the weasel and take these to see what happens in the morning". "You sure you wanna do this?" I asked. "What if we have a heart attack in our sleep?" "You"ve done speed before haven"t you?" he asked. "Why, yeah" I replied. "But, I never took them before I went to bed". "What's the worst that can happen?" he asked. "The shit will wake you up anyway. So, don't be a pussy and let's do this". "Ok" Georgie said. "But, I'm gonna need something to drink to wash them down with". "I'll be right back" Dave replied. Dave stood up and walked over to his kitchen and brought back two glasses of water. "Guzzle up" he chuckled. "We're about to go on the tweak express". We each took turns putting our capsules in our mouths and swallowing them in front of each other. Dave wanted to make sure nobody was cheeking them and trying to play it off. "That's right" he said. "No scheming to pretend. If I gotta take them, so do you guys". He shuffled over to a corner by the couch and came back with a couple of pillows and some blankets. Throwing them at us he laughed "Goodnight fellas. I'll see you in the morning". We situated ourselves on the carpet for the rest of the night while Dave insisted on sleeping in his recliner. I slowly drifted off to sleep and was hoping I would still wake up. Boy was I in for a surprise!

7am came and I could hear the distinct sound of birds chirping outside. I craned my neck to a picture window behind me and could see a beam of light shining down onto the floor. It was intertwined within the curtains and I could barely make out tiny dust particles dancing within its ray. Dave was stirring in his chair and began to stretch his arms out as he was awakening. I felt very tingly inside and my heart was beating a million miles an hour. I peered over at Georgie and he was still sound asleep. Dave turned his head to me and laughed. "That fucking kid can sleep through anything, bro. Even drugs don't affect him. I don't know about you, Ron but I'm speeding my balls off". "Me too, man". I replied. "What a way to wake up, huh?" "I guess we won't need any coffee" he grinned. "Because, I'm up and ready to go". "What about slow burn here?" I asked "What should we do with him?" "Wake his ass up" he instructed. "If we have to jet, so does he". I rolled over on my side and gave Georgie a gentle kick. "Wake up" I yelled. "Didn't you get off on those pills we took last night?" "I guess so" Georgie replied. "But, why did you kick me, man?" he asked. "I wasn't ready to get up yet". "Why not?" Dave asked aggravated. "I was having a cool assed dream" Georgie said. "I gotta hear this" I chuckled. "Tell us Georgie". "Well" he exclaimed. I was dreaming that I was in the shower at home. But, while I was in there, I fell asleep standing up and I was dreaming I was walking in the rain". Dave made a spitting sound with his mouth as if he was coughing something up. "What the fuck kind of dream is that?" he asked. "Did you dream you had soap too? Or, were you in a spa spraying yourself with lotion?" I was cracking up hysterically and waiting for Georgie"s answer. With one of those blank looks on his face he was known for, he offered "I don't know why I dream the dreams that I do. But, mine are always like that. They never make sense to me, man". "That's ok, Georgie" Dave laughed. "Because, you never make sense to anyone anyway you mumbling fuck". Dave turned to me "I think we've hit the jackpot with these, Ron. There's like 50 more of those babies in that bottle. I guess We're gonna be in a good mood for at least a week". "It looks that way" I replied. "And, thanks for giving them to us for free". "Oh, nothing"s free, bro" he howled. "You're both gonna owe me later". In the afternoon and farther on in the day, I went home to retrieve my PDR. On the prescription label I had read it said "Ionamin". I opened the book to research it and there it was, contraindications, suggested dosage, everything. On the last paragraph it read "Phentermine resin/amphetamine. Ionamin is a sympathomimetic amine with pharmacologic activity similar to the prototype drug of this class used in obesity, amphetamine (d- and dl-amphetamine). Actions include central nervous system stimulation and elevation of blood pressure." "Yup" I thought "Diet pills, just like Dave said". Later in the evening, we gathered back at Dave"s house for a round of cards. Dave absolutely loved the game and he was actually very good at it. There were more than a few times he had cleaned me out and had won the entire ante. On this night, we used Ionamin capsules to bet with. Dave wouldn't have had it any other way.

Ronnie E. and Mike W. had decided they wanted to enlist in the Navy. They asked me to accompany them to Loman"s Plaza in East Brunswick to do so. I had spoken to my father about it and he had assured me it might be the right thing for me to do. My dad was convinced if I became a professional musician or singer that I would always be poor and would probably amount to nothing. Taking him up on it, I decided to go with Ronnie and Mike to see what it was all about. As we entered the recruiting station, the three of us sat down and listened to the recruiter"s spiel about the benefits of being in the service. He went over pay grades, career classes, length of enlistment, the works. The man was obviously seasoned and was rather convincing with what he knew. He handed them their enlistment papers respectfully and was waiting for them to sign. After a few minutes, they went into a corner and were having a conversation I wasn't privy to. While they were conversing, I was going over the contract with a fine toothed comb. After a few whispers between themselves, they came back, took a pen, leaned over, and gave him their signatures on the bottom line. "What about you, buddy?" the recruiter asked. "Are you ready to serve your country and make the commitment?" While contemplating my answer, he kept trying to persuade me "You'll all be together for the entire enlistment" he said. "We can't break you guys up as per the agreement you sign between you and the United States Navy". He pointed to some line "It says so right here. You're on the buddy system. So, you have nothing to worry about. Here"s a pen, go ahead and sign, sonny" In between his sentences, I could hear faint whispers of laughter coming from behind my back. Ronnie and Mike were chuckling about something I knew nothing about. "What's so funny?" I asked. "Oh, they didn't tell you?" the recruiter replied. "Tell me what?" I demanded. "Well, they both receive a $500 bonus each for getting you to enlist with us". I immediately jumped up from my chair, threw the pen down on the desk, and asked them straight to their faces "Is this true?" "Well, yeah" Ronnie said. "What's wrong with a little something extra between friends?" "Friends?" I shrieked. "This is my life. How would you feel if I was making money off of you?" "We didn't bring you down here Ron just to make some cash off of you" Mike exclaimed. "You're making too much of a big deal out of it. We found out later that the Navy gives it to you anyway". "Why would we refuse free money?" Ronnie asked. "Well?" I asked the recruiter. "Do I get the same bonus too?" "Um, no" he answered sternly. "It doesn't matter which two of you get it. But, it can only be two". "So?" I asked. "I'm the odd man out then, huh?" "I guess so" Ronnie laughed. "Come on, man" he pleaded. "Join with us. It'll be fun". "I've changed my mind" I yelled. "You can forget this shit" "Well, that's unfortunate" the recruiter quipped. "I was looking forward to having the three of you". "You mean you were looking forward to your fee as well" I snapped back sarcastically. "It isn't about that" he said. "It's about serving". "Well, I'm gonna serve my ass right out that door" I chuckled. I got up, said "See you guys later" and left. So much for serving my country.

I had turned 19 and had been back at the vitamin plant for some time after my leg had healed. My father had been trying to persuade me into suing them as it was a clear case of negligence for them not repairing the forklift the way that they should have. Being so young and having already had bad luck with the N.J. court system, I was intimidated and wasn't really interested in taking it to a lawyer. It was a decision I had learned to regret later on. I had saved up a few hundred dollars and was in the market to purchase my first car. Hanging out over the Gulotta"s one afternoon, Billy F. overheard me talking to Dennis about it. "I'll sell you my car, Ron" he said. "I have a 62 Buick Skylark convertible". Knowing Billy, I asked "Does it run? And, does it need any repairs?" "I'll sell it to you for 80 bucks, bro" he replied. "It's been sitting in the parking lot over at Stewarts Root Beer on route 1 for a couple of days. The starter is shot. But, if you buy it from me and get a new one, I'll help you put it in. A starter is only 20 buck, man". "As long as you help me, you"ve got a deal" I said. "When can we go over there?" "We can go right now if you want" he said. "I'll stop by my house and get a few wrenches on the way there".

We arrived with the tools and I peered inside the car. I noticed right away that the ignition switch was missing. "What the fuck is this?" I asked. "How am I supposed to start the damn thing?" "Oh, that?" he said. "I bought it off the previous owner that way. You see those two buttons on the console above the radio? The left one turns the car on, and the right one shuts it off". "You mean you expect me to ride around like that?" I asked laughing. "If a cop pulls me over and sees that shit, he'll definitely think I stole it". "Nah" Billy said. "As long as you have it registered and insured the right way, they can't do anything as long as you show them the papers, bro. There's no law that says you need a key to start a car". "I dunno about this, man" I exclaimed. "The top is kinda raggedy and the car"s painted charcoal primer." "Come on, Ronnie" he begged. "You're not gonna get another running car for this price, man. Plus, I'm willing to help you put the starter in. I'll even stay with you to make sure it runs before you even pay me". "Ok, Billy" I replied. "As long as the damn thing runs".

After the starter had been installed, I cranked the engine and it came right to life. "See?" Billy asked excitedly. "I told you it was a good car!" "I guess so, Billy. I guess so" I said. "I just hope I don't have any more problems with it". I handed him his money and dropped him off. A few days later, I was cruising around with my girlfriend in Metuchen coming back from the Menlo Park Mall. As we passed the police station, a cop pulled up behind us at a light. As I attempted to turn right, he pulled us over. He gave me the usual documents request and started grilling us about "How come neither one of you are in school right now?" "Excuse me, officer" I replied. "But, I'm 19 years old and out of school and my girlfriend here is 17. She had no class today so we decided to go shopping". "Well, I pulled you over because I thought you looked younger than you are" he exclaimed. "Even if we were high school students, was that a reason to stop us?" I asked. "Actually, he replied. "I can detain you for whatever reason I feel is warranted". "So much for constitutional rights, huh?" I asked. "What do you know about that?" he asked. "You're too young even at your age to know what that is". "I'm well-read here" I said. "So, I know that you're not supposed to be able to do that"." Probable cause, son." he remarked. "For any reason I want too". "Well" I said. "If you're gonna give me a ticket for something, please give it to me so we can go. I have things I have to do today". Glancing more into the car, he smirked "Why don't you have a key for an ignition? I'd really be interested in knowing how you start this thing?" he asked. "How do I know you didn't steal it?" After giving him a demonstration with the buttons to prove that it was mine, he suggested "You should get it fixed to avoid a situation like this for the next time you come through my town". I thought to myself "That damn, Billy. Why did I listen to him? I knew this was gonna happen". Eventually from having over 165,000 miles on it, the Skylark"s engine blew. So now, I had to find another car.

Now carless, I was back to walking to wherever I needed to go. While taking a short cut home from the woods by the trestle, I saw a car on the dirt road that ran parallel to the train station. "I wonder who that is?" I thought. As I got closer, I could see that it was a Le

Mans and there was a long chain attached to its rear bumper. Scanning it with my eyes to its end, I could see that there was a telephone booth attached to it that it was smashed and lying sideways. "Some crazy bastard must have pulled this across the tracks" I mumbled. Just then, a tall figure appeared from the other side of the car with a screwdriver in his hand. When he got into enough light for me to see his face, I recognized that it was Jesse K. right away. "What the fuck is this all about?" I asked. How come you have a phone booth connected to your car by a chain, man? Did you actually wrap it around that thing and pull it all over the railroad tracks that way?" "I sure did" he laughed. "There's some money in that coin box and I needed it". "Why didn't you just pry it open while it was still standing upright?" I asked. "Because, there was a big spotlight over it and I didn't want anybody to see me" he said. "So, you pulled it off its moorings from the concrete just to get a little change?" I asked. "Listen Ron" he replied. "I don't have time for any of that bullshit, man. So, I figured I"d just drag it across the tracks to a place in the dark. Like where I am now, ok? Sometimes, these fuckers are hard to get open, bro. Since I'm in a place where I know no one can see me, I can take my time. See?" "Oh, I get it now" I chuckled. "But, you really smashed that fucking thing up, man. It's all mangled and shit". "I don't care about Bell Telephone"s property" he laughed hysterically. "All I want is some drinking money". I helped by keeping watch as he raided the machine. After about an hour of forcing it and knocking it around, he finally got it open. "How much did you get?" I asked. "We've been out here a pretty long time". "About 20 bux" he said disappointed. "But, it's enough for a few 6 packs and that's good enough for me". "Ok, man" I said. "It looks to me like you"ve got your hands full having to unravel that thing and put the chain back in your trunk. So, I'll see you later". "I'm not unraveling shit" he yelled. "Fuck that. I'm gonna unhook the lead from my bumper and I'm outta here". "You're just gonna leave this smashed up shit here where everybody can see it?" I asked. "Why not?" he asked. "They can just make calls horizontally if they want. They're not gonna fix it once they find it anyway". As I was leaving, he peeled out and I watched the dust rise up from the back of his vehicle. Months went by and the phone booth was never replaced. Ma Bell had done as Jesse predicted.

Ronnie E. and Mike W. sometimes came home from the Navy on leave. They missed home so much that they'd take the long 6 hour drive just to hang out with their friends and families on the weekends. One afternoon when I was hanging around Darios pinball joint, Ronnie pulled up in a car. He got out and started screaming at me "You're a fucking asshole, man. I told you in confidence about Mike and his girlfriend getting caught by the cops in Camp Kilmer naked and having sex in his car. Now, the whole town knows about it". He grabbed me off my feet, turned me sideways, and threw me to the ground. "I should punch you in the face for what you did" he said standing over me. "But since We're such close friends, I'm gonna cut you a break. Who the fuck did you tell anyway?" "I only told Lance D." I replied. "I thought I could trust him. I'm sorry I did, man. I guess he has a big mouth". "So, he's the one going all over town telling everyone?" he asked. "Just wait until I see him. Mike"s really pissed at me for this bullshit. So, I'm gonna beat Lance"s ass". "We're going down to the Edison boat docks later tonight" he said. "And, you're gonna buy us beer for what you did. I drink Michelob and We'll expect you to be there by 8 o"clock. You better show too, ok?" "All right" I replied. "I'll be there". "And, don't ever do that shit again" he said. "Or, our friendship will have problems".

I showed up like Ronnie asked with a case of Michelob bottles. Mike wasn't there and I was relieved. If they would have been together, I knew that it would have never ended. As I pulled up in my car, I saw a guy in the passenger seat who I didn't recognize. "Here"s your beer" I said as I handed it to Ronnie. "But, who"s that guy who is with you?" "Oh, him?" Ronnie replied. "His name is

Bob H. He's one of my shipmates. Go on over and talk to him and ask him about his older sister. He has a cool story about that" I went over to Ronnie's passenger"s side and began grilling the guy. "Hey, man" I said introducing myself. My name"s Ron too. It's nice to meet you. Ronnie says you're in the Navy with him and you have a funny story about your sister?" I asked. "Yeah, man" he said. My sister is Patti H. and she's a Playboy bunny. She's supposed to be in an issue as a centerfold soon". "Get the fuck out of here" I yelled. "No fucking way!" "Yeah, everybody on the base teases me about it" he said. "But, it's really true, I swear". A few hours went by and we all got pretty drunk. I left and told them I would see them the next weekend. A few years later, I read a story in a newspaper that his sister married Keith Richards of the Rolling Stones. I remember thinking "Fuck, I should have stayed in contact with him. I could have hung around with the Stones".

After searching around for a while, my older brother Robert had a friend who was selling a 1972 Oldsmobile Cutlass. It was a 6 cylinder and was in pretty good condition. The guy who was selling it was named Bruce G. and was a younger sibling of my brother's friend Carlos. I had met Bruce once or twice before. He was a nice enough guy and had a speech impediment that resembled the cartoon character Daffy Duck which I thought was hilarious. We settled on a price of $300 cash and exchanged the keys and the bill of sale accordingly. Being that I hadn't a license yet, he told me to drive home carefully as the car was still in his name. Fortunately, his house was right next to Stelton School. Therefore, my trip to Brookhill Rd. wasn't very far. My only problem now was passing the DMV written and driving test to procure a license to drive. My brother Robert"s girlfriend offered me the use of her 1974 Lemans should I be able to pass the written exam, and set up an appointment for me at the Rahway DMV driving course. After two attempts, I had passed and was giddy at the thought of my own personal open road experience. I showed up with her on the required date and time and passed the operator"s test with flying colors. I was now a bona fide licensed driver.

I had gotten into an argument at the vitamin plant with my immediate supervisor and had resigned. They had promised me a foremanship after my injury and had strung me along just enough to keep me productive and working. It didn't pay the best and was a boring, mindless job anyway. Cruising around in my car, it was refreshing not to have to depend on my friends for rides anymore. I could go wherever I wanted to whenever. The only immediate problem I had was how to come up with gas money? On one such day, Dennis G. and I got ahold of some lines of speed. We ingested it and were off to the races well into the wee hours of the morning. At around 3 am, I mentioned to him that we were running out of gas. "I know where we can get some" he quipped. "You know where me and Billy F. used to work at Vince"s Landscaping?" he asked. "Yeah, I know where that is" I replied. "The place on Jefferson Boulevard with the trucks and the fence around it". "That's the one" he said. "Stop by my house and We'll get a hose to syphon some gas from one of his trucks with. Its real dark in there any nobody will see us. But, you're gonna have to syphon that shit, man. Because, I'm not getting that gasoline bullshit in my mouth". "Ok, Den" I said. "As long as we get fuel, I don't care". We snuck my car up by Vince"s gate, hopped out and crept up to one of Vince"s trucks slowly. Dennis opened the truck"s gas cap and I inserted the hose. "Hurry up, man" he whispered. "Just take a little. You don't have to fill up this entire 5 gallon can we have with us here. I wanna do this quick and I don't want us to get caught because I used to work for him". In between spitting out mouthfuls of gas trying to get the liquid to flow, I finally received a steady stream. "I got it" I said. "Ulllhhhh" Dennis laughed "It's flowing now, bro". We took about half a can full, put the cap back on Vince"s fuel tank and went back to my car. "Don't put the gas in your car here, man" Dennis cautioned. "It's too far out into the street and it's too much risk for someone to see us. Put that shit in the trunk and we can fill your car at my house". I glanced around to see if it was safe and did as he suggested. We fueled up my vehicle by his backyard and continued driving around until dawn.

At about 5am, we were running out of gas again. "Already?" Dennis asked. "What the fuck, man? It's getting light soon, bro" he said. "We better hurry up if We're gonna try to get some more". "Should we go back to Vince"s again?" I asked. "Nah, I don't like to go back twice to the scene of the crime" he laughed. "We'll have to find someplace else". "I know of a place right on your street" I suggested. "Where"s that?" he asked incredulously "I don't know of any place to get gas at by my house?" "You know those two electrical contractor vans at the end of your street?" I asked. "I can back right up to one of those, open his gas cap in the back, open mine, and just run the hose between them. If we see anybody coming, we can just drive away". "That sounds pretty ballsy" he chuckled. "But, if you wanna try that, that's fine with me. But, it's all on you, bro. I'm gonna wait in the car. If the guy comes running out, I'm either gonna run or duck down. He's one of my neighbor"s here. So, I gotta be careful, man". "Understood" I replied. "I'll do it all myself". As Dennis tilted his head back on the seat"s head rest and was closing his eyes, I backed up and parked behind one of the company"s vehicles. I remember that they were white with blue lettering and they're gas caps didn't usually have locks on them. I specifically chose the one closest to DenniS's home in case we had to make a quick getaway. While Dennis attempted to nap, I prowled out my driver"s side door and approached the van with the hose in my hand. "This should be easy" I thought. "As long as I stay down about knee height, no one should see me". In between the two vehicles bumpers, I reached over and unscrewed the vans gas cap. I shoved the tubing in and put the other end facing my car. After opening my own car"s orifice, I sucked on the hose and waited for the familiar and nasty taste of the gas. Two attempts were enough before I finally got the flow I needed. "I hate this fucking shit" I mumbled. "And, it takes forever to get the smell off of you". When the opposing ends of the tube were set and I was sure neither side would fall out, I went back to my seat in the car. Dennis seemed to almost be asleep and had his feet up on the dashboard. "I'm coming down, bro. How about you?" he asked. "A little" I replied. "But, yeah. I'm starting to get tired some too". "I was seeing shadow people before, man" he muttered. "Shadow people?" I asked. "What are you talking about, Den?" "You know, bro?" he asked "After you"ve been up too long and you see people out of the corner of your eye walking across the street? Then, when you look back to make sure, you realize it was just a tree". "Are you hallucinating again, man?" I asked laughing. "Just how many days have you been up?" "Well" he said softly. "Before you came over with some crank, I was already up jetting for two days. So, I think it's time maybe I should crash." "Take a nap, man" I said. "And, I'll wake you when We're done". "That sounds good, bro" he exclaimed. "I'm gonna do that". "Within a few minutes, he was snoring and in a deep sleep. I was looking out the window of the car and hoping I would be done syphoning before the sun was fully up. The next thing I knew, I was hearing noises from the house next to the car. Apparently, one of the owners of the electrical company"s trucks was awake by his back door and I could see him through his window. I obviously had joined Dennis and had fallen asleep unintentionally. "Fuck!" I thought. "If this guy comes outside, he's gonna catch us". Contemplating my next move, Dennis woke up and asked me what was going on. "Why are we still here, man?" he asked nervously. "Its broad daylight, we better get the fuck out of here now!" "What should I do, Den?" I whispered visibly shaken. "Just start the fucking car man and get us out of here" he said. "The guy's not gonna know. He'll just think it's someone starting their car to go off to work. What the fuck is wrong with you, man?" he asked. "Did you fucking fall asleep or what? We were supposed to leave when you were done, man. I can't believe We're still sitting here with a hose between the two cars and you fell asleep. Drive away, drive away!" I turned the ignition and we were off. Luckily, we weren't caught. Talking about it a few days later, Dennis was describing to his brother Jeff how funny it must have looked with my car trailing a hose from behind as we were escaping down the street. "Imagine that guy's face if he would have come out and seen us driving away?" he asked chuckling. "I bet he would have been really pissed off". "At least we got more gas" I said. "Isn't that what it was all about?" "No" Jeff laughed. "It's about not getting caught, fool". "Ahhh, Ronnie's ok Jeff" Dennis snorted. "Just don't ever fall asleep in the car with him".

The band I was in was getting pretty good at rehearsals and Dave H. decided it was time for us to play out. The bass player Ted was having a party at his house and it was decided that it was the place where we'd make our debut. We were trying to decide on a name for the band and I had suggested Crysis. I had even drawn a logo using the alternate Y in the middle cascading down as a hook with three nibs attached on the end. I was very proud of it and thought it was amazing. Jim thought it rocked and couldn't believe I had drawn it. Ted and Donny were indifferent and Dave appeared to not be interested. Saddened by this, I put the graphic back into the trunk of my car and waited. Dave had come up with a suggestion "We should call the band Dead End" he announced. "What do you guys say?" Internally, I hated it and thought it carried a negative connotation. It was mostly Dave"s band though so I stood there and listened. Ted, Donny, and Jim said whatever Dave wanted was fine. Therefore, I was outvoted. Realistically, I was the last member to be indoctrinated so I had to respect that Dave was in charge. But, that didn't mean I had to like it. I kept my mouth shut and moved on. Most of the cover songs we were doing we agreed on except for the Stones. Dave didn't like the Stones and I think he felt that they were too simplistic and beneath his abilities. I under stood his feeling but was dismayed by his decision. The Stones have always been my first favorite band I've tried to copy and were a big contributor to my early influence musically. When I asked to do three or four Stones numbers, I was told we were only doing one. Again, I was disappointed. I didn't understand Dave"s disdain for their music as to me; they were part of white kids in bands emulating the blues.

The blues in my opinion are the backbone of rock and roll. I couldn't wrap my head around why he resisted and tried to find another band"s repertoire we could agree on. Thankfully, he liked Aerosmith. Aerosmith was my second group to copy and I was told that I did a pretty mean Tyler impersonation. Finally, I thought Dave and I had found common ground.

When our show opened, I was a nervous wreck. I was having trouble performing in front of people and couldn't understand why. I had sung in front of audiences before with the Velez brothers with no problem at all. But this time, I felt intimidated. I remember thinking "Wow, these guys I'm playing with now are really, really good. I hope I can sing to their expectations". There was that familiar low self-esteem issue popping its ugly head back up again. During the first three songs, like Jim Morrison had done with his maiden shows with the Doors, I refused to turn around. Dave was patient with me and came over to see what was up between numbers. "You can do it, man" he encouraged. "You sang in another band before and in front of people at practice. Just don't look at their faces. If it bothers you, close your eyes. But, you have to turn around, man. You're our front man". With Dave"s pep talk, I finally relented and faced our audience. Directly in front of me was a kid named Steady Eddie. He was Dave"s best friend and was taking pictures of us with his new expensive camera. I had met him at rehearsals before and he had always made me laugh making me feel at ease. I zeroed in on him and ignored all the listeners. The rest of the show went on without a hitch. I was finally in the zone and felt comfortable. After the party was over, I asked a few teens what they thought "You guys were pretty good, man" I heard. "But, you gotta turn around more and command that stage, bro. If you're gonna sing, sing. Get into it and don't just stand there. And, for the love of God, turn around next time". I took the criticism to memory and promised myself to improve my routines for the next show. The next time would come sooner than I had thought.

It was summer again and my favorite band The Rolling Stones were on tour. I procured tickets for Dennis G., Cliff G. and his girlfriend, my girlfriend, her best friend, and myself. It was the Miss You tour and we were all excited to attend. The day came and we followed each other in two cars to the show at JFK Stadium in Philadelphia. Being familiar with the venue, I felt comfortable that we knew where we were going and there would be no problem with entering and exiting. We took our seats on some benches toward the top, and waited for the show to begin. Peter Tosh was first and did a great rendition of the song about marijuana called Legalize It. The band Foreigner was next and did all their hits and some new songs from their Juke Box Hero album. While waiting in between stage set ups, it began to rain. It wasn't just a regular rain storm either, it was a monsoon. Anticipating the weather forecast, I had brought along some sleeping bags to cover us. But, they weren't waterproof and we got drenched anyway. Soon, The Stones came on to a round of thunderous applause. It was my first time seeing them and I was psyched thinking it would be a performance like their 69 tour. I was to become very disappointed. Jagger dancing on the wet stage announced "Everyone in the back is being very disrespectful. Just because it's raining some doesn't mean you can't get up and dance". "Man, this guy's got some balls" I thought. "He's got to be kidding, right?" He was reciprocated with a bombastic round of boos. Acting as if they were going through the motions and couldn't wait to get out of there, they only played for an hour and left. There was no encore and no apology, nothing. The crowd being fed up with waiting stormed the stage. I saw audience members clamoring over the fence in a barrage of bodies and pain. They were enraged and excited with revenge in their eyes and were ripping equipment to shreds. Most yelled they were taking pieces home as souvenirs. There were so many, they looked like a wave of army ants on the attack. "Whoa" Dennis said. "I mean, they sucked this time man. But, they're wrecking the stage. These people are crazy, bro". "Well" I replied. "I think the fans thought it was gonna be better than it was. I guess the band was just having a bad day" "Fuck that"

Cliff said. "We paid good money for these seats. They even made their stage into the tongue logo. And, we had to all sit here and get soaked in this fucking rain. Fuck The Stones, man. If they can't get it together, I'm never going to go see them again". When the stadium was empty enough for us to leave, we walked back through the mud and back to our cars. No one said much as it had become a miserable experience. "I told you, bro" Cliff said. "Next time, come with me to see The Who. Now, they never disappoint". "I hear that" replied Dennis. "Though it was cool to see Jagger prance around the stage, he didn't even do the rooster. I know Ronnie's disappointed too. Right, bro?" he asked. "I don't even wanna talk about it" I responded. "Let's just get out of here and go home".

CHAPTER 6

Nineteen & Trying

Once again I was over the Gulotta"s house early on a Friday afternoon. Ellis G. was there as well as Jeffrey, and Georgie Burns. Ellis got it in his head to introduce me to Tuinals. I knew some about Tuies as I had seen them previously down in their basement with Dennis much earlier. "We need to go to the city and get some of those bullets" Ellis said describing what Tuinals looked like. "Let's hop in your car Ron and go get some for our skulls". "I don't have the gas to go all the way to New York" I replied. "Unless you're gonna pay for it". "I have some money for gas" Georgie offered. "And, Jeff told me he'll pay for Tuies for all of us". "I don't like downers" I complained. "I'm an ups kind of guy". "You"ve never even tried them, Ron" said Jeff. "So, how do you know you wouldn't like them?" "I've seen people on them" I replied. "All they do is make you go to sleep. Fuck that, I wanna be awake if I'm gonna be high". "Check out Ronnie putting a crimp in our plans" Ellis said. "We're all gonna pay for it anyway. I don't see the problem?" he asked. "The problem is, I don't wanna drive on that shit" I replied. "I"d rather smoke some weed instead" "None of us have any weed" cackled Ellis. "But, I bet Georgie would buy you a bottle of pup instead?" "If Ronnie wants to sip on some booze instead of partying with Tuies, that's all right by me" he said. "I'll pay for it". "See, Ron?" Jeff asked. "You don't even have to do any. We can stop by the liquor store on the way and pick out whatever bottle you want. We just want to go to the city to get fucked up because we can't get Tuies here". I began to think about their offer.

I had to come up with a plan to be able to disguise the bottle in the car while I was driving. That was the only way I was prepared to go. I remembered that I had a thermos in my trunk that was clean inside and had been just sitting there collecting dust. "Ok, I'll take you guys" I said. "But, We're gonna put the alcohol in a thermos I have. We can pass it back and forth in our travels without the cops seeing what it is". "Stupendous!" Ellis screamed. "We can get skulled and Ronnie can be a souse puppy!" "Yeah, yeah" I replied. "Just don't aggravate me Ellis. You know how you can get on people"s nerves". "On clit's honor I won't scarf on you" he said. "It's city bound we go".

We stopped at the nearest liquor establishment and I picked out a container of Gin. Opening the trunk, I carefully poured the mixture into the thermos and threw the bottle away. "That will suffice" I mumbled to myself. "No cops would ever suspect this". Hanging out the front passenger window, Jeff was impatient and was yelling for us to go. "Come on, Ronnie. Enough with that shit. It shouldn't take you this long to empty a fucking bottle. Let's get rolling, bro" "Keep your fucking shirt on" I hollered back as I closed the trunk"s lid. "We'll get there when we get there". I jumped back into the driver"s seat and we headed for the Jersey Turnpike. On the way, we took sips of the Gin while I was forced to listen to their overzealous stories about what they wanted to do once they got there. "I'm gonna buy as many Tuies as I can" Jeff said. "But, you're only getting two each. I have to bring some home so I can make my money back off of them". I never understood why, but whenever people offered me drugs, it had always been two at a time and never more. "Perhaps they wanted to make sure they weren't responsible for anyone overdosing?" I thought. Ellis was speaking his own language again. I tried to turn the cassette player up to drown him out but it wasn't working. He was well into one of his incoherent rants. "I'll gonna get so skulled out tonight" he yelled excitedly. There's gonna be rainbow awareness in my corneal brain. I'm gonna get the nautical buzz. Who"s gonna ride the wave of medulishness with me?" "What the fuck is he talking about?" I asked laughing. "He's raving about some bullshit again". "Georgie?" asked Jeff. "You're burnt the fuck out, and you speak his language bro. Tell us what he's saying?" "I think he's saying something about his eyes seeing something inside his brain" he chuckled. "That's all I can figure out so far".

We finally came to the Holland Tunnel and made our way uptown. We parked close to 50th street and got out to walk around. Jeff was sauntering up to people he thought looked like drug dealers and was asking what they had for sale. Most of them wouldn't bite and Jeff was beginning to get depressed. "I think We're in the wrong area" said Ellis. "There's no skullishness to be had here". "We should go up toward Harlem" said Georgie. "Everyone knows the best shit is up there". "Perhaps he's right, Jeff" I replied. So, we hoped back in my vehicle and headed toward 112th Street. Once there, I pulled the car over to park again. "This place looks ghettoish" I said. "Do you guys really want to try to score drugs here?" "I'm not going home until I get my Tuies" Jeff demanded. "If you guys want, you can wait in the car. I'm gonna get out and go find me some". "That sounds like a good idea to me" I replied. "That way, we won't have to worry if the car is still here or not when you return". "Come on, Ellis" demanded Jeff. "You're coming with me. You're half black and nobody will fuck with you" "What kind of reasoning is that, Jeff?" I asked. "If you're gonna get mugged or ripped off, it doesn't matter what color you are?" "Ellis has relatives in Jersey City" Jeff replied. "So, fuck you guys. I feel safer if he's with me". "Why thank you for considering my aurical company" said Ellis. "And, I do have some experience in the citical ways". "Good" I said. "Take Jeff with you and Georgie and I will wait here".

Georgie and I watched as they scampered down the street to the front of a small convenience store. Concerned, I was hoping nothing would happen to them. "Jeff has a lot of balls for a little guy"

Georgie said. "I wasn't gonna go if they would have asked me. The city"s too crazy for us short guys". "Jeff can take a beating" I laughed. "You know how he is with his brothers". I could barely see them but noticed they were doing the obvious drug deal with the changing of the hands. There were two Latin looking guys in the doorway and a lot of head shaking in the affirmative. Eventually, I saw Jeff give them a handshake and him and Ellis began to return. Once back by the car, Jeff started to sing "I got Tuies fellas. As many as I wanted. All we had to do was find the right spot". They jumped back in the car and Jeff pulled them out of his pocket. "Feast your eyes on these, boys" he remarked proudly. He opened up a very small wrinkled paper bag and poured them out into his palm. The blue and red capsules tumbled out into a mound. "I bought thirty of them" he said. "So, eight for us, and the rest for sale when I get back home. I'll give you two each like I promised before we left. But, if you want more, you're gonna have to buy them from me. "Two is enough for me" Georgie exclaimed. "I won't need more than that". "If I take two, are these things gonna make me sleepy?" I asked. "It's like you took a couple of Valiums" Jeff replied. "But, I think its best you slow down on the Gin, bro. You might get more fucked up if there's booze with it". "It's a little late for that, Jeff" I said. "Half of that straight Gin is already gone. And, I've already got a small buzz". "It's up to you bro if you want to take them or not" he warned. "Don't say I didn't warn you, man". He held out eight capsules in his hand and put the rest back in the bag with his other. "Here you go, man" he said. "Take your two each". We took our doses and washed them down with what was left of the Gin. "What do we do now?" I asked. "Let's get out of here and go play video skulls at Fascination by Times Square" Ellis suggested. "I like how the bright lights fuck with my brain". "You don't need illumination for that, Ellis" I laughed. "The candle in your head went out a long time ago". "Be it that it may Mr. Ginical buzz. This chariot awaits you. Drive young man, drive. Before your Tuical effect proclaims us". "There he goes again" I replied. "And, I'm not even gonna ask anyone what he said this time".

We drove down to Broadway looking for the gaming parlor for some fun. After we found a place to park, we went inside to entertain ourselves. It was a short time later that I began to get bored. "Let's go drive around some more" I told everyone. "We don't have enough money to keep playing games here anyway". "Ronnie's right" Ellis said. "There's no more bahoots in our waloots to continue. Perhaps we should scarf someplace else?" "Ok" remarked Jeff. "Maybe we should start heading back home. Those Tuies are gonna hit us hard pretty soon". I steered the car toward 8th Avenue heading back to the Holland Tunnel. As I came to a stop sign, the downers started to affect me. I noticed right away that my equilibrium was off and we hit a curb. The right hubcap flew off into a ditch. Seeing this, I was intent on retrieving it. So, I jumped out of the vehicle with the door hanging open in the breeze. "Where the fuck are you going?" Jeff asked screaming at the top of his lungs. "You can't just stop here with all this traffic behind you?" I was undaunted by my task and insisted that I needed to put it back. As I ran back up the small ravine with the wheel covering under my arm, Jeff was really laying into me. "You better hurry up and put that shit back on" he yelled. Because if you don't, the cops are gonna come". Ignoring his request, I crouched down to tire level and began kicking the hub cap back in place. All the while cars were behind us honking their horns. "Come on asshole" one of them shouted. "Get the fuck outta the way". "Fuck you" I screamed back at them. "I'm almost finished and you can wait". After 3 or 4 attempts at centering it, I failed. I threw the hub cap into the back seat where it fell onto the floor. "He's skulled the fuck out" Ellis exclaimed. "We need to get out of here right now, Ronnie" Jeff demanded. "You're fucking crazy, bro". As I stepped on the gas to move forward, I realized I was seeing 3 of everything and I was having a very hard time keeping the steering wheel straight. Jeff had to grab my hand to keep it steady. Then, the car started to drift to the right forcing me to pull over. We were half in the road and half out. Jeff suggested that he should drive. "You're too fucked up, bro" he said. "You should let me take the wheel now. You're gonna get us all fucking killed". I became very belligerent and was convinced I was still in control. "You don't even have a permit, Jeff" I slurred. "Let me try one more time, man. If I can't do it, I'll give it to you". "Ok" he replied. "But, if you go off the road one more time that's it". Shaking off some of the Tuinals, I attempted to drive again. This time, I got into the street with no problem. While we were traveling, everything was fine until we came to a red light. Thinking I could beat it, I stepped on the gas pedal and hit 60 mph. Just as we hit the other side of the signal, the Tuinals kicked in harder. The car started to weave left and right again and I felt as if I was in a bumper car. Ellis was shrieking "We're all gonna die! He's a sick pup driver, a sick pup driver. He thinks this is the scrambler ride. He's tweaking I tell ya, he's tweaking" "Shut the fuck up, Ellis" I mumbled. "I'm the one driving here". Suddenly, the car veered to the left again. In front of us was a Dairy Lee milk truck. I didn't have the fortitude to stop in time and the left front quarter panel smashed into its bumper. I watched as it disintegrated into the street. Next, and obviously no longer in control, we careened to the right and directly into a Checker Taxi. The right quarter panel exploded and fell behind us in pieces. When I was finally able to steer straight again, and was in the center of the road, there was a brand new Lincoln Continental in the way. It still had its large sales sticker emblazoned on its rear left window and appeared to be parked illegally. It looked as if someone had run into a building for an errand and would soon return. I wasn't able to brake in time and remember seeing the hood crumble up in a V pattern right in front of me. We had come to a dead stop. Steam was wafting from the radiator and the tires immediately became flat. "Fucking Ronnie" Jeff screamed "You totaled your fucking car, asshole". A thin black man emerged from an alley way yelling that he couldn't believe what had just happened. "Hey, man" he shrieked. "That's my motherfucking car, man. I just bought that shit. What the fuck is wrong with you white boys? Didn't you see it stopped in the road?" Incoherent and barely able to speak, Jeff took over for me and explained the situation. "Hey, bro" he said. "You know the cops are gonna come here, right?" he asked acting concerned. "If you"ve got anything on you, you know They'll search your car. Now, wouldn't you rather just walk away like We're gonna do and you can just claim the insurance? Think about it for a second, man. Cash? Or, a night or two in jail?" "You"ve got a point there my little brotha" the man replied. "But, goddam that car was a peach". "You can always get another one" Jeff remarked. "But, you can't get out of a few years locked up". "True" said the man. He agreed to Jeff's suggestion and disappeared into the night. "What are we gonna do now?" asked Georgie. "We're gonna get the fuck out of here" said Jeff. "I'm not waiting here for no cops to arrive". We looked around and started to run away. Half way down the street, I had a change of heart and decided I wanted to go back. "I have shit in that car I have to go back for" I said. "Papers and stuff". "Well, I'm not going back" Jeff replied. "And, I don't advise the rest of us go back either". "I'm going anyway" I said. "Don't worry, I'll tell any cops that show up that I was alone". "You do that, Ron. You sick pup" added Ellis. "But, you're on your own". "You sure you want to do this?" Jeff asked. "Because, you could just say it was stolen after you got home". "I'll be ok" I said. "I guess I'll see you guys later. I'm straightened up some after the accident. I know what I'm doing now". "Ok" said Jeff. "We'll see you later then" and off they went.

I wasn't feeling the effects of the downers as much anymore. But, I did feel like I was somewhat drunk. As I teetered down the avenue back to my vehicle, I saw many New York City police officers around it doing an examination. I approached them trying to explain it was my car and that I had been in an accident. Immediately, I was grabbed from behind, had my left arm almost broken twisted up to the rear of my neck, and my face planted firmly on one of their patrol cars. "Where did you steal this car from?" an officer screamed. "You left the scene of an accident. We wanna know why you came back? Do you have drugs on you?" Speaking sideways out of my mouth with my cheek against the hood, I told them to check my wallet in my back pocket. "My license will match what's in the glove box" I said. "It'll prove the car"s mine". "Hold him there" another cop said. "I'll be right back". The officer handling me pulled my wallet out and retrieved my identification. The second cop came back and they compared their evidence for proof I was telling the truth. "He's right; it's his" he said. Upon hearing this, the cop holding me down released his grip and let me rise. A Sergeant who was supervising came over and asked me what I was doing in New York City this late in the morning. "We know you weren't by yourself" he said. "No kids your age come here this late by themselves unless they're looking for something. Its either women or drugs. Which one is it, Son?" "I don't know what you're talking about" I replied lying. "I took a wrong turn and ended up here". "Is that so?" he asked. "Bring me an eye chart card" he demanded from one of his subordinates. "And, hold his head up so I can see". He raised the laminated chart to my right eye and bleated "Yup, just as I thought. His pupils are dilated and he's high as a kite" What are you talking about?" I asked. "What's on that thing that makes you say that?" "This here son is an eye pupil chart" he said. "We use it to compare your eyes to what's on here. "Right here" he pointed. "At the middle one as a reference. You're definitely on something" "I was only drinking" I replied. "Sure you were" he laughed. "Why do all of you kids always have to come to our city to buy drugs?" he asked. "Can't you get anything in your own towns?" As the other cops laughed, he offered me a break. "I tell you what I'm gonna do" he said. "How much did you pay for this car?" he asked. "About $300 I replied. "Well, that's not a lot of money for a car" he joked. "Maybe not to you" I said. "But, it was all that I had". "You have two choices here" he advised. "You can take the plates off of your car and call it even or you can come with us and go to the tombs. Do you want to go to jail for a few days and get lost in there?" he asked. "I'm giving you a way out. So, hurry up and make your decision before I change my mind. In a few more minutes, I might not feel so generous. We have other calls we could be going to instead of doing stupid shit like this". I pondered his offer and reluctantly chose to take off my plates and go home. "A wise move" he said. "Now, gather anything you think is valuable to you from your car, and then leave. It's gonna be towed away for scrap and you'll never see it again". I was released to enter my vehicle and retrieve what I could. Just then, a guy walking by asked the cop if he could take what I had left behind. "Hey, officer" the man asked "Can I have that tape player in the dashboard before you take it away" "As long as the owner here doesn't care, neither do I" said the Sergeant. "But make it fast, I don't have all night" "Is it ok with you, man?" he asked. "I don't give a shit, go ahead" I replied. "Thanks, bro. You're the best" he remarked. "Yeah" I thought. "The best at cracking up my car".

After the cops let me go, I had no idea where I was. "The subway is down the street and not too far that way" one of the cops pointed. "We suggest you take that, and get out of here". In my hand was a plastic shopping bag. In it, I had my two license plates, my registration and insurance papers, and two copper pennies. That was it. Shuffling in the direction of the subway, I finally came to its entrance. "But, I have no money for a token" I thought. "How the fuck can I get home from here?" Out of nowhere, a tall Latin looking kid with a huge afro accosted me. "What's a matter, bro?" he asked. "You look pretty beat up, man". "I was in a bad car wreck" I said. "I have no money and I'm trying to get back home" "Where is that?" he asked. "Edison, N.J." I replied. "Whoa" he chimed. "That's a long way from here brotha. I think I can help you out though. The guy who runs the token booth is a friend of mine. Just follow me and wait by the turnstile until I have a chat with him. I'll see what I can do". I watched as he leaned down and spoke through the booth"s change receptacle and shook his head back and forth. He turned back and pointed at me and gave me a wink. When he was done, he came back and said "You're all set buddy. But, I have a word of advice for you man. You got to watch where you are this late in the morning, bro. Sometimes, people ain't as nice as me". "I appreciate that" I replied. "Because, I am kind of lost" "Yeah, you look it, man" he chuckled. "Now, jump on over the turnstile. I took care of it for you" "Thanks, bro" I said. And, I went down the stairs to catch a subway car.

Getting off as close to Penn Station as I could, I walked down 34th Street wondering how I was going to take the N.J. Transit train home. I was too dazed to beg or panhandle for money and it wasn't my style anyway. So, I came up with a plan. I would hide in the train"s bathroom as long as I could, and jump out at a station nearest Edison. I checked the train schedules just as the sun was coming up and took the stairs down to the corresponding track and waited. I must have looked pretty bad as I was getting multiple stares from commuters waiting to go to work. One old gentleman approached me and asked me if I was all right. "I'm fine" I replied. "And, thanks for asking". He walked away mumbling to himself and I didn't see him again. Once inside the train, I made a quick dash for the nearest lavatory, sat down on the bowl, and locked the door. My head was starting to pound and I was feeling nauseous. I leaned against the door and tried to wait it out. After a few stops went by, I was startled by the sound of keys in the door. As the lock turned, I heard a conductor"s voice asking if anyone was in there. "It's occupied" I yelled. "Please come back later". "I'm sorry" said the voice. "I was just checking". I didn't offer any more banter and heard his footsteps as he walked away. I remember trying to count the stops until Edison. My mind was fuzzy and I wasn't exactly sure. A couple of more stops went by and I heard the key in the door once more. "It's still occupied" I remarked. "You"ve been in there for a long time" the voice said. "I'm coming in to check on you". Not being able to stop him, the he forced open the door and stuck his head and looked down at me. He was obviously a conductor. "You can't stay in here without paying the fare" he said. Trying to play it off, I replied. "I've been in a terrible car accident. I'll be out as soon as I can. Now, could you please shut the door and go away". "I don't care what happened to you" he moaned. "You still have to pay the fare". "Yeah, ok. Whatever" I complained. "Now, could you please just go away? He slammed the door shut with an attitude and left. After about a minute, I could hear him through the door speaking to another conductor about watching me. "Rahway is the next stop" he said. "When we get there, don't let this kid off the train. Once we are idle, I'm calling the police on him for not paying for a ticket". When I no longer heard any voices, I pushed the door open a smidgen and stuck out my head. I could see the back of one of the conductor"s traveling to the front of the train to my left. There was also no one to my right. The one on the right was hollering as he walked "Rahway, Rahway next station. Rahway with continuing service to New Brunswick and beyond". Suddenly, the train came to a halt. "It's now or never" I thought. "I need to get out of here". Running to the left as fast as I could, I made it to the separation area between the cars to the open door and jumped. I could hear screaming behind me. It seemed as I was leaving the train, one of the conductor"s had spotted me and was furious. "Where are the cops?" he screamed "Where are the cops? I called them 10 minutes ago?" Ignoring him, I raced down Rahway Station"s concrete steps looking for an escape. I didn't even bother to use any of the steps, grabbed the handle, and slid down instead jumping over them. "I gotta find a place to hide" I thought. "Those cops will be here soon and They'll be all over me". I ran to my right at the bottom of the steps and found an area behind a bridge abutment to hide in. I knew this was a place where no one would see me. Looking out at the street, I waited for the police to arrive. Luckily, they never came. Shaken and nervous, I prowled slowly back up to the road seeing if I could find signs for route 1 south. Fortunately, it wasn't that far. When I got to the side of the highway, I stuck out my thumb hoping for a ride. To my surprise, a man stopped abruptly and told me to hop in. "Christ" he said. "What the hell happened to you?" "I was in a car accident in New York City" I whispered. "I had to leave my car there and come home" "Well, where are you going to?" he asked. "As close to Edison as possible" I replied "Is that where you live? Edison?" he asked. "Yeah, that's where I need to go" I replied. "Ok" he said "I'm going as far as Metuchen. I can let you off at that exit. The one by 287. That's almost Edison anyway". "That would be perfect" I said. "That's right where I need to be". After he dropped me off, I walked down the hill to a tree in front of the Mobil plant on route 27. There, exhausted and weak, I laid down against it and closed my eyes. I fell asleep for what felt like hours. When I woke up, I was being hit with the mid-day sun. All I could think of was if my friends had made it home all right. I found out later that Ellis had a relative in Jersey City and had let them stay there until the morning. His relative gave them train fare so they remained safe and sound. Walking home battered and beaten I thought to myself "I'm never doing Tuinals again".

After about a year and a half, my parents had made a deal with one of my father's brothers to buy a house in Kendall Park. Another brother of his had unfortunately passed away and left 6 kids and a wife that my father felt needed assistance. Since it was my father's sister in law, he felt obligated to help out so we moved. Being that I was out of a job, I was forced to go with them and had no other choice except homelessness. Living in Kendall Park and not knowing anyone was depressing and I despised it. Not because it wasn't a nice area to live, it was due to the fact that I didn't know anyone. Sure I had cousins around the block I"d hang out with occasionally, but it just didn't feel like home. Kendall Park was more spread out and more rural than Edison and in Edison I was able to walk everywhere. Without a car in that atmosphere, my social and love life was doomed. With money I would sometimes scrape up, I"d take the Suburban bus from the Shogun Restaurant on Route 27, get off at the New Brunswick train station, and hoof it to my girlfriend's house in Edison. Later, I would hope to find a friend who would let me stay over for the night. David G. and I had become closer friends at this time as he had just gotten a new girlfriend. So, he was gracious enough to help me out as my girlfriend and his had become friends. For almost a year on Friday to Sunday, I would sleep over his house with the four of us hanging out in his basement. When his brother Mike wasn't home, my girlfriend and I would share his bed. Most of the time, it worked out. Sometimes it didn't. There were one or two times when Mike would come home and kick us out to the small sofa. There, we were relegated to sleeping contorted and jockeying with each other for room. Dave had an extensive record collection and thoroughly enjoyed cranking up his Sansui turntable and humungous speakers to entertain us with. Most nights we'd listen as we sat around smoking joints and popping double barrel hits of mescaline. After the drugs hit our system, some of our conversations verged on the bizarre and insane. Dave"s family had a black Labrador dog named Shadow. Shadow was a very affectionate canine but always seemed to get into things he shouldn't have. While drinking large amounts of Pepsi to keep our buzz going, we all got into a conversation about insects. Dave insisted that common house flies made the sound fly, fly, fly as they flew passed you. As I was explaining that it was impossible for that to happen, his girlfriend broke in with a theory about ticks. "Oh yeah," she exclaimed "Have you ever heard them?" she asked. "They make the sound tick, tick, tick if you try to remove them". Laughing hysterically I replied "The only tick, tick, tick is the time bomb going off in your head". "She may have a point" Dave said trying to back her up. "Have you ever put your ear up to them to listen?" "You guys must have taken hits before we got here" I chuckled. "Because there's no way those bugs make any kinds of those noises". As I was finishing my sentence, Shadow had his nose near an ashtray. While sniffing, he let out a gust of air forcing cigarette ash to blow out everywhere. "Poof" Dave screamed. "Dogs go poof!" "I suppose they go poof, poof, poof like fly, fly, fly, and tick, tick, tick" I howled. "I think you need to take a valium, Dave". A few hours later, when the mescaline was really hitting me hard, I felt as if my body was burning up. "I need to go outside and get some air" I whispered to my girlfriend. "It's way too hot in here". "It's cold out there" she replied. "Are you sure you really want to do that?" she asked. "Absolutley" I said. And, I don't want my coat either. I'll be back in a little bit. Stay here and I'll see you soon". Once outdoors, I opened my shirt and let the cold air hit my torso. I was finally able to breath. When satiated with what I thought was enough to cool me down, I went back inside. "You look like you saw a ghost" Dave laughed. "Are you ok?" "I'm fine" I retorted. "But, you know how that tickling inside hits you when you do this kind of shit? I just had to get out of here for a bit". "Well, sit down and try to relax" he replied. "Because you"ve gotten us all worried. "I'll be fine" I replied. "As soon as I come down a little". As the hours turned into the early morning, my girlfriend and I laid down to try to fall asleep. I remember sweating so much that I felt I was in a pool of water. My back was soaked and my hair was wet. Just as I was almost able to drift off to sleep, I heard Dave"s father howling from above. "David!" he yelled. "Get up here and do what I asked you to have done yesterday". Dave ignored him at first. But, his dad was insistent. "David!" he screamed more profoundly. ""You better get up here right now!" Finally hearing him I heard Dave whisper. "I just fell asleep; I can't believe this fucking guy". I raised my head from the couch and replied. "But Dave, just tell him it was a fly who did it" "Shut the fuck up, Ron" he mumbled. "Flies really do make that sound". "Yeah, ok" I chuckled. "Remind me to get you more drugs later".

I had gotten some money from an income tax refund and was looking for another car. It was getting ridiculous constantly having to take a bus to New Brunswick and then having to walk every weekend. Fortunately, Dave"s brother Mike had a vehicle for sale. It was a green 67 Cougar and it was in pretty good condition. He wanted $300 cash for it and it was exactly what I had. I picked up the car and finally had a new ride. Dave and I liked to drive just about everywhere. So, one afternoon him, me, and my girlfriend took a ride to a place in the Watchung Mountains. It had huge boulders and a stream coming down that was very picturesque and was a perfect area to get stoned and enjoy our day. That was until my girlfriend started up with her attitude again. We usually got along, but when she was disagreeable about something we became the battling Bogarts. As she was babbling about a subject that had nothing to do with why were there, I grew weary of her incessant complaining and decided it was time for us to go. We got back into the car and she was still going at it. "Jesus Christ" I yelled "Give it a fucking rest already". For a small amount of time, she became complacent and shut up. "I'm getting kinda hungry, bro" Dave said. "There's a McDonald"s up there ahead. Can we go through the drive thru and get some grub?" "Sure" I replied. "I'm getting a little hungry myself". "What do you think?" I asked my girlfriend. "What do you want to eat?" She gave us unmitigated silence. "Well then, fuck you. Starve" I laughed. She continued to pout and look out the window. I retrieved the sack of food and handed it to Dave in the back seat. "Hand me my fish sandwich when you can" I said. "I'm gonna drive back home because little miss attitude here has gotten all pissy again". "I don't want you driving and eating a sandwich at the same time" she said. "And, I'm pissed because you didn't get me anything". "I asked you several times" I replied. "You decided to pout and not answer. So, tough shit, you get nothing". "I'll give you part of my burger" Dave offered trying to be nice. She shook her head no and declined. "I'm eating mine" I remarked. "So, I guess you're going without". Just as I was taking a bite from the corner of the bun, she turned and slapped me in my head. "Son of a bitch" I screamed. "You got tartar sauce all over my pants!" Enraged, and like the scene in the movie Public Enemy, I imitated James Cagney when he smashed a grapefruit in Mae Clarke"s face. I took the sandwich and ground it into her cheek accordingly. "You fucking hit me again you bitch, and you'll walk home" I yelled. Like a blind octopus, she started flailing her arms at me as bits of fish and melted cheese was dripping down her jaw. Screeching, she howled "I fucking hate you, I fucking hate you". Dave, torn between laughing and stopping us from getting into an accident tried to intervene. He was holding our arms from each other and yelling for us to stop. "Ron?" he screamed. "You gotta stop, bro. You're driving here". "Tell the psycho" I replied. "She is always mad at everything". Eventually, she calmed down enough to be reasonable. I bought her a Burger King meal instead as a consolation. Sometimes you have to compromise.

I had been working for a dry cleaners and tuxedo rental outlet as a delivery driver and was let go. It seemed in the summer months they had claimed to have been slow. So, they laid me off. I was fine with it as I was told that they would allow me to collect unemployment benefits. Receiving unemployment checks was sometimes regarded as a vacation as it was a break from the mundane and go nowhere drudgery for little to almost nothing hourly compensation. It was just enough money to subsist on while pretending to look for another job. Soon, I received a letter from them informing me that I was expected to show up in the unemployment office in New Brunswick for job training. "Job training?" I thought. "What the hell is this all about?" I called them and was told "Everybody has to do it and it's only a formality. We want to make sure you know how to fill out an employment application and be able to interview correctly". As I hung up the phone I muttered "Job interview? I've never had a problem with a job interview?" Still, under the threat of cutting off my checks, I was forced to go. I picked up Dave G. as I usually did and brought him with me so I wouldn't be bored. I parked the cougar behind Christ"s Church on Neilson Street and we walked on over for my appointment.

While Dave was sipping on a coffee and waiting for me in the lobby staring at the clock, I was inside listening to some boring speech about the do"s and don'ts of obtaining a job. After an hour had passed, I was finally free. What did they ask you about when you were in there?" Dave asked. "Are they gonna force you to get a job?" "Nah" I replied. "It was just some bullshit class to try to give you pointers and shit. It was a total waste of time". "So, what do we do now?" he asked. "I dunno" I responded. "I guess we go back to your house". As we walked back to my car, I saw that it was no longer there. It was just an empty parking space with some oil stains on the ground and some faint tire tracks from where it had been. I felt my stomach start to convulse and my knees getting weak. Standing in the parking spot, I began to spin around in circles with my arms in the air. "Where the fuck is my car?" I screamed. "I can't believe this shit! I do the right thing and go to their stupid job seminar and I get this? Dave laughing his head off interjected. "You"ve got the worst fucking luck of anyone I know, bro. You're always getting fucked. I guess someone stole it?" "Motherfuckers" I yelled. "I bet some junkie scumbags from the projects took it. "Well" Dave replied still chuckling "You did have a wing window on that car. As you know, those are easy to jimmy open". "I thought my car would be safe here" I replied. "I mean, it was parked right behind a fucking church?" "Look behind you" said Dave. "It's a 65 Mustang. It looks like they left it here and took yours. It wasn't here before, man. It's pretty beat up too". "You're right" I said. "That car wasn't here before. I bet they parked that shit here and hotwired mine". "Nothing you can do about it now" he chuckled. "Except to go and file a police report".

I went and retrieved a stolen vehicle report, gave it to my insurance company, and forgot about it. A week later, I got a letter in the mail from an attorney representing some cab outfit in New York City. They were accusing me of getting into an accident and they wanted compensation for damage and injuries. I immediately called them and advised them I was sending a report showing it was impossible for it to have been me. "Those scumbags must have used my registration as ID and said I was the one that caused it" I thought. "I don't fucking think so". I asked exactly where the car was and was given the address to go and check it out. My father drove me to a towing yard and we were allowed to enter to survey my car"s wreckage. When we got there, I did a thorough examination to decide if it was worth salvaging or not. Right away I noticed that my tape player and all of my tapes were missing. The inside appeared to have been set on fire and the front end of the vehicle had been smashed. "The tow truck guy at the front gate told me it wasn't that bad" I said. "What's this guy talking about?" "It's a total loss, son" my father replied. "He was obviously lying just to get you up here to pay his towing fees. Screw him. Hurry up and take off the plates before he sees us". I disengaged the tags, put them in a bag, and we headed for the exit. "Where are you going?" demanded the attendant. "You guys can't leave. You have to pay $150 in towing costs". "I'm not paying shit" I screamed back. "You lied to me and told me the car was ok. So, screw you. We're leaving". "I'm calling the cops; I'm calling the cops" he threatened. "Go ahead" my father replied laughing "We already have the plates. Have a nice day asshole". So far, I wasn't having much luck with cars.

It was early September and the band I was in was scheduled to do a gig in our bass player Teddy"s backyard. Teddy and Dave H. lived in the same area off of Aaron Rd. So, it was convenient for them and I understood why. His sister had just graduated from high school. So, it was a celebration of her achievement with food, kegs of beer, and other assorted substances. As I approached our make shift stage on a small hill in front of the house"s sliding glass doors, I was in awe of some PA system equipment that was on either side. I remember thinking "Man, those are huge. I've never sung out of anything like those before". Seeing my mouth agape, Dave approached and said. "See those, Ronnie? We're playing out of those tonight, man. They'll be able to hear us from here to Route 27". "I just hope we have a good show" I replied. "I don't want to have to puss out and not turn around like the last time". "I've been thinking about that" he said. "And, I have the perfect solution. I think if we ease you into it, it would be a lot better for you. So, We're gonna start with that Lou Reed rendition of that song Sweet Jane we do. You can lay back until my intro solo is done. Then, just leisurely walk up to the mic and start singing". "That's a great idea, man" I replied. "I think I'm gonna do that" "Good" he said. "We'll be doing sound check in a few minutes. So, don't go anywhere". As I stood upon the summit and peered around, I could see a guy named Julio playing with the PA"s sound board. There were also others milling around and setting up 55 gallon drums for insertion of beer kegs. Across from them on the right, were two long tables with hot dog and hamburger buns set upon them. There was a grill being fired up in the distance and looked as if it was waiting for guests to soon be fed. I turned to my left and saw a big guy we knew named Joe B. He was in control of another board and seemed to be in very good spirits. He smiled at me and gave me the thumbs up sign. Everything was in place. So, I sat down to have a glass of beer to calm my nerves when Steady Eddie walked by. "Hey Eddie? I asked "Are you taking pictures of us again tonight?" "Oh, yeah" he replied. "And this time, I'm shooting them in color". Remembering what had happened with my last performance, Eddie kept the inside band joke going "Just remember" he said. I cut him off mid-sentence "I know, I know wiseass. Just make sure to turn around, right?" "You got it" he replied laughing. "I don't feel like taking anymore pictures of your back or your ass". "Dave and I already have that problem figured out" I said. "So, you don't have to worry about that anymore". As he walked away, my girlfriend was babbling about something I didn't care about. All I could think of was wanting to have a good show and not to fuck things up again.

After our opening band C.C. Rider was finished, I went into Teddy"s bathroom and got ready for our show. Dave had Dead End stolen street signs attached to the back of Teddy"s home as our logo and we were almost ready to go. I went out to the front of the house and saw our friend Nicky with a cigar box in his hand. He was collecting a $4 admittance fee to cover the beer and the food. As he turned around, I saw my little brother Erik with his friend Jeff in tow. "This kid here says he's your brother" Nicky said. "Is that true?" "Looking over at Erik I winked and replied "Yeah, you can let him in. He just wants to come and see the show. He's all right, man". "Ok, then" Nicky said. "I'll let him in for free and only charge his friend half price. Is that cool?" "That's fine" I said. "How did you get here?" I asked my brother. "Because, I know there's no way the old man would let you come and see us play if he knew there was beer involved." "We rode our bikes" he replied excitedly". "All the way the fuck down here?" I asked. "I'm honored". "Don't get a big head" he laughed. "I haven"t seen you sing in your band yet. But, I know you sound pretty good around the house. So, Jeff and I came to see you". "Plus, there's beer here" Jeff remarked. "What's no to like?" "Ok, go ahead in and We'll be on in a little bit" I said. "And, don't get too drunk. I don't need the old man ragging on me later". As I turned to go in behind them, two police officers rode up in a cruiser. They got out and started asking "Who"s in charge? We've got some complaints that have come all the way over by Route 27 across from here. They said you guys are pretty loud and you have to tone it down". "I'm the lead singer in the next band to go on, officer" I replied. "I can assure you that according to local ordinances we won't be playing after 10 pm" "I don't give a fuck who you are" he boasted. "But, I'm telling you now, it's being turned down or the party is over". Knowing the law and that he was full of shit, I gave him the usual yeah yeahs and sent him on his angry assed way. While trekking back to the stage, I thought "Fuck those cops. Just for that, when we go on I'm telling Joe B. and Julio to turn it up louder". Behind Joe B"s console was a mirror with some lines of speed. He laughed and offered me some. "You know how energetic you get and how well you sing opening up your lungs with this" he said. "So, it's here if you want it". I walked on over and snorted them up. "We're all on it" he quipped. "So, have a good show and I'll be here if you need me".

As projected, we went on as soon as it got dark. The show was going well and I didn't even cut my mouth on my harmonica during our cover of Aerosmith"s song Somebody. Being pleased with myself, I looked over to my left and under a weeping willow tree was my brother and his friend. They were crouched down with beers in their hands and jumping up and down. I gave them the thumbs up and went back to play another number. By now I had been more into copying Steven Tyler and I was all over the stage. The amphetamine seemed to have helped it. As I spun to my left mid song, I hit Jim"s Gibson guitar with my mic stand causing his guitar to go out of tune. He didn't say anything and kept on playing the best that he could. After Dave gave me a break and did his solo acoustic songs with Jim accompanying him, we came back for a few more tunes and the encore. Since Aerosmith"s song Train Kept a Rollin" was my hardest to do, Dave always insisted we perform it last. It had something to do with him insisting that if we did it earlier that I would run out of breath. I had fun with the song and changed the lyrics to "This party"s gonna roll all night long". On the strum of Dave"s and Jim"s last chord, I fell down to my knees and slid toward the lighting rig in front of me. Dave was right; I was covered in sweat and exhausted.

After taking a much needed break while people were going home, I walked over to one of the kegs to get myself a beer. "Those are toast" Steady Eddie said. "They drank 2 entire kegs of beer?" I asked. "Yup" Eddie replied. "You don't know how many people were here, do you?" he asked. "I have no idea" I answered. "The only thing I could see through the lights was the tops of their heads". "You guys played in front of 500 people" Eddie chimed. "That's more than some nightclubs". "That many, huh?" I asked. "But, how did we sound?" "It was awesome" he said. "Better than expected. And, you…." "Turned around?" I asked. "No" he said. "I was gonna say you came out straight forward and never had to do that". "Finally" I replied. "Now, you'll leave me alone. "You gotta admit though, Ronnie. That shit was pretty funny" "You try it someday" I quipped. "It's not as easy as you think". "Fuck that" he exclaimed. "I'm the photographer and it's staying that way". "I guess it's time for me to help Dave and the others move some of this equipment inside" I said. "So, I'll talk to you later". "I'll be around" Eddie replied. "But, just remember?" he asked grinning "Yeah, yeah. I know. Turn around!" As I approached the stage again, I asked Dave how I could help. "Just grab a couple of these amps and put them in the first downstairs room you see inside the door" he said. "That way, we can get done faster". The sliding glass patio door was fully open and people were entering and leaving as I got close. Carrying a heavy amplifier, I placed it down on the floor in the room and headed back outside to grab more. While speaking to someone on the way out about how the show had gone on, I walked right into one of the panes. Suddenly, it disintegrated all around me and glass was flying everywhere. People began screaming. "Are you ok, man?" someone asked. "You better look at your hand, man. Its bleeding all over the place." Half in shock, and half in awe, I couldn't believe that someone had been stupid enough to have closed the door. They knew full well that we had been moving items in and out and there was absolutely no reason to have done so. I was annoyed more than concerned for my wound and let everyone know. "Who"s the fucking asshole who slid the fucking door closed?" I yelled. "Didn't you see all of us going in and out?" No one said a word. Soon, Dave came through the newly shattered opening with Steady Eddie trailing behind him. "What the fuck happened here, man?" he asked. "Are you all right, Ronnie?" Slightly laughing, he and Steady Eddie looked on shaking their heads. "How the fuck could you have not seen the door closed, Ronnie?" Eddie asked. "That just doesn't make any sense?" "It was really clear" I replied. "Teddy"s mom does a good job cleaning I suppose. It looked like it was still open to me. How was I supposed to know some douchebag closed it?" "He's got a point" Dave remarked. "But, We'll help with cleaning this up. I think you need to go into the bathroom upstairs and take a good look at your hand. You"ve got blood dripping all down your wrist, man". "Take Dave"s advice" Eddie added. "We've got this". I went upstairs and was greeted by a girl in the hallway. "I was just told what happened to you with the sliding glass door" she said. "So, let me help you take a look at that. I'm in school to be a nurse. So, I can at least wrap it up until you can get to the hospital in case you need stitches." "Thanks for your help" I replied. "I can't get it to stop bleeding." We entered the bathroom and she found a few butterfly bandages and some gauze to ebb the flow. We could both see upon examination that I had a large half-moon gash where some skin had been. "Yup" she advised. "You're definitely gonna need some stitches to close that up. But, I've gotten it to stop for now. I think you should go to the emergency room as soon as you get out of here and take care of it though" "Will do" I replied. "And, thanks for your help". The scar still remains.

Billy F. had gotten himself into a bad heroin habit and a predicament he couldn't get out of. He was full on addicted and would do anything to avoid withdrawals. He approached me one day talking about how he had the perfect scheme to make money. "Listen" he said. "Dennis G. and I need your car, man. I have a great scarf I've used a few times. If you drive us there, I'll give you a hundred bucks and fill up your car with gas. But, I can't pay you until we are done". "What's the scam?" I asked. "I'll tell you after we pick Dennis up" he exclaimed. "But, I think you're gonna like it because you don't have to do anything" "Like a look out?" I asked. "Something like that" he said. "So?" he asked. "Do you wanna do it or not?" "The risk sounds pretty good" I replied. "So, I guess I'm in". Once Dennis was with us in the car, Billy clued us in on what was happening next. "Drive to East Brunswick, bro" he said. "When you get by the Jersey Turnpike, pull into the neighborhood that runs along there and I'll tell you what We're gonna do next". "Ok, Billy" I replied. "But, I hope it's gonna be good". "Oh, it's good" Dennis remarked. "He's done it before. Billy makes a lot of coin this way". "As long as I get my cut, I don't care" I said. "You'll get your part" Billy assured. "Just do as I tell you and it'll all be fine".

I turned a corner with a row of homes that had backyards facing the Turnpike as Billy had asked. When we got to about midway on the street, he demanded I stop. "Pull over right here" he said. The white one in the middle looks good enough to me". "Good enough for what?" I asked. "You should know what Billy"s up to by now, Ron" laughed Dennis. "He's gonna do a B & E isn't he?" I asked. "You"ve got it" Billy chuckled. "You guys wait here and I'll be right back" "You sure you don't want me to go with you?" Dennis asked. "No, man. I've got it, bro" Billy replied. "It won't take me more than 5 minutes anyway. I'll be in and out nice and quick". Dennis and I watched as Billy carefully snaked up to the house"s front door and saw him give it a knock. He waited a minute or two and walked around the back. "His usual M.O." Dennis laughed. "He shouldn't be too long". We waited and listened to the radio. Dennis was spinning the dial and searching for WYSP. "There's gotta be some tunes on here for us to pass the time with" he said. "Maybe I can tune in some Trower". A few songs went by and Billy came running back from behind the house. He opened the back door, jumped in and yelled for me to leave. "Go man, go. Before somebody sees us!" I started the car and stepped on the pedal to get out of there as soon as possible. "Get out to Route 18" Billy howled. "And, take the exit going south". "What did you get?" Dennis asked excitedly. Billy was pulling a mass of credit cards out of his jeans pocket and waving them in our faces. "I got these, man" he bragged. "And, a few hundred in cash too. But what I really want is on the Turnpike. So, once We're on there, just keep driving Ronnie and I'll tell you when to pull over on the side of the road". "Ok" I replied. "But, I hope nobody sees us". "Nobody"s gonna see nothing" he said. "You're gonna pull over and I'm gonna pretend I'm getting out to take a piss. I threw something over that house"s back fence facing the road. I'm gonna run and get it and bring it back. Then, We'll go to the next exit and make a u turn". "So, that was your scam all along?" I asked. "I told you it was perfect" he laughed. "The less exposure to people, the easier it is to get away". "That's pretty smart, Ron? Isn't it?" Dennis asked. "That way, nobody will see you with a pillowcase running down the street". "You thought of this Billy?" I asked. "Yup" he replied. "It's just like Dennis said. All you have to do is throw shit in the grass over the fence and leave". "That's amazing" I exclaimed. "And, it's virtually foolproof". "You'll see" he laughed. "It's a piece of cake".

While Billy was showing Dennis the names of all of the credit cards in his hands, he pointed to an area just before an overpass and directed me to stop "Right here, bro" he demanded. "Stop the car and I'll be right back". Dennis and I watched as he tread into the tall grass on the bottom edge of some steel fencing that separated a yard from the highway. He bent over and retrieved a large mahogany box with ornate scripture carved into it. Picking it up with both hands, he straddled it against his waist and sprinted back laughing. We could see he had a smile on his face and was very pleased with himself. As he approached the car, he flung the box across the back seat and hopped in. "Ok, man" he beamed and out of breath. "Now, the u turn exit isn't too far from here. So, just take that and head for the city. Once we get to New York, We're gonna go to the diamond district on 47th Street. I'm gonna unload this shit there for some cash". "What's in the box that's so important?" I asked. He grabbed the containers edge and lifted it briskly. "Ullllhhhh" Dennis yelled. "It's a full on Sterling silver set. He should get some serious coin for that". "I've got these credit cards with a few grand on them I can use too" Billy remarked. "So, it looks like We're gonna have a good day". I turned around from driving to get a quick glimpse and marveled at the glint it was giving off in the sun. "That's a nice fucking set you"ve got there, Billy. I bet you'll get top dollar for that" "I've already checked" he replied confidently. "It's got the manufacturer"s stamp on it. So, I know it's not plated and it's real". "No wonder you were so freaked out to go get it" Dennis said. "You're gonna get a lot of money". "Why else would I do this?" Billy chuckled. "It's not to buy Christmas presents for poor people!"

After Billy chose a shop to park by to unload his wares, Dennis and I sat again waiting. Fifteen minutes later, Billy came back slightly excited and amused. "I got five hundred bucks for that set" he announced triumphantly. "It's way more than I thought I was gonna get. I had some diamond earrings in my pocket I didn't mention to you guys too. So, I've got 700 bucks". "Nice haul" Dennis exclaimed. "Way better than you expected, huh?" "Yeah" Billy replied. "I can pay Ronnie and still have enough for us to get off". He pulled out some currency and peeled off a one hundred and a twenty dollar bill. He handed it to me and said "Thanks for the ride, bro. I couldn't have done it without you. Maybe we can do it again sometime?" "Sounds good to me" I responded. "But, you don't want to take the same car there all of the time. The residents will eventually figure it out". "That's why I rotate friends with cars" he laughed hysterically. "I'm not stupid man. Anyway, start this pig up and take us to 112th Street in Harlem. I have to go visit somebody so I don't get sick". "Sick?" I asked. "Dope sick" Dennis replied. "If he doesn't get his dose, he's gonna get cranky". "Oh, ok" I said. "But, you're gonna have to show me how to get there. I've never been to that part of Harlem before". "I've been there many times" Billy leered. "I'll show you the way".Upon entering the street Billy was guiding me on, I noticed right away that it wasn't a neighborhood I was used to. Most of the buildings were old and dilapidated and looked like it was a war zone. "Ahhhh, the ghetto" laughed Dennis. "The premium spot to get your freak on".

We approached a large house with walk ups stairs and Billy told me to park. Not five minutes into it, a New York City police cruiser came by. He stopped, stuck his head out the window, and asked "What are you white guys doing in this neighborhood? I know you're only here for one reason. I'm going to drive around the block. If I see you when I return, you're walking home and your car"s coming with me". "Ok, officer" I blurted back. "We'll be gone in a few minutes. "I'm serious" he yelled. "Don't make me tow your car". The cop drove away and I looked at Billy perplexed.

"What do we do now?" I asked. "Let Billy run inside to see if the guy's got the dope first" Dennis said. "If he does, We'll go and park around the corner". Billy jumped out and bounded up the tall stairs. He wasn't gone very long and came back with a sly grin on his face. Addressing Dennis he advised. "He's got plenty, bro. He just got a new shipment in yesterday and it's supposed to be pretty good". "I don't know if I wanna leave my car here unattended, man" I said. "Nobody"s gonna fuck with your car" Billy said. "I know where to park it close so that doesn't happen. Like I've told you before, I've been here a few times. So, listen to me. The guy upstairs even has some coke too. I'll give you a twenty dollar piece for free if it makes you happy". Knowing that I liked cocaine, he knew exactly how to get to me. "Done" I replied. "But, I still don't wanna be in there for a long time". "What Dennis and I have to do in there will take about ten minutes" he chortled. "So, it'll be fine". We parked the car as Billy had offered and I followed them onto the third floor. "This must be what a shooting gallery looks like?" I thought. "I hope I don't get killed".

Billy reached a green door at the top of the landing and gave it a rap. A few seconds later, the door opened with a screech. A thin black man wearing dark sunglasses greeted us and motioned for us to come inside. As he closed the door behind us, I began to get very nervous. "It's Shorty White" the thin man said. "And, he's brought some other white boys we don't know with him". I looked to my right and there was a portly black man lying back on a couch with a Shar-Pei wrinkle skinned dog at his feet. He had a pillow with a palm tree embroidered on it in front of his stomach with his right hand hidden behind it. He was obviously the dealer. "Who be these guys with you, Shorty White?" he asked Billy. "They're friends of mine, bro." Billy replied. "They can be trusted" "Ok, man" said the large guy. "If you gonna vouch for them, that be on you. You know what happen if some bullshit go down. Now, what you need on this fine afternoon?" "I need a few jacks" Billy replied. "And, some works too" "You know the game" the dealer said. "Twenty each and three dollars for the rental". "Not being privy to the rental part of it, I thought "Rental of what? That's strange?" Billy then pointed at me and said "He don't jab, man. So, just throw him a twenty of coke". "Make no matter to me" the dealer said. "As long as you gots the green, you high ain't none of my business". "I'll take four jacks and one coke then" Billy requested and handed the man the money. After the exchange was done, Billy and Dennis went into a corner not far away to get their fix. Billy sifted through the envelopes and zeroed in on the one that was mine. He threw it at me and laughed. "Don't get too hyper" he said. "I might need you to drive me around again later". I opened the manila coin bag and peered inside. At the bottom was some shiny white powder that I knew would give me the rush I had come for. I spilled out a few granules onto a nearby table, rolled up one of the bills Billy had given me and snorted it up my nose. I felt the numbing chalky taste drip down my throat almost immediately. "Hmmm" I thought. "This stuff is pretty good" A minute or two went by and I walked over adjacent to the dealer to what appeared to be a large picture window. The only problem I saw was that it was devoid of glass with some shredded plastic hanging down that was flapping in the breeze. I turned to the dealer and asked "How come there's no glass in this window frame? And, why do you have your hand hidden behind that pillow with that cool assed looking dog in front of you?" The man glared over at Billy and was shaking his head. Billy looked like he had just seen a ghost. "What the fuck is wrong with you Ron asking my man questions like that?" he asked. "Don't you know where you are? Show the guy some respect, bro". Dennis didn't say a word and was staring at the door as if he was trying to figure out an escape route. The dealer was quiet for a moment and them him and his friend started to laugh loudly. "Check this motherfucker out?" he asked incredulously. "How old is you?" he asked. "I'm nineteen" I replied. "Shiiiiiiiit" he howled. "Dis motherfucker is just a baby. Since yous don't know the rules up in here. I"s gonna educate you for shits and giggles. I'm in a generous mood today". Looking relieved, Dennis and Billy went back to their session. "Look down yonder through that window opening down below" he instructed. "What do you see down there?" I stepped forward carefully as not to trip and fall. I stuck my head out and peered down into a partial dark abyss to the ground below. "I see nothing but trash, glass, and some rocks down there" I exclaimed. "Now you see why their ain'ts no windows" he said. He saw the look on my face and knew I was confused. "It's like this skinny white boy. If you OD while you is here, outs that window you go. I ain't having anyone die up in here. You feel me?" "Yes" I replied. "And, here"s another thing" he said. "I knows what you is gonna ask me next. So, here it is." He pulled the pillow away from his belly and was brandishing a small caliber handgun. "This is for fools like you who ask too many questions." he bellowed. "And, the dog is to get you if you try any funny shit to try to get it away from me. Is we clear now, white boy?" "Perfectly clear" I jammered. "Now, gets yo high" he said. "And gets the fuck out. I gots other paying customers who will be here soon enough". He then glanced over at Billy "Shorty White?" he asked "Is you done or what?" "Yeah, We're finished here, bro." he replied. "Would you like a taste back before we leave?" he asked the dealer. "That's a nice gesture". the dealer said.. "It'll be mah cover charge for yo ignorant friend here asking all those questions. Leave it on the table over there, and I'll see you next time. And next time, be here alone Shorty White. You don't know what could happen if I wasn't in such a good mood no more. You feel me?" "I got you" Billy responded. So, we gathered up what was ours and left.

While driving away, Billy wasn't satisfied with our visit. He was perturbed and nervous about how it went down while at the dealer"s house. "Go up the street some" he said. "You'll see a hospital. Right by there is a park with shale type cliffs and trees in it. We're gonna stop there so I can really fix myself up. And, you gotta learn to be cool more Ron. I thought that guy was gonna go off on us". "Yeah, Ronnie" Dennis exclaimed. "If there's a next time and you come with us, don't talk so much, man. They get suspicious and think you're a cop when you ask that many questions". "Hey" I said. "I didn't know. I was never at one of those before" "It's all good" answered Billy. "But, Dennis is right. You gotta learn to shut up sometimes. "Will do" I said. "I'll try to remember that". We parked by a tall metal gate that had a chain wrapped around its entrance and a padlock hanging down to deter future intruders. "How are we gonna get in there?" I asked. "It's easy" Billy said. "The gate isn't closed real tight where it meets on its edges. You just have one person hold it open enough and we can shimmy right through. I've done it dozens of times here". I followed them as we entered and we slid inside one by one. Billy had already picked out a spot before I was done and was sitting down and whipping out a syringe. I glanced down onto the orange dirt ledges and could see hundreds of used bottle caps under my feet. "This place must be popular" I quipped. "You get the beauty of the singing birds, the trees cascading down from above, and get to sit on a piece of shale and blow out your mind" Dennis laughed. "It is very pretty here though" he retorted. "I can see the irony in this" I laughed "It's an oxymoron in a way. A place of such beauty and possible death at the same time". "No need to get all philosophical on us" Dennis laughed. "It's just a place to do drugs, bro". By this time, Billy had already nodded out and was coming to. "You wanna try some, Ronnie?" he asked "I have plenty left over, man. I can tighten you up". Dennis approached me from behind and whispered in my ear "Don't do it, bro" he said. "He's just trying to get you hooked so he can use you for a car ride all of the time". "Nah, Billy" I replied. "That's ok, man. I don't like shit that makes me go to sleep" Agitated, Billy yelled "You would probably puke and couldn't handle it anyway. Fuck it, more for me then". "Thanks anyway Billy" I said. "You go on with your bad self" "Well" he replied. "At least you got your coke. So, you can't say I didn't turn you on". "Yes, and it was pretty good too. So, thanks for that". "No problem" he mumbled as he was becoming more awake. "Well, if you done here" I said. "I'm gonna go back home now. I have shit to do when I get back". I stood there as Billy motioned Dennis over for a quiet conversation I couldn't hear. When they concluded, Billy waved me over. "I'm gonna stay in the city tonight, man" he mumbled. "Dennis is gonna ride back with you, ok?" "All right" I responded. "Are you sure you're gonna be all right?" "He'll be fine" Dennis chuckled. "Billy was born for the city, bro. He knows all the ins and outs." "Ok, then" I replied. "If that's what you want, I guess We'll see you later". Billy motioned us away with his hand and said "Go on now. Go on and have a good time on me. I'll see you guys whenever and thanks again for helping me out. "No problem" I blurted as I waved goodbye. "Anytime".

I was invited to a house party at Jackie Boy G"s and brought along my girlfriend. Almost everyone from Edison was there and it was held in his basement. Soon after we arrived a guy named Joey D. asked me if I wanted to buy some diet pills. I declined from across the room as I didn't have any money on me. He instantaneously started to berate me yelling "You probably couldn't handle them anyway". I rolled my eyes at him and said "Whatever you say, you fucking weirdo". "What did you say, what did you say?" he asked shouting and trying to provoke a fight. As I stepped forward for a possible altercation, my girlfriend reminded me about the Edison judge"s promise to incarcerate me for any future offenses. "Shit" I said. "I really wanna fight this guy. But, I don't wanna go to jail either". I turned to leave and had to listen to him more "That's right, walk away, walk away". I gave him the finger behind my back and we went outside. After a while, I had to take a piss. So, I left my girlfriend in the front yard and searched for the ground floor bathroom. On my way there, one of Jackie Boy's younger sisters was having a hard time controlling some guests she had invited without Jackie Boy's knowledge. "You can't go upstairs or you have to leave" she screamed. "No one is allowed up there. I told you already". These kids were visibly intoxicated and looked like the jocks that all of my friends and I hated. Not about to listen, she flew down the cellar stairs to find her brother for assistance. Jackie Boy went up and reminded them that they weren't invited by him and weren't really supposed to be there. Right away they gave him attitude. "Fuck you!" the biggest lunkhead yelled. "We can go wherever we want" "No you can't" Jackie Boy replied. "You're gonna have to leave now". "We aren't going anyplace" another one said. "So, get lost". "Wait right here" Jackie Boy said. "I have a surprise for you". He returned to the basement and recruited some of us as back up. As I was walking out of the bathroom, I ran into the punks being forcibly removed. As they were being tossed down the front stairs, the one with the biggest mouth was screaming that they would be back for revenge. "Just get in your fucking car and leave you fucking losers" Jackie Boy warned. "You're lucky you didn't get your asses beat".

Returning back to the party, everyone thought that the dispute was over. We had seen the aggressors leave and thought that was the end of it. An hour later, we heard what sounded like bottles being broken from in front of the house. I was standing outside with my girlfriend by the large tree again when everyone came rushing out to see what the commotion was. The kids who had been kicked out previously had returned. But this time, they brought reinforcements. Seeing this, Jackie Boy held open the front screen door and screamed "Everybody out of the house. Right now! I need every guy up here to teach these assholes a lesson". "Assholes?" one of the punks yelled from a car window. "We'll show you who the assholes are!" Suddenly, all of the boys from their two cars jumped out and came running up the driveway. "Big mistake" JR G. said. "These guys are just asking for it". "Where the fuck are these clowns from?" asked his brother Dennis. "I've never seen them before". "I think my sister said they're from Dunellen" Jackie Boy replied. "Well, they're about to get some Edison street justice" Dennis laughed. The jocks came bounding over the hedges like fire ants looking for a victim. Immediately, they were outnumbered and met with superior force. I wanted to jump in to assist, but my girlfriend kept holding the court judge over me. She kept pulling me back by my sleeve and begging me to not get involved. "They're my friends. I have to help" I yelled. "So, back the fuck off a little". I was successful somewhat as I tripped one of them as he rounded the tree. He fell flat on his jaw making it easier for my friends to trounce him. As I watched, more and more Edison guys jumped on the enemy. Like intruders upsetting a hive, my friends were on them like wasps protecting their queen. I saw Dennis and JR"s fists pumping in and out of a circle on two Dunellen kids in the middle. Deservedly so, they were getting pummeled into oblivion. Seeing that they were being beaten with no hope of a victorious outcome, they waited for a loophole and escaped. Jumping back into their cars, Jackie Boy retrieved a rock from his yard. He wound up his arm and threw the projectile straight into the last vehicle"s rear window. With the sound of shattering glass, the jocks sped off in fear. Though they had lost terribly, they insisted on still running their mouths. We all watched laughing as they exited the cul de sac, never to be seen again.

I had what I didn't know to be our final gig with our band in the basement of a fraternity house at Ryder College in Lawrenceville. It seemed that our drummer Donnie was enrolled there and had secured a performance for us at a keg party opening for a band named Joker"s Wild. We did what I thought was a good show and I retreated to a lounge area to the right of the room. I had a blazing migraine and wanted to decompress before my ride home. Dave came in after a little while and asked me why I wasn't mingling with the crowd. I tried to explain to him that I was ill and I"d come in a little bit by the side of the stage for a view. "I'm watching Rosie Greer in some movie where he has two heads". I exclaimed. "I'll be out soon after". Satisfied with this, he left and I went on to watch the rest of the program with my girlfriend. I actually used that excuse as a diversion as my headache was getting progressively worse. Eventually, my girlfriend helped me out to spend a few minutes with the audience to hear that band. Unimpressed with them, I went back to the couch in the lounge and tried to close my eyes. It wasn't that Joker"s Wild wasn't any good; it was just that being sick I wasn't in the mood for them. I found them to be average and thought that our band was better than they were. When the party was over, I approached our band members and remarked that "do to my migraine" I was going home. I usually helped with load out of the equipment. But this time, I was incapacitated. Later on, I received some feedback from some attendees that insisted I was "stuck up with lead singer"s disease". They thought I acted as if was too good for everyone and it was the reason why I "escaped" to the lounge after the show. That was simply not true and I remember thinking when I heard that that those people were sadly misinformed.

A few days later at one of our rehearsals, I asked Dave what the people had thought of us. "They thought you acted way too Jaggerish" he said. "Perhaps you should tone it down some?". "Perhaps I should tone it down?" I thought. "How would you like it if I asked you to tone down your influences?" I was hurt by this. But as usual, I kept it to myself. Dave didn't like the Stones anyway. So, to approach him about it would have been a futile. We practiced some new cover songs we were working on such as Aerosmith"s Seasons of Wither and Bowie"s Ziggy Stardust. Ziggy was a disaster as we just couldn't seem to get the tempo together. Undaunted, I decided to try to sneak in a Stones tune again. Surprisingly, Dave relented and allowed us to perform Gimme Shelter. Elated by his decision, I wanted to give it my all. I've always been good at high falsetto parts so I did the background vocal in the middle as well. Ted was always aggravated by this and would beg me to leave it out. Complaining that it hurt his ears, I refused and would laugh it off as being part of the song. Soon, we made a demo tape that I submitted for a dance at my little brother Erik"s junior high school. I never heard back from them. So, I figured it was a wash. At our next band meeting, minus Donnie, I made suggestions that maybe we should explore playing clubs and writing our own songs. Dave wasn't interested and said he had something to tell us. I figured it would be good and couldn't wait to hear. "I'm breaking up the band" he said. "Donnie is going away to his college and won't be able to play with us anymore". Shocked by this, I asked him why. "How come you're breaking up the band now? We're just starting to get good? Can't we just get another drummer?" "I don't want to play without my brother in the band" he replied. "So, that's the end of it". A few months later, Dave started a cover band named Nursery Cryme that did nothing but Genesis songs. "So much for refusing to no longer play without your brother?" I thought. Toward the end of our band Dead End"s life, I felt that Dave was becoming more and more distant from me. I have always thought "Perhaps with the untrue grumblings of my "stuckupness", "lead singer"s disease", and "too much Jagger" that Dave might have thought it was becoming the "Ronnie" band? I felt it was a shame if that was the situation as it was definitely false. All I wanted to do was sing. It's unfortunate in my mind that we didn't stay together. I had high hopes for us and thought we would have done well. I guess Dave"s vision was different than mine.

CHAPTER 7

Work, Life, & the Pursuit of Sloppiness

I had been working a succession of go nowhere jobs and was getting a little depressed. Most of my friends had been successful procuring higher paying positions and I was becoming jealous trying to do the same. In Edison, you had a few choices. You could enroll at Middlesex County College (country club as we called it), or work at Ford, Revlon, Westinghouse, or Mobil. Those factories were the only establishments that paid a decent wage without having to finish high school. I was now age 20 and my prospects were getting smaller. I had applied at Westinghouse multiple times. But, I had never heard back from them. Ford was next to impossible to get into unless you knew a union representative, Revlon I wasn't interested in, and Mobil you had to depend on nepotism. Therefore, Westinghouse was my only hope. My friend Cliff G. worked there as well as Matt D. from my neighborhood, and an older guy named Walter L. who was a friend of my older brother. I attempted to apply again. But this time, I asked Cliff and Walter if I could use them as references. After they agreed, I jotted their names down on the application form, submitted it, and waited again. Surprisingly after a couple of months I was called for an interview. Giddy with happiness, I thought I was finally going to be able to make enough money to support myself.

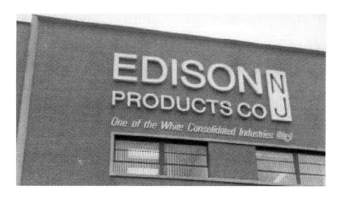

Where I Spent 8 Years Of My Life

The day came for my interview and I had to be there by 8am. I was so anxious to get a position that I arrived there at 5am instead. I waited patiently with hot coffee in hand while reciting my interview speech and refining it to the best of my ability. As the sunrise turned into morning, a few more people had shown up and began to form a line behind me. We made small talk about what it must be like to work inside the factory while we nervously waited our turn. Eventually, 8am came and we were called into an office in single file three at a time. "Sit right here on these chairs up against the wall" the receptionist instructed. "And, We'll be with you shortly". I peered around nervously and was wondering what position I might be offered. Since I was first, I was called in to be questioned. The interviewer went over my application diligently and asked me the usual questions. "Why do you want to work here? What can you contribute to our company? How do you feel about overtime? Do you realize you may be laid off occasionally? It was the usual standard bullshit stuff. When I mentioned that I was trying to get a position there for a couple of years and that I was the first in line, the interviewer wasn't impressed. He got an attitude right away. "Just because you were first in line doesn't mean you'll get to work here" he replied snidely. "We have a lot of applicants and we don't just go by how prompt you are" I immediately had a dislike for him. "What an asshole" I thought. "If it was me, I would be impressed if someone wanted a job that bad and was first in line". The interview ended and he told me if they were interested I would be called again. I walked out feeling defeated and didn't think I would get the job.

Six weeks went by and I was surprisingly called back to be hired. "Show up for an introduction" I was told. "We'll tell you what job you have when you arrive". I showed up on the required day and time and entered a room surrounded by many windows. In the middle was a long rectangular desk with many chairs around it. I was included in a presentation with about twenty other new hires and took a seat to listen. A woman employee went over our pay grades, positions and what was expected from us. "You will be instrumental in producing room air conditioners on one of our assembly lines" we were told. "After a probationary period, you will be asked to join the AFL CIO union". It all sounded good to me. But, I was really only interested in how much money I would be making. "Some of you will start as labor grade twos, while others will be labor grade fours" the woman said. "What is the difference?" I asked raising my hand. "About 25 cents" she replied laughing. "And by the way" she offered, "You're a labor grade four" "Excellent!" I thought. "I get the higher position pay". "You're all going to be sent for a physical and a blood test" she said. "If we don't call you by the end of the week, that means you passed and to show up next Monday at 7am. After that, you'll be taken to an area in the plant to start training. Congratulations and welcome to White Westinghouse". She handed us some insurance and tax withholding paperwork and we left for the day. The only thing blocking me now would be the physical.

The end of the week had come and gone and I didn't hear back from them. "I must have passed the physical and the education check" I thought. "So, I guess I show up at the beginning of the week". I went to Cliff G"s house and asked him if that was the usual procedure just to make sure. "You made it, man" he said. "You're worrying for nothing, bro. You're in". "They didn't tell me how much I'll be making an hour though?" I asked. "Its $6.97" he replied. "That's pretty good coin for a factory job" I said. "Yeah, it's not too shabby" he laughed. "That's why I work there. It's a cake job for the money". "I hope it goes well for me" I said. "I've been looking for a good job forever". "If you can deal with the repetition, you'll be fine" he chuckled. "Just do as they say until you get into the union. Once that's done, they can't fuck with you as much". "Cool" I replied. "Thanks for the heads up".

I showed up that Monday morning and was escorted to the back of assembly line 1. "This is where you'll be working" a resource manager said. "Your supervisor is a man named Bill L. You'll be in this corner here at the repair loop. When the units come down the rollers, you'll be reaching to your left and putting the fronts on the sets. All you have to do is press down on the two clips on the bottom and click the top in. It's an easy position. Congratulations on your new job. If you have any more questions, please refer to your immediate supervisor or your shop steward". A buzzer sounded signifying it was 7am and the assembly line had come to life. I watched eagerly as some units came toward me and thought "Look how slow these come down here? This job is gonna be cake". Unfortunately, it didn't last long and was all a ruse. The slow pace of the line lasted approximately a week. Soon, my job would be chaos.

> I made a friend with a coworker next to me named Roz. She informed me that this is the way it always is and not to be too worried about it. She said "As long as you don't miss too many, nobody will care. The bad ones get pushed into the repair loop anyway. If it's full, then the plant manager named Dave S. comes snooping around. He won't yell at you. But, he'll give you dirty looks. Just ignore him and he'll go away". On some days, it could get pretty crazy and frustrating trying to keep up. That's

when I found out half of the people working there were on speed. I asked around and wanted to know why? Though I dabbled with the drug in my past, I was totally oblivious for its need here. One employee informed me "You need to understand, most of the young people who start working here have no manual dexterity skills what so ever. It's the first job they"ve ever had. So, they snort that shit to keep up with the line. Well, at least until they're in the union anyway". During our lunch times, I had seen and smoked some weed in the parking lot and returned sufficiently stoned. Some of us even made a joke about it coming back inside "I guess we have to learn our jobs all over again". The crank however stayed mostly hidden. That was until more time went by. To secure a better position within the plant, you had to fill out a bid after the job was posted on a board near the cafeteria. If you were lucky enough to have the right level of seniority, the position was yours. I suffered out the two years of impaling the fronts and was promoted to a repair loop. I was fortunate no one above me had bid for it and was eager to learn how to fix them. At the back of line 1, it was an entirely different world. It was more like you were sub-contracting as an employee and they mostly left you alone. Most of the needed mending came in the form of stupid things. Like a missing corner post in a box, an upside down label, or a manual that had fallen on the floor. We'd push the rejected sets to our own loop on the left, do what was needed, and send them right back out again. Unless the line got backed up, then we had to put them on pallets. Pallet racking was very physically demanding. But, the company would do anything to keep the work flowing. During stressful times like those is when most of us took some form of accelerant type pills. There were two guys in front of the glue machine. The glue machine only did adhesive on the bottom, so they had to use a roller for the tops by hand. Their names were Gary and Joe. Joe was a huge guy and had the best sense of humor during a calamity. Gary was Robin to his Batman and they fed off each other"s jokes. Each morning, Joe would ask for "the word of the day".

Not surprisingly, it almost always had to with drugs. I"d ask "So? What's the word of the day, Joe?" "The word of the day is, upper" He'd reply. Then, He'd hand out pills named Robin"s eggs. They were speckled in light blue with brown flecks that would keep you going for hours. "Just what Dr. Joe ordered" Gary laughed. "Now, We're set for the day". It was comical watching them some days trying to keep up with the glue. But, they always made the best of it and I loved working with them. One day, I came into work and was told "Bill L. no longer works here. You have a new supervisor and she's from India". She was very hairy on her face and arms, and had a thick black mane that cascaded down her back to her waist. None of us were ever able to pronounce her name correctly. So, the workers simply deemed her "Wolf Pussy". The line was starting to have a high turnover rate and newcomers were sometimes brought in. I met a new guy who worked a screw gun named Pat S. Pat looked like Jesus and had a friend who got hired along with him named Kurt W. Both of them dealt speed. So much so, when someone needed amphetamine replacement, we'd send others to go see them. We named them "The Keeper of the Crystal and his side kick The Spoon". They had so much crank that half of the assembly line depended on them. They boasted that they made more cash from dealing drugs than they did from actually working. It was amazing that management never found out. It was that, or they simply didn't care.

The longer I worked on line 1, the more people I met. It was inevitable as when the plant was really cranking, there were over 2,000 employees on 3 shifts. There was a cast of characters who all went by various nicknames. It was like I was working but still in high school and some of them were quite hilarious. There was Johnny Handbag and Reed the Demon Seed from Keansburg, Brian Bulkhead who got his name because his head was shaped like a square, two black guys named Handsome Wayne the Self Proclaimed Mail Order Reverend and Muta Man the Incredible Compact Kid, Amphead (which was myself) Spliff (who was my friend Cliff G.), Squeaky (a girl who had a tendency to rat everyone out for no reason other than for personal gain), Step Dad, Baloo the bear, Alkahalsie, Shower (a dirty and disgusting girl who never changed her clothes) and many others. We also had names for management and supervisors that were equally as funny. They had such names as The Infamous Brow (Dave S. the plant manager. He had an arched eyebrow that would pop up pronounced when he was angry), Charlie the One Armed Bandit (he lost one of his arms in one of the machines), Al the Scowl (a German American guy who was always pissed off and spit on the floor as he passed by if you refused to work for him) Vin the Fin (a supervisor in the coils department), Bob the Slob (a supervisor on line 2 who would put his leg up on the rollers to try to show he was tough to impress young girls), and others.

By now, Wolf Pussy had given me a steady helper named Russell. Russell and I pretty much had full reign over our repair area as long as we kept our loop empty and clean. Wolf Pussy loved to show off to the plant manager Dave S. how efficient she could be. What she never knew was that when our loop was overflowing, we would hide pallets of broken sets inside the poly foam room. "Out of sight" we'd say, meant "out of mind". On one particularly busy morning, the assembly line was really popping. Units were coming down like termites rampaging from within a colony. Russell and I asked Wolf Pussy for some help. She sent us Johnny Handbag and Reed. Russell and I had made a napping area under our repair table by leaning large sections of cardboard against it and taping all of the corners down. It was flimsy and not permanent. But, it worked well when we didn't want to be seen. Inside, we had taken foam rubber strips with adhesive backings and stuck them to the floor to make a bed. It made a perfect hide out to get some sleep while others acted as a look out. I had some pills with me named

Elavil I had snatched from my mother's prescription bottle after she had mentioned that they would help calm a person down. If I was too wired on some speed, I simply ingested one or two to become normal. Reed had told me that he was very edgy and wanted to know if I would give him some. "Sure" I said. "I'll give you one. But, I have to warn you that they may make you drowsy". "I can handle it" he replied. "I've taken Quaaludes before. If I can handle those, I can handle anything". So, I handed him one from my pocket and he swallowed it without hesitation.

As the day wore on, Reed has disappeared. "Johnny?" I asked. "Where"s your friend at, man? Wolf Pussy is gonna be asking questions about where he is if he doesn't show his face pretty soon". "I haven"t seen him" he replied. "Go and ask Russell". I found Russell and asked him the same. He hadn't seen him either. "He's gotta be around here some place?" I thought. "Maybe he's in the bathroom? If we don't find him, he's gonna get fired or written up for leaving his work station". After a short lull in the assembly line, our loop had become packed again. "We better hurry up and get these fixed and off of here" I said. "Or, Wolf Pussy"s gonna be on the prowl". "Johnny?" I asked. "Could you reach down underneath the table and hand me a strip of foam please? This unit is missing one". He slid one of the large cardboard sections to his left and there was Reed balled up in a fetal position fast asleep. He was snoring and looked like a baby. We started to laugh hysterically. "What the fuck is he doing under there?" I asked. "No wonder we couldn't find him?" "I guess that pill you gave him earlier knocked him out" chuckled Johnny. Just then, Russell appeared. "I just came back from the bathroom looking for him" he said. "And, instead he's in here?" "Yeah, man" I replied. "I guess he needed to take a nap". "Don't you think we should wake his ass up? Russell asked. "Nah, fuck that" Johnny laughed. "Let him keep sleeping. I'm gonna teach him a lesson". "What are you gonna do to him?" I asked. "You know the large ink roller we use to add words to the tops of the boxes with stencils?" he asked. "Yeah" I responded.

"Watch this" he exclaimed. He took the roller to its indelible black ink pad and started soaking it back and forth to get it wet. "Watch for me" he said. "This is gonna be fun". Slowly and deliberately, he crouched down and pulled Reed to one side. He put the roller to Reed"s face and began to move it up and down on his nose. Russell and I started crying from laughing so hard. "He's going to kill you when he wakes up" I said. "He won't know it's me unless you tell him" he replied. "Do me a favor and don't say anything either. Let him walk around the rest of the day after he wakes up with it. It'll be great". When he was done, I glanced down between holding my side from laughing and Reed looked like a skunk sleeping in a burrow. "I'm gonna close this thing back up" Johnny exclaimed as he slid the cardboard back. "Make sure not to disturb him and let him wake up by himself". Russell and I agreed and left Reed alone.

Toward the end of our shift Reed still hadn't woken up yet. Our repair loop had become over full and there was no more room left in poly foam to stage the overflow. Chaos was about to ensue. "What the fuck are we gonna do?" I asked Johnny and Russell. "We don't have any more room left?" "We better tell Wolf Pussy about it" Johnny remarked. "So we don't have to take the fall for it". Since Wolf Pussy liked Russell the most, we sent him to give her the bad news. Suddenly, we heard the dreaded announcement over the plant's PA system. It was for The Infamous Brow"s extension. "Wolf Pussy, call 450. Wolf Pussy, (with angry emphasis) call 4-5-0 immediately!" We all knew when that call came that there was gonna be trouble. That meant that there was a problem and the line had stopped. In Westinghouse, the line was never to be stopped, ever. Wolf Pussy came running back to us "Get some more pallets and plywood and start stacking those units in the back" "But, Wolf Pussy?" we said. "There's no more room back there". "Make room!" she screamed. "Because, Dave S. is coming down here soon". We had a code with most of the employees on duty, if a higher up threatened us, we would purposely work slower just to piss them off. It was hard to write us up or fire us if the defect came from the front of the line anyway. The Infamous Brow knew this. So, he would come down and try to goad us along. We usually watched him and let him think he was teaching us "the right way" while all the while laughing at him behind his back. Putting new labels on boxes and adding a missing corner post wasn't rocket science. But for some reason, The Infamous Brow thought it was. I had always thought he was just obsessed with getting the line back on and thought he could intimidate us. But, it rarely ever worked. In the meantime, Reed was still under the table snoozing. Just as we had thought, The Infamous One showed up and was standing directly in front of the cardboard sleeve that Reed was sleeping behind. While Johnny, Russell, and I were on either side of The Brow, we struggled greatly trying not to laugh. We kept wondering if The Brow was going to catch him. We knew it would have been immediate dismissal for sleeping on company time. Johnny being the crafty manipulator he was, kept trying to get The Brow to another area to save his friend. It was comical watching him yell to The Brow to "please come here and help me" because "you're the boss and you know what you're doing better than me". Eventually, the surge let up and The Infamous Brow went away. About 10 minutes before it was time to clock out and go home, Reed had awoken from his golden slumber. He had been completely oblivious to what had transpired around him. "Really?" he asked confused when we told him. "The Infamous Brow was a foot away on top of me while I was sleeping under the table?" he asked dumbfounded. "That's right, man" Johnny replied as we tried not to stare at the ink stripe on his nose. "Well" Reed laughed. "Thanks for covering for me. That pill Ronnie gave me knocked me the fuck out!" "Obviously" Johnny laughed. "But, at least you didn't get caught". "Yeah" Reed replied. "I guess I was lucky this time". He arrived at work the next day with the same ink blotting on his nose, but it was slightly fainter. "You guys are fucking scumbags" he complained. "Nobody told me somebody did this shit to me until I got home. That shit is permanent ink. It'll never come off!" "You shouldn't fall asleep under tables when you were supposed to be helping us work" Johnny laughed uncontrollably. "Let that be a valuable handbag lesson to you". Reed came back each day with the stain more and more faded. It took a week until it was gone.

I had been offered another position in a third band and had accepted. I had known their drummer Tony K. for a long time through our mutual friend John H. and heard it through the grapevine that he needed a lead singer. I had liked the fact that he was from my home town and felt comfortable right away without question. When I arrived for our first rehearsal I was given an address I was familiar with. It was an old farm house with two floors that sat directly across the street from our old Zaffys nightclub hangout. To my surprise, Ronnie E. was living there and I had just found out that he had been recently been hired at Westinghouse. When I walked into the overly large living room, I was greeted by Tony"s lead guitar player George A. He was Puerto Rican like the Velez brothers so I sensed where he was coming from with his musical influences right away. He loved Santana and off style drum beats as well as most of the same tunes I had sung before. We got along after our introduction immediately. There wasn't a second rhythm guitar player with this band, so I was introduced to the bass player named Larry P. Larry I wasn't crazy about. He was overly arrogant, not particularly good looking, and generally thought his shit didn't stink. Though I let my resentment be known with Tony that I didn't like the guy, Tony insisted we keep him in the band as he was a half way decent bass player. Again, since I was the last member to be recruited, I was outvoted and Larry stayed.

We usually had rehearsals on the weekends as most of us had full time jobs. Most of the music we agreed on except that Larry would constantly badger us about doing more and more Judas Priest numbers. I had no problem with that as I could hit most of the high notes. But, Larry was beginning to grate on my nerves. At every practice and mid-way through, he would whine like a petulant child about how he deserved more input. When his fat girlfriend was there, he was even worse. During breaks, she would abscond with him into a corner and pontificate in his ear trying to convince him about how great he was and that without his contributions the band would go nowhere. After a while, I got tired of this and got into many drawn out arguments with him. It felt like I was debating with a child who had have tantrums when he didn't get his way. Eventually with much of George"s negotiating, we would come to some sort of compromise just to keep the sessions moving along. A day came where the band was asked to host a party within the house and Tony accepted. It was nice that we were playing inside in a living room atmosphere and I enjoyed the idea of us performing that way. "The more homier" I thought "the better". That was until some guests had arrived. Unknown to most of us, Ronnie E. had invited his biker friends. Now, I had no problem with bikers, it's just that they were known for getting a little more rowdy than the average American citizen. I didn't want to sing in front of people who may or may not decide to lug beer bottles past my head during our show. I had already gotten stitches from my last band mishap and I was hesitant in repeating it again. When I confronted Ronnie E. about it he laughed. "You don't have to worry about it, man. It's not like the fucking Hells Angels or The Breed are gonna show up. Its only gonna be a few of us. It's Hawk"s birthday man and we just wanted to have a little celebration for him". "A celebration?" I asked. "You don't think there's a possibility that it might get out of hand?" "Listen, man" he replied. "You watch too much fucking TV. We police ourselves. We're not stupid you know!" "I never said you guys were" I remarked. "I just don't feel like dealing with the cops if the party gets out of hand". "It won't" he said. "If it does, We'll just kick them out and bury their heads in the snow". "Ok" I chuckled. "I can live with that".

Of course more people showed up than were supposed to. The living room was packed with wall to wall revelers who were intoxicated into oblivion. I barely had enough room to spin my mic stand around let alone breathe. After a few songs, Hawk asked me if we'd play the biker anthem "Born to be Wild". I wasn't sure if the band knew it or not as we had never rehearsed it before. I knew all of the lyrics, so I whispered to Tony and asked him if it could be done. "Ask George" he replied. "He's the one We'll have to follow". As I glanced around the room, I wondered if it was a good idea to play the song as it had a tendency with some crowds to escalate wild behavior. I whispered toward George and asked "Hey, man. You know this number, right? Do you think we should play it or not?" While I was waiting for George"s response, the entire setup erupted into a chant lead by Hawk himself. "Play it!, play it, play it" they demanded screaming. "Play the fucking song!" they shrieked. "It's Hawk"s birthday, man!" " George looked back at me and asked mumbling "You know Ronnie, if we don't play this song you know what's gonna happen to us, right?" "They'll probably throw bottles at us and kick our asses?" I replied. "Seeing fear in George"s eyes, he nodded that he knew the tune and moved forward. At the stroke of his first chord, the crowd got on their feet and went ballistic. "That's right, that's right" they shrieked as I opened my mouth for the first verse. "Get your motor running, head out on the highway". It was instant pandemonium. With the little space on the floor that there was, people were singing along loudly with us while cajoling and dumping beers over each other"s heads. All I could think of was "Don't dare stop this fucking song or they're really gonna lose it". I made a circular motion with my right hand"s index finger indicating to the band to keep it going at all costs. Fortunately, George enjoyed doing Carlos Santana impersonations. So, at the mid break in the song, he decided to play a 10 minute solo. When we came to the end of the tune and stopped we were greeted with thunderous applause and ordered to play the song again. "Again?" I asked. "Don't you want to hear us play something else?" "Nooooo!" erupted the room. "Play it again!" Not wanting to risk being put in a position for a beating, we played it three more times. The only respite was we got a slight break after the second attempt by forcing everyone to sing Hawk the Happy Birthday song.

At the end of the night, he was quite moved and thanked us profusely. "We weren't really gonna do anything to you guys" he added. "We just wanted you to think that because we were having such a good time. And besides, you guys killed it. You did a really good job". "Thank you" I replied. "I'm glad you liked it and that your birthday party was a success. But, please do me a favor and don't ever ask me to play that song again!

Back at the factory, I put in for another bid after coming back from a layoff and it was accepted. I was told to report to the warehouse manager the following Monday morning. Most times an employee was supposed to give the supervisor of your present position notice that you would be moving soon. I had seen what had been done to some of my fellow workers where they would keep you there as hostage until a replacement could be found. Bound with that knowledge, I ignored that rule and went directly to my new post and reported. "You'll be driving a clamp truck on line 1 and bringing the stock back to the warehouse" the supervisor said. "I already know how to drive a forklift" I responded. "So, that shouldn't be a problem". As I mounted the truck and drove along between line"s 2 and 3, I ran into Cliff. He had put in for the same job as me and had more seniority. I was wondering why he was still driving screws into units and hadn't been relieved. So, I parked and went over to him. "What the fuck are you still doing here doing this bullshit?" I asked. "There were 6 positions open and I know you got one of them". "I know" he replied angrily. "I'm gonna get to the bottom of this shit as soon as I can". Feeling bad, I asked him if I there was anything I could do to help. "You know I sell some Coke on the side" he said. "But, I can't leave the line to supply people. If I have to stay here for a while longer, I'm gonna need you to bring it to them for me". "How have you been doing it so far?" I asked. "Well" he replied. "Anybody behind me on the line I can take care of. Each baggie has a different color twist tie. The amount inside is signified that way". "I still don't get it" I exclaimed. "It's like this" he laughed. "Say so and so down from me wants a half a gram, right? Well, a half a gram is a red twist tie. They wave at me from where they are and I simply place it somewhere inconspicuous on the unit and send it down the line. When it gets to them, they snatch it. Pretty ingenious, huh?" "But, how do they pay you?" I asked. "Oh, that" he responded. "I just catch them at lunch time". "That's fucking crazy, man" I said. "What if a supervisor sees it?" "They won't" he chuckled. "They're too busy trying to keep the line going. Besides, if they do, we create a diversion". "It's unbelievable the shit you think of" I said. "You have to be resourceful when you're trying to make money" he laughed. I drove away and pondered my next move.

The morning I reported for my new job on line 1 I was met by 2 others. One was Handsome Wayne and the other was a guy I had seen but had never met. He introduced himself as "Grady W". Cliff had seen him before and had deemed him "Cool Boy". Supposedly, Grady was known to have been a prankster and liked disappearing for long stretches of time. He would purposely let many rows of stacked units back up, and then breeze his way in to help us remove them at the last minute in what he called "Superman Style". There were more than a few times I had to laugh and caution him. "Look, man" I said. "If this shit backs up too much, they're gonna know We're fucking off. So, you have to show up here to help us more". "Work is my Kryptonite, bro" he laughed. "Don't I always show up? So, don't worry about me, man. Worry about your own self". "Ok" I replied. "But, there's only so many bathroom breaks I can tell them about you". "Solid" he said. "Let it be what it'll be". I waited for there to be no traffic on the lane we used, and I saw Johnny Handbag on a forklift whisking past me. "Where are you going?" I asked. "What department did you put in a bid for?" "I'm supplying the front of the line" he replied. "I got a job putting up metal parts". "Cool" I said. He looked around laughing and put his finger up to his lips and made the "Shhhh" gesture" What are you shushing for?" I asked. Is there something nobody is supposed to know about?" Pointing down to a large box on his forks, he giggled.

"Look inside the box and tell me what you see?" he asked. I jumped down off of my truck, lifted the lid, and peered inside. Lying on a bed of foam peanuts was Reed. He was asleep and oblivious to what was going on around him. "Again?" I asked. "He really likes to push the envelope, doesn't he?" "He's tired" Johnny laughed. "He can't help it". How long have you been driving around with him in there?" I asked "For about an hour" he replied. "Aren't you afraid somebody"s gonna open it?" "Nah" he chuckled. "They'll just think I'm resupplying the line. We do this all of the time". "Apparently so"I laughed. "Because, he didn't learn from the last time". "We have a motto when you're a handbag" he instructed. "And, exactly what is that?" I asked "Do as little as possible, whenever possible" he chuckled. "Is that why you guys are so lazy?" I asked. "Nah" he said. "The company doesn't care and doesn't pay us enough. So, we have to give them their money"s worth" "Ok, Johnny" I howled hilariously. I hopped back on my truck and went on my way.

Tony had booked us another gig in the backyard of some girl's house in South Plainfield on a Saturday afternoon. It paid $30 each and the food and beer was free. So, I accepted and was looking forward to it. Unfortunately, I had been at a Kinks, Joan Jett, and Loverboy concert the day before at JFK stadium. There, I had done way too much speed, it was hellaciously hot out, and I had become dehydrated. I was having so much trouble swallowing that no amount of cold soda, snow cones, or icy water could help me. Each time I tried, I was on the verge of panic. With my girlfriend and her friends begging me, I stuck it out until the ride back home. As we approached the entrance to the New Jersey Turnpike, I began to choke. The driver of the other couple became frightened and was asking what to do. "Do you want to go to the hospital?" he asked looking back at me in the rear view mirror. "Because, you have to tell me now before we get on this highway". "What do you want to do?" my girlfriend asked. "Just keep handing me those bottles of water you bought at the show" I replied shaking. "I think I can handle it until we get back". "Are you sure?" the driver said. "I can turn around right now if you want". "No" I whispered hoarsely. "I can make it. So, drive on". On the way back, I downed 3 or 4 bottles of water and had the driver crank up the air conditioner to freezing. Fortunately, just as we arrived home, my symptoms subsided. But, I was left with practically no voice.

The next afternoon, Tony kept calling my house leaving messages that I was due to show for the party. Not being in the mood since my throat was now raw, I got into a verbal altercation with my girlfriend. She was on another one of her attitude binges and I was refusing to respond. I kept shaking my head no until she lost it. "You have to sing at that that thing today" she screamed in my face. "You promised them" "Get the fuck away from me before I put you in the hospital" I screeched. "Can't you see that I'm sick?" I asked. "You're going, and I'm driving you there" she insisted. "So, get in the car and stop being a cry baby about it". "You don't understand" I said. "My vocals are shot. I can't hit any high notes at all". "You have to try" she replied. "Why?" I asked. "So, I can look like a fool?" "Nobody will care" she moaned. "It's only a stupid party". "Stupid for you" I screamed. "So, pull over this car because I'm getting out". She came to a dead stop and I flung open the door. "If you get out here" she said. "I'm not coming back for you". "Go fuck yourself" I shrieked. "And, you can kiss my ass too". I slammed the door closed as hard as I could and began walking down the street. I was on some lonely assed road in the old Camp Kilmer section not far from School House Lane. About a half an hour later, she came back for me. "I just went to where Tony is" she hollered. "He says you can't do this to him. He spent all morning making a stage for the band and nobody helped him. He says if you don't show up, you're out". "Fuck him and his band" I thought. "I'm in fucking pain here, seriously". After much begging, I relented and reentered the vehicle. "Take me to this stupid fucking show" I complained. "But I can tell you right now it's gonna suck".

We arrived and the band was already tuning up. I glanced over to my left and saw some other musicians I despised. They were in a group called Fortune and I thought they sucked. All they ever played were Van Halen covers and they thought their shit didn't stink. It wasn't so much that the guitars and drums were bad, it was their singer who had absolutely no range what so ever. All he did was prance around the stage trying to imitate David Lee Roth"s goofy shtick while desperately playing to all the ladies. He was the quintessential poser for sure. As I approached the stage, George asked me how I was. "I'll do the best I can" I replied. "You're late" arrogant Larry remarked. "We were supposed to go on 15 minutes ago" "Shut the fuck up and play" I warned him. "Or else, there might not be a show". I motioned for George to come closer whispering "Hey, man. Just play the shit that's easy for me to sing today, ok?" "Yeah" George replied. "We heard about what happened to you yesterday". We blew threw a couple of numbers and I had to take a rest. I turned out of ear shot of Larry and told Tony "Let that asshole sing a few songs, I'm gonna take a break and I'll be back in a little while". "Ok" Tony said. "I'll tell him". I gave the thumbs up to George and walked away.

Larry being his usual dickhead self, took over the lead microphone smiling. George got on the 2nd mic and made an announcement. "It seems our lead singer Ronnie here got a little too rowdy at the Kinks concert last night. So, he's gonna guzzle a few beers to ease his throat and he'll be right back". No one really took notice until Larry began to sing. He was doing a Judas Priest song and he was butchering it. "Damn, he sucks" I mumbled. "I really wish Tony would let us get rid of him". After a few more tunes, a tall pretty girl came over to me while I was resting on the grass. "Can you please make him stop?" she asked. "He's really terrible and all of us hate him". "I'll see what I can do" I replied. "I might be able to sing better now" "Please do" she said. "Because if not, We're probably going to leave". I stood up and went back to my mic while the band was in between songs. On the way there, I was approached from a member of Fortune. They were always scheming for gigs. So, I knew exactly what he wanted. "Your voice is gone today" he remarked. "Why don't you let us take it from here for you? I spoke to the girl's mother. We don't want any of the money and you'll still get paid. We just want to play. What do you think?" he asked. "No" I thought "You scumbags just want to try to upstage us". "I'll ask the rest of the guys if it's ok with them" I replied. "I'll be back in a minute". I walked over to Tony for his opinion. He gave me a resounding "NO" as a reply. "Fuck those guys" he said. "I don't like them either. It's our spot today. Let those idiots find their own show". Laughing, I strode back to the guy with an answer. "Tony says no, buddy. So, I don't know what to tell you". Annoyed, he replied. "Fuck it then, man. Do whatever you want.

When it was time for me to go on again, George went to turn his amplifier back on. He hit a few notes and it went dead. "Who"s the asshole who"s been fucking with the power?" Tony asked screaming. "Ronnie & Marie, Ronnie & Marie" some voices screamed from the audience. I knew right away it was the Fortune punks with their shitty, no talent singer. They were attempting to make fun of me by equating me to the Donny & Marie show. "Go in the house and check the breakers" Tony asked. I went inside and sure enough, they were tripped. I reset them and we continued. A few seconds later, it happened again. Tony rose up from his drummer"s stool and marched back into the house. He came back a few seconds later with the owner in tow. He breezed right by me and spoke into my mic. "Ok you fucking douchbags who want to act like children, this is our gig and you're no longer invited. So, it's time for you to leave". "Who said so?" asked a Fortune band member. Tony pointed to a middle aged woman in the doorway. "She does, you're all out". The woman looked over at them with anger on her face and swatted them away. "See you later, losers" Tony said. "It was nice knowing ya". After they were escorted off the property, I got up enough strength to sing a roaring rendition of Mountain"s Mississippi Queen. It was flawless and I had redeemed myself. Later, while settling up our pay, Larry arrogantly spoke up "You know, I should have gotten paid more for doing all of the work. I had to sing most of the songs. It's not my fault that Ron here lost his voice". Looking at Tony and trying to restrain myself I demanded "Get him the fuck away from me before I kill him. He has no business being in any band, period". As usual, Larry looked away with his fat girlfriend and fled.

Cliff and I had been making fun of our work environment and some people we were there with. We especially liked to parody famous songs and sing them while on the way back from our break times. One of his favorites was over a girl who worked on line 2 who never seemed to keep herself clean. We never knew her name, but Cliff had deemed her "Shower". So much so, that whenever we encountered her while walking back to our forklifts, he had changed the lyrics to the Rolling Stones song Shattered. "What are you humming there?" I asked him as she walked by in her greasy soiled jeans. "Shower, shower. Huh, shadoobie. That chick's all dressed in soiled rags. She's looking tattered. Don't mind the maggots. Ahuh!" That's a good one" I said chuckling. "What else have you got?" "Look at all the workers as we pass by" he laughed. "They all look like robots". "Robots?" "I asked. "As in how?" He started the first bars of a Who song. "Welcome to the plant, I guess you all know why you're here. Because you're losers, and there's no education near. If you want to make money here, you can't let units fall. So, pick up a screw gun, place in a wire, you know that this job"s a bore". It was hilarious and I couldn't stop laughing. Getting to the end of the factory was an arduous task and usually took about 10 minutes to go from one end to the other. Sometimes, we'd pass other friends like Matt D. who"d be singing his own parodies. We'd catch him on a corner on his hi lo singing a verse from a Fleetwood Mac song he had changed the words to. We cracked up as we heard him mumble "gimme lines, gimme sweet little lines". Not to be undone, Cliff would usually come up with more. As we climbed the stairs over one line to get to a thoroughfare, some units at the end on the rollers became bunched up in a corner. No one was attending to them and they began to teeter and fall on the floor. They were piling up and were starting to get damaged. Cliff saw this and another parody came out of his mouth that was from Simple Minds. "If you turn the line on, see sets falling, walk on by, sets keep falling, sets keep falling, down, down, down". By the time we mounted our machines; I was holding my side and crying. I think the point was since our work was so mundane and mindless; most of us would do anything to break the routine with comedy to have an easier day.

On one afternoon, I was called to water the batteries in all of the clamp trucks. Our supervisor usually rotated employees and we took turns accordingly. Cliff came by and mentioned that a coworker was in trouble. "Did you hear about Grady W.?" he asked. "No" I replied. "What did he do now?" "You know our one foreman named Mike?" he asked. "The one with the limp from an accident?" I replied. "Yeah" Cliff said. "That's him". "Apparently he and Mike got into it because Grady disappeared again". "So, They'll write him up. So what?" I asked. "No, man. You don't get it. Let me finish. Hop on your truck and follow me. You"ve got to see this". As we turned the corner to get into the lane we used for moving stock, Cliff stopped abruptly and pointed at a box that was stacked on top of another. "What does that say?" he asked laughing". Right across the middle of the container was a phrase emblazoned in bright red ink. It read "Mike is one of Jerry"s kids". It was alluding to the fact that Mike was like a disabled child that was usually seen on the Jerry Lewis muscular dystrophy telethon. "You know he's gonna wig and have Grady fired when he sees that shit" I said howling. "That's kinda cold and I can't believe he did that. Are you sure it was him?" I asked. "Oh, it had to be" Cliff replied. "Because him and Mike hate each other. But, there's no proof. So, they can't do anything. I just thought it was funny and wanted you to see it". Months went by and it remained. I guess Mike had never caught it. If he did, I was confident Grady would have been gone.

On a cold winter morning, I got to enjoy my first of many Westinghouse suspensions. I had reported for work but had a fever and wasn't feeling very well. All I wanted was a hot cup of tea before my shift was ready to begin. I approached the coffee machine in the cafeteria and deposited my 50 cents, pushed the button for what I wanted and waited. There was nothing. No sound of liquid being dispensed, no cup dropping down into position to be filled, no hot steamy beverage to soothe my throat, not even a trickle. I had suddenly become enraged. Since my older brother still worked at Automatic Catering, I was livid as he had told me about a scheme called a "coin jam". I felt I had become a victim. The route men he said would "purposely" stick a piece of gum in the coin chute blocking payment down into the coin box. That way, it facilitated a "pick up" that was untraceable for their pockets later on. If no inventory was lost, no money would be missing. The more I thought about it, the more infuriated I became. I was ill and wanted comfort. I wanted revenge. With the pent up emotion of a defense football player on a 10 yard line, I stepped back, raised my right leg, centered my heel over the coin return area, and kicked the machine to kingdom come. I was determined to get a refund at all costs. As the metal box swayed from side to side, the head of the Human Resources Department Tom A. had been skulking behind me. I hadn't seen him and didn't know he was there. "You have to come with me" he said. "For what?" I asked as I turned to him. "I'm sick and this piece of shit stole my money. All I wanted was a hot drink. It's happened to me before and they need to stop this thieving bullshit". "You can't go around breaking private property just because it took your quarters" he replied. "All you had to do was go to the register and fill out a form for that". "I don't have time for that crap" I yelled. "By the time I filled that out, the line would be on". "You still have to come with me" he demanded. "Because, you just can't act that way while working here".

He made me follow him to his office, made a few phone calls, leaned over his desk and blurted "You're going home right now and you're suspended for 3 days. We'll get in touch with you to let you know if you're terminated or not". "Terminated? I asked. "Over a cup of tea?" "No" he replied. "For breaking company rules and attempting to destroy another company's property". "Do whatever you have to do" I said. "But, I think you're ridiculous". He handed me a card with his idea of an infraction listed on it and I left. Three days later, he called me "Come into work as soon as you can" he said. "We have something we have to tell you and we can't do it over the phone". "Fuck" I thought. "I guess I'm fired". I arrived in his office and took a seat. I was sure I was being let go. Just then, a union representative named Ray W. walked in. "It's come to our attention that you were unlawfully suspended without a shop steward being present" he said. "Therefore, your alleged offense has been retracted and you'll also be getting 3 days retroactive pay on your next pay check". He looked at Tom A. and grinned. "Why did you even bother suspending him?" he asked. "Everybody kicks the coffee machine? Even I kick the machine?" "We stand by our decision" Tom A. replied visibly perturbed. "And, next time Ron" he warned. "I won't be so lenient". "Just do your job" I said. "And, follow the rules". "Get him out of my sight" he grumbled. "I don't want to see him anymore". I felt like I was back in Guzak"s office in TJ all over again.

Cliff and I were in the second cafeteria in the back that only had vending machines with no live attendants. He had come up with a scam to be able to get extra free food out of one of them without having to pay twice. "Watch this" he said as he slid open one of its doors. It was built with sections on each level with openings like the defunct automats that had been in New York City. Except this one spun in circles around a cylinder in its center. Therefore, each level and corresponding door could hold up to 5 items at a time. I watched as he paid the fee, opened a door for some pie, took out the dish, and with his opposing hand forced the door to stay open. "Take this shit" he demanded as he passed it to me. "And, watch the master in disguise" He pushed on the former pie"s chamber with his fingers until he got it just right. "Once there's enough centrifugal force" he said. "The cylinder in the center will get enough momentum. After that happens, the motor will move the box to the next item". "How did you figure that out?" I asked. "Easy" he replied. I was buying something one day and I saw that there was no stop mechanism. I noticed that if I pushed on it a little, it would keep going. So, I pushed really hard and I got instant free shit". "Wow" I laughed. "It's like two for one?" "Sometimes five" he chuckled. "That's pretty cool if you're low on funds". "It's not about funds" he said. "It's about their prices are too damn high for this mediocre food. So, fuck them. Have some pie and eat up. I'm gonna go back for another!"

During one of the plants layoffs where we were reassigned, an election was up for a new shop steward. Johnny Handbag won one of the nominations and was on a roll. Frightened by this, the union tried to deter his win at all costs. The last thing they wanted was a young partier with authority who would refuse to negotiate with the company rules. Of course all of us drug takers wanted Johnny for the future as we all knew it would be beneficial for representation later on. So, like a sweating Democrat at a reciprocal favored kick back party, Johnny went around the plant campaigning. Reed and I were working on the end of line 3 stapling up boxes of dehumidifiers when Johnny stopped by for a chat. "What's up fellas?" he asked. "You're gonna vote for me, right?" "You're gonna need a salute" Reed suggested. "A salute?" Johnny asked. "For what?" "To show your Handbag authority" he replied. "Just like the Romans and the Germans did". "What the fuck are you talking about, man?" I asked. "Like a Nazi salute?" "He'll never win with that". "No, no, no" Reed insisted "Like this". He held out his right arm, raised his fist up to the center of his chest, and beat on it twice. "Just like the Romans did, man" he laughed. "Except, you beat on your chest twice to show you have heart". This gesture made me laugh hysterically. In between breaths, I suggested. "How about you make it even better. Raise your arm up like Reed said, make the two beats, and then drop your arm back down and arch it like you're carrying a handle. "That's it!" Johnny howled. "That's exactly what I'm looking for". "Ok" I said. "So, anytime someone you see who you think supports you, give them that sign and They'll reciprocate their loyalty". "This is gonna be funny as fuck" said Reed. "But, you're gonna need a slogan next". "What should we use?" I asked Johnny. "It's your election". "Carry me, I have a flesh handle on my back" he chuckled. "I'm tired". "Perfect" yelled Reed. "It accompanies your other saying with gusto. I love it!" "Do as little as possible, whenever possible" Johnny replied. "Well, at least until all of us get a raise". "Wait a minute" Reed said. "We're gonna need a song too". "What kind of song?" I asked. "Let's make it a blues tune" he replied. "Make some guitar sounds, Ronnie?" he asked. As I voiced a few bars of music, he started to sing "Well, I woke up this morning. Da dum da dum. And, I was late for work. Da dum da dum. I grabbed my self a beer. Da dum da dum. And, a dirty shirt. Cause I'm a handbag, baby. H-A-N-D-B-A-G. Da dum da dum. And, if you ain't seen a handbag. Then you ain't a bag like me". It was quite comedic watching half of the plant give Johnny the Handbag salute and sing that tune for the remainder of the voting period. Of course the union fixed it so he never won. But, he kept his humor and was happy to have shaken them up temporarily for our cause.

Reed And I Working On The Back Of Line 3

Another morning on line 3 Reed had gotten to talking about one of the supervisors he disliked. "I hate that one armed bandit" he said. "Charlie who lost his arm?" I asked. "Yeah" he replied. "He rides around the plant on his three wheeled bike fucking with everybody for no reason. He only gets away with it too because he can't be fired". "I guess they gave him a lifetime job after he got hurt so he wouldn't sue" I said. Just then, he started singing a song by the Police. But, he was changing the words. "Don't point your, don't point your, don't point your stub at me". Suddenly and without warning, Charlie pulled up on his bicycle behind him. He put his finger up to his lips indicating he wanted the rest of us to keep quiet. It was obvious he wanted to observe what Reed was doing. All the while, Reed kept on singing "He's one armed, he's jealous, he's got no family. Sometimes it's not so easy, with one arm trying to pee. Don't point your, don't point your, don't point your stub at me". I began to make faces and nod my head to try to get Reed to turn around. But, he wasn't getting it. Charlie finally got off his bike and came over to him. Reed at first looked like he had seen a ghost. "So, you think your little song was funny, was it?" Charlie asked. I was trying so hard not to laugh that I dropped the staple gun on the floor. "Why, yes." Reed chuckled. "I think its good enough for the radio". "Just don't let me catch you doing anything wrong after that tune" said Charlie. "Because, I'll see how far I can stick my stub up your ass". "I"d imagine that would hurt" Reed said. "Especially since I don't know how long your injury is". "Just keep it up and you'll find out" Charlie grumbled. "Just keep on testing me". He got on his bike and drove away.

At our next band practice, George hadn't shown up and I wanted to know why. "What happened to George?" I asked Tony annoyed. "He's not coming" he replied. "He quit the other day and we've got a new guy" A new guy?" I asked. "What fucking new guy? George was perfect and already knew all of the material. Who"s boneheaded decision was that?" "Larry and I talked about it and we decided we wanted to go in a different direction" he said. "So?" I asked. "You made a fucking decision without consulting me first, right? What kind of shit is that if I'm a member of the band too?" "There's nothing we can do about it" he said. "The decision has been made. A new guy we got named Billy W. will be here shortly". "I'm telling you right fucking now" I howled. If I don't get along with this Billy guy, I quit". Larry who was off in a corner with his obese girlfriend mumbled "Good, then I'll get to sing instead of him". I ran over and got right in his face. "What did you say you fucking tone deaf loser? You couldn't sing yourself off of a ship if it was sinking". "My girlfriend and a lot of other people beg to differ" he replied. "They think I sing great" "Like at that party where my voice was out?" I asked sarcastically. "Yeah" he said "I was the star of the show that day". Laughing as hard as I was able and trying to catch my breath I chuckled. "No, man. You suck and have always sucked. You can't sing period. You screech like a cat in a blender. You only attempted it because your overly large girlfriend with the big mouth lies to you about your abilities to prop your as up. I had two girls come over to me that day while you were on stage begging me to get rid of you. I bet you didn't know that though, right?" "Nobody told me that. You're just jealous of me" he replied. "Yeah" I said. "Like I'm really jealous of a guy with a fat slob girlfriend who wears furry boots out in public with other weirdo clothes? You're pathetic, man". Tony, becoming concerned tried to referee. Surprisingly, he took my side. "Ronnie's our lead singer, Lar" he said. "And, he somewhat has a point" he added trying not to hurt his friends feelings with a compromise. "You can sing a couple of songs ok sometimes. But, Ronnie has the range". "You're fucking A right I do" I yelled. "And, it's about time your asshole friend here learns his place". Larry"s face began to look flustered and his cheeks were turning red. It was obvious has was pissed and wanted to fight. He took a step toward me with an attempt. As he got closer, his girlfriend ran out the back door crying. "Come on, man. Make your move" I warned him. "You're girlfriend isn't here to protect you anymore". His eyes were welling up from his anger and I waited for a response. Just then, Tony jumped up and was separating us with his arms. "Ok, you guys" he begged. "You can settle your differences later. I promise We'll negotiate and get to the bottom of it after rehearsal. Let's just all calm down and see what happens after Billy gets here". Larry turned away looking for his girlfriend while shaking his head and murmuring something. Then, the back door flew open. We were expecting Larry"s girlfriend to come back. But, it was the new guy Billy instead. He approached me and stuck his hand out for a shake introducing himself. "Hey, man" he said. My name"s Billy. You must be Ron, right? What the fucks going on in here? I can feel the tension in the air like it's a mortuary". "Just internal band bullshit" Tony replied. "But, We're over it now" "Good" Billy said. "Here"s my amp. Where do I plug in?" "Behind that curtain by the window there's a plug" Tony offered. "Once you tune up with Larry, I guess we can start then".

We went over a few songs we knew, and a couple Billy wanted to practice that we didn't. "So far", I thought. "He was good, but not as good as George". While taking a mid-rehearsal break, George emerged from the kitchen area. He had walked in like he usually did without knocking. No one knew how long he had been standing there. "Who the fuck is this guy?" he asked. "Is he going to be our second guitar player? "I thought you said George quit the other day? I asked Tony. "So, what the fuck is this crap all about?" "I knew if I told you the truth, that you would have followed him" he replied. "And, I didn't wanna lose you as the singer". "Quit?" asked George. "I didn't quit anything". "I'm not here to only be the rhythm guitar player" blurted Billy. "Nobody told me that. So, if I'm not the lead one. I'm out of here" "Good" George replied sarcastically. "I was in this band first. So, it's better if you leave then". "Say something,

Tony?" I asked, "Because, you're the one who did all this garbage". "You know what?" George asked. "Don't even bother, man. I left my amp here in the other room. I'm gonna grab it and I'm gone. Fuck you guys!" As I was attempting to coerce George into staying, he and Billy started trading more words. Eventually, Billy lunged at him and they began tumbling on the floor. Billy hit George first. But, George gave him a black and had gotten the best of him. "Break it up, break it up" I screamed. "You guys are gonna get the cops called on us". Recovering from his orbital wound, Billy had had enough. "This band is a fucking joke" he proclaimed. "Your friend here can have this band. It's not worth a fist fight with somebody I just met. I don't need this shit. So, I'm leaving". "Go soak your fucking eye, you fucking Gringo" George replied. "And, don't worry about this group. I'm leaving right after you anyway. Ronnie's the only one who has loyalty here". I watched as they loaded their gear into their cars and left. "Now, we have no band Tony, you fucking asshole" I said. "One of them will be back" he responded. "Because, before you joined, I went through this all of the time". "Well" I said. "Your time is no longer my time. Plus, I hate this douchbag Larry" I said pointing at him. So, I quit as well. I'll see you later, Tone." "And, goodbye to you and Miss Piggy as well" I quipped as I turned passing them laughing. While descending the porch steps leading out to my car, I could hear them arguing behind me. I never played in their band again.

Another layoff came. So, Cliff and I were sent to work in the coils department. In coils, we were assistants to the operators of the big machines that stamped out fins with holes in them. After the fins would pile up on some pins, we took a separate set of pins, inserted them on the edges, and pulled them off and set them in racks that were on wheels. I used to laugh at myself while working there as the racks always reminded me of having taken food from the back of the Jade Pagoda. The coils section was also very loud. Fortunately, we were allowed to wear headphones. Of course, Cliff found a way around the boredom of that and we used audio headphones instead. "You have a Sony Walkman, right?" he asked. "Yeah" I replied. "I have a copycat one that's just like it". "Good" he said. "Wear a hoodie like I do then. Put the Walkman in the big pocket in the front by your waist and snake the wire up through the back behind your neck. The hoodie will hide the headphones. Nobody will see it that way and you can listen to tunes for our entire shift". "Genius" I thought. Since we were allowed to sit in a chair in between sessions, he added "You can also position the racks around you in a U shape. That way, you have extra protection of not being seen by people like the Infamous Brow and Vin the Fin". Vin the Fin was our new supervisor in coils and was a very laid back person to get along with. His philosophy was "as long as you get your work done and don't give me any grief, I don't care what you do". Cliff and I loved this as if you needed a relief break to go to the bathroom, you usually had to wait for a stand in before they'd let you go. That way, we could take breaks as often as we wanted as long as we weren't too obvious about it.

We came in one morning for our usual shift and were greeted by some coworkers that we already knew. The Keeper of the Crystal"s sidekick The Spoon had just been transferred in and was assigned to the machine that cleaned the evaporators. Behind him, was a guy named Kevin who we gave the nickname Alchohalsie. He had a penchant for the drink and sometimes showed up half blitzed or with a hangover from hell. We were a group of substance taking handbags and just didn't care. None of us really saw our jobs there as permanent and were mostly just there for the ride. In our minds, even though some of us stayed working there longer than we wanted to, it was a mere stepping stone until we could find a place with better working conditions and wages. The one saving grace for us was the union. For without them, most of us would have been terminated long ago. Across from where Cliff and I worked was the Expander Department. Here, workers inserted evaporators into press machines that forced copper tubes to expand that set them permanently in place before being carted off for the assembly lines. To our surprise, one of them was Reed. I approached him when the shift started and asked "How come you're way back here with us? I thought you were going back to the dehumidifiers on line 3?" "I got punishment work" he replied. "What punishment work?" I asked laughing. "Do you remember when we were on line 3 before the last layoff and I went to lunch that time and took that license plate off of someone"s car to use on mine?" he asked. "Yeah" I replied. "I remember that. You got suspended for 3 days and almost got fired. Because you took the head shop steward Ray W"s license plate without knowing it. I heard he saved your job because he likes you". "Yeah, it was a fireman"s plate too" he chuckled. "We had a wake for you on the back of the line when that happened" I laughed.

"We thought you were a goner for sure. Johnny Handbag even folded up a paper American flag for you. And, I pretended to play taps". "I heard about that" he chuckled. "But, part of the deal for me to come back was that I had to come here. He pointed to the machine with a thick German accent and said "To Das Expander". "I can see where you would see this as torture" I said. "Due to being tethered to this damn thing all day". "You know what they say?" he asked. "Ist das ist da vey vee vork? Yes, das ist da vey vee work". Reed saw it as a concentration camp atmosphere and made fun of it to be able to cope.

Next to Reed at an identical machine was a guy named Kenny L. I didn't know him well. But, I knew his older brother Mike who had become an Edison Township police officer. Kenny had a great sense of humor. He was a large barrel chested guy with hands the size of oven mits and was about 6 feet 4. He hated the expander as much as Reed did. But like Reed, he made the best of it as he needed the paycheck to survive. One day, the press room manager Al H. was riding by on one of the plant's 3 wheeled bicycles. Al was a very unpleasant man and never seemed to be happy. Sometimes he would get angry if someone called out of work and he needed volunteers for the press room. A few times he asked Cliff and I and we declined. "I'll give you higher labor grade 6 pay" he shouted approaching us over our fin pressing machines. "It's not worth the 10 cents more you want to give us for a harder job" Cliff replied. "So, go find some other suckers". Al would shake his fist at us and then shout turning away "Bahhh! Sissies! You're all a bunch of sissies! None of you want to work!" "That guy is a real piece of work, Cliff" I said. "He doesn't like to be told no. He even spits on the floor when he leaves. What kind of supervisor does that?" "Fuck him" Cliff replied. "Look at his face. He has a dick for a nose" "A dick for a nose?" I asked. "That's hilarious, man". "It's true" he replied. "And, that's not even if it's a hard on. "I wonder how he sees when it's like that?" I asked. "Very carefully" Cliff laughed. "Very carefully". When Kenny found out about this, he would do anything to contribute to Al's misery. "Bahhh!" Kenny would scream bombastically as Al drove by. "Bahhh! I hate everything!"

Then, as Al turned the corner and Kenny knew Al had seen him out of the corner of his eye; Kenny would spit right toward him. "Bah!" Kenny yelled. "I don't wanna work! Bah!"

When lunchtime came, Cliff and I went outside by the parts department"s loading dock to waste some time. Adjacent to it was a ladder that went up to the roof. "I heard people go up there to get stoned sometimes and check out the view" he said. "We should go take a look up there and see. "What if somebody sees us?" I asked. "Nobody will see us" he replied. "It's too far in the corner". "I'll go up if you do" I exclaimed. "But, you have to go up first". "No problem at all" he responded. "Just follow me". I watched him grab the first rung and steady himself for the climb. We scampered up as fast as we could and turned to look around. Right in front of us was Frankie H. lying on a yard lounge with a silver piece of cardboard under his chin. He was holding it up by its corners and it was shaped in a V. "What's going on here?" Cliff asked. "I'm getting a suntan, man. What do you think?" Frankie asked. Seeing a stub of a marijuana roach in his hand, I asked. "Frankie? How long have you been up here? Have you been up here getting high all day?" "Well" he replied laughing "You're already high when you get up here because of the height. But, a little bit of weed adds to it I guess. And yes, I've been up here all morning. As you know, I work the baling machine. I'm all caught up. So, I figured I would get some sunshine". "You"ve got balls of steel Frankie" I said. "I could never take the chance of being up here for more than a few minutes". "Who"s gonna see him?" Cliff asked. The Brow and his friends would never come up here. They don't want to get their hands dirty". "Just enjoy the view, bro" Frankie suggested. "It's a beautiful day". We took a few pulls from his roach and went back down. After we reached the ground, I asked. "Now, Cliff? You don't see anything wrong with that?" "Nah" he replied. "It gives a whole other meaning to getting high. It's the Westinghouse way".

In the plant's bathrooms, there was a lot of graffiti being drawn. Most of it was done by a guy named Bob. S, Cliff, and me. I distinctly remember how upset all of us were when we heard that our union president named Carl had sold out to the company and had given back some sick days. So naturally, he ended up being the first victim. Being that there was a spot remover named Carbona that was sold at stores, I took it upon myself to parody him with it relentlessly. I drew a cartoon of a Carbona bottle but changed the logo to "Carlona spot and employee remover. Just one application and the worker vanishes instantly. Works on fraction days too". Following up with this was Cliff. Since he hated Al H. so much, he drew a cartoon of him on a three wheeled bike. He had a duck hanging down for a nose and was spitting onto the floor. Over his head were printed the words "Bah, sissies!" Not to be out done by him, I had to come up with something spectacular. So, I drew a picture of Dave S. the plant manager. He a large head, his hair parted to the side like Adolf Hitler"s, and a giant eyebrow that encompassed almost the entire left side of his forehead. Over it, I made the inscription "Beware! The Infamous Brow!" Bob though had a different style and didn't attack the management. He liked to use parodies from movies he had seen or something he had read in a magazine. After seeing the TV special The Day After, every bathroom in the place had a huge mushroom cloud with the lettering "Boom, and you're gone!" underneath it. Since he always seemed to be obsessed with anything to do with sex, he drew a big vagina with the words "Fuckfest 85" written over it. Another of his favorites that aggravated us later on was that he would scribble over all of our great artwork with the caption "The Terminator". He always denied it, but we all knew it was him and thought he was an asshole for his demeanor. The last graffiti I did was after I had been threatened with another suspension. On all of the beams that held up the ceiling on the thoroughfare that led back to the lines, I wrote on each one the letters "P-O-C-K-E-T U-N-I-O-N". There was no way anyone driving by wouldn't have seen it and I was very proud of myself for its inscription. For months after I had heard that the union desperately wanted to know who the culprit was. Of course they never caught me as I outsmarted them. Sometimes I think that people who try to screw other people are their worst enemies.

The recent layoff was over and we were we reassigned back to our clamp truck jobs. It was always a relief to go back as it was less physically demanding and a far more enjoyable work environment. Walking over line 3"s steps one day, I heard the supervisor Erlene C. talking to a loop repairwoman that was a friend of hers. The repairwoman asked "Erlene? I heard from a lot of the workers on our line that they are all doing drugs that make them all speed up". "Speed up?" Erlene asked. "What kind of drugs darling?" "They call it crank" she said. "It's supposed to make them work much faster and give them a lot of extra energy". Erlene, knowing that she received bonus checks at the end of the month for going over quota exclaimed. "Well, in that case honey. Turn the line up!" On line 2, my childhood friend Matt D. had been selling cocaine. I had found out that he had taken over Cliff's old territory after Cliff and I had been sent to the coils department. "You don't want that area back?" I asked Cliff. "Nah" he replied. "Don't you see how many drugs are being distributed in this place, bro? Everybody here is always on something. There's just the right amount of competition to not spoil it. As long as I still make my money, I don't care". With his analogy, I decided to tally up exactly how many dealers there were at a time. There were pot sellers, speed dealers, pill heads, cocaine entrepreneurs, and even alcoholics who would go to Knox Tavern down the street at lunch time and bring back 6 packs hidden in vinyl cooler bags. Anything could be bought if the price was right. It was ridiculous. The more I investigated, the more I found out. The factory had become a cornucopia of substance abuse. Even I had gotten in on the mix for a little while. It turned out Ronnie E. was on the front of line 3 preparing small compressors. When I bought from him for my own personal use, he informed me that he was the main crank dealer in the entire plant. I ended up having the same arrangement with him I had with Cliff with cocaine deals. If I took

Ronnie's bags to his customers throughout the plant, I was rewarded with free head stash and discounts. It was a beautiful thing. The only employees who weren't on something were the ones over 40. I remember thinking "It's amazing the employees produced anything under those conditions of value at all.

The Christmas holidays had come and the factory was running at full tilt. Winter time was our most productive period as management would produce as many sets as they could. Then, they'd stockpile them for shipment to retail establishments in the summer. During a morning coffee break, I drove my clamp truck to a spot by the pedestrian stairs closer to the cafeteria to park. Just as I had come to a stop, a woman grazed her shoulder on one of the clamps and said "Excuse me. I didn't see you, I'm sorry". She went on her way and I thought I had heard the end of it. Suddenly, as I was dismounting my machine I heard a shrill female voice screaming at the top of her lungs. "Did you see that?" she asked other employees walking by. "Did you see that? He almost hit her! I saw the whole thing!" I turned to her aggravated and replied. "What the fuck are you talking about? She ran into me? She even said she was sorry and let it go. What the fuck is your problem?" It turned out that I knew this girl because she was a known troublemaker who always seemed to thrive on other people"s business. "I'm going to HR" she screamed. "I'm gonna tell them what I saw". "You do whatever the fuck you want" I yelled. "But, you're fucking crazy. Now, get away from me before you get into even more trouble". "I'm gonna report you" she hollered. "I'm gonna report you for almost hitting that lady. And, everybody saw it". "The only people who saw anything are ghosts" I said. "So, be like one and drift away already."

A few hours later while on our afternoon break in the back cafeteria, I was watching Cliff put a hardboiled egg in a microwave. "I scarfed some free ones out of that machine" he said. "Watch what happens when I close the door". As he slammed it shut, he laughed and hit the on button. It made the familiar humming noise and then some crackling sounds. "Wait for it" he chuckled. "It's coming". "What's coming?" I asked. "Ready?" he responded. "1, 2, 3". Then, I heard a low thudding boom. "It's finished" he said as he opened the microwave"s door. "Ron!" he laughed pointing. "Look! It's egg salad!" "Who"s gonna clean that shit up?" I asked. "Not me" he said. "That's what janitors are for". Just as our break was over, a shop steward showed up as we were leaving. I was passing him in the doorway when he turned and called my name. "Ron?" he asked. "You have to come with me to the front office. There's been a complaint by someone that you almost hit them with your clamp truck. They want you to come up there and explain yourself". "Explain what?" I asked. "There's nothing to tell. The woman bumped into me after my truck was stopped. This is bullshit as usual". "You still have to go" he said. "Supposedly, there are witnesses". "Ron told me all about that" Cliff interjected. "I know exactly who it is too. It's that little fucking pixie looking bitch that everyone calls Squeaky. She's a fucking loser, rat fuck. She's always causing trouble. She's a fucking drama queen". "I think somebody dropped that skank on her head once" I laughed. "But, I guess I better go up there before I get it even worse". "You know where I am if you need me" Cliff said. "And, don't let those jerkoffs get to you either".

After the usual bullshit interrogation I was accustomed to, I was given another 3 day suspension. This time though, I was informed that I wouldn't be fired as long as I was more careful of my surroundings when traveling on my clamp truck in the future. When I came back, the charges were summarily dropped do to the woman Squeaky thought she was helping refusing to cooperate. The rumor I heard later was that she knew I was right and that Squeaky was wrong and the woman didn't want to accuse me of something I didn't do. Upset with the final outcome, Squeaky decided to perform revenge. She wrote a sentence on a row of boxes along one of the corridors. It read "Ronnie Arrow, payback is a bitch". "Payback?" I thought. "This bitch is delusional. The stupid fuck couldn't even spell my name right". A few days later while Cliff and I were in the back cafeteria, I took a very thick black magic marker and drew a large cartoon of a rat on one of the round table tops. Over its head with a balloon with words in it I wrote "Squeak, squeak. Beware!" When she saw it, she went crying to HR saying it was me. But, she had no evidence and it was squashed. So much for karma, eh Squeaky?

In my 5th year of employment, I explored the idea of going to night school to procure a certificate in Heating, Ventilation, & Air Conditioning. Cliff had already been going and was soon to graduate. I approached him and asked him for the low down "Who paid for your classes?" I asked. "Isn't it expensive?" "It would be if I paid for it" he laughed. "But, I'm on the free Westinghouse program. As long as I maintain a C grade point average, they pay for everything". "How hard is it?" I asked. "Does it take long?" "It's 18 months and the classes are cake. Most of the shit they teach we already know from working here. You should go, bro. It couldn't hurt to learn. What else are you doing besides fucking around in here all day?" "That sounds like a good idea" I replied. "I'll have to look into it". After I had filled out the papers to enroll, I was ecstatic about the possibility of actually having a trade instead of a lifelong position at a factory that went nowhere. In the meantime, I had been partying heavily on the weekends and the hangovers were becoming treacherous. Sometimes, I would come in still drunk from the night before. In those situations I made an agreement with Handsome Wayne my work partner. He would let me sleep it off in a giant box full of foam rubber strips from 7am until lunch at 11:30am. When we came back from lunch, we would switch and he would get the rest of the day off. Neither one of us minded doing double duty as we only had to hustle for 4 hours at a time. Soon, I became bored with the warehouse work and put in a bid for another position. There was an opening on 2nd shift and I decided to explore it. I had always loathed having to get up at 6am for work and thought it might be good to have a change. The bid came through and it was accepted. I was to start at 3:30pm the following Monday and report to the parts department on line 1. The job was relatively easy and I enjoyed the option of getting up for work later in the day. There was one problem though, and his name was Bob C. On my very first night, he accosted me and threatened "I know how you were on 1st shift with your sneaky crap. But, I'm in charge now and I'm not having any of your bullshit. You'll do your job and that's it. If I see or hear of you disappearing for anything other than a 5-minute bathroom break, you're out of here. I'll do everything I can to have you fired". "You can try anything you want" I replied laughing. "But, keep in mind that I'm not your little red headed girly friend who you tried to impress on line 2 with your leg up on the rollers. The only thing that"ll be rolling out of here is you if you think you're gonna try to accuse me of something I didn't do. You clowns tried it before and I'm still here". "We'll see about that" he mumbled annoyed. "Just do your work and I'm gonna keep an eye on you". "Just worry about yourself" I said. And, I drove away.

After 2 weeks of asshole Bob C.'s continual annoyance, I wanted back on 1st shift badly. The HR office told me that was fine. But, I would have to stay supplying line 1 and I couldn't go back to a clamp truck. Happy with their decision, I did as little as possible on the remainder of 2nd shift just to piss Bob C. off. Knowing that I was going, he surprised me by leaving me alone. The morning came to switch shifts and I had to report to Rocco B. Rocco was a very nice man who had an Italian accent and was very agreeable. His only concern was to keep the parts flowing to stop the Infamous Brow from calling him about the line not being on. "You supplied the compressors on line 1 before, yes?" he asked. "Now, this time you'll be bringing the metal parts instead. There are cages in the pressroom area that you will bring up here for me" He handed me a clipboard with part numbers on it and explained that all I had to do was match it to each bin and stack them with the forklift in the front of the line. "Sometimes, we may have a run for a few days" he said. "I don't mind if you drive around with nothing to do. But, don't make it too obvious my friend. All I ask is that if your name comes over the intercom that means there will be a change over and you have to come right away. "No problem, Rocco" I replied. "You can count on me".

While supplying thousands of parts to the line, I learned from others that I could "bank" the material and disappear. This came in handy when I found out there were card games going on behind tall stacks of boxes next to the warehouse in the back. One day, I moseyed in to see what was going on. "Ronnie?" Brian Bulkhead asked. "Welcome to the game. I guess you found out about us, huh?" "How long have you guys been back here doing this?" I chuckled. "A long assed time" he said. You want to ante up and play?" he asked. "It's poker you know? We have beers here too. But, you can only have one if you join in". "You have your own little private casino going on huh?" I asked. "Something like that" a guy named Pat C. said. "For those of us who can get away with it". I threw in a 10 dollar bill and grabbed a few hands. Fortunately, just as the booze was hitting me, I won. "I have to go and check my stock" I said. "Maybe I'll come back later". I scooped up my winnings and attempted to exit the maze. "Come on, man" barked Bulkhead behind me. "You didn't even give us a chance to win it back, bro". "Sorry" I replied. "Duty calls". I drove back to check in with Rocco and went for a break in the back cafeteria. On my way there, I ran into Cliff. "What's going on?" I asked. "Anything new?" "I've got a funny story, bro. Wait till you hear". "Go ahead, man" I said. "I'm all ears". "You know that tall blonde skank at the beginning of your line?" he asked. "Yeah" I replied. "I know which one you're talking about". "Well" he laughed "You know Bulkhead gets blowjobs from her in the parking lot during lunch break, right?" "No" I said grinning. "Tell me more". "From what I hear" he exclaimed laughing. "Brian doesn't make any noise when he comes". "What do you mean he doesn't make any noise?" I asked. "All guys make noises when they come". "Not according to that black woman by receiving" he said. "She got into a discussion about sex with Bulkhead about it. I was walking by and heard them. The woman was shrieking in front of everyone. She asked Bulkhead "What do you mean you don't make any noise when you come Brian? Everybody makes noise when they come. How come you don't make noise Brian when you come?" "What did Brian say?" I asked. "He didn't say anything, man. He just stood there with a smile on his face for a second and then left". "Crazy story, buddy" I replied. "I've heard a little about that blonde before". "Bulkhead told me another story about that chick once" he laughed. "Like what?" I inquired. "She came into work one morning with dried semen in her hair. She was also wearing the same clothes from the night before. Brian said she didn't know the white strip was there all day. All of the other girls on the line were making fun of her and she didn't know why". "Gross" I exclaimed. "So much for the women of Westinghouse".

While we were sitting at a table and munching on bags of treats, we glanced over to our right and noticed some management types hanging around by the edge of a wall. The wall was a barrier to a room behind it where Automatic Catering had kept their supplies and bags of coins they retrieved from their vending machines. As the supervisors moved away, we could clearly see that the aluminum barricade that once separated us had been curled up waist high. Apparently, someone with a forklift had slid the forks underneath, positioned them just right, and then lifted them up while crinkling it for access. "Someone did this last night" I heard one of them say. "It had to have been done on the afternoon or night shift". A rotund man wearing an Automatic Catering jacket turned to him and asked "Who"s going to reimburse us for this? You told us this was a secure area. Something has to be done right away". "We have the police coming to make a report" the supervisor chimed. "Depending on its contents, We'll take care of you". When Cliff and I got up to go back to work, I approached them and asked what had happened. I was quickly rebuffed. "Do you know anything about this?" The potbellied man asked. "Because, we just lost 3 sacks of money worth $3,000". "I haven"t a clue" I replied. "But, I wish you luck trying to find out" "Then, get out of here" he said. "It doesn't concern you". Cliff, being piqued with interest remarked as we walked away "I'm gonna see if I can find out who did that. That's an ingenious scam. It's too bad we didn't think of that". Months later, while sharing a joint in the parking lot, Cliff clued me in "Pat C. did that coin haul" he said. "How did he get all of that money out though?" I asked. "He hid the sacks someplace in the plant and took the coins out in his lunch box a little at a time" Cliff replied. "That must have taken him weeks" I exclaimed. "Supposedly, he says he did it in a week" Cliff said. "But, who cares? He's got 3 grand and we don't. I only wish I would have thought about it first". "Well" I chuckled. "Pat C. is pretty smart then. He told me a couple of months ago that he takes copper elbows from drums in the brazing area. He puts them in his pockets and stashes them at home a little at a time. When he has enough, he takes them to the metal recycler and gets cash for them". "See what I mean?" Cliff asked. "It's always something".

One Thursday night, I had stayed out a little too late and got highly intoxicated. Knowing that it could happen while working for Rocco, I had positioned 2 large cardboard containers beforehand deep into a row at the back of the plant that were hard for prying eyes to see. In the top half, I took a razor knife and cut a square in its floor on 3 sides with the 4th side acted as a hinge. On the front edge, I cut a small hole and slipped in a rope with a knot on the end that facilitated as handle. That way, it was easy to open and close. I made it just the right size for a human to be able to drop down to the other container below. In the bottom area, I cut another square on the left side with the same configuration as an escape hatch. If a nosey supervisor came milling about, I could awaken from my slumber and depart with ease. It was a perfect place to get in a few hours for a snooze.

In my final year of employment, a company named Electrolux had bought us out. They came in like gangbusters eliminating positions with time trials and reassignments throughout the plant. I have vivid recollections of their researchers standing by the lines with stop watches in their hands recording everything and anything in their attempts to boost maximum efficiency. But, they just didn't get it. The more workers they took away, the more the lines went down. We'd laugh it off and sometimes secretly sabotage them. Other times, we didn't do any work at all. Production and quality began to suffer. Soon, they asked for volunteers for Saturday overtime. There were stacks and stacks of units that had to be retested or repaired. Electrolux even changed the company name to Frigidaire to try to look fresh. They refused to believe that morale was low and we hated them. By now, I had taken a bid to work in the polyfoam room. There, I ran a huge Kohler General forming machine. One morning, I was sitting in a chair letting the machine do its thing. The pieces would drop below and an employee under me would stack and wrap them. There wasn't anything else for me to really do except to make sure the machine never jammed. I eventually got a new helper named Felix. In a way, he looked kind of like the old cartoon Felix the Cat and I told him so. After a few months, I started to get bored. So, I constructed a hidden room behind the vats that held the polyfoam beads that fed down to the machine. I took some plastic sheeting and fashioned a makeshift tent. Inside, I placed a builder"s horse and used the remainder of the plastic to make a bed out of foam peanuts for the floor. On the horse, I positioned an air conditioning unit I had taken from the line. I wanted maximum airflow to hit me so I would be comfortable. In the mornings, I had made a deal with Felix. It was the same agreement I had made with Handsome Wayne. I"d set the machine to run and warm up at 7am, and then crawl into my cave to talk a nap until lunch time. It was perfect and Felix and I swapped out for months. Until one day, I made the mistake of falling asleep in a chair before Felix had a chance to warn me. The former union president Chet P. had some health problems and had joined management as a turncoat. He had clearly sold us out to the company and seemed to no longer care. Next to the machine and with sunglasses on my head, I was snoring in the chair as he approached me. Since I was semi-conscious, I didn't at first hear him until the sound of him clearing his throat had awakened me. "What are you doing sleeping?" he asked roaring. "What are you talking about?" I replied startled. "I'm just sitting here watching this machine" "No you aren't" he howled. "You're wearing sunglasses. So, I know you were asleep". "Did you actually see me with my eyes closed?" I asked. "No" he replied. "But, I know you were". "I guess you must have x-ray vision then, eh Chet?" I questioned sarcastically. "Should we go to the office now? Or, do you want to drop it because you have no proof or witnesses?" "I'll get you sooner or later" he barked. "It's just a matter of time" "Yeah, yeah" I replied. "Same shit, different day".

A few weeks later, I had stayed outside in the parking lot a little too long at lunch time. I was 20 minutes late and had forgotten to clock in and out. On my way back in, I was seen by Chet. As I walked to the polyfoam area, he was trailing behind me. "I've got you now" he screamed. "You're done! You're 20 minutes late coming back from lunch. I was waiting for you and no one knew where you were. You're finished!" Like I usually did with overzealous authority figures, I ignore him and kept on walking. His rage became intense. "Don't you walk away from me." he yelled. "I'm taking you to the office right now!" "I'm not going anywhere" I replied. "Now, go away". He turned tail with crimson colored cheeks, hopped on his 3 wheeled bike, and headed straight to the front. I had obviously pissed him off and he was losing it. For someone who had claimed to have had a heart condition, he sure had fooled me. A few minutes went by and he came back with one of the HR directors and was hollering again "He was late from lunch and insubordinate. He refused my instructions completely. I want something done about it now!" "Ok, Ron" said the HR guy. "Come with us to my office and We'll try to figure this out". Sitting with Chet who was supposed to know better, I was suspended for 3 days without union representation. I knew he was wrong not affording me any, but I didn't say a word. I wanted a few days off and I knew that within a day or two the shop steward would find out and I would once again be victorious. Just as I had predicted, I was called back with an apology and retroactive pay. My shop steward made Chet tell me he was sorry and it had all been a big misunderstanding. The look on Chet's face was priceless and it made my day. He never approached me again except when I had given my two weeks" notice to resign after I had finished night school. Not knowing the exact date, he would try to act playful sarcastically and ask "So? When are you leaving? I hope it's soon". "I leave when I leave" I replied.

On a Wednesday afternoon, I went with a guy I worked with named Larry to help him go apartment hunting. He needed a new place to live and was trying to find a place that was closer to work. He found a rooming house in the newspaper that turned out to be close to Mary's Pizza. As we pulled up in his van he exclaimed. "This place is supposed to have a small apartment in the back. That"ll work for me as I don't really feel like living in some stupid room". "I guess you'll see when we get in there" I replied. "But you have to admit, this place would be ideal for you far as work goes". After entering, we met the superintendent who asked us to follow him. "It's right back here" he said. "And, it's nice and quiet too". "I don't give a rat's ass about being quiet" Larry said. "I only care about if it's a good fit for me and affordable". Upon entering, Larry had to bend way down just to be able to inspect the place. "This ain't gonna work" he grumbled. "Your ceilings are only 6 feet high and I'm 6 feet 4". On the way out, we looked to our right and there was a very pretty young teenage girl hanging clothes on a line. "Who"s that?" Larry asked the super. "Oh" he replied. "That's one of our neighbors. She's pretty hot, isn't she?" "She looks kind of young, man" I said. "I don't think you want any of that Lar. She looks like jailbait. "Yeah" he laughed. "If I lived here, I"d probably get in trouble trying to get with her anyway". Years later, I found out that the girl hanging the laundry was the little girl I had seen previously playing with the dough in Mary"s Pizza. It turned out that she was Mary"s granddaughter. Twenty years later, I married her.

Soon, I graduated from the technical institute in Clark. Though I knew I was going to miss all of my work friends at Westinghouse, I had felt it was time to move on. To Chet P's delight, I gave my two weeks" notice of my resignation. I had a lot of fun being employed there and felt it was a continuation of high school. It was a circus type atmosphere and every day was a laugh. In the end I had left on my own terms. "Still" I had thought. "I will never be beaten".